STAR CROSSED INDIA

STAR CROSSED INDIA LET DOWN BY LEADERSHIP

G.S. Bhargava

Publications

KALPAZ PUBLICATIONS

DELHI - 110 052

Star Crossed India : Let Down by Leadership

ISBN : 81-7835-422-5

Published in 2005 in India by
Kalpaz Publications,
C-30, Satyawati Nagar,
Delhi-110 052
E-mail : kalpaz@hotmail.com

Lasertype Setting by: Tact Computer Graphics, Delhi
Printed at: Salasar Imaging Systems, Delhi

Contents

Contents

Introduction

This book was intended to be published in the centenary year of Jayaprakash Narayan but because of certain unavoidable circumstances it was destined to be delayed. All concerned feel sad about it though it gave me an opportunity to revise the manuscript. At last, it is in the hands of the discerning reader. Historical figures like JP are not bound by time frame. I am sure it will stand the test of all time and the scrutiny of the history as well.

The genesis of the book was my experience in Government service as Principal Information Officer (PIO) to the Government of India during the Janata Party days (1977-1979). And its purpose was recording it My tenure started one year later in 1978 and lasted till January 1980. The 1975 'emergency', the 1977 general election which swept Indira Gandhi, her family and party out of power and put the makeshift Janata conglomerate in the seat of government, the disintegration of the Janata after just about 18 months in office and the return of Indira Gandhi to power was naturally the backdrop for my narration which is more perceptional and opinionated than historical. This core of the book has remained intact unaffected by more recent developments, which, In fact, underscore the thrust of the book that India is star-crossed because its leaders, undoubtedly great and promising individually, repeatedly failed the people. Leaving out the titans of our freedom struggle as well as the Nehru years including Lal Bahadur's short innings of eighteen months, we see from 1966 when Indira Gandhi was made prime minister by the Syndicate to her dastardly assassination in 1984 and till now an unerring pattern of leaders of great promise turning out to be persons with clay feet. For instance, Atal Behari Vajpayee hailed

Indira Gandhi as Durga in the wake of the successful handling of the 1971 Bangladesh war with Pakistan. The celebrated painter M.F. Husain depicted her as a goddess seated on a tiger! No person worth reckoning has questioned the wisdom of promoting secession of a deceased limb like the then eastern wing of Pakistan, instead of keeping it as a vulnerable target. That would have also put Pakistan on the guard against going haywire in Jammu and Kashmir. That has remained an 'if' of recent India-Pakistan history.

As stated, I worked on the book off and on. Except for the first draft of over a hundred pages written when I was at the Center for International Affairs at Harvard as a visiting Fellow, the work on the book was interspersed by long spells – running sometimes into several years – of inaction. When I was an active journalist — special correspondent or assistant editor– 'book writing' had naturally to take a back seat. After ceasing to be a 'working journalist' in the late 1980's I became a freelance journalist contributing articles and scripts for broadcasts. Only the periodical stints at universities abroad— they included, besides the one year 1973-74 at the Centre for International Studies, Harvard University, already referred to, another year (1976) at the International Institute for Strategic Studies, (IISS) London, and two spells (1980-81 and 1989-90) at Cornell University, Ithaca, New York, provided opportunities for working on the book. But at the IISS I had to work on my Adelphi paper *India's Security in the 1980's*, while during 1989-90 *I wrote a book on Afghanistan, South Asian Security After Afghanistan*, published by Lexington Books, Mass. US. in 1983. Similarly while at Moscow in 1990 as a scholar attached to the Institute of Oriental Studies I edited an English translation of Michel Gorbachev's speeches and writings on Perestroika brought out by semi-official Progress Publications.

The book brings out clearly that the Congress party has contributed most to India being star-crossed. One of the reasons for the popular resistance to the 1975 'emergency' was Sanjay Gandhi's bid to succeed his mother to the seat of power and Indira Gandhi's apparently helpless acquiescence in it. Still like the notorious Bourbons of early nineteenth century, the sycophants of the Congress party leadership conjured up a so-called Nehru-Gandhi dynasty or even clan. The reference is not to

Mahatma Gandhi but Ghandi that was Feroze Gandhi's family name corrupted into Gandhi. (During the 'emergency' *The New York Times* would remind its readers that Indira Gandhi was no relation of M.K. Gandhi.) In the process, they belittled Nehru's robust Republican spirit, which would not think of, much less brook, founding a dynasty. Then there was the Lal Bahadur Shastri interregnum which, if it had not been cut short to one and a half years, would have ruled out Indira Gandhi's succession. This was despite Nehru's conscious effort to annoint Indira as Congress party president. At the same time, at his last press conference in May 1964 Nehru had stoutly denied any intention to 'groom' his daughter to step into his shoes.

The reference to the so-called Gandhi-Nehru dynasty jars on our ears and offends our nationalist sensibilities because it disparages two hallowed names in our national history, Gandhiji and Nehru. Gandhiji's own sons were never in the run for political leadership because he set himself against hereditary leadership. The highest position one of his sons, Devadas Gandhi, held was managing editorship of the *Hindustan Times*. Even if uncharitable critics looked down on Devadas's professional ability, he was undoubtedly one of the great editors of the 20th century. In fact, hereditary leadership was alien to Indian political ethos. Thus, the highest position Sardar Patel's son, Dahyabhai Patel, could reach was leadership of the Swatantra party, an opposition group, in the Rajya Sabha. That, too, happened after the Sardar had passed away, confirming that he was no party to it. The Sardar's daughter, Manibehn, who was close to him, was secretary and political helpmeet rolled into one to him in his life time but faded away from public life thereafter. She was a spinster. (Incidentally, Indira Gandhi wanted to play a similar role vis-à-vis Nehru in his last days.) Another great national leader, perhaps on par with Gandhiji, Netaji Subhash Chandra Bose, died young, having been killed in an aircrash near Formosa. That was in 1945 when Nehru's tenure as Prime Minister had not even begun. (Of course, Netaji's acolytes refuse to accept that he had died in the plane crash. They believe that he is still alive and any statement to the contrary is blasphemy for them. A judicial commission has been verifying the matter for years). Later it came to light that Netaji had married a German girl but the family is out of our public life. The next leader, who was as great as Nehru, was Rajaji or Rajagopalachari. His son did not aspire for political leadership nor would Rajaji have promoted him.

Within the so-called Gandhi-Nehru parivar, Indira Gandhi was a great leader who imbibed many of her father's qualities even if Nehru's liberal temperament and democratic ethos had been alien to her. In an interview to Pupul Jayakar, one of Indira's acolytes, she recalls her childhood at Anand Bhavan in Allahabad when Motilal Nehru presided over the family. (Akashvani rebroadcast the interview on 31 October 2004 on the 20th anniversary of her assassination). It brings out unerringly the ethos, which marked Indira's upbringing and the deep sense of India's history that shaped her growing up. She also says that even as a child she felt a sense of responsibility for the family, primarily because her ailing mother was not able to look after her father. Against that background to project Antonio Maino AKA Sonia 'Gandhi' as her alter ego because she replicates Indira's mannerisms is an insult to her memory. Equally inappropriately, journalists loosely talk of 'first family' when referring to Sonia Gandhi and her children. Nothing can be more repugnant to Nehru's democratic spirit and the thrust of our freedom struggle, which was inconsistent with concepts like first family and royalty. There are no first families in parliamentary democracies. Even in presidential systems like those of the US and France, the 'first family' is merely the first among equals. If we have to have a first family in India it has to be that of our bachelor President, the genial Dr. A. P.J Abul Kalam. I have contrasted in the book Antonio Maino with some other women leaders in the country's public life, notably Jayalalitha, Mayavathi and Rabri Devi. Viewed against her mother-in-law, Antonio Maino sticks out like a sore thumb, so insignificant if not presumptuous. So much for her being a second Indira Gandhi!

Other fictions propagated equally sedulously by Sonia Gandhi's sycophants are that she had led the Congress Party to victory in the 2004 general election by campaigning single-handedly and after having been 'elected' leader of the victorious party renounced the crown and made Dr. Manmohan Singh the prime minister of the country. Of these legends, the only act of hers that deserves billing as national service – I mean to India, not Italy, — is the nomination of Dr. Manmohan Singh as Prime Minister. In him, the country has a perfect gentleman as Prime Minister, perhaps for the first time in its chequered history as an independent nation. The litmus test, in my assessment, is that he graciously called on P.V.Narasimha Rao to congratulate him on the quashing of corruption charges against him in the hawala and related cases. That was when Sonia and her henchmen abandoned Narasimha Rao. That speaks of the character of the man. I told him so in 2002 when he was the Leader of the Opposition in the Rajya Sabha and less inaccessible. And I shall say it again if I have an audience with him. Sonia also is aware of it. That was why even after dumping

Narasimha Rao and virtually jettisoning his policy of liberalisation of the economy in the 1996 general election, she has retained Dr.Manmohan Singh as a member of the Congress working committee and Leader of the Opposition in the Upper House. The Congress party would have returned to office in the 1996 general election if the Sonia faction had pulled its weight. In the light of Narasimha Rao's record of completing the full term of five years despite his lack of majority in the Lok Sabha, Sonia and her flunkies were afraid he would outlast them if the Congress party won the 1996 general election with Narasimha Rao at the helm. That would have obviated Narasimha Rao rigging up the United Front government with nincompoops like H.D.Deve Gowda as Prime Minister just to block the BJP from gaining office. In the process, he had brought under the Congress party's umbrella regional parties like the Telugu Desam Party (TDP) and the DMK, not to mention the Asom Gana Parishad.These regional parties being competitors for power in their respective States with the Congress party had until then tended to go along with the BJP.

As for Sonia's single-handed campaigning, as stated, she does not allow any other party leader to share the dais with her. The so-called road shows in front of television cameras are her exclusive exercise to hog the limelight. She knows that she owes her 'popularity' to the spin-doctor technique of photo opportunity. Being the wielder of the party's purse strings, she can afford to do it. Her 'election' as Congress party leader is fresh in the minds of all those who have seen the melodrama of Sonia's sycophants lavishing praise on her and insisting that she should lead the ruling party. Many of them like loud-mouthed Renuka Chaudhary of Andhra Pradesh reaped the reward by getting ministerships.

It is relevant here to take a closer look at the 2004 general election to the Lok Sabha. While it is churlish to deny that the Congress party and its 'allies', especially the Communists and Laloo Prasad Yadav's Rashtriya Janata Dal (RJD) have scored over the BJP and its dwindling flock of fellow travellers, an in-depth study of the election results puts the matter in perspective. The BJP contested only 364 of the 539 seats in the current 14th Lok Sabha or 67 per cent of the total. It showed either overconfidence that it would garner over 70 per cent of the contested seats or miscalculation. It proved to be the latter. The Congress party, on the other hand, contested 416 seats of which it won 145 which works out to a gain percentage of about 35 as against the BJP's 138 out of 364 or 37 per cent. In actual terms it is a loss of 34 seats for the BJP and a gain of 36 seats for the Congress party. The percentage of the popular vote of the Congress party at 26.64 is over four percentage points higher than that of the BJP. The larger number of seats contested by the Congress party partly accounts for it. The number and percentage of security deposits forfeited in the case of each party reinforces the larger picture.

The BJP 'lost' largely because its choice of electoral allies turned out to be flawed. Especially the TDP in Andhra Pradesh and Jayalalitha's A-I ADMK in Tamil Nadu failed to pull through. Together they account for 42 and 39 Lok Sabha seats respectively or a total of 81 seats. The BJP drew a blank in Andhra Pradesh while the Congress party bagged 29 seats; similarly the BJP got none of the 39 Tamil Nadu tally of which the Congress party had ten seats. In Andhra Pradesh, the BJP's electoral partner, TDP, lost heavily mostly on account of the separatist Telengana Rashtra Samiti (TRS) entering the fray in support of the Congress party. The TRS gained only five of the 29 seats it contested but it caused the debacle of the TDP outside Telengana also. The TDP, which had 29 seats in the dissolved Lok Sabha, won only five. This becomes clear from a look at the seats won by the Congress party and the TDP in the general elections of 1996, 1998 and 1999: they were respectively twenty-two, twenty-two and five in the case of the TDP and sixteen, twelve and 29.for the Congress party. The BJP tallies in 1996, 1998 and 1999 were respectively nil, four and seven. The Naxalites also were a factor in the electoral contest, ironically. They targeted the TDP and to a lesser BJP candidates and campaigners. Incidentally, a Naxalite attack on the TDP leader and former chief minister, Chandra Babu Naidu, in November 2003 precipitated the party's plea for advancing of the general election, which the Election Commission found it possible to conduct in May 2004, in mid-summer. The TDP group leader in the Lok Sabha, Yerran Naidu, contesting from his home constituency of Srikakulam in the extreme north of the State narrowly escaped injury or death in a Naxalite attack. In Tamil Nadu, the BJP had no other choice but to team up with mercurial Jayalalitha overlooking its bitter experience of alliance with her hardly six years ago. The BJP record in the 1996,1998 and 1999 elections was nil, five and four whereas that of the Congress party was nil, nil and two. The regional parties of A-IADMK and DMK shared the laurels winning a minimum of nil in 1996 for the A-IADMK and a maximum of eighteen in 1998 for the same party. The DMK's lowest score was five in 1998; it had 17 in 1996 and twelve in 1999. Now in 2004 it almost reached the 1996 figure with a tally of sixteen seats. The DMK along with its junior Dravidian allies had deserted the National Democratic Alliance charging the BJP-led Government with having armed Jayalalitha with POTA (Prevention of Terrorism Act) to ride roughshod over her political rivals. It was a tragedy more than an irony; The DMK was a party to the NDA Government's action in putting the draconian POTA on the statute book. Vaiko Narayanswamy.who was a minister in the NDA Government, too, had supported POTA to fall a victim to it when Jayalalitha used the law vindictively to keep him in detention for over two years! Vaiko, incidentally, is a gem of a politician, forthright and outspoken, which cannot be said of either Jayalalitha or veteran Karunanidhi.

Even in Gujarat claimed to be a stronghold of the BJP, the party did not fare well. It won only 14 of the 26 Lok Sabha seats conceding the remaining 12 seats to the Congress party. In the 1999 general election, the BJP had won 19 of the 26 Gujarat seats while the Congress party had seven. The corresponding figures for the 1996 and 1998 elections respectively were ten and seven for the Congress party and 16 and 19 for the BJP. In other words, the BJP's performance was the worst since 1996. In the National Capital Region of Delhi where the BJP had held office until it bit the dust on the issue of the price onions in 1998, it lost six of the seven seats. It was largely due to complacency and lack of diligent electioneering. Many of the BJP's potential voters did not apparently cast their ballots as shown by the poor percentage of voting, less than 40. Of course these factors do not alter the fact that the Congress and its allies are in power

Meanwhile, the unavoidable delay in the publication of this book is being turned into a blessing in disguise by drawing on more recent publications like B.G.Deshmukh's memoirs, From *Poona to the Prime Minister's Office, A Cabinet Secretary Looks Back* (2003, Harper Collins, New Delhi, in collaboration with *India Today*). It throws revealing light on some not-so-redeeming aspects of Rajiv Gandhi's prime ministership, notably the Bofors business and Sonia Gandhi's role in it. Deshmukh's account is personalised with the accent on first person singular, highlighting his role in developments. Still, it has nuggets of information, which are relevant. He introduces the Bofors affair with a mention of the Italian connection. He writes:" Sometime in October 1986 one of the security officers at 7, Race Course Road (the prime minister's official residence) said two or three of them would be going to Italy within a couple of weeks for special training. I was rather upset as I had neither seen nor cleared that proposal but Rajiv Gandhi said this had been arranged by the Prime Minister's House and 'the party would bear the expenses.'

(Deshmukh was then principal secretary to the Prime Minister). "I was not at all happy as the security force was not for Rajiv Gandhi but for the Prime Minister of India and, therefore, arrangements for its training and its expenses should be borne by the government. Rajiv Gandhi agreed and asked (for) my advice). I said the training could be in Italy as already arranged but that the funds should be made available by the Intelligence Bureau and to maintain secrecy I would speak to the comptroller and auditor- general to accept whatever explanation was given by the Intelligence Bureau

When I met him again he said the Intelligence Bureau should not bear the expenditure, as it was not at all a happy situation that the Prime Minister's security arrangements had been taken away from it. I suggested that I would ask RAW (Research and Analysis Wing) to bear the expenditure from its secret funds. Rajiv Gandhi said that I should discuss and resolve the matter with Captain Satish Sharma. Satish Sharma said that Joshi, director of RAW, could speak to a certain Italian, whom he named, and settle the details. When I asked who he was he had a hearty laugh and said Joshi would know him. Joshi was more diplomatic and said that it might have escaped my memory that this person was Rajiv Gandhi's in-law. (sic). Joshi came to me after a week with a curious follow-up report. When his Geneva office (sic) asked the Italian gentleman to pick up the amount in US dollars he said that Joshi himself should make arrangements to bring the amount in Italian currency and deliver it in Italy. Joshi was not all happy with this, as it would entail carrying about a quarter of a million US dollars in Italian currency in a big suitcase, which was sure to invite trouble. I told Joshi I would clarify this. I told Rajiv Gandhi that the arrangement suggested was not acceptable, specially because the amount asked for was so large. He flushed and told me to forget the whole affair. Later I learnt that the Prime Minister's House (PMH) was asked to be more discreet with me. The security officers were not sent to Italy for training but an Italian expert came to India. (Of course, he became rather unpopular with the security force for he would throw his weight around). I also realised that in the Mughal-darbar-like functioning of the Gandhis I had committed the cardinal sin of cross-checking with the king himself the message he conveyed to me through his aides". (Pages 219-220).

There is apparently some confusion. Was the person described as Rajiv Gandhi's in-law Otavio Quatrrochi, quite notorious in the CBI cases? If so who was the Italian expert who threw his weight around? It was said in those days that Quattrochhi would barge into defence ministry offices and try to browbeat officials, especially mild-mannered S.K. Bhatnagar, the defence secretary.) Further, Deshmukh says the Italian contacted his headoffice in Geneva. It should have been Rome if the reference was to Quattrochi's company or Sweden if Bofors was meant.

Deshmukh's narrative continues: "In the HDW submarine case I was told that the West German defence ministry had intimated to the German defence supplier.the amount of commission that would be required to be paid in selling the defence equipment. The Latin American and African countries were in the bracket of 10 per cent and above whereas we were placed in the bracket of 5 to 10 per cent. Incidentally, this clearly shows how cynical developed countries are in selling their defence products. Of course, they are also not entirely innocent as is evident from the scandal of US aircraft manufacturers trying to bribe a member of the royalty from the Benelux countries." (The element of hypocrisy in this comment stands out. When a non-aligned nations conference demanded that the developed countries should contribute up to 5 per cent of their GDP to the developing countries a British diplomat in Delhi asked me whether it would be over and above the money collected by Indian politicians and others in defence transactions!)

After recalling the circumstances in which the HDW submarine deal with West Germany was struck in December 1981 (Rajiv had not yet succeeded his mother as prime minister then), Deshmukh's account says that "in the first week of April 1987 the defence ministry was informed by our ambassador in West Germany that the HDW shipyard at Kiel was finding it difficult to reduce the price of the two submarines which we wanted since 7 percent commission had to be paid to the agent who had been involved in the original purchase in 1981 and whose contract with the shipyard was still in force. The defence minister V.P. Singh seriously objected to this arrangement as by that time Rajiv Gandhi had already decided there should be no commission agent involved in defence purchases. V.P. Singh also thought that payment of commission in 1981 would attract provisions in our income-tax laws and foreign exchange regulations. He sent a note accordingly to the Prime Minister but at the same time ordered an inquiry and had a press note issued. This naturally led to a public outcry especially when Parliament was in session.

"V.P. Singh's action in giving publicity to the whole affair was not proper as payment of commission for defence purchases was not banned in 1981. If there was any question of tax avoidance or breach of foreign exchange regulations it should have been referred to the finance minister who incidentally happened to be the Prime Minister at that time. It was generally believed that V.P. Singh wanted to settle scores with the Prime Minister who had made him leave the ministry of finance." (It is not improbable, in the light of Vishwanath Pratap Singh's subsequent behaviour as short-time Prime Minister and since as a disgruntled politician that he might have wanted a cut in the booty. The author of Mandal misadventure who had driven the country to the brink of civil war —just to save his rickety gaddi — would be incapable of nothing.)

Pointing out that the practice of taking kickbacks on defence purchases began with Sanjay Gandhi, Deshmukh concedes that Indira Gandhi was a party to it during Sanjay's life time and later. He quotes from B.K. Nehru's memoirs —presumably *Nice Guys Finish Second* — of a dialogue between Nehru and Rajiv on the day after Sanjay Gandhi's funeral. "I asked Rajiv whether the money Sanjay had collected allegedly for the Congress was safe. He said all they found in the almirah of the Congress office was Rs. 20 lakhs. I asked him how much Sanjay had collected. He held his head in his hands and said 'crores and uncounted crores.' There was another quotation in that context from the autobiography of the former President, R.Venkataraman, about a courtesy call on him by J.R.D. Tata. It reads: "Commenting on Rajiv Gandhi's statement on Bofors Tata said It would be difficult to deny the receipt of commission by the Congress party, He felt that since 1980 (when Indira Gandhi returned to power after the collapse of the Janata Government) industrialists had not been approached for political contributions and that the general feeling amongst them was that the party was financed by commission on deals".

As a matter of fact, cashing in on defence contracts was very much the practice when up to the 1970's India bought large quantities of Soviet weapons (the country was virtually dependent on military hardware from the then Soviet Union and other 'socialist' countries.) Indian officials, mostly from the ministry of defence production, would get expensive gifts in the shape of cut glass products and other specialties of those countries. Similarly, when officials of those countries visited India for transactions in rupee trade they would be lavishly entertained by being wined, dined and provided other comforts – not always available to them in their respective home countries. In the process, Indian Communists got crumbs from the table, which were often sumptuous.

To revert to Deshmukh's memoirs, a relevant extract from it was about Rajiv Gandhi's flip-flop in calling the Bofors company functionaries to Delhi to brief members of the Joint Parliamentary Committee (JPC) set up primarily to cover up the matter. He first wanted them to come to Delhi for the purpose and then cancelled their visit. Deshmukh continues to say: "I had an uneasy feeling that the Prime Minister's Office knew the names of the recipients and had communicated them to the prime minister. One could only surmise that the beneficiaries could be the Congress party or a close relation or friend of the Prime Minister's family. In August when the appointment of the JPC was to be discussed in Parliament Rajiv Gandhi made a statement declaring that neither he nor any member of his family had received any consideration in the Bofors transactions. All of us were impressed by the suo moto statement that clearly reflected not only his honesty and integrity but also the conviction that his integrity was beyond doubt that his image was unnecessarily being tarnished. A cynic remarked that the family mentioned in his statement did not include Sonia's Italian family."

Further, about Rajiv Gandhi's governance style and his commitment to values, Deshmukh writes fairly candidly but with caveats giving the benefit of the doubt to the then prime minister. First about what Deshmukh calls 'soft communalism': "His (Rajiv's) secular credentials were impeccable. Yet he could not resist political advice to reverse his stand in the Shah Bano case. The Supreme Court had decreed that as a divorcee she should get alimony under relevant ordinary law and not under the Muslim Personal Law. However to appease the Muslim community his government introduced a bill in Parliament that in such cases the Muslim Personal Law would apply, thus overruling the judgment. In the case of the Babri masjid at Ayodhya the BJP and other members of the Sangh parivar campaigned that the Mughals built this by demolishing the Ram mandir on the site which is the birthplace of Lord Ram. They therefore wanted to demolish the masjid and erect a Ram mandir in its place. A court case was filed. A proposal was put forward that the foundation stone for the Ram mandir, that is *shilanyas*, may be performed on the undisputed portion of the land till the court decided the case. Rajiv Gandhi could not explain why he acquiesced at all in the opening of the Babri masjid in February 1986 for worship of the Hindu idols inside. That was the beginning of the Hindutva onslaught that definitively and completely engulfed the Congress. Rajiv Gandhi became a helpless bystander. One could only say that his political inexperience did not allow him to overrule his advisers and boldly withstand the communal onslaught. He was persuaded to permit the shilanyas but it only whetted the appetite of the communal forces."

(Laloo Yadav could not have written a more biased and half-baked account of the event. Deshmukh wants his readers to believe that Rajiv Gandhi was pure as driven snow in the Shah Bano and Babri masjid capers because he had allowed himself to be misled by his 'nameless' advisers. In the Shah Bano case the crux of the matter was overruling a Supreme Court judgment rendered twice, the second time by a Bench headed by Justice Krishna Iyer. The entire Muslim community was not agitated as claimed by Deshmukh; only the orthodox elements were up in arms against it and because they controlled the bulk votes of Muslims or what is called the Muslim vote bank Rajiv was scared. In fact, modern minded Muslims were upset by the Government's action in denying adequate protection for Muslim divorcees through the new law superseding the Supreme Court ruling. They were also unhappy at the resultant widening of the gulf between Muslims and others on gender matters.

On the Ram Janmabhoomi issue also, it was an open secret that the then chief minister of Uttar Pradesh, Narain Dutt Tewari, wanted the masjid gates to be opened for worship of the idols smuggled in about a decade earlier. The argument of the protagonists of mandir was that while no namaz was being performed at the Babri structure the idols in the makeshift temple were being worshipped. Narain Dutt's formula was for winning the election by appeasing both the communities. For that purpose, to balance the Shah Bano surrender to the Muslim orthodoxy he got Urdu made a second language in Uttar Pradesh. Then the opening of the masjid gates to allow worship of the idols inside. The civil case mentioned by Deshmukh was as old as the hills, since 1949 to be exact, and was over a property dispute between a mahant and a Sunni Waqf organisation. The Allahabad High Court had been sitting on it for decades because of the delicate nature of the subject of the dispute.

Most importantly, the BJP and its 'parivar' did not ask for demolition of the masjid. Theoretically they stood for construction of a Ram temple at the site of the Babri structure on the ground that there had been a temple there before Babar's representative replaced it with the mosque. They also claimed it was the birthplace of Lord Ram. Advani's *rathyatra* in September 1992 also was for building the temple there. Demolition of the Babri structure was a later development on the fateful sixth of December 1992. Vandals among tens of thousands of persons allowed into the area by complacent

Kalyan Singh who was the chief minister of UP then attacked and pulled down the historic structure. In the process, Kalyan Singh had violated his assurance to the Supreme Court and the National Development Council. He was, therefore, dismissed forthwith by the Narasimha Rao Government that had been caught napping. The massive central para-military forces made available to the State had remained unused. Only Laloo Yadav has charged Advani with culpability in the demolition of the Babri structure. The eyewitness account of the outrage by the then Delhi correspondent of TIME magazine and Girilal Jain's account of Advani breaking into tears as the structure came down disprove or at least dispute the charge implicitly contained in Deshmukh's account. The disputed and undisputed parts of the Ayodhya land are fallouts of an enactment by the Narasimha Rao Government in the wake of the Babri demolition. It provided for acquisition by the Union Government of 0.313 acres of land on which the Babri masjid had stood, besides the adjacent area of 67 acres. The VHP had then come into the picture by challenging the land acquisition in the Supreme Court.in 1993. It claimed to be the owner of the land while doing it. At that time it was made clear from available documents that the VHP was only in possession of the land and was not its owner. The Sunni Waqf Board also challenged the acquisition but limited its challenge to the area on which the Babri masjid had stood. The Supreme Court disposed of the matter pretty promptly on 24 October 1994. The majority judgement of the court, with which the former Chief Justice, Justice A. N. Verma, was associated, drew the line qualitatively between 0.3i3 acres of land on which the masjid was sited and the adjacent area. (Justice A.N.Varma became chairperson of the National Human Rights Commission after retirement from the Bench.) They came to be called 'disputed' and 'undisputed ' land respectively. A subsequent court ruling and judicial clarifications had said that the so-called shilanyas could be performed on the 'undisputed' land.

A few more nuggets from Deshmukh's book about Rajiv Gandhi's governance style. "He reshuffled his council of ministers twenty-two times in thirty-nine months in office, a virtual merry-go-round in some of the ministries. There were more than three external affairs ministers; in the home ministry there were three cabinet ministers and seven ministers of state; in the commerce ministry two cabinet ministers and five ministers of state. This of course took a heavy toll on efficient government working and naturally created a powerful PMO and a coterie of strong bureaucrats who had worked their way into the Prime Minister's confidence."

An otherwise polite and polished person, even if wanting in formal education beyond the Doon School and training for being a civilian aircraft pilot, Rajiv had become notorious for publicly humiliating senior civil servants and ministerial colleagues outside the coterie. In the words of Deshmukh, " Rajiv Gandhi was more inclined towards suave advisers and officials who came from public schools, could write and speak good English and had a gloss both in appearance and presentation. He was impressed by short-term results and impatient when an officer tried to present a long-term strategy that inherently had to be a slow and steady one.... Something like this happened in the case of two senior civil servants, C.S. Sastry, agriculture secretary and D. Bandopadhyay, rural development secretary. An audio-visual presentation was arranged by them for Rajiv Gandhi. But he was not satisfied either with their technique of presentation or the contents. Bandopadhyay was shattered when Rajiv Gandhi said at the end, 'since I have no information I have no questions to ask.' When Sastri could not answer a question on an unrelated subject he asked him his State cadre and when he replied Andhra Pradesh, Rajiv said sarcastically, 'And how would you like to go back there.' Both secretaries behaved correctly and Sastri said he would 'not mind going back.'... Another well-known instance was his unexpected announcement at a press conference on returning from a visit to Pakistan that there would be a new foreign secretary. We were all left dumbfounded." The reference was to A.P. Venkateswaran who later joined the Centre for Policy Research as a professor.

Electoral reforms had been a topic of much discussion for several years before Rajiv Gandhi became the Prime Minister. Much groundwork had been done when Ramakrishna Hedge prepared a treatise on the subject for public discussion. State financing of elections was one of the remedies suggested for the play of money power in electoral contests. Over to Deshmukh again for Rajiv Gandhi's reaction to the idea: "Why should I give funds to the opposition parties to fight me, by which he meant the Congress as the party in power owned public funds." (Pages 174-176). Which reminds one of U.S. Deputy Secretary of State, Richard Armitage, meeting with Sonia Gandhi. Armitage was in Delhi to sell the American line on the Comprehensive Test Ban Treaty (CTBT) in the early days of the NDA Government in 1999. After serious negotiations with Jaswant Singh who was then the external affairs minister and a meeting with the Prime Minister, Atal Behari Vajpayee, Armitage had to call on Sonia Gandhi because she was the Leader of the Opposition in the Lok Sabha. Sonia did not have a ghost of an idea what CTBT was. As usual, after preening herself and wearing a designer sari and Gucci shoes she was ready for photo opportunity with the visiting dignitary. After the battery of TV cameras withdrew Armitage opened with an introduction on the US position on the CTBT. But finding the blank looks of the hostess he quietly veered the conversation to Gucci shoes and wondered why India with its highly developed footwear industry would not opt to produce similar shoes!

Finally, Rajiv Gandhi's attitude to opposition parties was overbearing and intolerant. According to Deshmukh, "his opinion about Jyoti Basu, chief minister of West Bengal, may not have been so unfavourable but he had little respect for N.T. Rama Rao, chief minister of Andhra Pradesh, Chaudhary Devi Lal, chief minister of Haryana, or Karunanidhi of Tamil Nadu whose DMK party completely routed the Congress in the State elections. At National Development Council (NDC) meetings there would be heated exchange of words and sometimes unpleasantness too... At one NDC meeting the unpleasantness reached such an extent that the opposition chief ministers walked out. Highly upset, Rajiv Gandhi asked the officers of those States to leave the meeting as well". (Page 175). I don't know whether it is a sign of insecurity or absence of urbanity. Even Indira Gandhi never behaved in that fashion towards her political opponents. Of course, there was no question of Nehru being rude to political opponents because primarily there was not much of an opposition to the Congress then and there was no opposition chief minister after E.M.S. Namboodiripad was sent packing as chief minister of Travancore-Cochin at Indira Gandhi's instance.

In the chapter, Gangotri of Gangrene, we have looked at some leaders, notably Chandra Shekhar, Madhu Limaye, Vishwanath Pratap Singh, Raj Narain et al, who pretending to be champions of 'secularism' lined their pockets, and /or put the country back by decades promoting hypocrisy and cynicism. A recent addition to the gang of five is Laloo Prasad Yadav, who puts all of them in the shade. Before recalling Laloo's metamorphosis from a student activist in the 1974 Jayaprakash Narayan's movement against corruption in Bihar to perhaps the most corrupt politician in contemporary India, let us look at a Ranchi report of 18 October 2004 citing details of the fodder scam in which Laloo is the principal accused. A fellow accused, Dipesh Chandak, disclosed in the court of CBI special judge, A.K. Sengupta, that Laloo "was paid Rs. 55-60 crores from Bihar Government treasuries during the early 1990s." Chandak had turned approver in the case, which related to payments from Ranchi treasury only. There were other payments from Patna treasury also. Chandak owned a fodder supply company "that existed only on paper." Chandak admitted, "he had been close to the alleged kingpin" of the scam, Dr. S.B. Sinha, the then assistant director of animal husbandry, "and had knowledge of the functioning of the department during the scam. He alleged that Rs.15 crore had been paid to (Laloo) Prasad in two instalments before the 1995 assembly polls in Bihar." (Published by *The Hindu*, 18 October 2004)

Laloo Yadav who contested and won the Lok Sabha election in 1977 retained his seat in the 1980 elections as well. He then moved to the Bihar State Assembly and became chief minister in 1991. He was then a State leader of Vishwanath Pratap Singh's Janata Dal. Chandak named Rajo Singh, Indra Dev Prasad Verma, Bhola Ram Toofan, Rajan Yadav and Maulana Asami as State politicians who were Laloo Yadav's accomplices in receiving bribes. On Sinha's direction, a supplier of fodder and medicine, M.S. Bedi had given Rs. 50 lakhs to former chief minister and another fodder scam accused, Jagannath Mishra. That was after Sinha had returned from Australia where he had gone for kidney transplant. Chandak also admitted that he and his wife had accompanied Sinha on the trip. Incidentally, the fodder scam came to light in 1996 before the BJP assumed office. Deve Gowda was Janata Dal Prime minister and along with him, other Janata Dal leaders, notably Madhu Dandavate and Surendra Mohan, asked Laloo Yadav to resign as chief minister until the CBI court investigated the corruption charges and exonerated him. Laloo refused to oblige and formed his own Rashtriya Janata Dal (RJD). When he was sent to judicial custody he made his wife Rabri Devi chief minister and started running the government on her behalf.

That was about ten years ago. To this day, November 2004, the trial has not even started in earnest. During this period, Laloo has been going from strength to strength; he was a member of the Rajya Sabha until May 2004 and now is railway minister in Manmohan Singh's Government, having been 'elected' to the Lok Sabha from, not one but two, Bihar constituencies. Earlier he had been to Pakistan as the *de facto* or *de jure*, depending on Mani Shankar Iyer's acceptance, leader of a delegation of MPs. During the Pakistan visit, he was reported to have fascinated no less a person that Pervez Musharraf and won the hearts of the common people as a 'true symbol' of Indian democracy! As stated, Laloo's political life started with Jayaprash Narayan's movement against corruption in Bihar in 1974 in the run up to the 1975 'internal emergency.' That was the time when "J.P" sought the help of the RSS in the agitation. Remember Raghu Rai's living picture of a police lathi descending on "J.P." s head with a RSS volunteer trying to ward off the blow by exposing his own head. Laloo, like other students, joined the "J.P" movement, as a 'secular' historian called the resistance to the 1975 'emergency' with a view to belittling its political and democratic significance. Laloo did not apparently mind the RSS in his company. He could not have also failed to notice that the Communists were with the regime. They organised an anti-fascist conference in Patna at which an effigy of "J.P" was hanged.

As stated, Laloo was elected to the Lok Sabha in the 1977 general election. He had by then completed his studies to be a lawyer but there was not much evidence of his later-day eloquence. He was also quiescent during Madhu Limaye's campaign to purge the Jan Sanghis from the Janata conglomerate. He joined the Janata Dal – formed by the marriage of Ajit Singh's Lok Dal with Chandra Shekhar's Janata Party to contest the assembly elections and became chief minister of Bihar in 1990. He remained in the post till 1997 even after the fodder scam came to light in 1996. Earlier, following L.K. Advani's rath yatra in September 1992 Laloo as chief minister stopped him in Bihar and formally got him arrested. He was also effective in curbing the parivar volunteers from provoking communal violence by their move to collect bricks from Muslim holy places to build a proposed Ram temple at Ayodhya. He rightly won national attention by his firm action. As a result Bihar escaped from communal violence following the demolition of the Babri masjid in December 1992. Mulayam Singh Yadav in U.P. also prevented mob attacks on the masjid earlier, with the parivar charging him with committing mayhem.

During his first stint as chief minister, Laloo was a frequent visitor to Delhi. His darbars at Bihar Bhavan became popular with journalists who were invited for sumptuous meals and also given rich presents. It seems Bihar political leaders have a flair for doling out gifts to press correspondents. One of Laloo's predecessors, Lalit Narain Mishra, had gifted suit lengths of imported cloth (a rarity in the early 1970's) to journalists who unknowingly wore suits of the same coloured and textured cloth for a function, betraying the source of the material. The expression, suit -length journalism, came into use then.

But Laloo's visits to the hair-cutting saloon at Ashoka Hotel were 'historic'. He would rain hundred rupee notes — in those days when money was not so cheap – all round, not merely to the barber who attended on him. If you happened to be a fellow customer at that time you could have had it. All the barbers would flock round the great man leaving you to yourself. Laloo has done it more recently also. During his pilgrimage in the south with wife Rabri Devi and their nine children he showered currency notes like manna at the temples he prayed in. Greatness had already been thrust on him as a ministerial colleague of upright Manmohan Singh. His 'popularity' in Kerala and Tamil Nadu matches it. Earlier, there were reports of his visits incognito to villages in Bihar when he similarly distributed money asking the recipients to have 'jal pani'

How does Laloo Yadav manage to avoid facing trial in any of the many criminal cases pending against him? The answer is gifted lawyers like Kapil Sibal with adequate cash for servicing court decisions or indecision. Sibal, for instance, was a member of the Rajya Sabha from Bihar – courtesy Laloo Yadav — until he won the Lok Sabha seat from Chandni Chowk in May 2004. The irony is that now Laloo Yadav is a senior cabinet minister holding the crucial Railways portfolio while Sibal is just a minister of state in charge of science and technology, which are Greek and Latin to him. No less importantly, what may be called networking among the accused in many of the scams and criminal cases. They are all Laloo Yadav's friends if not chelas. They are resourceful in their own way but together they are deadly. Like another minister in the Manmohan Singh Government, Taslimuddin, MP from Kishenganj, even when sent to prison they manage to travel to Delhi without even formal bail from the court. The court might tear its hair out but that was that!

No less importantly, winning an election from jail or when facing criminal charges is an effective prophylactic. Which court will have the will to pursue cases against MPs and ministers? Also, the CBI is under the Union Home Ministry and even if Shivraj Patil may not exert himself in favour of Laloo Yadav the CBI top brass will have to be circumspect in dealing with powerful ministers. Laloo Yadav's party with 26 MPs is the second largest in Dr. Manmohan Singh's coalition government (after the Congress party). The Communists and their allies are not coalition partners but support the Government from 'outside'. Laloo had even laid claim to the Home portfolio on that basis and the railway ministry was only a sop to him. Last but not least, electronic voting machines or manual balloting; Laloo has mastered the art of rigging the procedure. Lathi-wielding muscle men, his fellow crusaders for secularism, would chase away the opponents from the polling stations so that they could stuff the ballots in the box or ring the electronic voting machine in different names.

Next to muscle power comes money power as a resource for winning elections. A study based on the affidavits filed by candidates who contested the 2004 general election by a 'think tank' called Public Affairs Centre of Bangalore showed that over 50 per cent of the MPs have assets of over 50 lakhs each, " with an MP, on an average, possessing declared assets worth over Rs. 1.64 crores." The study was by Dr. Samuel Paul and Prof. M. Vivekananda. The operative word is declared because not all declarations are fool proof. For instance, Sonia Gandhi's assertion of having secured a diploma from Cambridge University (UK) in a subject which does not figure in the university curriculum and her mention of her landed property in Italy as practically of no monetary significance. The first assertion was in the *Who's who* of members published by the Lok Sabha secretariat and, therefore, not actionable, like the blurb on the jacket of a book. As for land prices in Italy who has double-checked them? It is relevant in this connection that the practice of paying from the taxpayer's money the constituency fund of Rs. 2 crores annually to MPs has been a source of some monetary substance to them. They are definitely better off than their predecessors are ten- twenty years ago when many MPs eked out a hand-to-mouth existence. Whether this has contributed to greater probity among lawmakers is a matter of opinion. Also, a whole row of buildings from India Gate to practically Man Singh Road has gone into trusts named after Indira Gandhi and Rajiv Gandhi and managed by Sonia and her family.

Reverting to the study reported by *The Hindu* (08 October 2004), the Congress party "has the largest proportion of crorepathi (multi-millionaire) MPs, 45 per cent, with its members accounting for more than 50 per cent of the assets of all the members." Considering that the Congress party has 145 members just seven more than the BJP, it makes a qualitative difference as well. But the Congress party had contested 417 seats or 43 more than the BJP. The study does not seem to have factored this input. Further, " the largest proportion of MPs with substantial agricultural assets are found in Laloo Yadav's RJD (43.5 per cent) followed by Mayavathi's BSP (Bahujan Samaj Party) 35.3 per cent." It is very good news that the Bahujans have crossed the poverty line and over a third of them who contested the elections are well off in terms of rural assets. Also, "the average value of assets owned by SC/ST (Scheduled Caste/ Scheduled

Tribes) MPs at Rs. 58 lakhs is much lower than the average asset value of other MPs." The study also sheds light on the incidence of criminality among MPs, which is a reflection on the muscle power they command. "RJD leads in the proportion of criminal cases with 43.5 per cent. There are no criminal cases registered against 83 per cent of Congress MPs and 80 per cent of the BJP MPs. There is a concentration of criminally charged MPs in a few States, notably Bihar, Uttar Pradesh, Madhya Pradesh and Jharkhand which account for 50 per cent of all MPs with criminal cases that could attract severe penalties of five years' imprisonment or more." Publicisation of the data has not had much effect on the MPs or their leaders. As with the fodder scam cases against Laloo Yadav the crux of the matter is the long arm of the law catching up with the accused. It is a pity that our criminal justice system has not been equal in wits to the accused. Perhaps it will have a salutary effect if upright leaders like Manmohan Singh and Atal Behari Vajpayee openly disown such persons!

Now a subject not much touched in the book, namely school textbooks and their qualitative analysis. The former HRD Minister, Prof. Murli Manohar Joshi, has been the butt of sustained criticism by 'secular' scholars and laymen and the favourite target of sharp criticism in the newspapers and the commercial TV networks. He was said to have got school textbooks, especially in history, rewritten with a view to purging them .of what he alleged was 'non-nationalist' bias. It is a long, long story with Arun Shourie exposing several eminent historians taking hefty sums of money as advance for writing textbooks and not fulfilling the commitment. Arun, as a Rajya Sabha MP had diligently collected the data through questions in the House and other official sources. The celebrities named by him did not respond to his charge presumably because it was based on official data but they zeroed in on Prof. Joshi when he became the HRD Minister in the Vajpayee-led Government.

Prof. Joshi's was an ideological approach as he called it. His targets were Lord Maucaulay who introduced English teaching in India during the East India Company days and Karl Marx whose philosophy, he thought, influenced the writing of the earlier textbooks. In the case of textbooks for junior level and higher secondary students ideology would not have much relevance. If Prof. Romila Thapar's critique of Prof. Joshi is an index it boiled down to acknowledging the contribution of the Mughals and other Muslim rulers during the 150 years they spread their sway over mostly north India. According to Prof. Thapar, the Mughal rulers, including such a bigoted emperor as Aurangzeb were not totally negative in their approach to promotion of India's 'composite' culture. But Prof. Joshi would not buy the idea of composite culture itself. He was for putting the clock back to pre-Mughal times when perhaps India was a collection of village republics or principalities. This broadbrush treatment of the controversy that festered for six years of the BJP-led government does not do justice to the subject but here the concern is with the political aspect of the so-called intellectual debate. Not many of the actual users of the textbooks, teachers and students, cared to join the debate. Instead the accent was on the personnel of the NCERT (National Council for Educational Research and Training) and other Government institutions in charge of education.

As it happened, Prof. Joshi was defeated in the 2004 general election to the Lok Sabha from his home constituency of Allahabad by the combined exertions of aggrieved academia and his political opponents, with the Communists in the vanguard. (Incidentally, the subtle distinction between the expressions 'Communist' and 'Leftist' is relevant in political debate. The word 'Leftist' has the intellectual aura of an alternate system of socio-political organisation whereas 'Communist' stands for an advocate of Statism .In the days of Soviet supremacy in the Communist world it represented an adjunct of the Soviet establishment. After the Sino-Soviet rift the CPI (M) became the pro-Chinese version while the CPI continued as a pro-Soviet instrument. After the Gorbachev period and the disintegration of the former Soviet Union, one cannot really place the ideological position of the CPI. In India, however, it is the poor cousin – older in age but poorer in pulling power – of the CPI (M). Both in West Bengal and Kerala the CPI (M) dominates the so-called Left Front with the CPI, the Revolutionary Socialist Party – almost a museum piece - and Forward Bloc (Marxist), also extinct everywhere except in West Bengal, as its hangers-on.

The origin of the expression 'Leftist' – as distinct from moderates and conservatives – is traced to the accidental seating of Deputies when the French Revolutionary National Assembly met in 1789 in a semicircular chamber. The progressives sat to the left of the Chair, the moderates in the centre opposite to the Chair and the conservatives to the right. Professor M. Venkatarangaiya, doyen of Indian political scientists, who was holding the prestigious Sir Pherozeshah Mehta Chair of Political Science at Bombay University, in his Introduction to my booklet, *Leaders of the Left*, discussed the pros and cons of characterising M.N.Roy as a Leftist. In that connection, he cited the "curious fact about Leftism in India. It is the split between the Socialist and Communist wings. The gulf separating these two sections seems to be much wider than that separating them from the parties of the Right and the Centre. It is this that threatens to make the world an arena of civil war. The fact of the matter is that a party, which is labelled Leftist, is not Leftist in all spheres of life. The Communists are Leftists in the economic sphere but they worship despotism and dictatorship in the political sphere. In matters of government there is nothing to distinguish them from the Czars of Russia. It is because of this that the Socialists who continue to cherish faith in democratic liberty part company with them." Incidentally, in 18th century Europe the legislatures were mostly housed in semi-circular chambers as distinct from the parliaments of the British Commonwealth that met in rectangular chambers. It is not known how our Lok Sabha chamber is semi-circular although it is a legacy of the British period. But the Central Hall where the Central Assembly would meet in the pre-Independence days is more rectangular than circular. The Ayub Hall in Rawalpindi where the Pakistan national assembly would meet in the 1960's — when Field Marshal Ayub Khan was experimenting with "basic democracy" —was not semi-circular either.

Reverting to the Communist flair for sailing under a Leftist umbrella, I vividly recall an open debate in Bombay in the late 1940s between my friend and mentor, Indra Sen. and wife of Rajni Patel, who was heading the Bombay Congress party organisation. Rajni was close to Indira Gandhi and a source of funds. He got the Bombay Master Plan changed thoroughly to enable property owners to grab public land and land set apart for non-building purposes. In the process, he set the style for making today's Mumbai a metropolis of slums. He would collect substantial sums of money, often running into crores of rupees, from the beneficiaries of his actions, while Mrs. Patel (her first name was Bakula)— was a crypto-Copmmunist. She would try to help the Comunists in their efforts, in vain, to whitewash their record in the Quit India movement. In a public debate in Bombay Indra Sen made her concede that Communists 'are not Leftists.' After the passing away of Indrajit Gupta and Mohit Sen (of the Dange faction) the CPI has been no match to the group headed by Harkishan Singh Surjit and Yechuri Sitaram with his striking record in organising the students of JNU as a Gangotri of "Leftists."

While Prof. Murli Manohar Joshi was, and still is, pilloried for his alleged saffronisation of history teaching, the curriculum of primary schools in Pakistan is replete with Islamist concepts of jihad (holy war against non-believers) and *shahadat*, or martyrdom. (The belief is that participants in the holy war will attain martyrdom if slain in battle). Najm Seth's Lahore publication, *Friday Times*, which enjoys a reputation for rational opinions, has shed light on the state of primary education in Pakistan in a recent article entitled "An endangered species, Who is going to save the moderate Pakistanis." The article says the National Curriculum of the Ministry for Social Studies for Classes I-V "formally endorses the following 'learning outcome': Recognise the importance of *jihad* in every sphere of life." Under the heading 'Evaluation', the officially certified direction to teachers and textbook writers is 'to judge their spirits while making speeches on *jihad*, Muslim History and Culture' while the 'affective objective' is 'concepts of ideology of Pakistan, Muslim Ummah and *jihad*.' Quoting Pakistan's Economic Survey 2003-04, the weekly said there were 17.4 million children who were attending primary schools, while about three million study in the 20,000 madrassas which churn out 40,000 graduates each year." The article was reproduced in *The Hindu* of 31 October 2004.

To most lay persons like you and me this may sound like double Dutch but the thrust is clear that the coming generations of Pakistanis will be staunch believers in what is loosely called Islamist philosophy. In the 1960s during a sojourn in what was then West Pakistan I noticed that Pakistani history books talked of six centuries of Pakistani history when its greatest emperor, Akbar, ruled over India! When grown up, not all Pakistanis might subscribe to the approach but the meaning is clear that non-Muslim India has again to be conquered. That was during the Ayub period, long before Zia-ul-Huque had introduced his idea of making Pakistan an Islamic State. More recently, in the early 1990s the Hurriyat leader, Syed Ali Shah Geelani, educated me in the Islamic idea that Muslims cannot accept non-Muslim Indian rule. He was fair enough to say that it is for the Muslims of India to decide their course of action but Kashmir cannot live with Indian rule. This, I think, is called the concept of *Nizam-e-Mustafa*.

It will be both appropriate and necessary, writing in late November 2004, to look at the first six months' record of the Manmohan Singh Government. That the curse of star-crossedness continues to haunt our unfortunate country hits you in the eye. First, contrary to convention and recommendations of the administrative reforms commission headed by K.Santanam in the 1950s and later by a similar committee headed by Morarji Desai, the prime minister and at least three key ministers, those holding the portfolios of home, external affairs, HRD, power, justice and law are from the Rajya Sabha. Of the key ministries, only the defence and finance ministers are from the Lok Sabha. There cannot be a worse disrespect for the House that votes supplies as they say in Westminster jargon. Which brings to mind the embarrassing situation in 1966 when Indira Gandhi succeeded Lal Bahadur Shastri as prime minister. She was a member of the Rajya Sabha.and so could not stay in the Lok Sabha when the House divided on money bills and/or other legislation. The rule is that when the division bell rings non-members should be 'ejected' from the House. That is why the division bell, as distinct from quorum bell, rings for a longer duration and also sounds shriller. Before the House divides, the Chair reminds non-members to leave the chamber and asks the watch ward staff the clear the lobbies but vis-à-vis Indira Gandhi Dr.Ram Manohar Lohiia and his fellow Socialist MPs — less than a handful in number – would chase her out shouting "out, out." The purpose was to humiliate her and rub in the fact that she was not a member of the Lok Sabha.

More recently, P.V. Narasimha Rao was not a member of either House when he became Prime Minister. He wanted to retire from parliamentary politics in 1991 when Rajiv Gandhi was assassinated and his widow was biding her time regrouping her supporters. The Congress party drafted Narasimha Rao to step into the breach. So within six months of his assumption of office he contested a by-election to the Lok Sabha from Nandyal (Rayalaseema) in his home State of Andhra Pradesh. The Telugus voted massively to elect their fellow-Telugu (*mana vadu* in Telugu or our man) to the Lok Sabha by a huge majority so that he could continue to be Prime Minister. That was the first time the Telugus had a chance to vote their man to occupy the highest political office in the country and they used the opportunity with gusto.

By the way, of the thirteen prime ministers the country has had to date, seven are from Uttar Pradesh (Nehru, Lal Bahadur, Indira Gandhi, Rajiv Gandhi, Vishwanath Pratap Singh, Chandra Shekhar and Atal Behari Vajpayee), one each from Gujarat (Morarji Desai) Karnataka (H.D. Deve Gowda) and Andhra Pradesh (Narasimha Rao) and two from Punjab, actually Pakistan Punjab of pre-partition period, (Inder Kumar Gujral and Manmohan Singh). Of these Charan Singh and Chandra Shekhar owed their elevation to manipulation. They ducked facing Parliament, while Manmohan Singh is dubbed by the BJP and other Oposition parties as 'selected' and not elected prime minister.

An 'iffy' caveat is in order here. If instead of Narasimha Rao Pranab Mukherjee had become prime minister after Rajiv Gandhi's assassination in 1991, he would have at least striven to eliminate the dynasty. Narasimha Rao tried to distance the family from office by introducing internal democracy into the Congress party and going in for organisational elections but was ultimately outmanoeuvred. He tried to finesse his way to the objective but pitted against him was the 'gang of five' (Arjun Singh, Natwar Singh, Shivraj Patil, Mani Shankar Iyer and Captain Satish Sharma. plus the family's war chest in the possession of Sonia Gandhi. In 1984 following Indira Gandhi's assassination the parliamentary board of the Congress parliamentary party had to endorse President Giani Zail Singh's action in naming Rajiv Gandhi prime minister. Rajiv was not the leader of the Congress parliamentary party then. Pranab opposed the move, which was endorsed by Narasimha Rao. Pranab was then handicapped by not being a Lok Sabha member. He is a Lok Sabha member now while the whole lot of them including Manmohan Singh are in the Rajya Sabha, as already noted. If Pranab had demurred to the extent of defying Sonia Gandhi he could have reopened the bone of contention about Sonia Gandhi's suitability to lead the party and thus becoming eligible to be prime minister. He could then team up with Sharad Pawar and others. As in 1969, if there were a split in the party which faction would have prevailed is anybody's guess. This is not wishful thinking or speculation. Pranab is visibly unhappy with the Congress party putting itself at the mercy of the Communists and their satellites — the so-called Leftists –because of the political compulsions in his home State of West Bengal. No Congress party leader of stature is happy with surrendering the State to the Communists and also teaming up with them at the Centre. Also, Pranab.had aspired to be home minister while remaining leader of the Lok Sabha in the present Manmohan Singh ministerial set-up but has been palmed off with the defence portfolio, held by George Fernandes in the NDA Government, Mulayam Singh Yadav held the portfolio in the United Front Governments in the late 1990s. The most high-profile holder of the portfolio in the Governments of Indira Gandhi and Morarji Desai was Jagjivan Ram, who was not number two in the team. By the way, was Sonia Gandhi's great act of 'renunciation' due to such apprehensions?

To get back to the record of the Manmohan Singh Government, on the face of it, the rate of inflation has been hovering between seven and eight percent since the Government took over in May 2004. It was near eight percent in November 2004. One of the contributory factors was Government inaction in the face of the ever rising crude oil price. The trend had begun early in the year but the outgoing NDA Government (as it turned out to be) could not deal with the problem for fear of losing the election and because the election commission keeps the country without a functioning government during the operation of the so-called model code of conduct. This year, the model code madness lasted nearly six months, an absurdity. As P. Chidambaram admitted while addressing the economic editors' conference in New Delhi on 18 November 2004, the inflation rate had never crossed the 4 per cent mark during the six odd years of the NDA Government. He also pointed out that cutting down levies on oil imports upset the budget calculation of revenue. Even if he tried to rationalise the decline in the expected GDP growth this year by saying that the eight percent growth last year was against the low base of four percent in the previous year, he could not cover up the virtual stagnation in the economic sphere since the present Government took over. The other alibis of drought and late onset of monsoon – trotted out by Dr. Manmohan Singh himself — also do not wash. For instance, the NDA Government's six years in office was marked by one year of drought, two successive visitations of floods, one of which ravaged Orissa beyond belief, plus the devastating Gujarat earthquake. (The Congress party critics of the NDA only harp on the Gujarat killings of 2002 to the omission of non-man-made calamities). More interestingly, Chidambaram's 1996 surrender to the Communists on the recommendations of the fifth pay commission continues to haunt him. He was finance minister then and had selectively implemented the commission recommendations at the dictates of the Communists. The salaries and allowances of Government employees at the Center (and in the States as a fall out) were steeply raised but the commission recommendation that the staff be progressively pruned was given the go by. At a conference of finance ministers in the middle of November 2004, the States demanded that the Centre should make up their fiscal deficit on account of that Tughlakian decision.

More striking were the Government's forays into foreign policy, especially India's relations with Pakistan and China. What Vajpayee and his colleagues had achieved in this respect will live in history even if the Manmohan Government tries to black it out. Vis-à-vis Pakistan the 6th January 2004 joint declaration by Atalji and Musharraf was a land mark because by it Pakistan has renounced its demand for application of the U.N. Security Council resolutions of the 1950s and also committed itself not to allow its territory or that under its control for terrorist activities against India, including their intrusion into Jammu and Kashmir and the rest of the country. It was a brief but very clear-cut joint declaration. In return India agreed to enter into meaningful negotiations with Pakistan on all outstanding bilateral issues, including Jammu and Kashmir. The joint declaration had not characterised Jammu and Kashmir as 'the core issue', nor did it say that the Kashmiris would be a 'third party to the dispute.'

Natwar Singh, brought out of the wood work by Sonia Gandhi to be the external affairs minister of the new government, opened his innings with a thoughtless reference to the 1972 Simla Agreement between Indira Gandhi and Zulfiqar Ali Bhutto in the wake of the 1971 Bangladesh war and the loss of its eastern wing by Pakistan. Pakistan's reaction was instantaneous and angry. General Musharraf called ex-prime minister Atal Behari Vajpayee in New Delhi to complain about what he thought was unilateral changing of the framework agreed to by the two countries in the January 2004 joint declaration. Normally even in presidential systems, succeeding governments start with maintenance of continuity in foreign relations before trying to build on it. But not Natwar Singh, whose pride and prejudice put him back in the 1960s.

After getting a rap on the knuckles from the prime minister, Natwar Singh piped down and tried to cover up his folly by saying that the new Government stood by the January 2004 joint declaration along with earlier Simla Agreement and the Lahore accord between Mian Nawaz Sharif and Vajpayee. Musharraf would not touch with a barge poll the Simla and Lahore accords to which civilian governments in Pakistan were parties. But he was mollified enough not to press the point at that time. Compounding the lapse, when Dr. Manmohan Singh met General Musharraf in New York in October 2004 on the sidelines of the U.N. General Assembly session the Prime Minister omitted to recall Musharraf's commitment on cross-border terrorism, made to Vajpayee in writing in January 2004. He just agreed to resumption of talks on Kashmir.

To make the most of India's half-baked conduct of its relations with Pakistan General Musharraf proposed demarcation of seven territorial zones in Jammu and Kashmir, including the Kashmir territory under Pakistan's occupation but leaving out what are called northern territories of Gilgit, Hunza, Nagar etc. According to the Musharraf plan, which he later said was not a formal proposal for India-Pakistan negotiations at different levels, the demarcated areas would be ultimately brought under India-Pakistan joint control or a United Nations administration. When Dr. Manmohan Singh said India would not stand for another partition of its territory, the Pakistan external affairs minister, Shaukat Aziz, chided him saying that such statements upset Pakistan. He further complained that Dr. Manmohan Singh was going back on his stand at the bilateral talks with Musharraf in New York! One is at a loss to know what the economist Prime Minister had said to the Pakistan President and how his external affairs minister had briefed him. But the fat will be in the fire sooner rather than later. Already Dr. Manmohan Singh himself had to describe stoppage of cross-border terrorism as Musharraf's commitment to Vajpayee implicitly admitting that he had not dwelt on it in his dialogue with the Pakistan head of State. But it sticks in the throats of other Congress party stalwarts to say so openly. The newspapers that make a song and dance about open diplomacy have not cared to question Dr. Manmohan Singh pointedly on the subject. (By the way, Inder Kumar Gujral as Prime Minister briefly in 1997 was perhaps the first Indian head of Government to visit Pakistan frequently and establish personal rapport with Mian Nawaz Sharif who was his Pakistani counterpart then. The Government spin doctors would build it up as growing India-Pakistan *bon homie*, even if Gujral would confine himself to recall in public the Urdu poetry (*shairie*) they mutually enjoyed in Lahore. It later turned out that Gujral's personal diplomacy was more poetry centred that real politick. Similarly, one would surmise that the good doctor, Manmohan Singh, might have been singing paeans of praise of his leader Sonia Gandhi because General Musharraf would not be interested in high economics.

Towards China also, Natwar Singh started his dialogue by recalling Rajiv Gandhi's visit to Beijing, in the middle 1980s! After that, P.V. Narasimha Rao, as Congress Prime Minister — though not of the family — had visited China and the Chinese leaders were also in our country. The former Prime Minister, Atal Behari Vajpayee, had established contact with Chinese leaders in Europe as well as in China when he visited that country. He also succeeded to put on a fast political track the dragging negotiations on Sino-Indian border demarcation. Ultimately, he prevailed upon China formally to recognise the fact of Sikkim being a part of India. Commonsense would suggest that the successor government would pick up the thread at that point but hubris stood in Natwar Singh's way. Further, J.N. (Mani) Dixit, a former foreign secretary, who has replaced Brijesh Mishra as Government's security adviser is a seasoned diplomat. He does not have to play second fiddle to the likes of Natwar Singh even if he, too, (Natwar Singh) belonged to the Indian Foreign Service long ago. I have known Mani Dixit since the mid-seventies especially when I was PIO and he was joint secretary and head of the XP (external publicity) section. As secretary of Indian Council of Cultural Relations, (ICCR), he did remarkable work in fomenting relations with the anti-apartheid movement in South Africa and educated our schoolboys and girls about the South African situation. Socialist leader, Asoka Mehta, who was close to the then external affairs minister, Atal Behari Vajpayee, spoke highly of Mani to me. I congratulated Mani Dixit when he joined the Congress party saying that the party needed somebody like him to guide it on foreign relations. That was before the likes of Natwar Singh were brought out of the woodwork and Sonia Gandhi assumed *de facto* control of the Government. So I was surprised when, without any provocation, Dixit delivered himself of high praise, almost flattery, of Sonia Gandhi. Apparently that is the new Government culture and Manmohan Singh repeatedly lauding the qualities of head and heart of Sonia Gandhi was on account of it. But even he, apparently, has not pursued with the Chinese leadership the second territorial matter of acknowledging Arunachal Pradesh in the northeast as part of India.

When the border dispute between China and us broke out as a military conflict in 1962 the skirmishes started in the Ladakh region with India taken by surprise about China building a road into Tibet through the Aksai Chin plateau. Chinese border guards saw Indian patrols in the area and asked them to leave the territory. When the matter was reported to New Delhi, the Government lodged a formal protest against it with the Chinese Government. That was how the dispute began. It did not take long to get politicised with defence minister V.K.Krishna Menon's rivals in the Congress party gunning for him and using the issue to embarrass Nehru. The skirmishes in the North-East Frontier Agency, (NEFA) as Arunachal Pradesh was then known, were only a sequel to the fighting in the west. In the circumstances, it would be appropriate for India to seek China's formal endorsement of Arunachal Pradesh as an Indian state, leaving in abeyance the delineation of the Macmahon Line. That would leave the border dispute to be sorted out through negotiations at the political and expert levels. The central sector, largely touching Uttaranchal and Himachal Pradesh, has already passed the muster of officials of the two Governments. The western sector is said to be the toughest requiring much political give and take mutually. So the eastern sector could be disposed of next. If the Vajpayee Government had not been replaced it would have in all probability taken it up with the Chinese Government. Will the new Government have the wisdom and will to act responsibly instead of standing on false pride?

Meanwhile a number of Communist women leaders including Captain Lakshmi Sahgal, Ahilya Rangnekar, Kanak Mukherjee, Brinda Karat, Saheba Farooqui, Primala Lomba and Suhasini Ali, among others, have assailed a move to enforce a two-child norm as a means of planning families. At the seventh national conference of the All-India Democratic Women's Association held at Bhubaneshwar on 18 November 2004, they adopted a resolution alleging that the two-child norm militated against the poor. One cannot comprehend the logic behind the argument. One would have thought that fewer children would help poor people to bring them up better and take care of their health and education. The days of larger families being welcomed as a source of support by the parents are gone. There were originally two factors for larger families: one the urge of the parents, especially the father, to have a male child and, secondly, the expectation of support from children, already mentioned. It also placed the premium on the male child because girls are not expected to undertake outside work even if they are hardy enough to work in the fields Then there was also the problem of dowry for girls to be married off. The result was the curse of foeticide, widely prevalent in Punjab and Haryana. Last but not least, too much childbirth, with or without miscarriages / abortions is injurious to mother's health. Against this background, one is surprised why the veteran women Communist leaders – the average age of those assembled at Bhubaneshwar must be in the late sixties — are against regulated families and disincentives against having more than two children which apply only for government employees and those seeking public office. This brings to mind the denunciation of family planning as fascist by the Communists in the early 1950's. The Socialist Party had advocated family planning even before the Government had taken it up in different forms, which infuriated the Communists. Those were the days when the Soviet Union and the countries in its orbit were honouring mother heroines with the largest number of offspring. So naturally the Indian Communists should adopt it. That those Governments were trying to make up the severe manpower loss in the war and that the Nazis also in their day encouraged large families did not strike the Communists!

Now a brief look at the internal security situation and the Manmohan Government's handling it. At the national level, bringing the separatist Hurriyat Conference in Jammu and Kashmir into the political mainstream through direct negotiations has been the task before the Union Government. N.N. Vohra, former Home Secretary has been the Government interlocutor in the effort. The present Government has wisely retained him, although he had worked with L.K.Advani in trying to tackle the Kashmiri separatists for some years. But there the connectivity seemed to end. After initial rounds of talks with the moderate faction of the Hurriyat in Jammu and Kashmir they were invited to New Delhi for further exchange of views. The job required plenty of patience and much perseverance because very often both sides would reiterate their known positions. A nuance here or a word there would sometimes provide an opening for a fresh initiative. After the Delhi round of talks Advani who became deputy prime minister then made them meet the Prime Minister formally. That meant, in the Hurriyat perception, Government commitment to the substance and style of the negotiations. Then came the general election and the failure of Vajpayee Government to return to office.

Shivraj Patil, who had a successful stint as Lok Sabha Speaker, following similar experience as Speaker of the Maharashtra Assembly in the late 1980s, was out of depth as Union Home Minister. The prime reason was his surprising defeat in the Lok Sabha polls from his home constituency of Latur in Maharashtra. Sonia Gandhi made him a Rajya Sabha member and put him in charge of the vital home portfolio. In the last (13th) Lok Sabha he put up with being Sonia Gandhi's deputy on the opposition benches. He would sit quietly as the Leader read out scripted speeches touched up by Mani Shankar Iyer. Iyer would also be prompting her from the rear bench with Patil as mute observer. The net result was Patil was not sure about his position while undertaking delicate tasks like negotiating with the Hurriyat leaders who are past masters in getting better of the other party Here again, if Patil has taken up the matter where Advani left it – Vohra had reportedly suggested it – there would have been headway. But following Natwar Singh's example Patil decided to start with a 'clean slate.' While the Geelani group of Hurriyat leaders would object to talks under the country's constitution, the 'moderate' Mir Waiz group demanded that they be allowed to go to Pakistan for talks with Kashmiri leaders on the other side of the LOC as a prelude to tripartite talks among India, Pakistan and 'Kashmir.'

Later the Prime Minister visited Srinagar and Jammu. His most striking concession to Pakistan, more than the separatists, was withdrawal of 20,000 troops from the State. This raises the basic question whether the source of threat to the life and limb of the Kashmiri people is the terrorist or the Indian security forces stationed there to curb the terrorists. After all, the terrorist menace in its present form began in the late 1980s when Rajiv Gandhi forced Farooq Abdullah's National Conference into an alliance and got the assembly elections rigged. Our troops, including the XVth corps, have been there for some decades now. The terrorist trouble was compounded later when Vishwanath Pratap Singh as Prime Minister (in 1990) put Mufti Mohammad Sayeed as his home minister and used Jag Mohan to ensure Farooq's resignation. It was Zia-ul-Haque as Pakistan President, who began to wield the terrorist weapon against India in Kashmir on the lines of the guerrilla warfare waged against Soviet troops in Afghanistan.

On the Indian side, terrorists kidnapped Mufti's daughter, not the PDP leader and MP, Mehbooba Sayeed, who is dynamic and very articulate, but a quiet girl called Rubiya and got the release of hard-core fellow-terrorists in return. More than the reinforcement of terrorists it meant, it represented surrender of the administration and put the terrorists on top. In the circumstances, the Prime Minister's decision to withdraw 20,000 troops from Jammu and Kashmir – as a gesture to Hurriyat and fellow-separatists would have been unexceptionable by itself if the security situation in the State, as adjudged by the chief of army staff and others, warranted it. But as a *quid pro quo* for expected co-operation by the separatists it can have dangerous implications. In this context, General Musharraf's idea of mutual demilitarisation is ominous. India should be careful to avoid the Prime Minister's gesture being linked with it. As for the General's threat of Pakistan going back to the 1949 UN Security Council resolutions, he should be reminded that the Dixon Plan —nearest to his idea of seven demarcated areas on either side of the LOC—stood for Pakistan withdrawing its troops from the occupied Kashmir territory while India would continue to be responsible for administering the State and maintaintining law and order in the territory.

Similarly, in the northeast, the long drawn-out peace talks with the Nagas are continuing with the Government wisely maintaining continuity. The Government interlocutor, resourceful K. Padmanabhaiah has also been retained. (Padnmanabhaiah, a Maharashtra cadre IAS officer, had retired as Union Home Secretary.) In the case of Manipur, Dr. Manmohan Singh seems to have had a better start than the predecessor Government, which was racked by agitation against apprehended inclusion of Manipur in a greater Nagaland, mooted by the Naga rebels.

Finally, a word about the chapter on the former chief minister of Andhra Pradesh, N. Chandrababu Naidu. He remains 'a new kind of leader' even if his party has been defeated in the 2004 assembly election. His steadfast rejection of populism in the shape of unwarranted handouts like free power supply which does not help the intended beneficiaries in the long run but bankrupts the State here and now. Similarly, his resistance to the vivisection of Andhra Pradesh – by formation of a separate Telengana State — evokes support and admiration of everyone who had either been witness to the long drawn-out struggle for formation of the State in the 1950s or is alive to the ethos and spirit of that struggle. It will only be a matter of time before the opportunism of the Congress party in promising to split Andhra Pradesh is exposed. The secession of Telengena areas is not like formation of Chattisgarh, Jharkhand and Uttaranchal in 2000. There is no linguistic principle involved, nor does it contribute to administrative efficiency. Meanwhile, the formation of Jharkhand in response to decades of struggle of the Jharkhand people and the aspirations of the inhabitants for shaping their own destiny within the Indian Union has been a big disappointment. As a result, Maoist extremists are gaining control within the State, holding the administration to ransom and stalling development. More alarmingly, from Telengana and northern districts of Andhra Pradesh through Chattisgarh up to Jharkhand and beyond into Nepal a Naxalite belt is being formed. The Andhra Pradesh Government, with the acquiescence of the Centre, has entered into a 'ceasefire agreement' with the People's War group, reinforced by alliance with the so-called Maoist Centre in Bihar, and has allowed the Naxalites to carry arms during political negotiations with the Government.

As for the Congress party's electoral commitment for formation of a separate State of Telengana as a prelude to poll alliance with the Telengana Reorganisation Samiti (TRS), the Manmohan Singh Government is having second thoughts. As recently as in mid-November 2004, the Prime Minister at a press conference in Hyderabad evaded a direct answer to a question on time frame for formation of the proposed State. He talked vaguely of a second States Reorganisation Commission to study the desirability of smaller States. There is nothing wrong in having experts to look at the matter in depth in the light of past and more recent experience. They should particularly pay attention to the Naxalite problem and the separatist tendencies it is fomenting. Also, such a study should not be an occasion for unleashing a Mandal kind of agitation as it happened when Vishwanath Pratap Singh landed the country in a civil war-like situation in 1990, just to retain his prime ministership.

Dedication

I first met 'J.P.' in 1946, when I was 21, barely exposed to life in a metropolis like Bombay. I had gone there a few months earlier straight from an Andhra Pradesh town, Vizianagaram. I was one of 'JP's' countless admirers, thrilled to meet him face to face. Such was my adulation for the simple, pleasant-looking man in his early forties that I did not know what to say on seeing him. I was then employed with *Forum*, a highly popular English weekly. Its editor, Joachim Alva, a doyen among the editors of the day, was a pioneer in introducing into India the *Time* magazine style of journalism, marked by pithy writing, with short sentences and picturesque phraseology. The magazine called "J.P." "Scarlet Pimpernel". I thought it was a glowing description little knowing that it meant a plant with small scarlet flowers. The plant was also known as the poor man's weatherglass because its flowers foretold approaching rain by closing their petals. There was another Scarlet Pimpernel, the elusive hero of Baroness Orczy's novel of the same name. He was against the excesses of the French Revolution which was seen as a forerunner of the October Revolution in Czarist Russia.The Scarlet Pimpernel ridiculed the bloodthirsty methods of the revolutionaries who sent several French revolutionaries of the stature of Robespierre to death after a summary trial in 1780. Apparently 'J.P.' was likened to him, although Baroness Orczy's novel dealt only with his exploits in rescuing from the gallows the members of the French aristocracy, lords and ladies. He would fearlessly go to France in disguise, save the lords and ladies and smuggle them into England. At the end of the operation, he would leave a note to the architects of the bloodletting, ridiculing them and signing himself as Scarlet Pimpernel, followed by the symbol of the flower, his trademark.

Most of us were moved by 'J.P's physical daring-do in dodging the British police for months and for the moral courage with which he faced torture, along with Ram Manohar Lohia. That was in the Lahore Fort, where he was locked up on his capture. I had, no doubt, read Telugu translations of "JP"s writings on the case for Socialism and the need to intensify the anti-imperialist struggle against the British. My colleagues and I also endorsed his reported rejection of non-violence during the 1942 Quit India struggle. We admired him more when the Communists, with whom we parted company on the 'people's war' issue, abused him as a social fascist. (The Communists had then denounced Netaji Subhas Bose as a Japanese agent.) The trouble with Telugu translation of Marxist classics was that it made understanding more difficult than the original text on subjects like dialectical materialism. The Communists crammed the text and unleashed it in discussions, just as pupils of the madrassas learnt by rote verses from the holy Koran without following their intent. As a result, we had, if at all, very little understanding of the tough subject, including why and how socialist transformation of the means of production and distribution was necessary for ridding the social system of disparities. During 1941 when the Nazis attacked the Soviet Union, 'JP', detained in Deolali detention camp in Maharashtra, had sent out a letter asking Socialists to support the Soviet Union. That was unknown to us because the newspapers did not report it. Nor were the documents available in Telugu. So we transferred our antipathy for the local Communists to the Soviet Union and hated it as well.

Reverting to the 1946 'encounter' with 'JP', I could only ask him for an autograph on a hesitantly produced piece of paper. When 'JP' remarked that I was too old to collect autographs I quickly tried to cover up my sheepishness by saying that it was for my wife and he gave the autograph. 'JP' was then putting up with Purshottam Trikamdas, a highly successful lawyer, in his opulent looking Malabar Hill apartment. From my lower middle class perspective and experience it looked like a palatial residence. Soon after, when Purshottam married for the second time, — a divorcee from Kerala — sending his plain Gujarati first wife to her village 'JP' stopped staying with him. This autobiographical introduction to one of India's greatest second-generation leaders was more to present the man, as I perceived him then and for many years later. It was not to beat my own drum, even if it might sound like that.

I don't think 'JP' had by then taken over the general secretaryship of the Congress Socialist Party (CSP), which at the Kanpur congress that year dropped the prefix 'Congress' from the party's nomenclature to indicate severance of parental link with the Indian National Congress. It was in the following year at the seminal Nasik party congress that 'JP' was elected general secretary. He then propounded his thesis on democratic socialism as distinct from both capitalism and Soviet style state 'socialism'.

He spelt it out in his path-breaking general secretary's report. At Nasik, the party broke free of parental Congress tutelage to become an independent political outfit as the spearhead of a larger movement. The CSP did not accept 'democratic centralism' in the party organisation. 'JP' dissected the principles of class war and dictatorship of the proletariat, stressing that the party was committed to a pluralistic society, without short-circuiting or subverting other parties. If there could be more than one capitalist party in the US, UK, France and elsewhere why could not there be two or more 'socialist' parties in the Soviet Union, he would ask. There was equal stress on democracy and socialism. If I remember right, the Communist Party - Marxist CPI (M) had not formally abandoned at least its theoretical commitment to dictatorship of the proletariat until perhaps the 1980s. That was notwithstanding the record of the CPI (M) - led government in West Bengal, especially in the long Jyoti Basu period. Even while saying that the party had not won power, but only the right to run the government, Jyoti Basu did not hesitate to steamroller opposition and conduct himself as if heading a single-party State. (The CPI or pro-Moscow Communist party, as it was known, formally gave up its adherence to democratic centralism at its Amritsar party congress in 1958) The Congress Governments at the Centre merrily put up with the CPI (M) tactics. Only Morarji Desai as Prime Minister for about twenty-eight months in 1977-79 had spoken out against the state of affairs in West Bengal. But the CPI (M) was technically an ally of the Janata Party. Straightforward members of the party like Jyotirmoy Basu and P Ramamurthy steadfastly stood by the Janata Party Government but some others were Janus-faced. Especially, Harkishan Singh Surjit was cheek by jowl with Madhu Limaye when he set out to topple the Morarji Desai Government and destroy the Janata Party. A crucial amendment to define 'secularism' included by Indira Gandhi in the preamble to the Constitution by the notorious 42nd amendment during the 'emergency' was defeated in the Rajya Sabha because of the double-dealing by the CPI M) leadership. The amendment spelled out secularism as "equal respect and treatment for all religions". The Congress was against spelling out its concept of secularism. 'JP' was not surprised but was sorry for the country saddled with the Indira Gandhi kind of secularism.

Going back to my socialist education, I owe whatever I know of the subject to my 'guru', Achyut Patwardhan who took over *Janata* (weekly) from Aruna Asaf Ali. She was running it on commercial lines, which cost the party about a lakh of rupees a month, which was a princely sum in those days (1951). Edatata Narayanan who left the *Hindustan Times* was the founder- editor of *Janata*; its office was located in the prestigious Odeon Building in the heart of Connaught Place in New Delhi. The Government had acquired it and gave it to the party on a nominal rent. But Narayanan and his retinue - including his wife and brother-in-law Viswanath — ran the publication, drawing salaries not commensurate with the monthly allowances of full-time party workers. I was getting Rs. 250 a month, which was also above the average. Worse still, the publication, supposed to be a party organ, echoed the views of Narayanan often voiced by Aruna Asaf Ali and not of the party. Aruna had already started distancing herself from the party and would not attend even national executive meetings. So she did not care to know and definitely not share the party's views and outlook. For instance, Narayanan was incensed by the party position that the Maoist takeover in China in 1949 was an extension into Asia of the Stalinist sphere of influence. He had written in *Janata* in his characteristic caustic manner, saying: "If Mao was a vassal of Stalin 'JP' was a stooge of Transport House" (headquarters of the British Labour Party). One could understand Narayanan and Aruna Asaf Ali disagreeing with the majority opinion in the party but there was a way of saying it, especially in the party publication. That was more or less the last straw that made the party decide to shift *Janata* to Bombay and make Achyut Patwardhan the editor. (Editorship for Achyut meant footing the bill of running the publication whereas in the case of Aruna Asaf Ali the party was reimbursing her to the tune of a lakh of rupees every month.)

Achyut made me the *de jure* editor of the party paper of which he was the chief editor by making me file the Declaration as printer and publisher. A few months later, when he moved to Pune practically severing ties with party politics, Rohit Dave was the resident editor being in Bombay as a Corporator. Rohit's main vocation was teaching; he gave tuitions to select students to supplement his meagre income as a Corporator. A voracious reader and an almost ivory tower intellectual, he spent most of his time in the libraries. As the printer and publisher of *Janata*, I was supposed to be the main contributor and the party's eyes and ears in respect of articles published. Indra Sen, formerly of the Trotskyist Bolshevik-Leninist party of India (BLPI), which merged with the Socialist party, specialised in economic and dialectical writing. Indra concealed a golden heart by a prickly tongue. He treated me as a younger brother and took upon himself my education in the Trotskyist version of Marxism. Achyut, on the other hand, made me read basic publications (mostly British) on

Marxism and socialism, especially the writings of Harold Laski (*Communist Manifesto a Socialist Landmark*) and Emily Burns (*Why Socialism*?). He would accompany me on the daily bus journey from the Gateway of India to Dadar and discuss serious issues with me. Achyut was not a Marxist and did not always share 'JP's' approach but he respected the elder leader. He was more a Gandhian. Having been virtually out of the party, he had no political ambitions. On the other hand, a convert to theosophist thinking Achyut had brought to bear on 'JP' to some extent his ethical approach to public life. Achyut was especially wary of what he would call 'sawdust socialism', saying that without adequate mental preparation and education socialists would not be able to bring about transformation of society even if they were in office. Supplementing my mixed bag of ideological upbringing were Asoka Mehta's erudite writings on the evolution of the democratic socialist idea from the Chartist beginnings to Leninist doctrines before and after the Stalinist takeover in the Soviet Union, a gold mine of serious political writing. It was later brought out in book form with the title *Democratic Socialism*. It was my good fortune to be with such titans, moved by the common thread of fellow feeling and, if I may call it, humanism. 'JP' was the greatest among them.

Two instances of my personal experience in this respect illustrate his generosity to a fault of a petty professional. The first was during the first Nehru Government. Sarat Chandra Bose had resigned from the Nehru cabinet charging Nehru with partiality for, if not infatuation with, Madame Chiang-ke Shek. Apparently, he wanted to launch a new party and had planned to visit Bombay in that connection. Rusi Karanjia of *Blitz*, who called himself 'Your Editor' and claimed direct access to Nehru and Nasser, had written a flattering letter to Achyut Patwardhan inviting him to join Karanjia in organising a reception to Sarat Bose. Achyut lost no time in rejecting the gratuitous invitation, saying he did not believe in forming opportunist alliances for the purpose of opposing the Congress party. Karanjia was demolished and decided to take it on Achyut and added me as a target. He published a report that 'JP' was concerned about the 'RSS line' being plugged by Achyut and Bhargava in the *Janata* and wanted to cleanse its editorial setup. The alleged basis for the insinuation was a meeting at Yusuf Meherally's residence where plans were chalked out for toning up *Janata*. Rafiq Zakaria, who was the *Blitz* correspondent in London and returned to Bombay with a barrister's degree and rich experience, was there, more on account of his proximity to Meherally. My grouse had been that party leaders did not write often enough for *Janata*.

Ashok, who was present, offered to share with *Janata* his weekly column in the *Blitz*. He wrote for the *Blitz* because of its reach to middle-class English-knowing Bombayites, as well as to counter Communist propaganda of which the *Blitz* was a ready vehicle; no less importantly because it brought him money which he needed. That was the crucial time when Communist-controlled trade unions were being overwhelmed one by one by Socialist (Hind Mazdoor Sabha) unions. The Indian National Trade Union Congress (INTUC) of Gulzarilal Nanda and Khandubhai Desai was no doubt a fly in the ointment but that was a different story. At one time Ashok was looking after as many as 150 trade unions, big and small, in Bombay and the Communists were on the run. Taking advantage of Zakaria's presence at the meeting it was agreed that he should spare time to advise me to tone up *Janata*.

Yusuf, in spite of his ill health, would write a weekly literary column, introducing books and authors of whom we had hardly heard in India. In response to Yusuf's personal letters to party leaders requesting their help in making *Janata* a first-class socialist weekly, many of them started writing for *Janata*. They included Kamaladevi who wrote on social and cultural issues and Professor M.L. Dantwala who regularly contributed economic articles. Acharyaji, too, had sent a few pieces. Only Lohia did not respond. When I complained, Doctor Sa'ab patiently explained his problem to me. First, he was always on the move. Secondly, he rarely wrote articles but if someone could prod him from time to time he would write, he said. I was afraid he would be offended by my cribbing but he took it in his benevolent stride and was extremely kind and nice. That was the beginning of a long 'friendship', which ripened when he was a Lok Sabha member and I moved to Delhi, giving up working for *Janata*.

Mixing up issues discussed at the meeting, Karanjia published the offensive report in the *Blitz* saying that fed up with Achyut and me 'JP' had asked Zakaria to revamp *Janata*. Achyut for his part treated it with the contempt it deserved but we were provoked. During 'JP's next visit to Bombay we brought it to his notice. He immediately wrote to Karanjia strongly denying the insinuation and adding, besides his respect and regard for Achyut's handling of *Janata*, he was also impressed by Bhargava, 'one of the promising fine journalists in India'. We wrongly concluded that Zakaria was the source of the mischievous report but it was not so.

The second instance was in 1948. A dispute was raging between India and Pakistan about the return to that country of its share of sterling balances. Sardar Patel was for squeezing Pakistan while others, especially Gandhiji wanted the amount to be paid promptly. Against that background, Satyanarain Sinha, parliamentary affairs minister in the Nehru Government, had come to Bombay. Staying at the Raj Bhavan, he invited K.K. Menon, a joint secretary of the party and a close friend of Sinha, for a cup of tea. Many Congress leaders had their eyes on Menon ('KK' to us), whom they wanted to entice into the Congress. But the invitation to 'KK' was essentially social. When 'KK' asked me whether I would like to go with him, I did not wait for a second invitation and readily accompanied him, although uninvited by the host. At the tea session at the Raj Bhavan, which lasted more than an hour, Sinha held forth on the Sardar's aggressiveness and Nehru's meek response. Among the 'instances' he cited was a reported suggestion by Sardar Patel that Liaquat Ali Khan should be arrested during his next visit to Delhi to make Pakistan disgorge secret documents of undivided India spirited away to Pakistan. A silent listener at the encounter, I could not contain my enthusiasm at landing such a peach of a 'scoop'. When I asked 'KK' whether it could be revealed; he saw no wrong in doing so without citing Sinha. So I wrote the story, vetted by KK himself and peppered by Indra Sen later. It was the lead story in the following week's *Janata*.

All hell broke Roose when the issue was out. All India Radio broadcast a strong denial in several of its news bulletins. Nehru wrote a personal letter admonishing Achyut. Achyut wrote a front-page apology to the Sardar. He also wrote a signed editorial disowning every word of the offending report. Rohit wrote another editorial, also signed, reinforcing Achyut's apology and denial. I felt miserable and asked Achyut to relieve me of the responsibility of running *Janata*. He refused point blank. Later 'JP', visiting Bombay, called me and asked me not to take it to heart. The purpose of recalling the murky incident is to show that even when Achyut was not involved, as in the earlier *Blitz* case, 'JP' felt the need to stand by an immature worker. It was a different matter that Madhu Limaye used it in cross-examining me in a Press Council case. It was during the hearing of Madhu's charge of misrepresentation against Arun Shourie in the 1980s. He wanted to show me as an unreliable witness.

Meanwhile, the Socialist Party made a serious effort to fight the first general election to the Lok Sabha in 1952. It contested more than 300 seats all over the country and came a cropper winning just a little more two dozen, even if its popular vote was as high as ten million. Even in Bombay, the party's stronghold, the Congress ran through the constituencies like a hurricane. Ashok and Ambedkar were humbled in a double-member constituency in the working class area. The main reason was lack of an election machine, which could translate support into votes. Also S.K. Patil & Co played tricks, like ballot rigging and manipulation of electoral rolls, with or without Nehru's approval.

Then the Sardar sent for Purshottam Trikamdas and said the Socialists should concentrate on Greater Bombay, build up the party and show their mettle. He said the Congress would leave the area to the Socialists to run in a model manner and develop a two-party system in one of the most politically developed parts of the country. The party, smarting under the electoral rout, rejected the suggestion out of hand. That was practically the beginning of 'JP's exit from electoral politics. There were divided counsels within the party leadership in reaction to the electoral debacle. While Ashok with his theory of 'political compulsions of a developing economy' was for a deal with the Congress, Acharya Narendra Deva and Lohia were for an opposition role for the party, urging beefing up the party organisation for the purpose. Achyut was out of the party. Yusuf was either too ill or had passed away. Kamaladevi was never in electoral politics. Before taking a formal holiday from party politics, 'JP' negotiated a merger arrangement with Acharya Kripalani's Kisan Mazdoor Praja party (KMPP) to form the PSP (Praja Socialist Party). That was done at the prodding of both Lohia and Ashok and proved deadly to the Socialist movement. Ashok's purpose in urging the marriage between the party and the KMPP was to break the entente in Andhra between T. Prakasam and the Communists. Doctor Sa'ab, on the other hand, had high regard for Acharya Kripalani acquired during his stint in the AICC as head of the foreign affairs cell and wanted the party to team up with the KMPP to face the Congress. Incidentally, this was perhaps the only occasion when Lohia and Ashok saw eye to eye with each other! Further, the 1950 effort to develop the Socialist party as a mass party on the lines of the British Labour Party with direct membership of trade unions, kisan organisations and cooperatives did not take off. The party had fallen between two stools. It was neither a party of select members, meant to influence national politics nor a pervasive movement to rival the Congress in the future. This could also be the reason for advocating the merger between the Socialist Party and the KMPP. But as it happened, the party became a pale imitation of the Congress, imbibing the pernicious Congress 'culture', except for individual members like Madhu Dandavate, Prem Bhasin, G.G. Parikh, P. Viswambharan, etc. who have remained steadfast Socialists.

Finally, an 'iffy' scenario: if JP had not been hustled into the merger with the KMPP and then into a negotiation with Nehru for a coalition; if the leadership had taken the 1952 rout in its stride and 'JP' had remained at the helm the Socialist movement would have been a living phenomenon now. Instead of going the whole hog in accepting administrative means for transforming society, the party would have stuck to 'JP's 1947 formulation of striving for transforming society and not merely for producing "well-fed, well-housed and well-heeled" politicians, trade unionists and others. Governmental machinery would still be important but not the only vehicle for change. Above all, 'JP' would not have hopped from partyless democracy, to Sarvodaya, to playing midwife in the birth of the stillborn Janata Party. Even if he had no stomach for partisan politics after 1952, he would have been the lodestar for generations of socialists. In the process, 'JP' had become prone to errors of judgement like accepting a person like Chimanbhai Patel in Gujarat to lead the anti-corruption crusade in 1974. Amenability to friends had also been a weakness of the great man. Thus, he had allowed himself to be drawn into the Congress for Cultural Freedom by Minoo Masani when it was being widely suspected of being funded by the US Central Intelligence Agency. Similarly, virtually on his deathbed in 1979, he sent out a letter suggesting (Thakur) Chandra Shekhar (Singh) for prime ministership after the Morarji Desai Government collapsed. The reason simply was that Chandra Shekhar had cadged it. If 'JP's post-1952 behaviour had been different, the socialist movement would have not been scarred by persons like Madhu Limaye, Raj Narain, Chandra Shekhar, Laloo Prasad Yadav and his blood brother, Mulayam Singh to wither on the vine ultimately. At the larger national level, a dynamic socialist party would, besides giving the country a healthy two-party system, forced the Congress to be either a Conservative party or a genuine liberal opposite number and not all things to all people. Parties like the Jana Sangh/BJP would have filled the vacuum in the centre, more like the Social Democratic Party in Britain. The upshot could also have been that caste and communal politics would not have been holding sway like today, at least not to the same degree because of the socialist corrective in the system. The likes of Vishwanath Pratap Singh would not be strutting about as born-again secularists and champions of social justice and affirmative action. Riff-raff like the Vishwa Hindu Parishad and Bajrang Dal would not perhaps have been there disfiguring the political landscape. The BJP would have been without its parivar barring the umbilical link with the Rashtriya Swayam Sevak Sangh (RSS).

As one looks back, 'JP' remains one of the greatest second-generation leaders of India, if not the greatest, with an unrivalled service to the country's social, economic and political development, who left his indelible mark on germane issues of governance and means of accomplishing objectives. Most importantly, he was an untiring crusader against corruption, tyranny and arbitrariness. His was a more rounded personality than Nehru's was because Jawaharlal did not have the Gandhian trait of compassion to the extent that 'JP' possessed it. 'JP' had no party or group to shield whereas Nehru was inhibited by his need to carry the Congress party on his back. Facing opprobrium for his advocacy of mutually satisfactory settlement of disputes with Pakistan and China, 'JP' said to me in 1961 that he had become a champion of lost causes. Firstly, they were not lost causes, in the long run. Further, only a leader of 'JP's moral courage could have undertaken them.

Would the situation have been different if 'JP' had remained in the Congress instead of leading his socialist flock out of the parent organisation in 1948? That would have put him next only to Nehru in the national leadership after the departure from the scene of Sardar Patel and Maulana Azad. The subsequent efforts to get him back into the Congress and the abortive negotiations for a Congress-PSP coalition on the basis of his famous 14 points were never destined to get off the ground. The Congress system had by then grown in such a way that even Nehru could not have successfully grafted 'JP' on it. The dynamics of power did not also require the Congress Party to seek the support of the PSP and that too, at a price. The Socialists' position in the country was not such as to tempt the Congress to welcome the prodigals back and kill the fatted calf for them. If 'JP' had not been a prisoner of loud-mouthed and shortsighted imbeciles in the ramshackle Socialist Party with which he was still associated at that time, he would have perhaps joined forces with Nehru without the 14 points. Years later when I asked him whether it would not have been wiser to join the Nehru Government unconditionally he replied that the 14 points were meant to make it easy for the Congress leaders to scotch the move. He added that Pandit Pant and others in the Congress did not want the Socialists back in the party as potential competitors for power. One does not know if Indira Gandhi also was similarly motivated but she, too, disliked the idea of rapprochement with 'J.P.' She also started befriending the Communists to queer the pitch for the effort to get close to 'J.P.' and subsequently raised the bogey of American money for the Socialists.

'J.P.' tried to silence the so-called radicals in his party by putting forward the 14 points as the basis for an accord with the Congress but it was doubtful whether they would have gone along with 'J.P.' even if Nehru had signed on the dotted line. After all, in Socialist professions and even implementation of some of the Socialist policies like nationalisation of banks and insurance and land reforms, Nehru did not lag behind the Socialists. He did not require the 14 points to establish his Socialist credentials. Nor did 'J.P.' need them personally. Above all, the 14 points would not have been a bar to putative Madhu Limayes throwing spanners in the works. 'J.P.'s greatness lay not merely in his commitment to democratic socialism but in his capacity to bring a breath of fresh air to public life already beginning to rot at the core. His transparent sincerity of purpose and unflinching commitment to basic values of human behaviour would have enriched the Government, as nothing else had done, not even Nehru's greatness. He did not covet power even in those days when he was still the leader of the Socialist Party and never contested an election not because, as some of his traducers claimed, he was afraid of being defeated but because he detested the electoral system built on money power. There was no dearth of critics of 'J.P.', who ranged from those (like the Communists) who doubted his patriotism to those who dwelt until his death on his preference for the system of basic democracy in Pakistan. His forays into active politics even after having joined the Sarvodaya movement and his advocacy of "anarchist" ideas like partyless democracy, not to mention his acceptance of support from the RSS (which polluted him in the eyes of heaven-born secularists), were sitting ducks for his vilifiers. At an international "anti - Fascist" conference held by the Communists (CPI) in Patna and hosted by the Government, an effigy of 'J.P.' was symbolically hanged during the 'emergency'. His motives were suspect as when he advocated normalisation of relations with Pakistan and China and links between him and foreign powers were alleged in 1975-76 when he was charged with being a tool for "destabilisation" of the Government of India, as it happened in Allende's Chile. A campaign of calumny was launched abroad, especially in Western Europe and West Asia, that in collaboration with the RSS 'J.P.' was endangering the interests and even lives of the minorities like the Muslims and the Christians. A move by world statesmen like Sir Philip Noel Baker to propose 'J.P's name for the Nobel Peace Prize was thwarted through Indian missions abroad. Earlier, in 1969, a proposal to draft him for Presidentship in succession to Zakir Husain was similarly nipped in the bud though there was no "confrontation" between him and the regime at that time. Presidentship, prime ministership or the Nobel Peace Prize would have been honours befitting 'J.P.' but being denied them did not detract from his greatness.

A White Paper published in July 1975 by the Government of India jeered at 'J.P.'s alleged lack of consistency. It said: "A study of Shri Jayaprakash Narayan's political career would show how, after having been at one time a votary of Marxism and Communism, then a Socialist and a staunch critic of Communism before moving to Sarvodaya from which also he seems to have strayed away." In 'J.P.'s own words, he has "journeyed from Marxism to democratic socialism to Sarvodaya not because he has been lacking in principles or fickle in thinking but because being dynamic in approach, he attuned himself to the changing needs of society. As General Secretary of the Socialist Party he said in 1949 that socialism and democracy are "by themselves incomplete; they are interrelated terms and, therefore, it would be wrong to characterise the Anglo-American system as democratic and the Soviet system as socialist. In the U.S. and Western Europe they have indeed introduced democratic methods like representative institutions and elections, but their democratic efforts are far from adequate. Likewise, Soviet Russia has abolished private ownership of the means of production and established planned economy, but she has centralised economic power and the mass of population is not only denied democratic freedom and civil liberties but also the full use of economic power". Subsequently, when he gave up party politics and dedicated himself to Sarvodaya, he wrote, "the bourgeois State has the monopoly of political power. The socialist State threatens to add to it the monopoly of economic power.... We must create and develop forms of socialist living through the voluntary endeavour of the people rather than seek to establish socialism by the use of the power of the State."

In 1954, in a letter to his colleagues in the Socialist movement he wrote: "It was not the ugliness of politics that repelled me, but the attraction of the new politics of Sarvodaya that drew me. Sarvodaya also has its politics. But it is politics of a different kind; politics of the people as I have called it, as distinct from the politics of party and power, *lokniti* as distinct from *rajniti*. The politics of Sarvodaya can have no party and no concern with power. Rather, its aim will be to see that all centres of power are abolished. The more this new politics grows the more the old politics shrinks, a real withering away of the State."

Finally, to clinch the issue of his inconsistency, he had said more than once: "My objective has not changed. It remains the same, as it was when I was young. It is the same as that of socialism or communism, a society free from exploitation, a classless society, a stateless society". If 'J.P.' had not left the Congress and wasted his time in trying to give an organisational shape to an amorphous mass of socialist doctrinaires weighed down by a group of feuding individualists, he would have been the natural successor to Nehru. He would have also in the process restored the balance between Nehru's preoccupation with day-to-day politics and his basic loyalty to the values of democracy and freedom. Even if 'J.P.' had lived only up to 1979 — his detention in Chandigarh in 1975 by destroying his kidneys had shortened his life — it would have meant two more decades after Nehru of purposeful leadership for India with the stage set for technology sensitive leaders to take over. It would have above all saved the nation the trauma of 1975 and the tragedy of 1977-79. We are lucky to be alive in this centenary year of the great leader's birth. The (NDA) National Democratic Alliance Government has allowed itself ultimately to be persuaded to instal his statue in a remote corner of the Parliament House complex. 'JP' had never been a member of Parliament, not even a legislator at the State level. So as in the case of Sri Aurobindo and Netaji Subhas Bose, he has been commemorated by a statue in the proximity, however remote, of the temple of democracy and not with a place in the portrait gallery in the Central Hall of Parliament. Among the parliamentarians and national leaders yet to be accommodated in the portrait gallery in the Central Hall are Acharya Kripalani and Nath Pai, two of the best and ablest.

October 2002

1
Unending Quest

India is star-crossed because its quest for committed leadership after Nehru has been unending. In the process the nation is reduced to the fate of Tantalus of Greek mythology, who was condemned to stand in Tartarus, a region of Hades surrounded by inaccessible water and fruit.[1] The lower he stooped to quench his thirst farther down went the level of the water. Similarly, the people of India who had set their sights high in the context of Gandhiji's approach to public life and had savoured Nehru's leadership for about two decades were prepared to make compromises both in the standard of leadership and its commitment to values. But even then the quest has remained unfulfilled. They are made to feed on half-baked puddings, one after another.

As time advanced it was not clear whether it was lack of leadership or erosion of institutions or both, not to mention the decay of the party system, that is at the root of India's not so enviable position at the dawn of the new millennium. More than fifty years have elapsed since the country chose to be a democratic republic. It is an accomplishment to be looked upon with pride and a sense of gratification for more than one reason. In the spreading desert of military and single- party dictatorships in the third world India has remained a steadfast adherent to the democratic system. In fact, by virtue of its being the second- most populous nation in the world, next only to totalitarian China, India prides itself as the world's largest democracy. It is both true and not so. The basic attributes of the parliamentary system with multiplicity of political parties, periodical elections, a free press and an independent judiciary are hallmarks of India's democracy it is undoubtedly a leader in the league. Its beneficial influence has also spread to neighbouring countries in South Asia notably Bangladesh, Nepal and even Pakistan (for some time) where the parliamentary system of democracy is highly fancied.[2] It has also been a psychological prop to Sri Lanka, the other South Asian State that has retained its democratic character despite the most virulent and fratricidal ethnic conflict aggravated by suicidal separatists. It was triggered by a short -sighted decision by J.R. Jayawardena to go in for the presidential form of executive. The island democracy has been struggling for the last about four decades to return to the parliamentary system with a view to promoting ethnic harmony among its people. There have been hopes lately of the end of ethnic strife with the Government and the Liberation Tigers of Tamil Eelam (LTTE) negotiating a future constitutional set-up.

India, as the next -door neighbour with democratic credentials, could have taken the lead in promoting an end to the conflict. In fact, Rajiv Gandhi, as prime minister of India, had tried his hand at it in the 1980s but hastily sent Indian troops to the Island in what was called the Indian Peace Keeping Force (IPKF). Ultimately, India had to take back the troops after suffering casualties because both the Sinhalese and the Tamils perceived it as a military threat from the larger neighbour and resisted it jointly. That compounded Indira Gandhi's ill-concealed complicity with the separatists in the early 1970s and the dirty tricks of the Indian intelligence agencies. Indira Gandhi had allowed Indian territory to be used to arm and train secessionist (LTTE) cadres. It was to placate M.G. Ramachandran (MGR), chief minister of Tamil Nadu who was a staunch supporter of the LTTE. MGR's A-I ADMK propped Indira Gandhi's central government by providing 39 Lok Sabha seats. Within the State of Tamil Nadu Ramachandran found the LTTE connection handy in beating the rival Dravidian party of DMK (Dravida Munnetra Kazagam) at the polls. Ironically, the LTTE bit the hand that had fed it by facilitating, if not carrying out, the assassination of Rajiv Gandhi in 1991. In the new scenario, the A-ADMK under Jayalalitha has turned a bitter enemy of the LTTE, while the rival DMK and some other smaller parties notably, Marumalarchi (progressive) Dravida Munnetra Kazagam or MDMK of Vaiko are tarred with the brush of being partisans of the LTTE.[3]

Thanks to Indira Gandhi's shortsighted Sri Lanka policy, India has not been able to play its due role in the latest ongoing peace negotiations between the LTTE and the Sri Lankan Government. Far-off Norway has been brokering the peace efforts, which would ultimately be in the larger interests of India and the entire region. The Sri Lanka Government has been magnanimously keeping India fully informed of the developments. India, too, has been reciprocally co-operative. Significantly the Bharatiya

Janata Party (BJP) heading the coalition National Democratic Alliance (NDA) government at the Central May 2004 had been going along with the Sri Lankan Government in evolving a peaceful solution to the ethnic problem. The BJP-led Government had also reiterated India's commitment to the territorial integrity of the island dispelling the apprehension that the presence in the NDA of pro-LTTE parties like the DMK would make its government side with the Tamil separatists in Sri Lanka. If the BJP had been true to its depiction by western observers as a right-wing Hindu extremist nationalist party, it should have taken a leaf from the policies of Indira Gandhi and her son in trying to impose Indian hegemony over Sri Lanka. But it had not done so. On the other hand, It has also convincingly shown itself to be different from Congress party leaders who tried to throw their weight around the smaller neighbours.

Similarly, in both Bangladesh and Nepal, the impact of the Indian democratic way of life has not been uniformly positive. In Bangladesh, in the birth of which India had played the midwife, the return to the democratic way of life has been intermittent and superficial. The long night of military dictatorship with sectarian elements swearing in the name of holy Islam and a series of political assassinations and military coups spanning over two decades came to an end in the late 1990s. Equally significantly, in May 1998, Shaikh Hasina Wazed, daughter of Bangabandu, Shaikh Mujibur Rahman, was elected Prime Minister of the Islamic Republic of Bangladesh, after about thirty years of political wilderness. She alone survived when the entire Mujib family was assassinated in 1975. But the bigots and remnants of the military junta unseated her after virtually holding the country to ransom through frequent recourse to general strike or *bandh* usually enforced through brute force. Begum Khaleda Zia, widow of a former dictator, Zia-ul Rehman, was the central figure in these protests. Unlike during her first stint in office, Begum Khaleda joined forces with sectarian groups, including pro-Pakistan Jamaat-i-Islami, the country's largest religious party, Islamic Oikya Jote and one of the factions of General Ershad's Jatiya Party to unseat Shaikh Hasina's Awami League Government in October 2001. The saving grace throughout these traumatic years was retention of democratic rule and return to multi-party parliamentary system. Its parliament completed two five-year terms without military coups and assassinations enabling both Begum Khaleda and Begum Hasina to complete their prime ministerial terms despite frequent hiccoughs. The Jamaat-i-Islami is committed to make Bangladesh a full-fledged Islamic State, with Koranic laws but has so far been unable to move in that direction.

The faith of the religious groups and the Jatiya Party factions in democracy is only skin deep. Shaikh Mujib's folly (aided and abetted by Indira Gandhi) in opting for the Pakistani model of presidential form of government capped by one-party dictatorship had been ended, for good. At the same time, unfortunately, India was dragged into Bangladesh's domestic politics because of Shaikh Hasina's efforts to improve relations between the two countries and promote mutual cooperation in the development field. Prospects of trade improved; there was a direct bus service between Dacca and Kolkata, to be followed by a direct rail link under consideration. Also on the cards was a Dacca-Agartala bus service.

Other projects like sale of surplus natural gas by Bangladesh to India and establishment of direct economic relations between Bangladesh and the northeastern States of India had also been on the cards, even if on an on-again and off-again manner. All these efforts which were in an advanced stage of consideration received a setback after Shaikh Hasina's electoral reverse but the new Government is gradually letting pragmatism prevail in its relations with India and so has been New Delhi. Further, the BJP Government had steadfastly jettisoned Indira Gandhi's vindictive policy. As stated earlier, within four years of the formation of Bangladesh, the founder of the nascent nation, Shaikh Mujibur Rahman, replaced the parliamentary system by a presidential form of government and imposed one-party rule on the country. (Since it coincided with the imposition of 'emergency' by Indira Gandhi in India, it seemed she had inspired the Dacca effort to snuff out democracy) That had given a handle to the dastardly assassination of Banga Bandhu, as Mujibur Rahman was endearingly called, and most members of his family, plunging the country into chaos and repeated coups and political assassinations. India did not rightly establish diplomatic relations with the military regime in Dacca. One could understand Indira Gandhi aversion for the perpetrators of the crime and even her refusal to have diplomatic relations with the government headed by them. But taking it on the people of Bangladesh by shutting off the waters of the shared Ganga river was Indira Gandhi's style of neighbourly diplomacy. While the short-lived Morarji Desai Government (1977-79) tried to undo the policy it was left to the United Front Government headed by Inder Kumar Gujral in 1997 to evolve an even-handed water-sharing policy, which has been working for the last eight years. In the process, sharing of the Ganga waters has ceased to be a bone of contention between the two countries. This is because the Vajpayee Government had kept it intact.

In the Himalayan kingdom of Nepal gone are the days when King Mahendra arbitrarily dismissed an elected government and put the Prime Minister in jail to turn the clock back to what is called panchayat democracy (1962). Now it is practically a constitutional monarchy despite the chequered interlude of political assassinations of the Head of the State himself and the entire royal family and repeated collapse of elected governments. When King Mahendra dismissed the B.P. Koirala Government and dispensed with the parliamentary system in the early 1960s, Nehru did not hesitate to upbraid the king's action even at the risk of straining India's relations with the kingdom. As it happened, piqued, King Mahendra began to cosy up to Pakistan and China to spite India, that, too, in 1962 when India landed itself in a border conflict with China and emerged a loser. Nehru's criticism of the Nepal king's action was not interference in the kingdom's domestic affairs but was a democrat's reaction to King Mahendra's arbitrary action. This is not to claim that India's attitude towards Nepal has always been altruistic and conducive to good neighbourliness. Even in King Tribuvan's time there were attempts by Indian diplomats (notably the then Indian ambassador C.P.N.Singh) and others to show off their clout *vis-a-vis* the Palace. It flowed from the fact that King Tribhuvan had sought asylum in New Delhi from the rampaging Rana regime. The restoration of his throne put India in a commanding position so to say but luckily the ugly phase in India -Nepal relations did not last long. This is not the place for recalling Nepal's recent history but suffice it to say that after King Mahendra, his son King Birendra encountered spirited popular demand for the restoration of responsible government and had to be content to become a constitutional monarch.

The bane of Nepal in recent years has been the brittleness of its main democratic parties and the growing pockets of strength of pro-China Communists playing the parliamentary game. After the death of the legendary Bishweshwar Prasad (B.P) Koirala, the Nepali Congress has been at sixes and sevens, with feuding factions fighting for its control. His nephew Girija Prasad Koirala had to resign although his Nepali Congress enjoyed a majority in Parliament because of intra-party feuds. At the policy level, while Girija Prasad Koirala set out to wage a full-scale war against insurgents in the western districts by deploying the army against them, his successor Sher Bahadur Deuba, toned down Koirala's policy. He pursued a policy of carrot and stick as long as he lasted in the hot seat. There have been intermittent negotiations between the Government and the insurgents for a peaceful settlement of the essentially law and order problem. It also seemed that the Palace was finding the problem handy to replace prime ministers according to its political convenience and the king's personal whim. One silver lining is that there is no evidence of military support from other countries to the insurgents, while India has been beefing up the Nepali army's fighting capability. The ultra-Left activists calling themselves Maoists reject the prevailing constitutional monarchy in the kingdom, whiie at the same time holding the parliamentary democratic system also unsuitable. More than their perception of future Nepal, their violent methods of functioning and establishment of a so-called parallel government in remote areas make them a menace to Nepal's orderly progress and territorial integrity. Meanwhile, there was a ghastly massacre of the entire Royal family in 2001, like the one in Dacca in 1975 when the then Bangladesh President's family was virtually liquidated. The massacre in Kathmandu royal palace was said to be the work of the crown prince due to a family dispute. King Gyanendra, the late king's sole surviving brother, has since been crowned king and Nepal has been steadily recovering political stability. In short, all the three countries — Sri Lanka, Bangladesh and Nepal — had earlier suffered in different degrees on account of hegemonic attitude of Indian leadership towards them. The most shamefaced was Rajiv Gandhi's cold war against the Himalayan kingdom in the 1980's because the authorities of Pashupathinath temple in Kathmandu would not allow his Italian-born wife into its *sanctum sanctorum*! Apparently, neither Indira Gandhi nor her son realised that domestic democratic values suffered on account of such misadventures abroad.

Reverting to the practice of democracy within India, it has been a mixed bag. This is because the system is being deliberately run down. Beyond the ritualistic routine of periodical elections democracy lately has been a shell without substance. When the founding fathers of the Constitution opted for the parliamentary system in preference to the presidential form of government the overwhelming urge was for accountability of the Executive. The stability associated with the presidential form did not appeal to the Constitution makers even though the country had just gone through the traumatic experience of partition, massive migration of population and bloodletting on a large scale. While the danger of fissiparous forces threatening the integrity of the country had made the constitution makers go in for a quasi-unitary polity, rather than for a federal structure: they did not allow this consideration to sway them from their preference for the parliamentary system. As Bhimrao Ambedkar, the architect of the constitution, said the accent was on accountability of the Executive, which parliament was expected to ensure by virtue of its being elected on the basis of adult franchise every five years. Further, in a country of India's size and diversity, the presidential system would have accentuated divisive tendencies.

The presence of leaders of the stature of Nehru, Patel and Azad and the availability of Nehru to guide the country for the first 18 years of independence had, no doubt, taken care of stability. Unfortunately, however, transparency or accountability of the Executive has remained only on paper especially after the Nehru-Shastri years. It was because the successors did not share Nehru's democratic temper and outlook and also because other democratic institutions like an independent judiciary and a free press were slow in blossoming, presumably because of personality-oriented politics of the Nehru period. The predominant public feeling during the Nehru years was that he would do no wrong. The belief had led to indifference towards institutions to promote democracy at different levels and also take care of good governance. Nehru's towering personality and his absolute credibility as a leader dedicated to the betterment of the country ironically caused public complacence towards the central issue of governance. Compounding the phenomenon, Nehru also preoccupied himself with his pet passion to keep the East-West cold war from hotting up. In the process, he would objectively steer clear of desired domestic agenda. He would set the style for national debate highlighting larger international issues like Panchsheel,[4] or non-alignment or verbal concern for peace in a cold war riven international system. He personified the country's desire for peace in the world. No doubt, India had a vital stake in the avoidance of East-West hostilities because its development would be hampered in the event of outbreak of war between the Soviet and Atlantic blocs, with sensitive issues like Korea, Berlin, etc. perennially on the boil. A large number of Asian, African and Latin American countries shared his outlook and approach. In the process, the non-aligned movement spread far and wide with leaders of the stature of Gamal Abdel Nasser (Egypt), Kwame Nkrumah (Ghana), Soekarno (Indonesia), not to mention Josip Broz Tito of Yugoslavia, perched precariously between Stalinist Russia and mutually hostile US, swelling the non-aligned ranks. As long as it lasted, it was the grandest concert of newly independent and freedom-loving nations. No wonder, it stirred the people of India to their depths. It was believed to be the golden age of Indian political renaissance. It seemed what Nehru had dreamed and set out in his monumental work, *Discovery of India*[5] was happening.

But it was easier wished than accomplished. Keeping peace between the Soviet and Atlantic alliances by avoiding military alliances was easy as long as the territorial integrity and sovereignty of the non-aligned nations was not threatened. When it happened the policy had to be diluted. First, Tito started leaning on the West, as Stalin became more and more intolerant of non-conformism in his Communist church and military threat from Moscow developed. Similarly, threatened by Anglo-French forces out to undo the nationalisation of the Suez Canal, Nasser was forced to seek Soviet military support. India's day of reckoning dawned when the border dispute with China assumed military proportions Meanwhile, Nkrumah was deposed as leader of Ghana and Soekarno started scripting his own version of nonalignment

Looking back from the narrow domestic perspective, national needs like population planning, promotion of literacy and establishment of a viable national health care system had never figured either in Parliament discussions or the writings in the newspapers in those two decades. If there had been concern for the building blocks of a thriving nation among the leaders or the led the situation today would not have been so uninspiring. Our population would not have grown to unmanageable levels, literacy levels would not have plummeted and public health would not have been sadly neglected. Above all, institution building is a difficult and time-consuming task, which required dedication and creation of congenial national temperament. It was absent. More importantly, the sinews of national defence proved frail, due to over-confidence in the efficacy of the psychological weapon as a means of national security. In retrospect, if Nehru had pressed into service his stature and influence to evolve a population policy, to launch literacy campaigns and build a national health care system, India would have been a different nation now. For instance, India's population of 300 plus millions in 1947 had doubled in the next forty years with attendant spread of illiteracy and ill- health. As Nehru himself stressed in the *Discovery of India*[6], population planning, massive literacy and a functioning national health service would have made the democratic system with adult franchise more meaningful denying caste and religion their present salience in shaping the country's political landscape. Because of massive illiteracy and backwardness among the people, caste and religion have vitiated the democratic system.

Another problem was that Nehru would not delegate responsibility for such domestic tasks by taking every thing under his wing. The resultant centralisation of initiative did not impair democratic institutions in Nehru's time because he abhorred arbitrary governance and was a great stickler for democratic norms. But his daughter and other successors proved different. At another level, the dominance of the Congress party both numerically and in terms of the appeal of its leadership virtually crippled the system because the conventional two-party or multi-party system was nowhere in sight. It was the Congress *Vs* nothing, with the different groups trying to forge ramshackle pre-election combinations which would collapse soon after the polls. Those ploughing their lonely furrows were equally decimated at the hustings. In short, the first-past-the post electoral procedure vitiated the democratic system by denying the smaller parties their due political space. Further, electoral considerations determined the policies and actions of political parties, including the Congress Party. The Communists seemed to be different even after they opted to fight elections and run the parliamentary system. The Communist Party of India (CPI) had formally fallen in line with the concept of political plurality at its Amritsar Congress in 1958. But the Communist Party (Marxist) (CPI (M), is not formally committed to uphold a pluralist polity nor has it eschewed its ideological proclivity for dictatorship of the proletariat. At the other end of the political spectrum, the Bharatiya Janata Party (BJP), as well as its earlier avatar the Bharatiya Jana Sangh, promised to be parties with a difference viewing elections only as milestones to reach their larger political and social objectives. But while the Jana Sangh at least had tried to keep principles, right or wrong, above power politics, in the case of the BJP the upshot is depressing. After five years of its assumption of office at the Centre as the head of a disparate coalition of as many as 23 parties and groups, it is in a worse position than even the Congress party. Infighting and group rivalries mar the once cohesive organisation.

Caveats, however, are in order in this context. A practice has developed especially since 1998 that the ruling party or group of parties has to be constantly on guard to maintain numerical majority in the Lok Sabha. Otherwise, all the other parties irrespective of their mutual incompatibility would gang up to pull down the government and precipitate a fresh election. That a party or the alliance led by it should have a majority in the Lok Sabha to be invited by the President to form government is understandable. However, once that happens, it is reasonable to expect a tacit agreement that the Government should be allowed to run and implement its projected policies and programmes. Only in an extreme case when the ruling combine runs rough shod over democratic principles, trampling over opposition rights and privileges, should it be challenged to a trial of strength. Otherwise the country will become ungovernable as it has been lately. In 1996, a BJP Government headed by Atal Behari Vajpayee lasted just thirteen days because all the others, many of them mutually warring, combined to vote it down. Once bitten, the BJP has since been going out of its way to cajole its coalition partners and other supporters to stay on course. In the process, even budgetary levies were rolled back, making the Government vulnerable to threats from within and outside. To compound the tragedy, the budget sessions of the Lok Sabha were disrupted for three consecutive years in 2000, 2001 and 2002, with the Opposition MPs invading the well of the House, shouting slogans and forcing adjournment of the proceedings. The legislative business of the country's supreme legislature remained stalled. Any issue was good enough for such protests; its relevance to Parliament being least important. For instance, the U.S. invasion of Iraq, which started on 20 March 2003, was used to demand suspension of normal business of the Lok Sabha two weeks later! In other words, the commitment of the political class to democracy is skin-deep, while their concern for development is spasmodic.

Ironically, the Congress party which spearheaded the country's freedom movement and established and ran the democratic system for about twenty years under Nehru and then very briefly under Lal Bahadur Shastri, became a mere election machine under Indira Gandhi, setting the pattern for other parties. In 1966 when Indira Gandhi became the Prime Minister it seemed she was set to promote the objectives which her father and Lal Bahadur Shastri had upheld. The dynastic dimension of the political transition was submerged by the groundswell of public support for the new leader. That was how Indira Gandhi was able to overcome the challenge of party managers to her leadership and assume unquestioned sway over the party. Apparently, the popular adulation and the success of the intra-party manoeuvre had turned her head and made her recklessly jettison the cherished values for which Gandhiji, Nehru and other national leaders had laboured. The 1971 military conflict with Pakistan was a watershed in Indira Gandhi's career as well as in India's political history. Indira Gandhi was at the pinnacle of glory and popularity. Atal Behari Vajpayee who was then a leader of the Bharatiya Jana Sangh hailed her as Durga or goddess of strength and power. She perceived herself as the monarch of all she surveyed. The general election in 1971 in which she trounced the opposition and established the supremacy of her Congress party practically all over the country was the climax. If she had the vision to use her immense power to transform India into a fast developing nation, the history of both Indira Gandhi and India would have been different. But at that crucial moment when history beckoned to her she fumbled and reduced the once-vibrant Congress party into a lap dog, besides pushing the country's democratic political system to the brink of disintegration.

The bane since the breaking away of Indira Gandhi's followers from the parent body in 1978 had been manipulation of organisational elections. Enrolment of bogus members was the rule, with names copied from voters' lists, telephone directories and the like to outbid rivals. Whoever could muster a larger number of such supporters would win the election if and when it was held. To avoid such a hassle, Indira Gandhi dispensed with party elections altogether. She would nominate State Congress committee presidents who would in turn name their lower-level counterparts. Loyalty to Indira Gandhi and her cohorts was the sole criterion. With money collected from various sources — very often it was 'black' money, meaning income concealed from tax authorities—the general elections were fought and won with money power, reinforced in some cases with muscle power. The party thus remained in power because it had a well-oiled election machine. On the flip side, it led to intense faction fighting from top to bottom in the party. When a leader of the stature of Indira Gandhi, with her prime ministerial authority undisturbed for eighteen long years, was at the helm, the feuding groups could be kept under control. Indira Gandhi had her own faction, association with which was highly sought after. But her successors were not equal to the task. Indira Gandhi herself failed to consolidate the massive mandate she had received in the 1971 general election. It was frittered away in four years, with the emergency of 1975-77 lending a dangerous dimension to the Prime Minister's travails[7].

The Janata conglomerate was voted to power with a massive two-thirds majority in the Lok Sabha in 1977 and roused great expectations. But its leaders nursed a death wish of mutual destruction while bringing the party down and causing the collapse of the first attempt to form a coalition of non-Congress parties at the Centre. The Janata Party, incidentally, was Jayaprakash Narayan's brainchild. Lying ill in Jaslok Hospital in Bombay, he brought together the Congress (O) of Morarji Desai, Charan Singh's Lok Dal, the Socialist Party and the Bharatiya Jana Sangh, all of which were targeted by Indira Gandhi during the 'emergency.' Acharya Kripalani, a veteran freedom fighter and Gandhian, and a contemporary of Nehru and Sardar Patel was present at the birth of the Janata conglomerate and blessed it. He had to resolve a conflict for the leadership of the new party by preferring Morarji Desai to both Charan Singh and Jagjivan Ram, the other contenders. Many of the leaders of the coalescing parties like L.K. Advani and Madhu Dandavate had been in the same jail during the period. Charan Singh, incarcerated in a Delhi jail, had several RSS stalwarts as companions and reportedly was impressed by their commitment and zeal. Still they could not pull together, disproving the assumption that power was a lasting remedy to ideological and temperamental differences. In late 1978 when Janata Party President Chandra Shekhar was lying ill in a New Delhi hospital, Indira Gandhi called on him. In the course of the conversation, she reportedly asked him almost casually, "Chandra Shekharji, what do you think of the state of the nation?" Sensing the implicit dig at the squabbling in his party, Chandra Shekhar replied that India seemed to be star-crossed. (He could not naturally foresee that the Janata Government would collapse within a year). Chandra Shekhar incidentally was close to Indira Gandhi when he was heading the Young Turks in the Congress party to advocate radical economic and social policies. Still, he too, was detained during the 'emergency.'

The quest, therefore, has to go on. What kind of leadership is India after? We can find the answer to the question only by a process of elimination. It cannot be of any of the existing parties, however cohesive they may be, but individual leaders, with established dynamism and unalloyed commitment to national development, like, for instance, Atal Behari Vajpayee and Lal Krishna Advani, may yet lead the country out of the woods. It is not because the party system has come unstuck but because no party, however monolithic, can unilaterally accomplish the national tasks, which we shall enumerate presently. Power politics has so deeply permeated the system that governance has become a hurdle race. After the defeat of the Janata, political pundits had begun to sing requiem for the party system itself. Their approach was empirical and the reasoning simple. See what happened to the Janata experience. Here was a party which in 1977 seemed to be a historical necessity, public support for which was spontaneous and overwhelming and which had accomplished what was once thought to be impossible, namely the displacement of the Congress from power at the Centre. Within three years, it had not only lost power but had nearly withered away. Was it not a symptom of the decay of the party system? It also begets another theory as a corollary that the resurgence of the Congress (I) is due to the personality factor. Conversely, by bringing about the metamorphosis in the Janata fortunes by her charisma (an extremely overworked expression) Indira Gandhi had shown that personalities, and not parties, counted in India

The factors responsible for the collapse of the Janata become relevant in this connection. In one of her election speeches Indira Gandhi was reported to have said that having come together to grab power the Janata constituents were falling apart without that cement. Even the most uncharitable critic would concede that power did not prove an adhesive to the Janata Party. Not that the constituents were not after power. In fact some of them seemed to be mad about it. But there was no method in their madness. That was the tragedy. Even the fear of losing power, achieved after long years of coveting, and trying unsuccessfully, did not inhibit them from pursuing their separate paths to annihilation. Ironically for nearly three decades it was the single effort of all of them to replace the Congress monopoly on power and yet when it happened their individual ambitions drove some of them back into Indira Gandhi's parlour. To fathom the reasons for such behaviour one has perhaps to stray into the realm of psychology. As for the personality factor, the Janata Party was second to none in that respect, although none of its too many leaders would measure up jointly or severally to Indira Gandhi's stature. So if it is a case of individuals putting the party system in the shade the Janata experiment should have been the exception and not the rule.

But the Janata Party did not have an ideology, it was contended, as if the Congress (I) had a cast-iron one. There are no doubt the well-worn slogans of socialism, secularism and democracy which are repeated *ad nauseam* to this day as if set to cheap music but they do not constitute an ideology even assuming that there is a genuine commitment to them by the party. On the other hand, the economic policy statement of the Janata Party hammered out after much discussion was a cogent document. Did anyone ever mention it even, when tearing up the party brick by brick? Against this background is it right to cast the horoscope of the party system in India on the basis of the experience of such a party? In my view what happened to the Janata underscores not the decay of the party system but the pulling power of power-oriented groups or parties, the resistance of narrow, inwardlooking loyalties on which the Janata constituents were built for absorption into an organisation which had once the glow of a national movement. Because the constituents would not allow themselves to be contained in a larger framework the Janata collapsed. A better yardstick for evaluating the durability of the party system would be the pre-Janata experience of political parties. Until Independence the Congress was a national forum, a movement for the struggle against the British. Even after 1947 it did not become a party in the dictionary sense of the term. The Socialists and Communists had been hounded out on a charge of dual membership i.e. that they could not be members at the same time of their respective parties and the Congress. But that did not make the Congress homogenous or monolithic.

Gandhiji was so distressed by the state of affairs in the Congress that a few weeks before his assassination he suggested its disbandment and the formation in its place of a social service organisation. What was it that upset Gandhiji so much? Not individual indiscretions of Congress leaders of which there were many; not even the influx into the organisation of opportunists to the chagrin of idealists because Gandhiji knew that it was inevitable in the context of its accession to power. But being a staunch believer in people's power, which meant pressure from below to prompt social- economic change, Gandhiji was disturbed by the tendency to lay store by administrative action from the top. And the Congress operated from the top without worrying about action at the grassroots level. The transformation of the Congress, as desired by Gandhiji, did not take place whatever be the reasons. After the 1952 general election Rajaji also pleaded for reorganisation of the Congress to make it less heterogeneous but Nehru did not go along with him. Still, the Congress had not been reduced to a mindless election machine of more recent years. It remained a cross between the Gandhian concept and the Western practice. In his disputes with Purshottam Das Tandon and Acharya Kripalani, Nehru no doubt established the supremacy of the governmental wing of the party but he did not make it a mere instrument of power. That happened after the 1969 split whatever be its ideological overtones,

Even then, Indira Gandhi had soon after taken back into the party even those opposed to her personally, thus restoring to the Congress a part of its comprehensive character. But the 1978 split put paid to it. Considering her stature it was not surprising that Indira Gandhi should tower over the rest. But the institutionalisation of the fact that the party would be a mere instrument of power manipulated from above was the villain of the piece. The Janata experiment, if anything, showed the shortsightedness of such an approach. No doubt, single-minded dynamic leadership can make it durable, but for what purpose? "Charismatic" leadership in our conditions should mean capacity to stir the people not merely to flock to the polling booths but for action at the grassroots level. Raising astronomical sums of money for election purposes, building a party machine and winning votes with populist slogans are, no doubt, great skills, but there is no dearth of such talent in India. What is needed is sincerity of purpose and dedication to values—not slogans-and speeches.

Let us recall here what Professor Raj Krishna, who was influenced by 'J.P's thinking and was personally close to Lohia said in an article published on January 31, 1980[8]: "The basic parameters of the performance of the Indian economy have proved to be stubbornly resistant to the coming and going of politicians of various persuasions. The promises of these politicians have been almost identical; and their average knowledge/ ignorance, sincerity / insincerity and performance / non- performance have been depressingly similar. Inflation, unemployment, poverty and inequality are too deeply rooted in the politico- administrative structure of India to be affected by the charisma of 1980 any more than they were by the charisma of 1971 or the charisma of 1952. After all, Mrs. Gandhi presided over this unreformed structure for a whole decade in which the economy recorded its normal low rate of growth (about 3.5 per cent a year), a decade in which we lived through hyperinflation, mounting poverty and unemployment, and progressive concentration of rural land and urban wealth. Techno-economic measures for solving these problems do, of course, exist. But the civil service, with its limited lights and entrenched interests, on which all Indian prime ministers have exclusively relied, is not likely to implement these measures in the absence of sufficient non-official pressure of the right kind. The new-style politicians will, of course, be pressuring the bureaucracy relentlessly. But they would be demanding favours for their followers and supporters among landlords and businessmen. They would not be asking and getting much for the rural and the urban poor, for they do not really represent the poor, although the poor have voted for them"

Raj Krishna, who as the principal draftsman of the aborted Sixth Five- year Plan (1978-83), spelt out the development strategy in the document, which was adopted by the Janata Government. It flowed from the objective situation that although a lot had been accomplished in the previous 30 years and an infrastructure had been raised much of the benefits from it accrued largely to the relatively affluent sections. No Government is likely to implement these measures in the absence of sufficient non-official pressure of the right kind. "Our pattern of investment, particularly in the provision of social infrastructure has been biased in favour of urban areas. Thus, though the output of doctors is numerically adequate and the urban well-to-do have reasonable hospitals to go to, the rural areas continue to be poorly served in respect of access to medical services."

The slogan of *garibi hatao* (banish poverty) electrified the country in 1971. Nearly 10 years after even a strategy to tackle the problem had not been worked out. (Indira Gandhi after returning to power in 1980, discarded without batting an eyelid the Janata strategy evolved after plenty of study and discussion). Raj Krishna went on to say: "unemployment, poverty and inequality are related phenomena so that a dent in any one of them will mitigate the other. The concept of poverty includes not merely those who are unemployed and poor but also those who, fully or partly employed, earn very little because of low productivity or low wages... According to a recent estimate using norms of caloric consumption, the percentage of population below the poverty line in 1977-78 may be projected at 48 in the rural areas and 41 in the urban areas. The total number of poor, so defined, would be 290 million. About 160 million of these fall below 75 per cent of the poverty line."

Describing the Sixth Plan approach, he wrote: "The strategy, in a nutshell, was to provide gainful employment to as many of the poor as possible by creating avenues for it in the very villages where they live instead of drawing them to the urban slums. Absorbing them in the heavy industry sector will require massive investment, which is not available. Small-sized, labour- intensive industries, irrigated agriculture, dairying, forestry, fisheries, poultry farming and the like are some of the means of stimulating the employment augmenting capacity of the economy with reasonable investment. The plan was to generate employment also through the expansion of infrastructure and social services like road construction, electrification, water supply, rural schools and community health services. Once the poor are productively employed in the villages and not as migrants to the swelling towns, the increase in their consumption will create additional employment for wage goods, which can be produced by labour-intensive methods. The paradox of glut in stocks of food grains and cloth while millions go hungry and naked will cease. The irrigation, power and housing programmes also imply a massive increase in construction activity with a corresponding expansion of employment opportunities. The Minimum Needs Programme was revised to include elementary and adult education, housing and urban development and nutrition. Unlike in the Fifth Plan adequate outlay was provided for the programme."

The crux of the new development strategy lay in its accent on distributive justice. It was candidly admitted that the rural and urban poor have to be organised so that through the strength of their unity and vigilance the benefits of various laws, policies and schemes percolate to the people. The document realised that "critical for the success of all redistributive laws, policies and programmes is that the poor be organised and made conscious of the benefits intended for them. Organised tenants have to see that the tenancy laws are implemented. Organisations of the landless have to see that surplus lands are identified and distributed to them in accordance with the law within five years. Local leaders of the poor have to ensure that all area plans and sectoral plans designed for the benefit of their localities and target groups are effectively administered. The general lesson of the experience so far is that because of leakages in delivery systems and ineffective administration, rural programmes fail to improve the distribution of income. The Planning Commission is proposing a massive shift of resources in favour of rural areas with an in-built redistributive character in almost every programme. But whether the larger resource will have the desired equalising effect will depend on the extent to which the organised pressure of the beneficiaries counteracts the weaknesses of the administration and the opposition of vested interests". Never before did a five-year plan envisage such grassroots' level action in support of socio-economic objectives. At the practical level, the Janata Government faithfully carried out its programme of augmentation of irrigation potential at the unprecedented rate of 2.8 million hectares annually. Further, extension of drinking water supply to problem villages, food for work, fisheries, social forestry, *Antyodaya*, enlargement of Operation Flood and the National Adult Education Programme were among the ingredients of the massive nation - building enterprise of the two years of Janata rule. But governance was not the issue in the highly politicised atmosphere of 1980. The issue was the incapacity of the Janata constituents to pull together. They could not hang together. So they hanged separately.

Within three years of a veritable electoral rout in 1977, Indira Gandhi bounced back to power in 1980, in an election precipitated by the break - up of the Janata party. Meanwhile, she had also purged the Congress party of elements not totally loyal to her and her family, bringing into being Congress Party-Indira or the Congress (I). Nevertheless, it was the same story again, with the party suffering in popularity in State after State within three years. Among the contributory factors to the decline and fall of the great leader and the party she led were absence of internal democracy in the party, erosion of checks and balances in the political system and disregard of moral values. As the party began to lose popular support and lost control of several State administrations, even if it retained power at the Centre, Indira Gandhi began to adopt desperate damage control measures. In the strategic border State of Punjab, sensing loss of public support for her party, she first created the Frankenstein of Bhindranwala to outflank the Akali Dal and then sent troops into the holy Golden Temple to weed out armed terrorists led by him.[9] Simultaneously, there was an indiscriminate witch-hunt against Sikhs in Punjab, Haryana and Delhi in the run up to the much-hyped 1982 Asian Games in New Delhi. In the process, the Sikh community was outraged and alienated. Young men and women began to swell terrorist ranks which, in turn, led to a cycle of violence and counter-violence. It seemed that Punjab, India's sword arm, which has always stood by the country in the past military conflicts with Pakistan, might now be compromised. Pakistan naturally fished in the troubled waters supplying weapons to terrorists from Punjab and training them on its territory. If Indira Gandhi had not been cruelly assassinated and become a martyr, the Congress party might have lost the 1984 general election to the Lok Sabha. Indira Gandhi's murder, however, sent shock waves throughout the country and enabled Rajiv Gandhi to score a landslide win in the 1984 election on a massive sympathy vote. More importantly, there was no opposition worth the name to Rajiv's succession in spite of the inherent dynastic character of the changeover. Just as the silent majority had accepted Indira Gandhi as the successor in 1966, the country, shaken by the assassination of Indira Gandhi and its aftermath, heartily endorsed President Zail Singh's action in swearing Rajiv in as prime minister even before he was formally elected party leader. Interestingly, P.V. Narasimha Rao who was then a member of the Congress Parliamentary Board went along with the choice of Rajiv while Pranab Mukerjee, with his own prime ministerial ambitions, demurred.

Rajiv Gandhi's record in office was, however, far from edifying. From the word 'go', he seemed lost and groping. At the organisational level, he frittered away the massive majority that his party had garnered in the 1985 general election. The sympathy wave had resulted in the party winning a whopping 401 of the 508 seats in the Ninth Lok Sabha. But by 1989 he managed to bring down the tally to 197 seats or a loss of more than 50 per cent of the1985 mandate. Once the apprehension of threat to national security in the wake of Indira Gandhi's gruesome murder waned, Rajiv was on his own to lead the party and run the Government. As party leader, his effort was not equal to the task; in fact, his record was galling. In his home state of Uttar Pradesh, the Congress strength had come down from 84 to 15, (which Narasimha Rao further brought down to five in 1991). In the other Hindi states of northern India, like Bihar, Madhya Pradesh and Rajasthan, too, the Congress record was equally bleak. It was understandable that Rajiv, new to politics and burdened with the awesome responsibility of governing a country of India's size and problems, should lack self-confidence but he was also wanting in vision and political drive and determination. It was said he would follow the advice of the last person he consulted and that invariably happened to be his wife. The result was disaster. India Gandhi, too, had been short of vision but she was second to none in drive and determination. She had become a past master in manipulative politics as the Punjab tragedy showed. But Rajiv fumbled from the word 'go'. He first adopted the high-minded approach of distancing himself from 'power brokers' but soon retraced his steps and fell in line with them, that, too, with a vengeance. Some of the characters he had collected around him stand out for their many-sided notoriety. No need to mention names because some of them are still in the higher echelons of the Congress party.

His response to the irrelevant Rama temple issue catapulted to centre stage by the BJP was even more opportunistic and damaging. Aided by Narain Dutt Tiwari, who was then the Congress Chief Minister of Uttar Pradesh, Rajiv pursued the zigzag path of appeasement of rival sectarian elements. The two leaders first allowed the gates of the Babri Masjid to be opened for the worship of the idols smuggled into it and then bestowed the second language status in U.P. for Urdu, as if Urdu is the language exclusively of the Muslims. To crown the chain of false steps, he launched the Congress election campaign from Ayodhya with the slogan of Ram Rajya. Earlier there was the Shahbano disaster when the Government set aside a Supreme Court judgment allowing due compensation to a divorced Muslim wife. When orthodox Muslim opinion was up in arms against the court verdict, Rajiv got the judgment superseded by new legislation accommodating conservative opinion. In the process, divorced Muslim women were left at the mercy of charitable institutions like the *waqfs* instead of being able to claim alimony from their former husbands. Enlightened women of all faiths throughout the country were outraged by the opportunism. Similarly, Salman Rushdie's controversial book, *Satanic Verses*, was banned outright without going through the due process for such proscription. The purpose was again appeasement of intolerant

Muslim opinion. As a result while the book was widely sold in the black market, the issue of its arbitrary proscription along with Ayatollah Khomeni's *fatwa* for Rushdie's death needlessly became a controversy in domestic politics. For instance, ruffians egged on by a former Congress minister at the Centre hounded out the vice-chancellor of the renowned institution of learning, Jamia Milia Islamia, on the alibi that he had not joined the vilification campaign against Salman Rushdie. In short the Congress party under Rajiv Gandhi did not have the social awareness to understand the forces at work in the country and to cope with them. So they indulged in pathetic rituals at the cost of national cohesion and religious harmony. The BJP, not to be left behind, became a champion of Rushdie's right to be read merely because it offended Muslim opinion.

Rajiv Gandhi's prime ministerial tenure also was marked by two man-made, avoidable national tragedies. He opened his account, so to say, with the Bhopal gas disaster, which claimed nearly ten thousand lives, including about seven thousand condemned to slow death years after the leakage of poisonous gas from an insecticide factory in the Madhya Pradesh capital. That happened in December 1984, within weeks of Rajiv becoming Prime Minister. Blinded by partisan considerations and overwhelmed by Arjun Singh, Rajiv did not care to find out how the insecticide factory had come to be set up in an inhabited area of Bhopal and what the terms were for its establishment. Did the State Government, also manned by the Congress party and then headed by Arjun Singh, subsequently an inveterate Sonia *bhakt*, (devotee) swing it and was the Central Government also a party to it? Worse still, the chief executive of the offending factory was allowed to escape to the US, beyond the reach of Indian criminal investigation agencies.[10]

The second was the massacre of Sikhs mostly in Delhi following Indira Gandhi's assassination, which led to Rajiv succeeding her. Because Indira Gandhi's Sikh bodyguards were said to have killed her to avenge the army assault on the Golden Temple, an anti-Sikh pogrom was mounted. It might have been initially a spontaneous emotional outburst sparked by canards of Sikh conspiracy to destabilise India. The entire community was sought to be implicated in the crime of two or three misguided young men. About 4,000 Sikh men, women and children were killed in cold blood or burnt alive and their belongings looted. They were all housed in rehabilitation colonies and therefore became sitting ducks to sectarian frenzy. Quite a few local Congress party leaders had a hand in the outrage but all of them have gone scot-free. First, the police remained silent spectators while the carnage was going on. Secondly, the judiciary was manipulated to save them from trial and punishment. Although Narasimha Rao was nominally the Home Minister at that time, Rajiv Gandhi called the shots in letting the ruffians have their criminal way. He virtually condoned the brutality likening his mother's murder to the uprooting of a giant tree, which would lead to disturbance of the soil.[11]

The subsequent terrorism in Punjab was partly triggered by the massacre. Incidentally, the anti-Sikh pogrom had shades of the Jallianwala Bagh massacre of 13 April 1919. It was said the outrage tolled the death knell of British *raj* in India, which ended in 1947. One thousand six hundred and fifty rounds of .303 rifle fire was directed for ten minutes at a gathering of about 15,000 people trapped in a maidan with narrow exit and entry points at Jallianwala Bagh near Amritsar.[12] The toll was about 300 lives lost, including women and children. General R.E.H. Dyer, the architect of the massacre, was censured by the Hunter Committee, which investigated the atrocity. He was also deprived of his command and soon after his career in the British army had come to an ignominious end, even if racial and imperial impulses spurred some Britons to raise money in his support. The British House of Commons endorsed a resolution charging Dyer with 'error of judgment,' with Winston Churchill speaking in support of the motion. In terms of both fatalities and cold- bloodedness the Jallianwala Bagh massacre pales in heinousness before the 1984 anti-Sikh pogrom promoted by some Delhi Congress party leaders with the tacit connivance of Rajiv Gandhi and his colleagues. There is another dimension also to this tragic denouement, which sharpened the contrast between image and reality. It is the perception of the kind of leadership that the people thought the country needed. There was, firstly, the tendency to look upon the youth of the country as *per se* better endowed with a sense of public morality. No doubt, that was a reaction to the people's disgust with some of the old leaders who were strutting on the national scene for decades with what seemed an abundance of hypocrisy. Secondly, in a country like ours where the youth outnumbers the rest of the population it is natural for a young leader to be welcomed as a messiah. Thirdly, professional politicians have as a category become untrustworthy. Rajiv Gandhi was a technocrat who reluctantly joined politics. He thus satisfied all the criteria of a promising leader. He was thought to have reluctantly joined politics after the tragic end of his younger brother to help his mother brave the trauma of bereavement. In short, all the ingredients of an ideal leader were there: non-involvement in the dirty business of politics; perceived flair for cleanliness in public life and preparedness to stand by his mother when she badly needed support.

In 1987, within two years of Rajiv Gandhi's resplendent rise to public acceptability and consequent promise of an almost millennial change in India, the scenario came unstuck. For the first time since India's independence the Prime Minister of the country was widely perceived to be lacking in integrity. He was alleged to have accepted kickbacks from the Swedish supplier of Bofors howitzers.[13] There were charges of corruption against Indira Gandhi and Morarji Desai also. But the situation then was qualitatively different. Probity was not Indira Gandhi's strong suit. Her greatness did not rest on a reputation for honesty and incorruptibility. In fact, she promoted a kind of cynicism, especially among her numerous supporters that corruption, being a global phenomenon, was unavoidable. In the case of Morarji Desai, the impression was that he tolerated or connived at his son's indiscretions, not that he was privy to the peccadilloes. Moreover, not many tears would have been shed at Desai's downfall if it had not also meant the end of the Janata experiment whereas a mountain of hopes had been built on Rajiv Gandhi and his perceived mission to cleanse our public life.

The upshot was that, as stated, Rajiv Gandhi's party managed to get just 197 seats in a House of 505 members in the 1989 general election. It was the single largest party in the Lok Sabha even if technically short of a majority by nearly sixty seats. Even then Rajiv could have formed the government with the support of others, which would have been available for love or money. That could have also preserved political stability, which would not be forthcoming otherwise. He did not do so because of bruised ego and an urge to avenge the defeat at the hands of Vishwanath Pratap Singh who was then his *bete noir*. Pique has no place in a parliamentary democracy as P.V. Narasimha Rao showed by forming a minority government in 1991 and keeping it going for the full term. The BJP at the head of the NDA Government in 1998 was also buffeted by repeated challenges but Atal Bihari Vajpayee had been able to weather the storm for five years. That is statesmanship. Instead of doing his duty as the leader of the single largest party in the Lok Sabha, Rajiv let Vishwanath Pratap (VP) Singh's Janata Dal form the government. The Janata Dal with 142 seats was the second largest party in the House but it had 58 members less than the Congress party. That it was not an altruistic gesture by Rajiv was clear as daylight. Nor was it a sign of respect for the electorate's verdict against the Congress party because he strutted about as a veritable victor. It was just a ruse to let a minority Janata Dal government come into being and then precipitate a fresh election by pulling it down.

V.P Singh cobbled a coalition with the 86-member BJP and the CPI (M)-led Leftist parties with a total of 55 members supporting his government from outside. It seemed many regional parties had come together to lend a federal colour to the government and it was hoped V.P. Singh would build on it to evolve a national alternative to the Congress party. But it was not to be. Thus, the hopes built around the second non- Congress government at the Centre in nearly fifty years evaporated before they could be felt. V.P. Singh seemed to have an in-built flair to hasten his own downfall. Even if his Government lacked a majority on its own his image as an honest leader stood out. His campaign against corruption, pinning down Rajiv Gandhi on the Bofors issue made him a veritable national hero. He was riding on the crest of a wave of public approbation and support. But within his Janata Dal he faced opposition from Chandra Shekhar, who coveted prime ministership. Towards that end, he forced an election for the leadership of the Janata Dal Parliamentary Party. If V.P. Singh had taken him on, he would have won hands down in a straight contest; Chandra Shekhar himself knew he had no leg to stand on. So he was trying to manipulate a situation which would obviate an election. Singh walked into the trap. Instead of clinching the issue there and then, he staged a stupid, self-defeating manoeuvre of nominating Devi Lal as the leader of the party and Devi Lal in turn returning the compliment. In the process, instead of being the elected leader of the parliamentary party he became a protege (and potential victim) of *tau* (uncle in Hindi) as Devi Lal was endearingly called by his admirers. Earlier, he made Devi Lal his deputy prime minister.

In fact, bringing in the wily Devi Lal, who was a past master in manipulative politics, as deputy prime minister was a grave mistake. Instead, he could have made N.T. Rama Rao (NTR) the deputy prime minister and reinforced his position in the southern States. NTR had been defeated in the State assembly election and was visibly dejected. A berth at the Centre would have revved him up; his Telugu Desam Party (TDP) was already solidly backing V.P. Singh On the other hand, as expected, Devi Lal spelt trouble with a capital T from the day he was taken into the Cabinet. He started a subtle blackmail policy by organising massive rallies of his supporters in Delhi, to campaign for subsidies and reservations for Jats. Renting crowds and carting them in hired vehicles for political demonstrations is a Haryana specialty. As a result V.P. Singh's leadership of the Janata Dal was under threat. Singh was in a fix. He could not sack the deputy Prime Minister nor could he quietly put up with his open challenge to his leadership. So he hit on the bright idea of implementing through an executive order the recommendations of the Mandal Commission providing for reservation in employment and education for what are called other backward castes (OBCs).[14]

In the process, perhaps unwittingly, V.P. Singh unleashed a social revolution which nearly fifty years earlier had changed the political face of the southern states of Tamil Nadu, Karnataka and even Andhra Pradesh to an extent. The vibrant Elavas in Kerala similarly organised themselves for political and social action. The upsurge generally owed itself to the philosophy of social egalitarianism as propounded by Periyar E.V. Ramasamy Naicker, founder of the Dravidian Movement in the shape of Dravida Kazagam (DK). Its offshoots, the DMK) and the A-AIADMK have been alternatively in power in Tamil Nadu for 40 years without a break. Congress leaders like K. Kamaraj, (Tamil Nadu), Devaraj Urs (Karnataka) and Brahmananda Reddy (Andhra Pradesh) had responded to the challenge of the Dravidian parties by bringing backward castes into leadership positions in the Congress party. In Karnataka, Devraj Urs as chief minister had also undertaken fairly radical land reforms benefiting actual cultivators; in Tamil Nadu security of tenancy has been a boon to farmers in Andhra Pradesh, the Firka Development Scheme of Prakashm in 1946 was similarly motivated.

Cumulatively, the measures awakened backward classes and led to their empowerment, very often at the expense of the upper castes. More significantly, Ramaswami Naicker in the south, like Mahatma Jotiba Phule in Maharashtra and Ambedkar at the national level, became the prophet of social revolution as India advanced into the twenty-first century. This is the positive aspect of the Mandal phenomenon, although the peremptory decision to implement the commission recommendations, without preparing the people for the drastic change was an invitation to chaos and anarchy. There was not also an adequate explanation of its implications to the public, except for the distorted writings in the newspapers. So middle class non-OBC job- seekers felt deprived, cheated and enraged. Even V.P. Singh's party members did not know what it was all about and were stunned into inaction as anti-social elements, masquerading as champions of the upper castes, let loose mayhem. Some misguided young persons were also made to immolate themselves in public demonstrations to inflame passions further. It seemed several parts of north India, Delhi included, were in the throes of a caste war. The Congress party and the BJP quietly fuelled the flames of the chaos, the BJP to safeguard its Hindutva flanks and the Congress to spite V.P. Singh for having virtually put Rajiv Gandhi on the mat. Thus went up in smoke the hope of a second non-Congress government at the Centre surviving its full term much less, delivering on its promise of clean, efficient and responsible goverrnment. It seemed Rajiv Gandhi's calculation that V.P. Singh's Janata Dal would soon fall apart and necessitate a fresh election was coming true. He hope the Congress party would do better in the event, whatever it might cost to the nation in terms of repeated electrions and virtual absence of governance and development. Even as V.P. Singh was hurtling towards his downfall, Rajiv induced Chandra Shekar and his supporters to defect from the Janata Dal and form a rump government with 'support from outside' of the Congress party.[15] The irony was that Rajiv was the author of what is called the anti-defection law in enacting the law, Rajiv had personally promoted defection of legislators, that, too, at the national level, taking technical shelter under the imprecise letter of the law. The Chandra Shekhar phase lasted just four months, with the 'prime minister' and his colleagues setting a record in corruption. The slogan was that what the Congress party could do in 40 years (in amassing wealth both individually and as a party), Chandra Shekar and his colleagues would do in four months. The economy was in a shambles; the balance of payments position was critical, was resources adequate for just for for week of imports. The nation's gold reserves were mortgaged to the Bank of England. (It was left to P.V. Narasimha Rao and his chosen finance minister, Dr. Man Mohan Singh, to retrieve the situation later when Narasimha Rao stepped into the beach caused by Rajiv Gandhi's dastardly assassination.) To their eternal credit, Narasimha Rao and Manmohan Singh put India on the road to speed economic progress. But that Government was not allowed to last longer than one term that, too, with repeated brushed with parliamentary challenges. The BJP and the Communists ganged up to try to pull it down on two or three occasions. In the process, Narasimha Rao had to 'induce' purchasable MPs like Ajit Singh (Charan Singh's son) and members of the Jharkhand Mukti Morcha to back the Government.

Earlier, after Rajiv's murder, when P.V. Narasimha Rao took over the reins of Congress party leadership in 1991, he was shrewd enough to realise that the retain control of the party he would have to change its hierarchical structure. It was partly because he lacked the dynastic crutch; also he is more an intellectual and committeeman than a mass leader. So he set out to democratise the party structure and succeeded partially in 1991. Even if his motivation were self-centred his efforts would have restored the Congress party to health. The conventional procedure was for the lower level Congress committees to be elected by party members and they in turn to elect members of district and State or provincial Congress committees and so on to the apex level. But it was not to be because the entrenched factions within the party made him beat a hasty retreat. In the process his idea of distancing the dynasty from the party went by the board. In respect of internal democracy in the party, he had to drop the move for direct election of the party president by A-ICC members through secret ballot. Instead, he stuck to the practice of retaining the presidentship of the party while being the party leader in the Lok Sabha and therefore Prime Minister, in contravention of the rule that a person could hold only one post at a time. (The rule was largely honoured in the breach even in Nehru's time). Traditionally, the Congress President would nominate members of the working committee, or the national executive, the idea being that he or she should have a homogeneous team to work with. That provision was amended to provide for partial election of working committee members, with the Congress president having the veto on who should be elected and who should be nominated. Thus, while nominating members of the Working Committee Narasimha Rao rubbed Arjun Singh - an old-time power broker and Rajiv loyalist — on the wrong side by first setting aside his election to one of the posts on the committee and then retracing his steps. Here again, Narasimha Rao was aware that Arjun Singh was being backed clandestinely by Sonia Gandhi, who despite her pretense of disinterest in politics while mourning her husband's death was secretly conspiring to keep a finger in it. Still, he did not want openly to confront Sonia Gandhi and draw her out. Instead, he played her own game, quietly trying to end the dynastic domination of the party.

In the process, India as an independent nation of 50 plus years, instead of being a mature and self-confident democracy capable of evolving its own remedies for the problems besetting the polity, presents a picture of absolute poverty of leadership and paucity of positive thinking. Nothing illustrates this bleak picture more starkly than the elevation to the leadership of the Indian National Congress or the Congress party, in existence for 114 years, of Rajiv Gandhi's Italian born widow.[16] There could be a no more nauseous spectacle than that of party functionaries falling at Sonia Gandhi's feet and imploring her to lead their party and "save the country." If she had been a person of sterling virtues like commitment to India's integrity and development and experience of promoting its democratic institutions there would have been nothing wrong in her being asked to lead the Congress party. But she is wanting both in values and commitment and is a total novice to politics and political institutions. Especially, she is totally bereft of social values and ethical considerations. Her only claim to be made the leader of the party is that she had been married to Rajiv Gandhi, who later became Prime Minister of India, or that she could be a tool to promote a dynasty repugnant to the republican character of the Indian polity. If the British conservatives after the drubbing they received in the 1997 general election had approached Princess Diana to assume the leadership of the sleaze- soaked party the situation would not have been far different. Princess Diana, even if of plebeian origin, had a whiff of royalty by virtue of her marriage to the heir to the British throne, whereas Sonia, having married Rajiv Gandhi, is believed to have entered the portals of the dynasty disfiguring Indian democracy. Diana, if her BBC interview was an index, was better informed, more worldly-wise and definitely articulate compared to the older Sonia whose forays into Indian politics have been farcical while being destructive of the democratic system. She may have overcome after two years the problem of acquaintance with either Hindi or English by reading out written speeches and statements but is that what is expected of a potential prime minister of India? No serious student of politics in Britain would argue that accession of an attractive leader would put life back into the Conservative Party and restore unity and purpose to its functioning. But not the Congress leaders in India; they are pining for "a charismatic" leader to win votes for them in future elections and put them back in power at any cost. Having been out of office for six years since 1996, they were desperate for the fishes and loaves of power. When Sonia turned out to be zero they started seeking her married daughter, Priyanka and even her infant son. They are not worried about policies and programmes. They have the least interest in inner party democracy and the need for accountability of the leadership to the members. They are mentally living in the nineteenth century of feudal overlordship.

In 1998 when both Narasimha Rao and his successor, Sitaram Kesri, were unceremoniously elbowed out, the scramble among party leaders to claim credit for prevailing upon Rajiv Gandhi's widow to join the party was, as already stated, nauseating. As a matter of fact, she did not need persuasion because she was bent on making the most of her marriage to Indira Gandhi's eldest son. Initially, as daughter-in-law of the then prime minister she had a lion's share of perks and privileges She also shared in the booty when Sanjay Gandhi mulcted the tax-payer with his so-called people's car project. She was managing director of one of the Sanjay rackets in the Maruti automobile enterprise drawing a monthly salary of Rs. 10,000 (in the 1970s) for signing on the dotted line whenever required.

Later when Rajiv succeeded his mother as Prime Minister, she became the first lady by default because the wives of a succession of Presidents preferred to keep away from public gaze. After Rajiv was assassinated she inherited the same perks as his widow plus a security cover costing over Rs. 100,000 a day for the taxpayer. One cannot be an active politician while enjoying such privileges at the people's expense. Sonia has managed to reconcile the contradiction thanks to the servility and greed of her hangers-on. She is basically deficient in flair for serious issues. Clothes, perfumes, shoes and the like are her *forte.* As Amar Singh, an associate of Mulayam Singh Yadav, put it, she cannot name five rivers of India. Or for that matter, she might be equally unaware of the geography and history of her home country of Italy.

It would be instructive to compare Sonia Gandhi with other women political leaders at the helm of affairs in the States. Of them, Jayalalitha in Tamil Nadu is streets ahead of her. The Tamil Nadu chief minister is articulate, intelligent and a past master in political manipulation. Regaining the mantle of leadership of the A-AIADMK from M.G. Ramachandran's widow, she consolidated her position and reduced the party to a tool in her hands. She, too, is unscrupulous, like Sonia Gandhi but a thousand times more thorough and smooth. At another level, Laloo Prasad Yadav's wife, Rabri Devi, a homespun housewife, pitchforked into chief ministership of Bihar is sniffed at by the sophisticated for her uncouthness and ignorance of public affairs. But she has robust commonsense. She has been conducting herself fairly well despite the journalists' hostility towards her. If Sonia had been subjected to the treatment meted out by the media to Rabri Devi, she would have packed her suitcase for Italy. Instead, Sonia is a creature of the media, with both television channels and the newspapers trying to build her up. A retinue of retainers always guards her and the press has no access to her except when the spin-doctors unleash her for photo opportunities. The most disgusting spectacle was her so-called half-dip in the confluence of rivers at Khumb in January 2001, when she was said to have renounced her birth religion of Christianity and become a Hindu.[17] A more pathetic pursuit of opportunism is difficult to recall in the long history of Indian politics. At another level, Mayawati, leader of the Bahujana

Samaj Party (BSP) and off-and-on chief minister of the politically sensititive State of Uttar Pradesh has braved taunts and insinuations from the media to hold her ground. For a person of Dalit origin, she is very articulate, worldly wise and quick on the uptake of even intricate issues. She has become adept at playing power politics She has ability to match her overarching political ambition.

Still, Sonia's sycophants promote the absurdity of her becoming Prime Minister of this unfortunate country. The super leader of the Communist Party (Marxist), Sardar Hari Kishan Singh Surjeet, supposed to be the last word in principles and theories, was the prime mover in the direction in 1998 when it seemed Sonia had nearly made it. First, the fall of the BJP-led coalition government had been contrived by weaning away Jayalalitha, whose A-I ADMK was the second largest constituent of the coalition at the Centre. When the BJP Government was ultimately voted out of power by a solitary vote, there was a veritable conspiracy to make Sonia prime minister of India. What the *quid pro quo* was nobody knew; the charitable assumption being that that it could be for the CPI (M) to exploit the resultant situation for political purpose, as the rival CPI had tried to do vis-a -vis Indira Gandhi in the 1970s. Indira Gandhi was a leader with mass appeal and a born political manipulator. She pretended to go along with the Communists (CPI) until she regained electoral support when she dumped the CPI. Sonia being a novice in politics and a veritable babe in the wood might be easier to handle for the CPI (M). On the pretext of preventing the 'communal' BJP from returning to office, Surjeet tried to rig up a 'secular' front of power-starved parties and personalities in support of Sonia.

At the same time, Surjeet reportedly promised the top job to the AI-ADMK boss Jayalalitha. That was evidently to defeat the BJP's opportunistic alliance with Jayalalitha when her A-I ADMK became a coalition partner of the Vajpayee-led Government. The hype at the time of Sonia cynically grabbing Sitaram Kesri's gaddi after using him as a stool pigeon was that her "charisma" as Indira Gandhi's daughter-in-law would put the party back in power. The first victim of the propaganda was Sonia herself. She would imitate the dress and mannerisms of Indira at stage-managed public meetings where she would fumble through written speeches. Primed by her public relations managers through the usual means of spin-doctors, the media were full of her public appearances. Even the BBC was taken in by it presumably because of Sonia's European origin. A white leader for India might have stirred nostalgic memories of the *raj* in the British breasts. After displacing Narasimha Rao as party president in a veritable coup, stage-managed by Sonia's coterie, Kesri was equally servile to her until she gave him the Narasimha Rao treatment. Poor man in the months preceding his death in August 2000, he would rue before visitors the day he betrayed the "good Brahmin" meaning Narasimha Rao. In spite of claiming to be a champion of the backward castes, Kesri shared the traditional attitude of bowing to Brahmins as a superior caste. Leaving out the dying generation, there are many younger leaders in the Congress party like Rajesh Pilot, who as party president could have put Sonia in the shade if not sent her packing to Italy. But he died prematurely in the prime of his life, in a road accident. Sprightly Madhavrao Scindia, scion of the Gwalior ruling family, who showed promise of putting the Congress party back on its feet, also met with an accidental death in a plane mishap. The epidemic of death in the party, which claimed better and more deserving people, has been a godsend for uninspiring Sonia. More than Sonia's lack luster personality and lack of commitment to India and its people, she has not made herself a part of India even two decades after marrying into the Indira Gandhi family. The wives of the former British viceroys of India, just as the members of the British royalty in England, would involve themselves in philanthropic and welfare activities, Sonia had no time for such diversion from her essentially socialite pursuits. Consequently, after her assumption of the leadership of the Congress party she has been sticking to the sterile path of politicking and electioneering like her husband, Rajiv Gandhi. So the question arises whether the Congress under the leadership of the much-vaunted Sonia will join this mainstream or be swept away by it. As has been pointed out, there is no inkling of Sonia's flair, much less commitment, to such a change. She is content to play vote bank politics.[18] Kesri was in fact on a better wicket to project a pro-Dalit image for the Congress but he had other fish to fry as Sonia's stool pigeon. His opportunism in bringing down the Deve Gowda Government was in fact a command performance to facilitate Sonia's elevation to prime ministership. It was repeated when the Gujral Government was pushed out on the flimsy issue of DMK's participation in the United Front Government. The third attempt that nearly succeeded was when the Vajpayee Government was voted out through bribery and deception in 1998.

In short, instead of evolving policies suited for the socio-economic purposes of contemporary India the Congress party leaders harp on the so-called Gandhi-Nehru dynasty (Gandhi for Ghandi in Feroze Ghandi's name). In the process, they misuse the Mahatma's name and denigrate

Nehru as a promoter of dynasty instead of a full-blooded democrat that he was. Although Indira Gandhi's succession as Prime Minister was widely accepted some observers regarded it as the beginning of dynastic rule. Making her the Congress Party President by allowing himself to be persuaded by K. Kamaraj towards that end was both the first step and the index of Nehru's mind, they said.[19] Ram Manohar Lohia suspected it in the 1950s itself. In the monthly journal *Mankind.* He wrote that the saving grace of such succession would be seeing a pretty face on the front pages of the newspapers everyday. The reflection was as much on the penchant of the press to publish Nehru's pictures more frequently than necessary as on the socialist leader's uncanny eye for a pretty face. Indira Gandhi was personable in her own way especially before she started flaunting the hairstyle with a dyed white patch in the front. Compared to her, her daughter-in-law, Sonia Gandhi has neither looks nor personality. Still, every time she reads out a written script or her spin-doctors issue a statement in her name, we have her picture in the newspapers.

Indira Gandhi's biggest qualification for the job, first of Party President and then of Prime Minister was no doubt being Nehru's daughter. But there were also complementary factors. She had nation-wide visibility, not entirely by the publicity in the newspapers and bore a cosmopolitan outlook. Even if lacking formal education, she was widely read and a good conversationalist. Not being associated with a clan or group, she had a national stature. She was modern in her thinking and had the advantage of growing under Nehru's direct attention, especially after 1947. Between 1967 and 1969 when battling party bosses whom she ultimately humbled, she evoked widespread sympathy and support not so much because she was the prime minister as because she had overrun a group of power-brokers some of whom were notorious. By the same token, when in 1975, she went the whole hog to remain in power, jettisoning everything which a national leader should value and cherish, she fell from the pedestal. Disfiguring the democratic content of the Constitution, tampering with the Republican character of our polity by striving for dynastic succession, putting herself above the law on the lines of the feudal rulers of former princely states, whom, incidentally, she cut down to size, self-aggrandisement and misuse of state power for purely personal ends cost her the image which she inherited as Nehru's daughter. In retrospect, there were also two other contributory factors for Indira Gandhi's decline and fall in moral terms. The Congress Party, which was hell bent on staying on in power, was already rotting with some despicable characters gracing its leading ranks. Secondly, her two sons having come of age started interesting themselves in public affairs in the name of looking after their mother. Both the albatrosses weighed down Indira. Sanjay's record is well known and has been written about elsewhere. Rajiv, often projected as a reluctant politician, was worse, being inept also. Long before he succeeded his mother as Prime Minister, he was overbearing. For instance he did not hesitate to humiliate. Air Chief Marshal Moolgavkar, the then Air Chief, on the choice of aircraft for the Prime Minister's domestic travel. Rajiv was then only an airline pilot, not very distinguishable from scores of them.

End Notes

1. A king of Lydia, in Greek mythology, son of Zeus and a nymph, and father of People and Niobe. He was punished in Hades (some say because he stole nectar and ambrosia for mankind) by being near fruit and water, which drew out of his reach whenever he tried to satisfy his everlasting hunger and thirst. Rajaji with has vast erudition and learning would often mention the story in response to British offers to dominion status in India.
2. As a correspondent in Pakistan during the Ayub period, I would feel flatterred when Pakistanis while discussing Ayub Khan's "basic democracy" system, would speak highly of democracy in India and adult franchise and one men, one vote.
3. A former Union minister and member of Lok Sabha, Vaiko Narainswami, had been in detention from June 2001 until mid-2004 under the Prevention of Terrorism Act (POTA). According to his counsel quoted by NDTV news Vaiko was denied the use of fan in jail.
4. Panchsheel or five principles of peaceful coexistence based on Buddhist precept formed the basis of India-China relationship when Nehru and Chou en-Lai signed the 1950 treaty by which India renounced its extra-territorial interest in Tibet.
5. 1946, Signet Press, Calcutta.
6. *Ibid.*
7. According to P.V. Narasimha Rao, who was then general secretary of A-I.C.C., then, the reason for the decline in Congress popularity was failure to carry out basic land reforms as promised in the 1971 election manifesto. Narasimha Rao wrote the critique of the emergency at my instance and for my use. Responding to my whining about the destruction of democratic institutions by the 'emergency' he asked me to write a paper on it. When I did it he rejected it as one-sided and largely political and wrote the counter-paper.

8. *The Times of India.*The date is significant because Indira Gandhi resumed her prime ministership after the Janata interregnum about a fortnight earlier.
9. For a military dimension of the Blue Star tradegy, see *OPERATION BLUE STAR* The True Story, Lt.-Gen. K.S: Brar, 1993, UBS Publishers, New Delhi. The Shiromani Gurdwara Prabhandak Committee (SGPC), the supreme Sikh religious body declared Jarnail Singh Bhindranwala a martyr or saint in July 2003 on the ground that his body was not found in the debris of 1982 Golden Temple assault.
10. There were reports early in 2003 that the chief executive Anderson had been sited in the US.
11. In 1998 his widow, as Congress party president, read out a letter of apology at a public meeting at Amritsar.
12. See *Jallianwala Bagh* V.N. Datta, 1969 Ryalte Book Depot, Ludhiana.
13. For a thorough expose of the Bofors cover-up see Chitra Subrahmanyam, *Bofors, The Story. Behind the News*, 1993, Viking, New Delhi. For a whitewash of the Bofors cover-up see Vir Sanghvi, in the *Hindustan Times* 24 Aug. 2003. It was journalistic writing at its worst.
14. The Mandal Commission was set up ten years earlier when Charan Singh was Home minister in the Morarji Desai Government. Its report remained on the shelf during the intervening decade until Vishwanath Pratap Singh decided to implement it through an executive order.
15. "Support from outside" had become an over used ruse to put the supported Government on the tenterhooks and then pull it down when it suited to supporter. Rajiv Gandhi pulled the rug from under the defector regime in February 1990 on the alibi that 'spies' from the Harayana police has been shadowing his residence at 10 Janpath. Chandra Sekhar would lament that his Government had not been allowed 'to pass the motion' of thanks for the President's Address when it was pulled down.
16. Antonio Maino, of Italian origin, married Rajiv Gandhi in the early 1970s but retained her Italian nationality until 1983. Brahmachari, meaning celibate, who was 'spiritual guru' of Indira Gandhi and her family, rechristened her Sonia when she took her under his wing. Another version was that Harivanshi Rai Bachchan, the celebrated poet and father of Amitabh Bachchan gave her the name.
17. The *Times of India* had gone to town in highlighting the spectacle with a picture also.
18. According to information available on the Internet, Antonio Maino had met Rajiv Gandhi at Oxford – not university – where Rajiv was training to be an

airline pilot. There is no reference to her educational pursuits there, if any. Considering her command of English even 2003 she could not have studied at Oxford.

19. Rebutting whispers of acquiesence in dynastic succession, Nehru had vehemently denied any such intention at his last press conference in May 1964. He was ailing then. Incidentally it was a memorable press conference by the great leader, which all those like me who attended cherish to this day, forty years later.

2

Gangotri of Gangrene

The attention and space devoted to the Congress party in the foregoing chapter is not on account of any unhealthy obsession. Nor is it driven by ideological aversion for the party as Jaipal Reddy, one of the very few straightforward and cerebral leaders in the Congress party, alleges. My first exposure to politics as a 16-year-old youth was to the Indian National Congress. Apart from Gandhiji, Nehru was our idol whose *Autobiography*[1] was Bhagwat Gita and Bible to us. Gandhiji's *My Experiments with Truth*[2] moved us not so much to emulate his difficult example but to revere him and shine in his reflected glory by virtue of our fascination for the freedom struggle. Secondly, to evoke ideological attachment, the Congress party has to have an ideology. After Nehru, practically, it ceased to have anything resembling ideology. It has been all things to all men and women. For instance, the Communists, then united in the Communist Party of India (CPI) were the bitterest critics of the Congress during the freedom struggle and in the early years of independence. They charged it with being pro-capitalist and pro-landlord and even being allied with imperialists. They caricatured its class character as comprador bourgeois. When the then Soviet Union and China acclaimed India's world role, they conveniently divided the Congress party into progressives and reactionaries. Now, both the CPI (M) and the CPI find the Congress uniformly progressive enough to team up with. The CPI led the way in Indira Gandhi's time and now the CPI (M) has fallen in line during Sonia Gandhi's presidentship! So ideology has no relevance in either opposing or supporting the Congress party.

More seriously, the party had been in office for more than forty years of the last fifty-plus post-independence years of the 20th century. Its record, therefore, is a perennial point of reference for judging governments and political leaders. Last but not least, what is called Congress culture has come to afflict all political parties, including the BJP, which once called itself the party with a difference. Congress culture roughly translates itself into crass opportunism, ducking accountability, saying one thing and doing another. Every political party, not only in India, suffers from dichotomy between precept and practice. Also, no government in a pluralist democratic environment lives up to what it promises to deliver. In the case of the Congress party, however, both precept and practice vary from time to time, depending on their suitability for garnering votes. For instance, when P.V. Narasimha Rao initiated the programme for liberalisation of the economy with Manmohan Singh as the architect, the Congress party flaunted a pro-reform visage. At the time of the 1996 general election to the Lok Sabha, however, finding the reforms difficult to sell one section of the leadership jettisoned it while Narasimha Rao single-handedly campaigned on its basis.[3] But for the divided approach, the party would again have emerged as the single largest party in the new Lok Sabha. True, the stabbing of Narasimha Rao in the back was also for promoting Sonia Gandhi's political fortunes. If the party had returned to power, even if without an overall majority in the Lok Sabha, Narasimha Rao would again have become the prime minister and again managed to last the full term. That would not suit Sonia Gandhi's political agenda. As it happened, Narasimha Rao, caught in the coils of a number of criminal cases, mostly on corruption charges, was dumped unceremoniously like a wet sponge. But Manmohan Singh was made a member of the party's working committee so that the corrupt in the party hierarchy could hide behind his clean image. This is also a manifestation of Congress culture which, one still hopes, will not spread to other parties to the same extent. The degeneration did not engulf the Congress suddenly or in one gulp. It had been there even in Nehru's time and he would try to stem it by stratagems like the Kamaraj Plan. Simultaneously, Nehru reconciled himself to keeping the party as a well-oiled election machine, *sans* a larger socio-economic purpose. He concentrated on foreign policy and kept India steadfastly on the nonaligned path. The socialist pattern of society with which he loaded the party in fact meant reinforcing centralised economic planning and imposition of a licence permit *raj*. Crucial land reforms were conveniently overlooked with the result that the rural scene presents a bleak picture to this day.

The Sixth five-year plan, authored by some of the most perceptive economists of the day, including Professors Lakdawala and Raj Krishna had showed that after nearly thirty years of planning the problems remained the same, although magnified many times, and that similar solutions were being suggested. Raj Krishna's famous aphorism was that the fifth five-year plan was the fifth version of the same plan! The purpose of recalling the sixth five-year plan (1980-81-1984-85) was that it had tried to break new ground. But it did not take long for Indira Gandhi to abort and bury it after her return to power in 1980. But two decades later in 2001-2002, Yeshwant Sinha's third budget attempted many of the tasks listed in that Plan document. The glaring omission was the stress on mobilisation and organisation of the rural poor. Technology-oriented politicians like Chandra Babu Naidu, former chief minister of Andhra Pradesh, said that it would be possible to do *via* the Internet what Raj Krishna had intended organisations of landless labourers and other wage earners to accomplish. There can be no quarrel with the proposition, although physical mobilisation has a different, deeper feel. However, the issue is not the means but the objective. Thanks to the spread of awareness among the people and the advent of what is called communication revolution, the poor can no longer be kept cowed and ignorant. Of course, they can be misled into ways destructive of their own welfare and of the country. That larger question has to be dealt with separately. Meanwhile, the Congress party being the Gangotri or source of national political attributes of cynicism and opportunism naturally deserves pride of place in this discussion.

The foregoing kaleidoscopic review of the first fifty years of our independence has brought into focus the factors contributing to our not-so-enviable position. Central to the malaise is erosion of values. It will be instructive, in this context, to identify personalities who contributed to the downgrading, if not destruction, of ethical standards and moral and social values, while sanctimoniously mouthing pious platitudes. The effort is to spot them, even if it involves recalling once again the course of events already described. To start with, let us take Chandra Shekhar, one of the stalwarts who dominated the political landscape during the dark decades. He became a member of the Lok Sabha from Ballia (UP) representing a one-member party called Samajwadi Janata Party (Rashtriya) or SJP (R). He had written in October 1989 a foreword for a centenary volume brought out in honour of Acharya Narendra Deva. Narendra Deva, a contemporary and close friend of Nehru was a scholar, a Marxist and above all a humanist. Even Nehru was no match to him in upholding principles and living up to social and ethical values. Chandra Shekhar had written in the course of the foreword: "Of late, politics has come to denote the race for power and pelf. To some people, capacity to manoeuvre, prevaricate and befuddle the masses are its attributes. Such people do not hesitate to adopt even questionable means to reach positions of power. The result of this is the all-round degeneration of democratic institutions and erosion of the cherished values of our national life." Literally, a few months after he wrote the trenchant denunciation of politics of power, Chandra Shekar became the 'Prime Minister' of benighted India, by breaking up Viswanath Pratap Singh's Janata Dal and forming a rump government with the support of Rajiv Gandhi's Congress party. Chandra Shekhar had shed his caste prefix, 'Thakur' and suffix, 'Singh' as marks of rejection of caste in politics in the late 1950s. But instances are not rare when he deployed the caste factor to win elections. Keeping him company in the noble enterprise was no less a person than Raj Narain who was Charan Singh's Sancho Panza in fomenting caste-based politics and practising politics of defection. The thrust of Chandra Shekhar's appreciation of Narendra Deva was the moral dimension he (Acharyaji, not Chandra Shekhar) had brought to bear on the political scene. In that context, Chandra Shekhar recalled how while quitting the Congress in 1948 "because of ideological differences he (Acharyaji) also resigned from the UP Assembly and tried to establish a healthy norm for our nascent parliamentary democracy."[4] His subsequent criticism of the Congress leadership which "could not appreciate the value of the ethical precedent" is not relevant here.

Compounding the irony of Chandra Shekhar heading the committee to celebrate the hundredth anniversary of Narendra Deva's birth, his 'friend', Madhu Limaye was put in charge of 'editing' the volume. The purpose of dwelling on this episode is not to score easy debating points but to set the focus on hypocrisy masquerading as socialism and morality. Secondly, quotations, however weighty, of pandits and others, Indian, British or American, do not lend moral weight to happenings. Karl Marx, Gandhiji and Lenin at one level and Chandra Shekhar and Rajiv Gandhi at another can be cited in support of any argument. For instance, such a staunch advocate of liberty as John Stuart Mill has laid down the limits of it by declaring that in pursuit of his liberty the individual "must not make himself a nuisance to other people," namely society. In the Indian context, as Chandra Shekhar has highlighted, the issue is degeneration of democratic institutions and erosion of cherished values of our national life. His thesis was that by promptly quitting his legislative post on resigning from the Congress, Acharyaji had set an example in thwarting the politics of defection eating into the vitals of democratic institutions. Narendra Deva along with eleven of his fellow-MLA's in Uttar Pradesh had resigned their seats when the Socialist Party, of which they were members, decided to snap its parental link with the Congress. That was in 1948. In the ensuing by-election the Congress candidate who claimed to be a true representative of the Hindus as against 'atheistic' Narendra Deva defeated Acharyaji. Narendra Deva was a Marxian and agnostic and not an atheist, as alleged but that is not relevant here. Nehru was alive then and was the supreme leader of the Congress and the country. Yet he allowed the UP Chief Minister, Govind Ballabh Pant, to have his way in 'putting' Acharyaji 'in his place', which was political wilderness. In other words, principled politics did not help either the first generation Socialist leaders or their party. Many of them, like Jayaprakash Narayan, Ram Manohar Lohia and Achyut Patwardhan, the tallest of their kind in those days, are strangers to present generation Indians. As for the Socialist party, it withered away leaving behind offshoots of doubtful character like the Praja Socialist Party (PSP) and the Janata Dal. The lesson seems to be that principles have no place in a polity where the dominant elements have their own exclusive ethical code. For instance, the Congress party today sniffs at the Hindu outlook of the BJP while donning the fig leaf of secularism but even in the hey-day of Nehru years in 1948 it had stooped to play the Hindu card to prevent a great man like Acharya Narendra Deva from re-entering the legislature.

Reverting to Chandra Shekhar and his sermon on political morality, it was significant that he had omitted in his denunciation of defection politics "the right of a legislator to exercise "his independent judgement through his enlightened conscience", which was Madhu Limaye's *mantra* when he opposed, at the introduction stage itself, a bill to prohibit floor crossing.[5] That was in 1979, when the Janata Party Government was on its last lap, so to say. Limaye was then the general secretary of the ruling Janata Party. Needless to say that the Bill collapsed partly because the then Law Minister, Shanti Bhushan, was ill and the minister deputising for him was raw. Limaye knew that such a bill would come in the way of Charan Singh, he and others who were planning to defect from the party and bring down the Janata Government. As Bernard Shaw said of the British, Limaye did every thing on principle. He sabotaged the first attempt at enacting a law against floor crossing on the principle of the right of legislators 'to exercise their independent judgment through enlightened conscience.' In the following year, in 1979, with a possible hurdle against defections out of the way, he helped Charan Singh to split the Janata Party, again on the principle of secularism. At that time, the overriding principle was aversion to the 'communal' character of the Jana Sangh, the forerunner of the BJP, because with a hundred odd MPs in the Lok Sabha it stood foursquare behind Morarji Desai and the Janata Party. It had taken two years for Limaye and his accomplices to discover it. The seeds sown by Limaye were not new, even if the fruits are in vogue even today. In 1969 when Indira Gandhi decided to break the Congress party because she had no control over its leadership, she had tarred the then Congress President, S. Nijalingappa and his colleagues with the brush of consorting with communalists. Then she used the slogan of 'conscience vote' to defeat Sanjiva Reddy in the presidential election. Reddy was the official candidate of Indira Gandhi's Congress party and she was his principal proposer. 'Conscience vote' was also the argument used by Limaye to thwart the anti-defection legislation.

The legitimacy of the actions and their outcome are the issue, irrespective of their constitutional veneer, said (Sir) C.Y. Chintamani, a great liberal leader and thinker.[6] Trying to justify a wrong action is rationalisation and not conscientiousness, he added. Conscience should not be a cover for crookery, he meant. Besides being one of India's tallest editors, Chintamani, hailing from Vizianagaram in Andhra Pradesh, had become education minister in UP. Such a development could not even be imagined today. But about a hundred years ago, in Uttar Pradesh, one of the cradles of caste and religion -determined politics now, talent and worth had their recognition and a man from the south could be made a minister. Pandit Pant who was then the leader of the opposition had acknowledged that Chintamani more than matched his own legislative acumen and eloquence. That was India of Indians and not of UP, Bihar, Andhra Pradesh, Gujarat, etc. Memory of Pant, a stalwart in many ways, brings into focus his contribution to today's Ayodhya imbroglio. It was during his chief ministership of UP in 1949 that miscreants broke open the locked doors of disused Babri masjid at Ayodhya and smuggled an idol of Rama inside. Pant would not undo the mischief, especially after he realised the popularity of the district magistrate who connived at the piety by stealth. The district magistrate's wife, attractive Shakuntala Nayar, was elected to the first Lok Sabha in 1952 on a Hindu Mahasabha ticket on the basis of the Hindu support her husband garnered by sneaking the Rama idol into the mosque. There was no doubt a formal police complaint registered under the Criminal Procedure Code but no accused was named in the case

Reverting to defections, the issue is not conflict between an electoral mandate and individual judgement but the political requirement, if not the moral obligation, of giving up an elective post while crossing the floor in a parliamentary system and facing the electorate for endorsement of the action. Until the advent in the late 1960s of the *aya* Ram and *gaya* Ram - meaning one Ram, a legislator in this case, has come and another has bolted (no disrespect meant to Ram) phenomenon in Haryana it was the practice to abide by party discipline and respect the whip at the time of voting. The Haryana practice has spread all over the country over the years. In the pre-Independence days, the Indian National Congress enforced it as a basic principle of legislative activity by its members and blacklisted offenders like Khan Abdul Qayyum Khan[7] of the N-W.F.P. (In contrast, the Unionist Party in Punjab specialised in enticing legislators from other parties. It was said that Sir Sikandar Hyat Khan would ask the seekers of his party ticket to fight the election first so that the winner could be given the ticket.) After Independence, too, there were notable instances of legislators resigning from the legislature on parting company with the party or in the event of disagreement over policy. V.V. Giri as Union Labour Minister quit the Nehru Cabinet (on the bank award issue) while Chintaman Deshmukh as Finance Minister left on the question of a separate Maharashtra State. T.T. Krishnamachari had done it in a different context, after having been asked by the then prime minister following the exposure of the Mundhra deals by Feroze Gandhi. They all followed in the footsteps of Acharya Narendra Deva without making much ado about it.

But Chandra Shekhar, when he switched from the PSP to the Congress, did not give up his membership of the Rajya Sabha. It not only depressed PSP leaders like Acharya Narendra Deva who had felt it deeply but also politically hurt the PSP to an extent, when one of the few MPs it could send to the Rajya Sabha deserted it. The Congress, on the other hand, could have easily accommodated lateral entrants like Chandra Shekhar among its scores of Elders. But it did not bother to make him surrender the PSP seat. That was the genesis of the rot in the then ruling party, which over the years has acquired several alphabetical suffixes and developed proxies for political convenience. It spread to other parties over time so that there is not much difference today between the different parties in the matter of expediency overriding principles. It has come to be known as Congress culture. We had a weed known as Congress grass in Delhi. It was death to healthy plants and polluted the atmosphere. There is no remedy short of uprooting it, root and branch. That has not happened in the political sphere. Instead, it has spread to other parties as well, including the BJP, not to mention the Telugu Desam Party in Andhra Pradesh, the two Dravidian parties, DMK and the A-I ADMK, in Tamil Nadu and of course the Shiv Sena of Bal Thackeray. There is internal democracy of sorts in the BJP and with the erosion of cohesion for which the party was once known discipline is also discriminatingly enforced. But in the other parties, the self-appointed supremo is above reproach and beyond reach. He or she is also irreplaceable. In the Congress party, the role model in this respect, there had been no organisational elections for decades nor any vestige of internal democracy. Sheerly by virtue of the numerical weight of its adherents and material resources of its election machine the party continued for five long decades to be the dominant factor in our political life. The semblance of change in 1991 when Narasimha Rao became prime minister, albeit by default, was short-lived. Rajiv Gandhi had been killed in a suicide attack by terrorists. There was, in addition to grief, desolation also in the bereaved party, not because there were no other leaders worthy of the mantle of leadership but because Rajiv's widow, Italian-born socialite Sonia, would not yet step into her husband's shoes. The accidental (or providential?) break with dynastic leadership in the party opened the prospect of reviving internal democracy and holding organisational elections. They had become luxuries since Indira Gandhi made herself the party boss in 1978. Narasimha Rao revived the practice of organisational elections and went some way with the effort until Sonia Gandhi's underground supporters like Arjun Singh tried to use the opportunity to unsettle Narasimha Rao. There the effort ended. Now with Sonia back at the helm "Madame's word " is the norm.

To return to Chandra Shekhar and the health of our democracy, the expectation after the 1989 general election was that the democratic institutions would be revived or at least their degeneration, which Chandra Shekhar had bemoaned, would stop and that the accent would shift to "the cherished values of our national life". Vishwanath Pratap Singh's Janata Dal managing to form the Government at the Centre was a break. He had made an issue of corruption and evoked enthusiastic middle class support for his charge that Rajiv Gandhi was guilty of accepting kickbacks from the Bofors company when the Government bought howitzers from the Swedish firm. He had also set out to probe the 'scandal', although it remains unsolved to this day, fifteen years after.

But V.P. Singh's 'election' as leader of the Janata Dal and prime minister-designate left a bad taste in the mouth. Teaming up with Devi Lal, Singh outmanoeuvred Chandra Shekhar, who 'owned' the Janata Dal, having bought the Dal part of it in a barter deal with Ajit Singh, Charan Singh's son. Not content with the Pyrrhic victory, V.P. Singh unleashed a veritable civil war in the country in the name of social justice. He unearthed the Mandal Commission report, lying dormant for ten years, to provide for reservation in Government appointment for 'other backward classes' and implemented its recommendations through an executive order. The provocation was a threat by Devi Lal to outflank him from within. As Nehru had noted in a different context hunger for jobs was the driving force in public life. Threatened with deprivation of their main means of livelihood, the urban-based upper castes resisted it violently. For the lower castes, called 'other backward classes', it was an opportunity not to be lost. The two clashed in the cities and many large towns in UP especially. Urban unemployment has been a continuing bane because of stunted economic growth - 'Hindu rate of growth' in the words of Professor Raj Krishna. It was so at the dawn of independence and the situation worsened yearly. The main reason was emasculation of private enterprise in the name of establishing a socialist pattern of society. The resultant public sector saddled with all kinds of responsibilities from baking bread to running luxury hotels became unaccountable. For the tax payer's money it guzzled the return was meagre. Almost as a rule, the efficiency of the public sector undertakings was poor, and productivity appalling. Losses mounted requiring increasing budgetary support year after year. So Government employment was much sought after and highly valued. 'Reservations' thus became a violent bone of contention.

The chequered history of the short-lived Janata Dal Government has already been described adequately. More important is the effect of the cynical practice of floor crossing on the democratic institutions for the health of which Chandra Shekhar has professed concern. It is both natural and right for politicians to seek power, individually or collectively but the survival of the democratic system demands constraints on its pursuit. Chaudhri Charan Singh was at least honest, if that word can co-exist with the Lok Dal leader, when he confessed that his ambition to be the prime minister had been fulfilled by toppling the Morarji Desai Government in 1979. To try to clothe such action with high-sounding principles is nothing short of hypocrisy. Which was what Chandra Shekhar did and does to this day. Chandra Shekhar was lucky in teaming up with a celebrated economist, Dr. Brahmananda. Picking up phrases and words from him, Chandra Shekhar specialised in projecting an image of extreme radicalism. If Indira Gandhi was Left of self interest, Chandra Shekhar was farther Left of her. In the pre-split Congress, he targeted Morarji Desai, who was deputy prime minister holding the finance portfolio. Chandra Shekhar, incidentally, started his political career as a democratic socialist, and an acolyte of Acharya Narendra Deva. That was in the wake of the 1942 Quit India struggle in which he participated, like most socialists of the time. An ardent socialist, he was keen to discuss issues and enlighten his followers and friends like me. He was not an ideologue but well read and well informed. As general secretary first of the Socialist party and then the PSP in UP he was a good organiser and a budding national leader. But Raj Narain as a Lohiaite was a pain in his neck until the parting of the ways between the two parties. Within the PSP Narain Dutt Tewari, a skilled parliamentarian and Genda Singh a leader of the sugarcane growers were his rivals and contemporaries in the State party hierarchy. All the three had found themselves in the Congress, following Asoka Mehta's action in reverting to the parental fold as a compulsion of the country's backward economy. Chandra Shekhar became a member of the Rajya Sabha, while Narain Dutt confined himself to the State legislature to become chief minister and later union minister, and Genda Singh went in for a ministership in the State.

Although Chandra Shekhar had followed Asoka Mehta into the Congress, he did not share his senior's social democratic outlook. He remained a radical committed to nationalisation of key industries and abolition of 'vestiges of feudalism' like the princely rulers and their privileges. Paradoxically enough, both Asoka Mehta and Chandra Shekhar were close to Indira Gandhi initially. But when Indira Gandhi realised that to be a successful prime minister she would have to be seen to be left of centre, she began to distance herself from Asoka Mehta, although not until after the devaluation debacle. Chandra Shekhar, meanwhile, became her secret weapon against her rivals in the leadership, notably Morarji Desai. As a member of the Rajya Sabha, he would rain philippics on the Birlas, among the business houses, and implicate Morarji Desai in favouring them. Morarji Desai once even formally protested to the Prime Minister, implying that she was instigating the attacks on him but his protests had as little effect as his charge subsequently that she had unleashed Madhu Limaye to level corruption charges against his son, Kantibhai Desai. Apparently,Chandra Shekhar's crusade against "blood-thirsty" capitalists had a tactical dimension. By singling out one business house it encouraged the business rivals to sustain the campaign in more ways that one. It showed, incidentally, that capitalists, too, could be divided and ruled. In the process, he perfected the technique of transcending class and other loyalties among victims by pitting one group or one person against another. When Indira Gandhi split the Congress in 1969, Asoka Mehta and Chandra Shekhar found themselves in opposite camps. Asoka was with Nijalingappa, Kamaraj and others of the Organisation Congress, ultimately to be made its president, while Chandra Shekhar went with India Gandhi.

From his home State of UP, Hemvati Nandan Bahuguna was among those who joined forces with Chandra Shekhar as supporters of Indira Gandhi but the Young Turk - which he was by then - was somewhat uneasy in their company. Yeshwantrao (Y) B. Chavan from Maharashtra, C. Subrahmanyam from Tamil Nadu, Babu Jagjivan Ram and Fakhruddin Ali Ahmed (who had fired the first shot in the battle of the split) at the national level were among the stalwarts in the new party. Each was a match to the other. But the proximity of idealistic Mohan Dharia and Nandini Satpathy with her Leftist credentials sharpened the radical image of Chandra Shekhar, whereas most of the others were identified with power brokers. Further, Chandra Shekhar's political base was narrow and nearly eroded by his preoccupation with national level politics. In his own constituency of Ballia he began to need the backing of strong-armed supporters some of whom had an underworld odour. Shrewd politician that she was, Indira Gandhi sensed the possibility of Chandra Shekhar proving a potential danger to her position, especially in collaboration with 'Babuji' and others. So she decided on pre-emptive action by denying him re-nomination to the Rajya Sabha. But a noisy campaign by 'progressives' of different hues saved the seat for him ultimately. In the run up to the 'emergency', the chasm between Indira Gandhi and Chandra Shekhar widened. Sanjay Gandhi was proving a thorn in his flesh. Correctly reading the writing on the wall, Chandra Shekhar revived his old filial relationship with Jayaprakash Narayan, although almost until he was bundled up for detention he was guarded in his endorsement of 'JP's' anti-corruption drive. The post-emergency situation pitchforked him into the position of an elder statesman, virtually on par with Morarji Desai, Charan Singh and Jagjivan Ram. When there was a tussle for prime ministership especially between Morarji and Charan Singh — with the Jana Sangh group rooting for Jagjivan Ram — 'JP' toyed with the idea of proposing Chandra Shekhar for the job. But Morarji put his foot down and that was the end of the matter. He had the consolation prize of party presidentship.

Despite his antipathy for Morarji, Chandra Shekhar was never close to Charan Singh. Babuji and Bahuguna were his allies in the power struggle in the party and were closer to him than even a fellow-Young Turk like Mohan Dharia. The reason was obvious; Dharia is too straightforward to be a politician. In fact, Morarji was surprised when Chandra Shekhar opted for the party post instead of putting himself forward as a representative of the former Young Turks in the composite cabinet. It was a clever or wise decision because as a cabinet minister he would have been one of the fifteen or so and would also be expected to deliver on his profound professions. At the formal onset of the Janata leadership struggle, Chandra Shekhar along with Babuji and Bahuguna was for dropping Charan Singh without a qualm. But when the drama of rapprochement between Morarji Desai and Charan Singh opened, he, too, joined the chorus of peacemakers. Ultimately in 1979 when the government was coming unstuck and Morarji would rather go down with the ship than give up the prime ministership, the ever-obliging Badoria couple was despatched to Patna to seek the 'advice' of ailing 'JP'. The great man was only clinically alive then but such was his fondness for Chandra Shekhar that he gathered enough strength to write a letter to the Janata leadership suggesting Chandra Shekhar as the ideal choice for the top post at that critical time. But there were no takers for the leader's advice and Chandra Shekhar did not become Prime Minister. May be, if he had taken over the Congress-I would have tolerated him better than it did Charan Singh.

End Notes

1. *An Autobiography*, Jawaharlal Nehru, first published 1936, London, Bodley Head Ltd. Current edition, 2004, New Delhi, Penguin Book India (P) Ltd.
2. *My Experiments with Truth*, M.K. Gandhi, 1927, Ahmedabad, Navjeevan Press.
3. Sonia Gandhi's supporters in the Congress party did not endorse the economic reform and sabotaged the party's chances in the 1996 general election to the Lok Sabha.
4. *Acharaya Narendra Deva* published by Acharya Narendra Deva Centenary Samoroha Samiti, 1990, Radiant Publishers, New Delhi. (The volumes were published in Hindi and English.) Narendra Deva's role has often been cited not only by the likes of Chandra Shekhar and Madhu Limaya but Nehru, too.
5. There have been several attempts since then to end the menance of floor crossing or defection until it ended in Rajiv Gandhi's half-baked attempt in 1985 to add the Tenth Schedule to the Consitution.
6. Chintamani was not only pathbreaker among Indian editors but also author of a seminal publication, *Indian Politics since the Mutiny*.
7. Author of a devastating critique of British Government policy in the North West Frontier Province, viz, *Gold and Guns on the Pathan Frontier*, Qayyum Khan changed sides in the run up to the partition and joined the Muslim League. In the 1960's he set up law practice in Lahore and defended H.S. Suhrawardy hauled up by Ayub Government on treason charges.

3
Values *versus* Power

Dynastic succession was a factor in the repugnance for and resistance to the emergency. But hardly a decade later in 1984 when Rajiv Gandhi succeeded his mother as prime minister without being a member of the Government or having been formally elected leader of the ruling party, there was practically little public opprobrium. Indira Gandhi's assassination was no doubt a factor, which benumbed the nation and generated a sense of helplessness. But that did not by itself prepare the mood for acceptance of Rajiv Gandhi. If so, it would have been a mere rationalisation of Giani Zail Singh's exercise of his presidential discretion in Rajiv Gandhi's favour.[1] More than his adoption as leader by the Congress party's parliamentary board the outcome of the subsequent general election to the Lok Sabha showed overwhelming public support for the young prime minister.[2] It was a definitely positive endorsement of the succession in contrast to Sanjay Gandhi's debut into politics at the time of and following the imposition of the 1975 'emergency'.[3] According to Indira Gandhi, Sanjay had entered the fray only to help her face the onslaught of her political enemies following the Allahabad High Court judgment setting aside her election to the Lok Sabha on largely technical grounds. The first phase of Sanjay Gandhi's political career was marked by a ruthless drive against his mother's political opponents. He perceived it as a no-holds-barred fight. No political leader worth the name, including Jayaprakash Narayan to whose memory Sanjay paid homage during a visit to Patna a little while before his own death, was spared from detention without trial. All the institutions relevant to democracy, Parliament, judiciary and the press[4] were immobilised and brought under the political executive which was, in effect, himself and his sycophants. A shrewd judge of the Indian mindset, he realised that excessive force was necessary to instil fear in the people. With an oppressive pall of terror hanging over the country there were excesses and aberrations even if their magnitude had been exaggerated. As the Prime Minister's son and confidant, he wielded boundless power, unencumbered by accountability or responsibility. That was why some of the laudable programmes he projected proved counterproductive in the long run.[5] The officials had only to achieve the quantitative targets by whatever means. How they did it did not matter. The result was that the programmes suffered and Sanjay got a bad name in the bargain. The subsequent abandonment of the family planning drive was not entirely due to Raj Narain's myopia and incompetence because Sanjay, too, had not taken it up after his mother's return to power in January 1980. The clearance of urban slums also was erratic. The poor had suffered by being deprived of gainful work within their easy reach, while the operators in real estate had thrived on unauthorised construction of dwellings and shops. As for tree planting (it is called social forestry) and adult literacy, they recalled to mind the countless earlier exercises that degenerated into rituals. There was no sustained effort. The policeman and the revenue official are not cut out for nation building activities. The Youth Congress (I) cadres are more cheerleaders and sycophants - to this day - often doubling as thugs and musclemen than workers at the grassroots' level .In other words, what remained of the opening phase of Sanjay's dazzling career was a sense of all pervading fear. But fear does not do away with human wickedness and social injustice. It only drives them underground. It also induces adulation in some that see in it a short cut to escape punishment. There were also some that used his name and his accessibility to reinforce their bargaining power in society.

The next phase in Sanjay's transient career began with the assumption of office by the Janata party. It was totally and destructively negative, which was natural perhaps considering the perception of being victims of persecution which both he and his mother got by the words and deeds of leaders like Charan Singh and Madhu Limaye.[6] (Incidentally both these leaders and their accomplices did not hesitate to seek her support to topple the Morarji Desai Government in 1979. Sanjay played his cards adroitly by encouraging them in their illusion and after the fall of the Janata Government discarded them like spittle.) That the due processes of law had been adhered to in the conduct of the Shah Commission did not mitigate the veritable horror of being involved simultaneously in a series of criminal cases. All the while, Charan Singh as Home Minister was goading the officialdom to pursue Indira Gandhi and her son relentlessly, though, in effect, his progress towards his fell intentions was a big zero.

But for the army of clever counsel Indira Gandhi had engaged and the resources she commanded, she could have been in trouble, Sanjay's reaction to the persecution mania of the Janata stalwarts was true to form. He let loose his acolytes to invade courtrooms, browbeat magistrates and judges and manipulate the course of justice. He cast himself in the role of an iconoclast of what Marxists would disdainfully describe as the bourgeois legal system, though he did not share their concept of class war and class justice.

The last phase in Sanjay's meteoric political life dawned with the victory of the Congress (I) in the January Lok Sabha poll. But the process of regaining power was not complete or nearly so until the party gained majorities in eight of the nine State assemblies where elected governments were dismissed *en bloc*. Sanjay realised that more than the Central Government the States constituted the key to wielding and exercising power. In fact, he wanted to be anointed as chief minister of UP after the June 1980 general election. But his mother vetoed the proposal. Soon after he was cruelly killed in an air crash. As a result, he had no time or opportunity to bend his unbounded energy and drive to larger purposes. Putting the political opponents in their place (which in 1975 was jail), resisting legal action by strong-arm tactics, egging power-mad Janata myopics to fall apart and winning the Lok Sabha and Assembly elections had become his objectives. They were by no means insignificant accomplishments but did not add up to the leadership qualities required for uplifting our people. Sanjay did not lack the qualities, which was the case with his elder brother, but he was denied the time and opportunity to show his mettle by premature death.

In this connection, nothing illustrates more strikingly the poverty of philosophy in the political class as a whole than the homage paid to Sanjay on his death. He was compared to Karl Marx, Gandhiji, the Buddha, Jesus Christ, Alexander the Great, Che Guevara and Ho Chi Minh, all rolled into one. He was pictured as an apostle of truth and non-violence. In other words, the people whom he stirred deeply, in life as well as in death, did not know the reason for their being moved so intensely. So they lavished on him the attributes normally associated with greatness. (I am not referring here to professional eulogists of persons in power). If his career had not been cut short, Sanjay might have overgrown the earlier phases of his political life. He had at the time of his death both power and responsibility that would have begun to weigh on him as time passed. Despite his innate impatience with bureaucratic procedures, he would have realised the unavoidability of the bureaucratic means and even their usefulness on the long haul in the context of the administrative system we have in the country. It was called the steel frame in the British period and was fairly productive in carrying out the then Government's purposes. Similarly, Sanjay would have put the Babus on their toes and made them sweat. He would have gradually got tired of his hero-worshippers as leaders invariably do and would have cut himself loose from the hordes of favour-seekers. It could have been a different Sanjay then.

In that case, Sanjay would not have been the first leader to reconcile himself to procedures and means which he detested heartily and temperamentally. It happened with greater leaders like Nehru and Sardar Patel. Panditji, especially, would chafe at the Government's slow moving ways but ultimately settled down to it. The Sardar, who was every inch a plebian and committed to integrate the princely States with the rest of the country, had gone about it with remarkable finesse and tact. He enjoyed co-existing with the princes thus reassuring the former rulers of the States that the Government was not vindictive. In the process, he accomplished the near miracle of unifying the country But for his leadership, India would have splintered and disintegrated. At another level, the first communist Chief Minister of a State, E.M.S. Namboodiripad, in what was then Travancore-Cochin, a dyed-in-the-wool Marxist, succeeded remarkably in functioning within the system which his philosophy was pledged to overthrow. When he arrived at Udyog Bhavan as Minister of Industry, George Fernandes, seemed to be bent on setting the Yamuna on fire but very soon he was content with poring over Government files until midnight. They were not false to their professions. They also succeeded in achieving their objectives in their different ways. They brought to bear on the administration the imprint of their dynamic personalities. But they all realised the limitations of government, especially in a country like ours with its vastness and variety added lately by venality. The same with power. The very process of wielding it generates limitations on its exercise. Ignoring the constraints only breeds disequilibrium and worse in the system. What Prince Matternich and Viscount Castlereagh -- Henry Kissinger's role models — said applies to the domestic sphere also. The emergency experience was a fire-fighting operation. It would never be durable. So, all those who admired Sanjay and expected of him miracles ranging from punctuality on the railways to regularity of the monsoon were either naïve or dishonest.

There was no doubt that his style of operation, just as Indira Gandhi's, was basically different from that of Panditji. Sanjay's technique was and would have been at variance with what the country had been used to. That was less important than whether in the long run it would have made much difference to policies and their effective implementation. Whether it be due to Nehru's 'indecisiveness' and penchant for democratic norms, or because of his 'faulty' approach to economic development the country had been stuck in what Professor Raj Krishna called the Hindu rate of growth under his prime ministership. The consolidation of the democratic political system and achievement of political and social stability in the country, which were the principal blessings of the Nehru era, were not reflected in the economic sphere. That was despite the fact that the Congress party wielded unchallenged power at the Centre and in all the States and first generation party leaders honed in freedom struggle were at the helm. Whether Sanjay's methods throwing democratic norms to the winds would have put India on a faster track to growth was the issue. And it could only be hypothesised because Sanjay did not live long enough to pursue his policies. The situation was no different - as far as economic growth was concerned — during Indira Gandhi's 11-year regime from 1966-1977. It remained stagnant despite her style of leadership and adoption of Soviet methods of planning.

Finally, what about Sanjay's ideas and ideology? It was claimed by some of his admirers that he had no corpus of commitments and that was why he was so dynamic in action. Luckily for the country and for himself, Sanjay had ideas even if they were nebulous. He had set himself certain priorities and went about striving for them unmindful of the means deployed. He was convinced that the public sector was a waste of national resources and that without the profit motive the individual could not be stirred. A sizable section of the urban middle class youth was drawn to him but it would not be right to read ideological affinity into it. The advent of Gandhiji on the national scene at the dawn of the century had gripped the youth of the day, especially the educated, with his mission to make India free of foreign rule. Nehru was one of those who reinforced that attraction by adding an egalitarian dimension to it. Those were the days of intellectual fallout from the October Revolution. During and after the Quit India struggle, there was the Left nationalist magnetism of Socialists like Jayaprakash Narayan and Ram Manohar Lohia. But more recently the youth either tilts towards the Naxalites or the Hindutva type of politics. In economic matters it plumps for the American model of a society of opportunity. Disenchantment with the socialist pattern as it obtained in the country was at the root of both these extreme reactions. Sanjay personified it. He also reflected the imminent failure at the global level of regimented economy and centralised planning which were called socialism Above all, he seemed to presage the advent of massive technological changes which would make nonsense of theories and ideologies.

The secret of Sanjay's success lay in his bluntly honest manner of going about his work. He did not indulge in the traditional Congress party practice of sanctimonious lip-sympathy for Gandhian values. His mother and other Congress party leaders pretended to be adherents of Gandhian values while in practice their actions represented the exact opposite. They were hypocrites of the first waters. Sanjay, on the other hand, jettisoned not only external symbols of Gandhism - like khaddar, austerity, self-denial of privileges which are beyond the reach of most of our people and, above all, compassion and love for one's adversaries but also basic principles like compatibility between means and ends. It will be unfair to charge that Sanjay had been untrue to Gandhian values as if they were prevalent in the country until he emerged on the political scene. They were being steadily eroded and distorted. He gave them a decent and open burial. During Gandhiji's lifetime itself, Nehru, Sardar Patel and some other close followers of the Mahatma had reservations about his commitment to non-violence. Nehru said it was only a policy and not a creed for him. The idea was to enable independent India to have armed forces and the police and be organised as a modern State. Gandhiji might not have objected to it perhaps but his creed of non-violence would not have gone with the type of State Nehru and his successors have gone in for. True, Gandhiji had endorsed the despatch of troops to Kashmir at the time of the Pakistan invasion in 1948. He had also defended his participation in the ambulance corps during the Boer war in South Africa as consistent with his philosophy of non-violence because it meant rendering service to one's opponents. As for truth, it has come to be taken for granted having been coined into the slogan *Satyameva Jayate* or truth only triumphs to proclaim a national value. It adorns all official institutions and there ends the commitment to it. At another level, in the name of speedy industrial development, Nehru abandoned the Gandhian approach of decentralisation and small-scale technology. Instead, he opted for the Soviet system of State socialism, as a result of which India found its capital formation inhibited and burdened with problems of glaring economic disparities, large-scale unemployment and endless social tension, plus massive poverty. That was after decades of planned development. But in his conduct Nehru tried to reconcile Gandhiji's approach with his own predilections. He did not consciously practise deceit. By his commitment to the democratic way of life he lived up to the Gandhian precept of non-violence in thought. Let me explain this conundrum. He tolerated dissent. Even when his political opponents did not play the parliamentary game according to Westminster rules, he did not throw them in gaol or burn down their houses. In other words, he ensured to a large extent that means and ends were inter-related.

Indira Gandhi represented the transition from Nehru to Sanjay. She had no qualms about rejecting totally everything that Gandhiji or even her father had stood for but she would always swear by them. It ranged from the relatively least important prohibition to the most crucial norms of public behaviour. For instance, in 1975, she met Vinoba Bhave at his ashram in Wardha and issued a circular to the State Governments asking them to enforce prohibition strictly. That was in connection with that year's Gandhi Jayanti celebrations. At the same time, the Government of Haryana, headed by her close confidant, Bansi Lal, was consciously promoting consumption of alcohol by establishing breweries and opening liquor shops. Her role during the 1969 Presidential election, at the time of the split in the Congress party, and while imposing the so called internal emergency in 1975 needs no recapitulation. Sanjay had taken it to the logical conclusion. It is believed to be the Western materialistic approach to life as distinct from our spiritualistic ways. But that was an over-simplification. Sanjay was, no doubt, an addict to what the Americans call the work ethic and profit motive; there is no escape from hard work in his scheme of things. It is claimed that the work ethic is enshrined in the Bhagwat Gita also. In a way yes, but indifference to the outcome or the fruits of labour which the Gita is said to preach has distorted our approach, even in the case of the microscopic minority which takes the Gita seriously. It is more often recited than acted upon. Gandhiji was worldly wise enough to link toil with its outcome. He had always striven for a cause, not merely for the sake of striving. So did Nehru. There was the famous saying of his that *aram haram hain* (loosely translated as idleness or rest is sin.) Sanjay, like his mother and her contemporaries reduced the concept to narrow personal ends. They translated it specifically into raising a motor car factory from scratch with minimal personal investment, striving to keep one's prime ministership at any cost as Indira Gandhi did, promotion of what is called licence -permit raj and amassing wealth for the family and the party. The instances are too many to be listed. It had been going on during the first fifty odd years of our independence, by big men and petty bureaucrats and the country is still paying for it. But Sanjay made it into a fine art and lent it the force of a religion. He made no bones about it. There was nothing sanctimonious about him.

The following incident is an index, at a somewhat frivolous level, of his tastes and interests and how the officialdom had attuned itself to them. In 1979 I had visited Bikaner as Principal Information Officer (PIO) to the Government of India. Being of additional secretary rank (at that time) I was honoured by the head of the district administration receiving me at the railway station and putting me up at the renovated circuit house. He recommended me to the renovated bedroom specially done up for Sanjay's stay during the emergency. It was a spacious suite, with a very sprawling bedroom, a dressing room besides bathroom and lounge. The furniture was specially made in the image of traditional Rajasthani woodwork and the bed was almost oceanic in proportions. I felt like a frog in a well but slept comfortably and luxuriously. The following morning at breakfast I thanked my host profusely for the luxury but said the only omission was a reading lamp to meet my need of reading myself to sleep. "We were never asked to provide reading lamps in Sanjay's bedroom", he replied.

Does it mean that Sanjay's detractors are angels? Did those like Charan Singh and Raj Narain, to mention the stalwarts, practise the means-and-end theory with the violation of which they charged Indira Gandhi? If there is any difference between Indira Gandhi and her son on the one hand and their traducers like the Lok Dal luminaries on the other it is that Sanjay never stabbed his own supporters in the back, whereas the latter had done so. Political Pundits call this duplicity populism. If Indira Gandhi's populism was abominable because of the price the nation had to pay for it for decades, the Charan Singh variety was no better and the cost the country had paid for it was equally enormous. It was also contagious. He specialised in lavishing large subsidies in his budget for rich peasants who were his supporters and penalise the urban middle class who were with the former Jana Sangh; he would manipulate the sugar policy with a view to raising money for election purposes. It was supposed to be beefing up the growers of west UP's main cash crop. It was his reply to Indira Gandhi winning elections with the slogan of *garibi hatao* (banish poverty) when she knew she had no intention or capacity even to move earnestly in that direction. It was only in 1991 nearly four decades later that P.V. Narasimha Rao and Dr. Manmohan Singh took the first step towards reducing poverty and releasing the potential of Indian entrepreneurs, peasants, and middle classes for nation building.

There was also another qualitative difference between the two varieties of populism. Indira Gandhi and her second son were efficient in what they set out to achieve — whereas the Lok Dal crowd was uncouth, clumsy with a tough exterior to their liquidy opportunism. They have landed the country in the lap of subsidies, which no finance minister could do away with to this day. There is one more basic difference between Sanjay and Gandhiji, which is crucial for the nation. It is the attitude to the rule of law. Gandhiji and Nehru did not use the coercive apparatus of the State for narrow political purposes. The political opponents, be they Communists, zamindars or RSS men, were not locked up in jail without trial or chargesheet even though Nehru had a preventive detention law promulgated, jailed several communists and had got scores of RSS workers arrested in the wake of Gandhiji's assassination in 1948. More importantly, Gandhiji who had in his last years lost his faith in the fairness of British justice in India nevertheless abided by the verdicts of the courts. His famous Ahmedabad trial, like its internationally renowned counterpart, the Dimitrov trial, showed up the accuser as the real accused but there was no invasion of courts by muscle men, beating up of judges or tampering with court papers.[7] Nor did they try to override court judgments by political means. The practice of political leaders taking recourse to technicalities, like avoiding the service of summons, filing false medical certificates - which are the stock in trade of cheap criminal lawyers - was also unknown in those days.

At one extreme there are the Naxalites and their fellow travellers who believe that the parliamentary system is doomed and that the country's salvation lies only in a kind of Maoist revolution. There are no doubt variations in this theme with some of the Naxalites practising individual terrorism against landlords and other 'class enemies' in the name of establishing dictatorship of the proletariat. Some like the People's War Group in Andhra Pradesh do not also hesitate to take protection money from 'class enemies'. The urban middle class goes along with these groups up to the point of disenchantment with the working of the democratic system. Beyond that there is a parting of the ways. A growing number of young men and women have come to believe that private enterprise with the profit motive will be far superior in efficiency to the State socialist pattern of society. They chafe at controls and bureaucratic delays and red tape, even while they cut their way through them by greasing the palms of officials. This applies to such trivial matters as obtaining reservation of a berth on the Railways as well as major problems, like securing industrial licences. The kind of trade unionism developing in the country also discomfits the young people engaged in trade and industry. They want a strong Government to put down frequent work stoppages for political purposes so that along with productivity profits also will go up. The two and a half years of Janata rule was marked by assertiveness on the part of the organised working class and frequent strikes in industrial and business establishments. That had made most middle class people plump for the type of strong Government which Indira Gandhi promised but which they knew Sanjay Gandhi would have provided. As the emergency excesses did not affect men of property and influence they had no aversion for the type of regime which prevailed during those days.

In this context, the hypocrisy in the approach of Sanjay's critics should not be overlooked. They would not like others to do vis-a-vis themselves what they did or intended to do to others. This is best illustrated in the writings of Khushwant Singh who faithfully mirrors the urban elite with all its contradictions. He once wrote in his weekly column: "The way our legal system operates it is virtually impossible for the prosecution to prove crimes committed by dacoits. In the areas where they operate they create so much terror that only the bravest have the temerity to give evidence against them. There are many instances of prosecution witnesses and their families being wiped out by members of dacoit gangs who had eluded the police. Dacoits usually have enough looted money to hire the best lawyers to defend them and have leverage with local politicians who in their turn influence the judiciary to grant small discretionary favours like granting them bail. Once out of handcuffs and fetters the dacoits can silence opposition with their guns. They only way the police can eliminate them is to put them beyond the pale of the judicial system. This may sound very highhanded, arbitrary and undemocratic but in the circumstances that prevail in our country it is by no means wholly immoral. This is exactly what the police have been doing over the last 200 years or more".

It was with reference to an incident in 1976 in the district town of Baghpet in Meerut subdivision where three persons suspected to be dacoits were shot dead by the police and their woman companion disrobed and dishonoured. Khushwant Singh was presenting the other side of the medal to counter the political campaign against police high-handedness launched by Charan Singh and his associates. If one looks back, the police were in an exactly similar predicament in 1978 when the *Kissa Kursi Ka* case against Sanjay Gandhi and V.C. Shukla, former Minister of Information and Broadcasting was being tried in a Delhi Court. The charge against them was that they had conspired to destroy a movie depicting politicians in a lurid light, as it was believed to be a satire on Indira Gandhi's rule in 1973-74. The producer, Amrit Nahta, a member of the Lok Sabha at that time, was originally a Communist. He joined the Congress Party and was elected to Parliament in 1971. Subsequently, he turned a critic of Indira Gandhi when he produced the film. He followed it up by joining the Janata Party for some time in 1977-78. He quit that party also in 1979 and returned to the fold of Indira Gandhi's party *via* the Lok Dal. On a complaint from Nahta that the film produced by him when submitted for clearance to the censor had been taken to Sanjay Gandhi's Maruti factory and destroyed there by burning, the case was launched against Shukla, Sanjay and others. Even though the Janata Party was in power scores of prosecution witnesses turned hostile during the trial. There were also attempts at tampering with court records. At one stage Sanjay Gandhi had to be sent to jail on a charge of interfering with the course of justice. All the while an army of well-paid counsel was defending Sanjay pressing into service all the technicalities available in the legal legerdemain. According to Khushwant Singh's logic persons facing trial who indulge in such tactics to short-circuit the course of justice should be dealt with summarily. But in Sanjay's case the mere attempts to expedite the case and bring about his prosecution were dubbed persecution. In fact, the judges who finally quashed the proceedings against him waited for the results of the January 1980 Lok Sabha election to pronounce their verdict!

Of a piece with this mentality is a kind of false national pride which makes people push under the carpet the seamy side of our existence, be it poverty, backwardness or superstition. The celebrated film star, Nargis Dutt, a nominated member of the Rajya Sabha, had criticised Satyajit Ray for projecting an image of destitution and hunger about India. She did not deny that Ray's portrayal was real but complained that it lowered the image of India in the eyes of foreigners. The logic seems to be that since amelioration of the lot of the poor is going to be a difficult and time consuming process the destitutes should be kept out of the foreigners' range of vision. When thousands of families of slum dwellers were hounded out of Delhi and Agra and other places during the 'emergency' the idea was that the poor should not spoil the picture of urban beauty and gaiety.

The storm of protests, which greeted Louis Malle's superb documentary, "Phantom India", was also a reflection of this attitude. Many Indian residents in London told me that when the BBC screened the documentary they looked small in the eyes of their British neighbours who became acquainted, through the feature, with the abject poverty and squalor of many of our people in India. There was such an uproar against the BBC's action that its correspondent was thrown out of India even before the emergency.

Earlier during the Bihar drought in 1966-67 when foreign philanthropic organisations like Oxfam and CARE tried to mobilise relief from outside the country Indira Gandhi was very angry. Jayaprakash Narayan was blamed for publicising a domestic disaster and seeking help from abroad. International assistance during floods, droughts and earthquakes is common. Except in the case of former Communist countries such aid is enthusiastically given and warmly received. Even Communist Kampuchea - under Vietnamese control - had accepted relief supplies from abroad. The Stalinist regime in North Korea too had sought and accepted international assistance to tide over acute food shortage within the country. China, too, accepts aid from abroad in times of natural and other calamities. The Taliban perhaps was the only exception. It is also unavoidable that because of the spread of communications reports of such calamities are widely publicised abroad. Only a false sense of national pride would look askance at these facts of life. It is true that perennial poverty like that which afflicts thousands of our villagers is not the same as a stray natural calamity. It is also not denied that self-reliance in meeting such crises should be developed and encouraged. Foreign reaction to such publicity has also a sting of contempt for us. But any attempt to hide the fact of India's massive poverty would be self-defeating. Herding the destitutes out of the cities where they eke out a miserable existence and where their services are essential for the relatively better off inhabitants was nothing short of a callous crime. A young civil servant of Maharashtra who was holding a key position in the State's Housing Department was horrified when he visited the trans-Yamuna colonies in Delhi in 1976. The colonies were products of Sanjay's dynamic slum clearance drive in pursuance of which hundreds of families cluttering the Jama Masjid area were overnight uprooted and transshipped like cattle to places beyond the Yamuna while their ramshackle dwellings were bulldozed. There was, no doubt, the carrot of a small patch of land on which each of them could build their own dwellings. But without infra-structural facilities like water, electricity, drainage and roads in the new colonies their existence became worse. It merely amounted to lifting the slums physically from the heart of the city to its periphery. Further, the inhabitants who plied their trades in the city or who were employed there had to trek long distances to earn their livelihood. Apparently these considerations did not weigh with the policy-makers whose only objective was to rid the city of the eyesore.

In this context, India is made up of two nations, those who are born to affluence or have made their way up, who despise not only poverty but also the victims of the social situation and those with no means of amelioration and so resign themselves to their lot, blaming a cruel fate for it. The latter are steeped in ignorance, superstition, disease and squalor. Their abysmal poverty makes them cynical and forces them into all types of crime. There are not many Mother Teresas to wipe the tears from their eyes. The division between these two nations will be more explosive in the long run than the religious differences magnified and exploited by Qaide-e-Azam Mohammed Ali Jinnah. They are more deep-seated than the caste loyalties on the crest of which politicians like Chaudhri Charan Singh for the Jats and Mayawati for the Dalits sail to power. This dichotomy cannot be ended by cosmetic measures like burning down slums and beautifying the urban areas. In his autobiography Panditji (Nehru) wanted to see the slums of Kanpur burnt down but as Prime Minister he was content to strive for the betterment of the slum dwellers. The problem cannot be wished out of existence by shutting out Louis Malle or castigating Satyajit Ray for their faithful portrayal of the Indian reality. Presumably because of his immaturity Sanjay Gandhi had sought such short cuts to social goals and coteries of admirers had egged him on to do so.

A third dimension to this tragedy is the reaction generated in patriotic hearts by Western criticism that India is a soft state. Indira Gandhi was extremely alive to such comments by Western and other observers and thought strong-arm methods could dispel the impression. To the extent that her Government stood firm on its decisions refusing to be deflected by agitations it was a positive trend. Otherwise, India would cease to be governable as it has been lately. But Indira Gandhi had also got into the habit of arbitrary behaviour because of her flair for wielding power. Eminent sociologists like Samuel Huntington of Harvard University were all praise for the former Shah of Iran for the strong leadership he provided to that country in the sixties and early seventies. They contrasted Iran's progress under the Shah with the muddling through by India under its parliamentary democratic set-up but before the end of the decade while the Shah and his leadership had been wiped out Indian democracy is still surviving, despite the beating it received in 1975-77. Given a Nehru type of leadership the democratic system can deliver the goods even in India though the pace may be slow and the process cumbersome.

Reverting to the Baghpet incident of alleged assault by the police on the woman companion of three suspected dacoits, the tendency on the part of the police to seek extraordinary powers and to resent intervention by the courts was aggravated during the emergency. Thanks to MISA (Maintenance of Internal Security Act) and COFEPOSA (Conservation of Foreign Exchange and Prevention of Smuggling Act) a citizen could be thrown into goal for an indefinite period without trial or even a charge sheet at the sweet will of middling police officers. Simultaneously, in the name of combating Naxalite violence the police let loose terror in the affected villages killing all those who came in the way of their arbitrariness and reporting them as encounters. The newspapers would either publish skimpy accounts of such "encounters" or black them out altogether. Sometimes, such incidents found mention in the press only for highlighting the meritorious record of the police. Courts were prevented from acting because even the right of habeas corpus remained suspended. Subsequently with the restoration of the rule of law under the Janata Government the police found themselves handicapped. Organisations like the people's Union for Civil Liberties (PUCL) with which eminent jurists like justice V.M. Tarkunde were associated began to exert themselves to expose police high-handedness. Newspapers also started publishing vivid accounts of such happenings. As a consequence it was claimed on behalf of the police that the security forces were demoralised. The reported spurt in crime during the Janata days was the result of such "demoralisation". Indira Gandhi exploited it fully to garner urban votes with the promise of putting an end to the alleged lawlessness but the first six months of her prime ministership showed that she had no magic wand for the purpose.

The converse of this mentality was the attitude of political leaders like Charan Singh, Raj Narain and Madhu Limaye. Although the Baghpet police had acted on suspicion that the three victims were dacoits, these leaders demanded summary punishment of police officers whom they held guilty of murder and rape. They would not be prepared to await the outcome of the judicial investigation, which the U.P. Government had instituted into the outrage. Nor were they willing to have a people's commission of inquiry to bring out the facts of the case. Their aim purely was political to exploit the caste factor at the local level because the arraigned police officer was a Brahmin while the victims were Jats. They hoped thus to break out of their self-inflicted wilderness on an evocative issue like dishonour to womanhood. This is the other side of the Sanjay medal. This also sharpens the trend towards two nations.

India is not like most other Third World countries where ambitious Generals or clever politicians seize power and perpetuate themselves and their families in it by muscle strength or recourse to craft and cunning. As the only developing country to have successfully experimented with the democratic system, India stands apart from such States and will remain so. The argument that a distortion of national values in the shape of an authoritarian government was necessary for the promotion of socio-economic progress was exposed as hollow long ago. Indira Gandhi did not usher in Socialism or Communism during the 'emergency'. If anything there was a stark departure from some of the egalitarian policies pursued from Nehru's time. Popular revulsion for Indira Gandhi's behaviour reinforced by the attraction of the values and ideals with which the Janata Party was born led to the landslide victory of the Janata in 1977. Notwithstanding all that has happened since then, the revolutionary significance of that popular upsurge through the ballot box cannot be ignored. It was not like any other general election, including the 1937 election under the Government of India Act of 1935 (on the basis of restricted franchise) which served notice on the British to quit India. The Janata was welcomed not for the greatness of its individual leaders nor for its policies and programmes but for the values, which it epitomised, and for the leadership of Jayaprakash Narayan with which it was identified at birth. That in practical terms it came to be translated into the prime ministership of Morarji Desai was a tragedy because, first, Desai lacked vision and secondly because his principal rival for the position, Charan Singh, was outright close minded and blatantly opportunist. In spite of his obsessive emphasis on moral values, Morarji Desai lacked the elementary honesty to acknowledge that the Janata victory in the 1977 elections and his own prime ministership were the handiwork of Jayaprakash Narayan. He began to conduct himself as if he had won - on a recount - the contest against Indira Gandhi for prime ministership, which he had lost in 1966. He remained immune to all that had happened during the intervening decade plus between 1996 and 1977. Although he was among the leading lights kept in detention for eighteen months in 1975, he would not move even his little finger against the 'emergency.' He thought remaining in detention was enough to undo the 'emergency.' For instance, while in detention only his family members were allowed to meet him once a fortnight. When his son, Kanthi Desai was persuaded to take with him documents on the developing political situation Morarji flatly refused to look at them even saying that he would not be a party to defiance of detention rules. That was when he himself acknowledged that the detention was malafide and spurred by political motives. He generally lacked vision but where he had it myopia blinded it. He could not see a nail without hitting his thumb. The less said about his successors the better. India hit the nadir in the quality of its leadership when Charan Singh's excursions to get into the prime ministerial chair succeeded for a brief while mostly due to the machinations of the then President Sanjiva Reddy. In short, after Nehru and Shastri India has been ill served by its second-generation leaders.

In this context, a word about Sanjiva Reddy's Presidentship is relevant here. Turning the spotlight on the person of the President does not and should not in any way mean demeaning the Presidency, which we are all committed to respect. The purpose of this reluctant task is also partly to stress the need for circumspection in electing the President of India. Catapulting any person into the high office on specious grounds of his or her caste or community will only devalue the Rashtrapati. Secondly, the Janata Party's brief tenure in office had seen involvement in the murky goings-on of the Head of the State himself. The starkest lapse of Sanjiva Reddy was that even when he was made the President of India he could not rise above his provincial outlook notorious for manipulation and satisfaction of personal needs. Most strikingly, Sanjiva Reddy had a very small mind, which could not rise above the Syndicate mentality of 1969 when a few state leaders ganged up to manipulate succession to Lal Bahadur Shastri with a view to retaining a whiphand on national affairs. It was qualitatively different from the subsequent efforts of regional parties to come together to forge a coalition to run the Government at the Centre. This is federalism even if not perfect, whereas the Syndicate in 1966-69 tried to exploit the perceived malleability of Indira Gandhi to run a proxy government in New Delhi.

Sanjiva Reddy was a self-serving person, who used the party for his own purpose. For instance, during the 'emergency', George Fernandes who had been 'underground' went to Anantapur where Sanjiva Reddy had a bungalow. George wanted to stay there for a while since Reddy's residence was not under police surveillance. Reddy did not hide his nervousness and did not hesitate to pack George off saying that his position would be compromised if he were seen to be harbouring a fugitive from the law. That was his commitment to resistance to the 'emergency.' Reddy was in charge of the Janata Party's election campaign in 1977 in the southern States, where the Janata Party had virtually drawn a blank. In his home State of Andhra Pradesh, he managed to win a single seat, his own, (of the total of 42. (It was alleged that the election had been rigged).

If Morarji Desai was an individualist who could not identify himself with the Janata Party and the larger socio-political purposes it was expected to serve, Sanjiva Reddy as the Speaker of the Lok Sabha tended to use his office to buttress anti-Morarji elements like Madhu Limaye because they had contributed to his elevation to Speakership. The situation within the Janata Party in 1977 was aggravated by the total absence of rapport between Desai and Reddy. Morarji never made a secret of his conviction that Reddy did not deserve any position at the national level. Once when I asked him whether in view of the poor showing of the Janata party in the south he should not have taken advantage of the presence in the parliamentary party of a leader like Sanjiva Reddy by making him Deputy Prime Minister or entrusting him with a key portfolio like Home Affairs, Morarji' s reaction was sharp. "He is a corrupt person. Lal Bahadur committed a mistake by making him the Transport Minister at the Centre" he said. The reference was to an adverse judgement by the Andhra Pradesh High Court on the nationalisation of bus routes by the State Government and Sanjiva Reddy owning moral responsibility for it and resigning as Chief Minister in 1965. Sanjiva Reddy's perception of Desai was no more flattering. In 1979, Morarji Desai had to resign as Prime Minister following defection from the Janata Party of Charan Singh's supporters. Soon after, however, the A-I ADMK in Tamil Nadu and the Akali Dal in Punjab had offered to co-operate with the Janata Party in forming a government, which would have been a coalition of sorts. But Sanjiva Reddy, as President, while assessing the different parties for being called to form the government refused to give a second chance to Desai. His justification was that Morarji not only condoned but also connived at his son Kanthi Desai's money- making activities from the prime minister's house. In other words, instead of exercising his constitutional position as President during a political crisis he had brought to bear on the issue his moral judgment, or personal prejudice as the case might be. More than the charges and counter charges of corruption harboured, if not traded between the leaders occupying high positions in the polity, their readiness to develop attitudes on the basis of the perceptions and prejudices was a reflection on both Desai and Reddy. Reddy also did not forget or forgive Desai's unwillingness to let him be the President of India.

Desai's choice for Presidentship was Dr. Rukmini Arundale, the celebrated Bharata Natyam artiste of Kalashetra fame in Chennai, who would have perhaps made a very good Head of State. She had all the virtues, which the President of India needed; she was alive to the contemporary situation in all its aspects without being a party to partisan politics. But Madhu Limaye as Secretary of the Janata Party had successfully stymied the move and launched a campaign for Reddy on the ground that an active political leader should be the President. Desai had to bow to the majority opinion in the party and Reddy was elected unopposed. Desai was far from pleased. His ego overshadowed his acquiescence in the will of majority opinion in the party. He put the blame for it as much on Madhu Limaye as on Reddy.

To compound the situation, in the name of being above party politics Sanjiva Reddy began to assume an attitude of equidistance towards the Janata Party and Indira Gandhi's Congress (I). His favourite theme was that all national leaders including Indira Gandhi, Desai and Charan Singh should work together. That was at a time when "his" government was trying to prosecute Indira Gandhi on charges of corruption and violation of the Constitution. That had reinforced the suspicion of Desai and others that Sanjiva Reddy was keeping open his lines of communication with Indira Gandhi. Finally, he allowed Charan Singh to form a minority government consisting mostly of defectors from the Janata Party on the basis of a secret pledge of support to the government by Indira Gandhi. When Charan Singh ducked facing the Lok Sabha for a confidence vote, he let him continue in office for six months, pending fresh election. Charan Singh was thus India's first unelected prime minister, even if for six months. Chandra Shekhar was the second for four months in 1990. The most charitable construction on Sanjiva Reddy's action was that since there was no provision in the Constitution for President's rule at the Centre, he had to allow the government to stay on as a caretaker regime. Reddy's explanation was that having become President he had jettisoned his party label and was striving for political stability. The Congress party was then riven into two factions led by Indira Gandhi and Yeshwantrao B. Chavan. Chavan and his supporters joined the Charan Singh group to form a coalition government, while the Indira Gandhi faction assured support from outside to the regime, primarily to induce the President to agree to its formation. The over-arching purpose was to spite the Janata Party.

Incidentally, Yeshwantrao had been very close to Desai, having been his understudy in Bombay. He had also succeeded Desai as chief minister of Bombay when Morarji moved to the Centre in the 1960s. Yeshwantrao said to me that if only Desai had asked him for support after the defection of Charan Singh's group he would have readily agreed either as a partner or from outside but Desai would not do it. Significantly Reddy who never missed an opportunity to disagree with the Desai government and had fought a relentless battle for turf with Desai, meekly surrendered to Indira Gandhi when she returned to power following the 1980 general election. The most striking instance of presidential subservience to the Prime Minister was the readiness with which Reddy had signed an Ordinance, just one day before the commencement of Parliament session, for nationalising Sanjay Gandhi's auto workshop called Maruti Udyog. The purpose was to transfer the massive liabilities of the company to the national exchequer. Sanjay had borrowed heavily from industrialists in the launching of his "small car" venture. He did not apparently intend to repay the amounts because he believed that as Prime Minister's son he had the right to touch industrialists who depended on the Government for licences and permits. Perhaps the industrialists had parted with their money either to curry favour with him and to encash the obligation into licences and permits or out of fear that not keeping Sanjay in good humour might jeopardise their businesses, if not their lives. The first act of Indira Gandhi after resuming prime ministership in 1980 was to nationalise the massive debts of the Maruti Company so that the taxpayer could pay for Sanjay's exercise in entrepreneurship. The Government of India inherited the liability as a result of the so-called nationalisation.

Reverting to Indira Gandhi's return to power in 1980, there was hope that she might retrieve the promise of 1966 but it was blighted from the beginning. Thanks to Charan Singh's strategy of inflicting physical punishment on Indira Gandhi and her family members - by implicating them in criminal cases - her first priority after returning to power was to extricate herself and her associates from the web. Whatever be the rhetorical overtones of her election campaign her main objective in trying to regain power was saving herself from liability to criminal prosecution. In the case of Sanjay, she candidly admitted that he re-entered politics and contested the election only for self-preservation. Having accomplished it, the next step was to eliminate all threats to their position so that there would be no recurrence of 1977. A country of India's size and diversity of problems could not be led by persons with such limited purposes in life. History will not specially forgive Indira Gandhi for killing, out of sheer pique, an adult literacy programme initiated by the Janata Government. In quantitative terms alone, it would have brought literacy to 100 million people by 1982. Meant mainly for persons in the 15-35 age group, it was to benefit those above 35 years also. The Planning Commission was particular that 50 percent of its outlay of Rs. 2000 million should be spent through the state governments. While chicken-sexer "experts" picked holes in its conceptual framework, the politicians set out to kill it with the stick of the R.S.S. The Planning Commission had rightly stressed that non-official agencies and voluntary organisations including trade unions would have to be associated with such a massive developmental programme which could not be implemented through official machinery alone. Remember Raj Krishna's fervent plea for mobilising beneficiaries of welfare schemes so that the bureaucracy could not distort them into the familiar sources of middlemen enrichment. The so-called secular critics interpreted it as a ploy to pump money into the R.S.S. as if mere money power would have built a cadre-based organisation. Indira Gandhi started the campaign of calumny with the pro-Moscow Communists constituting the chorus. As PIO, I approached some eminent journalists (including my benefactor Kuldip Nayar) to look at the programme, discuss it with officials, educationists and others, probe the charges against it and write about it but they had no time for such "heavy writing" because the fissures in the Janata were a ready and endless "food for thought" for the celebrities! In short, no successful or success-seeking person be he (she) a politician, journalist or publicist has stomach for persevering with work which does not yield quick and striking dividends, be they power (legislatorships, party posts, hangers-on in the vicinity of the great) and self-promotion through publicity. The leadership, which India deserves, and needs, has to be different from this tribe.

Apocalypse is another dimension of the national scene. It consists of prophesying doom highlighting caste, religions, and language and sex disparities among our people and playing on their problems of poverty and backwardness. Spreading divisiveness by pitting one section against another to form vote banks has been a feature of the country's politics since Nehru. Indira Gandhi, in her *avatar* of an opposition leader in a hurry to retrieve power, played that role as do many who go by the name of opposition leaders today. Recurring incidents of violence on account of caste, religion and language animosities naturally make news, which sets foreign observers to pronounce that India is a soft State doomed on account of its feuding populace.[8]

End Notes

1. P.V. Narasimha Rao unhesitatingly endorsed President Zail Singh's action in naming Rajiv Gandhi as successor to his mother but Pranab Mukerjee dumurred. Mukerjee was then a Rajya Sabha member and had later distanced himself briefly from the Congress paty.
2. R.S.S. chief, Balasaheb Deores, rightly read the writing on the wall when he said the nation felt bereaved and insecure at the assassination of Indira Gandhi and favoured a respite from party politics. He, therefore, advised the BJP not to oppose the Rajiv-led Congress in the impending general electrion. But the BJP could not abide by his advice. Professor Deores explained the rationale of his approach when I called on him in Hyderabad.
3. For a graphic account of the 1975 'emergency' see L. K. Advani *A Prisoners' Scrap-book*, (Foreword by Morarji Desai) 1977, Arnold-Heinemann, New Delhi.
4. For a detailed account of the crackdown on the press and journalists see *Misuse of Mass Media During 1975 Emergency*, ed. K.K. Das, ICS, 1977, New Delhi, Government of India.
5. Population control was the most important, which objectively sought to overcome the lapse of Nehru and Indira Gandhi. But an exaggerated campaign of misrepresentation saying that the Muslims were exclusively targeted killed it even before Raj Narain as health minister in the successor Janata Party Government scrapped it.
6. There was no method in the madness of Charan Singh and Madhu Limaye unless the purpose was to make martyrs of Indira Gandhi and Sanjay Gandhi by ineffectively trying to persecute them. The administration was so porous that hours before punitive action was mounted against Indira Gandhi she had information of it. See also L.K. Advani, *The People Betrayed*, 1979, New Delhi, Vision Books.
7. For a stirring account of Gandhiji's trial by C.N. Broomfield, District and Sessions Judge, Ahmedabad, on a charge of seditious writing on 18 March 1922, see Louis Fischer *The Life of Mahatma Gandhi*, 1950, Jonathan Cape, London. Fischer called it "The Great Trial."
8. For a persuasive and positive account of growing divisiveness on caste, language and religion in India. See Selig S. Harrison, *India The Most Dangerous Decades*, 1960, Madras, Oxford University Press.

4
The Gods Who Failed

The short-lived Janata Dal dispensation (1989-90) had shown promise of resurrection of the failed Janata Party experience. It was thought the circumstances in which the Janata Party had been born had also condemned it with fragile existence and doubtful survival. As L.K. Advani said to me in 1979, if, instead of winning a whopping two-thirds majority in the 1977 general election, the Janata Party had just scraped through or even failed to get a majority in the Lok Sabha, it would have had a sobering effect on many of the party's leaders, especially power-mad characters like Charan Singh. The reference to Charan Singh is my annotation because even in his freest moments Advani is not a gossip nor did he cast aspersions on his political rivals. It could not be because he did not trust me enough. Far from it. In January 1979, for instance, there was an international film festival in Delhi. The avalanche of requests/demands for passes had to be seen to be believed. Among the celebrities whom I had to oblige was Khushwant Singh. He sent me a note saying that besides the invitation he would get in the normal course he needed one more pass. Apparently Advani, too, must have been snowed under by such requests. So when he suggested that we should go to the Andamans for a week, I jumped at the idea and off we left for Port Blair, with a stopover in Calcutta. Not that he did not like watching movies. In Paris, during the UNESCO session for which he was leading the Indian delegation — I was a member—he had noticed that one cinema house was showing the English movie of Agatha Christie's 'Murder on the Orient Express.' It had taken some effort and time to locate the theatre in a remote part of the French capital but we managed it. For functionaries of the Information and Broadcasting Ministry, which we were then, the pleasure of seeing good movies during the festival was offset by endless demands for 'passes.'

That was the barometer of our 'friendship ', as he would put it. When he was the editor of *Organiser*, we would often meet in the Parliament press gallery or the Central Hall. That remained the basis of our relationship even after he became a minister and I had my only stint as an official when I became the Principal Information Officer (PIO) to the Government. I owed the honour or headache to George Fernandes and Kuldip Nayar in that order. After the formation of the Janata Government in June 1977, George started urging me to be the PIO. He had also spoken to Morarji Desai about me. Initially, Morarji did not place me. He also wanted some other correspondents for the post; one of them, Kamal Bhat had also the plus point of having been arrested during the 'emergency'.

Ultimately, when Morarjibhai was reminded by good old Tonpe, his principal private secretary and life-long companion, that I was correspondent of the Socialist weekly *Janata* during Morarjibhai's chief ministership of undivided Bombay State, he knew who I was, but without much enthusiasm There were quite a few occasions when he found my presence at his press briefings unpleasant and avoidable. Still, he did not reject George's suggestion. The wheels of officialdom started to move with their usual speed. Nothing happened for some months, partly because I was not too keen on the job although being an assistant editor of the *Hindustan Times*, with Hiranmay Karlekar as editor was not very pleasant. For Karlekar, who is undoubtedly gifted — he is a product of the Presidency College, Calcutta, and was brought up in an intellectual atmosphere by his mother who was a noted Royist—it was career first and profession next. To have become the editor of the *Hindustan Times* when he was still in his thirties was doing a Kennedy in journalism, he would rightly say. Well connected, he moved from being one of the many assistant editors of the *Statesman* to the editorship of the *Hindustan Times*. It was no small jump and he wore the elevation on his sleeve. If the 'emergency' helped in his career, he did not mind. It was said Siddarth Shankar Ray recommended him for the job. He was, and is, well informed, tolerably well read in the context of editors whose only reading is their weekly column. The *Hindustan Times*, in those days, was more loyal than the king. Hiranmay did not believe in half measures, apparently. He went the whole hog in 'selling' Indira Gandhi and Sanjay and blacking out even the names of the resisters. He would not trust assistant editors like me a mile and virtually pensioned us off. I don't think I did even one edit during the six months I worked 'under' him.[1] He would buy 'edits' from T.N. Ninan, now editor of the *Business Standard* who was then on the staff of the *Hindustan Times*.

The topics would be technically economic but could by no stretch of imagination be linked to the politico-economic situation in India. It must have needed some effort by Ninan to cover his natural lucidity under the bushel of obfuscation and jargon. Outsiders, too, contributed editorials on payment.

The editor concentrated on news, ensuring that nothing even remotely 'objectionable' seeped into the newspaper. He would spend three to four hours every night in the newsroom supervising the bringing out of the main city edition. Indira Gandhi's picture was a permanent fixture on the front page. *The Times* (London) noted that for twenty-nine days in a month of 30 days the paper carried Indira Gandhi's picture on the front page to wonder why it had been omitted on the remaining day. Hiranmay would not take me into confidence in the matter to this day! Hiranmay's charm lay in making light of the dirty job of subordinating professional requirements to political necessity. He stayed with the sub-editors every night, lavishing tea and snacks on them to make it a co-operative effort in collaboration. It was difficult to get angry or find fault with the man although when he claimed to be an upholder of press freedom in the post-emergency days one tended to get emotional. His logic, if meant to be taken seriously, was disingenuous. It was that by overdoing the 'emergency' he had brought it into disrepute! I have written, week after week, 'attacking' him but he does not hold it against me. He had achieved the ambition of joining the ranks of editors and it was no small career development, well deserved by his gifts and talent.

Secondly, while N.C. Menon, who let down his colleagues resisting the ouster of B.G. Verghese from editorship of the *Hindustan Times* could not survive as editor for more than a few months - it was the management's reward for his playing Judas - Hiranmay thrived in the hot seat for years. A mischievous dimension of Hiranmay's impish personality was showing off the wounds on his thighs, received in fistfights with Naxalites and the Communist- Marxists at the Calcutta Presidency College. He revelled particularly in thus entertaining women visitors to the editor.

Reverting to my PIO-ship, nothing happened for about ten months after Fernandes got the Prime Minister's assent for his proposal. Then Kuldip Nayar, who was editor of the *Indian Express*, asked me to meet Advani saying that he was keen to have me as PIO. Still, hesitant, I sought a meeting with Advani. I explained my misgivings to him. I said that I could join only if my terms were accepted. He asked me to give them in writing.

They were primarily freedom to professionise the Press Information Bureau without interference from the I & B Ministry. Advani readily agreed and said I could report directly to him sidestepping the Secretary. The PIO then had the rank of additional secretary, full one thousand rupees 'below' the salary of the full-fledged secretary. It has since been raised to Special Secretary's status with the salary several times the amount I was drawing. In effect, however, Advani's assurance to me did not work because the 'system' required routing the files through proper channels, which meant through the secretary. Ultimately I became the PIO in June 1978, when the Janata Government was already experiencing death pangs.[2] While I do not look back with pride or pleasure on my two years in Government service, it gets mentioned in my career assessment more prominently than my over forty years as journalist!

Working with Advani, was, however, an experience. We hit it off famously, although he would often allude to my 'socialist' past and caution me against being blacklisted as a RSS convert. Both temperamentally and intellectually, RSS ideologues are difficult to get on with. During the emergency when the RSS cadres bore the brunt of repression, we worked together in my field of publicity. I would argue for hours with the RSS personnel in my team about the political approach to fighting the totalitarian set-up. They would insist on including Nehru among the Congress leaders to be pilloried but I would argue that the rot started with Indira Gandhi and her dynastic agenda. They would not trust even Nikhil-da (Nikhil Chakravartty) dismissing him as a Communist whereas I admired and still admire liberal Communists. True, liberal Communist is a contradiction in terms but, as Richard Crossman said in his brilliant introduction to *The God That Failed*[3], turning anti-Communist to the point of compromising with the *status quo* is admission of defeat in the mission which would move Communists in those days of decay of capitalism in the West. The RSS, technically, is an ultra-nationalist phenomenon, which got sidetracked by the Muslim League politics in pre-partition India and the division of the country in 1947. As they saw it, the mischief was the making of the Muslim League, virtually a creature of British imperialism, who acted as its tool until the last. My guru, Achyut Patwardhan who co-authored with Asoka Mehta the seminal study, *The Communal Triangle*[4] shared the sentiment towards the Muslim League. So did Sardar Patel and Nehru, too. But following especially the partition riots the RSS started identifying the League with Muslims *per se* and grew more and more sectarian in its championship of Hindu nationalist interests. Ram Manohar Lohia, who was once closest among socialist leaders to the RSS, advised the Jana Sangh to be anti-Pakistan but pro-Muslim. Still, the RSS largely lives in the days of M.S. Golwalkar and Hedgewar, its founders, whose mindset was shaped, as I said, by the pre-independence political situation.

There were two factors influencing their outlook, the opposition of the Muslim League to British withdrawal from India due to the apprehension that the Hindu majority would ride roughshod over their interests in an independent India, and the partition of the country ultimately. The tragedy was that the Muslim League leadership underestimated the numerical and other strength of the Muslim population. Secondly, to buttress its claim to be the sole representative of the Muslims of the country the League dismissed the Congress as Hindu. True, many Congressmen shared the distrust of Muslims voiced by the Hindu Mahasabha and the RSS but the leadership was genuinely non-sectarian. Perhaps, it was a tactical ploy of M.A. Jinnah to strike a hard bargain with the British and the Congress and extract optimal concessions. But it worked not always because the Congress was keen to compromise but because the British Government was adept at playing the game of divide and rule and then divide and quit. Some of Nehru's statements during the pre-1946 period days were very sharply critical of the Muslim League and Jinnah with the result that Jinnah retaliated by using foul language against Panditji. The Hindu Mahasabha and the RSS thought that the Muslim League was gaining from co-operating with the British colonial power whereas the Congress policy of denial of support to the British was costing Hindu youths opportunities of careers in the army and the Services. So like the Muslim League, the Hindu Mahasabha, too, asked Hindus to join the war effort and get military training and arms. They not only did not support the Congress-led freedom movements, including the 1942 Quit India struggle, but also opposed it.[5] The RSS of the 1970s inherited this intellectual baggage, which was largely bankrupt and bereft of vision. Their acquaintance with the Hindu religious works was also very limited. That was also their attraction for the lumpens who had no patience or capacity to study and think. If a learned person of the calibre of Arun Shourie faults Ambedkar for collaboration with the British, not caring to understand the problems of the Dalits in Hindu society, it is no wonder that the average RSS operative is so raw.

My views on the philosophy, if that is the word, and thinking of the RSS remain the same to this day. But individuals like Advani, and Atalji, to mention only a few, despite their upbringing in the RSS, are some of the most decent specimens of Indian leadership. One would wish one could say the same thing of Madhu Limaye or Viswanath Pratap Singh, among others. There were instances during my brief tenure as PIO when I had to choose between my political association with a gem of a person like Madhu Dandavate and Advani. And I opted for Advani, despite his caution that I might be tarred with the brush of communalism if I did so. I was unaware of the internal working of the bureaucracy and the wheels within wheels in it. I owe the enlightenment in the matter to Upendra, then known as Upendra Chaudhry, who was a deputy director in the Railways[6]. It was never too late to learn.

I am afraid that what is meant to be a historical account of the collapse of the Janata experience has developed autobiographical overtones, unavoidably of course. In this unfortunate episode, the gods who failed were Madhu Limaye and to a lesser extent, George Fernandes. Madhu, while fast growing to be a leader of promise, had in those days shown himself as a petty politician more driven by ego than by the larger consideration of consolidation of anti-Congress forces to develop at least into an alternative to the Congress party and its self-serving leadership. For one, he was not prepared for the different constituents shedding their individual identities and emerging as a single entity. Admittedly, more than the Congress party the Janata conglomerate would be heterogeneous but it would have enabled the centre-left elements in the polity to assert themselves. Preparatory to formation of a single party a membership drive had been launched. Chandra Shekhar was the party president and among the secretaries were Ramakrishna Hegde, (Congress-O) Rabi Ray (Lok Dal), Madhu Limaye (Socialists), and Nanaji Deshmukh representing the Jana Sangh. (Nanaji soon after gave up parliamentary politics and took to land reform in Gonda district of UP). Land reform was one of the responsibilities of Rabi Ray because of Charan Singh's perceived championship of kisan interests. I had made it a point to meet Rabi Ray frequently to know about the progress of land reforms. None. Even broad guidelines for changes in land tenure and distribution of land among landless labourers had not been there because the Lok Dal leaders were more interested in sterile power politics. Any number of agrarian experts, including top notchers like Prof. M.L. Dantwala were available for guidance. There was also Prof. Lakdawala, who was deputy chairman of the Planning Commission. Prof. Raj Krishna was also a member of the Planning Commission. Where else could one find so much talent and experience. In fact, I had called on Prof. Dantwala during a visit to Bombay to sound out his views. He said in disgust the Janata Governments in the States and at the Centre were not interested in the vital issue of land reform. Instead, they were jostling for positions in the governments and the party. Charan Singh was after gaining control of as many State governments as possible, which the Jana Sangh would not allow. The socialists wherever they had physical presence were ambivalent, sometimes going with Charan Singh, sometimes opposing him even at the cost of teaming up with the Jana Sangh.

In contrast, the CPI (M)-led Government in West Bengal, headed by Jyoti Basu, embarked on basic land reform. Hare Krushna Konar, a remarkable peasant leader, who was revenue minister, was the source of the reform. I was lucky to meet him briefly during a trip to Calcutta and try to understand his strategy. It was a pity that Charu Majumdar, the Naxalite leader, had allowed political differences with the CPI (M) to cloud his commitment to land reform and pitted himself personally against Konar. I called on Majumdar at Siliguri and was surprised that the dreaded peasant revolutionary was so gentle and benevolent looking. He could be another Jayaprakash Narayan. Thanks to Konar's initiative and drive, the CPI (M)-led Government reaped for more than four decades the rewards of its land reform programme by remaining in office to this day, while none of the Janata Governments lasted even twenty-five months! . P.V. Narasimha Rao, in an unpublished critique of the 1975 emergency pointed out that the failure of the Congress State Governments to live up to the promise of fixing ceilings on land holdings with a view to distribution of the surplus land among the landless had led to erosion of the party's strength in the rural areas and the imposition of the 'emergency.'

To compound the failings of the Janata leadership, Madhu Limaye introduced the red herring of dual membership of the Jana Sangh members who retained their ideological links with the RSS. As Madhu told me candidly, 'they' could not afford to have organisational elections in the new party because the Jana Sanghis would swamp them. He wanted 'consensus' in the choice of office-bearers at all levels, which was against the party's constitution approved by his faction also. Madhu's tactics snowballed into a split in the party, first with Charan Singh pulling out his supporters who, in collaboration with Indira Gandhi and Sanjay, tried to form a short-lived puppet government. Then the Janata Party virtually disappeared when the Jana Sanghis were sought to be driven out on the alibi of their allegiance to the RSS. That was the end of the brief chapter of diverse democratic forces coming together to resist Indira Gandhi's authoritarian ways. George Fernandes had initially seen through Madhu Limaye's game but soon after staged a somersault. It was said that Raj Narain, the architect of destruction of Jayaprakash Narayan's political dream, had "blackmailed" George into acquiescence.

Viswanath Pratap (V.P.) Singh launched the second experiment of anti-Congress front, nearly ten years later, in 1989. Singh had no ideology or commitment worth the name. But he seemed an honest Congressman, which is a rare animal. He is also a bundle of plus and minus virtues, but over all he is good for nothing. Made chief minister of Uttar Pradesh by Sanjay Gandhi, he remained unaffected by the emergency, which wrought virtual havoc on a large scale in Agra and elsewhere in UP, particularly the remote areas of the sprawling State. Today, he pretends that his heart bleeds for slum dwellers thrown out of their makeshift habitats. But as chief minister of U.P. during the 'emergency' he did not bat an eyelid when thousands of slum-dwellers were uprooted in Agra, Kanpur and elsewhere. But he stood out as a Central minister in Rajiv Gandhi's time by exposing governmental corruption at the highest level.

Indira Gandhi and her sons had perfected a new strategy of collecting kickbacks from armament manufacturers on military hardware acquired by India. It would amount to millions of dollars and also remained stashed away in safe havens overseas. It obviated dependence on Indian businessmen and traders for handouts. It could also enable the party to sound revolutionary *vis-a-vis* captains of industry. It had been happening in most foreign countries with even a socialist government in Sweden implicated in such deals. During the British colonial days the practice was for the commander-in-chief of the British Indian Army to receive commission on equipment acquired for the army from invariably British firms. There was no corruption in the transactions because the choice was limited to a few British companies. After Independence, when military deals were largely with State enterprises in the former Soviet Union and the east European countries the raking was often diverted to party coffers plus personal pockets. Jagjivan Ram as defence minister for long years had the reputation of having amassed large sums that way. At least Indira Gandhi had charged him with it when he broke away from her regime on the eve of the 1977 general election to the Lok Sabha. He told me that he would always depute large delegations of officials and military top brass for negotiating arms deals abroad. That would obviate anybody making money, he said. But the then Chief of Air Staff, Air

Chief Marshal I.H. Latif let the cat out of the bag when he acquainted me with the other side of the medal.

Against this background, V.P. Singh, as Rajiv Gandhi's finance minister, caused a veritable revolution in business circles by presenting a relatively capital friendly budget for 1985-86. It was the first of its kind by a Congress minister and reportedly owed itself to Rajiv Gandhi's conversion to market-oriented economy, turning his back on licence-permit *raj* and his mother's populist Leftism. The policy of recklessly raising tax rates and augmenting black money through tax evasion was reversed. He was naturally acclaimed as a new trendsetter in economic policy making. He presented two budgets consecutively in 1985 and 1986, both of which were well received. In fact, they made a splash, with Nani Palkhiwala hailing them. Apparently, the applause had gone to Singh's head and he launched indiscriminate income-tax raids on business magnates. Among the victims was a highly respected industrialist of Pune, the venerable Kirloskar who, despite his advanced age, was sent to jail. When the honeymoon between Rajiv and his finance minister abruptly ended it was thought the reckless drive against tax evasion put off the Prime Minister. Singh was stripped of the sensitive finance portfolio and sent to defence. If, as claimed by Singh, he had come across indications of hanky-panky in defence deals and had launched an investigation through an American firm into the matter, Rajiv Gandhi must be extremely naive to give the defence portfolio to him, unless he expected Singh to swallow the scams he noticed.

Even compared to a shifty character like Rajiv Gandhi, Viswanath Pratap Singh does not stand out as a steadfast person. The way he landed the country on the brink of a civil war in 1989-90 to save his prime ministership from a threat from Devi Lal, the creature of his own opportunism has been described elsewhere. What is not so well known, however, is his meanness in moving heaven and earth in 1996 to pull down the Vajpayee Government which was just thirteen days old. The result was a general election within one year at great cost to the nation, both in opportunity and resources. The motive is said to be avenging the BJP's withdrawal of support to his minority government in 1990 on the temple *versus* Mandal issue. Even then his Government would have survived because the BJP, I know from reliable sources, did not want to move a censure motion against a non-Congress Government. It was Rajiv Gandhi who led the onslaught with a no-confidence motion. He had also won over Chandra Shekhar and his fellow defectors to ditch the government of their own party. Architect of the so-called anti-defection law, Rajiv masterminded the vile manoeuvre. It was no secret that Rajiv Gandhi had spent crores of rupees (of apparently black money) in inducing Janata Dal MPs to cross over. The rump Government had initially the backing of the Congress party. Even a blind man could see that Rajiv would pull the rug from its rickety feet whenever it suited him. Within four months he started playing the wolf and the lamb game alleging spying on him by Government secret agents.

The most reprehensible aspect of VP Singh's behaviour, as stated,, was in pulling down the Vajpayee Government. There was no prospect of an alternative Government. Even after Jayalalitha had been roped in, courtesy the machinations of Dr. Subrahmanian Swamy, and Mayawati had been neutralised, they were not sure of their numbers. So VP Singh prevailed on poor Saifuddin Soz of the National Conference to defy Farooq Abdullah's whip and vote against the Government. He had also promised Soz, a personal friend of mine, that the Sonia Gandhi Government, which would be formed, would amply reward him. When that did not happen and Soz was left high and dry he approached Singh for help in retaining the bungalow he occupied as minister in the United Front Government. The BJP Government let him stay on in the bungalow even though Soz had ceased to be a minister. But when Abdullah promptly sent him out of the National Conference, on his defiance of the party whip, he had to move into a flat as an ex-MP. VP Singh sitting pretty in his palatial bungalow did not move even a little finger to help Soz. Joining the Congress party in Jammu and Kashmir, Soz has since managed to rehabilitate himself as a Rajya Sabha member with a bungalow to stay in.

End Notes

1. An 'edit' I did on the lifting of emergency in Northern Ireland went into the wastepaper basket without a second look because Hiranmay saw an unseen link between the Ulster and Indian situations.
2. L.K. Advani *The People Betrayed Ibid* describes in detail the emergency Cabinet meeting convened by Prime Minister Moraraji Desai to consider Charan Singh's outburst against his colleagues denouncing them as 'a pack of impotent people who cannot govern the country.' The reason, according to him, was 'failure to put the former prime minister (Indira Gandhi) behind the bars by now. 'I opened my unhappy innings as PIO with the task of briefing the Press about the meeting. It was quite a fiasco with nobody to tell me what happened because the Cabinet Secretary and other officials did

not attend the meeting devoted to party matters and party president Chandra Shekhar, as special invitee, later spilling the beans to PTI to trigger Charan Singh's expulsion from the Government.

3. 1950, Hamish Hamilton, London.
4. Achyut Patwardhan and Ashok Metha, *The Communal Triangle in India*, 1942, Allahabad, Kitabistan.
5. Atal Behari Vajpayee was a rare exception. He participated in the Quit India Struggle and was arrested.
6. Upendra minus his caste affiliation of Chaudhry has been a dynamic personality despite his later-day flair for party hopping. He was special assistant to Madhu Dandavate when the latter was railway minister in the Janata Party Government. He was then a deputy director, public relations, in the Railways. Later he left Government service to join N.T. Rama Rao to become general secretary of the Telugu Desam Party (TDP). Nominated to the Rajya Sabha by the TDP he was the de facto leader of the opposition in 1985 when the TDP was the largest opposition group in Parliament by eclipsing the group leader in the Lower House. He left the TDP in 1989 to join V.P. Singh and become the minister for information and broadcasting. He then revived Advani's Prasar Bharati Corportation even if as a halfway house to autonomous public broadcasting. He joined the Congress party to become MP in the late 1990s but Sonia Gandhi made no secret of her dislike for him because of the blunt speaking about her leadership. His son, a thriving businessman, became a Congress MP from Vijiayawada in the 2004 general election.

5

If the "Emergency" had Lasted Longer

About six months after the end of the "emergency" in 1977 I was stuck for petrol on my way to the airport in Delhi. It was a cold winter morning and the petrol pump attendant was in no mood to brave the weather and help me out. It is not the time to open the pump yet, he pronounced, covering himself up with the blanket. It is an emergency, I pleaded. Pat came the reply: 'The emergency is long over'. This aspect of the "emergency" - compliance with the law — will hardly figure in our recollection of the nightmarish experience three decades ago. The in-thing is to recall its horrific face and bemoan its occurrence as if it was an unrelieved enactment of zoolum by the authorities. In fact, recent instances of police highhandedness and perceived violation of human rights in Kashmir and elsewhere have been projected as imminent or actual recurrence of the "emergency."[1]

Against this background of freewheeling use of the expression, a word about the origin and meaning of the 'emergency' is in order. According to Article 352 of the Constitution a 'threat' to the security of the country or any part of the territory is central to proclamation of emergency. Thus, there had been emergencies during military conflicts with Pakistan in 1965 and 1971 and at the time of the border war with China in 1962. The 1971 'external' emergency was still in force in June 1975 when Indira Gandhi reinforced it with an 'internal' emergency on June 25 on the ground of 'internal-disturbance' in the country or a part of it, as facilitated by the Constitution. Incidentally, there was no emergency during the 1999 Kargil operations. The immediate provocation for the June 25 'emergency' was the Allahabad High Court judgment setting aside Indira Gandhi's election to the Lok Sabha on technical grounds. She had also been disqualified from being a member of Parliament. That was interpreted as another emergency. The Congress party was unable to countenance the situation by electing another leader in her place. Meanwhile, the non-Communist opposition parties launched agitations demanding her resignation.

The 1975 'emergency' was marked most notoriously by precensorship of the newspapers and a blanket ban on the dissemination of any information unpalatable to the authorities. An iron curtain of sorts descended on the country. Other democratic institutions like Parliament and the judiciary had also been drained of autonomy. Independent-minded judges of the Supreme Court were superseded and replaced by malleable ones. As Justice Jeevan Reddy, Chairman of the Law Commission, recalled subsequently, piqued by the Allahabad High Court judgment, Indira Gandhi set out to snuff out the independence of the judiciary itself. The civil service was already 'committed.' In short, a one-person rule was established and she was made unaccountable. In the process, the executive had been enabled to get away with whatever it did with the people being kept in the dark about blatant denial of civil rights. In other words, it was not so much the misdeeds of the administration as their being shielded from the public view and the absence of relief from the courts that marked the 'emergency.' The Supreme Court ruled in April 1976 (in a case called ADM Jabalpur) that 'a proven malafide' detention of a person could not be challenged in the courts during emergency. Misgovernance and police highhandedness were there before the 'emergency' and they have been there since. For instance, West Bengal had the dubious distinction of the largest number of custodial deaths among the States of the Indian Union during the 1990s. . But there was no hush- hush about the incidents; the courts had pronounced in several of the cases. So, to say that an emergency situation prevailed or had been prevailing in CPI (M) -rule in West Bengal would be a misnomer. Or for that matter in UP, Jammu and Kashmir or even Bihar.

At the political level, the popularity of Indira Gandhi who had been nearly deified after the 1971 Bangladesh war was perceptibly dipping. More than the divided opposition, dissidence within the Congress party had begun to pose a threat to her centralised leadership. Thus, when the court quashed her election to the Lok Sabha she could not afford to step down temporarily and name a substitute for fear of being outmanoeuvred. The idea of dynastic succession was also mooted so that her second son, Sanjay Gandhi, could take over from her ultimately. That had brought into the picture Sanjay (Gandhi) who was seen as the principal instrument of the 'emergency.' Sanjay had both political and non-political objectives. At the political level, he set out to silence critics as well as potential rivals of his mother, paving the way, in the process to his own expected succession. He continued to play the role even after the establishment of the Janata Government in 1977 by taking the law into his own hands. He and his followers would break into the courts and assault policemen and officials to resist arrest and trial. His non-political agenda had a larger purpose, whether intended or otherwise. Controlling the country's burgeoning population was its centrepiece. It could even be called the second phase of the 'emergency', as though having accomplished the political objective of securing his mother's leadership, Sanjay had embarked on the second task. Enforcing the small family norm, even in the normal circumstances and without recourse to force, would not be evocative. It was far from populist. That it had been taken up showed that the threat perceived to Indira Gandhi's prime ministership had abated.

Sanjay apparently realised that a problem of such gigantic proportions could not be tackled through speeches and seminars and needed a direct assault. So he got down to it in earnest unmindful of the implicit political risk. It was alleged that the sterilisation drive launched at his instance was indiscriminate and ruthless and had alienated the people. The Congress party's rout in the 1977 general election was attributed to it. There were no doubt instances of mishandling of the programme by overzealous officials. But a sizable number of couples welcomed the programme and benefited immensely from the plots of land given in reward for undergoing vasectomy and in the long run from having to bring up fewer children. Proportionately the excesses were fewer even if they had received much play at the hands of the vested interests. I have come across in western Uttar Pradesh scores of families who are better off in consequence. If the programme had not been jettisoned, with a person like Raj Narain setting the style for the Janata party, perhaps the BIMARU (meaning ailing) States of Bihar, Madhya Pradesh, Rajasthan and Uttar Pradesh would not have got the dubious appellation. The socio-economic conditions of the people would have been far better than what they are today, with fewer mouths to feed and relatively larger employment opportunities. The country as a whole would not have been so weighed down by galloping baby boom. Some eggs might have been broken, unavoidable for making the omelettes.

As noticed, law breaking and hypocrisy marked Sanjay's post-emergency *avatar*. He became the typical Indian politician brought up on what is derisively called Congress culture. But during the emergency he was a stern enforcer of the law or what he had laid down as law. He put the fear of god in the notoriously sluggish civil service and brought discipline to bear on the proverbially inefficient public sector undertakings. In short, at that rate he would have made India less ungovernable than it is today. His down-to-earth approach to public life made short shrift of slogans of socialism and other opportunist gestures, which his mother had popularised to wriggle out of the Allahabad court verdict. The successor Janata party government did not stem the impression that resistance to tyranny did not mean lawlessness and licence. Thus, if Sanjay had his way and the 'emergency' had lasted longer the mindset of the people could have changed, with shibboleths yielding place to ground reality.

More relevantly, it would have turned the spotlight on a crucial social problem, namely uncontrolled growth of population and the people's duty to overcome it. Until then airy slogans like *garibi hatao* (banish poverty) held the field with the leaders making tall promises and conjuring up visions of prosperity for people who were without the elementary requirements for decent existence. Given more time, not only would the programme have stabilised and spread but it would have also affected the agenda of public life in the country with the people seeking tangible improvement in the quality of their life and not falling for catchy slogans. We, in India, are today victims of slogans covering up opportunism and venality. For instance, social justice has become a shield for rampant indulgence in caste division, while secularism has come to mean soliciting votes in the name of every conceivable kind of separatism. Viswanath Pratap Singh landed the country in the lap of a virtual civil war in 1989-90 by his Mandal fiat, primarily to prolong his shaky tenure as prime minister. There is also the legacy of leaders like Laloo Prasad Yadav and Mulayam Singh Yadav as a fall out from Singh's many-splintered Janata Dal. Democracy has been reduced to periodical or frequent elections that are not seen as contests for political legitimacy but life-and-death struggles. In the process, the country has been living from election to election with the politicians doing their damnedest to stay in power. A caveat to this state of affairs in the 1970's and 1980's is in order. In the 2003 assembly elections, for instance, the focus has been on governance and the quality of life of the people, which is a healthy change for the better. It is obviously on account of the success of the second generation of economic reforms initiated by the Vajpayee Government, which had taken up the thread of liberalisation of the economy launched by P.V. Narasimha Rao and Man Mohan Singh in 1991.

It is not my contention that Sanjay was fired by an altruistic purpose of reforming the Indian political scenario. His actions were objectively leading in that direction, even if unintentionally. But if the 'emergency' had lasted longer, what about the muzzling of the Press and the snuffing out of the citizen's fundamental freedoms? As it happened, Sanjay had prematurely died in a plane crash in June 1980. So, even in the worst case scenario, the 'emergency' would not have lasted beyond five years at the most, assuming that no other leader in the Congress party would have the stomach for it. Keeping it going for five years would have been extremely arduous because by the end of 1976 itself its fury had abated and the characteristic Indian inertia had begun to surface. Also, as Mark Tully put it, India is a highly porous society not built for an iron curtain dispensation. So the curbs on the press and the citizens would have begun to dissipate. Meanwhile, with the 'emergency' sifting fair weather champions of freedom from the rest, the resistance to censorship would have stiffened. It happened in Pakistan which has a relatively more limited experience of the democratic way of life and where the military has been the ruler. In fact, Indira Gandhi opted for the 1977 general election not out of concern for democracy but because the 'emergency' regime was becoming unmanageable. She did not know how to dismount the tiger. Sanjay would have done it a few years later with better results for the country.

Among the indirect benefits of a longer spell of "emergency" would have been a genuine thirst among the people for open society and the democratic way of life, which is largely absent now, thanks to the venality of the politicians. It was so in Pakistan after the Ayub and Zia-ul-Haque dispensations. In our country, on the other hand, there is election fatigue among the people put off by the general run of politicians. So the voters are sought to be swayed in the name of religion and caste. That trend would have subsided at least for some time. Democracy and the rule of law would have returned to centrestage as in 1977 without the need for a mandir (temple) or Mandal for voter mobilisation. Having resisted and overcome the curbs, the Press would have been more robust and professional than it is today. Look at our Pakistani colleagues. They know the value of freedom of the Press and cherish it!

The foregoing retrospective defence of the 'emergency' is notwithstanding some revealing accounts of the politics of vengeance practised during the first phase of the emergency when Indira Gandhi's perception of threat to her political life had not abated. The reference is to the diaries of Professor P.N. Dar, Secretary to the Prime Minister and P.N. Tandon, a civil servant who was additional secretary in the Prime Minister's Secretariat. There is also the account of M.G. Devasahayam, district magistrate of Chandigarh in 1975 where Jayaprakash Narayan was kept in solitary confinement at the Post-Graduate Medical Institute. It had taken such a heavy toll of 'J.P's " morale that he stopped eating, living on *upma* for breakfast, lunch and dinner. Devasahayam's revealing account, *India's Second Freedom: An Untold Story*. Shows Sanjay's dominant role in inflicting heartless treatment on 'J.P', wanting to see him dead.

End Note

1. The most grotesque was an allusion to the alleged persecution of Tarun Tejpal, editor of *Tehelka*, in an article in the *Hindustan Times*, which had supported the 'emergency' through anmd through.

6
A New Kind of Leader?

The common complaint, which had been widespread, against Chandrababu Naidu, ex-chief Minister of Andhra Pradesh, was that he did not have his feet on the ground. In the Indian, especially Andhra Pradesh context, deploying high-tech means like the computer and the Internet to bring efficiency and transparency to bear on governance is starry-eyed. That was the thrust of the charge against Chandrababu Naidu. Andhra Pradesh, the southern State of India, is predominantly agricultural and is high in the ranking for backwardness. More than half the State's population of seventy million is illiterate. It ranks 26th - just above notoriously misgoverned States like Bihar and Rajasthan - among the 35 States and Union Territories of generally unlettered India. The Untouchables (Scheduled Castes), who are sizable, and the tribals (Scheduled Tribes), who are not many and dispersed, are the worst among the illiterates with the bulk of them without schooling. The women among these sections of the population are at the rock bottom of the literacy ladder. Urban infrastructure and services are woefully inadequate and the rural people have limited opportunity to participate productively in the economy. Urbanisation in this context has meant migration of landless people to towns for work as wage labour, swelling the slums of the already unhygienic towns and cities.

More importantly, until Chandrababu came on the political scene, either through good luck or by manipulation, delivery on the promises made to the people was unheard of. An encounter I had with a village woman in Andhra Pradesh, almost on the extreme tip of northern Srikakulam district, was revealing. That was in the late 1970s. The Congress party had been governing the State uninterruptedly since its formation as a separate entity in the late 1950s. But very often the State Government was being run by remote control from New Delhi by Indira Gandhi. Sycophants in the media, mostly the newspapers, worked overtime to create the illusion that

Indira Gandhi had a special affection for Andhra Pradesh and that she would also contest from one of the constituencies in the State in the next Lok Sabha elections. Then came the celebrated *garibi hatao* or remove poverty slogan, which won her the 1971 Lok Sabha election with a convincing majority. It was against that background that I had gone to that village. The poor woman whom I had met wanted to discharge the hostess's duty by offering me water to drink because I was visibly thirsty due to the heat outside. But the water was so muddy as to be nonpotable. She put the paste of a seed in the water and kept it in a pot to drain it of mud and other pollutants[1].

I hesitated to drink but she assured me that they had been drinking the water for years. Then she broke into praise of Indiramma, who, she claimed, had promised to eradicate their poverty. "Why can't she start with giving you clean piped water to drink", I jibed. "That will also come. She can do it in no time. She is a maharani with plenty of wealth," she educated me. Apparently, she and others had been brainwashed by Congress party bandicoots to win their votes. And the voters had never cared to ask when their poverty would be eradicated and how. It was only when Chandrababu became chief minister that the focus was shifted to delivery on promises. N.T. Rama Rao, who ended the Congress party's monopoly on government in 1984, did not have to face the problem. He promised subsidised rice at the rate of Rs. 2 a kilo and gave it unmindful of its cost to the exchequer and the economy of the State and benefit or lack of it in the long run to the people themselves. For the rest everything remained as before, no schools, no health care, no clean drinking water. With his cinematic charisma and flair for filmi rhetoric he could silence his Congress party rivals by sheer eloquence and credibility which he enjoyed in good measure.

Among Congress chief ministers there were those like P.V. Narsasimha Rao and Vengal Rao to a lesser extent who tried to live up to their election promises. The quality of chief ministers varied. Those like Narasimha Rao diligently tried to follow the party's policies in the rural sector, including imposition of ceilings of land holdings and distribution among the landless of the surplus land thus obtained. The objective simply was to put an end to the non-productive feudal system of land ownership and make land a tool of development. For a predominantly agricultural state it was very essential. Earlier, the Communists tried it through their violent agrarian revolution, which at least sensitized the administration and the thinking people of the problem of absentee ownership of large areas of farmland while the tenants and agricultural labour were in dire need.[2]

The educative value of the Communist agitation was evident when the brother-in-law of Sanjiva Reddy, the then chief minister and future President of India, became a Communist committed to agrarian revolution. He was Nagi Reddy who was also leader of the Opposition in the State assembly in the early 1950s during the penultimate stage of the evolution of Andhra Pradesh as a State of the bulk of the Telugu-speaking people. At that time only the Telugu-speaking districts of the former Madras Presidency had been carved out to be called Andhra. Later the Telengana region of the former princely State of Hyderabad was merged into it to form the present Andhra Pradesh. Nagi Reddy's younger brother, Rajasekhar Reddy joined the Communist Party (Marxist- Leninist), also called Naxalites. Rajasekhar Reddy was killed apparently in a police encounter. At the political level, Narasimha Rao, too, had a bad turn when he embarked on a programme to impose ceilings on land holdings in the State. Although it was part of the Congress party's election manifesto for the 1972 general election Indira Gandhi ditched him when he set out to implement the reform.[3]

Against this background, to visualise Andhra Pradesh as among the most educated, productive and thriving States of India in less than twenty years (2020 AD) sounds like day dreaming. It is not. Contrary to the chorus of his critics, mostly hidebound power politicians of Sonia Gandhi's Congress party, Chandrababu—he was popularly called by his pet name of Babu and rarely uses the caste suffix of Naidu with his name—was highly perceptive and cent per cent down to earth. His argument, simply, is that since the people are so neglected with a depressing quality of life that it is necessary to undertake measures of modern governance to lift them by the bootstraps, so to say. I posed this question of how the "basic needs" of the people can be fulfilled by his "hi-tech approach" at my first meeting with Chandrababu in Hyderabad in November 1999. That was also the gist of the charge against him by the intemperate leader of the Congress party, Rajasekhar Reddy whom I had met earlier. Chandrababu's response was loud and clear[4]. The basic problem is creation of gainful occupation for the rural people. The Government has allotted four million acres (.405 hectare per acre) of degraded forest and another ten million hectares of barren land for cultivation by the landless people. They are being provided inputs including implements through co-operatives. Rural handicrafts are being streamlined and given access to profitable market through e-commerce. Similarly fishermen and toddy tappers are being helped to pursue their occupations without harassment and exploitation by officials. In that context, he narrated an interesting instance of the bureaucratic methods of extorting bribes from unlettered labourers. The Government had dispensed with the practice of issuing annual permits for toddy tappers. Yet, at the grass roots level, it was translated into three-year licences to be endorsed every year. That would mean that the toddy tapper would have to go to the official at least every year for the so-called endorsement of the permit and grease his palms. As soon as the chief minister heard of the twisting of the order he issued specific instructions to ensure that the licencee need go to the officialdom no more frequently than once in three years!

There is also a systematic effort to involve the people in a big way in both the preparation and execution of development schemes. Chandrababu calls it micro-level planning. Every village will develop its Vision targets within the framework of Vision 2020 prepared for the Government by the well-known management consultants, McKinsey & Company[5]. "From the village level this will be consolidated to the mandal (group of villages) level, and further to the district level and then on to the State level." University students are drafted to spend two weeks in every academic year in villages of their choice and within their easy reach as part of the curriculum. The students are to interact with the villagers to prepare village-level development plans taking the local conditions into account. The physical and financial targets of development will be fixed in relation to the needs and ability of individual villages. Half of the funding has to be local, with the Government finding matching finances. The priorities, however, will be those laid down in the Vision document, namely education, public health and gainful occupation of the local people.

The execution of the programme will be the responsibility of the panchayat chief, or elected head of the local self-government agency. The gram sabha or village council will review the plan in the light of progress of the schemes contained in it every three months. The officials will have no role in the effort, except to see that the government contribution is not misspent. The officials, of course, will not like the arrangement but will have to lump it in view of the determination of the chief minister to keep development at the grassroots level autonomous. Simultaneously, measures are on the anvil to streamline the bureaucracy. Manuals containing government circulars and regulations are being simplified and updated. Many of them are full of anachronisms so that petty officials can take shelter behind them to thwart decisions. In this context, Chandrababu cited examples of mutually contradictory orders remaining in the manual. Years ago, a lower-level official had leased out ten acres of prime land in the dried up Hussain Sagar lake in the centre of Hyderabad. When the Government needed it for laying roads and development of the city it was realised that the land had been on perpetual lease for 99 years. Thanks to computerisation of land records in and around the capital it was discovered that the lease had been effected some years earlier under a regulation of the erstwhile Nizam administration. When the Government rescinded it the lessees went to the court and got it set aside on technical grounds. Leave it to the lawyers to argue in the air, quoting chapter and verse of obsolete laws to get forward-looking legislation struck down. The judges also, by and large, lacked social outlook, barring a handful like Krishna Iyer, N Venkatachalaiah, Chinnappa Reddy, Jeevan Reddy and the like. But the matter did not end there. The matter had to be clinched in the Supreme Court of India. This is the fate of many reform measures. The aggrieved, mostly vested interests, knock on the doors of the courts, with distinguished lawyers like Kapil Sibal, K.F. Nariman, Ram Jethmalani and their likes readily lending their costly legal skill. (Their fees usually ran into more than Rs. 500,000 per day). There are a million Government employees in the State. They include 200 Indian Administrative Service (IAS) officers and another 120 Indian Police Service (IPS) officers, belonging to the Central cadre. The State Government cannot discipline them. They can at the most be transferred to remote areas as punishment. In fact, transferring officials is the most favourite pastime of State level politicians, particularly legislators. It has become a scandal in some States with upright officers being shunted from place to place every few weeks.

Chandrababu had appealed to his party legislators to desist from the game. He told them candidly that some officers transferred in the run up to the recent Lok Sabha election, in the hope that the replacements would favour the ruling party candidates proved false. They were inclined towards the Congress in the impression that the party would form the next government in the State. The transfers in some cases were also on the basis of what is called consensus. It implied that the officer was asked to choose among two or three options. Bitterness is contained in the process. The snag in the matter, however, was that the state finances have been in the red for about ten years. The parlous financial position was on account of thoughtless subsidies, on electricity, water and even food grain rations, plus leakage and laxity in revenue collection.

Chandrababu's father-in-law N.T. Rama Rao, called NTR in the south Indian cinematic style, was a charismatic movie star. He founded the ruling Telugu Desam Party (TDP) and led it to power initially on a plank of self-respect of Telugu-speaking people who felt marginalised by the north Indian leadership of the ruling Congress party at the Centre. He then added the populist promise to provide subsidised rice ration to mostly town-dwellers. To balance it, free electricity for agricultural operations was offered. Then, finally, in his last phase as chief minister, he introduced prohibition, or outlawing of possession, consumption and making of alcoholic beverages. The net result was a big hole in the State's finances. Revenue from excise was lost on account of prohibition, while bootlegging and corruption thrived. The subsidised grain and free electricity also were widely misused, brakrupting the Government. Chandrababu, who succeeded him as chief minister, abolished all the schemes at the cost of being dubbed anti-people and of having "stabbed" his father-in-law in the back. In fact, he had virtually to depose N.T. Rama Rao because the legislators and party functionaries were restive at his drift and non-governance. The first two years of Chandrababu's chief ministership were thus spent in warding off the emotional threats to his leadership on these counts. NTR's second wife led a raging, intemperate campaign against Chandrababu, charging him with every crime in the calendar. English newspapers published from Delhi and elsewhere projected her as a potential Jayalalitha!

Incidentally, NTR was totally innocent of governance. His *forte* was mass appeal. When Chandrababu as general secretary of the party put the names of district functionaries of the party on the computer the old man put his foot down. He ran both the party and the Government as personal fiefdoms. The opposition Congress party took up those populist slogans and offered free power and waiver of electricity arrears in its election manifesto for October (1999) general election to the Lok Sabha and the State legislature. Chandrababu narrowly escaped defeat at the hustings because of the Congress party's populism. Congress party leader Reddy's intemperate pronouncements and personal attacks on Chandrababu -he said he would dump Chandrababu in the Bay of Bengal - put off the saner voters. An electoral alliance with Atal Behari Vajpayee's BJP further saved the situation for the Telugu Desam Party. With the urban voters being moved by Vajpayee's charisma and transparent sincerity the Congress party's electoral edge in the towns was neutralised. That was in 1999.

Finally, Chandrababu's *Deepam* (light) scheme by which the villagers were offered free supply of cooking gas to wean them away from burning wood and waste as fuel clinched the matter. The Election Commission vetoed it on the ground that it amounted to unduly influencing the voters after the election process had begun. That made it more evocative. Another asset of Chandrababu was his deep friendship with Prime Minister Vajpayee whom he regarded highly. He has thus very cordial relations with the Federal government. In the process, he would also strike meaty deals with the Centre. First, the TDP with less than two dozen MPs got the plum post of Speaker for its nominee. The Lok Sabha Speaker not only has the rank of a Cabinet minister in the order of precedence but is also the fourth in succession for Presidentship. In the most unlikely event of the posts of the President, the Prime Minister and the Vice-President falling vacant simultaneously the Speaker becomes President. There was, in fact, a love-hate relationship between Chandrababu governed Andhra Pradesh and the Centre under Atal Behari Vajpayee's prime ministership. In the circumstances, why dont the two parties come to an arrangement like that between Indira Gandhi and M.G. Ramachandran in Tamil Nadu in the 1970's? According to it, the Congress left the assembly seats to the A-I ADMK and concentrated on the Lok Sabha seats. Of course, the deleterious effect of the deal was that the Congress party in the State withered. But it assured the party of all the 39 Lok Sabha seats from Tamil Nadu in the 1980 and 1984 general elections. In Andhra Pradesh, on the other hand, neither Chandrababu nor the BJP would opt for such an arrangement. Chandrababu wants TDP presence in the Lok Sabha because it provides leverage vis-a-vis the Centre. Both during the United Front days and during BJP rule sizable presence of the TDP in the Lok Sabha had been yielding good political dividend to Chandrababu. He was the kingmaker when the feuding constituents of the United Front could not agree on any policy matter. In return he got a lion's share of ministerships for his party at the Centre. By cleverly staying out of the National Democratic Alliance while supporting its government, Chandrababu often drove very good bargains with the Centre.

There are two reasons for the Central Government's vulnerability in such matters. First, more wearisome allies like Mamta Banerjee's Trinamool Congress, which believe in sharing power without a wee bit of responsibility spelt worse trouble. Secondly, the NDA's majority in the Lok Sabha was relatively small, thus making TDP support to it essential. BJP leaders hope that once the syndrome of unstable governments and repeated elections is broken it would be able to fare better in the next general election so that dependence on allies in a future coalition would be manageable. At the same time, the BJP seeks to grow on its own in the States, including those in the south. It had remarkable success in Karnataka but the party suffered badly in the 1998 elections to the State assembly as well as the 1999 general election to the Lok Sabha. It does not even have pockets of strength in Kerala where the RSS has been making its presence felt in fistfights with the CPI (M). In Tamil Nadu, too, its growth has been limited and also inhibited by the alliance with the DMK and an assortment of Dravidian parties. In Andhra Pradesh, it has a presence, which is the reason for its reluctance to leave the assembly seats to the TDP in return for all Lok Sabha seats. Chandrababu, it has been noted will not have it either. So both the parties are doomed to the present ambivalent relationship.

Among Chandra Babu's Emeginative programmes is *Janmabhoomi* meaning motherland. It is a programme of rural development through voluntary participation of villagers, students and academics, with the officials chipping in with support and advice from time to time is a novel experiment in rural communication. It was initiated on the first of January 1997. Each phase would last eight days and the venue is shifted to another location sometimes in another district. The effort had been to cover the entire State. It is modelled on the South Korean experiment of *Saemaul Undong* or new community movement, but adapted to the conditions in Andhra Pradesh. *Saemaul* in Korean implies diligence, self-help and co-operation. Narasimha Reddy, a communication expert with long innings in the Government public relations department, has made a study of the *Janmabhoomi* Programme. Incidentally, by the time Chandrababu Naidu became chief minister, Narasimha Reddy had sought voluntary retirement from Government service to devote himself to academic work. Working with N.T. Rama Rao with his eccentric style of leadership had browned off Reddy and hastened his intention to call it a day from 'babudom' The loss to bureaucracy by Reddy's action has been a bigger gain for academia and research in media matters Reddy published an on-the spot study of the *Janmabhoomi* Programme in his book[6]. He writes: "As part of Janmabhoomi,. . .development oriented action plans were launched... Singannaguda, a medium-sized village in the backward district of Medak, became a participant in this novel programme of self-help when the chief minister launched it on January 1, 1997, by joining the villagers in self-help programmes... They included road laying and whitewashing of the panchayat building. As many as 56,366 habitations, each with a population of more than 200 and less than 1, 500 were covered. The action projects centred on providing basic services such as safe drinking water, access to primary health service, universal primary education, provision of public housing to (the) the shelterless poor, extension of the midday meal scheme programme in primary schools to all economically backward sections, streamlining of the public distribution system and social security in rural and urban areas."

Narasimha Reddy's narrative adds: "A novel feature of the programme is the close association of students and teachers... A team of ten students headed by a college teacher.. and assisted by a local official .. was assigned to a habitation. In the beginning the students familiarised themselves with the people of the assigned village and interacted with the president of the village panchayat, ward members and people's representatives of a mandal (cluster of villages). The students also got an idea of micro-level planning. The girl students took an active part. To cite an example, 230 girl students from Sri Padmavati Mahila Viswavidyalayam, Tirupati, participated in 75 habitations under Tirupati (rural) mandal... they whitewashed school buildings, cleaned drinking water tanks and drains besides motivating the people in the 'clean village' concept. Yet another example: ten students from the Andhra Pradesh Residential Junior College, Bhongir in Nalgonda district worked at Brahmanapalli of Bibinagar mandal, where they dug a model compost pit and also put up a boiling water pot system for demonstration ... of the need to have a compost pit in every house to keep the surroundings clean and to drink only boiled water for better health. They also laid an approach road to the school building. An interesting feature of their interaction was that 90 per cent of the village womenfolk were aware of the importance of family planning with two children. Most of the women who are accustomed to using open-air toilets expressed the need for financial assistance from the Government to have covered toilets."

Finally the political dimension: let Narasimha Reddy wind up: "The difference between Brahmanapalli and Anantaram villages, which are five kilometers apart, was that the sarpanch (President) of the village panchayat of Brahmanapalli who belonged to the(opposition) Congress party neither participated in the Janmabhoomi programme nor extended any cooperation in the successful implementation of the scheme, while the sarpanch of Anantaram who represented the Telugu Desam Party was an active participant, lending a helping hand to the students. This testifies that politics and party affiliations can hinder village development programmes.

The success lies in taking all political parties together. There should be a national consensus that party politics should not interfere with development-oriented programmes. Otherwise, political parties opposed to programmes like *Janmabhoomi* will not only keep themselves off the schemes but also begin a disinformation campaign."

End Notes

1. It is called *Induva pikka* or seed of Induva plant in Telugu. The paste of the seed is put in water and the pot allowed to settling until it drains the mud and other pollutants and makes the water potable. In thousads of Andhra villages without drinking water the practice is in vogue.
2. P. Sundarayya *Vishal Andhralo Praja Rajyam* (people's rule in Vishal Andhra), 1946, Vijayawada, Vishal Andhra Publishing House.
3. For an allegorical account of the travails of P.V. Narasimha Rao as chief minister of Andhra Pradesh who tried conscientiously to implement land reforms by enforcing ceiling on the land holding see see *The Insider,* 1999-2000, New Delhi, Penguin Books.
4. Rajasekhra Reddy is the present chief minister of Andhra Pradesh. He was an intemperate critic of Chandrababu Naidu whom he threatened to dump in the Bay of Bengal.
5. *VISION 2020 Swarna Andhra Pradesh* (Golden Andhra Pradesh), Jan. 1999. Government of Andhra Pradesh, Hyderabad.
6. *Public Relations and Communications Handbook*, 1999, CVN Public Relations Foundation, Hyderabad.

7
Two Bogeys

Two bogeys have been haunting India for the past about 50 years. As policies they are not only unexceptionable but also extremely desirable, for a country like ours with its traumatic experience with partition, growth of Pakistan next door as a theocratic State built on the two-nation theory, a large Muslim population and the massive poverty of the people requiring speedy remedial action on egalitarian lines. But reduced to bogeys, they have done more harm than good to the country and the people. They are 'secularism' and socialism. It is to Nehru and his vision that we owe the two principles of a non-denominational polity (secularism) and economic justice (socialism) as national policies. To what extent Nehru might have, perhaps unwittingly, contributed to their distortion into instruments of condemning the largest minority to a milch cow of block votes (secularism) and economic stagnation and bureaucratic corruption (socialism) is debatable. As stated, the emergence of the theocratic State of Pakistan in the northwest (after the 1971 birth of Bangladesh, ironically with India playing the midwife), the problem was multiplied by two. A non-denominational State policy was necessary to maintain harmony between the majority Hindus and the large minority of Muslims. Otherwise, the country would have been condemned to perennial civil strife. Also, without an even-handed approach to the development and growth of all the people of the country irrespective of their religious faith, there would have been no economic growth worth the name. As it was, with the Muslims lagging behind in the socio-economic sphere, there have been glaring disparities leading to tragedies like the anti-Muslim pogrom in Gujarat in 2002. Similarly, when India became independent in 1947, it had no heavy industry worth the name and there was not enough entreprenuerism available to undertake the task of industrialisation of the country. So the State had to establish and run machine-making industries, promote mining, develop ports, explore for oil and even build and operate power plants.

The state sector was thus born. But Nehru was naive in expecting these objectives of maintaining social harmony and achieving speedy economic development to be accomplished largely by the British-trained bureaucracy, steeped in civil service culture. He could not be unaware that the political leadership barring himself, was devoid of appetite for social change and nation building. Still, he stuck to his starry-eyed idealism. Unable to reshape the instruments of contemplated change Nehru had perhaps resigned himself to living with them. Most importantly, jettisoning Gandhiji's basic approach, Nehru and the Congress party wanted to accomplish societal changes implicit in a secular polity and a just social order through governmental action which at the most could be auxiliary. First and foremost are required reformers to attune society to the desired destination. Even in Nehru's time the Congress was not awash with such talent. With State control of the commanding heights of the economy leading to centralisation, bureaucratisation of operation and skewed development, young educated people who should have been manning the State enterprises have come to despise them as inefficient, wasteful and corrupt. At the same time, a new class of managers has grown with a vested interest in enriching themselves at state expense. At the political level instead of trying to restore to health the enterprises in which millions of rupees have been invested the tendency has been further to extend State control. The purpose was nothing else than promotion of political interests and lining one's pockets. It was what the great Yugoslav political thinker and socialist, Milovan Djilas, had diagnosed as the emergence of a New Class. Even production of bread and running of hotels were not spared. In short, there has been replication of the Soviet pattern of State capitalism. For instance, in 1969, Indira Gandhi, bent on wresting control of the ruling Congress party from her rivals, nationalised fourteen commercial banks, with dire consequences to the country's banking system. The banking sector of the economy has not to this day—nearly fifty years later — recovered from the havoc wrought by the populist action.

At the other extreme, there has been an upsurge of anarchistic tendencies among the poor, which in the name of ushering in revolution has taken to virtual terrorism. The phenomenon is called Naxalism. Instead of acknowledging that indiscriminate nationalisation of the means of production and distribution is at the root of the malaise, they blame gradualist change for the malfunctioning of the economy and skewed distribution of the national product. According to them, a total overhaul of the system by violent means is the panacea. In the process, the socialistic pattern of society has fallen between two stools. At the political level it became a competitive slogan for garnering votes. Nehru had gone in for all the measures which are the stock in trade of doctrinaire socialists—establishment of heavy industry in the public sector, exclusion of private enterprise from key areas like mining, oil prospecting, power generation and distribution, nationalisation of life insurance and labour legislation to restrict rationalisation of employment among others.

In the process, because of these measures the socialists and communists felt ideologically naked. So instead of owning that indiscriminate nationalisation or promotion of State capitalism was the villain of the piece they would clamour for more of the same. The most crucial issue, on which he could have been faulted, namely land reform to put purchasing power in the pockets of the rural poor escaped their attention. At least it was absent from their radical rhetoric. Acharya Narendra Deva, the socialist patriarch, was perhaps the only exception. His painstaking critique of the zamindari abolition law in Uttar Pradesh was almost prophetic in envisaging the topsy-turviness of the reform. Dr. Lohia and at his instance Karpoori Thakur in Bihar among a few others had stood consistently for land reform. If the bulk of the Socialists had not been largely urban intellectuals and trade unionists, they could have organised the peasantry to bring pressure to bear on the establishment from below on behalf of landless labour. Thus, it has become the happy hunting ground of terroristic Naxalites. The Congress Governments enacted laws setting ceilings on land ownership but the reform was short-circuited by landowners fraudulently transferring surplus land through bogus transactions.

Andhra Pradesh was perhaps the sole exception to this make-believe land reform. The much-maligned P.V. Narasimha Rao as chief minister of the State, set out diligently to implement the land ceiling law. But he was thwarted first by *benami* (fraudulent) transfer of surplus land and, secondly, by a campaign to bring him down from chief ministership. There was a spate of bogus divorces to facilitate transfer of land to the supposedly estranged spouses. There were also instances of land transfers to cattle, named after the deities, with the collusion of the government functionaries at the village level. The pull of land-owning interests in the ruling Congress party was another impediment. Dr. Chenna Reddy spearheaded them. He was reinforced by the caste factor, which had bitten a section of shortsighted socialists also. It was alleged that Narasimha Rao being a

Brahmin had brought forth the legislation to punish the non-Brahmin castes of Kammas and Reddys. Indira Gandhi, despite her radical image and oral endorsement of land reform, sided with the opponents of the reform on the ground that the Congress party would lose the support of the powerful Kammas and Reddys. Narasimha Rao was removed as chief minister. He was kicked upstairs and made a functionary of the Congress party at the national level. Later he was taken into the Central Cabinet to become ultimately one of the more successful Prime Ministers of the country. He was not allowed again to head the Government in his home State.[1] It is strange that persons claiming to be socialists should put caste-based reservation of jobs in the Government and the public sector undertakings above land reform in the list of priorities. The reason was that job reservation on the basis of caste would be more visible, easier to implement - through an executive order - than land distribution. It is, therefore, more fetching electorally. The paradox was complete when Indira Gandhi who got the country's constitution amended to include socialism among the objectives of the State beat the Socialists in their game of one-up-manship in radical slogan mongering. At her hands, nationalisation of fourteen commercial banks became the high watermark of socialism. Even Sanjay, her second son, who did not conceal his aversion for socialism, got a few more banks nationalised in May 1980 because one of them handled the money of several Sikh enterprises and had to be kept under the thumb for political reasons.

The second bogey, secularism, strictly means irreligion or rejection of religion *per se*. But Nehru visualised it as a non-denominational approach to public life, which in practice became equal respect for and treatment of all religions. Fair enough. The State has no religion of its own nor does it patronise one. Conceptually, it flows from the fundamental right in the Constitution enshrining freedom to profess, practise and propagate one's religion. The inclusion of propagation in the guaranteed religious freedoms has upset the balance, especially in practice. The argument in its support was that since book-based religions like Christianity and Islam believed in and thrived through conversion of others to the respective faiths, it had to be safeguarded. Which reminds me of Anatole France's aphorism that every French citizen had the right to sleep under the bridges. It no doubt enables the homeless to survive the winter but for the opulent that kind of equal treatment has no meaning except that it perpetuates the disparity. I was blind to the implications of the constitutional provision in the early 1950s when the Constituent Assembly was deliberating on the constitution because I had no experience of propagation of religion. But B.H (Hanumantha) Rao, who was the first non-European chief reporter of the *Times of India* in Bombay, made me alive to the provision and its implications. Joachim Alva, although a Christian by birth, shared the apprehension and allowed me to write on it in his magazine, *Forum*. To many of us religion did not mean much except for an occasional visit to the temple and performance of rituals connected with the anniversaries of dead ancestors. As students in 1941-42 we tried to organise prayers in temples, mosques and churches for the welfare of Gandhiji who was fasting inside the Aga Khan Palace in February 1943. The temples readily complied with our request and our programme began at about 6 .am at a three-temple complex in Vizianagaram, my birthplace. There was one big mosque and a large church in that one-horse town. The authorities at the mosque turned us out saying that only Muslims could offer *namaz* within its premises. Secondly, there could be no special prayers for any one; only the regular recital from the Koran. At the church, too, we were told there could be no special prayers but the head of the institution would include the name of Mr. Gandhi when he made a general prayer for the well-being of the sick and the ailing. His calling Gandhiji Mr. Gandhi outraged us and we picked up a quarrel with him. At the mosque, however, we tamely accepted the ruling of the Maulvi lest there should be a communal disturbance. In retrospect, I would say that putting up with the bluff and bluster of Muslims who did not account for even one percent of the population of towns like Vizianagaram was the genesis of the later-day 'secularism', which has been working havoc with our polity

A few years later, what had awoken me to the seriousness of the matter was the sharp reaction from some Bombay Muslims to the plea against proselitisation. The problem could have been obviated, perhaps, if Dr. S. Radhakrishnan's idea of religion-based secularism had been accepted. It would have first recognised the secularist dimension of Hinduism with its commitment to plurality of faiths and countered the argument of self-professed Hindu zealots that secularism is anti-Hindu. Gandhiji also represented such secularism, although he never called himself one. In fact, he was proud to be a Hindu, as his controversy with Dr. Ambedkar on the caste system would show. The cover of the annual number of the *Mainstream* (1993) quoted from a speech of Gandhiji at a prayer meeting in Patna on March 12, 1947 in the run up to Independence and partition. There was large -scale Hindu-Muslim violence in several parts of the country. With the H.S. Suhrawardy regime in Bengal condoning, if not fuelling, attacks on Hindus, there was retaliation against Muslims in neighbouring Bihar. Gandhiji had undertaken the nearly impossible task of quenching the fires of religious hatred by moving from place to place on foot and offering solace to the victims of the onslaughts. In that connection, Gandhiji said: "Those who desecrated the mosque were not men but devils; because mosques, temples or churches are houses of the Lord. I have come here today to convey to you my grief. You may perhaps be smiling and thinking that whatever happened was all very good. But I assert that is potent injustice. I have grieved when I heard that Muslims have desecrated a temple. Should I retaliate by damaging a mosque? How can such damage save the temple or benefit the Hindu religion?" Dr. Radhakrishnan reinforced the pluralist approach of Hinduism to religion from a higher philosophical perspective. The germinal conceptions of Hinduism', declares Radhakrishnan, 'are contained in the Vedanta standard. ... The Vedanta is not religion, but religion itself in its most universal and deepest significance."[2]

As Lal Krishna Advani pointed out later, secularism came to be accepted in India because of its Hindu majority and tolerance synonymous with Hinduism in theory. The political shape of secularism, however, has tended to be more and more opportunistic. As already stated, partition failed to solve the Hindu-Muslim problem, for which it was offered as a panacea, especially in the case of India. The non-Muslim minority in West Pakistan had been steadily squeezed out in preparation, as it were, for the dominant Punjabi elements in the bureaucracy and the army to reduce the Bengalees, the Sindhis, the Baluchis, the Pathans and the Mohajirs into virtual second class citizens. In the process, Pakistan might have become homogeneously Muslim but the so-called homogeneity bred ethnic and linguistic intolerance. Barring perhaps the Bengalees who were the single largest ethnic entity in Pakistan, the others were late in realising the dangers of letting the Punjabis hold unfettered sway. The Mohajirs, who are now the loudest in protesting against domination by the Punjabis, remained silent spectators of, first, the anti-minority crusade and then the expulsion of the Ahmediyas from the Muslim community. Similarly, the Pathans were a party to the abortive attempt to annex Kashmir through armed infiltration soon after the birth of Pakistan. Most importantly, the death of the parliamentary system with adult franchise and one-man one-vote principle in operation was precipitated by the Punjabi dominance. Given the democratic principle, the Bengalees who outnumbered the others would have had a natural weightage in numbers in the Pakistan polity. That was nullified when the different States of the western region, namely Punjab, Sindh, Baluchistan and the North-Western Province (NWFP) were arbitrarily merged to form a single unit. Thus, the preponderance of East Pakistan in terms of population was neutralised. Part of the problem was inherent in the emergence of Pakistan as a sovereign State. The Muslim League, which led the Pakistan movement, was more an *ad hoc* arrangement than an organised party. It had the support of the vast majority of Muslims in Uttar Pradesh, Bihar, Bombay and other non-Muslim majority areas, which remained in India. The Muslim League in what was later East Pakistan was a formidable organisation but it was autonomous under leaders of the stature of Fazlul Huq and H.S. Suhrawardy. They regarded Mohammed Ali Jinnah as only the first among equals and not the supreme leader. The NWFP under the Khan brothers, Khan Abdul Ghaffar Khan and his elder brother Khan Saheb, had been with the Congress and against partition. The riff-raff under the likes of Qayyum Khan put up to destroy Badshah Khan's Khudai Khidmatgars (servants of god) was no party. Similarly in Sindh, after the assassination of Allah Bakhsh, there was neither leadership nor organisation.

In the circumstances, the formative years of Pakistan saw the emergence of bureaucrats and middle-level army officers into leadership positions. Under the towering personality of Jinnah with Liaquat Ali Khan occupying a distant second position, ex-bureaucrats filled the gap. A veteran Uttar Pradesh leader like Khaliq-uz Zaman was eclipsed and elbowed out. I had an opportunity to meet him in Pakistan in 1961. He was a bitter man; feeling betrayed by Jinnah himself. Ibrahim Chundrigar from Bombay managed to squeeze himself in largely due to his proximity to the Quaid-e-Azam. Even then, if Jinnah had not died prematurely and Liaquat Ali Khan had not been assassinated soon after, the democratic system would have perhaps survived. But it was not to be. Similarly if Pakistan had not split in 1971 when East Pakistan seceded to become sovereign Bangladesh, there would have been some restraint on its becoming a theocratic State on the lines of Saudi Arabia and the like. It was not because the Bengalees were less religious minded but their cultural identity with the Bengali language diluted fanaticism. After 1971 whatever countervailing forces might have been there were overwhelmed. Pakistan became an Islamic State and Bangladesh, too, followed suit formally. India, alone in the sub-continent, is non-denominational, which was unavoidable with the Muslims accounting for over 110 million. According to the 1991 census the Muslim population of India had gone up from 46.9 million in 1961 to

95.2 million in 1991,more than double. In percentage terms, the figures were 10.7 and 11.7 respectively, which shows a general increase in population across the board. The corresponding figures for the Hindus were 83.5 per cent in 1961 and 82.8 per cent in 1991. Although the gross Hindu population has nearly doubled from 366.5 million in 1961 to 672.5 million in 1991, as a percentage of the total it registered a nominal decline. It showed that the rate of growth of population among the Hindus was more manageable than among the Muslims. Even if the Hindu population has been stabilising due to the Hindus being relatively better developed in socio-economic terms it will be ludicrous to talk of Muslim domination in India. Similarly, India can never be a theocratic Hindu State without exposing itself to endless religion-based civil strife

The moral is loud and clear. Neither majoritism nor minorityism will be conducive to political and social stability in India. By the same token, a tilt in the direction of any community, majority or minority, will unleash backlash and unsettle inter-community harmony. With the Constitution assuring, in theory, equal rights and equal opportunities to the practitioners of all faiths, incentives for any one section to overcome backwardness in socio-economic terms have to be non-denominational, based on universal criteria. It is ridiculous to differentiate the poor and the socially repressed on the basis of religion or even caste. When the likes of Mulayam Singh Yadav talk glibly of reservation for Muslims they compound the damage to social cohesion and national unity done by Vishwanath Pratap Singh in the name of affirmative action. There is no parallel with the US in the matter. First, the black-white divide over there is racial, compounded by practices like slavery. Therefore, affirmative action on behalf of the blacks seeks to redress the injustice. But it should be remembered that quotas and reservation are taboo in the US. In our country, on the other hand, they are the stock in trade of politicians. They may benefit the targeted groups or sections of them but, at the same time, they reduce whole sections of people into vote banks, vitiating their democratic rights as citizens. They make them moronic pawns in caste and communal conflicts.

It was because of Nehru that India awoke to the secular ideal, which was an article of faith with Gandhiji. When in the wake of partition riots and large-scale migration of Hindus and Sikhs from Punjab, Sindh and the NWFP the aggrieved refugees and others had sought to take it on helpless Muslims who stayed behind in India, Nehru stood by the threatened people courageously, sometimes risking his own safety in the process. Gandhiji extended his magnanimity to Pakistan, the root cause of so much death and destruction in both countries, and insisted on payment of Pakistan's share of the partition debt - in sterling - putting his precious life on the line. If even a section of the leadership of Indian Muslims had reciprocated the emotional gestures of Gandhiji and Nehru by abandoning sectarian politics and joining the mainstream the entire community would have been better off today. Instead, they converted themselves overnight into followers of the Congress party for electoral purposes without shedding their sectarian identity for a share in the spoils of political power. The essence of democracy and pluralism in a multi-religious country like India is political uniformity of followers of all religions and not religion-based politics. It jars on one's mind to see over fifty years after independence organisations like the Indian Union Muslim League (IUML) and its leaders like Banatwala, otherwise sensible, continuing the sectarian politics of the past but with secularism on their lips. Very few of them, if at all, are guilty of ameliorating the lot of the common run of Muslims through reform of social conditions and promotion of opportunities for development. They are for an extremely orthodox kind of Islam, not available not only in progressive countries like Egypt, Syria, Malaysia and Indonesia but even in Pakistan.

A sizable chunk of Muslims, who could not migrate to Pakistan, the perceived homeland of Muslims of the subcontinent, were relatively poor, especially in UP, Bihar, and other Hindi-speaking States. The predominantly Muslim Kashmir Valley is an entirely different kettle of fish. In Maharashtra, Gujarat, Andhra Pradesh, West Bengal and Karnataka, among a few other States with a noticeable Muslim population, the relatively better off also did not opt for Pakistan. First, there was no threat to property and life of the Muslims in these States. Secondly, they had property or business to take care of. In some cases, like my friends from Hyderabad, some members of the family moved to new Pakistani pastures while the others remained behind. But for the unending tension between India and Pakistan, this would be the ideal arrangement and also a way of healing the wounds of partition. There were other paradoxes, too. The Communists, as a party, were the staunchest supporters of the Muslim League demand for Pakistan invoking the misconceived principle of the right of self-determination. But many of its Muslim leaders preferred to stay back in or opt for India, instead of moving to Pakistan where they could have provided much-needed balance against religious fanaticism and feudal obscurantism. The most illustrious Muslim Communists or radicals, who remained in Pakistan, were the Iftikhar-ud-Dins — Mian and Begum —, Faiz Ahmed Faiz, J.A.

Rehman and Manzur Qadir, among others but they were mostly property owners or ideologically committed. As long as the Iftikhar-ud-Din couple lived they stood by their convictions, paying the price for it.[3] After them, their son Arif Iftikhar-ud-Din kept the flag of defiance flying against repression and persecution of individual leaders. I can never forget the warmth of friendship for "an Indian", which he exuded when I ran into him at Murree in 1961. Karachi and to a lesser extent Lahore were cosmopolitan enough to house Left-minded political leaders; Rawalpindi, where I was forced to stay, and its successor Islamabad are comparatively dreary deserts of orthodoxy.

Reverting to 'residuary' Muslims in India, the majority of them needed to be reformed socially. There was crying need for a Sir Sultan Ahmed who would have provided liberal education to them to enable them to fulfil their potential as the largest minority accounting for over a hundred million people or 12 per cent of the Indian population. Compounding the misfortune of the death in the prime of his life of a dynamic personality like Rafi Ahmed Kidwai, (who rose to be a great non-denominational national leader after Maulana Azad and Asaf Ali,) there were Congress Muslims like Fakhr-ud-Din Ali Ahmed who grew at the expense of their community and the country. They lacked the vision to strive for social reform within the Muslim community. They were content to be manipulators and powerbrokers. In the 1952 first general election to the Lok Sabha, the main threat to the Congress party was from Hindu and Sikh extremists who reflected the emotions of millions of people who had to flee Pakistan leaving behind their vast property or large businesses. They were loath to accept that Muslims should be full-fledged citizens of India enjoying rights and privileges which the Hindus and Sikhs could never have expected in Pakistan. Nehru had to wage a veritable crusade against such "communal forces." The Muslims thus began to look to him as a saviour, overcoming the prejudice against the Congress and him. Electoral support to Nehru's Congress party had become an insurance policy for Muslims needing security.

That was a negative approach to building a non-denominational State in India. It was perhaps unavoidable in the circumstances but had to be followed up by positive measures to ensure that no religious group, big or small, vocal or quiescent, was disadvantaged as an entity or promoted on a sectarian basis. One way of going about it was to absorb into the Congress denominational organisations like the Muslim League and the Shiromani Akali Dal so that they would cease to project their past philosophy of sectarianism. The other— least desirable alternative — was to proscribe organisations linked directly to religion. Neither was done. True, banning religion-based politics would drive sectarian elements underground without combating their approach. The Socialist leader, Asoka Mehta, pleaded for the formal merger of the Muslim League and the Akali Dal in the Congress. According to him, where the Muslim League was strong as in Kerala as well as Punjab, the home of the Akali Dal, the Congress would speak their language but in a non-communal voice. Individual leaders like Master Tara Singh of the Akali Dal would be better able to realise their personal and community aspirations through the Congress than outside in opposition to the Congress. But the Congress party in post-partition Punjab was so hopelessly riven by clashes of personalities and factional feuds that a new entrant like Master Tara Singh would have found himself out of place without teaming up with one of the factions. So it did not attract a towering leader like Tara Singh with a live-wire organisation like the Akali Dal at his command. True, factions developed in the Akali Dal, too, but they were not of the magnitude of the warring groups within the Congress. Also, the internecine differences in the Akali Dal were often fuelled from outside by the Congress and the State Government led by it. Only junior operatives like Swaran Singh and more recently Buta Singh joined the Congress, initially as individuals.

As for the Muslim League, in Bombay S.K. Patil admitted them as members of Fourth Party, their new label after partition. In Kerala, on the other hand, the change was even more cosmetic; from All-India Muslim League it became Indian Union Muslim League (IUML), indicating autonomy from Pakistan's ruling party. More than severance of ties with the old Muslim League, the IUML became a regional or State party, which was significant. Not that it ceased to be 'communal' as Nehru and Pandit Pant certified. Soon after the Kerala State Congress party accepted it as a member of the anti-Communist coalition. It remained an exclusively Muslim-centric outfit, while toeing the Congress line at the national level. That could be partly out of a guilty conscience for having worked for the partition of India. In course of time, both the Communists and the Congress began to woo the IUML and in return agreed to the division of a Muslim majority district to make it a pocket borough for the IUML. The IUML also meanwhile started fragmenting, imbibing the Kerala trait. As long as Nehru lived and led the Congress party, there was no necessity to cash in on the Muslim vote bank to keep the party in power especially at the Centre. But at the hands of Indira Gandhi, after a brief interlude under Lal Bahadur Shastri, it became the only shield against defeat at the hustings. More than that, it became the criterion for the secularist claim of the party. For a time it was a mutually convenient arrangement for both. The Muslim vote, available in bulk and controlled by leaders, enabled the Congress party not only to clinch marginal constituencies where the Muslim vote was decisive but also to swell its popular vote at the national level. A classic illustration of the new secularism was the manoeuvrings of Indira Gandhi and her supporters in 1969 when she made a bid to wrest the leadership of the party. Aging Nijalingappa, brought up in the Congress tradition, was first stupefied and then bowled over by the 'secularist' tactics of Indira Gandhi. She charged him with partiality for, if not partnership with, the Jana Sangh and the Swatantra Party because he had appealed for support from the two parties to the Congress Party's Presidential candidate. Her propagandists began to claim that because of the electoral support for Indira Gandhi from Muslims and Harijans—she was the best bet for India's survival as a secular State.

But the chain of disturbances in several parts of northern India, starting with Moradabad in UP, and enveloping even Delhi, showed that election-oriented secularism could be a double-edged weapon. The Moradabad riot had been described as 'the worst in recent history.' It might or might not have been so in terms of its toll in life and property but it set the pattern of the minorities and the law-enforcing agencies clashing. Over the years there have been several such instances in different parts of the country. Some of them like those in Ahmedabad (1969), Osmanabad in Maharashtra in 1974, Aligarh, Jamshedpur, Srinagar and Hyderabad in 1978-79 were similarly described. A number of senior journalists with unimpeachable secular credentials have looked closely at the riots in Moradabad and other towns of western UP and written perceptively about them. The newspapers include the *Times of India*, the *Statesman* and *The Hindu*, none of which can be accused of bias against one community or another. They have all established that the Moradabad trouble started with a premeditated and planned assault - with firearms - by some members of an Id congregation on the unprepared police. It was also brought out that there were about 22,000 "licensed besides unlicensed firearms " with individuals in the district. In the words of N.S Saksena, a former Inspector General of Police of the State, there were " more firearms with individuals in Moradabad district than in the whole of United Kingdom or Japan."

The then editor of the *Statesman*, S. Sahay, had also pointed out that there was 'continuing tension' between the police of the area and the legislators of the constituency—both MLA's and MP's — who got the district magistrate transferred only a few days earlier "because he refused to oblige them" in the issuance of arms licences, among others. The Lucknow correspondent of *The Hindu,* who visited Moradabad, reported that when the police refused to remove a pig, which strayed into an Id congregation " there was an altercation and policemen were manhandled. Some persons from the crowd stabbed a few policemen and the armed constabulary men. If the senior leaders of the minority community had tried to pacify the mob and control the situation it would not have taken an ugly turn. Heavy brick batting (hurling of bricks) followed. Arms from policemen were snatched. A police constable was shot dead with the rifle snatched from him. The violent mob dismantled a huge wall nearby and took out bricks to hurl at the police and the majority community." Then followed theories galore. Some saw the hand of foreign powers, hinting at Pakistan and even the US. A few Muslim leaders argued that *agents provocateur* had been planted in the congregation by "communalists" with a view to pitting the minority community against the custodians of law and order. If so, how could they have roused the mob to tear up a brick wall for the use of bricks as ammunition against the police, unless they were sizable in number? How did they manage to store arms in a place of worship? How did the huge congregation and their leaders allow it to happen under their noses? Using deductive logic, others contended that since the minority community suffered the most in the violence its members could not have started the riot. But it was proved in Aligarh in 1961, Ahmedabad in 1969 and Osmanabad in 1974 that the provocation often came from the ultimate victims. In their frenzy they would not pause to ponder the consequences. Secondly, the persons who set off such conflagration have no concern for the lives, property and honour of their co-religionists. They are interested in creating situations, which will establish their leadership on people who may otherwise be weaned away from narrow religious sentiment. A judicial inquiry into the Osmanabad violence had established the role of Communists in fomenting trouble for purely political purpose.

I was in Pakistan when rioting broke out in Aligarh on 3 October 1961. It was sparked by a university union election. The victors, Muslims, took out a procession, which was attacked by the rivals, Hindus: a perfect setting for an inter-religious fracas. While the university authorities failed to control the situation, outside the campus the police stopped a large-sized mob bent on avenging what happened in the university. The disturbances, which claimed a toll of ten killed and 39 others injured in Aligarh, spread to twelve other UP towns in the next few days. They assumed grave proportions in Meerut, the stronghold of the then Home Minister of U.P., Chaudhry Charan Singh. Fourteen persons were killed there and the troops had to be called out to quell the violence. In a prepared statement after visiting Meerut, Charan Singh traced the trouble to "the parties opposed to the Congress." The reaction in Pakistan was nothing short of hysterical. President Ayub Khan said the riots "could not have happened without the connivance of the Indian administration." Agha Hillaly, who was Pakistan High Commissioner in Delhi, conveyed to the Government of India "Pakistan's concern at the organised killing of Muslims in India by Hindu communalists." The Press unleashed a campaign insinuating complicity by the UP and the Central Governments in the "massacre."

Under the Nehru-Liaquat Agreement, a Pakistani diplomat, Deputy High Commissioner, Agha Shahi, visited the affected areas and prepared a report for the Pakistan Government. The implication of official agencies in the violence suddenly stopped after Agha Hillaly personally brought the inquiry report to Rawalpindi. So did the demand for raising the matter at the United Nations. Ayub Khan ruled out such a step saying it would be counter-productive. Intrigued by the change in the tune of professional India-bailers like the then editor of *Dawn* (Altaf Husain), I tried to find out what was in Agha Shahi's report. A Bengali officer in the Pakistan Home Ministry - who is now no more - let me have a glimpse of it on condition that I would not report it. Having seen it, I pleaded with him that not reporting it would be a waste of all my effort. Also, the tendency of some Pakistani publicists to blame the authorities in India for the actions of others would go unchallenged. Ultimately, he relented, provided the source was not cited and the report did not carry Rawalpindi dateline. I travelled to Amritsar, using up one of my three visas, to file the report for the *Hindustan Times*. It said, in sum, that the provocation for the trouble in Aligarh came from the Muslims and the Hindus retaliated in force, inflicting a larger number of casualties. To make it appear that it was not based on the findings of the Deputy High Commissioner, but mere deductive reasoning, I pointed out that if Agha Shahi had found even an iota of proof of official connivance in the riots, it would have been leaked out to the Pakistani media. It would have then gone haywire with its campaign against India on the issue. On the other hand, the anti-India hysteria dried up after the receipt of the report by the Ayub Khan Government. It was to be a New Delhi-datelined report without my byline. But the *Hindustan Times* news desk, in their wisdom, ignored my request for anonymous publication of the report and used it with my byline and Rawalpindi dateline.

Thus, by the time I returned to Rawalpindi, after a two-day sojourn in Lahore, the fat was in the fire. I was summoned to the information ministry and asked to disclose the basis of my report. In fact, there had been frantic calls for me earlier before I returned to Rawalpindi. My wife told me that the vigil around our residence had also been tightened, with every visitor being watched closely and our servant repeatedly grilled. I said that as the Government had dismissed it as a fabrication, it could only be speculative, without any basis. The Information Secretary's reply was that I did not deserve the visa if I was wont to indulge in dangerous speculation. The *Dawn* wrote an editorial asking for my expulsion if the report was wrong. Otherwise, it said the Pakistan mission in New Delhi had to be revamped. The *Hindustan Times* editor, Sri Mulgaokar, who passionately wanted better India-Pakistan relations, thought my conduct was at cross purposes with the policy of the newspaper and asked me to wind up my Rawalpindi innings. I could not face my 'source' in the Home Ministry again before leaving Pakistan for good a few months later. Subsequently, I heard that he opted for Bangladesh and died after a few years. Interestingly, when I happened to meet the President's Secretary a few days later, his admonition to me was that by my "rash action" I had caused a setback to India-Pakistan friendship. The Pakistan Government had deliberately put the Agha Shahi report under the wraps to cool down the temperature, while I did the opposite by speculating about its contents. I don't know if it was a case of scoring Brownie points against a reporter or whether the Ayub establishment was desirous of good relations with India.

In retrospect, I am convinced that what had been shown to me as Agha Shahi's report was genuine and that the pattern of a section of the minority provoking trouble and endangering the lives of a large number of their co-religionists had been persisting. I saw the same thing happen in Ahmedabad in 1969, although it came in handy for the Indira Gandhi Government to discredit the Congress (O) Government in Gujarat. In the case of Moradabad, it gave rise to the charge that the police and the para-military forces were contaminated by communalism and targeted the minority in the name of maintaining law and order. The suggested remedies against the perceived police bias against the minority included proportional representation for Muslims in the security forces. That could be worse than the disease. The recruitment into the security forces should be non-denominational. What would be of help in enabling more Muslims to join the force would be opportunities for them for education and training. Additional facilities including scholarships for them would help.

A similar mis-perceived secularism had led to the Rashtriya Swayam Sevak Sangh (RSS) being readily blamed for the Aligarh and Jamshedpur riots of 1978-79. The Janata Party was in power then both at the Centre and in UP and Bihar. The theory was that with the Jana Sangh as a constituent of the Janata Party being in power, the RSS with its links with the Jana Sangh was entrenching itself through an anti-Muslim crusade. Raj Narain, who was Charan Singh's chief lieutenant for splitting the Janata Party and bringing down the Morarji Desai Government, led the anti-RSS chorus. The purpose was to bring pressure to bear on Morarji Desai to expel the Jana Sangh from the conglomerate. Since the Jana Sangh was the strongest of the Janata Party constituents its expulsion would, first, enfeeble the party and, secondly, put Charan Singh's Lok Dal in a position of strength in the combine. The Lok Dal could then dictate terms to Desai. In that context, a demand was made for the Jana Sangh to delink itself from the RSS or make the RSS admit Muslims also as members. With a large number of Jana Sangh members-including top leaders like Atal Behari and Advani, having graduated from the RSS and still being nominally associated with it, disassociation from the RSS would mean disowning their ideological parentage. No self-respecting public person, much less committed leaders like Vajpayee and Advani, would do it. The RSS having Muslim members would be a novelty, because it claims to uphold the Hindu ethos and Hindu culture. Would any conscious Muslim be with such an organisation? How could he/she reconcile it with the rigidly exclusivist outlook of the followers of Islam? Such a member would practically cease to be a Muslim. By the way, the Rashtra Seva Dal, the socialist volunteer organisation, launched by Sane Guruji, too, had no Muslims among its members, although there was no bar to their joining it. The reason simply was that the way the Muslim mind was being developed the community had, and still has, no stomach for mainstream organisations; it cannot rise above its sectarian outlook, barring a few honourable exceptions like Yusuf Meherally, Moinuddin Harris, Adam Adil and others in pre-Mumbai Bombay. But that generation has passed out. So the RSS throwing its membership open to all communities would be either cosmetic or a thinly veiled essay in deception.

The issue has again been in focus more recently since 1999 when the BJP was able to put together an unwieldy coalition of nearly two dozen parties from different States to form the National Democratic Alliance and head a difficult even if generally stable, — definitely working— coalition. The countervailing factors against the cohesion of the coalition are distrust among the constituents, largely on account of the image of the BJP as antithetical to minorities, not merely the Muslims, and its being the dominant party in the grouping. Meanwhile in the run up to the demolition of the Babri masjid at Ayodhya in December 1992 and in its wake, the RSS has spawned more offspring, largely of the scum of society. They include the Vishwa Hindu Parishad (VHP), a front organisation set up for propagating Hinduism overseas and at home, as if Hinduism has to be propagated in India.It was a contradiction in terms because Hinduism has never been propagated. Seers like Shankaracharya and Vivekananda merely spread its message of peace and harmony, as they perceived it. The maths established by the Shankaracharya and the temples launched by him at Sringeri, Kanchi, Srinagar and Kathmandu among others were not like churches and mosques. So the VHP should not have been established at all; maybe the RSS thought it required a tool to carry out its programme of "recovering" the temples at Ayodhya, Kashi (Varanasi) and Mathura. In the case of Ayodhya it required uprooting the mosque-like structure reportedly raised by Babar at the site where a Rama temple was once believed to have stood. At Kashi and Mathura, mosques stood cheek by jowl with the temples. The RSS wants the mosques to be re-located so that the temple could have more land for expansion. The VHP in turn begot illicit offspring like the Bajrang Dal, a so-called volunteer organisation, but a mob of lumpens, who wrought the vandalism at Ayodhya in December 1992. Compounding the tragedy, self-seeking and ambitious persons put themselves in command of these riffraff to set the agenda for the BJP. Several of them had their pound of flesh in the shape of membership of assemblies and Parliament and the benefits flowing from it. It was a vicious cycle: the more the BJP accommodated them the more was their appetite whetted. Brought up on the delusion that rabid anti-minorityism is the surest ticket to continued power they have been plugging the extremist line, whether it be forcible construction of a Rama temple on the debris of the Babri mosque or repeating the outrage at other sites like Mathura and Varanasi.

In short, while responsibility inherent with power and political maturity natural to committed political workers have made the BJP shed some of its angularities — like rectification of presumed historical wrongs of Muslim rule over India—the VHP, the Bajrang Dal and their likes live in the past. The purpose largely is to wrest more power for themselves at the expense of the BJP. The irony is that none of these outfits is in a position to win an election by itself; they have to ride piggyback on the BJP. The more responsible the BJP tends to become the greater their recourse to blackmail. Even elementary commonsense shows that the bulk of Hindus have no appetite for emulating the fundamentalist elements among Muslims and Christians. It is clear from the aversion these elements and their leaders evoke. For some journalists, however, they yield saleable copy. So there is a race to highlight their rabid views and weird actions. The volume of newspaper space wasted on a character like Pravin Togadia of the VHP, who sounds to be mentally ill, is a reflection on today's journalistic standards. For the self-appointed leaders of the VHP, Bajrang Dal and even Shiva Sena's Bal Thackeray, any publicity is good enough to keep them in public view and enhance their nuisance value vis-a-vis the BJP. True, BJP leaders like Atal Behari and Advani also started their public life in the RSS and grew in its ranks. Their driving force was amelioration of Hindu society and promotion of what were perceived as Hindu interests. The collaboration of the Muslim League with the British Government during the freedom struggle and the ultimate partition of the country as the price for British withdrawal reinforced the average Indian hostility to the Muslim League. It got extended to Muslims as a whole at the hands of the RSS, which began to demand that the Muslims and other minorities identify themselves with the majority and shed their separate identity in political terms. The demand for a uniform civil code flowed from it. A uniform civil code by itself is not a heinous reform as made out by some critics, although narrow politicisation has now put it beyond the pale of realisation. Dr. S. Radhakrishnan also favoured a uniform civil code

It is included in the Constitution in the chapter on Directive Principles of State Policy, like the State's obligation to provide compulsory primary education to children up to the age of eleven within ten years of the coming into force of the Statute. In the case of elementary education, the apex court, taking a dim view of the failure of successive governments to fulfil the constitutional obligation for forty years declared it a fundamental right, which can be enforced through intervention of the judiciary. The court felt strongly for a common civil code also and endorsed it more than once. But by clubbing it with avoidable issues like scrapping of Article 370 of the Constitution for the presumed purpose of integration of Jammu and Kashmir with the rest of the country, and worse still, construction of a Rama temple at the site where the Babri mosque had stood, the BJP eroded the acceptability of common civil code. No wonder, even its partners in the National Democratic Alliance look askance at it. Surprisingly for a mature party, with perhaps the best human material at its helm, the BJP has a knack of making controversies of otherwise unexceptionable subjects and landing itself in avoidable scrapes.

Similarly, it did not deem it necessary to din sense into the heads of RSS leaders who started raving against Christian missions just when there was a spate of attacks on their personnel and property. A Church leader was brutally burnt alive along with his two children, while there were reports of violence against nuns and other functionaries of the Church. Naturally, there was widespread concern abroad, more than at home, bringing the fair name of India and its record of religious tolerance under a cloud. That was the time chosen by the RSS leaders to campaign against proselitisation through dubious methods. Riffraff outfits like the VHP and the Bajrang Dal seemed to be calling the shots on the issue. Although it was ultimately found out that the anti-Christian violence was the work of *agents provocateur* the BJP had volunteered to pocket the stigma. Such was the public disgust with the Sangh parivar that even legitimate criticism of the Christian missions had come to be identified with intolerance of others' faiths by Hindu fanatics. The demolition of the Babri mosque was a watershed in the thinking of many Hindus. Until 1991 there was widespread feeling that the demand for establishment of a Rama temple at Ayodhya was both justified and necessary. They accepted Advani's analogy of the restoration of Somnath temple in the 1950s and thought the Government should similarly undo the wrong supposed to have been done in Babar's time. This was irrespective of the perceived contribution of Advani's rath yatra to the party's electoral success in 1989 especially in southern States like Karnataka and to a lesser extent in Andhra Pradesh. The irony was that in 1992, both in the run up to the vandalism at Ayodhya and following the demolition of the structure, the support for a Rama temple at the Ayodhya site diminished considerably. A large number of Hindus felt betrayed and cheated of their pride in the cosmopolitan character of their faith by the tactics of the VHP and its ilk. The fulminations of the VHP leaders have put off most thinking people, including those who were proud to call themselves Hindus. The name of the 'parivar' was mud among saner sections of the Hindu society.

The reasons are twofold. First, the calculated appeasement of Muslim communalism in the name of secularism but solely for nursing the vote bank had stopped after the end of Congress rule at the Centre practically in 1991 and actually in 1996. Consequently, the backlash it used to generate has also ended, even if the Congress and other parties still flogged the dead horse of their kind of secularism. Secondly, there has been growing realisation that socio-economic development of the country and growth of the liberalised economy should have priority over gimmicks like temple building. The credit for this change in public attitude goes to the BJP Government and its single-minded pursuit of the economic agenda. Paradoxically, its links with outfits like the VHP even indirectly cannot jell with the new popular mood. The BJP realised it but has been unable totally to disown its ideological legacy. That is the major dilemma of leaders like Vajpayee and Advani. The BJP was also shortsighted in its initial reaction to violence against Christian institutions and even personnel. When a clergyman was burnt alive with his two little children in Orissa in 1999 neither the party nor the Union Government demonstrated the kind of shock and revulsion for the culprits it merited. Nor did it firmly reprimand those rationalising such barbarism on any ground. It sounded to be defensive, presumably out of apprehension that it could be the work of an outfit like the Bajrang Dal and denouncing it roundly might recoil on it. At the same time, it denied that any of the RSS outfits was responsible for the crime. That added to the scepticism among uncommitted persons in the capacity of the BJP to rise above sectarian considerations. In the process the real culprits, *agents provocateur* or foreign agents, had an opportunity to put the blame for their actions on the Sangh parivar members. Not until the Karnataka police cracked the conspiracy behind attacks on churches in Andhra Pradesh, Goa and Karnataka was the air cleared.

As for the RSS demand for a national church, articulated by its chief Dr. Sudarshan, the media made it appear like the height of religious intolerance. Far from it. "The natural allies of the exploiters were the Christian missionaries". This quote is from Dr. Sarvepalli Radhakrishnan, former President of India and renowned philosopher and thinker. He knew because he had observed at first hand the missionaries at work in south India during his scholastic years. In the last quarter of the nineteenth century, the number of converts to Christianity in the south more than tripled. Christianity in India is as old as St.Thomas; but with the coming of the Europeans it became inextricably bound up with imperial domination. As a functionary of the indigenous Church put it, Christianity did not make the empire Christian but the empire made Christianity political. When C.F. Andrews was sent to Delhi as a conventional young clergyman in 1904, he was told by the British community: "Never, under any circumstances, give way to a native, or let him regard himself as your superior. We only rule India in one way—by safeguarding our position."[4]

The prospective Deenbandhu was not cut out to be an accessory of imperialism in the garb of a man of religion. He called it a day. To this day we revere his memory. In Calcutta, Raja Rammohun Roy had to fight a running wordy battle with the Serampore missionaries when he embarked on his mission of reform of Hindu society. Dr. Sarvepalli Gopal sums it up in his father's biography: "Stripping bare the mind and spirit of the people fortified imperial rule; and missionaries did what they could do to help in the process of damaging the identity of the Indian people." Thus, while the indigenous Church (the members of which later came to be known as Syrian Christians) thrive as a national institution, the Roman Catholic, Anglican, Baptist and related versions were engaged in sustaining imperialism in areas outside politics and administration. The missionaries would not have Dr. Radhakrishnan's early writings as textbooks in the Madras Presidency because of the accent of Dr. Radhakrishnan on religious plurality and rejection of uniqueness of Christ.

It was not the first time that the 'guilt' by association with the RSS was used as a political weapon against the BJP. It happened first in 1979 before Charan Singh split the Janata party to pull down the Morarji Desai Government. Madhu Limaye had asked the Jana Sangh to sever its links with the RSS at peril of being thrown out of the Janata conglomerate.[5] He also served notice on Morarji Desai to choose between the Jana Sangh and prime ministership. Advani, who was minister of information and broadcasting then, issued a rejoinder on behalf of the Jana Sangh members. I was the Principal Information Officer Although it did not concern me officially, he showed the statement to me to elicit my reaction. I asked him why he should be so categorical about the ideological origin of the Sangh in the RSS. He cited three reasons for it. First, they did not feel apologetic about it and so no need to soft-pedal the issue. Second, having had their upbringing for public life in the RSS they would be untrue to themselves to deny it. Thirdly, denying the link would hardly carry credibility.

There had been very few instances of the RSS taking a public position on a political matter. The first was perhaps during the 1975 emergency when the then RSS chief, Balasaheb Deores, had entered into correspondence with Indira Gandhi on the advice of "friends" to plead for lifting of the ban on his organisation. It was perhaps tactical. There were also indications that the RSS initiative was in response to 'advice' from

Congress leaders who did not like the Communists exploiting the 'emergency' to entrench themselves in key positions. The Jana Sangh leaders were locked up in jails and had no hand in the move. Again after the assassination of Indira Gandhi in 1984, the RSS perceived a threat to national security and wanted the Government and the Congress party to be supported. Professor Deores articulated it.[6] His argument was that the assassination of the Prime Minister and the upsurge in terrorism supported by Pakistan spelt national peril. Only a strong Congress Government could face the situation. The BJP, on the other hand, was in no position to win a majority in the Lok Sabha nor could it provide a strong government. The BJP disagreed and was left in the lurch in the 1984 general election. The party had no identity devoid that of Hindu nationalism, which was diluted due to absence of full backing of the RSS cadres. That was the time when th BJP ended up with just two seats in the Lok Sabha, both from Andhra Pradesh and that too through the courtesy of N.T. Rama Rao. Only Rama Rao and his Telugu Desam Party could withstand and overcome the Congress juggernaut. All the others including Ramakrishna Hedge in Karnataka were swept away by the flood of pro-Rajiv sentiment. There was a groundswell of sympathy for the young leader bereaved of his mother in extremely outrageous circumstances. As already stated, Rajiv Gandhi, for his part, had initially shown promise of being different from his mother.

The BJP and the RSS being on different wavelengths is not an impossibility. A near parallel is the Communist movement in India. Years after the CPI had taken to parliamentary politics, it continued to pledge theoretical commitment to Leninist tactics including dictatorship of the proletariat until the Amritsar party congress in 1958. The CPI (M) does so even now. It means that when the party gains power, may be with adequate majority to change the Constitution, it will do away with the bourgeois practice of free elections and seek to establish one-party state. At the height of Sino-Soviet rift, Moscow nudged the CPI to distance itself from the CPI (M), which was seen to be toeing the Beijing line. If tactical differences of lasting political significance are possible in the Communist church at the zenith of its orthodoxy and power, why can't the RSS and BJP disagree, as they do now on a number of issues? The former BJP president, Bangaru Lakshman, had spelt them out.

Even when the CPI (M) cadres are running amuck in West Bengal, nobody has questioned the credentials of the party to participate in elections and form government. Its claimed ideology is not held against it. Instead it aspires to lead the 'Left and democratic forces' to provide an alternative to the NDA. But the RSS is judged differently and the BJP has to treat it as an untouchable. And when the BJP says it does not go along with the RSS on some issues, there is hunt for 'a hidden agenda'. When Bengaru Lakshman as BJP President tried to build bridges to the Muslims the 'secularists' feigned outrage. Obviously, the proof of the pudding would lie in the eating. If the bulk of the community dismisses the effort as a gimmick it will mean that the BJP cannot have credibility among the Muslims There is no question of the party being able to hoodwink a relatively cohesive section of the population. The bulk of the Muslims may be relatively backward on the socio-economic scale of development but they are not babes in the wood to be taken for a ride *en bloc*. That, too, when more experienced hands are working over time to keep them apart.

The refreshing aspect of the BJP approach is its pragmatism. Bangaru Lakshman conceded plainly that even with saturation support from committed Hindus the BJP vote share was stuck in a plateau. At the same time, the Muslim community has found itself out of the political mainstream because of its exclusiveness from a national party, like the BJP. In short, they both need each other. Most interestingly, he did not even once talk of secularism, the key to Muslim electoral support. In the pre-Independence period the Muslim attitude to the Congress had not been different. It was dubbed a Hindu party. Its proportion of Muslim support in States like Punjab and Bengal was miniscule. But the situation changed soon after independence. Then came the practice of professional secularism, which meant using the slogan to nurse the Muslim vote bank. Not that the Jana Sangh and the BJP to a lesser extent are not insensitive towards minority feelings. In the process, the BJP has become a prisoner of its own propaganda. It had come to believe that the enlargement of its Lok Sabha strength from two in 1984 to 86 five years later was the miracle wrought by Hindutva. The truth is different. The party's share of popular vote rose from 7.4 per cent in 1984 and to 11.5 in 1989. The increase, although sizable, did not warrant a forty-three times boost in the seats tally. The reason simply was that in 1984 following Indira Gandhi's assassination, a shocked country flocked to the Congress as the saviour of national security. Even the then RSS chief Deores was on record that weakening the Congress in the name of democracy would impair national unity. In 1989, on the other hand, Bofors put the Congress in isolation with the major opposition parties working together. There was a whopping rise of eleven percentage points in the popular vote of even the makeshift Janata Dal. The BJP ceased to be untouchable, which was heady wine for a party used to being shunned. Beguiled by its own propaganda, it hit on the Rama temple idea, little realising that there were others in the field who would hijack its programme. Riffraff like the Bajrang Dal and Vishwa Hindu Parishad spewed by the RSS, plus Bal Thackeray's Shiva Sena started setting the agenda. The P.V.Narasimha Rao Government which had pulled Dr. Murli Manohar Joshi's chestnuts out of the fire by providing logistical support from the army to enable him to hoist the national flag at Lal Chowk in Srinagar let the BJP stew in its own Ayodhya juice. There was no cheap martyrdom; instead there was a high price tag for sectarian intolerance of the minorities. It is not that a sensible stand on the temple issue will unleash a flood of Muslim support to the BJP. But if liberal Hindus, constituting a quarter of the community, who are put off by the BJP's obsession with temple and sectarianism, are reassured it will be no small gain. That may also open the door to enlightened Muslims. As for the Muslims, the BJP can ameliorate their condition without treading the forbidden ground of uniform civil code. For instance, the National Commission for Women (NCW) has asked for a ban on instantaneous triple talaq (divorce) on the basis of public hearings on the status of Muslim women in India,. Its report on the subject narrated numerous instances of men pronouncing the three words in a single breath without reason or warning. If the BJP acts on the NCW recommendation to resist and stop the practice it will go further to prove its *bona fides* vis-a-vis the community.

End Notes

1. *The Insider,* P.V. Narasimha Rao, *Ibid.*
2. *Radhakrishnan, A Biography*, Sarvepalli Gopal, 1989, Oxford.
3. When Nehru visited Pakistan in 1959 to sign the Indus Waters Treaty with Field Marshal Ayub Khan, he wanted to meet Begum Iftikhar-ud-Din, widow of his pal, Iftikhar-ud-Din, who was a Congress leader before partition. The Pakistan police, however, said she was no longer living in Lahore. Nehru then offered to locate the Iftikhar-ud-Dins' ancestral house in old Lahore, when the police allowed the Begum to meet him at Government House where Nehru was put up.
4. *Radhakrishnan,* Sarvepalli Gopal, *Ibid.*
5. *The People Betrayed*, L.K. Advani, 1979, Vision Books, New Delhi.

8

An Abode for Rama

Gandhiji said the 1934 Bihar earthquake was punishment for the practice of untouchability in Hindu society and the oppression of Harijans or untouchables. Less generally, he would have called 2001 Gujarat earthquake advance retribution for what the State witnessed in the wake of the dastardly arson attack on the Sabarmati Express train at Godhra. The larger irony is that ever since the revival of the Ram Janmabhoomi agitation in the1980s, especially after the demolition of the Babri Masjid in December 1992, the very mention of a Rama temple at Ayodhya conjures up visions of strife and bloodshed. Devotees of Maryada Purshottam or gentle colossus, as Rama was widely portrayed, should ponder this portent. If one looks back at the origin and history of great temples, in north or south India, the preparatory stage was marked by peace and penance, particularly by the promoters. Even in the case of the Somnath temple, the restoration of which was performed by the head of State himself, there was festivity and celebration before and after the occasion. That was despite the reservation of some national leaders, including reportedly Nehru, about reviving historical controversies, which could fester. The spirit of Mohammed Ghazni, who sacked and looted the original shrine centuries earlier, was exorcised. If it was a correction of a historical wrong, it was done with grace and without malice. Besides K.M. Munshi, N.V. Gadgil and Lal Bahadur Shastri, the then Jam Saheb of Nawanagar was associated with the project, consecrated by the President of India.

Can a similar situation be replicated in respect of Ayodhya? Not if the conduct of some of its vociferous protagonists is an index. Sri Rama Janmabhoomi Nyas or trust, which the Shankaracharya of Kamakoti says, is the rightful party —not the Vishwa Hindu Parishad — to negotiations on the site at dispute at Ayodhya has brought out a glossy publication called FACT (Focused Awareness and Complete Truth) on the Mandir (temple) issue. Instead of stating its case, it projects it as a *mandir* vs. masjid (mosque) dispute and seeks to preach to the converted. Its propagandist style and substance, with needless jibes against Marxists, puts one off, even if he or she were for a Rama temple at Ayodhya. My virtual Guru in journalism, Madhav (M) V. Kamath is perhaps the most vocal and unambiguous votary of building a Rama temple at the site of the demolished Babri *masjid* at Ayodhya. His thesis has been oft repeated and long. For the present, let me quote from a passion-packed article by him in the RSS journal, *Organiser*[1] "There were no secularists when Ghazni Mohammad invaded India 13 times, smashed the *lingam*[2] in the Somnath temple and took the pieces to be scattered in the front of a masjid in his home town for his Islamic kinsmen merrily to trample over. Nor were any secularists living when, during the long Islamic reign over many parts of India, over three thousand temples were demolished without so much as by your leave. It was considered part of medieval behaviour and so to be taken in one's stride. If not Babar, it was his General, who destroyed a temple in Ayodhya and despite the hysterical denials by our demented historians, a temple did exist where the Babri structure once stood and there are enough records — an architectural evidence — to prove the fact. Only the determinedly blind people will argue otherwise and refuse to accept the testimony of many Muslim writers themselves, like Mirza Jan (1856), Mohammad Asghar (1858), Mirza Raja Ali Beg Sarur (1787-1867) and Sheikh Mohammad Azmat Ali (1869) who have had no reasons to tell a lie."

Historical evidence is of course binding but sometimes it can also be interpretative. None of the authorities cited by Kamath was witness to or contemporary to the existence of a Rama temple and its destruction at the instance of Babar. Be that as it may, there were many horrendous actions attributed to Mongol and Muslim invaders of India. It was the practice in those times to proclaim one's victory in battle and sway by humiliating the vanquished. There were incidents of violation of women's honour, demolition of shrines, sacred to the defeated and killings on a large scale. It was said that the Hindus had meted out similar treatment to the Buddhists and Jains when Hinduism recovered from the renaissance spearheaded by Mahavira and the Buddha. Here again, Dalit scholars cite what they regard as Brahminic brutality towards the lower castes who were beaten in battle. It may be true or it may not be true, despite the conviction of the Dalit scholars, who speak as if they were witness to the alleged Brahminic aggression. One should respect the deeply held belief and faith of Hindus in regard to the demolition of temples by Muslim invaders. Even then does it warrant Hindus imitating the Muslims five centuries later? First, Hinduism is projected as a faith free of violence, coercion and intimidation. It does not provide for conversion or at least it did not until the Sanatanists started the ritual of re-converting people from other faiths into Hinduism. Our Constitution distinguishes between Hinduism and other religions by guaranteeing freedom of not merely observance but propagation, which are characteristic of both Islam and Christianity. In other words, the defenders of the demolition of Babri masjid and construction of a Rama temple at the site wish to borrow a leaf from the invaders whom they depict in lurid colours. This will be a greater affront to Hinduism than what it had received at the hands of intolerant and medieval invaders of India.

To resume Kamath 's theory, "But even if for the sake of argument, there was no temple in Ayodhya, it ill behoved anybody, let alone a murderous marauder like Babar to build a masjid in what is considered a Hindu holy city any more than a theoretical Hindu invader of Saudi Arabia would have in building a temple in Mecca, close to or on the site of the Kaaba. Sri Ramachandra is as much meaningful to Hindus as Allah is to Muslims, a point that needs to be stressed. The Babri structure was specifically raised in Ayodhya to tell the Hindus who the rulers were. The VHP does not have to be apologetic to anyone, least of all to the secularists, for wishing to raise a temple to Sri Ramachandra at a site they believe he was born."

The absurdity of the approach is apparent. As mentioned earlier, it was the practice in the medieval times for the conquerors not only to inflict on the victims their suzerainty but also their faith. Those were the days of religious wars, in Europe as well. Christianity was given a fillip with the help of the sword of Christian chieftains and monarchs. The Crusades were a glaring instance. But in the late nineteenth and the twentieth centuries - not to mention at the dawn of the twenty-first century - there is firstly no physical conquest of militarily vulnerable nations and peoples. The supremacy is established in other, very often subtle but no less galling ways. The treatment meted out to Iraq and its President, Saddam Husain, after the 1991 Gulf War by the Americans is there for everyone to see. In the name of United Nations' sanctions against Saddam Husain's involvement in efforts to produce weapons of mass destruction, Iraq was denied full access to its own oil resources for rebuilding itself after the US-UK bombings. Iraq was thus punished for its aggression against Kuwait for more than ten years. Not satisfied the US and Britain set out in 2003 to devastate the country and occupy it militarily. In the case of Japan, the US did not impose its religious faith on the Japanese people, but after killing at least two million of them in Hiroshima and Nagasaki established political domination over the isles through democracy imposed through General MacArthur. To this day, Japan despite its economic prosperity and industrial growth is alive to US strategic interests in the region as well as in other parts of the world. Sometimes, it seems to be more loyal than the king as when following the 1998 Pokhran nuclear tests by India, it was quicker than the US in clamping economic and other sanctions on India. The sanctions were not lifted until much later even after the US had largely ended them.

Kamath goes on to write: "Let this be stated; what happened in Ahmedabad is not different from what happened in Delhi when Indira Gandhi was assassinated or what happened in Punjab following Partition. The Gujaratis are as law-abiding a people as anyone else and don't deserve to be maligned. Does anyone remember Rajiv Gandhi's remarks about the wholesale killing of Sikhs following Indira Gandhi's death? Did (the) Congress pull him up for his thoughtless comments? The Ahmedabad rioting was not pre-planned unlike (the) Godhra killings by Muslim fanatics or the killings of the innocent Kashmiris by ISI-supported jihadists? Granting that any violence is not to be condoned one has to assess the Ahmedabad rioting in its proper context."

Thank god for small mercies. Madhav has graciously conceded that violence is not to be condoned in any circumstances. But he has mixed up so many things that it is necessary to untangle the web of genocidal crimes to consider them adequately. Whether the orgy of killings which took place in Gujarat between 27 February and beyond the end of March 2002, including the Godhra carnage was preplanned or spontaneous, the toll in human life and suffering was not qualitatively different. Granting that the Godhra outrage was preplanned while the subsequent mass murder in other parts of Gujarat were a spontaneous reaction to it, the former would be more heinous but would not cleanse the subsequent mass killings of their guilt. Secondly, how could the 'spontaneous' reaction last weeks and weeks claiming nearly 900 innocent lives, including women and children? One could understand outbreak of violence when the news of the Godhra arson spread and the charred bodies of the victims were taken to Ahmedabad for cremation. It should have petered out within seventy-two hours - which was Narendra Modi's time frame for claiming success for his anti-riot operations! How could it persist day after day, gaining in intensity and beastliness, infesting villages and even tribal areas of the unfortunate State, if not planned, executed and sustained by organised criminal gangs, in this case of VHP and Bajrang Dal activists? Kamath has bracketed the Gujarat killings with similar atrocities elsewhere. The only crimes which he had not listed in the catalogue are the Nazi holocaust against Jews and the latest Israeli violence against Palestinians within their hearths and homes. No congressmen could pull up Rajiv Gandhi because the party has never had that much internal democracy as to enable ordinary mortals to criticise openly the leadership. But Commissions have gone into the 1984 anti-Sikh pogrom and the accused Congressmen have been dodging trial through legal subterfuge. After eight years the BJP government at the Centre had set up another committee to go into the crime. In the case of 'Operation Blue Star' in Punjab, Rajiv Gandhi's widow had to apologise to the Sikhs publicly before the Congress party could return to active participation in the politics of the State. The partisan killings are a horror and nobody has condoned them. As Kamath himself noted, two or more wrongs do not make a right. The Gujarat carnage cannot be rationalised by reference to similar or worse happenings in other parts of the country in the past. The issue is not to judge the people of Gujarat or Gujaratis, as Kamath calls them, and pillory them. The tragedy is that the VHP and its parivar have driven even law-abiding and peaceable people like the Gujaratis mad by their communal frenzy. The Germans as a people are not bloodthirsty by nature, but the Nazis made millions of them into veritable fiends. The Jews having been victims of the holocaust know what it means to be subjected to sectarian violence, but Ariel Sharon has been using similar tools to hunt down the Palestinians.

The Rama Janmabhoomi issue comes into the picture because it is the background against which the Godhra outrage, pre-meditated or provoked by the behaviour of some of the kar sevaks travelling in the ill-fated train, took place. That brings the VHP into the centre of the trouble. The short point really is whatever the desirability of building a temple for Rama, the way the VHP has been going about it is marked by violence and bloodletting. It has been so from the word go. The demolition of the Babri masjid, whether it was a structure or a disused place of worship, was the beginning of the wrong approach. It was also done by deceit. The then Chief Minister of Uttar Pradesh Kalyan Singh had solemnly assured P.V. Narasimha Rao, who was the Prime Minister in 1992, and the Supreme Court that the proposed kar seva at Ayodhya would be formal and go off peacefully and that no damage would be done to the structure. The commitment was brazenly violated forcing Kalyan Singh to resign before he was given the order of the boot.

Meanwhile, the publication of the Ram Janmabhoomi Nyas, 'FACT' has selective quotations of Hindu saints and scholars not to bring out the essential peaceable quality of Hinduism but to suggest the absent aggressive dimension. The seers mentioned range from Swami Vivekananda to Ramdas, a devotee of Rama who embezzled 'emperor' Tanisha's money at Golconda (near Hyderabad) to build a temple for Rama and faced jail and torture. Ramdas, incidentally, is claimed to be Shivaji's guru. Vivekananda's famous message of peace and friendliness of Hinduism towards all religions, unfolding a civilisational perspective, is thus glossed over. So is Ramdas's willingness to suffer hardship for his cause. At another level, we have Tulsidas with his immortal *Ram Charitra Manas*; representing Rama as ever gentle and forgiving, even when Sita was spirited away and he was pitted against Ravana in battle. There was a reference in the work to Ravana's wife Mandodari's plea to Rama to spare her husband's life even if he had committed an evil act and Rama's sympathy for her. Nowhere in the epic chronicle does one find venom or hatred. Thyagaraja, saint composer of magnificent Carnatak music, paints the picture of a Rama who is benevolent to one and all. The traditional picture of Rama is one of sweetness and light whereas the drawing on the cover of FACT shows a ferocious-looking warrior shooting an arrow. In short, that is the visage of the deity which the authors of the publication wish to project.

In our generation Gandhiji died with "*hey* Ram" on his lips while his assassin Nathuram Godse had no mind for lofty sentiments after performing the fell act. Apparently, the VHP and the Nyas have chosen to opt for a Godse-like Rama alien to most other devotees of the deity. The way they have been going about their plan to build a temple at Ayodhya, it seems they want it to house such a god and not what most other Hindus see Rama as.They have been emulating the Mughal rulers charged with demolishing temples and building mosques in their place. Bloodshed and strife have been their constant companions. If such a temple is built will it be a worthy abode for Rama universally visualised as a personification of perfection in humanity, with the spark of divinity lighting his personality? The latest pogrom in Gujarat following the burning alive of VHP activists returning from Ayodhya adds to the poignancy of the situation.

The Sikhs are very choosey about the way a gurdwara is built so that it will be worthy of their great gurus and the holy text of their sayings.

If the *kar seva* going into the gurdwara construction does not tally with the ordained ritual they reject the structure. At the pilgrim centre of Tirupati in Andhra Pradesh, there is a discarded temple. The belief is that the deity had rejected it because the builder was 'impure' in raising it. He was said to have worked out the cost of its construction sitting in a the lavatory! In other words, can an outfit like the VHP with its hands dripping with the blood and tears of hundreds of people be a worthy builder of a Rama shrine? Will such a structure if raised by the VHP be a temple or a tomb? To get over the problem, either the VHP should be totally and for ever kept away from the temple project or the temple idea should be kept in abeyance until the strife-torn prelude is overtaken by events and a congenial atmosphere created in the country for such a lofty effort.

Appropriate to his mindset and thinking Kamath ends his defence of the VHP with a peroration: "The nation is heading for a crisis of unprecedented proportions that would make the Ahmedabad riots pale into insignificance. The secularists are warned. They are driving a frustrated people to desperation. And when that comes to pass, logic and good sense are stood on their head and the entire nation will suffer. And then let not the kar sevaks be blamed for what is not their fault. There has to be a limit to secular pig-headedness." Bravo! That the nation is the target of all the frenzy is clear enough. The economic reforms initiated by Dr. Manmohan Singh in 1991 received a setback in December 1992 after the Babri demolition. The pace of liberalisation did not pick up after that, until Yeshwant Sinha embarked on his second generation of economic reforms in 1998. Hardly had the process started than the 11September 2001 terrorist attack on the World Trade Centre sent the world economy into a tailspin and virtually halted growth in most countries. India too suffered from it. A few months later, when the economy was seen to be recovering from the September 11 shock, the VHP started its new phase of Ayodhya agitation. If as Kamath warns "the nation is heading for a crisis that would make the Ahmedabad riots pale into insignificance that would be the fittest atmosphere for the VHP's Rama temple!" In other words, the proposed temple by the VHP will be built on the ashes of India.

The sense of urgency given to the project bereaves belief. If the Hindus could wait 500 years to redeem the honour supposedly besmirched by Mogul invaders, if during the fifty odd years of independence there was no urgency to build the temple, if there was no talk of the Ayodhya project even at the time of the Somnath restoration soon after independence, why couldn't it wait till the economic situation improves, when the country is not ravaged by communal violence and an atmosphere congenial for negotiations with Muslims is created?

In the same context, Khushwant Singh[3] has quoted from an Urdu poem by a celebrated Delhi poet, Gauhar Raza, which as quoted by Khushwant reads:

"A temple built with mortar soaked in human blood,
Its bricks fired and baked in kilns made of burnt down huts,
Its bells pealing with screams, sighs and sobs,
A temple whose foundations are laid
By uprooting from the earth its glorious past,
Whose walls are plastered with savagely torn off stones,
And coloured with sindhoor taken from heads of married women;
Its stones are carved out of flesh of innocent people
Let an aged man whose hopes are dead
Like the last gasp of a young man who has been bled
To name a temple raised thus
Will be an unpardonable sin.
You have made this into a habit
But we will not let you Shri Rama defame
By giving such an edifice, bear his sacred name."

Not that we are blind to the Hindu-Muslim controversy on Ayodhya and related matters. A number of other writers have been championing the cause of the VHP but not in the cut-and-dried way of Madhav Kamath. Among them stand out S. Gurumurthi, an established chartered accountant who was once very close to late Ramnath Goenka, Varsha Bhosle, apparently a NRI, or non-resident Indian living in the US and Arvind Lavakare, both of whom write for *Rediff-on-Net*.[4] Gurumurthi recounts the history of the Ayodhya dispute in the court, which is fascinating because it is not widely known. Following the demolition of Babri Masjid on 6 December 1992, the Narasimha Rao Government enacted a law acquiring, besides the 0.313 acres of land on which the Babri Masjid had stood, the adjacent area of 67 acres also. The VHP claimed ownership of the adjacent land, though according to experts conversant with the documents the VHP was only in possession of the land and not its owner. That was in 1993. Both the VHP and its associates on the one hand and the Sunni

Waqf Board on the other challenged the acquisition in the Supreme Court. The Constitution Bench of the Court consisting of five Judges disposed of the case on 24 October 1994, pretty promptly. It was in the shape of minority and majority judgements. The minority judgement struck down the entire take over and restored the land to its former owners, both Hindu and Muslim. But the majority of three judges headed by the then Chief Justice, Justice A.N.Varma, distinguished between the 0.313 acres of the land, described as 'disputed' land, and the remaining 67 acres. The Court ruled that the disputed land should be in Government custody, with the Union Government as a Receiver. It was to be handed over to the winner of the civil dispute pending in the Allahabad High Court for decades, since 1949 to be exact. Calling the rest of the land as the 'adjacent' land or undisputed land, the judgement said it was needed for the purpose of ensuring "the enjoyment of the disputed land on which the disputed mosque stood, should the Muslims win the case finally". It also left it to the government to decide what part of the disputed land it should retain and what part it could part with. The successor Central governments did not bother to make the decision and so the entire land remained in the custody of the Union government.

Although the BJP-led Government at the Centre had been charged with having a hidden agenda to ensure the construction of the Rama temple at the Babri site, it too did not, during the first four years of its tenure, decide the matter and return the unrequited land to the VHP. The VHP came into the picture because it questioned the validity of its acquisition by the government, whereas the Sunny Waqf Board had limited its objection to the area on which the demolished structure stood. The VHP, of course, had challenged the acquisition of that part of the land also. One would have expected the BJP -led Government to have parted with the undisputed land or a good part of it to buy peace when the VHP revived the temple agitation in 2001 if it had a surreptitious intention to facilitate construction of the controversial temple on the sly. On the other hand, the then Prime Minister had bent over backward not only to be correct but also appear to be so. His response to the repeated ultimatums of the VHP was that the matter would be settled before the deadline of March 2002. According to the critics of the BJP, by keeping the matter in suspense during the Assembly elections in Uttar Pradesh in March 2002 the BJP wanted to cash on the Ayodhya issue. If so, it had come a cropper. As a matter of fact if the VHP had been off the BJP's back it could have fared better in the elections. Either the BJP was extra cautious not to offend its NDA allies, because any suspicious step would have brought the media and the Opposition on its throat or the leadership had not applied its mind to it.

The claim that the Rama temple issue had helped the BJP at the polls in 1989 as well as in 1998 and 1999 general elections is without foundation. But it had been so widely and loudly voiced that the BJP also had begun to believe in it. Close scrutiny of the matter would have saved the BJP from being hamstrung on the Ayodhya issue while being subjected to suspicion and motivated propaganda. The 1989 election was fought by the BJP in the company of Viswanath Pratap Singh's Janata Dal although VP Singh did not endorse the Ayodhya demand and did not have joint campaigning with the BJP. The construction of a Rama temple at Ayodhya was no doubt an item of the BJP's election manifesto. But it was not the most pressing one. Corruption and Rajiv Gandhi's alleged involvement in Bofors kickbacks overshadowed all other issues. It moved the electorate throughout the country and not merely in UP with the result that VP Singh emerged as an un-compromising crusader against corruption. When the electoral verdict left neither VP Singh nor the BJP in a position to form a government even in conjunction the novel idea was put forward of V.P Singh being supported by both the BJP and the Communists from outside. For the purpose, V.P. Singh fabricated the National Front of regional parties spread all over the country, from Punjab to Andhra Pradesh, Orissa, Karnataka and Tamil Nadu. In that election, the BJP's tally had shot up from just two seats in 1984 to 89 in the Ninth Lok Sabha. Most facile commentators attributed this spurt in the BJP strength to the Rama temple 'magic'; so much so, the BJP also came to believe it.

But in 1984, following Indira Gandhi's assassination and the groundswell of sympathy for the bereaved new Prime Minister (Rajiv Gandhi), there was a landslide win for the Congress party. For the first time since the parliamentary system was introduced in 1952, the Congress party not only secured a massive three-fourths majority in the Lok Sabha, but also a majority in popular vote. Until then, even in Nehru's time the Congress party did not score 50 per cent of the popular vote. The BJP also was swept away by the current. The only party which withstood the surge of sympathy for Rajiv was the Telugu Desam Party (TDP) in Andhra Pradesh, because N.T. Rama Rao pitted his own cinematic charisma against the sympathy wave. It led to the novelty of the TDP emerging as a single largest group in the Lok Sabha with the so-called national parties taking the back seat. Even after L.K. Advani's *rath yatra* in 1989 and the rupture of the power sharing arrangement with V.P. Singh, the BJP could not win a majority of seats in the 1991 general election. The Congress party was the single largest group, enabling P.V. Narasimha Rao to cobble up a makeshift working government. That was despite Rajiv Gandhi himself campaigning for his party. Following Rajiv Gandhi's assassination near Chennai, the election process had to be suspended to be resumed after a few days. The Congress party scored appreciably better in the second phase of the polling, making it the single largest group. The BJP was in no position even in the first phase of the polling to emerge as the winner. In other words, if the Rama temple card was such a vote getter, why did it not put the BJP in power on its own in the 1991 election?

It was as though the people were testing the BJP to monitor its maturity single-handedly to rule the country. As it happened, it was a fairly sobered-down BJP, which assumed office in 1998, for a brief 13 days and again in 1999. It was also defanged by having to bank on similarly placed anti-Congress regional parties like the DMK, the Trinamool Congress and the Akali Dal in Punjab. More surprisingly, the National Conference in Jammu and Kashmir joined the NDA, while the TDP offered outside support to the ruling coalition. Instead of being shunned and isolated, the BJP was acceptable as a partner in power to many parties. The arrangement acted as a check on the party being misled by irredentist elements in the Sangh parivar. That a party hitherto believing in a unitary form of government had to seek the support of parties in the south and the east where the BJP lacked electoral support and form a multi-hued coalition government was the lesson. The BJP was quick to learn it and also respect it. Not only had it been seeking the support of parties not belonging to its genre, like the DMK, the Trinamool Congress and the National Conference, but except in Jammu and Kashmir, it had also been accommodating its allies by surrendering even safe seats to them at the time of elections. It was especially so in UP. Short of a majority to form a Government in the state, the BJP had wooed a number of non-descript parties, rumps of the Congress and the Bahujana Samaj Party, to form a BJP-led jumbo Government. In the subsequent election to the State assembly in 2001 the BJP not only failed to retain power even as the single largest party in the Vidhan Sabha but was relegated to the third position, after Mulayam Singh's Samajwadi Party and the BSP. So the BJP had to enter into a coalition with the BSP, with Mayawati calling the shots. Elsewhere too, the BJP had to cut down the number of constituencies it would contest from to let the allies run there. Very often they would lose as in 2002, thus reducing the party's overall prospects in crucial States. In the process, the party realised the imperative need to pursue economic reforms. The apprehension that the clock might be put back on the path breaking 1991 liberalisation process was dispelled.

Reverting to Gurumurthy's argument that the VHP plea for return of the "undisputed" Ayodhya land in March 2002 did not require further approval of the Supreme Court, it was as though the VHP had been losing sleep because of non-availability of the land for organising the puja. After the 1992 vandalism at Ayodhya and the betrayal of the Supreme Court and the country at large by the VHP there were no takers for its *bona fides*. Gurumurthi might be on a strong wicket in purely legal terms that the 1999 judgment said, "it is permissible", even "desirable" to return "any part of the land at any stage "even before the suits are finally decided. " It said the Hindus can force the return of the land." The only point to be decided by the Government, as mentioned, was which part of the land should be restored to the VHP. The clarification issued by the Court subsequently in response to the Advocate-General's plea on the grounds cited by Gurumurthi amply vindicated the Government's inaction in the matter. With profound apologies to the eloquent champions of the VHP case—Kamath, Varsha Bhosle, Gurumurthi *et al*—the bulk of the people, mostly Hindus do not share the urgency for either the return of the land or the construction of a temple on it. That is the sum and substance of the situation since April 2002.

End Notes

1. March 6, 2002.
2. A phallic symbol of Shiva.
3. From weekly column in the *Deccan Herald,* Bangalore 14 April, 2002.
4. 8 May, 2002.

9

Gujarat 2002

The Sabarmati Express[1] returning to Ahmedabad from Ayodhya was stopped at Godhra railway station in Gujarat and two of its compartments torched. As many as fifty-eight persons were burnt alive. They were mostly the so-called kar sevaks (also called Ram sevaks) returning from Ayodhya after agitating for erection of a Rama temple at the site of the mosque demolished in December 1992. That was on 27 February 2002 on the eve of the presentation of the Union budget in the Lok Sabha. There were several versions of the provocation for the outrage. The then Prime Minister, Atal Behari Vajpayee, said that the kar sevaks were raising provocative slogans while the train halted at Godhra. Others said they refused to pay for what they had taken from the vendors at the railway station, yet another report was that they misbehaved with and insulted a Muslim woman travelling by the train. Whatever be the provocation burning people alive was a ghastly act, which could not be reconciled with any religion, Muslim or Hindu. More importantly, it was apparently not a spontaneous retaliation on the spot for the kar sevaks' allegedly offensive behaviour. It was organised and even premeditated because the train was forcibly detained a few meters from the railway station and scores of persons armed with tools for breaking down doors and setting the inmates afire descended on it. The mayhem could not be thwarted, or interfered with, because fire tenders summoned to dose the burning train were prevented from reaching the spot. It was said that the hawkers and miscreants were from a nearby slum colony peopled by Muslim lumpens and hotheads.

With a judicial commission inquiring into the outrage, gingerly though as if it were an unpleasant task, it would be improper to dwell on the crime or hazard a guess about the provocation for it. The Manmohan Singh Government has, however, extraordinarily got a retired judge to conduct another 'inquiry' into the outrage on the plea that a departmental probe had not been made by the railways. Worse still, an 'interim' report of the 'inquiry' was publicised on the eve of the Bihar assembly elections in February 2005! The Vishwa Hindu Parishad (VHP) similarly did not hesitate to conclude, then and there, that the arson in the railway compartments was directed against the kar sevaks travelling by it and was a riposte to the agitation for construction of a Rama temple at Ayodhya. Of course, the VHP neither hastened the construction of a Rama temple at Ayodhya nor created public opinion even among Hindus normally desirous of such a temple. It succeeded only in unleashing horrendous violence in Gujarat on a scale witnessed only during the partition riots. As a matter of fact, the VHP and its rag tag associates were never keen on the temple project becoming a reality.

Their only objective was to disturb public peace, distract national growth, add to the drain on national wealth, bring discredit to the country in the comity of nations with a view to some of their leaders making a quick buck and strengthening their bargaining position vis-a-vis the BJP and the Government led by it. Already some of the VHP leaders were members of Parliament courtesy the BJP. Perhaps they wanted more. Like the jihadis said to be trying to pull down the Musharraf regime in Pakistan so that a more rabidly pro-terrorist establishment could replace it, the VHP & Co would like the BJP-led Government to fall, creating conditions for its likes to thrive. Perhaps, they were also hoping that overthrown from power the BJP would again embark on a Rama temple misadventure so that it could jump on the bandwagon.

Meanwhile, it seemed that the Pakistani ISI (Inter-Service Intelligence) was one step ahead of the VHP; it could trigger a veritable Hindu-Muslim conflagration. The VHP had been periodically reviving the demand for a Rama temple, partly for political and commercial reasons and partly to put the BJP-led Central Government in the wrong and objectively provide a handle to its opponents. Godhra has a notorious history of Hindu-Muslim strife. In 1947 at the time of Independence, when the people of Junagadh rebelled against the nawab's accession to Pakistan there was similar carnage. The victims were Muslims who supported the nawab's action precipitated by the diwan, Shah Nawaaz Bhutto, father of Zulfiqar Ali Bhutto. Samaldas Gandhi emerged as the hero of Godhra for spearheading the movement against Junagadh becoming a part of Pakistan. Quite a few of its residents had even migrated to Pakistan; I met some of them in Karachi in 1961 when I was correspondent of the *Hindustan Times* in Pakistan. Apparently they were middle-class Muslims not directly involved in the disturbances and were able to restart life in the country of their adoption. Whether they were happy with Pakistan's progress in the first decade of its formation was a different matter.

They came to be known as Mohajirs by the 1970s when Punjabis and Pathans in large numbers settled in Sindh claiming a lion's share of its resources. The intruders often displaced the earlier settlers. (practically all Hindu Sindhis had fled to India after partition. They were traders and in a few cases landowners). The emigrants from India, including Godhra, helped themselves to the assets left behind by the Hindus forced to flee to India. Very soon Pakistani Punjabis and Pathans descended on Sind and began to appropriate to themselves the properties and positions of the Mohajirs.

When Field Marshal Ayub Khan seized power in 1958 he shifted the country's capital from Karachi, the nerve centre of activity of Urdu-speaking Muslim migrants from India, to Rawalpindi, a garrison town in Punjab. Ironically, the brunt of the agitation for Pakistan was borne by the Muslims of States like UP, Bihar, Gujarat and Bombay. They shifted to Pakistan in the hope of cashing in on their political activity. But the Punjabis, Pathans and Sindhis who were residents of the provinces forming Pakistan naturally had an edge over them. The conflict spilled into the political sphere with the Punjabis and Pathans using muscle power and weapons to keep the migrants from India down. After the death of Quaid-e-Azam Jinnah (who was from Bombay) and the assassination of Pakistan's first prime minister, Liaquat Ali Khan, (who was from UP), the Punjabi-dominated army started asserting itself. That was one of the factors in Ayub Khan's *coup*, the first in Pakistan's rich history of military takeovers of State power.

Reverting to Gujarat and Godhra, the agitation against Junagadh's accession rekindled the latent anti-Muslim sentiment among the Gujaratis. Among the early rulers of Gujarat Mulraj set up the Solanki dynasty in the 10th century A.D It culminated in what was known as the golden age of the Solanki dynasty. The Gujaratis' dream of a Gurjar Desh or Gurjara Rashtra, or Gujarat incorporating present-day Saurashtra, particularly Junagadh, Kutch and Malwa was realised during the over one hundred years of Solanki dynasty . It was followed by a 76-year spell of Vaghela dynasty. That was all shattered by the invasions of Mohammads of Ghazni and Ghori. Ghazni attacked and pillaged a magnificent temple of Somnath at Prabhas.[2] He was said to have put to sword 50,000 Hindus who tried to save the shrine of the guardian deity of the Solankis. Ghori followed in his wake and inflicted more depredation and indulged in loot and arson The outrage got embedded in the Gujarati psyche. It created an anti-Muslim attitude and outlook over the years.

The 1947 struggle against the accession of Junagadh to Pakistan was marked by animus against both Pakistan and the Muslims of Godhra who supported the Nawab's accession. The anti-Muslim sentiment thus got identified with deep-seated feelings against Pakistan. As a frontier State Gujarat has also been bearing the brunt of Pakistani attacks and incursions. The Pakistani occupation by stealth of the Rann of Kutch in 1965 and the way India was forced to come to terms with it at the instance of the then British Prime Minister Harold Wilson did not improve matters. More recently when Pakistan unleashed low-intensity conflict in several parts of India, the situation became grave. The proxy war has been no doubt targeted mainly on Jammu and Kashmir through infiltration of hundreds of trained and armed terrorists since 1989 but other parts of the country including Gujarat are also affected by it. There are reports of protagonists of *jihad* being active in Godhra; specially. It was claimed that the slum-dwelling Muslims near Godhra railway station were bristling with such elements. The judicial commission established to go into the attack on the Sabarmati Express at Godhra is expected to confirm whether it was the handiwork of such elements.

But the VHP and even the BJP heading the Gujarat administration did not hesitate to let the impression spread that it was the handiwork of sectarian elements. In the process an atmosphere for retaliation against local Muslims came to be created. A large number of them, including women and children, were killed or burnt alive. As many as "800 lives (some estimates put the toll at 2000 lives),[3] untold brutality inflicted on women and children and property worth hundreds of crores of rupees destroyed. Over 1,50,000 Muslims were rendered homeless and kept in refugee camps in extremely uninhabitable conditions. More alarmingly, people have been overcome by insensate hate. The Hindus had largely left the walled city in Ahmedabad. Their improved means enabled them to move to less congested and more homogenous localities. Consequently, there has been 'ghettoisation' of the Muslims remaining behind. Against that background television visuals showed Muslim women, donning traditional dress, telling their tale of woe in the killings.

Most startlingly, a Hindu woman explained that being educated the women were able to understand their dharma (duty) and exert themselves for it, implying resort to sectarian violence. According to a colleague in Ahmedabad, after the attempt to blow up Parliament House in Delhi on 13 December 2001 the national mood of perceiving Pakistan infiltrated terrorists as a security threat aggravated Gujarati distrust of Muslims. They did not distinguish between being anti-terrorist and being anti-Muslim. Further, ever since the 1947 sack of Godhra in the wake of the Junagadh crisis anti-Muslim bias in attitude and action had come to be seen as a patriotic duty of Indians. The latent sectarianism has been breaking out periodically especially in 1969, (when Indira Gandhi was battling the Hitendra Desai Government) again during 1989-90 anti -Mandal disturbances, and in 1992 after the demolition of the Babri masjid. The Godhra train attack was a spark that needed to touch off the conflagration.

A stark reminder was an email message from Varsha Bhosle, a scholar now in the US. She said, alluding to the Godhra outrage: "The Muslims, despite their economic backwardness and in short-sighted glory behave badly as they did at Godhra. The Hindus react poorly." It evoked a response from Rafiq Dossani of Stanford University pointing out that it would be wrong to identify Hindus or Muslims with vile acts. He blamed the media, especially TV " for indiscriminately showing violence". At another level, the Samata party leader, Jaya Jaitley, and some BJP leaders said the failure of the Congress President and her Communist allies to condemn the Godhra outrage was partly responsible for the subsequent mass killing of Muslims. That showed that the party and its allies were far from being remorseful for what has shamed most Indians at home and abroad.

Mind you, the literacy rate in Gujarat is 61 per cent. Thus, it is the educated and relatively better off sections that were seething with anti-Muslim sentiment. If it were only the masses the situation could have been controlled by a show of force whereas now the rot had seethed deeper. The Gujarat administration, wilfully or through characteristic inertia, failed miserably tackle the problem by physical means as well as by political persuasion. In fact, it objectively fuelled the flames of anti-Muslim violence. First, fifty-four of the fifty-eight charred bodies were taken to Ahmedabad, the termination point of the ill-fated train, the same evening. The much-maligned police commissioner objected but was overruled on the plea that the victims belonged either to the Gujarat capital or its neighbouring areas.

Even so, it could have been done without public demonstration. After all, death, even if violent, is a matter of sorrow and not demonstration. It is not a marriage or a political event .The BJP leadership in Gujarat is culpable on this count. The remaining bodies were sent there on the following day. It was nothing short of spreading the virus of hate .In other words, the impassioned elements in these areas, especially those who viewed the Godhra outrage as an organised Muslim riposte to the Ayodhya agitation, did not need live television coverage for getting worked up.

Compounding the crime, the VHP called for a statewide bandh on the next day, with the support of the ruling BJP. One can understand local BJP politicians, with their narrow vision, expecting to garner Hindu votes by such tactics but why didn't the central leadership of the party educate and discipline them? A party in which different State units put their local interests above the national sentiment is not much of a 'national' party. If the Congress party is run from the centre as a machine without even a semblance of local initiative the BJP, once regarded as a party of cohesion and discipline, is now a picture of chaos. The Communists, no doubt, make no distinction between the State and the party. In West Bengal, the party would organise a bandh and the Government would enforce it

Looking back at the Gujarat mayhem and the way political parties, including the BJP, used it for vote garnering it was one of the most disgraceful chapters in the country's history. The Gujarat riots were compared to the Hindu-Muslim mutual killings in the wake of partition in1947. It was not an exaggeration, although Gujarat did not experience much of it except for the sack of Godhra after the Junagadh nawab's provocative 'accession' to Pakistan. What happened in Godhra then had left the Congress leaders in a quandary. They had theoretically accepted the division of the country on the basis of religion. At the same time, leaders like Nehru and Sardar Patel did not subscribe to Jinnah's two-nation theory. Further, acceptance of religion-based sectarianism as the determinant of Statehood would have been self-destructive for India with over 110 million Muslims (at that time) as its nationals.

But mere verbal repudiation of the two-nation theory did not help. Active and consistent efforts to knit India into a single nation.were needed. That required separation of religious practice and ritual from nationhood; people of all faiths should have full religious freedom but essential attributes of nationhood like common civil law and shared commitment to national values would have to go with it. The eminent security expert, K

Subrahmanyam, writing in the *Times of India*[4] has candidly declared that "India cannot be termed either a secular state or a democracy" because it does not have common civil law and, as in a genuine democracy, all its citizens do not have equal rights and are not treated equally under the rule of law. Subrahmanyam has spelt it out that even though the US had proclaimed itself a secular and democratic State in the last quarter of the 18th century it became a truly democratic and secular State only in the last quarter of the 20th century with the passing of the civil rights law. His bottom line is: secularism should be properly defined and applied and not reduced to a slogan. Subrahmanyam also blames the situation to the faulty electoral system of first-past-the post saying by giving rise to vote bank politics it has obviated deliberate and conscious cultivation of tolerance and harmonious existence of divergent faiths.

To put a positive construction on Nehru's thinking and action, he thought that once rid of the troublesome Muslim Leaguers India could concentrate on nation building and development on non-sectarian lines. Gandhiji abandoning the leadership of the Congress and going on his mercy mission to quench the fires of communalism in Bengal and Bihar also handicapped Nehru. An additional nuisance was the Communists' support to partition raising the bogey of the right of self-determination of Muslims, obviously at the instance of Moscow. The Communists' mundane calculation could have been that given the ideologically bankrupt leadership of Pakistan they could have gained control of the new State. As it happened, many of the Muslim Communist leaders had to return to India to survive physically and pro-Communists like Faiz Ahmed Faiz had no political role in the country in spite of their academic brilliance and universally acknowledged talent. Even the far fewer socialists operating in Karachi as trade unionists had a rough time until they were silenced. India being always tolerant did not hold it against the Communists that they contributed to the formation of Pakistan. Of course, when the Congress itself opted for partition how could the Communists be blamed for putting a gloss on downright sectarianism.

In this context, those who call themselves secularists and denounce the BJP as communal would do well to recall Maulana Azad's agony. The Maulana held the second position in the Nehru cabinet and was education minister until he passed away. From his book, *India Wins Freedom*[5], one could understand how deeply he had felt what he perceived as incipient anti-Muslim bias in the Congress party and the Government. Not wanting to hurt the image of the country and cause pain to his pal Nehru, he saw to it that the last chapter of the book was withheld from publication for twenty-five years until after his death and that of Nehru. The short point is that sensitive Muslims even then were worried about the state of affairs with the Hindus developing fast and mastering skills to keep up with which the Muslims would find it tough. First, there were no reformers of the calibre of Sir Syed Ahmed Khan to promote quality education for Muslims. The Central Government was helpless in reforming the prevailing practice of resourceful persons setting up teaching shops for Muslims and claiming State assistance under the constitutional provision regarding educational institutions for the minorities managed by them. The managers of such institutions were not equal to the task by and large and contributed only to segregation of Muslims from non-denominational educational institutions.

Further, the orthodox Muslims and clerics who opposed Jinnah's concept of a home land for Muslims on the ground that a modern state was antithetical to the Islamic tenets carried weight in India because of their proximity to Congress party leaders. The germ of vote bank politics was already raising its head, although the Congress commanded Muslim votes in States like UP and Bihar also. Most importantly, the definition of secularism as envisaged in the Constitution had ingredients of sectarianism.

As Dr. Radhakrishnan pointed out, secularism in Indian conditions has to be rooted in the Hindu approach of equality towards all religions and equal rights and responsibilities for practitioners of all faiths. That would have obviated the present day distortions and the phenomenon of Muslims being kept as a backward vote bank depending on Government and Congress support. In the process, independent growth of Muslims as equal citizens of India with equal rights and responsibilities was generally thwarted. Compounding the matter, Laloo Yadav, Viswanath Pratap Singh, Mulayam Singh Yadav et al further vitiated it, giving rise to equally unhealthy Hindu backlash.

In this context, the veteran editor and thinker, N.J. Nanporia, has brought out the fetish about 'secularism.' He has recalled that "ever since Indira Gandhi inserted the word in the preamble to the Constitution in 1976 it has achieved the status of a mantra dutifully chanted by all politicians across all divides.“His charge against the BJP ironically is that it has forfeited its claim to be a party with a difference by "willingly giving lip service to secularism". True, the BJP draws the line between its version and the 'pseudo-secularism' of its opponents whereas even a person like

Sonia Gandhi, who least understands these formulations and their nuances routinely reads out speeches denouncing the BJP as communalist and fundamentalist. Apparently, Nanporia's point is that in the face of such a campaign the BJP, instead of joining the crowd by denying the charge and professing its commitment to the 'secular' values of Indian constitution, should have brought out the confusion and worse attending 'secularism.' This is despite BJP's simultaneous allegiance to Hindutva.

Nanporia's punchline follows: "Secularism as shaped in Indian conditions has been reduced to a device for garnering votes. But meanwhile the BJP has the difficulty of somehow reconciling the Gujarat tragedy with secularism however defined. It is a difficulty it has chosen to ignore. Yet no 'justification' of post-Godhra developments in Gujarat is even remotely possible without the BJP boldly rejecting secularism. Is the fact that it hasn't done so a glimmer of hope for the future and the restoration of some political sanity?" Nanporia's thesis almost sounds like a tongue-in the-cheek dig at the BJP. But it doesn't seem to be so, not because he has a soft corner for the party but because of his disgust with politicians trading secularism for cheap votes. It is also possible that the apprehension that the BJP might fish for a share of 'secular' votes got the goat of parties already squabbling for bulk Muslim votes. The Congress party has been straining at the leash to get back the Muslim electoral support it had lost after P.V. Narasimha Rao allowed the Babri masjid to be demolished and a makeshift temple put in its place without lifting his little finger. Mulayam Singh Yadav, who thinks he is a legitimate claimant to the vote because of his efforts in 1990 to save the Babri structure from being brought down, naturally does not like it.

He has also to give crumbs to Harkishan Singh Surjit and his hangers-on who dutifully bleat secularist slogans in the name of a mythical People's Front. Even H. D Deve Gowda is in the run with his version of Janata Dal. If the Muslim vote, even if cast in bulk, gets dissipated among so many aspirants it will be no different from the fractured Hindu vote. So they all combine to keep the BJP out; then they squabble among themselves for cornering as much of the vote share as they could lay their hands on. They are united only in demonising the BJP as communal, Fascist etc.

This was what happened in Gujarat in March-April 2002. First, for over ten days without a break both Houses of Parliament were not allowed to function demanding dismissal of Narendra Modi as chief minister of Gujarat. (The irony is that during Indira Gandhi's prime ministership in the wake of the 'emergency' there had been frequent recourse by the Centre to Article 356 to dismiss elected State governments not to her liking. The Sarkaria Commission was set up to go into the problem and suggest remedies. The Inter-State council has accepted its recommendations after detailed and deep discussion.

The result is a system of restraints on recourse to Article 356. Now the non-BJP and non-Congress parties including Communists joined hands with the Congress party to demand dismissal of a State Government that had not lost majority support in the State assembly.) That would leave the option of the BJP changing its chief minister at the bidding of other parties. Neither the Prime Minister nor the Home Minister was allowed to speak to dilate on the situation and try to evolve a mutually acceptable solution. The strategy was for a few MPs to invade the well of the House - forbidden for entry according to rules of parliamentary procedure - and start raising slogans. The presiding officer, the Speaker having been killed in a plane accident, the Deputy Speaker in the Lok Sabha and the Chairman himself in the House of Elders would have to adjourn the Houses for the day. The MPs presumably collect their sumptuous daily allowance, hold forth in front of private TV cameras at the Parliament gate, eat lunch in the Parliament canteen - run by the Railways and subsidised by the Government —and go home for their afternoon nap.

Meanwhile, in the towns and even villages of Gujarat there would be mayhem, initially by Hindu mobs provoked by the Godhra outrage and organised by the VHP and its associates. It was evident that in the last two days of February 2002 and early in March the State Government let the thugs carry on their killing spree. The thinking among many Hindus especially in Ahmedabad and other urban areas of Gujarat was that the Muslims deserved a stiff dose of the medicine they administered in Godhra. In actual practice, professional killers armed with all kinds of lethal weapons wreaked mayhem on innocent Muslim, men, women and children. The only crime of the victims was that they happened to share faith with the alleged perpetrators of the Godhra massacre. Scores of members of the traditionally trading Bohra community were killed and their businesses worth millions of rupees looted and destroyed. Incidentally, Mohammad Ali Jinnah, founder and first governor-general of Pakistan, was a Bohra; so were many associates of Mahatma Gandhi in South Africa. At that stage, the State administration apparently tried to control the situation but it had gone out of hand. The local police force was demoralised and immobilised. Army troops had to be deployed in some strength and constantly for over a month. It was unhealthy for regular defence forces to be so deployed; a succession of army chiefs of staff have repeatedly spoken against frequent use of the defence forces for such tasks. It was against that background that a number of para-military organisations were launched; they have over the years proliferated but still the army was being used.

The politicians who allowed such a situation to develop had no concern for national security. In this context, Gujarat, more than other States, seems to have a tradition of groupism and internecine squabbling among political leaders. Even in Gandhiji's time, his former personal secretary, Indulal Yagnik, turned against him and politicised the differences. Sardar Patel, too, had to face the problem; he would either call the dissidents into his presence to silence them by a severe tongue-lashing or send them packing from the party. Similarly, Nehru had to rehabilitate U.N. Dhebar from political wilderness into which his rivals had cast him by elevating him to Congress presidentship. Dhebar had been dislodged as chief minister of Saurashtra. In 1969 Indira Gandhi allowed nasty communal riots to be fomented to spite Morarji Desai by bringing a bad name to his protege Hitendra Desai. Hitendra was then chief minister of Gujarat He had to go finally and later switched over to Indira Gandhi's group deserting Morarji Desai. The same was the case with Balwantrai Mehta, who as secretary of the A-I.C.C. laid the foundation for a far-reaching decentralisation programme through the panchayat raj system. He could not get along with Dr. Jivaraj Mehta. In 1975 Morarji Desai went on a fast unto death when corruption was brought into the dispute between Chimanbhai Patel and his rivals. The Congress indulged in the luxury of rampant groupism and infighting when it had no opposition worth the name. The BJP tried to fill the gap and soon grew into a fairly strong outfit. Then it too fell into the rut when Sankarsinh Vaghela ousted venerable Keshubhai Patel as chief minister. Vaghela ultimately left the party to end up in the Congress. Most recently in 2000, Narendra Modi was brought in to replace Keshubhai who, it was said, failed to grapple effectively with rehabilitation of 1999 earthquake victims.

To complete the gory story of Gujarat killings, there was evidence of their having been carried out with a sinister political motive. To what extent Modi was personally a party to the cynical plan was not clear but being the chief minister he could not be unaware of it and should, therefore, be held accountable. A plausible surmise - to be confirmed by the Nanavati and K.G.Shah judicial commission if its report ever sees the light of day — was that the VHP calculated that organised mayhem against Muslims would swell the BJP vote in a future election and put the party at its mercy. Most of the anti-Muslim violence was in the constituencies of Congress leaders like Vaghela and Solanki. The BJP strongholds were relatively unaffected. The large-scale participation in and support to the pogrom by the Hindus of these areas suggested that they had switched over to the BJP. Sensing the people's mood, the Congress, too, changed its tune and endorsed the anti-Muslim violence. To recall the cynical politics of the post-carnage situation, first, the BJP leaders tried to advance the assembly elections.

The Modi Government resigned in July 2002, after recommending dissolution of the State assembly and the Governor readily complied with the suggestion. The idea was to cash in on the continuing anti-Muslim sentiment among large sections of Hindus. That had made the Congress party not only to tone down its criticism of the anti-Muslim violence but also virtually to go along with it. Meanwhile, the Election Commission put its foot down and thwarted the BJP plan of a snap election. It ordered a six-month respite for tempers to cool down and the electoral rolls to be updated. Then, the national executive meeting of the BJP held at Panaji in Goa in the last week of May went along with the State party leaders' plans. Earlier at the end of April when the Prime Minister visited Godhra and Ahmedabad and spent some time at the Muslim refugee camps, he was shocked beyond words. He gave Modi a piece of his mind and thought in terms of replacing him as chief minister. In fact, the move for a change of guard in Ahmedabad was already afoot in Delhi.

Arun Jaitley was despatched to Ahmedabad to prepare Modi for the blow and to make him offer to resign. But the sustained campaign for the sack of Modi by the opposition with the Congress party in the lead and with the media in chorus put Vajpayee's hackles up. The Congress party, too, was speaking in two voices. While in Gujarat the party had reconciled itself with the anti-Muslim sentiment of the Hindu voters, outwardly it was trying to enlarge its Muslim vote bank. The Prime Minister was fed up with the intense politicisation of the human tragedy and fell in line with the party hotheads. Giving in to the demand for dropping Modi would land the BJP between two stools, it was thought. While there was no prospect of the BJP getting Muslim electoral support worth the name it would lose the backing of Hindu hard-liners, it was calculated. Ultimately, the BJP national executive, while rejecting Modi's 'offer' to resign, asked him to prepare for an early assembly election. It was supposed to be in support of the theory that since his resignation was rejected on the plea that he enjoyed the support of the legislature it was to be put to the test in an election. The most blatant demonstration of the Congress party's cynicism was the leadership vetoing an agreement by the Punjab Government to spare commandos and trained police personnel for deployment to quell the rioting in Gujarat. K.P.S. Gill as security adviser to the Gujarat Government had approached his former colleagues in the Punjab police and got them to agree. The State Government too okayed it. By then, the Gujarat violence had changed qualitatively into Hindu-Muslim fighting with Muslims employing terrorist technique. It was either a backlash to earlier one-sided killing of Muslims or due to involvement of Pakistan-sponsored agencies. So neither the army troops nor general police could handle it effectively. Those with experience of overcoming terrorism in Punjab would have been a great help. But Sonia Gandhi & Co. would not have it because they were afraid peace might return to Gujarat diluting their vote bank.

End Notes

1. Madhu Dandavate as railway minister in the Janata Party Government in 1977 gave the evocative name to the train since its destination of Ahmedabad was the location of Gandhiji's ashram on the banks of the Sabarmati river.
2. K.M. Munshi *The Story of Somanatha,* 1948 Bharatiya Vidya Bhavan, Bombay.
3. Humanitarian needs assessment report facilitated by Oxfam and Bangalore Institute for Peace and Relief, PTI report in the *Deccan Herald*, Bangalore 2 May, 2002.
4. March 2, 2002.
5. 1950, Asia Publishing House, Bombay.

10

Foreign Policy: First Fifty Years

Nehru was his own Foreign Minister, which was as it should be. Even before Independence, he took intense interest in international developments and forged links between the Indian National Congress and anti-colonial and anti-Fascist movements abroad. He was India's *de facto* foreign minister even before India became free and could have a foreign policy of her own. As head of the pre-Independence Interim Government, Nehru took important decisions concerning India's relations with the then Soviet Union by establishing diplomatic presence in Moscow. Gandhiji would refrain from commenting on international developments - the only exception being his advice to Britain to face the Nazi onslaught nonviolently - saying Jawaharlal was knowledgeable about them and he would defer to Nehru's assessment. So was Sardar Patel, although on the India-China agreement on Tibet he had pointedly differed from Nehru and made his position clear in a private letter to the party leader. After Independence, the declaratory content of Nehru's pronouncements and the Congress resolutions on foreign affairs were reinforced by the opportunity and capability to act on them. In the effort, he had to draw heavily on the inherited Foreign Service - with an outlook and approach entirely different from his own - and a few trusted and knowledgeable colleagues like V.K. Krishna Menon.[1]

Of the contemporary Congress leaders very few had Nehru's flair for and interest in foreign affairs. Similarly, very few leaders had the ability to head Indian missions abroad, the exceptions being Vijayalakshmi Pandit and Sarvepalli Radhakrishnan. Asaf Ali as India's first ambassador to US was a disappointment. Radhakrishnan in Moscow and Krishna Menon in London were the kind of non-career diplomats free India needed, though there was the complication of Vijayalakshmi Pandit's foray into the foreign policy arena and her antipathy for both of them. Nevertheless, she proved a successful chairperson of the U.N. General Assembly and had very cordial relations with leading US and other diplomats and journalists. Abe Rosenthal who rose to be the managing editor of *The New York Times* regarded her highly, having struck a friendship with her during his stint in Delhi as the newspaper's correspondent.[2]

Once, I asked Ram Manohar Lohia who was Nehru's choice to head the foreign affairs department of the All-India Congress Committee (AICC) before independence, what would have been the result if he had not parted company with Nehru and had been drafted by him to assist him in shaping free India's foreign policy. Instead of flaring up at the blasphemous (retrospectively in the light of his anti-Nehruism) implication of the hypothetical question, Lohia replied without passion: "Vijay Lakshmi and Indira would not allow it." It is difficult to visualise the result if the impossible had happened and Lohia had teamed up with Nehru in shaping the country's foreign policy. But leave aside involving his former followers like Lohia in foreign policy; Nehru did not train young members of his Congress Party for taking the responsibility from him ultimately. Even bright Congress Party MPs like Sadat Ali Khan and Dinesh Singh were not fully groomed for the task.

There was, no doubt, criticism of Nehru's foreign policy especially by the Socialists and other opposition groups like the short-lived Swatantra Party and the Jana Sangh, but most of it was ill informed because barring a few like Lohia the others did not have an understanding of foreign policy. The critics were largely chicken-sexers lacking Nehru's grand sweep. For them the microdot was paramount. Even Jayaprakash Narayan's criticism of India's stand on the Soviet invasion of Hungary in 1956 was morally motivated and overlooked the global situation in the light of the simultaneous Anglo-French invasion of the Suez Canal area. Secondly as it became clear when some of the Nehru papers of the period were published, much of what he did and said in the sphere of foreign policy remained hidden from the public view. The critics knew only what Nehru had said for the record. Finally, Krishna Menon who had been closely associated by Nehru in the conduct of foreign policy was a prickly personality with nothing but contempt for most of his critics. He thus rubbed many in the wrong way and they included Congress leaders like Morarji Desai. Their approach to foreign policy had thus become warped by the personal factor.

Foreign policy was foreign for Lal Bahadur Shastri. As Prime Minister, he had announced at his one and only press conference in 1964 that a medical mission would be sent to South Vietnam. That would have been a change from Nehru's policy of keeping aloof from Vietnam as long as the US military involvement in the country lasted. So, I approached the spokesman of the External Affairs Ministry, I.J. Bahadur Singh, and (an expert in his own right on many foreign policy issues) for particulars of the medical mission. "Forget about it," he shooed me away good-naturedly. The reason was that the Prime Minister had confused Laos with Vietnam! Subsequent induction of Swaran Singh (than whom there could be no more painstaking non-professional) as external affairs minister improved matters.

Indira Gandhi had the advantage of closeness to Nehru when he formulated India's foreign policy. She knew many of the world leaders personally and had rapport with statesmen like Gen. de Gaulle by virtue of being Nehru's daughter. Until 1969 she pressed home these advantages. The seasoned experts in the ministry took care of the declaratory dimension of foreign policy. For instance, her repeated advocacy of withdrawal of foreign troops from South Vietnam and a political rather than a military solution of the problem was backed by an unassailable case prepared in South Block. The situation, however, began to change after 1969. Domestic political requirements began to influence foreign policy postures. A kind of pro-Soviet orientation began to manifest itself because Indira Gandhi's minority government needed the support of the Communist MPs in the Lok Sabha to avoid embarrassing situations.

The Indo-Soviet Treaty of Peace and Friendship of 1971 was a striking example, though the circumstances in which it had been signed concealed its unsavoury aspects and whetted the nationalist expectation that it was a prelude to the liberation of Bangladesh. Instead of promoting India's objective in East Pakistan, Moscow used it to restrain India in the interest of Soviet regional interests in South Asia. That apart, the concept of an Asian security system, propounded by Alexei Kosygin in Kabul, was the larger background to the treaty. A series of similar treaties between the USSR and other countries of Asia and Africa and the move for a chain of inter-locked arrangements (which became manifest after the Indo-Bangladesh friendship treaty) should have made India more circumspect. For instance, as the Yugoslavs pertinently pointed out, the commitment of support to the treaty partner in the event of outbreak of hostilities was too sweeping. They cited the hypothetical case of Soviet military action against Yugoslavia (on the plea of a threat to Soviet security from "reactionaries" in Belgrade or interference from outside in Yugoslavia's internal affairs) and said that under the treaty India would be required to support the Soviet action. I was one of those who laughed away such fears.

But the Soviet invasion of Afghanistan on 2 December 1979 and what followed it have shown that such apprehensions were not totally unfounded. Let us look back at the Afghanistan development. The monarchy there was overthrown in a *coup* staged in July 1973 by Mohammed Daoud, a cousin of the deposed king Zahir Shah, and a member of the Muhammedzai family.[3] Daoud who proclaimed himself President of Afghanistan had to lean on the Progressive Democratic Party (PDP) formed in 1965 on the lines of a Communist Party and with close links to Moscow. But the PDP had by then begun to call itself the Parchami (flag) party, following a split in its ranks in 1971. Babrak Karmal, the incumbent president, was the leader of the breakaway Parchami Party. While supporting the Daoud Government the Parchamis managed to gain influence in the administration and the armed forces. A few years later the Parchamis lost Daoud's favour and had become like the CPI in India after Sanjay Gandhi's advent. But by 1977 they merged with the dominant Marxist faction of the PDP led by Nur Mohammud Taraki. About a year later (April 1978) Daoud was toppled and killed with many members of his family. The PDP gained power as a result of the military *coup* and its leader Nur Mohammud Taraki took over as Prime Minister. When Morarji Desai visited Moscow in June 1979 — a few weeks before the collapse of the Janata Government in India— Afghanistan figured prominently in the discussions he had with the Soviet leaders. A joint statement signed by him and his Soviet host, Alexei Kosygin, said: "India and the Soviet Union declare their desire to develop friendly relations and cooperate with the Democratic Republic of Afghanistan. They express themselves firmly in favour of the aspirations of the people of Afghanistan for the preservation of their national independence and economic development." It was a foreign office draft, which stuck in Morarji Desai's throat, but it was too late to amend when he discovered it. Also, he would not have been satisfied with stylistic changes because he did not fundamentally endorse the Soviet attitude towards Afghanistan. Thus when Leonid Brezhnev said the USSR could not "look on indifferently" if Pakistan continued its "incursions" into Afghanistan, Morarji Desai observed that the Kabul Government "should try to acquire credibility among the Afghan people instead of blaming Pakistani interference for its troubles." Morarji Desai also openly questioned the Soviet celebration of the Saar revolution (resulting in the overthrow of the Daud regime) saying it was no business of the Soviet Union to prescribe solutions for Afghanistan's domestic problems. Soon after - on 14 September 1979 - Taraki went the Daoud way, overthrown and bumped off. According to the Soviet media, Taraki paid the price for his "anti-people policies". There was no mention at that time of "intervention from outside". Hafizullah Amin replaced Taraki. Exactly three and a half months later Amin, too, was deposed and executed on 28 December 1979. Babrak Karmal stepped into Amin's shoes. But meanwhile on 27 December 1979, a massive airlift of Soviet troops to Kabul began. According to Western estimates about 40,000 Soviet troops entered Afghanistan by New Year's day in 1980.

The looming crisis in Afghanistan provided Charan Singh with an opportunity to live down his reputation of unelected Prime Minister who had ducked the Lok Sabha vote on the legitimacy of his coalition government. He accomplished an A-one feat that, too, in the field of foreign policy, which was as alien to him as scruples. He sent for the Soviet ambassador in New Delhi and asked him to convey to Moscow India's stand that the Soviet troops should withdraw from Afghanistan. Not content with it, the spokesman of the External Affair Ministry (Mani) J.N. Dikshit issued a statement on 31 December 1979 recalling the Morarji-Kosygin joint statement six months previously in which both sides "opposed any interference by outside forces in the internal affairs of Afghanistan" and calling for the withdrawal of Soviet troops from that country. That was India's formal response to the message conveyed to the Foreign Secretary, Ram D. Sathe, in the small hours of December 28, 1979, that an indefinite number of Soviet troops had moved into Afghanistan to counter "external threats" to the host country. There was no mention then of the reported request for Soviet troops by Hafizullah Amin before he was overthrown and executed. The Soviet ambassador's pre-dawn call on Ram Sathe to acquaint him with the *fait accompli* of Soviet invasion of Kabul was in pursuance of the 1971 treaty which required either party to keep the other informed of its military actions outside its territory. In effect, it was no more than a formal confirmation of the Soviet 'invasion' of Afghanistan. In contrast, in December 1971, India had alerted Moscow even before our troops moved into what was then East Pakistan.

Further, a 1926 treaty between the then Afghanistan ruler Amanullah and the Soviet Union provided for what was called Reciprocal Neutrality and Non-Aggression.[4] Under the treaty, both sides had undertaken to observe neutrality towards each other in the case of war or military action between one of them and one or more third parties. This was different from the provision in the Indo-Soviet treaty, which committed the treaty partner to involvement in such hostilities - a blow to the spirit of non-alignment. The Soviet-Afghan treaty did not thus justify the induction of Soviet troops into that country. That the Soviets were not pleased with Charan Singh's cheek in ticking them off like that in public goes without saying. Nehru in his time had told more blunt truths to Brezhnev's predecessors. So did Shastri to Kosygin. Even Indira Gandhi let the Kremlin know her mind when in 1967-68 Moscow started shipping arms to Pakistan. But those moves were never publicised. The Russians are extremely sensitive to open diplomacy and that is their main grouse against the Americans.On January 3, 1980, more than 50 UN members, including Bangladesh, Indonesia, Pakistan, Sri Lanka and Nepal signed a motion calling for an urgent meeting of the UN Security Council "to examine the situation in Afghanistan and its consequences for peace and international security". The French President for the month of the Security Council convened it on January 7 when the Soviet Union vetoed a resolution calling for withdrawal of the Soviet troops from Kabul. Thirteen members including Mexico, Norway, Portugal, Bangladesh, Jamaica, Niger, the Philippines, Tunisia and Zambia plus the four veto-wielders - China, France, the UK and the US - voted for the resolution. East Germany and the USSR voted against.

Following the killing of the resolution by the Soviet Union, the UN General Assembly was convened on January 10, 1980, in an emergency session, the sixth of its kind until then in the history of the world organisation. A resolution urging the "immediate, unconditional (and) total withdrawal of foreign troops" from Afghanistan was adopted by 108 votes to 18. India was one of the countries, which abstained while Romania and Bhutan were among the countries that absented themselves from the voting. Besides the other members of the Soviet *bloc*, such non-aligned countries as Cuba, Afghanistan (under Karmal) Ethiopia, South Yemen and Vietnam opposed the resolution.

Indian abstention though at variance with the position of our Asian neighbours and a majority of the non-aligned States was nothing compared to the remarks of India's spokesman, Brajesh Mishra during the discussion. He said: "India could not remain indifferent to the efforts of certain foreign powers to interfere in the internal affairs of Afghanistan by training and arming subversive elements and encouraging them to spread trouble in the country… We have no reason to doubt assurances from the Soviet Union that its troops will be withdrawn from Afghanistan as soon as possible."[5] The obvious reference to Pakistan might have pleased the

Soviet Union because it tried to shift the focus from its invasion of Afghanistan to long-standing Pakistan-Afghanistan tension. For South Block it was sticking to India's general anti-Pakistan policy and doing its bit for the Soviet Union. Non-communist opinion in Afghanistan, however, did not relish it. At that time, the people's main concern was the Soviet military presence and everything else was secondary to it. Indian policy also objectively contributed to Pakistan using the occasion to get back into American good books and receive sizeable economic and military aid. It cemented America- China-Pakistan *entente* in the name of resisting Soviet threat to South Asia, with most of the Islamic countries, particularly Saudi Arabia, pouring in their oil money to build a potentially terrorist infrastructure in Afghanistan. For the US smarting under its humiliating military defeat in Vietnam it provided an opportunity to settle scores with Moscow, short-sightedly no doubt. The ultimate result was the emergence of the Taliban backed by US weapons, Saudi money and Pakistani manpower.

Though not yet sworn in as Prime Minister, Indira Gandhi had been involving herself in guiding our UN mission in the matter. It appears Triloki Nath Kaul, former Foreign Secretary who had subsequently turned a publicist for the Kremlin was the author of India's "tilt". He was being tipped to be Indira Gandhi's Principal Secretary but Sanjay was said to have scotched the move. However, Indira Gandhi asked him to draft the President's Address for the opening of Parliament a few days later and to look after the Afghan issue. Kaul also had contributed the brief references in the Congress (I) election manifesto to foreign policy. He always poured scorn on Janata's "genuine" non-alignment to correct which he showed his hand so clearly on the Afghanistan issue.

After he was entrusted with the External Affairs portfolio, P.V. Narasimha Rao tried to live down the effects of the Kaullist *coup*. His forthright statement on a visit to Pakistan offering co-operation to safeguard mutual security was an instance in point. He had also advocated the withdrawal of the Soviet troops. But as it happened it was too little and too late. India could have seized the opportunity to evolve an India-Pakistan joint policy towards Afghanistan and the big powers, although it was doubtful if the Islamabad establishment was in a mood for such a potentially beneficial policy. It had already set its mind on partnership with the US. The Indian official mindset was similarly shortsighted. The 1980 annual report of our Ministry of External Affairs, after referring to the "developments" in Afghanistan, said the subcontinent is "in danger of being converted into a theatre of great power confrontation and conflict, threatening the security of India". Then followed a critical account of the moves by China, Pakistan and the US to counter the Soviet military presence in Afghanistan making it appear that the Soviet action was a lesser evil. It was deliberately overlooked that the root cause of the developing security threat to India was the extension of the Soviet military frontier to the Khyber Pass which led to a virtual revival of the East-West cold war and the debilitation of *détente*.This is not to swallow the favourite theme of many Western analysts that the Soviet drive into Afghanistan was a continuation of the Czarist strategy to secure warm water ports. The allusion in the Molotov-Ribbertrop talks of October 1940 to "a natural sphere" of Soviet influence "extending in the general direction of the Indian Ocean" was not conclusive. Professor Geoffrey Jukes, no apologist for Moscow, has adduced historical evidence that Czar Peter, the Great, was primarily interested in the Black Sea littoral for his southern warm water outlets and that Molotov had clearly stated that he did not fall for Ribbentrop's bait to push Russia in the direction of the Persian Gulf and India.[6]

Equally unfounded was the Soviet alibi that the massive thrust to the Khyber - a consummate military manoeuvre with a horrendous prospect for potential victims - was to forestall Sino-US engineered intervention in Afghanistan. One is reminded by it of AJP Taylor's jibe about the seizure of the Chinese port by the German navy in 1897. He said: "The ostensible motive was that Germany needed a coaling station for her non-existent fleet - and thereafter a fleet to protect her coaling station."[7] Moscow needed a malleable Afghanistan on its southern flank to counter an imaginary threat and having accomplished it by installing the Karmal regime in Kabul it had to stay put there militarily to protect the regime!

How should Pakistan react to the disappearance of a buffer - however hostile - between its northern frontier and a Super Power with which its relations were for the most part unfriendly? How did we feel when China established its control over the Roof of the World, although Tibet had always been a part of China? Further, what would be the implications of the advance of the Soviet military border to less than 300 kilometres from our frontier? There was premature jubilation in New Delhi when Gen. Zia-ul-Huq turned down military aid offered by the Carter dispensation in Washington as "peanuts". As subsequent developments showed, it was only to get a much larger package from the successor Reagan establishment. Hypothetically speaking, if General Zia -ul-Haque or his successor had made their peace with Moscow to learn to live as a compliant neighbour of a Super power how would it affect the security scenario in the region? Field Marshal Ayub Khan who had taken Pakistan into SEATO and CENTO had no difficulty in mending his fences with the Soviet Union and receiving military aid from it in the post-Tashkent period. There was then some congruity between Soviet and American interests in the region, with both of them pitted against China and so the regional sub-system was not much affected. It was not the case in 1980. It was also too much to expect that the Soviet Union would use its benign influence to bear on India-Pakistan relations. No doubt, the character of the regime in Pakistan was a complicating factor. General Zia was trying to convert the curse of Soviet occupation of Afghanistan into a blessing for his military rule. As a result, his political opponents tended to take a pro-Soviet position on Afghanistan, making it more tempting to stage a volte face when the situation demanded. But none of these detracted from the fundamental fact that the Soviet military frontier had moved south towards our territory.

"Didn't we express the 'hope' that the Soviet forces will withdraw from Afghanistan," the draftsmen of the report would ask? Would it have been desirable for India to join the anti-Soviet chorus of reactionary elements? If geographically Afghanistan were Czechoslovakia or Hungary, academic expression of regret and a pious hope for withdrawal of troops would have sufficed. Secondly, without identifying itself with what was dubbed as an anti-Soviet chorus, India could safeguard its interests. The first requisite for that would be a correct perspective, which did not go hand in hand with Indira Gandhi's practice of involving India's relations with other countries in domestic politics. In 1975, for instance, when she was fighting to save her position and started subverting our democratic system for the purpose, she welcomed comments like the following from the Soviet official media. Hailing the imposition of press censorship by Indira Gandhi, *Pravda* wrote that it "normalised the work of the press and subordinated its activity to the higher interest of the country and the people". Nothing brings out so starkly the global perspective behind the Soviet occupation of Afghanistan as Andre Fontaine - an admirer of de Gaulle and Nehru - noted in an article in *Le Monde*. He wrote, "The Russian invasion of Afghanistan did not mark what is generally understood to be a 'change of policy' on the Soviet Union's part. Afghanistan is simply the latest addition to a list of countries, which has included, over the last few years, Vietnam, Kampuchea, Laos, South Yemen and Ethiopia and which has suggested, to more than one observer, an inexorable advance towards a very Russian-flavoured brand of socialism. What has changed as the

French communist daily, *L' Humanite*, rightly pointed out on July 2, is the global balance of power. When it is favourable to their enemies, the Soviets are capable, if need be, of giving up space in order to gain time, as Lenin taught them at Brest-Litovsk in 1918. Just as long as they remain convinced that the 'imperialists' have not yet got their second wind—and that, by any calculations will take several years — the Russians will try to turn the situation to their own advantage."[7]

In December 1971 when the hostilities with Pakistan were on Indira Gandhi addressed a public meeting at Ramlila grounds in Delhi to hurl defiance at Richard Nixon's decision to send a Seventh Fleet task force into the Bay of Bengal. It was a fitting reply to the US 'tilt' towards Yahya Khan. It was an instance of personal grit of the leader projecting the country's foreign policy options. Overcoming her aversion for Jayaprakash Narayan, she had requested him to go round the world capitals explaining the situation in East Pakistan and the security and other implications of the influx of refugees into India. But where China was concerned, India needlessly sided with the Soviet Union in the Sino-Soviet mutual quarrel, although it should have been no concern to us. In the process, New Delhi missed many an opportunity to improve relations with Beijing. It was a mistake because China, having lost caste with the Soviet Union, was keen to warm up to fellow-Asian countries, especially those not in the American bag.

Thus, when the Janata Party Government came into being with its professed policy of 'genuine non-alignment' and India's relations with the Soviet Union lost some of their former warmth, China started making overtures to India. As a result the external affairs minister Atal Behari Vajpayee undertook a much postponed but crucial visit to Beijing in 1978, the first since the Sino-Indian rupture in 1962. But while he was still in their country the Chinese launched an invasion of Vietnam, a close ally of India's traditional friend, the Soviet Union. Not content with it, Deng Xioaping rubbed it in by recalling the "lesson" taught to India in 1962. (Subrahmanian Swami, the perennial 'Janata Party president' was then a Janata Party MP and very close to Morarji Desai but bitterly prejudiced against Vajpayee. He could not contain his glee at the Chinese treatment of Vajpayee. Regarding it as personal humiliation of his *bete noir*, Swami issued a gratuitous statement saying that but for Vajpayee's flair for sight-seeing the External Affairs Minister would have been out of China by the time Beijing launched its nine-day military incursion into north Vietnam.) While there were too many foreign policy makers in Morarji Desai's Government, the South Block resumed making the policy in respect of

China after the fall of the Janata Government in mid-1979. The *de jure* external affairs minister in the Charan Singh regime, Shyam Nandan Mishra, was a mere titular head. Madhu Limaye was the *de facto*, if not ad hoc, external affairs minister. Suddenly one fine morning it was decided to recognise the Hang Semrin regime in Kampuchea, unmindful of the affront it meant to China. There was absolutely no provocation for the pro-Soviet and anti-Chinese demonstration unless as a return gesture to the Soviet Union, which had been wooing Limaye when Moscow's relations with the Morarji Desai Government were rather cool. The casualty was the normalisation of India-China relations, which started gingerly under Morarji Desai, with the prospect of a *quid pro quo* on the border dispute

The following sequence of events suggests sinister significance. On June 22 and 23, 1979, the Vietnamese army launched a major offensive against Khmer Rouge rebels and others pitted against the Heng Samrin regime in Kampuchea. It was a deft military manoeuvre — as Vietnamese "police actions" always had been — and seemed to have destroyed several rebel bases, though in the process the Vietnamese had violated the Thai border. What did it matter? Didn't South Africa repeatedly attack SWAPO sanctuaries in Angola and their troops even stayed put on Angolan territory? The same is the case with the Israel military might always getting away with violations of the international law. As a pre-monsoon military operation, the Vietnamese action was successful. But before the rebels could re-group and take advantage of the onset of monsoon — which would impede the Heng Samrin forces, international recognition was necessary for the regime. On July 2 and 3 1979, there were high-level talks in Moscow between Soviet and Vietnamese leaders, with Brezhnev, Kosygin, Phan Van Dong and Gen. Giap, among others, participating. According to the *Economist*,[8] the Soviet Union had been pouring into Vietnam military and other aid of the value of two million dollars a day since the Kampuchean adventure eighteen months earlier. It was a heavy drain even for the Soviets. More importantly, the Vietnamese had not been able to stabilise the Heng Samrin regime. It was still unable to survive without the 200,000 Vietnamese troops backing it. (A close parallel to the Afghan situation requiring the Soviet troops to keep Humpty Dumpty on the wall). The conclusion of the Moscow meeting therefore was that a massive drive be launched for getting recognition for the Kampuchean Government. On 5 July 1979, New Delhi received a letter from Brezhnev. Two days later followed the announcement of the recognition. It would have suited the Soviet book even better if the timing of the Indian decision on Kampuchea had been seen by Beijing as a slap in its face just when the normalisation process was getting warmer. In short, while reinforcing the hostility towards Pakistan, the Government also ensured that a China-India entente was ruled out. It seemed we couldn't sleep peacefully unless we had hostile neighbours on either side of the country. It was only after Rajiv Gandhi became Prime Minister in 1985 that efforts were made to build bridges with Beijing. Rajiv cemented it by a visit to the Chinese capital, hailed as a breakthrough in India-China relations, which remained frozen practically since the 1962 border conflict. But by then the Sino-Soviet standoff had begun to thaw and China had no particular compulsion to make up with India, as it was the case in the late 1970s. If the 1978 effort had succeeded we could have possibly been on the way to writing finis to the border dispute by now.

While the Soviet connection has had beneficial consequences for India, especially during the Cold War years, the other side of the coin should also be noticed. In Afghanistan, for instance, India lost an opportunity to play a role which could have obviated the problem of the Taliban if only Indira Gandhi had not gone the whole hog in endorsing Soviet occupation. In the process the divergent forces resisting the Soviet occupation were sucked into the American orbit. The CIA and the ISI jointly pumped sophisticated weapons to the Mujahideen in the name of beefing up the anti-Soviet resistance. The US especially was bent on putting the Soviet Union in the same position in which it had found itself in Vietnam. Of course, the Soviet Union was not routed in Afghanistan; its troops made an orderly and planned withdrawal leaving in the lurch the Soviet supported regime in Kabul. If only India had an independent role, distinguishable from that of Moscow regarded as an aggressor by the bulk of the Afghanistan people, the denouement in that hapless country would have been perhaps different. First and foremost, the field would not have been left open for Pakistan to develop Afghanistan as a satellite country in the name of acquiring 'strategic depth' against India. With the Americans pouring in lethal equipment through the ISI conduit, Pakistan had full sway over the situation. It siphoned off some of the equipment including the deadly Stinger missiles into its own armoury. It played favourites with the Afghan resistance groups, like fattening the extreme right wing Hukmetyar faction and its allies and starving the others of military supplies. In the process the civil war that followed the Soviet withdrawal from Afghanistan ultimately led to the right-wing forces gaining virtually complete control of the territory.

What came to be known as the Northern Alliance of 1980-81 subsequently, led by Ahmed Shah Masoud first fought its way to the top, but its policy of ruthless elimination of ideological enemies landed the country in bitter strife. (Masoud was murdered by Taliban agents one day before the September 2001 carnage in the US) The Afghanistan people had borne the brunt of the Northern Alliance's sectarian policies and turned against it, virtually welcoming the Taliban. Pakistan began to see it as an opportunity to fight a proxy war against India through its creature, the Taliban, which was largely officered by Islamist Pakistan army officers, and manned by the products of several madrassas run by the Jamaat -ul-Ulema-i-Islam. The prospect of King Zahir Shah returning to the country to establish a broad-based constitutional monarchy evaporated in the result. The Pakhtoons who were allergic to the Uzhbek dominated Northern Alliance gravitated towards the Taliban. The Northern alliance was pushed into the mountains to wage a fruitless war for over two decades. The Taliban, meanwhile, was captured by the Arab elements led by Osama bin-Laden and his fellow Wahbi Saudis. They deployed terror first to establish their unquestioned supremacy in the country and then as a tool of foreign forces, with Pakistan providing the military muscle, as well as diplomatic and 'moral' support.[9] In the process Taliban and Osama grew to their present (2001) size. For Pakistan the bonus was the availability of Taliban trained terrorists for *jihad* in Jammu and Kashmir. While Gen. Zia-ul-Haq had an ideological bias in favour of the Jamaat, successive Pakistan prime ministers during his regime and after, Benazir Bhutto and Nawaz Sharif, turned a blind eye to what was happening in Afghanistan at the instance of the ISI. The ISI was so powerful and perhaps still is — and beyond the control of the Pakistan Government that Benazir had admitted that even when aware of the massive infiltration of foreign terrorists into Punjab and Jammu and Kashmir she kept quiet. Presumably to rationalise her inaction and inability, she mounted an anti-India campaign on Kashmir. Surprisingly, that was despite friendly noises she was making towards the Rajiv Gandhi Government in India.

Nawaz Sharif, despite his subsequent participation in the aborted Lahore process, was a less unwilling party to the ISI policy towards India and Kashmir. In fact there had been a race in belligerence between Benazir and Nawaz Sharif on the issue, until in 1994. Nawaz Sharif realised the futility of undiluted hostility towards India and changed track. His party, the Pakistan Muslim League, had won two-thirds majority in the 1996 National Assembly election in which Kashmir had been on the back burner.

Benazir fought the elections making bellicose speeches on Kashmir finally to rue her shortsightedness, although she did not seem to have learnt the lesson. She subscribes to this day to the superstition that a tough anti-India policy in Kashmir was necessary for any Pakistani political party to win public support.[9] The Lahore process at the instance of Nawaz Sharif fell victim to the subsequent Kargil operation, which was the thin end of the wedge to dump Shariff. The army is back in Government and Pakistanis are happy!

Whereas the West had been the principal cold warrior, with ethnic, strategic and economic interests in West Asia, its involvement in South Asia had been, and continues to be intermittent and uneven. The general perception of most Western scholars is that "Indians and Pakistanis regard their security environment as basically hostile mutually." It was once as deeply rooted in the Western conventional wisdom as the inability of Arabs and Israelis to co-exist in harmony. The principal reason for this phenomenon is the stereotyped view of their mutual relations that both Indians and Pakistanis have presented to the world during the last several decades. It can be compared only with stereotyped US perceptions of the backwardness and poverty of South Asia and the propensity of the elites of India and Pakistan to squander their limited resources on armaments while their peoples starved and went naked. In the South Asian section of Olin Library at Cornell University, one of the best equipped of its kind in the United States, there were in 1990 no less than 200 volumes by Indian and Pakistani authors, all depicting each other's country as demons. There are also a sizeable number of books by US scholars, bemoaning the almost congenital incapacity of the two countries to see the light. There are no doubt variations on the theme, disputing the wisdom of the United States in allying itself with a military dictatorship like Pakistan, disparaging India's record first as a 'pacifist' and non-aligned country and lately as a nuclear capable and aggressive promoter of conflict. Surprisingly, except briefly in 2001, Pakistan's assiduous encouragement of terrorism was not much discussed. There were also schools of thought that if India, as the larger of the two, had been accommodating towards Pakistan's territorial claim on Kashmir; South Asia would have been free of strife. This is without counting a veritable library of studies on the nuclear dimension of the India- Pakistan relationship. Their main theme was that South Asia was a nuclear flashpoint and that the only way to reduce the risk was for India and Pakistan to accede to the Comprehensive Test Ban Treaty (CTBT). This point of view was the dominant one in the early 1990s, when PV

Narasimha Rao deftly disarmed India's critics by joining the US in sponsoring a UN resolution on termination of production of nuclear fissile material. He had also toned down Rajiv Gandhi's negative rhetoric on CTBT. Incidentally, the CTBT was in the forefront of international strategic dialogue in the late 1990s reaching a climax in 1996-97. That was the time of Arundhati Ghosh's eloquent rejection of the treaty at the Geneva Disarmament Conference. Her dramatic action and speech, which virtually killed the treaty as far as Geneva conference was concerned, made her a heroine in Indian middle-class circles. Ironically, in 1998, when the BJP government took the logical follow-up action by undertaking nuclear tests there was not similarly wide-spread enthusiasm among the earlier admirers of Arundhati's diplomatic *coup*. The reason could be the widespread Western resentment against India's nuclear tests and the inevitable economic sanctions by the US, Japan and other member-states of the Western bloc.

Before India gained independence from the British, the Indian National Congress, which spearheaded the freedom struggle, had virtually no policy for safeguarding the security of the country to be liberated. This was unusual because Nehru had definite ideas and preferences about conducting free India's foreign relations and had made himself felt in international relations even before India became independent and he took over the prime ministership. The reasons for the absence of a security policy could be (one, a naive impression that the policy of friendship with both the USSR and the West, coupled with solidarity with anti-colonial and anti-imperialist movements abroad, would insulate India from security threats from abroad. Secondly, distaste for the British Indian Army — the naval and air wings were mere appendages of the army at that time — which was often deployed in support of the British civilian administration and against the freedom movement, and, three, the influence of Mahatma Gandhi's pacifist outlook. Incidentally, talking of Gandhiji's promotion of pacifism or non-violence as he distinguished it from inactive pacifism and his massive influence among the people, after Gandhiji's assassination in 1948 and more blatantly since the 1980s India's internal security scenario has been vitiated by internecine conflict and blood-letting. The reference is not only to recurring Hindu-Muslim riots, but also the tendency of petty quarrels to more serious economic and political disputes to end up in public disturbances. The frequency of such incidents and the readiness with which competing interests use violent means to settle disputes or even score points, Indian life had not been so cheap as it has become over the recent years. There was a marriage of distorted Gandhian technique with propensity to take the law into one's hands and provoke violence. For instance, most agitations begin with a fast or satyagraha during which there would be violence followed by the usual cycle of killings and bloodletting.

The first Indian national leader to draw the military into the freedom struggle was Subhash Chandra Bose. He founded the Indian National Army (INA) composed largely of Indian troops taken prisoner in Europe and Southeast Asia. The military worth of the INA may be a matter of opinion but there can be no doubt of its psychological impact on the struggle against the British. Coupled with the 1946 'mutiny' by the ratings of the navy and the refusal of units of the air force to obey the orders of their British commanders in the winter of 1945-1946, the organisation of Indian National Army and the prosecution of some of its leaders by the British government on charges of treason and disloyalty to the Crown hastened the departure of British rule from India. Another important contribution of the INA was its inculcation of the nationalist - as distinct from Hindu or Muslim - sentiment among its members. The British Indian Army also was by and large free of Hindu-Muslim antagonism among its ranks, despite the British policy of categorizing Indians into martial and non-martial races and organisation of the regiments on a caste basis. By 1947 however the poison of religious bigotry and mutual hostility between Hindus and Muslims had seeped into the Army, and troops belonging to both the communities participated in the massive killings that accompanied the partition of the country. But members of the INA remained uncontaminated throughout. During a professional visit to Burma in 1952, I found former INA personnel, settled in that country and belonging largely to the Muslim community, deploring the partition of the country and extolling the concept of free and undivided India as projected by Netaji Subhash Chandra Bose. Significantly, some of my Muslim interlocutors had opted for Pakistan and were awaiting repatriation to that country, five years after the partition. The treason trial of the INA leaders and the revolt by the naval ratings were occasions for nationalist propaganda in India that the military would join the 'final struggle' against the British. Both the Indian National Congress and the Muslim League set up committees to organise the defence of the arraigned INA leaders. While the Muslim League chose to defend only the Muslims among them the Congress defence team which included Nehru himself pleaded for INA leaders of all faiths, Hindu, Muslim and Sikh.

It is obvious that the officers and most ranks in the British Indian Army to be handed over to the new dominions of India and Pakistan were far from happy with the glorification of persons who, in their assessment, violated the pledge of loyalty and the honour of the military. Thus, despite the moral commitment of Nehru to absorb the INA personnel in the regular Indian Army, the former could not re-enter the military. Some INA leaders came to occupy important positions including membership of the Central Cabinet, but their demand for the reinstatement in the Army was not met. This might have been partly due to the realisation by the political leadership that their induction into the army would impair the morale of the troops, politicise the fighting forces which were essentially professional and put a premium, even if indirectly, on violation of discipline. The charge of breach of discipline by the INA was largely technical. They continued to observe army discipline even as prisoners of war, and later when they joined Netaji Bose's campaign to free India of British yoke by force of arms. The charge against the INA was that in violation of the pledge of loyalty to the British Crown they had crossed over to the Japanese side, because the INA was an adjunct of the Japanese onslaught against British colonialism At the same time, the motivation of freeing India from British rule was an asset which the British Indian Army did not possess. It was a different matter that after the transfer of power and the circumstances in which the country was partitioned with massive Hindu-Muslim killings along the border the army had also got conditioned to the nationalist sentiment. Subsequent generations of army leaders and ranks were free of the slur of being tools of the British administration in India.

Two factors need to be stressed in this context: one, compulsory military training for the youth of the country as part of the educational curriculum would have toned up the community and countered the spread of sectarian thinking and outlook. But the Nehru Government had never even tried it. The University Training Corps (UTC) was not even an apology for mandatory national service for the youth. Two, inculcation of military training even for a couple of years would have countered the spread of divisiveness among the youth and made them more involved in larger national affairs. Lately middle rank military officers are being bitten by the bug of commercialism and tending to drop out through voluntary retirement to pursue business careers. The intake into the defence forces has also been suffering on account of the clamour among the youth for more lucrative openings in business and industry. The tradition in Punjab, and Maharashtra to a lesser degree, of sons following their fathers into the army has practically ended. Last but not least, the spread of professional politics among the younger generation would have been also checkmated by military training. Incidentally, one of the attractions of the Rashtriya Swayamsevak Sangh (RSS) was the provision of physical training and inculcation of military-like discipline among its members. In the pre-independence days, the Congress also had its Seva Dal drawn from the youth. Netaji Subhash Chandra Bose was famous for his organisation of volunteers for the freedom movement before he became the Congress President. But after independence, the Congress has virtually abandoned the practice. The so-called youth Congress launched by Sanjay Gandhi consisted mostly of thugs manned by lumpen elements and driven by careerist / opportunist motivation. Similarly, organisations like the Bajrang Dal of the BJP were havens for goons bent on sectarian violence.

The outbreak of hostilities with Pakistan soon after independence and the role the Army played in repulsing the Pakistani attack on Kashmir strengthened the position of the military vis-avis the political leadership. First-generation Indian Army officers like Generals (later Field Marshal) Cariappa and Thimaya became household names, because they spearheaded the sword arm of India in preserving national security. In contrast, the plight of INA personnel who opted for Pakistan had been pathetic, though their number was limited to a dozen or so. Once the euphoria of the Muslim League's participation in the defence of the INA 'heroes' had evaporated the former INA personnel who went to Pakistan were left to fend for themselves. The primary reason was the hold of the military on the Pakistani administration practically from the inception, and the deep aversion for the INA among the military officers. Unfortunately, this professionalism of the Pakistan defence forces did not extend to their keeping out of politics and undertaking periodical forays into the political sphere. The deep feeling among Pakistanis of a security threat from India has been a factor for the army's predominance in that country's public life. Whoever might have been heading the government in Pakistan, he or she had looked upon the Army more as a shaper of Pakistan's policy towards India. It had been so in its formative years when General Iskander Mirza and Ayub Khan paved the way for military involvement in politics. General Pervez Musharraf is the latest representative of this tribe, as in 2002. Interestingly, India did not simultaneously reciprocate the Pakistani perception of a military threat from Pakistan. In fact it had taken many years before Pakistan came to be regarded as an unrelenting adversary of India.

Against this background, at the dawn of the new millenium, India's initiatives in international relations have transformed the situation. First and foremost, there has been a breakthrough in relations with China. Beijing's reservations about acknowledging Sikkim as part of India have been overcome. China has virtually accepted the ground reality and a new transit route to Tibet through Sikkim will be in place soon.[10] Simultaneously, there has been advance in sorting out the border dispute. Political level talks between the two Governments have been going on. Trade and economic relations are proceeding satisfactorily. A direct air link between the two countries is operational. At the same time, relations with the U.S. and Russia are on firm footing. Strategic and political relations with both the countries are reinforced, with co-operation in defence matters continuing. Nearer home, Myanmar has ceased to be a security headache and a haven for insurgents from the northeastern States.

Strategic and political relations with Israel have been formalised – taking to the logical conclusion P.V. Narasimha Rao's initiatives in the early 1990s. Despite a recklessly politicised campaign by the Opposition parties, including the Congress party, the warmth of relations with Palestine and the Arab States has not dimmed. The Government has unequivocally reiterated India's support for an independent and sovereign Palestine State within secure borders and cessation of Israel-directed terrorist activity. The Prime Minister's visit to Syria, the first by an Indian head of Government in many years, had upgraded Indo-Syrian relations. Similarly, there has been a successful opening towards the Asean States. Japan and Germany, the economic giants, are in our friendly grasp. As in Nehru's time, not a week passed without a foreign dignitary visiting India or India hosting an international conference. In short, a picture of confidence and drive has replaced the slump in India's world image after the Nehru years. Above all, the starry-eyed Nehru approach to international relations has been reinforced by economic and practical underpinning. Further, India had then virtually ignored the States in our immediate neighbourhood, notably Sri Lanka, Nepal and Burma. The Vajpayee Government had avoided that mistake. Relations with Nepal and Sri Lankahave been cordial and mutually cooperative. In short, there is no country or grouping of States like ASEAN and the European Union with which India's relations are not smooth. If the Prime Minister's repeated and untiring efforts to normalise relations with Pakistan yielded fruit, step by step, its spin-off effects would be felt both at home and abroad. There is, however, one difference with the Nehru era. At that time, Nehru was the monarch of all he surveyed. The muted criticism on specific issues by some groups, as noted, hardly mattered. During Atal Behari Vajpayee Prime Ministership, on the other hand, obstructionism had been the norm of the Opposition parties. At every step there was a hurdle.

End Notes

1. Peter Stursberg *Agreement in Principle* 1961 Toronto, Longmans Green and Company. Stursberg covered the British Cabinet Mission negotiations with Indian leaders in the run up to the transfer of power in 1947 as a correspondent of the *Daily Herald*, the daily of the British Labour Party. A Canadian journalist Stursberg specialised in reporting on international developments including the Korean peace talks. He was a great admirer of V.K. Krishna Menon whose diplomatic skill he praised in the book.
2. Abe Rosenthal, who was *The New York Times* correspondent in India soon after Independence was highly complimentary of Vijayalakshmi Pandit when she a minister in the G.B. Pant Government in Uttar Pradesh and later rose to preside over the U.N. General Assembly when I met him in New York in 1980. He had not yet become managing editor of the newspaper then.
3. See G.S. Bhargava *South Asian Security after Afghanistan,* 1983, Lexington Books, D.C. Heath and Company, and Lexington, Massachusetts.
4. Vartan Gregorian, *The Emergence of Modern Afghanistan* 1969, Stanford, California, Stanford University Press.
5. Brajesh Mishra's statement was a reiteration of the then Soviet President, Leonid Brezhnev's declaration, Keesing's Contemporary Archives, Vol. 26, 1980.
6. Dev Murarka, Geopolitics of Brezhnev's Visit, *Mainstream,* 13 Dec. 1980.
7. *Ibid.*
8. 20 June, 1981.
9. John C. Griffiths, 1981, *Afghanistan, Key to a Continent,* Boulder, Colo. West View.
10. *Strategic Survey*, 1996, IISS, London.

11
Soft State Syndrome

A new slogan had become popular in the media in the 1970's. It is that India is a soft State. The connotation in political science is that the State, not merely the Government, has lost the capacity to stand up for what it regards as national interests but will succumb to pressure and blackmail. The talk of a soft state syndrome is not new but it was not so openly voiced earlier. Indira Gandhi, interestingly, used the argument to justify curbs on citizens' rights and liberties, ultimately ending up in the 1975 'emergency'. It is not that her Government had failed to enthuse the people to participate in nation building but that the people were apathetic and slothful. (Like the joke that if the people don't go along with the Government change the people.) Inculcating discipline in the people is not the same thing as riding roughshod over their civil and political rights. Acharya Vinoba Bhave used the euphemistic expression, discipline, to voice his anguish at the 1975 'emergency.'

From the days of Rajiv Gandhi's prime ministership, the favourite question by newspaper persons of a Prime Minister returning from the US had been whether Washington was pressurising India to join, first, the nuclear non-proliferation treaty (NPT) and later the comprehensive test ban treaty (CTBT). The stock answer of the leaders was naturally 'no', but it would be taken as a proforma denial and not an honest statement of the factual position. Implicit in the question and its perennial pursuit is the mindset that subscribing to international treaties seeking to contain spread of nuclear weapons technology and the weapons — the NPT and the CTBT respectively — would be *ipso facto* at the instance of a power like the US and not of India's own volition. If the bulk of the nonaligned States had subscribed to the treaties, it was because they thought their national interests were served that way. They had no stake in keeping out of them nor did they feel it was their international duty to keep out. In the case of

India, on the other hand, retaining what is called the nuclear option was necessary for acquiring nuclear weapon capability which was seen as essential for national security. With both China and Pakistan, in our neighbourhood, flaunting nukes India's conventional military strength might come to naught in a test of wills. Incidentally, no Chinese leader would be asked by journalists whether the Government was being pressurised to sign or not to sign a treaty because they would regard it as unthinkable. But not Indian journalists whose vision is limited to assuming that the Government was amenable to pressure. To this day, 'globalisation' is seen as an imposition.

The argument against joining the CTBT was that abjuring nuclear tests might thwart India's ability to acquire weapon capability, not that India would wage a nuclear war. Arundhati Ghosh, as India's representative at the CTBT talks in Geneva, put up a one-person resistance to the US, China, Russia and other nuclear weapon powers in 1997. Her act of defiance of the CTBT lobby, more than the logic behind it, caught public attention. She became a heroine, like Karanam Malleswari after she won the bronze medal in weight lifting at the Sydney Olympics. All those sniggering at the soft state syndrome had then felt proud of being citizens of not a soft State but a hard State.

Surprisingly, there was no similar elation when in May 1998 India conducted a series of nuclear tests. That was despite the fact that the Shakti tests had achieved the objective of the objection to the CTBT articulated by Arundhati Ghosh. The logical consequence could be that just as China and France, after years of opposition to the NPT, joined both NPT and CTBT after conducting tests to fine-tune their capability, India, too, could subscribe to the CTBT without fear of impairment of its deterrence capability. Especially, when India has committed itself against conducting any more nuclear tests. Also, if the experience of India and Pakistan were an index, going in for more tests in defiance of the treaties would amount to opting out of the international system. Still, there will be few cheers when and if India signs on the dotted line. In other words, strength is identified with foolhardiness.

There is also a subterranean sentiment. While vocal resistance to the treaty in 1997 had no repercussions on the country, the Pokhran-2 (Shakti) tests evoked the wrath of the US, Japan, Germany, and even the European Union to an extent and also naturally China. Economic and other sanctions were clamped on the country by the US and Japan particularly. The 'sacrifice' involved does not jell with our new national character. We want to be heroes without any cost, absolutely free as the advertisements say. Further, while the BJP in opposition in 1997 had endorsed the then Government's resistance to the CTBT as it did not suit the party's policy of going for more nuclear tests, (and earlier hailed the 1974 Pokhran 'peaceful' test)the Congress party in opposition in 1998 was afraid that the BJP might reap the electoral harvest of its active nuclear policy. The Congress leadership contended that the tests were premature, not necessary for India's security and were motivated by the BJP's electoral politics.

Dr. Manmohan Singh's first budget speech in 1991 was famous not only for its initiation of economic reform but also for his eloquent plea against what he called the East India Company complex. The reference was to the deep-seated distrust of international organisations including the United Nations. Ironically, India has been drawing liberally on the World Bank for both technical assistance and credits and had also signed the Indus Waters Treaty with Pakistan, brokered by the International Bank of Reconstruction and Development. Yet, it is seen as surrender of national sovereignty if Government accepts its advice and assistance. This is the East India Company complex, implying that just as the British who had come as traders remained for about two centuries as rulers international investors and the World Bank and IMF would circumscribe India's choice of economic policies, if not political sovereignty itself. International diplomacy is largely a matter of deploying whatever clout a country has for accomplishing what it wants. It is not always true that the big powers alone take recourse to it. A relatively small neighbour like Nepal can get from India what it wants for, otherwise, it might go along with Pakistan on an India-Pakistan dispute. In the late 1950s, Nehru was outraged by the dismissal by King Mahendra of an elected Nepali Congress Government (headed by B.P. Koirala) and replacing the parliamentary system with what was called panchayat democracy. And he said so openly. The Nepal king was wild. In retaliation, he first, began warming up to the Chinese, proclaiming neutrality in the India-China border dispute, which had led to the 1962 conflict. Then he joined Field Marshal Ayub Khan's chorus that the parliamentary system did not suit the people in the hot climates like south Asia and that 'basic' or panchayat democracy based on indirect election of the chief executive was the remedy.

Nehru was scandalised. But he was forced by the need to face what was perceived as a security threat from China into putting up with it. Lal Bahadur Shastri was sent to Kathmandu to humour the king and accept

Tulsi Giri, a Nepali Congress defector picked by the king to be Prime Minister, as a legitimate head of government. Koirala was then languishing in detention in Sunderijal fort. Nobody then called India a soft state, because it was not. India had bowed to the circumstances, which showed realism. However, in the run up to the 1975 'emergency', Indira Gandhi would justify repression against opposition as a necessary antidote to the soft state syndrome.

Take the nuclear Non-Proliferation Treaty (NPT). For nearly twenty years the resistance to India's accession to it was not merely that it was unequal and weighted against non-nuclear weapon states but that it would subject our nuclear power programme to international oversight. The attitude was extended to the CTBT when the US ultimately opted for it in 1994.That Nehru had hailed and wholeheartedly supported the partial test ban treaty about thirty years earlier and that the CTBT was a natural sequel to it did not matter. The same was the case with the agreement regarding cessation of fissile material production. During the prime ministership of P.V. Narasimha Rao, India in 1993 had co-sponsored with the US and others a UN resolution in favour of cessation of fissile material production, which was seen as largely beneficial to India, while Pakistan cribbed that it was weighted against it by allowing India to keep intact its stockpile of fissile material.

Against this background, the Congress party's reaction to the Government's decision that India would not stand in the way of the CTBT becoming operational is opportunism. (It was said Sonia Gandhi did not know what CTBT was and fumbled when a visiting US official met her to "discuss India's attitude to the treaty". Further, both the Rajiv Gandhi Government and its successor headed by Narasimha Rao pursued efforts towards a nuclear weapons test. They did not put an end to India's ongoing efforts in that direction following the 1974. Pokhran-1 'peaceful' test. But it was done on a low key, especially during Narasimha Rao's prime ministership. He had gone out of the way to be one with the US for termination of fissile material production. Presumably the strategy was to approach CTBT negotiations from a position of demonstrated or acknowledged nuclear weapons capability. The BJP-led Government fine-tuned it and carried it to the logical conclusion of Shakti tests in 1998.

There was, however, a sharp change in the Government stance during the years of the United Front Governments headed by Deve Gowda and Inder Kumar Gujral. Firstly, external affairs ministry hotheads had a free hand to reverse the position on both the CTBT and cessation of fissile missile production. Arundhati Ghosh's Geneva outburst was a manifestation of it. Simultaneously, again due to inertia at the higher levels of policy making the preparations for a possible nuclear test were downgraded. It might also be the result of the backfiring of a move by the Narasimha Rao Government to conduct a test in December 1995. It was reportedly leaked out to American intelligence sources and there was pressure on the Government against undertaking the test. The belief in knowledgeable circles in New Delhi was that Arjun Singh masterminded the leak, with or without Sonia Gandhi's knowledge. In retrospect, Narasimha Rao might have hit on the nuclear test idea on the eve of the 1996 general election to regain his lost position. Opposition by Congress factions to his liberalisation programme and his loss of face over the December 1992 Babri masjid tragedy had made it clear to him that he would lose the election. In fact, the Congress party already drifting into the hands of Sonia Gandhi's sycophants had virtually jettisoned him in the elections.

As for the pros and cons of going along with the CTBT, there are both technical and political factors to be weighed. Incidentally, the urgency for India making up its mind has abated with domestic politics in the US having mothballed ratification of the treaty. There is hopefully no prospect of the treaty coming to the fore internationally for some years even if the European Union feels strongly about it. According to our nuclear scientists, including those outside the Atomic Energy Establishment, Pokhran-2 has given us sufficient experience of subcritical tests obviating the need for more explosions. At the same time, it has been conceded that if the scientists are wrong and more tests are needed signing the CTBT will deprive us of the right to do so. Let us assume that the scientists have overestimated. Even without signing CTBT can India undertake more nuclear tests? The Congress party leadership should answer this question without quibbling because of the record of its Governments cited earlier, including that headed by Rajiv Gandhi. If there had been more tests to accompany Arundhati Ghosh's rhetoric the situation would have been easier. Some foreign Governments, including that of the US, had a suspicion that the tests were the result of the BJP's ultra-nationalist approach to national security and that coming down on India would isolate the Government from the people. In this connection, Deve Gowda as former prime minister played a comical role. He did not know from Adam what it was all about. But BJP bashing was his natural wont and he came down heavily on it denying there was any potential threat from China. That must have been music to the ears of US critics of India. The Saddam Hussain syndrome, even if unsaid, was in the air. More importantly, considering the reaction of Japan, G-8 nations and even Russia to Pokhran-2, can India hope to undertake more tests? Following the Geneva disarmament negotiations where Arundhati Ghosh demonstrated her emotional eloquence, the UN General Assembly endorsed the treaty by an overwhelming majority of 158 to three (India, Bhutan and Libya). It is thus even more hazardous than in 1998 to risk another test. Barring Pakistan, which has the luxury of tacking on to India in a bilateral parity game, no other State has kept out of the CTBT. Of the three threshold States, Israel had already fallen in line. North Korea, too, has been tamed and Libya is not much of a nuclear weapon State, even potentially. As for those recognised as nuclear weapon States by the NPT there will be no incentive for undertaking more tests because they have mastery of the sub-critical test technology.

If we look back at the situation which culminated in the passage of the CTBT at the Geneva Conference both China and France had carried out series of underground tests, in defiance of world opinion, before acceding first to the NPT and then to the CTBT. The US, which pretended to be outraged by Pokhran-2, silently connived at them. Thus all the nuclear weapon States have acquired the technology of carrying out sub-critical laboratory tests. In other words, India's desire to see the end of nuclear weapon testing is being fulfilled, even if in a weird way. Elimination of nuclear weapons is, no doubt, a different matter but that will take time. So the question arises whether India should face the consequences of keeping out of the CTBT for the sake of the ideal of a nuclear weapon-free world. When Arundhati Ghosh rhetorically declared at the 1996 Geneva disarmament conference " not now, never," and cast India's vote against the treaty, the situation was qualitatively different. Mention has been made of US connivance at Chinese acquisition of sub-critical test capability in the run up to its adherence to the CTBT. Then both of them, along with the UK, virtually conspired to put India in the wrong by including India among countries which have mandatorily to accede to the treaty before it can come into force The purpose obviously is to deny India a demonstrated nuclear weapon capability. Pokhran 2, code named Shakti tests, defeated that.

In this context, P.K. Iyengar co-architect with Raja Ramanna of the 1974 'peaceful' explosion, thinks that ' the secondary fusion device' could have burst only partially, ' perhaps less than ten percent' in the Shakti tests. That meant that the tests were not adequate for credible thermonuclear capability, much less ability to weaponise He has, therefore, argued that joining the CTBT at this stage would leave India's weapons capability incomplete and to that extent affect the efficacy of minimum deterrence policy.[1] At the same time, he admitted that to go or to go in for more tests with a view to weaponiising is a political decision. According to K. Subrahmanyam, however, thermonuclear capability or weaponisation is not necessary to deter a nuclear attack on the country. It is enough if the potential adversary is convinced that India can inflict unacceptable damage in retaliation. If it were so, why did India undertake the 1998 tests at all? That is the nuclear dilemma.

Still, as Stephen P. Cohen noted, the alternatives are grim. He wrote: "since its birth as a nation 50 years ago, India has seemed poised on the edge of two very different futures. On one side lay greatness, on the other collapse. That drama has now ended and a new one has begun. The spectre of collapse has passed and India is emerging as a major Asian power, joining China and Japan. The 1998 nuclear tests in the Rajasthan desert that announced India's entry into the nuclear club only served to underscore the nation's new stature. India has begun economic reforms that promise at last to realise its vast economic potential."[2]

End Notes

1. Personal Interview.
2. Statement at Nimrana Workshop 1998.

12
The Israeli Connection

Anwar El Sadat, who succeeded Gamal Abdel Nasser as President of Egypt, caused a veritable revolution in the Arab world in November 1977 when he unilaterally visited Israel, still the mortal enemy of the Arabs. He followed it up with signing the first Camp David peace treaty with Israel, under American auspices. As a result, Egypt got back the Sinai Peninsula occupied by Israel in the 1976 war. Although Sadat was assassinated, he was the path breaker for subsequent peace efforts in the region. It took India, nearly twenty more years, to delink relations with Israel from the conventional extremist Arab position that there could be no truck with countries dealing with the Jewish State. It was only in 1992, fortyfive years after the establishment of Israel and its formal recognition by nascently independent India that the P.V. Narasimha Rao Government established relations and exchanged ambassadors with that country.

More recently in July, 2000 Jaswant Singh, became the first Indian External Affairs Minister to visit Israel, thus taking to the logical conclusion the formal step taken eight years earlier. The visit also followed closely Home Minister Advani's tour of Israel a fortnight earlier. So it aroused unusual interest internationally. Meanwhile, much water has flowed in the Nile with the Palestine Liberation Organisation under Yasser Arafat, dealing directly with Israel and negotiating return of occupied territory for integration with the proposed Palestine State. The unsuccessful Camp David meeting between Arafat and the then Israeli Prime Minister, Ehud Barak, was the last in a series of negotiations brokered by President Clinton. As a result, the nucleus of a Palestine State was formed with Israel surrendering the occupied Gaza Strip and West Bank. Jordan and Morocco have followed Egypt's lead in establishing formal diplomatic relations with Jerusalem. Saudi Arabia deals with it through the back door. Only Saddam Hussain's Iraq and Gaddafi's Libya, among the Arab States, and

Iran have stuck to their uncompromising refusal to recognise the Jewish State. Even Syria, for long the most implacable enemy of Israel, had been negotiating with Israel under its former President Assad.

In other words, the situation in the 1950s and 1960s, when Israel was a pariah State to Arab countries, most of which would not even acknowledge its existence and vowed to destroy it is no longer there. Still, there was some cosmetic flutter, both within India and abroad, over the visit and some of the reported pronouncements of the then Indian external affairs minister. Some members of the Congress party took exception to Jaswant Singh's reported statement that the long delay in establishing relations with Jerusalem was on account of the domestic compulsions of the Congress party then in power. It was apprehensive of losing the Muslim vote, its main stay for decades. The theory was that if India-Israel relations annoyed the Arabs its impact would be felt on Muslims who were emotionally attached to their co-religionists abroad. There was also fear that there might be negative fall out in a Muslim majority State like Jammu and Kashmir. More importantly, Pakistan would exploit it for anti-Indian propaganda in Muslim countries as also among Islamists in India. That was what happened following. L.K. Advani's visit to Israel in June 2000. A canard was floated that there had been an agreement between the two countries for cooperation in development of nuclear weapons. Even before the establishment of India-Israel diplomatic relations in 1992, Pakistan would periodically cry wolf about the two countries conspiring to attack it with Israel helping India to launch a pre-emptive strike at Pakistan's nuclear facilities. The basis apparently was Israel's success in preempting development of nuclear weapon capability by Arab States like Iraq. But Pakistan is geographically next door to India, which would not need Israel's technical collaboration to mount such attacks if New Delhi wanted to. Naturally, there were no takers for such stories but this time India had to deny formally that the nuclear issue figured in Advani's talks in Israel.

Still, the Arab League office in Cairo went through the motions of lodging a formal protest with the Indian Ambassador to Egypt. Subsequently, a senior official in the External Affairs Ministry in New Delhi briefed envoys of eighteen Islamic countries of Middle East and North Africa, dispelling misapprehensions about growing India-Israeli relations. About newspaper reports of Advani's mission to ensure bilateral cooperation with Israel to combat 'Islamic fundamentalism' it was explained that the cooperation being developed, not only with Israel, was to counter international terrorism. India has been striving for international action in the matter so that Governments sponsoring and promoting terrorism in the name of religion are isolated and thwarted. It has no exclusive Israeli angle.

Before landing in Israel, Jaswant Singh met Yasser Arafat, Chairman of the Palestine Authority, at Ramallah, on the West Bank. During a stopover at Gaza, he inaugurated an India-funded Mahatma Gandhi Library-cum-Students Activity Centre, meant to spread awareness of India among the Palestinian youth. He also opened a library named after Jawaharlal Nehru at Al-Azhar University at Gaza City. During these formal occasions and in his talks with Palestinian officials, Jaswant Singh reiterated India's support to the "inalienable Palestinian right to reside in internationally recognised territories" which amounted to endorsement of a Palestine State. There was also a tangible commitment of Indian credits for development of tele-communications, power and information technology related projects in Palestine. Indian private investment in the to- be- born State is also on the cards .In other words, no effort was spared to convince the Palestinians that India's expanded relations with Israel would not be at the cost of its traditional support to Palestine. That was why perhaps Palestine was not one of the West Asian entities, which showed concern at India and Israel coming closer.

Long before the establishment of formal diplomatic relations with Israel, India had been after Israeli know-how in water management and modernisation of agriculture. State Governments had been sending study teams to Israel for the purpose and there were also business deals. For instance, Appasaheb Pawar, elder brother of Sharad Pawar, leader of the National Congress Party, told me at Baramati in Pune district that he had been to Israel more than once to study their lift irrigation system and its suitability to India. Arid areas in India, like west Rajasthan and Baramati in Pune, are attracted by Israeli success in irrigating the Negev desert and want to acquire the technology for the purpose. In fact, a part of Baramati has been turned green through scientific management of water from the Neera River and intensive irrigation of the adjacent area. This has been independent of diplomatic relations between the two countries. Now with both countries coming closer the trend will be strengthened. India is also interested in Israeli border defence methods to study which Advani visited Israel. Indian fascination for Israeli defence system has been long standing. A former Israeli defence minister, Moshe Dyan, architect of the 1967 Israeli victory over the combined Arab forces, had visited India secretly in 1978 during the tenure of the first non-Congress government at the Centre. The then prime minister, Morarji Desai, had met him.

As for Arab apprehensions, they are a hangover from the times when Israel was at war both in theory and in practice with all its Arab neighbours, Egypt, Jordan, Syria and Lebanon. Israel also would not part with Arab territory acquired in war, in the name of security. The Arab-Israeli conflict was also partly an offshoot of the East-West Cold War, with the former Soviet Union backing the Arabs and selling huge quantities of arms to them and the US standing by Israel. Thus came into practice the Middle Eastern version of the 'Hallstein Doctrine' according to which West Germany would break ties with countries extending 'full recognition' to East Germany. Interestingly, the USSR was exempt from application of the doctrine. Bonn could not afford to have a formal diplomatic rupture with Moscow. Similarly, the then Soviet Union had diplomatic relations with Israel without its Arab allies batting an eyelid. Just as the 'Hallstein Doctrine' lost its bite with the passage of time, until Willy Brandt as West German Chancellor, ultimately dumped it, so had the Arab anger at countries dealing with Israel begun to abate. For instance, visas to Arab countries were not available to travellers who had been to Israel. One had to have different travel documents to be able to go to both countries. But as long ago as in 1970 when I applied for an Egyptian visa, the consular officer simply tore off the page showing my visit to Israel years earlier and issued the visa for Egypt.

According to Moshe Sharret, a leader of the Israeli Mapai (moderate socialist party) if the 1956 Suez crisis had not intervened, Nehru would have probably opened formal relations with Israel long ago. In our neighbourhood, Burma, Nepal and Sri Lanka had diplomatic relations with Israel then. It was felt that Israel as the only democratic State in the region, had much more in common with India than single-party dictatorships and feudal establishments in the Arab world. It was not uncommon in the early 1950s for Israeli intellectuals and others to visit India and also be allowed to meet Nehru. Sharret was a classic example. He led the Mapai delegation to the first Asian Socialist Conference held in Rangoon. On his way back to Israel, he was to stop over in India for some days and also have a meeting with Nehru. But following Nasser's nationalisation of the Suez Canal Israel joined France and Britain in launching a military attack on Egypt. It happened just then and put the clock back. India was in the vanguard of the States demanding UN action against the aggressors. The twain did not meet for about forty years.The Arab States' hostility to carving out of a Jewish homeland from Palestine and their unsuccessful efforts to thwart it did not make India withhold recognition from Israel.

Nehru had a large number of friends among intellectuals of Jewish origin in the US and elsewhere and shared their sympathy for Israel virtually surrounded by intolerant Arab neighbours. That was the time (in the 1950s) when Israel, isolated internationally, was looking for friends .It had diplomatic relations with Burma (Myanmar now), Ceylon which Sri Lanka was then and Nepal in India's neighbourhood. The socialist governments of the three countries had fraternal relations with the ruling Mapai in Israel. The 1952 Asian Socialist Conference in Rangoon was the high point in this respect.

Ironically, Israel had objectively facilitated the death of feudalist regimes in Arab countries like Egypt, Libya, Iraq and even Syria but the resultant military dictatorships were more intently bent on undoing the Jewish State in their midst than their former feudal rulers. There was thus much sympathy for the beleaguered State but its military collusion with France and Britain destroyed it. The Eisenhower Administration in Washington had come down like a ton of bricks on London and Paris - later sending the Anthony Eden Government packing - but towards Israel it remained a constant bulwark. Indian Military top brass who would have liked to acquire some Israeli defence equipment was aware of the bottlenecks because of US links with Israeli defence establishment. Washington would not have allowed it because India was seen as being on the other side of the fence in the raging East-West cold war. Thus, among the factors contributory to establishment by India of diplomatic relations with Israel in January 1992 was the end of the cold war and the disintegration of the former Soviet Union as well as the Madrid peace process. As a result Tel-Aviv overcame the myopia of treating Yasser Arafat and the Palestine Liberation Organisation as terrorists and refusing to enter into negotiations with them. While India-Israel relations are independent of each other's external relations, efforts towards peaceful settlement of the Middle East crisis will provide a congenial milieu for them. Raging conflict in and around the Palestine area and growing estrangement between Israel and the Palestine leadership have their own imperceptible effect on India-Israeli relations. According to Farah Naaz,[1] although Israel is a late entrant in diplomatic relations with India, it has emerged as an important partner, particularly in the military field. Such a partnership is based on India's realistic assessment of the global and regional security environment as well as technological requirements. India is accelerating its self-reliance programme. Given the problems with Russian purchases, there was need to diversify sources of India's defence equipment. Many looked at the Israeli offer in this context. India could seek Israeli technology and expertise in both lethal and non-lethal areas in which Israeli has credible achievements. It included weapons systems as well as support equipment like radar, electronic warfare equipment and a range of engineering items used in border fencing. The biggest advantage of seeking military co-operation with Israel lies in the fact that its technology is largely indigenous and facilitates technology transfer with no end user problem." This is the crux of India- Israel defence co-operation, which is still in its starting phase.

End Note

1. Research Scholar at the Institute for Defence Studies and Analyses, (IDSA), New Delhi.

13

Water Management*

Where exactly has our fifty years of independence gone sour? A farmer in the field will put his finger on the spot and say in our failure to husband our once ample water resources. That was what Appasaheb Pawar told me at Baramati, in western Maharashtra, in 2000, a few months before he passed away. He should know because he was not only a quintessential agriculturist but has also wrought a veritable revolution in rural development in his area, which is a taluqa of Pune district. Although an elder brother of Sharad Pawar, leader of the Nationalist Congress Party, Appasaheb had no appetite for politics of any variety. He was not apolitical, though, because as the inspiration and moving spirit behind the Agricultural Development Foundation (Krishi Vikas Prathistan), which has transformed Baramati he was a wide-awake and sharply discerning public person. The litmus test to which he put the political leadership of the last fifty years and found it wanting was that while large parts of the country suffered from shortage of water, the rivers emptied themselves into the sea or devastated the countryside through periodical floods. Nearly sixty percent of our hydroelectric potential has remained untapped, while the country is reeling under growing shortage of energy, which is as vital as water, for moving us forward. Nehru had described hydroelectric projects like Bhakra-Nangal and Hirakud as our new temples but today's leaders are more interested in resurrecting temples said to have been replaced by mosques under the Moghuls. So they want to pull down masjids and raise ''grand'' non-productive temples in their sites. Further, when mega projects like Narmada and Tehri are taken up self-centred busybodies bog them down in artificial controversies.

I realised the cost to the nation and to posterity of these petty politics during my visit to Baramati. To begin the story at the beginning,

---

* Appa Saheb passed away in April 2000.

long years ago, in 1959 to be exact, I was swept off my feet to see the Negev desert in Israel blooming, literally. There was profusion of fruit and flower, all geared for export. They even grew mangoes, thought to be the exclusive product of our sub-continent. Eating a mango in Hamburg in Germany, my pride in its having come from India was neutralised when the hosts said it was an import from Israel. Those were the years of a 'socialistic pattern of society' leaving India short of everything, especially food grains. The joke, not so funny, was that the US farmer produced wheat for India, which was shipped to our shores under the Public Law (PL) 480 or as currency for influence, to put it crudely. Israel under a socialist Mapai-led Government practised private enterprise in agriculture. Above all, it pioneered in drip cultivation productively using the water from the Jordan River carried by a pipeline to the Negev area wrested from the Arabs in the 1948 war. Under the Arabs it was arid and mostly fallow.

The provocation for recalling my experience of about fifty years ago was watching drip irrigation, again in action, at Baramati. A third of India is deficient in rainfall and of that another quarter is perennially and acutely short of water for irrigation and even for drinking by humans and animals. Broadly, the average annual rainfall in India varies from 350mm in the west to about 1,000 mm along the middle range to nearly 6,000-mm in the northeast. Except in the northeast where the Khasi-Jaintia Hills receive as much as 2,500 mm of rain on an average, there are sharp variations in rainfall within a district or even inside a taluqa. (It is a different story that even at Cherrapunjee in Meghalaya, which is the wettest place in the country with an average rainfall of 11,314 mm there is shortage of water, thanks to mismanagement.) In Maharashtra the variations in rainfall are striking: while Ratnagari in the Konkan area records an annual rainfall of 2,500 mm, in the case of Solapur it is just 500 mm. At the same time, Satara gets 6,000-mm rainfall in a year. No wonder, it grows the finest quality grapes in the country and has come to be known as the country's potential Champagne, the wine country of France. The taluqa of Baramati, lying between Solapur and Pune is also largely arid. The northern two-thirds of the taluqa is parched like Jaisalmer or Barmer in Rajasthan or Rayalaseema in Andhra Pradesh But visiting Baramati township and its surrounding areas one gets the feeling it is flowing with milk, fruit and sugarcane. It is green and bountiful everywhere with bird and beast in fine fettle. All this is not because the water is plentiful but because it is prudently husbanded.

This is the miracle wrought by Appasaheb Pawar and the Foundation he had built into an unparalleled institution in the last three decades. As

Amartya Sen has empirically established, the British period in our chequered history was marked by periodical famines caused by drought. One such famine in 1876 laid western Maharashtra waste provoking food riots at Baramati and its adjacent areas. The then British administration of Bombay Presidency undertook to build dams on the Mutha River at Khadakvasla and the Krishna at Khodsi as well as dig a canal on the left bank of the Neera River to take water to the dry belt. Even the British administration realised the gravity of the situation, something akin to what is now prevailing in the Kutch area of Gujarat, western Orissa and parts of Rajasthan, and undertook the projects "on a war footing", as the cliché goes. Instead of sticking to the procedure of building the dam first and then proceeding with the canals both were started simultaneously. By the 1950s, however, about 40 villages in the Baramati area stopped getting water from the Neera left-bank canal and steps had to be taken to overcome the situation. That was the time the foundation established by Appasaheb Pawar came into its own. It weighed different alternatives to ensure water supply to the affected villages. Among them was lift irrigation, which was rejected as expensive. Ultimately it opted for the difficult but self-sustaining method of saving every drop of water from the ten to 12 inches of annual rainfall, meticulously planning the management and use of water, digging wells, growing vegetation in the vicinity of Peza tank, etc. These, along with farming on a no-profit no-loss basis, elimination of middlemen, recourse to modern technology in both farming and water management constitute the objectives of the foundation. For industrialisation, a chain of co-operatives was started to make use of the high quality sugarcane grown in the area. Education and health of humans have been provided for. The foundation acknowledges the assistance of two Christian missionaries from Australia in its establishment and growth.

Today, the activities of the Pawar demonstration farm include recourse to drip irrigation to optimise the use of water, farming with modern methods, horticulture for growing export quality fruit, dairy and poultry farming, sheep rearing, sericulture and wine making from high quality grapes grown in the farm. The wine made with technical collaboration from McDowell is supplied to the defence forces. There is provision for technical education, including use of computers. The accent is on girls in this respect to ensure gender justice. Mixed bred cows yield enough milk for being pasteurized and sent to other parts of the State. Most importantly, more and more private farmers learn from the demonstration farm and adopt modern methods of agriculture sometimes with its help.

In short, the success of this entire effort rests on prudent water management. Even if one of the many schemes for water management through linking rivers (the so-called Garland scheme) had materialised, or if riparian States had not been wasting time and money on disputes over water sharing India would have been spared the ordeal of water famine and subsistence farming. This was the background to Appasaheb Pawar's aversion for politicians who have let down the people. This is the story of water with a difference, not a polemical one that hit newspaper headlines.

14

Corruption Incorporated*

The simplest definition of corruption is improper or selfish exercise of power and influence attached to a public office or a position in public life. In other words, any act of commission or omission, to repeat the cliché, by a public servant for securing pecuniary or other material advantage directly or indirectly for personal or family benefit or to favour friends and relatives is corruption. In a democracy like ours, countervailing forces have an opportunity, theoretically, to fight corruption relentlessly because of its accountability to the electors, whereas in a dictatorship the evil is driven underground. I happened to be a correspondent in Pakistan following the seizure of power in 1958 by Field Marshal Ayub Khan who had dispensed with the parliamentary system inherited from the British days and scrapped the legislature. His complaint was that the politicians by their mindless pursuit of power had virtually institutionalised corruption. There was some basis for his charge because the political leaders had not been able to complete the constitution-making process even after ten years since the transfer of power. In India, on the other hand, a democratically evolved constitution had come into force within three years of independence. The Ayub regime had also put down petty corruption with a heavy hand. Officials who had earlier to be humoured with presents and the like for doing their duty would not think of even suggesting that they expected illegal gratification. Even on festive occasions like Eid they would be circumspect in accepting gifts. But corruption at the higher levels had been far from eliminated. When ultimately Ayub Khan had to give up office in 1968 after having been virtually deposed there were charges of

* Text of author's Narla Memorial lecture delivered in December 1997 at Dr. B.R. Ambedkar Open University, Hydrabad, Andhra Pradesh. The Vice Chancellor, Professor Mohammad Afzal, presided over the funtion.

his family members having enriched themselves. So were other military top brass involved in administration. In fact whenever dictators do away with elected establishments or replace each other as in some African countries, they bandy charges of corruption though very soon they themselves fall into the rut. But in a democracy, unchecked corruption cuts at the root of the system and impairs public faith in it. When our Constituent Assembly opted for the parliamentary system in preference to a presidential form of executive, the main consideration was "daily" assessment of responsibility. As B.R. Ambedkar, Chairman of the Drafting Committee told the Constituent Assembly on 4 November 1948: Under the presidential system of America, the President is the chief head of the Executive. The administration is vested in him. Under (our) draft constitution, the President occupies the same position as the King under the English constitution. He is the Head of the State but not of the executive. He represents the nation but does not rule the nation. He is the symbol of the nation. His place in the administration is that of a ceremonial device on a seal by which the nation's decisions arc made known. Under the American Constitution the President has under him secretaries in charge of different departments. In like manner, the President of the Indian "Union has ministers in charge of different departments of administration. Here again there is fundamental difference between the two. The President of the United States is not bound to accept any advice tendered to him by any of his secretaries. The President of the Indian Union is generally bound by his ministers. He can do nothing contrary to their advice. The President of the United States can dismiss a secretary at any lime. The President of the Indian Union has no powers to do so, so long as his ministers command a majority in Parliament.

The Presidential system of America is based upon the separation of the Executive and the Legislature so that the President and his secretaries cannot be members of Congress. Our draft Constitution does not accept this doctrine. The Ministers under the Indian Union are members of Parliament. Both systems of government are, of course, democratic and the choice between the two is not easy. A democratic executive must satisfy two conditions : (a) it must be a stable executive and (b) it must be a responsible executive. Unfortunately, it has not been possible so far to devise a system that can ensure both in equal degree. You can have a system, which can give you more responsibility but less stability. The American and Swiss systems give more stability but less responsibility. The British system, on the other hand, gives you more responsibility but less stability. The parliamentary system differs from a non-parliamentary system in as much as the former is more responsible than the latter but they also differ as to the, time and agency for assessment of their responsibility. The daily assessment of responsibility which is not available under the American system is, it is felt, far more effective than the periodic assessment and it is far more necessary in a country like India. The draft constitution, in recommending the parliamentary system of executive, has preferred more responsibility to more stability."

In other words, the founding fathers clearly opted for day-to-day accountability of the executive besides its need for a renewal of its mandate when it falls short of majority in Parliament. They were apparently apprehensive of stability vesting untrammelled power in the executive, which will not be directly accountable to an elected legislature. Dr. K.M. Munshi, a member of the drafting committee added his voice to Dr. Ambedkar's persuasive explanation. Comparing the working of the American and British systems of executive, he said : "We know that the Constitution in America is not working as well as the British Constitution for the simple reason that the Chief Executive is separated from the legislature. The strongest government and the most elastic executive have been found to be in England and that is because the executive powers vest in the Cabinet supported by a majority in the Lower House which has financial powers under the Constitution. As a result, it is the rule of the majority in the legislature for it supports its leaders in the Cabinet which advises the Head of State, namely the King or President. The King or President is thus placed above the party. He is made the symbol of the impartial dignity of the Constitution. The government in England in consequence is found to be strong and elastic under all circumstances. The power of the Cabinet in England today is not a whit less than the powers enjoyed by the President of the United States of America. By reason of the fact that the Prime Minister and the whole Cabinet are members of the legislature, the conflict between the authority wielding the executive power and the legislature is reduced to a minimum; really there is none at all because at every moment of time the Cabinet subsists only provided it carries with it the support of the majority in Parliament. It is that character of the British constitution which has enabled the British Government to tide over the many difficulties which it has had to face during the last 150 years".

That the accountability of the government in recent years has been far from what it should have been under our parliamentary system, while inadequacy of stability has been more obtrusive than anticipated by the constitution makers, is a different matter. We will look at the likely factors responsible for our falling between two stools, so to say, later. More than the incidence of corruption which perhaps has not been eliminated in any society from time immemorial, attitudes of the public, and more importantly of those vested with administrative and political power, to the prevalence of the malaise and measures to counter it are crucial. The attitudes vary from ideology to ideology, from culture lo culture, from generation to generation and from one mental approach to another. Except in extremely rare cases, nobody in authority will formally and openly condone corruption. It has been so throughout human history, it appears. But when it comes to recognising the evil and taking effective and visible steps to counter it, there is no such universality. The Communists, for instance, would argue that the capitalist system is the fountainhead of corruption. They look upon it as an unavoidable attribute of acquisitive society, which is true. But unfortunately the evil has not disappeared in communist or what they call socialist systems. Following the denigration of Stalin in the former Soviet Union came revealing reports of institutionalised corruption. So was the case in eastern Europe and even in China. But among the factors that had attracted millions of Chinese to the Communists in the 1940s and earlier was their reputation for probity, as it has been the case with Communists of the early years. Dean Acheson as Secretary of State of the United States was on record that what had enabled the Communists to identify themselves with the popular demand for change in the conditions prevailing in Kuomintang China was the image they projected of being inveterate opponents of corruption in public life. He said : "I know from my own personal experience that large numbers of young Chinese college graduates have gone over to the Communist party not because they favoured the ideology of the party but because of their complete disgust with the corruption among the officials of the Chinese (Kuomintang) Government. In the opinion of these young men, the Communist party was trying to do something for the common people and no one accuses the Communist leaders and officials of personal graft."[1]

The western experts, on the other hand, contend that regimentation and concentration of economic and political power breed corruption and that the free enterprise system has countervailing forces against it. There is undoubted validity in the argument but how effective are the countervailing forces and why does corruption prevail, despite dispersal of power and absence of regimentation and concentration of power in the democratic systems? According to Peter H. Odegard corruption is in a sense a product of the way of life of an acquisitive society where "money talks", where what 'works' is justified, and where people are judged by what they have rather than what they are".[2] That would suggest that spiritual values as distinct from material pursuits are an antidote to corruption. By that yardstick, we should, be the least corrupt in the world because spiritualism is said to be the crux of Hindu religion and philosophy. I don't think any of us, including Chandra Shekhar, former prime minister who has taken up cudgels against corruption, will make such a claim. Even the holy places like pilgrim centres and so-called godmen are not free of the curse.

Developing societies are more transitional than traditional. Transitions involve institutional and cultural contention. Conflict among competing elites, cultures and institutions has characterised periods of corruption and scandal from the fourth century Roman empire to the late 19th century America. In early modern Europe sale of office was justified on grounds of efficiency. While it would be looked down upon today as graft, the patrimonial system of government of those times considered office as the property of the office-holder who could sell it to the highest bidder. Social and economic modernisation, even at the pace at which it is taking place in India brings corruption in its wake. Political life in 19th century America was said to be more corrupt than in the preceding centuries. Similarly, in the case of Britain, the high point of corruption coincided with the impact of the industrial revolution and the emergence of new classes in the eighteenth and early nineteenth centuries. When modernisation is said to breed corruption, the reference is not merely to the industrial society which, "offers prizes for doing evil: money, position, power" but also to the attitudinal changes it induces in the system. Now loyalties and new identifications emerge among groups and individuals and the concept of equality before the law takes shape. Groups who are most affected by such a change in the basic values of the society, the intelligentsia and the professionals mostly, begin to judge the old society by new norms. This can be an explanation for the widespread impression of a quantum jump in the incidence of corruption in public life in the recent years. As the Harvard sociologist, Samuel P. Huntington put it, "corruption in a modernising society is thus in part not so much the result of deviance of behaviour from accepted norms as it is the deviance of norms from the established patterns of behaviour."

At the same time, the challenge to old standards and norms initially undermines the legitimacy of all standards, which leads to a kind of free-for-all as far as adherence to the values of society is concerned. This seems to be the phenomenon of India in societal transition. This can be an explanation for public preoccupation with highlighting corruption in public life. very often as a tool of political warfare. That modernised, as distinct from modernising societies, take it in their stride underscores the point. For instance, it was nearly proved that some Conservative members of Parliament in Britain had accepted money from interested parties to table questions in Parliament but the issue hardly figured in the election campaign, except perhaps at the local level. Similarly, in the U.S., questionable campaign contributions are talking points in the slanging matches between the Republicans and the Democrats within Congress and outside but they seem to fade out of currency in the run up to the Congressional and presidential elections.

Further, modernisation sharpens the distinction between public welfare and private gain. While it thus brings into question the traditional approach of identifying the family with the State it also stimulates such identification because those threatened with erosion of their position will reassert themselves by traditional means. In Haryana, for instance, when politicians like Om Prakash Chautala, Devi Lal's son and Bhajan Lal, among others, are known to have enriched their families, their constituents do not abandon them. Instead, they expect to be similarly benefited depending on their position in the semi- feudal society. Even those who have no means of emulating them do not agree that enriching one's family is corruption. There is an interesting incident, not at all apocryphal, about Bhajan Lal when he was Janata Party chief minister of the State. A German tractor company opted to set up a manufacturing unit in the State and was duly welcomed with availability of ground and infrastructural facilities. When the factory was being established the chief minister sent for the top official of the company and recounted to him how the Stale Government had speedily, met with the requirements for launching the enterprise. "What do we get from it ?" he asked the company manager, making himself clear without committing himself.

Either on account of his ignorance of the practices in India - those were the hey-days of licence-permit raj - or feigning incomprehension, the German entrepreneur started to reel out the benefits which will accrue such as fillip to industrialisation of the State, employment opportunities and increased tax revenues." But how does that all benefit me?" the chief minister blurted out.[3] Most other politicians, arraigned for malfeasance, notably Pratap Singh Kairon in undivided Punjab, Bakshi Ghulam Mohammad, in Jammu and Kashmir, Krishna Ballabh Sahay in Bihar, among others, similarly resisted introduction of achievement standards which did not suit their traditional family interests.

There is also a dichotomous dimension to the prevalence and spread of corruption in India. While the system of privilege largely associated with private enterprise economies is at the root of most political corruption, in our country and some other developing societies, the so-called underprivileged are more prone to use political power for pecuniary purposes. Bakshi Ghulam Mohammad and Pratap Singh Kairon, among others, were millionaires of middle-class origin. Former South American dictators like Batiste in Cuba, Perez Jimenez in Venezuela and Trujillo in the Dominican Republic were commoners before they enriched themselves in office. In Thailand and Philippines, similarity, the mobility from poverty to riches was facilitated by misuse of political power. There is 'also another qualitative difference between corruption in public life in India and that in countries like the U.S. called modernised societies. In the U.S., for instance, money power invariably plays a role in politics and is a source of political power, but rarely does political power yield money power. Men and women who want to make money go into business where opportunities for success are plentiful. But the rich enter politics where their wealth bestows an advantage on them in enlarging their power. It is a different matter that contributors to campaign funds are rewarded without any inhibition. In India, on the other hand, political power is often a means to economic power and enrichment of individuals and families at the expense of the public.

Politics in India is not an art or science of government but a national obsession. This was an asset in the pre-Independence days because it had provided the nation with a single-minded determination to free itself of foreign political domination. When leaders like Motilal Nehru, Sardar Vallabhbhai Patel, Rajendra Prasad, Subhas Chandra Bose and Tanguturi Prakasam were drawn into politics to give up their avocations they had brought into public life the virtue of sacrificing private gain for public weal. While it is understandable that public life today may not similarly involve abandonment of personal interest, the present-day accent is on persons, with or without any other claim to recognition, seeking personal advancement by purely political means. Kwame Nkurmah's parody of the Christian watchword, "Seek ye first the kingdom of politics" has become the main driving force in public life. Every aspect of national life agriculture, industry, commerce, administration, even literature, the arts and sports has a political projection. This has endowed politics with an unhealthy aspect of a vehicle for personal aggrandisement in more ways than one. There have been two kinds of consequences of this situation. First, politicised corruption has cast its pall on other spheres of activity, including administration. Thus, legislative and other measures to cleanse the administration end up in political roadblocks. Secondly, fighting corruption is politicised so that bringing the corrupt to book assumes the aspect of inter-party and intra-party feuds. The Committee on Prevention of Corruption (it is better known as Santhanam Committee after its chairman) was the first of its kind in independent India. Lal Bahadur Shastri who was Home Minister established it in June 1962. According to its terms of reference, it was to examine the working of the vigilance units in the ministries and departments of the Government and the Special Police Establishment (SPE) and suggest measures further to improve their functioning. It was also to suggest changes in the Government Servants Conduct Rules and the rules relating to disciplinary proceedings against officials, to ensure speedy trial of bribery, corruption and criminal misconduct. Although political corruption was specifically beyond the purview of the committee, it had taken advantage of one of the terms of reference asking it to recommend measures "that would conduce to the creation of a social climate both among public servants and in the general public in which bribery and corruption may not flourish."

Despite the negative tenor of the term of reference, the committee rejected the contention that at the political level "ministers, legislators and party officials were free from the malady." Advocating prompt action to improve the image of the public man the committee lamented evaporation of the idealism and moral values which characterised freedom struggle under the leadership of Mahatma Gandhi. Recommending 'preventive and punitive' measures to ensure 'absolute integrity on the part of ministers at the Centre and in the States it wanted a code of conduct to be prescribed for ministers putting them on par with other public servants 'in the matter of acquisition of property, acceptance of gifts and disclosure of assets and liabilities.' The prime minister at the Centre and the chief ministers in the State were to be responsible for enforcing the code. (Incidentally, it has been the contention lately of legislators and ministers facing corruption charges that they are not public servants for application of anti-graft laws).

Dealing with charges of corruption levelled against ministers, it suggested that when a minimum of ten members of Parliament or a State legislature made a written complaint against an incumbent minister and forwarded it to the prime minister or a chief minister through the respective presiding officers, the charges should be immediately referred to a committee for investigation. The Government turned down the proposal saying that it would put a premium on legislators bandying charges. As a result, instead of legislators owning responsibility for charging ministers and others with corruption by putting them in writing and submitting the documents to the presiding officer of the legislature of which they are members for onward transmission to the head of the government, the practice has grown of their making sweeping charges orally against occupants of the Treasury Benches without the obligation to stand by their complaints and face the consequences. Thus, what the Government feared would happen if the Santhanam Committee recommendation had been acted upon has come to pass but without the Government having to investigate even valid complaints. Referring to the Government's proposal of the head of the government investigating the charges to establish a prima facie case before ordering an investigation, Santhanam pointed out in a newspaper article that 'corruption of this kind should not only be checked but it should also be seen to be checked'.[4]

The Santhanam Committee stressed the need for creating a social climate against corruption. It meant that in addition to punitive and preventive measures against graft an atmosphere should be created in which the corrupt-including those not cleared of corruption charges by an appropriate court of law - could not thrive. The proposed changes in the election law for rejection of nomination papers of candidates facing corruption charges are an instance in point. Political parties have to be made to distance themselves from such persons and not entrust them with responsibility. Whatever be the real reasons for the Congress leaders blackballing P.V. Narasimha Rao for involvement in corruption cases, it was a positive development, so was the dropping of Sukhram from the Congress party even if the Himachal MP could not be disqualified pending conviction. The former chief minister of Bihar, Laloo Prasad Yadav, had been forced to resign when he was prosecuted in the the fodder scam case 1997. First he left the Janata Dal to form his own Rashtriya Janata Dal and put his wife in the chief minister's chair. He had been thriving in more senses than one since then, dodging the courts and rigging elections. He is now a Cabinet colleague of the 'clean' Prime Minister, Dr. Manmohan Singh.

There have been recurring instances in our country, as in many other developing countries, of the high and mighty stooping low to make money at the expense of people who repose faith in them and elect them to public office. Many explanations arc offered for the phenomenon. First, most of the newly independent States of Asia and Africa have been telescoping centuries into decades. What the industrialised countries of the west did in 500 years, that, too with colonial possessions to fall back upon, Asian nations are set to accomplish in 50 years. It entails inadequate attention to details and procedures evolved by the colonial powers to ensure accountability of officials and their political masters. The procedures are also cumbersome in some cases and can lead to avoidable litigation on technical grounds. For instance, while inviting tenders for execution of public works is an accepted method of ensuring transparency, rigid insistence on it in all situations can also be counterproductive to the larger purpose. For instance, Biju Patnaik, as chief minister of Orissa, got the deep sea port of Paradeep on the Orissa coast built in about two years, a record achievement, especially compared to more than two decades which the then British Government had taken to develop the Visakhapatnam port. If one computed the opportunity cost of extended completion of projects and the economic and other benefits accruing from their speedy execution, it will be wrong to harp on the technical irregularities in the completion of the Paradeep project. As B.G. Verghese passionately argued in the *Times of India*, "Paradeep is a symbol of the effete 'system' to which the country has become prisoner and of the outmoded norms and codes that constitute the current framework of development... The Press, politicians and the private sector never tire of complaining of bureaucracy, red tape and inefficiency and delay.... Initiative, however, entails, breaking out of the system and the moment this is done every fury is let loose: there is immediate cry for heads on charges of irregularity, procedural impropriety, suspected corruption and worse.... Political vendetta has also blinded the vision."[5]

The other side of the medal is that in the absence of transparency and adherence to procedures, talk of corruption overshadows the positive side of development. This has led in our country to the dichotomy of the Government highlighting the development projects and the opposition publicising the 'corruption' that goes with them. The result is a negative psychological atmosphere for a developing economy. The most glaring instance in Andhra Pradesh was the tendency of the Opposition Congress politicians to level wild charges of corruption and mismanagement in connection with the *Janmabhoomi* programme of the Telugu Desam Government. The charges are often sweeping and general and there has been no effort, it seems, to have them investigated by either a legislative body or an appropriate judicial authority. If the Santanam Committee proposal, cited earlier, had been accepted the legislators would have been loath to make wild charges against all and sundry and when a minimum of ten of them made written complaints to the chief minister through the presiding officer of the legislature they would have to be investigated to the satisfaction of the complainants.

During the freedom struggle days, Mahatma Gandhi was an unrelenting enemy of corruption. While he missed no opportunity to expose corruption implicit in the colonial system of administration, juxtaposing the extravagant ways of the rulers with the poverty of the mass of people, he never made a specific charge without satisfying himself of its tenability. Secondly, he linked corruption to vulgar consumption in a society marked by abject poverty and advocated curbs on wants. That was how the first Congress ministries in the provinces (as the States were then called) had voluntarily scaled down their salaries to Rs. 500 from Rs. 5,000 and had to lead austere lives. He made himself the watchdog of public behaviour of his followers even at the risk of overshooting the mark and punishing the innocent. The ruthlessness with which he enforced standards of public behaviour would be hard to fathom in these permissive days. For instance, he objected to the Lion of Andhra, Tanguturi Prakasam, being made the premier (chief minister) of the presidency even when he enjoyed the support of the majority of the legislators. The reason was, in his assessment, Prakasam did not live up to the standards of rectitude he expected from his followers. His crime was that he had diverted Rs. 30,000 from a purse presented to him as Congress leader to buy a car for his personal use. Gandhiji argued that purses presented to political workers should go into party coffers and not used for personal purposes. When Prakasam volunteered to reimburse the amount, Gandhiji pertinently asked him how he proposed to raise the money. Even if there was no formal *quid pro quo* in his being the head of the provincial administration, his finding the money from his 'friends' would be suspect. In short, he condemned the great man who had given up a roaring practice at the bar when he plunged into the national movement and had reduced himself to virtual penury.[6]

Many of us then had attributed motives to the Mahatma for pillorying a personification of sacrifice like Prakasam. But in retrospect, Gandhiji was right even if he was unduly harsh. After the Mahatma's assassination and during Nehru's prime ministership, the pendulum had swung to the other extreme. Standards of rectitude in public life came to be determined by political considerations. Thus, when V.K. Krishna Menon was put in the dock by the public accounts committee of parliament on charges of irregularities in the acquisition of jeeps for the army, Nehru unilaterally absolved him of responsibility for the lapse and claimed that by winning a bye-election to the Lok Sabha from North Bombay Krishna Menon had vindicated himself before the higher tribunal of the electorate. The argument has become common in recent years.

There were other instances also of politicians charged with corruption not being made to face trial. Among them were the former chief ministers of Punjab and Jammu and Kashmir, Partap Singh Kairon and Bakshi Ghulam Mohammed respectively. The argument, perhaps valid in the light of their perceived indispensability for stability in the strategic frontier States, has over the years become a convenient alibi for shielding suspect politicians. Accountability has been a casualty in the process. Paradoxically, when P.V. Narasimha Rao, as prime minister reversed the trend in 1995 and allowed nearly a dozen members of his council of ministers, besides a respected BJP leader like Lal Krishna Advani, to be prosecuted in the hawala cases, he was seen to have been guided by vendetta and partisan motives. It was widely felt that he had been hoist with his own petard when he was hauled up in criminal cases involving corruption. It is the first time in independent India that a former prime minister faced trial on criminal charges of bribery and cheating. Although Rajiv Gandhi was implicated in the Bofors scandal. He got himself exonerated by a handpicked joint parliamentary committee. Even after many years there is no prospect of the case being clinched when he was dastardly assassinated and the matter ended. The Congress party is shy of getting his name cleared by a courty of law for its own reasons.

When the 1989 general election to the Lok Sabha was fought mostly on the Bofors issue and led to the rejection of Rajiv Gandhi's party by the electors, it was thought that an effective antidote to corruption might employ the ballot box to counter it and, failing that, public opinion would grow cynical saying 'plague on both your houses' to the different contenders for power. But, this kind of public opinion is less effective than it ought to be in a democracy, as long as there are a large number of electors to counterbalance it, to whom corruption causes no great concern, either because they do not understand it or because they take it for granted: they do not see why a man should take the trouble of getting himself elected unless there is some thing in it for him, and if there is something in it for them in the shape of a bribe everyone is happy.

It may sound cynical but it reflects the ground situation in populous democracies like ours with millions of illiterate voters being swayed by caste and religion and the credibility of most of the contestants is low. Electoral reform in the shape of Sri Krishna Kant's idea of majority replacing plurality so that the present system of first past the post gives way to insistence on the winner polling more than 50% of the vote, if necessary through repeated balloting, can be a remedy. Caste and religious considerations will cease to be effective in such a situation because practically in no constituency—especially for the Lok Sabha—can they clinch the issue. The second requirement is publicity of corruption cases. The newspapers have done a good job lately bringing the issue before the courts and forcing the executive to act. But there is the attendant risk of the press overdoing it like for instance condemning persons even before they are tried and presenting charge-sheets as proven cases. The former Chief Justice of India, Justice J.S. Verma, had been cautioning journalists against trial by the media, which will compound the problem by making corruption a political weapon. In short, there is no simple answer to the question of competition in public life nor can there be a single remedy. But once the problem evokes public awareness there is every hope of its being contained by a judicious combination of measures and persistent efforts by you and me, the people of the country.

End Notes

1. Extract from State Department publication, *U.S. Relations with China*, 1944-49, 1950 Washington DC.
2. *Political Corruption—United States* by Peter Odegard quoted in *Corruption: Control of Maladministration*, John B. Monterio, 1960, Bombay, Manaktalas.
3. Narrated to me by the Indian director of the German company.
4. The *Times of India*, 20 October, 1964.
5. The *Times of India*, 7 June, 1965.
6. Ramnath Goenka who had personal knowledge of Prakasam's economic condition told me that the Prakasam couple often did not have two meals a day in those harrowing days.

15

Punishing the Corrupt?

On the face of it, the conviction of a former Prime Minister of India, P.V. Narasimha Rao, on charges of bribing members of Parliament should have been an earth-shaking event. It was said to be to win their support for his government facing a parliamentary challenge. Despite rule of law and equal justice for all being enshrined in the Constitution, in practice the experience has been that some are more equal than others even in the eyes of the judiciary. It is not because the judges are squint-eyed but the judicial process gives the powerful and the rich ample latitude in, first, escaping detection and then in ducking punishment. Against this background that the law, even if it has ground slow, has ground finely and caught up with one of the biggest fishes, is no small reason for excitement. But except perhaps a handful of his personal adversaries in the Sonia Congress party, the others see no reason to rejoice. They are unmoved. Even the chattering classes are relatively quiet, while for the 'common man' it might have happened in the Philippines or Indonesia. In fact, there was comparatively more perceptible public interest when President Clinton was in the dock for impeachment for having had an affair with a White House employee and lied about it on oath. The reason simply was the publicity attending the Clinton trial, before, during and after the Senate proceedings. Equally, man-woman relationship at that level has mass appeal.

In Narasimha Rao's case, on the other hand, in the context of widespread perception that present day MPs are often on sale, his crime pales into the common place. The Supreme Court itself has ruled that being bribed is no offence for a legislator. The motive, saving his government against parliamentary censure is even more unexciting. It is the done thing always and perhaps everywhere. Most importantly, the incumbent government today is neutral. It has no axe to grind either in Narasimha Rao's conviction or acquittal, even if ardent supporters of L.K.

Advani within the BJP, who were outraged by their leader being charged in a hawala case by the Narasimha Rao Government, might have felt avenged. Biter bitten, they would have revelled like the editor of a Delhi newspaper who spoke for Madhavrao Scindia, another alleged victim of Narasimha Rao's supposed vendetta against potential political rivals.

Let us, for a moment, conjure up an 'iffy' - to borrow President Eisenhower's over-used expression-scenario; in fact, a multi-'iffy' scenario. If Rajiv Gandhi had been guilty of receiving kickbacks in the celebrated Bofors howitzer deal, and if, after having been investigated in the teeth of a massive cover-up, had been ultimately convicted, there would have been an orgy of action and reaction. The reasons: Rajiv was the first prime minister to be defeated in a general election on corruption charges, defeated in the sense that from a whopping two-thirds majority in the Lok Sabha his party had fallen short of qualifying to form government in the 1989 general election. The people were actively involved in the raging campaign for weeks on end. Viswanath Pratap Singh had led his makeshift Janata Dal to power on the issue and promised to unearth the scandal within a year. After long years the Bofors case is still hanging fire with high voltage accused like Quattrochhi and the Hinduja brothers evading appearance in the court. Conviction in such a 'lost case' would have stirred people's emotions. Also, the posthumous accused, Rajiv Gandhi, was a dynast, unlike Narasimha Rao who had been initially seen as Prime Minister by default. As stated, the Congress party cannot resign itself to seeing the Bofors case disposed of. At least two governments had been toppled to stall the prosecution.

In 1998, when the Vajpayee Government was voted out by one vote, with Sonia Gandhi and Jayalalitha making common cause for the purpose, it was widely believed that the driving force was prevention of crucial action in the Bofors case. As for the Viswanath Pratap Singh Government in 1990, it would not have collapsed within one year, if it had not been feared that the CBI investigation in the Bofors case was closing in on Rajiv Gandhi. Similarly, if Indira Gandhi had been held to have struck the HDW submarine deal with Germany for its pecuniary fallout for her party through her, there would have been a national convulsion. In 1975, when her election to the Lok Sabha had been set aside on technical grounds and she was on the verge of losing the prime ministership, she imposed emergency on the country, gagged the press, put thousands of political opponents in jail and unwittingly precipitated her own 1977 downfall. The world's largest democracy was at work, both positively and negatively. A born fighter, Indira Gandhi would not have tamely acquiesced in her conviction for felony, or like Narasimha Rao pleaded for clemency on grounds of old age and long political record. In the process, the country would have witnessed a many-sided upheaval.

Even if Narasimha Rao's conviction has been a tame affair relatively, it is not totally devoid of significance. Cynics might contend that while Narasimha Rao has been caught, there are many who escaped detection and punishment, not merely the co-accused in the same case like Bhajan Lal, Satish Sharma and his own nephew. His bitter experience could put his blood brothers on their guard to thwart the law from taking its own course. For instance, it was an open bazaar for Janata Dal MPs in 1990 when Chandra Shekhar brought down the wobbly V.P. Singh Government to make himself 'Prime Minister' of a rump party. Rajiv Gandhi facilitated the change 'from outside,' apparently fine-tuning the strategy, if not oiling the defections.

Nevertheless, the widespread feeling that when it comes to the crunch the law does not take its own course for those who can manoeuvre to stay out has received a deserving jolt by Narasimha Rao's conviction. It is a huge institutional gain. No law is foolproof and no remedy fail-safe. To fault a positive development on the ground that it is not perfect smacks of negative thinking. Still, Narasimha Rao's distinction that he is the first ex-prime minister to have been found guilty of political corruption for what he has done in the high office is dubious. Here again, his record is by default. Among his illustrious predecessors, Indira Gandhi perfected the art of staying in power. She imposed the emergency and sought to put herself beyond the reach of law in 1975 when her election was quashed by the Allahabad High Court and the Supreme Court would not restore her position. During the Janata period, an army of muscle-flexing supporters made capital out of Charan Singh's folly in arresting her. More originally, the very same Rajnairain who defeated her at the polls was won over - by what means only Sanjay Gandhi knew -to sow the seed of destabilisation of the Morarji Desai Government. Winning over MPs was no crime then, presumably because it was to bring down a government and not prop one.

Her son and successor, Rajiv, moved heaven and earth to ensure a gigantic cover-up, worldwide, when he found the Bofors bribes case developing. Later, while in opposition, how he ensured that a Government trying to crack open the mystery of Swiss bank accounts came crashing down has been mentioned already. As long as Rajiv was Prime Minister he used his party's massive majority in the Lok Sabha, won on the crest of a sympathy wave in 1984, to block even a free discussion on the Bofors scandal. The Opposition parties stupidly led by Viswanath Pratap Singh retaliated with wrecking tactics. It was not filibuster in the sense in which the tactic is understood in the US. It was not even the method popularised by the Luddites in the UK - and borrowed by Maniram Ram Bagri, Rajnairain and Madhu Limaye in our Lok Sabha in the late 1960s. In 2000, the outnumbered Opposition groups in the Lok Sabha adopted the same tactics to disrupt proceedings for days on end to harass the incombent government. That was despite the BJP-led Government's readiness to discuss issues. They did not want any debate. They wanted to reduce Parliament into a bazaar with the presiding officers meekly succumbing.

Reverting to the corruption charges against Narasimha Rao, the first requirement of avoiding his fate is to have a supportive government to rein in the CBI. After the 1996 general election, the only way of Narasimha Rao doing it was to keep the BJP out of office and put a Deve Gowda on the gaddi, owing his survival to the Congress party. But the internal dynamics in the faction-ridden Congress party gave a handle to Sonia Gandhi to manipulate Narasimha Rao's ultimate downfall. First, they facilitated Sitaram Kesri's *coup* and the subsequent bad blood between Kesri and Gowda. It did not take long for Kesri to be administered a dose of his own medicine and be elbowed out ignominiously. Then the choice for Narasimha Rao was between a government headed by Sonia Gandhi or a return of the BJP to office after an election. The situation would have been perhaps worse for Narasimha Rao if Sonia Gandhi's game plan had worked and Mulayam Singh had not strayed out of the team. The BJP Government at least was neutral and would have perhaps allowed the CBI to have its way. There was still a chance of the prosecution not being able to establish the charge to the judge's satisfaction. But it was not to be. In other words, Narasimha Rao did not have the political props, which helped Indira Gandhi and her son before him.

Even if the good is oft buried with one's bones, Narasimha Rao's record as Prime Minister needs to be recalled, when the evil will live after him. He breathed life into an ailing economy by opting to do away with licence-permit raj and liberating productive forces from the stranglehold of bureaucracy. Dr Man Mohan Singh, who was the architect of the reform with Narasimha Rao's approval, is one of the few Congress leaders who has not abandoned him in his trauma. It speaks not only of the economist's culture and good breeding but also of the bond of affection between him and his past leader. Narasimha Rao's advent as Prime Minister marked the end of the cold war and the eventual collapse of the Soviet Union. India having been over-dependent on Moscow's political support and economic relations in the shape of vital defence supplies, the transition to a unipolar international system was tricky business. Narasimha Rao handled it deftly, slowly building bridges with the US. While he did not eschew the nuclear option, either openly or otherwise, he also did not believe in wearing it on his sleeve. So he was able to make common cause with Washington in promoting a regime of a comprehensive ban on nuclear testing and end to missile production. The smoothness with which he established diplomatic relations with Israel, forty-four years after India recognised the Jewish State, without antagonising Yasser Arafat and moderate Arabs is a lesson in diplomacy. For the Congress party, he restored internal democracy and held organisational elections for the first time in two and a half decades. True, it was not a smooth affair and the remnants of earlier practices persisted, requiring him, as party president, to pack the executive and offend ambitious rivals. Above all, he set out to end dynastic leadership in the party. Given time, he would have perhaps accomplished it. That would have also meant a different end to his story. But it was not to be and he has paid the price of the attempted reform.

Ironically, Narasimha Rao would modestly recall after having become Prime Minister that his ambition was to follow in the footsteps of his father and become a lawyer at a district court in Andhra Pradesh. Instead, he rose to the highest political position in the country. The success did not go to his head but it rendered him blind to the wealth-amassing activities of his kith and kin. It was said he gave a free rein to his nephew, who was ultimately his undoing, out of gratitude to his uncle who helped him in his youth. Even when it was public knowledge in Hyderabad and elsewhere that his sons and the nephew were making too much hay, with impunity, as it were, he remained unconcerned, as he did when vandals brought down the Babri masjid at Ayodhya and undercut minority support to him in December 1992. Finally, notwithstanding the conviction for corruption, Narasimha Rao's place in history will not disappear, only it will be blurred, and may be touched by tragedy. For the Sonia Congress party which condones the corruption of Jayalalitha and Laloo Prasad Yadav without batting an eyelid and which stood by Indira Gandhi and her son in similar circumstances, the double-speak on Narasimha Rao's plight will mean further loss of middle class esteem. There should be honour even among thieves and the thieves who fail in the test are brigands.

16

The Caste System

How far and with what assurance has the Indian constitution in its working in the last fifty years lived up to the promise of the fundamental human rights enshrined in it, ushering in a humane and human rights-prone society in the country? The crux of the answer to this question is the success of the Statute and those entrusted with its working in mitigating societal wrongs like the caste system in Hindu society. For countries, which go by the nomenclature of Islamic or for that matter countries with theocratic qualifications, to claim to be republics or democracies can be a mixture of contradictions. Islam in theory is a highly egalitarian faith free of the curse of the caste system marring Hindu society. The practice, however, is different. They are rarely democratic in the sense of endowing every citizen, man and woman, with the right to vote and to be entitled to equality before law. Gender discrimination is the rule, rather than the exception. Persons belonging to non-Islamic faiths are denied equal opportunities, especially in the political sphere. No non-Muslim can be elected president or Prime Minister in an Islamic State.

In India, both Islam and Christianity further complicate the situation in practice by being contaminated by the caste system. Persons belonging to these faiths cannot shed their pre-conversion caste label. I have seen in Pakistan that *bhangi* (*sweeper*) Christians cannot go in for inter-marriages with their fellow Christians. The only saving grace is that during Id and other religious community feasts they are not excluded even if they do not mix with better-off or upper caste guests. I was told that it was due to class differences, rampant in the semi-feudal social system. It is so to an extent in Anglican and other non-Catholic theocracies. But when they are constitutional monarchies like the United Kingdom or countries of Scandinavia and northern Europe (Norway, Sweden, Denmark, the Netherlands, Belgium etc.) the problem is simplified due to the practice of dynastic succession of the constitutional Head of State. Since the custodian of executive authority, the prime ministership, is a political office open to all citizens they are democracies. In the democratic republic of the United States of America, as Dr. Henry Kissinger ruefully noted, birth as a US citizen is necessary for seeking the Presidentship[1]. Naturalised Americans like the celebrated former Secretary of State are barred. Still, eyebrows are raised when a Roman Catholic or a Jew is on the slate of nominees for the posts of President and Vice-President. Blacks, once victims of racism and slavery, have graduated to top military and other positions. So might Hispanics and Asian Americans in the not too distant future, thanks to the vibrant dynamism of the system and the social mobility engined by a free enterprise economy.

In India, on the other hand, form outshines facts of life as determinants. We have had two Muslim and one Sikh of Heads State. Non-Hindus have held top positions in the defence Services. The view that only persons of Indian birth should be eligible for the top elective posts of President, Vice-President and Prime Minister has been under intense discussion in the recent years. If it is motivated by a desire to exclude non-Hindus, by making it virtually communal, it will be obnoxious. But if the purpose is to stall dynastic succession to political positions in a republican democracy it is to be welcomed. In the name of keeping open the top positions in the polity to all faiths and persuasions, a backdoor cannot be opened to perpetuate feudalistic dynastic practice in the polity, thus vitiating the basic republican structure of our polity.

The Fundamental Rights Chapter (III) of our Constitution covering equality before law (Art.14), prohibition of discrimination on grounds of religion, race, caste, sex or place of birth (Art. 15), equality of opportunity in matters of public employment (Art.16), abolition of untouchability (Art.17), protection of certain rights regarding freedom of speech (Art.19), protection in respect of conviction for offences (Art.20), protection of life and personal liberty (Art.21) and freedom of conscience and free profession, practice and propagation of religion (Art.25), to cite the vital privileges of Indian citizens, is a veritable Magna Carta of human rights culture. According to Subhash Kashyap,[2] "coming closely on the heels of the Universal Declaration of Human Rights, inclusion of a bill of rights in the Constitution of India accorded with the contemporary democratic and humanitarian temper and constitutional practice in other nations of the world. It reflected in no small measure the anxiety of the founding fathers to incorporate and implement the basic principles enunciated in the

Universal Declaration of Human Rights. Also incorporation of a charter on Fundamental Rights in the Constitution became necessary in view of the special problem of minorities and the need to assure them of the fullest protection of their rights."

In retrospect, however, some of the guaranteed rights like that to propagate religion have in practice vitiated into licence for proselitisation. It is incorporated with a view to ensuring India's continuance as a secular State, free of a State religion. The idea as elaborated by Pandit Nehru and other founding fathers of the Constitution was to keep India non-denominational, not 'secular' in the western sense, which requires religion "not to interfere in State affairs". It will mean equality for all religions, incumbent and new, named and unnamed, to be practised without let or hindrance. It also implies that no religion should interfere with the practice of other religions through pressure and other tactics by its practitioners. Such secularism could have been better ensured by making it rooted in the Hindu pluralist approach, as Dr. S. Radhakrishnan has said. "An ample expression of all sides of human nature in their highest forms, economic organization animated by community feeling, a democratic system supported by education and striving for the least inequality of opportunity and the fostering of oneness of outlook and feeling as the basis of international relations, these were the goals of a truly religious person, whatever his denomination."[3] The question of relevance of secularism and its operation in India to human rights culture will naturally arise. The answer is simple and straightforward. Inter-religious disharmony and strife flowing from it are least conducive to human rights culture. It is evident in India for the last few years. First, the right to propagate religion enshrined in the constitution of secular India has become grist to persons claiming to be followers of the incumbent Pope, His Holiness Pope Paul. His theme of the 21st century being the millenium of christianisation of Asia was sought to be achieved through religious conversion by all means. Its backlash among intolerant Hindus has been on expected lines of fanaticism and fantasy. They even want us to believe that Christians who now constitute less then two percent of India's one billion people will one day overwhelm the Hindus accounting for about eighty percent of the population! Egged by anti-Christian propaganda there have been incidents of violence against Christian institutions and personnel. The resultant tension and turmoil have vitiated the prospects of human rights culture being promoted.

Meanwhile, the state policy of secularism has been professionalised and debased into a tool of power politics. The Ram Janmabhoomi movement and the subsequent outrage of the demolition of Babri mosque at Ayodhya would not have been possible but for the widespread feeling among even educated Hindus that Muslims were being 'appeased' for their block votes as a community. This will be evident from the aversion for temple politics in recent years - since the BJP formed coalition governments at the Centre — as distinct from its endorsement by the silent majority in the late 1980s and early 1990s. The BJP would not have dropped it from its governmental programme if it enjoyed the salience of the 1980s responsible for its elevation to the party with the largest voter support in the country. In fact, the Vishwa Hindu Parishad (VHP) as an irredentist offshoot of the RSS owes itself to the conversion to Islam of sizable Dalits in Tamil Nadu. Over the years, the VHP has grown into a veritable Frankenstein. The spread of separatist Muslim politics also has the stamp of 'secularist' approval. In other words, an atmosphere of inter-religious antagonism reminiscent of the Middle Ages cannot go hand in hand with human rights culture.

Maybe, the Constitution *per se* is not responsible for the state of affairs. It is more the failure persons working the Constitution. In the ordinary course, considering the use being made of the letter of Article 25 of the Constitution it should have been possible to make its purpose and scope explicit. But being a part of the basic structure of the Constitution, the fundamental rights chapter is beyond amendment according to the Keshavanand Bharati judgment of the Supreme Court. In the prevailing surcharged atmosphere it is not also possible to touch any statutory provision or law concerning Christians or Muslims. If the reigning Pope had been a liberal like his predecessor, His Holiness Pope Pius who had spoken of the greatness of Hinduism and put all faiths on par in his address at the Eucharistic Congress in Bombay in 1965 his help could have been forthcoming in redeeming the situation. But Pope Paul, presumably on account of his role in shaping the minds of the majority of Roman Catholics in Poland during the last phase of the East-West cold war, has a different attitude to co-existence with non -Christian faiths. As for professionalising the policy of secularism and using it as a vote catching device at the expense of the Muslim community as well as the health of the polity that is a sign of degeneration of politics after the Nehru-Shastri period. If the Constitution, after fifty years of operation, is found wanting in fostering a climate of human rights culture the blame should be laid at the door of political leaders who are tragically revered as martyrs because of their violent death. As stated at the outset, in judging the Constitution as a means of promoting human rights culture in the country the focus is naturally not on the document and its provisions but the way the leadership of the country worked it. The founding fathers of the Constitution can be faulted, if at all, for not anticipating the caliber of men and women into whose hands the baton might fall. Dr. B.R. Ambedkar and his colleagues treated it as an intellectual exercise, examining the suitability of American, Irish and other republican systems to India. It has in retrospect proved to be - at least in parts - an ivory tower exercise because they did not seem to have paid enough attention to the Indian society and its social, economic and moral failings.

Dr. Ambedkar, especially, had first hand experience of the havoc wrought by the caste system among Hindus and its oppressive effect on the Dalits, or the untouchables as he called them to counter Gandhiji's term of reverence, Harijans. He had suffered personally as well as at the community level and had even been thinking of opting out of the faith. Still, he was content with including in the draft Constitution a fundamental right abolishing untouchability in all forms and provision of reservation in the legislatures and in respect of employment opportunities in Government service for the Scheduled Castes and Scheduled Tribes. He had rightly realised that empowerment of the socially oppressed was the surest, even if somewhat slow, way of their emancipation. In retrospect, he is right. Several million Dalits have benefited from the weightage even if it has not always been faithfully implemented in Government service. The Dalits have found their voice, which, unfortunately, does no longer speak Dr. Ambedkar's language. Like Mahatma Jotibha Phule, Dr Ambedkar was a man of peace and law abiding. He did not lay store by extra-constitutional methods of political action. Above all, he was an intellectual who preferred debate and discussion although, like Gandhiji, he was a constitutional and non-violent agitator. As we will see later, while Dr.Ambedkar was an uncompromising opponent of the caste system which he wanted to be rooted out of Hindu society, his later- day followers, notably Kashi Ram and Mayawati, are working for its fortification. For instance, when Dr.Ambedkar felt that there was no hope of reforming the Hindu society by ridding it of the pernicious caste system he decided to renounce his faith. He then weighed the merits of other religions he could join and rejected both Christianity and Islam because, in his assessment they were no better and were also contaminated by caste-based discrimination. So he chose Buddhism.

It might also be true that Indian society was not so disfigured and ugly three decades ago, as it has been lately with the scum of sectarianism showing up. The prevailing situation of division and sub-division of Hindu society is the harvest of leaders like Viswanath Pratap Singh and his political progeny, Mulayam Singh Yadav, Laloo Prasad Yadav, etc. balanced by the likes of Kashi Ram and Mrs. Mayawati. The objection is not so much to their language and behaviour as to the mindset. V.P. Singh had so distorted the idea of affirmative action that instead of promoting egalitarianism in thought and action it fostered sectarianism and strife. One does not know whether Chaudhary Charan Singh, by no means a champion of the Dalits, had like V.P. Singh ten years later looked upon the caste card as an easy vehicle to durable political power, when he set up the Mandal Commission as Union Home Minister. Its mandate of ensuring empowerment and employment opportunities for the so-called Other Backward Castes (OBCs) has in effect brought about fragmentation of Hindu society as it moved out of its feudal moorings. By no stretch of imagination has the Mandal Commission unified the OBC ranks. Above all, it exposed the vulnerability of such reform to cynical exploitation for narrow political ends. The upshot has been a setback to promotion of human rights culture in the country. You cannot foster culture through civil war. The assertion of Dalit rights has evoked from the OBCs an extremely unhealthy reaction of violence and counter- violence and competition for reservation of legislative seats. In the process, the Dalit movement also has shed the positive visage of Ambedkar and Phule. In parts of Tamil Nadu, for instance, the Dalits and Thevars (OBCs) are prone to fight pitched battles on the streets. They resemble rival war camps. Instead of the accursed caste system melting or being diluted, it has become more rigid than ever before. Ironically, some contemporary Dalit scholars swear by the caste system to the delight of the spirit of its originator, Manu. Ambedkar, Gandhiji and Phule have become back numbers.

Could the caste system have evaporated or withered away if the Constitution had formally abolished it as it did untouchability?[4] The experience with the proscription by law of the practice of untouchability speaks for itself. It is mostly a paper reform because the community has no reformers to prepare the ground for the law to operate smoothly and effectively. Making its violation a cognisable offence will not also help. Even a police state cannot enforce it faithfully. A sustained effort over the years to educate the upper castes in the inhumanity and counter-productiveness of practising untouchability might have helped but once the British rulers were replaced and Indian leaders came to occupy positions of power the tendency has been to depend solely on the administration for accomplishing even social reform. A more unwholesome rider is the easy way out of blaming every evil on the ubiquitous bureaucracy. In short, the socio-political milieu is hardly conducive to promotion of human rights culture. It shows the magnitude of the task of reforming Hindu society and bringing it in tune with human rights culture.

End Notes

1. In contrast the Congress party raised a rumpus when the NDA Government set up a committee in 2000 for the review of the working of the Constitution with a highly respected jurist and former chief justice of India, Justice Venkatachellaiah, as chairman. Former Lok Speaker, P.K. Sangma's inclusion in it as a member was interpreted as a move to debar non-Indians from top constitutional postions of President, Vice-President and Prime Minister and by implication block Sonia Gandhi from becoming prime minister of India. Against that background one cannot fathom the 'renunciation' of the top political post by her in 2005 and the hype about it. The party not only did not co-operate with the committee but also waged a relentless propaganda war against it.
2. Dr. Subhash Kashyap, *Our Contitution*, 1994, New Delhi, National Book Trust.
3. *S. Radhakrishnan Biography*, Sarvepalli Gopal, *Ibid.*
4. See *Annihilation of Caste, (An undelivered speech)* B.R. Ambedkar, edited by Dr. Mulk Raj Anand, 1990, Arnold Publishers, New Delhi.

17

Jharkhand and its Sisters

On three consecutive days in one week in August 2000, the Lok Sabha passed bills for reorganisation of Madhya Pradesh, Uttar Pradesh, and Bihar by carving out of them smaller States of Chattisgarh, Uttaranchal and Jharkhand respectively. Of these, Madhya Pradesh and Uttar Pradesh are respectively the largest and most populous in the country. Together with Rajasthan, the three States being split up have earned from economists the collective sobriquet of BIMARU, or stricken in Hindi, on account of their backwardness in growth as well as human development indices. Equally distressing, the political leadership in these States, irrespective of their party affiliation, has been either politicising development or unashamedly neglecting it. It was a record of sorts that there had been a relatively smooth passage of the bills in the Lok Sabha. It is because both the BJP and the Congress were committed to the creation of the new States and stuck to their stand in the face of distractions. Paradoxically, while senior members of the Congress party were in the vanguard of the pre-lunch disruption of the House proceedings on two occasions, the party was supportive of the reorganisation bills in the afternoon. This augured well at least as far as enactment of the legislation went. This was despite some constituents of the National Democratic Alliance (NDA) being tempted to ride their hobbyhorses of territorial claims on the States being reorganised through the Bills. The Akali Dal, for instance, opposed the inclusion of Udham Singh Nagar in Uttaranchal while the Biju Janata Dal demanded transfer to Orissa of Saraikela and Kharsuan areas of south Bihar which are now part of the new Jharkhand State.[1] So, at the political level, the shared approach of the two principal parties was central to the new States coming into being. This could be a pointer to the improbable but nationally desirable prospect of the two parties pulling together on issues that have no electoral mileage. Such a larger vision, however, is too much to expect in India's conditions even at the dawn of the new millenium.

Possibly if the two-party system, even if in the shape of two combinations of coalition parties, stabilises, there can be joint effort by them on issues without electoral dimension. Interestingly, the veteran Akali Dal leader, Surjit Singh Barnala, was the first Governor of Uttaranchal. This was despite his party, the Akali Dal's reservations on the inclusion of Udham Singh Nagar in Uttaranchal.

On the surface, each of the bills disposed of by the Lok Sabha in a single, even if extended, sitting has on average ninety clauses. But most of them are consequential to the proposed division of the concerned State. In fact, except for details, the bills are identical. For instance, in the statement of objects and reasons, there is the common assertion that the proposed reorgainsation will meet the democratic aspirations of the people of the States. Two of the new States, Chattisgarh and Jharkhand, are preponderantly tribal in population which will be roughly one-fourth of that of the residuary State. In exact terms, the population ratio on the basis of the 1991 census was 176.2: 485.7 between Chattisgarh and Madhya Pradesh. In the case of Jharkhand, of the 864-lakh population of Bihar, the eighteen southern districts, which form Jharkhand, account for 218 lakhs. Uttaranchal will be the smallest of the new States, with a population of only 70.4 lakhs, a fleabite on the existing 1391 lakh population of Uttar Pradesh. The residuary State still has over 132 million people, retaining its position as the most populous in the country. Its Lok Sabha tally of 85 members has marginally declined to 80, the remaining five going to Uttaranchal. In the Rajya Sabha, too, only three of the 34 Uttar Pradesh members are designated as members of the new State.

The urge for administrative union of the members of a linguistic group was recognised by the British Government itself. That was how the Simon Commission recommended the formation of Orissa as a separate State. The Indian National Congress, as the platform for the freedom struggle, formally accepted the principle of linguistic States at its Kakinada annual session in 1920. The Communists and Socialists were in the forefront of agitations for the creation of such States. During the passage of the bills, the CPI (M), however, opposed the reorganisation of the States, with Mulayam Singh Yadav, flaunting the socialist label, dittoing. So did Laloo Prasad Yadav. As late as at the end of 1945, the Congress party had renewed the pledge of linguistic States in its election manifesto for the pre-independence general election under the Government of India Act, 1935. But the Linguistic Provinces Commission headed by S.K. Dar in 1948 rejected it as the 'sub-nation' theory. It said that the prevailing British-created provinces, as the product of two centuries of British rule, had stood the test of time and taken root in the minds of the people. That was the beginning of the post-Independence trend of aversion to redrawing State boundaries on the basis of the language of the inhabitants. The idea behind the formation of linguistic States was that a linguistically homogeneous administration would be closest to the people. The size of the State and the quality of governance did not count in that emotional atmosphere. Nehru, who seemed initially to go along with the Dar Commission view, had to have second thoughts on the subject in the 1950s following the death by fasting of a Telugu leader, Potti Sriramulu.[2] He had consented to carving out an Andhra State from the then Madras Presidency. Then came the States Reorganisation Commission and the linguistic redrawing of administrative boundaries of mostly southern States. Sardar K.M. Panikkar, who was a member of the commission, suggested the splitting of Uttar Pradesh although it was homogeneously Hindi speaking. The reason: it was too unwieldy to be governed well. That should be the crux of the exercise

Referring to the demand for more States by members who spoke on the Bills, the then Union Home Minister, L.K. Advani, said that if the legislature of a State advocated its division the Centre would go by the will of the people. Apart from the cultural dimension, the abiding consideration was effective government. The new States of Chhattisgarh, Jharkhand and Uttaranchal satisfied that criterion. It was also the fruition of democracy in action, as Michael Brecher[3] described the Indian experience in the 1950s. If, as alleged, the BJP was motivated by the narrow purpose of retaining or regaining power in the affected States it proved short-lived. It had lost to the Congress party the majority in the Uttaranchal Assembly in the March 2002 assembly election. Narain Dutt Tiwari, who has remained steadfast as a Congress leader — he had defected to the party from the Praja Socialist Party (PSP) in the 1950s —took over as its chief minister The demand for a separate Uttaranchal State, which grew rather late and had been initially sluggish was soaked in blood when the police, egged on by the Lucknow administration, had run amuck during a peaceful demonstration and people's march for the new State in 1999. Men and women were pounced upon and badly beaten; many of the women were also raped. There were a number of deaths. But most of the victims were unknown common people and remained so after the formation of the new State. Only a few politicians reaped the harvest. Narain Dutt Tiwari, who assumed charge of the Uttaranchal administration less than three years later, was, if at all, lukewarm in his approach to the Uttaranchal State demand, while Nityanand Swamy, the first BJP chief minister, was a Congressman at heart.

Madhya Pradesh, the parent State of Chattisgarh, was itself relatively new, having been formed in 1956 during the half-hearted reorganisation of States by Nehru. The urge for a new State remained submerged because Ravi Shankar Shukla, the first chief minister of Madhya Pradesh, was himself a big landlord in the Raipur area. He was a typical feudal lord but not venal or blood sucking. He was a "Gandhian" His sons, Shyama Charan and Vidya Charan, branched off into industry and diversified their interests while remaining active politicians. So diversified are their interests now that the family tending to split over and over again has a finger in every pie, including modelling, film making and allegedly smuggling. The agitation for a separate Chattisgarh State started in earnest in the mid-1960s - when Shyama Charan Shukla had fallen from Indira Gandhi's grace and had been at loggerheads with his younger brother Vidya Charan. Dr. Khubchand Baghel, who was then a Congress member of the Rajya Sabha, spearheaded it. Then Shankar Guha Niyogi, a trade unionist, launched the Chattisgarh Mukti Morcha. He was killed in 1991

Ajit Jogi, whose claim to be a tribal, converted to Christianity, was disputed, became its first chief minister. He had been an active member of Parliament and very close to Sonia Gandhi. Not finding avenues for promotion at the Centre he moved to his home base. A shrewd politician, he had won over BJP legislators with ministerships to reinforce his majority in the state legislature and preempt any toppling efforts from inside. He had come into prominence when he opposed the privatisation of profit yielding State-owned aluminum industry, BALCO (British Aluminum Company Limited). In the process, he also earned strictures from the Supreme Court.

Of the three new States formed in 2002, Jharkhand has a long and vicissitudinous history of a movement for a separate, predominantly Adivasi State. The Jharkhand region consists of 18 districts in undivided south Bihar, three in West Bengal, four in Orissa and two in Madhya Pradesh. However, over the last half-century, through the avenue of political negotiation, the Jharkhand movement came to concentrate on 18 districts of south Bihar. These districts are Bokaro, Chatra, Deoghar, Dhanbad, Dumka, East Singhbhum, Garwa, Giridih, Godda, Gumla, Hazaribagh, Kodarma, Lohardaga, Pakur, Palamu, Ranchi, Sahebganj and West Singhbhum.

The Jharkhand region tribes speak a number of languages. None of them has a written script. Tribal folklore has been communicated down the generations with the help of a strong oral tradition, but the written form is largely in the Devnagari or the Roman scripts. The interaction between tribals and non-tribals has been widespread. Consequently, most tribals also speak Hindi and a variety of related dialects. The Jharkhand movement and the related political developments began with the efforts of a student of St. Columbus College, Chaibasa—an important centre of tribal political activity in the region. The student, J. Bartholomew, along with Anglican missionaries established the Dacca Students Union in 1910 to deal with the problems faced by poor tribal students. The early activities of this organisation were limited and ambiguous. It was a religious society, a cultural organisation, a discussion forum and students' union, all rolled into one. The Dacca Students Union organised religious discourses, discussions and seminars, staged plays and generally represented the interest of the students. The success of a play staged by the union at Ranchi in 1912 proved a landmark in the development of the movement for a Jharkhand state. The staging of the play was for the ostensible purpose of raising funds for the union but it highlighted the urge for unity among the tribals. It was followed by a meeting of all Anglican and Lutheran students that established a branch of the union at Ranchi for mobilisation of tribal students to demand better educational facilities, economic development and job opportunities. In 1918, the educated Christian tribals with active help and encouragement from the Anglican Bishop of Ranchi reorganised the Union and renamed it the Chota Nagpur Improvement Society.This new body championed the cause of adequate protection of the tribal population and their cultural identity and emphasised the pressing need to create avenues for rapid politico economic advance of the region. Ten years later, a deputation of this organisation met the Simon Commission to put forward what was perhaps the first demand for the creation of a separate province of the Jharkhand area. But the Simon Commission did not go along with the demand in the political sense confining itself only to the administrative aspect.[4]

The same year the Chota Nagpur Improvement Society was renamed Chota Nagpur Unnati Samaj, which represented the earliest political organisations in the Jharkhand region. The period of activity of these organisations along with their radical and progressive ideas, also saw the emergence of social reforms among the tribal population on the lines of the 19th century of Indian renaissance. The next step was the formation of the Adivasi Mahasabha. Tribal leaders like Ignis and Baniface Lakra, who won the 1937 legislative assembly election in Bihar, were convinced that pan- India parties like the Indian National Congress would not be able to serve the interests of the tribal people. That was following a brief legislative stint. It was for the tribals themselves to look after their interests through an organisation confined to the region. At the same time, the landslide victory of Congress in the election impressed on the tribal leaders the need for denominational unity and they decided to float a joint body.

At this time, Dr. Jaipal Singh, who remained a key personality in the Jharkhand movement for over forty years, entered the arena of tribal politics. He joined the Adivasi Mahasabha in April 1939. The social base of the Adivasi Mahasabha also changed over the years. Until the fifties its membership was restricted to the tribals (Christian and non-Christian of south Bihar). However, it was realised that it could not develop into a movement without the support of the non-tribal settlers in the region. While sizable numbers of tribals migrated outside the region as labourers there was large-scale influx of skilled workers into the region to run the rapidly growing industries. Soon these 'outsiders' who had settled in the region outnumbered the tribals by almost two-to-one. To get over the dilemma of representing the entire region while safeguarding the interests of the tribals the Adivasi Mahasabha became the Jharkhand party (JHP) in 1949-50. It also succeeded in securing the support of the Chota Nagpur Separation League that was powerful among the depressed classes especially Muslims and the Miners' Association of Santhals. The Jharkhand Party while becoming a full-fledged party also retained its cultural identity as Adivasi Mahasabha. Dr Jaipal Singh became its President and Ignis Beck was appointed as Secretary.[5] The Jharkhand Party in some ways represented the translation of the essentially tribal identity of the people into a regional identity drawing on the uniqueness of the region's tribal heritage. Its cultural aspects were construed to represent the geographical region instead of any specific social group. By successfully bringing together the various tribal denominations (Christians and non-Christians) within the region under a cohesive political platform, the Jharkhand Party gradually evolved into a full-fledged movement, commanding support from all sections of the people.[6]

Paradoxically, the Muslim League that was thinking in terms of a corridor through the Jharkhand region to link the western and eastern wings of its proposed Pakistan supported the demand for a separate Jharkhand province or state. The idea apparently was that it would be easier to clinch such a deal with a regional body rather than the entire Bihar province. The JHP also supported the British war effort during the Second World War. The purpose was twofold: to obtain employment and opportunity for military training for the Jharkhand youth and, politically, to induce the British Government to concede the demand for a separate Jharkhand province.

Although led by highly educated and articulate leaders, the JHP failed to mobilise the masses adequately. It fared poorly in the 1946 election to the Constituent Assembly, which was unfortunate because the party had thus lost an opportunity to represent its case in the Constituent Assembly. However, for the first general election in 1952 under the new Constitution, the JHP had prepared itself well. First it widened its social base to include not only non-tribals in its ranks but also opened its doors to the *dikus* (money lenders-cum-landlords, hitherto regarded as enemies of the tribals). The *dikus* also were keen to find political space in the region where they had been virtual aliens until then. The JHP choice of the cock as its election symbol was also imaginative and evocative. "The cock is a revered tribal symbol since it is not only the favourite sacrificial animal but also signifies the dawn of a new day as well as the creative God and His all-pervading power. Further, it did away with formal membership on the plea that all tribal people were its members by birth and there was no need for recruitment of members separately or collection of membership fee from them. The net result was that the JHP emerged as the principal opposition in the Bihar State assembly formed after the first general election. It repeated the feat in 1957 as well, establishing its identity as a representative of the Jharkhand region. Taking advantage of its record in the 1952 and 1957 assembly elections it staged massive demonstrations at Ranchi and Dumka during the visit to the State of the States Reorganisation Commission (SRC) in support of its demand for a separate Jharkhand State. The executive committee of the party also submitted a memorandum to the SRC stressing the economic, socio-political and cultural grounds for carving a Jharkhand State out of Bihar. But the SRC was not impressed. It weighed the issue only on a linguistic basis. Since the region had a multiplicity of tribal languages it concluded that there was no basis for a separate State based on language. The larger cultural and socio-economic factors did not matter in the SRC's reckoning. Coupled with the rebuff from the SRC, a severe reverse in the 1962 assembly election demoralised the party The entire edifice of the Adivasi movement seemed to have caved in. The result was a decision to merge the JHP in the Congress, practically giving up its claim to speak exclusively for the people of the Jharkhand region.

The merger, as expected, proved an essay in expediency. Jaipal Singh and other leaders opting for the merger did not even care to get the JHP executive committee to endorse it[7]. So when the executive committee rejected it, there was embarrassment and confusion. The Jharkhand movement was in the throes of division. Compounding it, the inclusion of Jaipal Singh as a Cabinet minister in the Bihar Congress ministry had given rise to the charge that he had been won over with ministership. A senior leader of the movement, N.E. Horo, spearheaded the opposition to the merger. He and his supporters reflected the widespread sentiment in the movement that its identity should not be submerged. The Christian tribals also were against the merger because they saw a threat to their influence from the Congress. In extenuation of Jaipal Singh and his supporters, they thought in good faith that their being in the Congress and joining the Government would further the prospects of a separate Jharkhand State. They felt that they would be neutralising the Congress party's opposition to a separate State by being a part of it. But they did not reckon with the rampant factionalism in the Bihar Congress party, which made matters worse. For instance, while Binodananda Jha the incumbent chief minister played a key role in bringing about the merger of the JHP in the Congress the rival claimant for the job, K.B. Sahay had other ideas. He set out to fish in the factional waters of Jharkhand politics and started backing S.K. Bage, a tribal leader also supportive of the merger but opposed to Jaipal Singh. As a result, the Jharkhand movement suffered in elan.

The next spurt in the movement was in 1972 when the Santhal leader Shibu Soren formed the Jharkhand Mukti Morcha (JMM). In response to its campaign for a Jharkhand State, the Jharkhand Area Autonomous Council was set up in 1992 – after twenty years–as a half-way house to a full-fledged State. By then the Congress party in Bihar was virtually disintegrating due to groupism and infighting. Simultaneously, the BJP struck roots among the Adivasis and had been winning a considerable number of reserved tribal seats in both assembly and Lok Sabha elections. But Laloo Prasad Yadav, who was a promising leader of the Janata Dal in the 1980s, meanwhile became a tinpot casteist dictator, populist to his fingertips. He purged potential opponents from the party and made it a family fief. With the backing of the Congress party leadership and with the help of clever lawyers he has been surviving a series of criminal cases on charges of corruption. He was bitterly opposed to separation of Jharkhand from Bihar. The primary reason was that the State of Bihar had been exploiting the Adivasi resources, while keeping the people backward. According to Amit Prakash, the development policies pursued by the Bihar Government first under the ambitious Community Development Movement of the Centre and then on the basis of the more focused Modified Area Development Approach (MADA) of the Planning

Commission failed to have perceptible effect on the tribal population of Jharkhand. The MADA was a sharpened version of Integrated Tribal Development Programme (ITDP) operational throughout the country. In pursuance of MADA, districts in the Jharkhand region with more than fifty percent of tribal population (that is where the tribals constitute more than half of the district population) were identified for concerted development effort. Advisory committees of local officials and non-officials were set up to oversee and aid project officials in formulating policies and their implementation.

It was apparently not a mere reflection on the general administrative laxness in Bihar but also the failure of even some dedicated officials to deliver because of political interference. To continue with Amit Prakash's study, " the local communities became passive beneficiaries of the State's development policy instead of being active partners. There were very few efforts, if any, to involve local communities in the generation and maintenance of development programmes and projects. Consequently, there was no perception of improvement on the part of local communities, and whenever matters worsened, the local population simply looked up to the State for more handouts instead of making joint efforts with the development policy machinery to ensure better availability and management of resources". The point made is that without greater administrative and political autonomy for the region it will not be possible to harness local initiative. More than betterment of the conditions of the people the perception of such improvement has to be created through political reforms.

The States Reorganisation Commission, as noted, did not entertain the plea for a separate Jharkhand State on grounds that were fairly valid then. First, the development profile of the Jharkhand region vis-a-vis that of Bihar was better at that time. It was only subsequently in the 1960s to the 1990's that it either deteriorated or did not compare favourably with that of the State. Secondly, it noted that the tribals or Adivasis were divided on language basis and did not unanimously support separation from Bihar. Further, in response to the argument advanced by Jharkhand leaders like Dr Jaipal Singh that the region was being denied its due share of resources, the State Government started pumping funds into it as if to drown the autonomy plea in a flood of allocation of resources. That, without catering to the urge for political autonomy of the people, development will be tardy even if resources are there did not weigh with the State or even Central political leaders.

The Commission on Centre-State Relations, better known as Sarkaria Commission after its chairman, Justice Sarkaria, was another landmark in the movement for formation of smaller States like Jharkhand. That was in 1987. Of course, the commission did not dwell on the subject of splitting up of large and populous States like Madhya Pradesh, Uttar Pradesh and Bihar because its terms of reference did not cover that aspect of Centre-State relations. Indira Gandhi set up the commission after her Government dealt arbitrarily with States ruled by opposition parties like Andhra Pradesh and Jammu and Kashmir. The Sarkaria Commission was supposed to salve the anger of opposition and preempt a movement developing from widely felt public opinion that Indira Gandhi and her son Rajiv were aiming at a one-party State in the country as a whole. But the response of political parties notably the Jharkhand Mukti Morcha (JMM) to the Sarkaria Commission questionnaire shed insightful light on the prevailing opinion in the Jharkhand region of Bihar.

There is a significant statement in the JMM's response to a question on decentralisation. It said: inter alia, "decentralisation should not be (merely) between the Centre and the States but also between district and district considering heterogeneity, uneven development and multi-cultural character of the State itself with specific mention of the hilly and tribal areas of Bihar, now existing (as) an internal colony of both the State and the Centre." In another context, the JMM tried to liken its demand for an autonomous Jharkhand State to the nationality question in the former Soviet Union. The Communists were fond of citing it to support their stand that India is a multi-national country, from which flowed their endorsement of the demand for Pakistan in the late 1940's. But the JMM, apparently wise after understanding the existential position in the former USSR, avoided reference to it. Subsequently it realised that the constituents' right to autonomy, not to mention separation from the Union, was only in theory. In practice, it was the most centralised country in the world. The same was the case with Marshal Tito's Federal Republic of Yugoslavia, the five constituents of which had fallen out after the passing away of Tito. The cement of the League of Communists, said to be different from the Communist party in the USSR, dissolved in the heat of inter-ethnic rivalries between the Serbs and others, particularly Croats and Bosnian Muslims. There was severe bloodletting before the republics separated, no doubt with the European Union and Germany prodding the disintegration of what was once a model Socialist State.

But, as Amit Prakash brings out in his study, the JMM did not see the all-India Services as detrimental to the autonomy of the contemplated Jharkhand State and in fact asked for an adequate number of Central Service personnel with the proviso that they should not be from the parent State of Bihar. It was no doubt a necessary precaution because even the most upright officers can be swayed by considerations of State and ethnic loyalty. That is why south Indian officers are preferred in many north Indian States, particularly, Punjab, UP and Bihar. The Centre further bided for time by setting up a Committee on Jharkhand Matters (COJM) in 1990 under the Ministry of Home Affairs. While the JMM might have seen it as a move to accede to its demand for a separate State — because such committees were not set up in the case of Uttaranchal and Chattisgarh — it amounted to delaying a decision on the subject by at least a decade. (The reason obviously was that the Congress party government at the Centre did not want to let down the Bihar Government, which was its ally.

More encouragingly, the committee favoured establishment of a Jharkhand State for the development of the region. It claimed that the Central and State governments had been engaged in ameliorating the conditions mainly of the scheduled tribes inhabiting the Jharkhand region. This was despite the development profile for the region vis-avis that of Bihar deteriorating between the 1950s and 1990s. It concluded: "Notwithstanding these and various other steps taken, it would appear that the discontent of the people of the region has not only continued to simmer but has also shown a tendency to rise. The demand for a separate State of Jharkhand falls into that pattern." The index which made the committee discern simmering discontent in the region was the fact that the BJP had been gaining in electoral popularity in the region, winning both assembly and Lok Sabha seats.

One result of the unstable political and social situation in the Jharkhand region between 1967 and 1970 especially was the birth and rise of radical groups like the Birsa Sewa Dal, (BSD) Krantikari Morcha (or KM) meaning revolutionary movement) and Chota Nagpur Parishad (CNP). While some were urban pressure groups the others were industrial political bodies. Jaipal Singh was associated with the BSD as patron saint to guide it in the direction of forging an independent tribal organisation. Meanwhile, unnoticed at the surface extreme radical groups wedded to violence and pillage began to strike roots in the rural areas of Hazaribagh and other places. They came to be known as Maoist Communist Centre (MCC) and an assortment of Naxalite groups, operating in different areas. The MCC especially has grown into a thorn in the flesh of Jharkhand polity. In the 30 odd months following the formation of Jharkhand State in November 2000, the MCC has spread its tentacles to 16 of the 22 districts of the State. As many as 400 persons including nearly 150 police personnel were killed in its depredations up to June 2003. Its modus operandi usually is kidnapping officials and professionals working in road construction and other activities in the tribal areas and extracting ransom for their release. Sometimes the victims are killed in cold blood as police informers. There was a sensational incident of the MCC kidnapping a busload of passengers to demand the release of its arrested activists. To compound the situation, the BJP government in the new State was soon enveloped by infighting . One chief minister had to be dumped to save the government. In contrast, the Maoists despite their group rivalries are growing in strength. In sum, even if the progress of the new States formed in the new millennium has not been uniformly positive it is no small compensation that the people of the States have a greater say in their administration than was the case when they were within larger States

End Notes

1. The two parties which are constituents of the National Democratic Alliance (NDA) put up token opposition to the legislation.
2. The change in Nehru's attitude to reorganisation of the States and his ultimate reconciliation with the formation of an Andhra State by carving out Telugu speaking districts from Madras are described by Michael Brecher, *NEHRU Political Biography*, 1959 Oxford University Press, London.
3. Brecher *Ibid.*
4. The Simon Commission conceded the formation of only two States, Orissa, carved out largely from Bihar and including the Oriya speaking northern areas of Madras Presidency and Sind or Sindh taken out of the Bomaby Presidency of satisfy the demand of the Muslim landlords of Sindh.
5. See Amit Prakash, *Jharkhand–Politics of Development and Identity*, 2001, Hyderbad, Orient Longman.
6. Amit Prakash, *Ibid.*

5. Highly educated and motivated leaders like Dr. Jaipal Singh and his wife contributed in no small measure to the development of the Jharkand movement. Dr. Jaipal Singh was born in an animist priest family of the Munda tribe in the village of Takara near Ranchi. An Anglican missionary converted him to Christianity. He studied at Oxford where he excelled in shorts and games as well. He won a Full Blue in hockey and captained the Indian hockey team at the 1928 Amsterdam Olympics. He was also a member of the first Press Commission set up in 1952.

18

Terrorist Jitters

At the commencement of the holy month of Ramazan in November 2000, the then Prime Minister, Atal Behari Vajpayee, made a unilateral gesture in respect of Jammu and Kashmir, despite the setback suffered by his bold peace initiative in the shape of a bus trip to Lahore a few months earlier. The qualitative difference between the Lahore peace initiative and the Ramazan 'cease-fire' of November 2000 was that while the Lahore initiative was directed towards Pakistan the Ramazan gesture was to a section of our own people. Miscalled cease-fire in journalistic shorthand, it consisted of stopping preemptive action by the security forces against militants in the State. Flowing from it, cordon and search operations in civilian areas to ferret out hidden terrorists were suspended. But the security forces were free to act in self-defence and retaliate against terrorist attacks. About six months earlier in July, the militant outfit, Hizbul Mujahideen, had come out with a surprise offer of 'unconditional cease-fire' for three months. The Central Government readily responded and there was widespread sense of relief among the people of the State. But after 15 days the 'cease-fire' offer was withdrawn, again unilaterally, leaving the Union Government high and dry. But the people of the State, by and large, realised that while India was keen for a negotiated settlement of the 'problem' Pakistan was not. It was also clear that the Hizbul offer was not a flash in the pan but reflected the ground situation in Jammu and Kashmir and the overriding urge of the people for a return to the pre-1989 days of peaceful lives. Apparently, the basic consideration of the Government in responding so promptly to the Hizbul move was that the people, plagued by insurgency for over a decade, were desperately yearning for an end to the cycle of violence and counter-violence and the Government should reflect their urges. Mao Zhe-dong likened terrorists or guerillas, as he called them, to fish in a pond. They have to stay with it to survive. By the same token, countering terrorism requires isolating them from the people. The immediate result of the official reaction was to sift the no-changers in the All-Parties' Hurriyat Conference (APHC) and the Hizbul Mujahideen from the pragmatic elements.

It was significant that the Prime Minister's move to win over indigenous insurgents followed his bitter experience of the previous year when Pakistan virtually invaded the Kargil area of Ladakh within three months of the signing of the Lahore Declaration in February 1999. Apparently, a line had been drawn between bilateral State relations with Pakistan, with their perennial ups and downs, and the winning over of alienated Kashmiri youth from the path of terrorism. That the Pakistan Government was sticking to the mindset that prompted the Kargil misadventure was evident from Islamabad's reaction to the Hizbul offer. It made no secret of its embarrassment. In fact, it was rattled perceptibly that its own creature, the Hizbul, should stray from the path and talk in terms of conditional stoppage or suspension of terrorist activities in Jammu and Kashmir. One way of looking at the development was to watch the current affairs programmes on the State-run Pakistan television—beamed pointedly at Kashmir. Day after day, ex-diplomats, retired Generals, academics and journalists were fielded to denounce India's 'sinister' ploy to isolate Pakistan from the Kashmiri 'struggle.' How could there be talks between the Government of India and the militants without Pakistan being the third party at the table was their refrain. It was as though New Delhi had prompted the Hizbul offer! Pakistan had reason to be upset because the Centre's efforts to wean indigenous terrorist organisations from the path of violence to the negotiating table did not suit its strategy. As long as India viewed and tackled the problem only as one of law and order, civilian casualties in the counter-terrorist operations were grist to Pakistan propaganda. The Government remained isolated from the insurgents. Now it was trying to open the lines of communication with the 'rebels.'[1]

Secondly, the Hizbul was, and is, essentially a creature of Pakistan.It was fostered and promoted to sideline and destroy the Jammu and Kashmir Liberation Front, (JKLF) launched initially to militarise the Kashmir autonomy movement. That such an organisation should think of a respite in its killing spree affected Pakistan's strategy of using terrorism as a weapon against India. Apparently, the Hizbul initiative was the result of a conflict of interest between the local militants and Pakistan. What might have happened was that the Central (Indian) Government agencies established contact with sections of the Hizbul with a view to engaging them in dialogue and the Hizbul leadership, conscious of the ground situation in the Valley, had fallen in with it .The Hizbul leaders might have also felt the pinch of the new "pro-active" security policy on the line of control with more and more infiltrators being killed. At the same time, the ISI (Inter-Services Intelligence) Directorate of Pakistan and the *jihadi* elements holding a whiphand over the Islamabad establishment forced the Pakistan Government into stopping the Hizbul from pursuing the 'cease-fire' proposal. It will be interesting to recall here how the Hizbul offer had come to be made and how it had to be rescinded. Abdul Majid Dar, the top commander of Hizbul Mujahideen in Kashmir, made the 'unconditional three-month cease-fire' offer in July 2000. Defending his action, apparently prompted by 'talks' with some Central Government officials, Dar told an interviewer in December 2000: "The militancy cannot throw out the army and the army cannot eradicate the militancy. Because of this there has to be a political solution".[2]

The *Strategic Survey* report adds: "The Hizbul Mujahideen is Kashmir's largest and most indigenous militant group. Its readiness to accept an unconditional cease-fire undercuts the position of 'guest' militants and their Pakistani hosts. Indeed, if the Hizbul Mujahideen were prepared to suspend *jihad* and if it were in tune with public sentiment then on whose behalf would militancy continue to be waged? Leaders of the All Parties Hurriyat Conference (APHC) — political dissidents receiving strong backing from Pakistan — were now suddenly stuck with an outdated stance." So, the Hizbul supreme commander based in Pakistan, Syed Salahuddin, chaired a meeting of Pakistan-based militant groups to repudiate the cease-fire and expel the Hizbul Mujahideen from the United Jihad Council. The Jamaat-i -Islami, Pakistan's largest religious party and the Hizbul Mujahideen's parent political organisation, severed its ties with its wayward progeny. On 8 August, fifteen days after Dar made the "unconditional" cease-fire offer Salahuddin formally announced its withdrawal. As if to save the face of his Pakistani masters, he harped on conditions like tripartite talks among India, Pakistan and 'Kashmiris' while terminating the 'unconditional three-week ceasefire ', two weeks after it had been announced by Abdul Majid Dar.

If the Hizbul cease-fire had been tactical and meant to regroup forces, the people would see through the game. Terrorist organisations elsewhere like the IRA (Irish Republican Army),in Northern Ireland, ETA (*Euzkadi ta Azkatasuna* or movement for homeland and liberty) in the Basque region of Spain, and LTTE (Liberation Tigers for Tamil Eelam) in Sri Lanka resorted to it more than once. In Northern Ireland, even before the ink on the Good Friday Agreement in April 1998 was dry there were the Omagh killings claiming 29 lives and a succession of bomb attacks. The LTTE in Sri Lanka, similarly, agreed to a cease-fire at least thrice in the last decade (1990-2000), every time to break it after the lull in fighting served its tactical (military) purpose. The last false start was in mid- 2000 when the Government rightly let go of a cease-fire proposal by the LTTE because it was poised to overrun the entire Jaffna peninsula. (More recently, since 2002, however, cessation of hostilities and talks for a political solution of the ethnic problem have been progressing, even if by fits and starts.) Invariably the tactics claim attrition from the terrorists also. Every time a terrorist group called for and broke a cease-fire it lost supporters. There were splits in the extremist outfits. In other words, a cease-fire, whatever its motivation, is worth considering, especially if the ground situation is favourable. Nothing had come out of an earlier cease-fire proposal in Jammu and Kashmir itself by a paper organisation called Quami Mushawati Council early in 1999 because no terrorist group was associated with it. Lacking in credibility, it was ignored by the Government.

While announcing the Ramazan 2000 peace initiative, the then Prime Minister invited for negotiations all indigenous militant organisations that were prepared to lay down arms and enter into talks. He nominated Krishna Chandra Pant, veteran politician and Planning Commission Deputy Chairman, to represent the Government in talks with militants willing to enter into a dialogue with the Government. Pant visited Jammu and Kashmir for talks with different sections of the people but drew almost a blank, not unexpectedly. To make matters worse, over a hundred civilians, including Amárnath-bound pilgrims, were massacred. The increase in the intensity of terrorist activity first following the Hizbul offer and later in the wake of the Prime Minister's gesture was not unexpected. Still, the situation had the potential of a breakthrough. It was also a pointer that the policy of clamping down on the terrorists and keeping the door open for negotiations with those who wished to abandon the cult of the gun was yielding results, even if haltingly. That the other terrorist groups did not go along with the Hizbul Mujahideen and that the All-Parties Hurriyat Conference —a Musharraf lap dog —was hostile to the idea made it more complex. Meanwhile, persisting with the gesture, the Prime Minister extended the 'cease-fire' first through two monthly extensions to March 2001 and then until the end of May 2001. Just as the cycle of violence and counter-violence has a momentum of its own so has the 'cease-fire'.

To get back to the days of confrontation and conflict would require extraordinary circumstances, a large number of terrorists were being killed in encounters with the security forces in the first two months after the November 2000 initiative was unveiled, showing that Pakistan was using its terrorist weapon desperately to undo the "cease-fire". That the so-called *jihadis*, or mercenaries operating in the name of Islam, would not be moved by the cease-fire gesture was expected and obvious. This, in short, was the perspective of the policy decision. The response to it was admittedly mixed. Some indigenous militant groups had welcomed it. So did the people of the State by and large. Among the *jihadis*, like the followers of the Jamaat-e Islam, many believe that a Muslim majority State has to be absorbed by an Islamic country like Pakistan. There could be no talks with them. The All-Party Hurriyat Conference, as an umbrella organisation of diverse elements, had been humming and hawing. Some of its leaders generously and gratuitously offered to broker talks with Pakistan. A whole lot of them had sought travel documents to go to Pakistan as if their frequent confabulations with the Pakistan High Commissioner in Delhi were not adequate. The Government downsized the matter, which did not please the Hurriyat bosses and their backers (among journalists and 'experts'.) It was made clear to the Hurriyet leaders that there was no need for mediation by anybody, including the Hurriyat Conference, even when the subject is Kashmir. The two Governments had discussed it in the past and will do so again when a conducive atmosphere for possible headway is available. Tripartite talks have never been on India's agenda because they will be a recipe for outbidding and bargaining. Why can't the Hurriyat Conference leaders, for a change, draw out the military rulers of Pakistan on their intentions vis-a-vis the large Kashmir area in Pakistan's occupation? Islamabad has quietly incorporated in its territory the former principalities of Gilgit, Hunza, Nagar and other parts of what are called Northern Areas. 'Azad' Kashmir leaders demanding their return to Pakistan-Occupied Kashmir (PoK) were arrested in Gilgit. Pakistan ignored a PoK court ruling that the Northern Areas formed part of Kashmir. So a clear-cut enunciation of Pakistan's stand on the issue might clarify its policy which is confined to platitudes about the right of self-determination of the people of the Valley.

Starting with Sheikh Abdullah's Plebiscite Front, there have been several organisations disputing the finality of the State's accession to

India and demanding reopening of the issue. After the 1975 agreement between the Sheikh and the Union Government and his return to office as chief minister, others had appropriated the slogan. As chief minister the Sheikh had lost the glow of popularity in which he basked as a champion of independence from India. But it was still an agitation and not an insurgent movement even if it used weapons to press its point. First by supplying modern weapons like AK-47s to the agitators and then by training them in guerrilla warfare Pakistan made it into an insurgency. Pakistan was uncomfortable when the JKLF raised the slogan of *azadi* (independence from both India and Pakistan) and said its objective was to make the former princely State of Jammu and Kashmir, including the area under Pakistani occupation, a composite and independent entity. So, in 1989, the Hizbul Mujahideen was launched, as the armed wing of the Jamaat-e - Islami, just as the Irish Republican Army (IRA) is the military face of Sinn Fein. In fact, the Hizbul Mujahideen had originally seen birth as Al Badr speaking for militants seeking the State's merger in Pakistan as against the JKLF stand of independence The Jamaat-e-Islami in Kashmir was an offshoot of its Pakistan version, with no links with the Indian counterpart. It had been engaged in opening and running *madrassas* (religious schools) to indoctrinate the youth. In the Kashmir case, it meant weaning the people away from Sufism towards orthodox Islam and the doctrine of *Nizam-e-Mustafa*, which ruled out a Muslim from being a citizen of a non-Islamic State. Listening to captured or surrendered militants, many in their teens, at Kupwara some years ago, I was struck by the sway of the indoctrination. Of course, they had learnt the theory by rote and could not explain what it meant but their conversion into supporters of Pakistan was undoubted. They were mostly school dropouts who underwent religious instruction at the *madrassas*. Sheikh Abdullah as chief minister of the State was worried by the multiplication of the *madrassas*. That was in the early 1980s. He prohibited the establishment of new *madrassas* which angered the Jamaat-e-Islami. But it was one thing to ban the launching of new religious schools but quite another to carry out the order. There was no administrative infrastructure for it. So, ironically, the social welfare measure of providing free universal education - up to the university stage —in Jammu and Kashmir had been twisted into a tool of religion.

Flush with resources, especially AK-47s, the Hizbul Mujahideen did not take long to sideline the JKLF, starved of supplies by Pakistan. Lieutenant-General Arjun Ray in his *Kashmir Diary* published in 1997 called it "AK-47isation of a political movement." The rise in the movement for assertion of Kashmir's identity, based on the distinct culture of the people, Muslim or Hindu, and the spread of liberal education, got twisted into ugly terrorist activity. They were also the years of bungling by the Centre and consequent political instability in the State. Indira Gandhi was peeved by Farooq Abdullah's refusal to prostrate himself before her and so engineered defections from the National Conference. The Prime Minister then got the Farooq Abdullah Government dismissed. The gamble failed even if it softened Farooq Abdullah to enter into an alliance with the Congress party in the elections to the State assembly in 1987. Dogged by the Bofors scandal and desperate to win the 1989 general election in the country, Rajiv Gandhi had no time for Kashmir. His successor, Viswanath Pratap Singh, let his Home Minister, Mufti Mohammad Sayeed, wreak havoc with the State. Pakistan's proxy war strategy matured during the period when Mufti as Union Home Minister let his personal prejudices and political whims prevail over larger security and political considerations. Jammu and Kashmir Liberation Front (JKLF) militants kidnapped Mufti's daughter, Rubiya Sayeed, and demanded the release of five hard-core JKLF terrorists in return for her 'freedom.' The Government capitulated. That was virtually the note on which V.P.Singh and the Mufti inaugurated their Kashmir 'policy' at a time when terrorism was developing into a formidable weapon in Pakistan's anti-India armoury. Ironically, the JKLF was then in the doghouse as far as Pakistan's support for terrorist outfits was concerned. Islamabad had already started building up the Hizbul Mujahideen at the expense of the JKLF as a punishment for the JKLF demand for an independent and unified Jammu and Kashmir state. At the domestic political level, V.P. Singh and the Mufti drove Farooq Abdullah to resign and got the State legislature dissolved. As B.K. Nehru recorded in his memoirs,[3] "From 1953 to 1975 chief ministers of that State had been nominees of Delhi. Their appointment to the post was legitimized by the holding of farcical and totally rigged elections in which the Congress party led by Delhi's nominee won by huge majorities. What Mufti Sayeed, M.L. Fotedar and their followers really wanted was that Kashmir should revert to the *status quo ante*, that the Indira Gandhi-Sheikh Abdullah accord of 1975 should be scrapped and that Farooq Abdullah should be dismissed."

That was the transition, so to say, from a pro-independence political movement to armed insurgency. Among the heinous crimes of the Hizbul were the assassination of Mir Waiz, Maulvi Mohammed Farouq (1992), the burning down of the Muslim shrine of Charar-e-Sharif (1995) and the slaughter of 23 Kashmiri Pandits, including nine women and four children (1998). All these are repugnant to what is called Kashmiriat, Sufi-based eclectic Islam. So they were blamed on the security forces, particularly the much-maligned Border Security Force (BSF). Presumably Pakistan wanted to test how far the Hizbul would go in straying from Kashmiri culture. Equally probable was the claim that they were the work of Pakistani and other mercenaries. Soon after, there were clashes between locals and foreigners within the Hizbul, which led to the formation of Al-Badr as an exclusively mercenary outfit. But that did not help because the mercenaries controlled funds and weapons and if the Hizbul had to stick to terrorism it could not afford to let go of their backing.

For Pakistan, promoting and sustaining terrorism across the border is a low-risk operation. It began in the late 1980s in an entirely different situation following the Soviet withdrawal from Afghanistan. There was euphoria that if a Super Power could be tackled by guerrillas or mujahideen (soldiers of God) how could the upshot be different *vis-à-vis* India. It was fondly believed that the strategy of 'a thousand cuts' would bleed India white and force it to surrender the Kashmir Valley.[4] When it did not happen in ten long years there was naturally rethinking among the agitators who were not professional terrorists. A sizable section of the Hizbul had taken to terrorism in the mistaken impression that it would force India to cede the Valley. After that they could not get out of the Pakistani grip. For Pakistan, however, it was a means of punishing India at the cost of Kashmiri lives. Thus, when the supply of Kashmiri recruits began to dry up it started deploying more and more mercenaries. There was a candid admission of the situation by Air Marshal Asghar Khan, leader of the Tehriki Istaqbal, in the late 1990's when Nawaz Shariff was Prime Minister. He told a meeting of non-resident Pakistanis: "We are in a no-win situation in taking up the Kashmiri *jihad.* Pakistan cannot attain Kashmir by *jihad.* People in Pakistan who talk of *jihad* are either naïve or are outright stupid or hypocrites. Pakistani politicians are using Kashmir to whip up sentiments for their own selfish ends." He added that the ISI had assumed a stranglehold over the governing and political systems in the country. Another professional military person, Air Marshal Noor Khan confirmed it. He wanted Pakistan "to stop considering Kashmir as its jugular vein and allow Kashmiris to settle the contentious issue themselves."

Going back to Vajpayee's Ramazan peace initiative to indigenous militants, another point of criticism, voiced in the newspapers was that it was no more than a ploy to win international acclaim or a mere public relations gimmick. India definitely welcomes world opinion rallying round its view that India-Pakistan talks need a proper milieu and that continuing cross-border terrorism cannot produce it Beyond that, nobody expects or even wants international actors —including the International Monetary Fund (IMF) and the World Bank— to bring Pakistan to its knees and make it opt for talks with India on our terms. It will be unrealistic to do so. Does not India resent such outside interference? Expecting Pakistan to be so treated will set a precedent for third party meddling on Kashmir. It has been India's demonstrated policy since the 1960s, especially when the then US President John F. Kennedy, deputed Averrel Harriman to play the role of broker during the doomed Swaran Singh-Bhutto talks in 1962-63. Nehru did not conceal his displeasure but had to go along with it because India was then desperately seeking US military support against anticipated Chinese military attacks. As for the US 'pressurising' Pakistan on the Kashmir issue, it will be more unrealistic and counterproductive. Also, as the Anglo-American policy towards Iraq has shown in Operation Desert Storm in 1991, excessive pressure—military or economic —from outside makes a martyr of even a regressive regime and rallies public opinion around it. Thus, it is again fatuous to expect the Musharraf establishment to succumb to pressure from outside and fall in line with India.

So what next after the 'cease-fire', it will be asked. Had it not been for the incidents at Haigam in Baramula and Srinagar, leading to firing on mobs of protestors, there would have been a steady stabilisation of opinion in the Valley in 1999 itself in favour of substantive talks with the Centre. The disturbances were a setback to the effort but it was hoped that after a brief lapse of time the situation would calm down with more and more people abandoning the path of armed struggle and opting for talks. The National Conference and the State Government were naturally to be at the vanguard of such discussions. There was already on the table a plea for return to the pre-1954 position in the State's constitutional position within the Indian Union. The Centre had rejected it but kept the door open for talks. By designating KC Pant to conduct the talks with whoever was willing to sit round the table, the Government carried the situation forward. That was the long-term perspective of the policy. But in the immediate wake there had been so many almost earth-shaking developments that the long-term aspect was nearly snowed under.

The year 2002 saw a spurt in terrorism with the qualitative addition that it followed the pattern set by Osama bin Laden and his gang of international extremists. Pakistani terrorists launched suicide attacks first on the Jammu and Kashmir Legislative Assembly in October 2001 when the House had been going through its budget session. Luckily the Chief

Minister, Farooq Abdullah, was not in the chamber. Thus, the terrorists had to be content with killing over fifty innocent persons. They could not get their target, Dr. Abduliah. Then followed a similar attempt on the Parliament of India in New Delhi in December 2001. India retaliated with deployment of troops on the border and a warning to strike at terrorist bases in Pakistan and its occupied part of Jammu and Kashmir The crisis was at its peak until June 2002 with the 'unprecedented' deployment of defence forces along the Pakistan border. As the pressure began to tell on Pakistan, the US led the world community in leaning on Pakistan to live up to its pledge to end permanently terrorist operations against Jammu and Kashmir and the rest of India. As Britain's experience in Northern Ireland shows, finding a political solution to causes of insurgency is as arduous and fraught with setbacks as using force to contain terrorism. Even a decade after the 1994 Easter cease-fire with both the Irish Republican Army and its political wing, Sinn Fein, terrorist strikes continued right in the heart of London It was not a unilateral gesture as in Kashmir but a bilateral arrangement. Further, in Jammu and Kashmir, Pakistan has a vested interest in promoting terrorism from across the border through the Kashmir territory under its occupation.

The prospect of a political settlement within Jammu and Kashmir had given rise to a crop of domestic critics and politicisation of the issue. The Congress party and other Opposition groups were apprehensive that if Vajpayee were able to pull off a Kashmir settlement with sizable sections of the militants, they would be left without a juicy 'election issue.' Even a section of the terrorists had come to realise that armed struggle cannot be an end in itself especially for those who claim to have been forced to wage it in the absence of avenues for negotiated settlement of their grievances and demands. Similarly, for the security forces counter-terrorist action is only a means to control terrorism and create conditions for political solution of basic issues. The then Prime Minister's offer followed an assessment by the security forces, including the army, that proactive measures like cordon and search operations could be suspended without adverse security implications even if costly in casualties At the same time, it was made clear that the security forces would defend themselves.

Following the 1975 accord between Indira Gandhi and Sheikh Abdullah and the Sheikh's assumption of chief ministership of the state, the Kashmir Government had set up a committee to draw up a catalogue of its grievances for redress by the Centre. Primarily, the Sheikh's complaint was that during the years of his political wilderness when Bakshi Ghulam

Mohammad, Shamsuddin and his successors, notably Ghulam Mohammad Sadiq, were in office the Centre had extended to the State several laws in violation of the letter and spirit of Article 370. The Kashmir Governments under the Sheikh and Dr. Farooq Abdullah had prepared a report on the subject, which would have to be examined as a first step towards enlarging the State's autonomy within the Indian Union. Some of them like the jurisdiction of the Election Commission and the Comptroller and Auditor-General were beneficial. For instance, the Election Commission conducted the 2002 State assembly elections with credibility and fairness writ large on them despite determined Pakistani attempts to disrupt the polling and target candidates and even voters. For the first time, there was electronic voting throughout the State. The international media was there in full measure to watch and report. There were also observers from the diplomatic missions of Britain, the European Union and the US, among others. In the process, Pakistan had with impunity defied US advice that the elections should not be interfered with. Especially against the background of General Musharraf's rigged referendum in Pakistan, the conduct of the Kashmir assembly elections with a fairly sizable turn-out was a political setback to Pakistan. At the larger India-Pakistan bilateral level, the first priority was ensuring that cross-border terrorism and infiltration stopped for good. The Prime Minister has suggested a joint India-Pakistan committee to verify the situation on the ground for a reasonable period of time.

Of course, the Hurriyat hardliners were unhappy. Their fear of facing the electors was confirmed, although they would never miss an opportunity to claim the status of 'true representatives of the Kashmiri people'. Having swallowed the camel of Musharraf's referendum in Pakistan the Hurriyat pretended to strain at the gnat of the State elections. They need not be taken too seriously. But the cowardly assassination of Abdul Ghani Lone in May 2002 was a setback to peaceful transition to elimination of gun culture from the politics of Jammu and Kashmir. However, General Musharraf in his much- hyped 'broadcast to the nation' on 24 May 2002 had insinuated that supporters of India assassinated Lone. Even a tyro in politics would know that a live Lone was more useful for India than a dead one because he had been favouring participation in elections and renunciation of gun culture. He had also been on record that foreign mercenaries had no place in Kashmir's 'struggle' So it would suit Pakistan and its stooges in the Hurriyat Conference like Abdul Ghani Bhat more than it would India if Lone was removed from the scene. Until he opted for armed action and seeking Pakistani arms and logistical help in 1989, Lone was a typical Kashmiri politician honed on the Indian pattern. He was with the National Conference and was also a minister in one of its pre-1975 governments. But Sheikh Abdullah could not stand him and sent him out. Lone then joined the Janata Party of Morarji Desai and contested the 1977 assembly elections. When Chaudhry Charan Singh, as Home Minister in the Morarji Desai Government, visited Srinagar for campaigning, Lone approached him with a plea that the Centre should wink at rigging the elections at least in some of the constituencies. Wasn't the Congress party government at the Centre helping the National Conference in that manner in the past? Charan Singh had no problem about it but Morarji Desai following him to Kashmir put his foot down. He said he did not mind if Sheikh Abdullah won the election even if he was a *de facto* member of the Indira Gandhi's party but would not be a party to ballot rigging. I had a long chat with Lone in Srinagar after he joined the Hurriyat and started openly questioning the state's accession to India. He claimed to me that if the 1987 elections had not been manipulated and if the Muslim United Front, which he and others launched, had been allowed to win at least some seats, he would have remained a supporter of India. After the election had been rigged he had become a convert to armed struggle instead of democratic politics. He admitted to going to Pakistan to seek armed help from the regime and said many of his followers had gone to Rawalpindi in 1989-90 to obtain arms. As stated, during the short-lived V.P. Singh Government when Mufti Mohammad Sayeed, a convert from the Congress to VP Singh's group, was Union Home Minister there was chaos in the Valley. There was through traffic to Rawalpindi across the Line of Control. Operators of the vehicles, usually trucks and tempos, would solicit passengers to Pakistan saying they would get AK-47s free as bonus! B.K. Nehru in his memoirs recalls Lone calling on him in 1984 to protest against Indira Gandhi's move to dismiss Farooq Abdullah as chief minister. He reportedly told Nehru: "I hate the Abdullah family. I would like to kill both the Sheikh and Farooq with my own hands if an opportunity arose. But he is heading an elected government and should not be dismissed!" Incidentally, Lone did not recognise Nehru as Governor.[5]

Meanwhile, the Jammu and Kashmir political scene saw a generational change with Dr. Farooq Abdullah handing over the baton of leadership of the National Conference to his young and articulate son, Omar Abdullah. In the light of hardened prejudice against Dr. Abdullah let us recall B.K.Nehru's assessment of Dr. Farooq. Nehru writes : "Farooq was the first honestly elected leader of the Kashmir people, who felt himself totally

Indian, who was not neutral about Pakistan but definitely anti-Pakistan, who, unlike his father, repeated ad nauseam to audiences in Kashmir the fact that the accession of the State of Jammu and Kashmir to India was final, that Kashmir was an inalienable part of India and anybody who did not like it could lump it. As for his communalism, the fact is that in spite of his foolish electoral alliance with the Mir Waiz, religion to him was totally irrelevant. His ignorance of the beliefs and practices of Islam was the subject of jokes in the Valley. He was totally unaware of even the prejudices from which his co-religionists suffer. He once visited a temple in Srinagar and took part in the *aarti* ceremony, an act which among Muslim fundamentalists would have immediately caused him to be declared an apostate. Once he went to Vaishno Devi, came back with a bag of prasad and a stock of *roli* then went to Jammu Secretariat in the morning and as the people came to work decorated every one of them - Hindus and Muslims alike —with a teeka and presented them with prasad. His only son, Omar, was at school in Sanawar in a totally non-Muslim atmosphere instead of going to school in Kashmir or in England. The latter was in spite of Farooq's wife being English and unlike the practice of many of our super-patriotic netas. Omar among other things was studying Sanskrit. To cap it all, he eventually married a Hindu girl."

Which reminds me of the Sheikh's ambivalence on the State's attitude to Pakistan. In 1964, Nehru on his deathbed wanted to undo the wrong to his friend, the Lion of Kashmir. So D.P. Dhar, who was Home Minister in the Ghulam Sadiq Government went to work, got the Sheikh freed from detention preparatory to ultimate quashing of the cooked-up conspiracy case against him and allowed to return to the Valley. But the Sheikh being essentially a showman decided to go to Srinagar by road *via* Banihal, covering Doda, Bhadarwah and other Muslim populated areas of Jammu Province. He would address meetings at every stopover and there were overnight stops at some places. Wherever he went there was tremendous ovation, which tickled his vanity. A group of us journalists accompanied him because he was 'news' and also because he needed to be projected positively in the Indian press. But some of the correspondents would needle him asking for his stand on relations with Pakistan. The Sheikh would never commit himself, although he was careful enough to guard himself against his 'enemies' who would paint him as a pro-Pakistani or as plumping for an independent Kashmir.

B.K. Nehru narrated other instances of the Sheikh's insensitivity to Indian interests. Among them was a move to facilitate the return to the

Valley of Kashmiris who had migrated to Pakistan and also ensure return of their property. Nehru as Governor had to threaten to deny approval of the legislation to make the Sheikh pipe down. That was despite the 1975 agreement with Indira Gandhi. Incidentally, the Sheikh resisted formally recognising the State's accession to India until after the 1971 war when Pakistan was cut to size, more than geographically. When Kashmiris like the Sheikh saw Pakistan virtually defanged they settled down to living with reality. Even now, if India either prevails over Pakistan in - god forbid — a military confrontation or is able to clinch a mutually acceptable and beneficial political settlement with Pakistan, the average Kashmiri attitude to Pakistan would change. So much for the so-called alienation of the Kashmiri people which is grist to the mills of anti-Centre propaganda.

What next in Kashmir, then? Let us first see what could General Pervez Musharraf's contribution be for the consummation. The General has proved himself a good gambler. Until 11 September 2001, he had been the patron saint of the Taliban and the al-Qaeda. Following the US President's stern warning that those who were not with the US in its war on terrorism would be treated as against it, he quickly changed sides. George Bush unhesitatingly welcomed him and as in the Biblical story killed the fatted calf to fete the prodigal. True, Pakistan was necessary for effective military operations against the Taliban in Afghanistan. The result was a plenitude of goodies for Pakistan in the shape of IMF and World Bank credits and military and economic aid from the US.But terrorist attacks by Pakistan-sponsored marauders continued against India. Public opinion in the country was naturally outraged; there was widespread feeling that the US war on terrorism was selective and that India had been left high and dry. The Government was also faulted for rushing to pledge support to the US drive against terror without corresponding guarantees of security for India.

The then Prime Minister and the Defence Minister, among others, said that India would continue to fight terrorism as it had been since the mid-1980s and that being with the international campaign against terrorism was part of the country's duty. India had been demanding in the United Nations and outside comprehensive international efforts to curb terrorists worldwide. They included banning of identified terrorist outfits and choking of avenues of monetary support to terrorists.and drug traffickers. The UN resolution on the subject was a fulsome recompense for India's efforts. Accordingly, India mobilised its defence forces on its western border and enforced diplomatic sanctions against Pakistan. Soon came the General's much-hyped speech of 12 January 2002 in the course of which he pledged termination of support to terrorists operating from Pakistan. Although he was coy about mentioning India by name it was inferred that Pakistan-sponsored terrorist operations against Jammu and Kashmir and the rest of India would end. He also acknowledged the attack on Parliament as a terrorist act and formally banned Lashkar-i-Taiba and Jaish-e-Mohammad.

For nearly four months thereafter a game of hide and seek ensued with General Musharraf making anti-terrorist pledges to visiting US officials but denying them or omitting to repeat them in his public pronouncements. The alibi, gratuitously voiced by do-gooders in the media, was that since the General was vulnerable to violent opposition by Islamic extremists within Pakistan he could not be seen as conceding India's demands. If it were really so, it is a self-defeating policy. If the Pakistan leader is genuinely bent on changing Pakistan from being an epicentre of terrorism and taking it on a modern Islamic path like Egypt or Syria he should bite the bullet and summon up the moral courage to own it openly Exporting terrorism anywhere, including India, should be eschewed. In the process, he should prepare his people to face the consequences.

As Vajpayee embarked on a fresh peace initiative towards Pakistan in June 2003, General Musharraf was back at centre stage of South Asian politics. While continuing to be remiss in announcing compliance with Indian demand for permanent disbandment of terrorist infrastructure in Pakistan and its occupied Indian territory, he had been expecting to be rewarded for having done it. If the Pakistan Government genuinely stops exporting terrorism for good it is no favour to anybody, though it would let the people in India to live in relative peace. It is the duty of all member States of the UN not to make terrorism an instrument of foreign policy. By starting to do it, Pakistan will live down its ugly past. In return India would not have to take measures it would have taken if terrorist attacks continued. In this context, the European Parliament's stand on Kashmir, as shown by its resolution of December 2002 on the subject is refreshing. So is the position of France, which apparently inspired the European thinking. It said it would not take note of the human rights situation in Jammu and Kashmir in the context of continuing cross-border terrorism. At the same time it asked Pakistan to put an end to it permanently.

End Notes

1. For an excellent analysis of the terrorist strategy, whether indigenous or directed from outside, see *Low Intensity Conflicts in India*, Lt. Gen V.K.

Nayar, 2000, United Service Institution of India, New Delhi. In the context of the need to isolate terrorists from participants in other kinds of agitations, even if violent, the Indian media practice of loosely calling terrorists militants, and thus glorifying them is counterproductive.

2. *Strategic Survey,* 2000, London, IISS.
3. *Nice Guys Finish Second, Memoris*, 1997, Viking, New Delhi.
4. For a revealing account of Pakistan strategy of using terrorism against India see *The Bear Trap* Muhamad Yousaf and Mark Adkin, 1992, Lahore, Jang Publishers.
5. In a chat with me in Srinagar in September 1995. Earlier I heard him at a meeting in Kupwara where he emotionally exhorted his supporters to seek Pakistani armed support for detaching Kashmir from India. In a freewheeling chat lasting about an hour Lone, while being unapologetic about the change in his stand explained the factors which made him an insurgent from a democrat.

19

The Kashmir "Problem"

What is loosely called the Kashmir "problem" or "issue" has several aspects and over time has got complicated. In a way it is a byproduct of the partition of India into India and Pakistan. The Muslim League and its supreme leader, Quaid-e-Azam Mohammad Ali Jinnah, wanted the predominantly Muslim areas of the sub-continent to be carved out to form Pakistan. The Indian National Congress did not formally concede the two-nation theory or that religion should determine the nationality of people but acquiesced in the formation of Pakistan to facilitate and hasten the end of British rule. Besides what was called British India, which had been split into India and Pakistan, there were about 570 princely States or Indian India – as they were called—left loose after the end of British colonial rule. The bulk of the princely States embedded in or contiguous to the territory of India were integrated into the mainland by Sardar Patel.[1] The great statesman and nation-builder saved India from Balkanisation to prevent the spread of fissiparous tendencies by first clubbing clusters of states into unions of states and then absorbing them into contiguous territory. The relatively fewer princely States bordering Pakistan, notably the Baluch principalities under the Khan of Kalat and the State of Bahawalpur were incorporated into Pakistan by coercive means, with British civil servants and military officers playing the midwife. On 15 August 1947 when the British left India and Pakistan only three States, Hyderabad, Jammu and Kashmir and Junagadh in the Kathiawad region of Gujarat remained undecided. The Indian Independence Act passed by British Parliament provided for rulers of the States to accede to either Dominion or to remain independent. There was also provision for the State rulers to enter into standstill agreements with either or both Dominions pending final decision about accession. Lord Mountbatten laid down criteria for accession of the States such as geographical contiguity, viability, security and 'practical considerations', which implicitly meant the religious composition of the people of the state. But nowhere was the will of the populace even hinted at in so many words.

There was a sharp difference of opinion between the Indian National Congress and the Muslim League on the basic issue of lapse of paramountcy. The Indian Independence Act of 18 July 1947 laid down that the end of British colonial rule also meant that the 'suzerainty of Her Majesty the Queen of England' over the Indian States would lapse simultaneously and that the states were free to decide their future political status. While the Congress did not agree that paramountcy as far as the Indian States were concerned had lapsed in the sense that the State rulers could unilaterally decide the political future of their territories, Jinnah supported the view that it had indeed lapsed leaving the State rulers free to join either Dominion without involvement of the States' peoples in the decision-making[2].

As a way out Lord Mountbatten suggested that the States could accede to either dominion if they did not want to be independent. Accession meant that the State or states would cede to the chosen Dominion control over its defence, external relations and communications. The legal framework for independence also provided for rulers to enter into standstill agreements with a view to maintaining the *status quo* with either or both the Dominions. Maharaja Hari Singh of Jammu and Kashmir, accordingly, offered to enter into standstill agreements with both India and Pakistan, apparently to bide his time and possibly to opt ultimately to remain independent. Here again, India would not sign the standstill agreement on the ground that the representative of the State's people, Sheikh Mohammed Abdullah, could not be involved in the process. Abdullah was then in detention in connection with an ongoing agitation by his National Conference for responsible government in the State. (The National Conference was affiliated to the All-India States' Peoples' Conference of which Nehru was president and which had close political ties with the Congress). Pakistan entered into a standstill agreement with the ruler of Jammu and Kashmir on 14 August 1947 when it emerged as an independent political entity but violated its commitments like continuing the supply of essential articles like petrol and salt. It also snapped telecommunication links with the State and stopped supply of currency and coins. Until Partition, Kashmir's links with India were through what had become Pakistan. The highway linking Rawalpindi *via* Murree to

Srinagar was the main means of commerce and travel. The Jammu-Srinagar highway through the Banihal Pass was not there. There was a rail link between Jammu and Sialkot, which went to Pakistan and was ultimately terminated. The *de facto* or undeclared blockade was a prelude apparently to invasion of the State first by tribals provoked and armed by Pakistan and then by Pakistani troops themselves. The Maharaja, finding the State in siege and its security and integrity gravely imperilled, sought Indian military assistance to repel the raiders. Legal accession of the State to India had thus become necessary for India to move troops into Jammu and Kashmir. Accordingly, the Maharaja acceded to India on 26 October 1947 and Lord Mountbatten on behalf of the Government of India accepted the accession promptly. At the same time, Nehru wanted the State's accession to be reinforced by the people through the National Conference and its leader Sheikh Abdullah. The Sheikh was set free from detention and associated with the administration first informally.

Meanwhile, as Indian troops beat back the raiders Pakistan committed its regulars for fighting in Jammu and Kashmir. The result was a full-fledged India-Pakistan military conflict within six months of the birth of the two States. As the fighting raged for over six months, India approached the United Nations Security Council on the first of January 1978 under Chapter VI of the UN Charter charging Pakistan with aggression. Ironically, the move came at a time when the Indian troops had a military edge over the Pakistanis and it seemed given a few more weeks the Pakistan military could have been dislodged from the Kashmir territory it had occupied.[3] The official justification was that it was to preempt reference to the UN under Chapter VII of the Charter presumably by the Western Powers supporting Pakistan. Chapter VII provided for 'action' whereas the Indian move under Chaoter VI, as already stated, merely called for recommendation of 'appropriate procedures or methods of adjustments' for the pacific settlement of disputes. In other words, if there had been a reference to the UN under Chapter VII, there would have been binding action by the Security Council[4]. (Whether the situation also warranted going to the UN without taking into account the military situation on the ground was not clear.)

True, the future status of the State was to be decided by a plebiscite to which India had agreed. But the ground had to be prepared for the plebiscite according to a plan prepared by UN representatives. One of them, called the Dixon Plan after the Australian diplomat who headed the team of UN observers, provided for Pakistan withdrawing its troops and tribal raiders from the Kashmir territory overrun by them and the territory returning to Indian administration through the Government of Jammu and Kashmir. A plebiscite would then be held under UN auspices. But Pakistan was not prepared to let go of the real estate grabbed by its troops and there the matter remained. The deadlock was compounded by Pakistan joining Western military alliances, SEATO (South-East Asian Treaty Organisation) directed mainly against China and CENTO (Central Treaty Organisation or Baghdad Pact to subserve Western strategic interests in the Middle East and generally favour Israel against the Palestinians).[5] In the entirely changed circumstances, India rejected the idea of plebiscite because the East-West cold war had been brought into the India-Pakistan region The Western Powers, especially the US, started openly siding with Pakistan in the 'dispute'.[6]

The net result is that the cease-fire line, renamed Line of Control after the 1971 war, has over the years, virtually become the boundary of India and Pakistan in Kashmir with angularities in its configuration, like the Pakistani garrison atop the crucial supply line to Ladakh at Kargil, largely intact. But the change in nomenclature signified, first, the termination of UN involvement in the Kashmir 'problem' along with the *de facto* elimination of the old cease-fire line and, secondly and more importantly, a transition from a military line separating the two armies brought about by the UN-arranged cease-fire in 1949 to a political divide which could evolve into a boundary. The new Line of Control, (LOC) was demarcated and delineated by representatives of India and Pakistan, Lieutenant-General P.S. Bhagat and Lieutenant-General Abdul Hamid Khan respectively, following the Shimla Agreement of 1972. The agreement describing the LOC and specifying its configuration was signed at Suchetgarh on 11 December 1972. But Zulfiqar Ali Bhutto, who negotiated the Shimla Agreement with Indira Gandhi, went back on his commitment ultimately to recognise the LOC as the boundary. The perennial tension and exchange of mortar fire, plus frequent skirmishes sometimes with several fatalities on either side of the LOC, are the harvest of the situation. Pakistan has also been taking advantage of the strategic advantage it enjoys at places like Kargil to sneak into and occupy Kashmir territory. That was what had happened in 1999 when a major conflict broke out between the two countries.

During the 1965 India-Pakistan hostilities, what stood out even more than the grit and determination of the defence forces was the people's morale. Private transporters with trucks, lorries and other kinds of motorized vehicles had taken care of transport of infantry equipment and other material to the frontiers of Punjab and Rajasthan, braving enemy action Similarly, troops on their way to the front were feted and fed by the local people *en route*. Haryana and Punjab particularly rallied round the nation.[7] It was so heart-warming and infectious that reporters shed their customary detachment to fall in line with the national mood. (A typical instance was what my colleague, Asha Spaak, and I did while working for the French news agency, Agence France Presse, (AFP) at that time. In its early drive against India, Pakistan had managed to overrun a shaft of Indian territory which it began to advertise widely as a gain against India. Foreign correspondents were taken there to report with the provocative dateline, "from Indian territory with Pakistan." When the Pakistan-based AFP correspondent filed such a report it did not take us long to hit back with stories from the relatively larger Pakistan territory in India's adverse possession. The dateline was 'from Pakistan territory with India!')

In retrospect, it might appear juvenile but at that time it reflected the fact that newspaper correspondents, too, were one with the surcharged national mood. If the Pakistani intrusion had been stealthy the open military offensive in its wake was massive. It was said that India's setback in the Rann of Kutch fighting earlier in 1965 had encouraged Pakistan to embark on a larger scale repeat performance in Kashmir. In the Rann of Kutch, too, Pakistan occupied disputed territory in an area where the boundary between the two countries remained to be finalised. When it ended in a military deadlock India had to agree to arbitration by the British Prime Minister, Harold Wilson, indirectly giving in to Pakistan's strategy of sneak attack to internationalise bilateral disputes between India and Pakistan. In Siachen, in 1985, and in the Kargil area in 1999 Pakistan adopted similar tactics, as if to say that possession was nine points in international law too.

Reverting to the 1965 hostilities, almost providentially a few of us, Delhi-based journalists, had a ring-side view of the launch of the Pakistani attack across what was then the cease-fire line in Jammu and Kashmir. We had been on a trip by road from Udhampur to Leh and beyond organised by the Army Service Corps. We were to travel by three-ton and ten-ton vehicles like the Shaktiman trucks used by the troops on the mountain roads to negotiate sharp hairpin bends on some of the highest passes in the world. Colonel Victor Longer, who was the army public relations officer then, had hit on the idea to give journalists a taste of what the troops experienced in Kashmir. The massive trucks shook one's bones to make mince meat of the body unless one had a sufficiently strong physical frame. We set off from Udhampur as programmed and reached Srinagar on the third day through the Banihal pass. During a two-day stopover in the summer capital of Jammu and Kashmir we heard 'rumours' of infiltrators from Pakistan sneaking into the State but there was no definite information. We resumed our odyssey on to Zojila and beyond, stopping over on the way. At Kargil we saw the Pakistani highway almost running parallel at an altitude and looking down on the Srinagar-Leh lifeline or National Highway (NH1). Vehicles and men on the road would be sitting ducks for Pakistanis manning their garrison on the other side of the cease-fire line. When the 1947-48 hostilities in Kashmir ended in a cease-fire on the first of January 1949, the dividing line between the two parts of Kashmir was determined by the location of the rival armies bar some mutual sparring in the run up to the cessation of hostilities. Neither the security of the residents on either side of the line nor the defence requirements of the two administrations was taken into account in the Karachi Agreement of 27 July 1949, which delineated and demarcated the cease-fire line. It was signed by Indian and Pakistan military commanders as well as by representatives of the United Nations Commission for India and Pakistan (UNCIP), established after India approached the Security Council with a complaint that Pakistan had invaded its territory. The assumption was that the cease-fire line would be a temporary arrangement to be replaced by a permanent accord between India and Pakistan worked out by the United Nations. But to this day Pakistan has not carried out its commitment to the UN to withdraw troops from the territory of Jammu and Kashmir. Instead, what is called Pakistan –occupied Kashmir (PoK) or 'Azad Kashmir' has been incorporated in the territory of Pakistan.

To resume the story of our being unintended witnesses to the 1965 incursion, after a couple of days at Leh and the adjacent Changla pass leading to the world's highest highway, as the India-Tibet road is called, we learnt that the reports of Pakistani incursions had been confirmed and that it was on a fairly large scale. *Bakrwallahs* or goat grazers on the mountain heights noticed the intruders and carried the tale to the State government authorities through the local administration. That involved some time and so by the time the Kashmir Government brought it to the notice of the defence authorities Pakistan came into the open with an armoured thrust in the Chhamb sector in Jammu. The plan was to intercept the Jammu-Srinagar road link and isolate the Kashmir Valley from the rest of the country. It was at that critical moment that the pint-sized new prime minister of India, Lal Bahadur Shastri, belying Pakistan's assumption of weak-kneed leadership, ordered the defence forces to launch a counter-attack against Pakistan in Punjab across the international border. Nehru had been warning Pakistan that an attack on Kashmir would be treated as an attack on the whole of India and dealt with accordingly but it was left to Lal Bahadur to live up to that warning. The effect was electric. The nation rallied round his leadership.

Our team of correspondents on the road trip to Leh and beyond was stranded at the Ladakh capital when the balloon went up. The defence authorities did not want snooping journalists around when they had the important task on their hands of preparing for hostilities with Pakistan. Also, ensuring the security of the correspondents not all of whom were adaptable to trying conditions was the last problem the defence authorities had wanted on their laden plate. So we were packed off in a transport plane straight to Chandigarh from there to be bundled off to Delhi. Unlike the more sophisticated American counterparts, the Russian transport plane (AN 12) was meant mainly to ferry equipment including battle tanks and armoured vehicles. Only a dozen seats in the front of the aircraft are air-conditioned for officers on urgent trips. Other ranks going on leave are also accommodated to facilitate their reaching Punjab faster. Road journey from Leh to Jammu or Pathankot would take three days at the minimum. But they have to squat at the rear along with the equipment. Flying by a non-air-conditioned aircraft is like being roasted alive. So the squatters at the rear move to the front crowding the area. Years later in 1990 on a trip to Moscow on an Aeroflot commercial flight I had a similar experience. There was no reservation of seats, although the passengers had to go through the formality of booking their flights in advance. Once aboard the aircraft there is a scramble for seats and those not lucky enough to land a seat have to make do with standing in the aisles or at the rear. Those were the last days of Communism, incidentally!

As already stated, India was caught off-guard by the Pakistani sneak attack. Mobilisation of troops and positioning them at the front, in this case Kashmir would take at least three weeks. But thanks to the availability of private trucks it could be cut short. Troops with light arms were rushed to Punjab and Rajasthan borders while heavy equipment moved separately. Meanwhile Indian military advance into Pakistan Punjab made Pakistan pause to fortify its rear. Even then Indian infantry troops with armour and artillery raced towards Lahore within ten days crossing physical impediments like the Icchogil canal. They were on the outskirts of the Punjab capital where they halted because the purpose was never to attack a civilian centre, that, too, a densely inhabited city like Lahore with its historical treasures and heavy Pakistan defences. The purpose of the move was basically psychological.to make Pakistan feel the pressure of Indian defence might. Simultaneously, our troops moved towards Sialkot from Jammu, wading through a forest of wheat fields with the harvest still on the ground.

The hostilities lasted twenty-one days, which was the limit of Pakistan's war fighting capacity although it had the advantage of modern American equipment like Patton tanks and F-47 jet aircraft. India's mainstay was the sturdier but less modern Mig-21 and Second World War vintage armoured vehicles. Driven to the wall, so to say, our troops acquitted themselves so creditably that the Pakistani Pattons were immobilised by the score both through armour attacks and by hits from the air by Indian air force bombers .The US which had been an alliance partner of Pakistan refused to take sides without acknowledging Pakistan as aggressor. It equated India and Pakistan and stopped military supplies and economic aid to both countries. Since India received no military aid from the US – commercial purchase of Western military hardware was not always within Indian means — the US action did not affect India. In the case of Pakistan, however, it had the effect of stopping supply of spares for the aircraft and ammunition for armour. So the war ended in a deadlock - militarily speaking- with Pakistan unable to seize Kashmir by force for the second time in twenty years.

The then Soviet Premier Alexei Kosygin brokered the truce with the United Nations also in the picture. Thanks to the developing US-Soviet *entente* against growing aggressiveness of Beijing, Washington let Moscow handle the India-Pakistan conflict, offering to lend moral support to it. That was the time the US was caught in the Vietnam quagmire and the then President Lyndon Johnson was in a no-win situation. More than the military cost of salvaging South Vietnam was the political price of Lyndon Johnson's ambition to go in for a second term as US President. The effort, therefore, was to buy Soviet acquiescence in US efforts to cut down the mounting cost of the Vietnam operations and bring the boys back in time for the Presidential election. As it happened, Lyndon Johnson had to give up the idea of seeking a second term, partly to pacify public opinion at home, which was worked up by the mounting cost, in terms of body bags especially, of the Vietnam war.

The purpose of recalling in some detail the 1965 war with Pakistan is to highlight the short-sightedness of militant Hindu leaders, including a section of the Jana Sangh, the forerunner of Bharatiya Janata Party. They tended to identify Pakistan with Muslims and adopted an attitude of suspicion, if not hostility to the community as a whole. That Muslim majority Kashmir stood solidly behind the defence forces fighting back Pakistani aggression did not register with them. Delhi and other cities had black out due to the risk of Pakistani air attacks. Driving on dark nights, an ordeal by itself, became a nightmare with the so-called Jana Sangh volunteers taking the law into their own hands to enforce the lights -out requirement. It was especially so for correspondents like me who had to work late and drive home in the wee hours of the morning. The so-called volunteers would stop vehicles every few meters to satisfy themselves about the bona fides of the occupants. Even the Press label on the windshield was no guarantee against the harassment. In some old Delhi areas they would adopt strong-arm methods to enforce their version of black out. In localities inhabited mostly by Muslims it was a veritable enemy action against the dwellers. Still, luckily, there were no incidents of Hindu-Muslim violence anywhere in the country. More insidious was a rumour spread by overzealous Hindu 'patriots' that an IAF plane piloted by a kinsman of the then President Dr. Zakir Husain, a Gandhian and a sterling patriot, had been taken away to Pakistan. An extremist Hindu member of the Rajya Sabha — not belonging to the Jana Sangh—had even voiced the calumny in the House. The Upper House was shocked into silence until the Prime Minister rose to deny the canard. Atal Behari Vajpayee who was leader of Jana Sangh MPs added his voice to the Prime Minister's to caution against such rumour mongering and the weakening of the morale of the people and the defence forces.

Thirty-three years later, in 1999, when the country was coping with a similar Pakistani sneak 'invasion' of the Kargil region of Ladakh the 'Sonia Congress' party tried to politicise the issue of national defence and gain political mileage. It was first alleged that importing sugar from Nawaz Sharif's factories in Pakistan had blinded the Government to the intrusion until it came into the open. The Government explained that sugar imports from Pakistan under open general licence were on the basis of global tenders and were through private traders. The Government had no hand in them. Also, once the Kargil invasion had come to light the imports were stopped. The controversy had led to widespread allegations in the newspapers that there had been a grave intelligence failure in unearthing the Pakistani intrusion and that as a result the defence forces had to fight bitter battles at snowy heights to evict the intruders. It was further implied that the Kargil intrusion could have been prevented if the Government had not lowered guard and made the defence forces follow suit. The relatively heavy casualties among Indian troops, including many junior commissioned officers and some commissioned officers as well, were also blamed on the Government. In contrast to such cynical politics, there was spontaneous public support for the operations. Contributions for the Prime Minister's national defence fund had poured in from even persons with moderate means. Never before, not even in 1965, did the country rally round the leadership so enthusiastically. One reason was that for the first time round-the-clock television reports from intrepid correspondents stationed at the front brought the fighting on the snowy ridges into people's homes As it happened, the cheap propaganda recoiled on the 'Sonia Congress' party which fared badly in the following general election to the Lok Sabha.

In retrospect, the 1966 Tashkent agreement brokered by the Soviet Union was marked by strategic uncertainty and political fluidity within both India and Pakistan as well as the relations between the two countries. It was because the 1965 India-Pakistan hostilities ended in a military deadlock, which was aggravated by the terms of the peace accord. That Pakistan had failed in its second attempt in less than two decades to grab the territory of the entire Jammu and Kashmir State by force was the only definite outcome of the military encounter. But the aggressor was rewarded, so to say, by the requirement that India return strategic passes like Haji Pir captured during the 21-day fighting.

As a result the angularities of the Cease-fire Line remained unmitigated. Cumulatively, the situation had a negative impact on the security of Jammu and Kashmir and the physical safety of the inhabitants of areas along the Cease-fire Line They were condemned to constant vulnerability to sniping and mortar attacks from across the border, even if incursions of armed intruders had not been frequent or large in number. Of course, there was the overriding psychological asset of India having lived down the 1962 military reverses in the border fighting with China and the Rann of Kutch skirmishes. The army regained its morale and the chaos and manipulation of the pre-1962 days were a thing of the past. Virtually a new generation of leaders were at the helm of the defence forces, represented by General (later Field Marshal) Sam Manekshaw, Admiral Nanda and Air Chief Marshal P.C. Lal.

Within Pakistan Zulfiqar Ali Bhutto who as Ayub Khan's foreign minister had engineered the 1965 misadventure (of incursions into Jammu and Kashmir) used the Tashkent arrangement to whip up sentiment against the Field Marshal and ultimately to get him deposed. Healthwise, too, Ayub Khan was in poor shape and so stepped down in favour of his nominee General Yahya Khan. General Yahya Khan held the number two position in the army hierarchy and was Ayub's trusted deputy. But he was known more for his weakness for women and liquor than military prowess, if any. Further, having been in power since 1958, the army was becoming less and less professional. The net result was a senseless military involvement in the struggle of East Pakistan for political parity with the west in the wake of the 1971 general election. Bhutto was again in action blocking a political settlement and forcing the Awami League in East Pakistan to take to agitation. The humiliating defeat of the Pakistan army in the 1971 hostilities with India, the atrocities of the Pakistani military on the people of what was then East Pakistan and its ultimate secession to become Bangladesh are too well known.

End Notes

1. For grahpic account of Sardar Patel's painstaking effort to weld over 500 princely States into India see *The Story of the Integration of the Indian States,* V.P. Menon, 1956, New Delhi, Orient Longman.
2. Press statement dated 18 June 1947.
3. *Slender Was the Thread: Kashmir Confrontation, 1947-48,* Lt.-Gen. 'Tiger' L.P. Sen, 1969, Bombay, Orient Longmans.
4. The retrospect, if the Indian complaint had been under Chapter VII, (binding action) the upshot would have been possibly far different in the light of the U.N. Council resolution of 29 April 1957. It read, inter alia: "The UN Representative for Jammu and Kashmir, reporting to the Security Council, acknowledged on 29 April 1957 that "in dealing with the problem under discussion as extensively as I have during the period just ended, I could not fail to take note of the concern expressed in connection with the changing political, economic and strategic factors surrounding the whole of the Kashmir question, together with the changing patterns of power relations in West and South Asia. The Council will, furthermore, be aware of the fact that

implementation of international agreements of an ad hoc character, which has not been achieved fairly speedily, may become progressively more difficult because the situation with which they were to cope has tended to change." Cutting through the circumlocution one understands that the U.N. Representative noted Pakistan's admission to Western military alliance, notably CENTO, as well as its acknowledgement of direct military involvement in Kashmir. Pakistan, which initially claimed that the raids into Jammu and Kashmir were 'a spontaneous expression of Muslim sentiment following reports of killing of Muslims in Jammu and Kashmir', had to admit that its regular troops were involved in the invasion of the State. Accordingly, the United Nations Commission for India and Pakistan passed a resolution on 13 August 1948 saying that "as the presence of troops from Pakistan in the territory of the State of Jammu and Kashmir constitutes a material change in the situation... Pakistan should "secure the withdrawal from the State of Jammu and Kashmir of tribesman and Pakistani nationals not normally resident therein, who have entered the State for the purpose of fighting."

5. After the *coup* in Iraq led to the deposition of its king and ascension of Saddam Hussain to power, its original name Baghdad Pact was changed to CENTO, because Iraq ceased to be a member.

6. As a result of backing by the U.S. and U.K for geopolitical reasons in the light of the raging Cold War, Pakistan had rejected the Council resolution with impunity and failed to create conditions conducive to the holding to the plebiscite. At the same time Pakistan had continued to maintain that a plebiscite was the crux of a solution of the Kashmir 'dispute'.

7. (cf). "Following the emergence of America as an independent State as a result of the American war of independence in 1781, Britain found itself humiliated and outnumbered both at sea and on land by its potential enemies. With a war against France looming large on the horizone, Britain "struggled to re-arm itself. The nation was called to arms in a dramatic speech to Parliament by Pitt, the young Prime Minister, in March 1794, and throughout the country, gentlemen formed themselves into military regiments of volunteers who bought their own uniforms, supplied their own horse, paid their soldiers from their own pockets and drilled twice weekly, to remarkable effect and with a minimum of Government help") *Military Intelligence: The British Story,* Peter Gudgin; 1989 London, Arms and Armour.

20
The Kargil 'War'

The Kargil experience lasting eight weeks after 11 May 1999, when 15 Corps "had acquired sufficient information" about the nature and extent of the intrusions was costly in terms of casualties, even if the purpose of evicting the Pakistani intruders had been effectively served. Besides, as many as 474 officers and men of the defence forces, including many junior commissioned officers and quite a few commissioned personnel, were killed. There were civilian fatalities also and over a thousand (1, 109) defence personnel were wounded.

The established defence expert K.Subrahmanyam headed the Kargil Review Committee[1], set up by the Government on 29 July 1999, within weeks of the successful conclusion of the military operation. Its members were a retired lieutenant general of the army, K.K. Hazari, a senior journalist B.G.Verghese and a civil servant, Satish Chandra, secretary of the National Security Council Secretariat who was also the secretary of the inquiry committee. Its broad terms of reference were: "to review the events leading up to the Pakistani aggression in the Kargil district of Ladakh.... and to recommend such measures as are considered necessary to safeguard national security against such "armed intrusions". While the Government called the Pakistani action in the Kargil area 'intrusion' the report said it was nothing short of long-prepared invasion and described the military operations as "the fourth Kashmir war."[2] The report was the most exhaustive of its kind and was submitted to the Government in a record time of four and a half months. It was also published almost completely but for a few portions, which the committee itself declared sensitive on account of their bearing on defence operations. The report looked deeply at Intelligence generally to spot any deficiencies in its collection and assessment that found India unprepared for the aggression. Among the important findings of the committee was that the Kargil invasion was not preventable in the strict sense of the term because trying to plug loopholes in the Line of Control and man all and every post along it would not be cost effective. To quote from the prologue to the report in this connection: "The LOC from Manawar, on the international border near Jammu to Gurez, above the upper Kishenganga (river) is closely held with the two armies virtually confronting one another eyeball to eyeball. The hills are gullied and densely forested and provide infiltration routes of ingress with suitable cover. Beyond Gurez, moving east through Ladakh, intermittent posts separated by "unheld gaps" of ten to 45 kilometres mark the LOC. So grudging and virtually impassable is the terrain here that both sides have traditionally maintained just temporary summer posts, from which they launched patrols, only to withdraw from them variously between November and May when General Winter resumes command.

"This is a country that would dare a bold ibex at the best of times. Come winter and the Westerlies bring 10 to 20 to 40 to 60 feet of snow and crashing avalanches. Only trained mountaineers, specially clothed, shod, equipped and rationed, would venture to risk a passage through nowhere to nowhere." Further elaborating on the military, political and other cost effectiveness of trying to avoid "Kargil," the report said in chapter 12: "Had the Indian army sought to plug all conceivable loopholes to frustrate every eventuality, howsoever foolhardy, and attempted to safeguard "every inch of (unpopulated) territory," it would have meant the 'Siachenisation' of Kargil along a wider front with correspondingly higher annual human and material costs. This would have been neither militarily nor politically cost-effective and would have resulted in large forces requiring complex logistic support systems being dissipated in penny packets. Such a posture would have invited criticism and enabled Pakistan to bleed India."[3]

Secondly, the report noted intelligence lapses due to, among other things, multiplicity of organisations involved in the task and lack of adequate coordination among them. One glaring failure was inaction by the authorities on a report by the Intelligence Bureau of movement of men and supplies on the other side of the LOC. It is pertinent, in this connection, to look at military intelligence as it has developed globally and to recall instances of its lapses on a number of occasions. The illustrious British author, Peter Gudgin,[4] has given a lucid account in layman's language of the British experience in establishing institutions for gathering and dovetailing military intelligence. It dispels at the outset the image of James Bond —type of glamour and mystery attached to military intelligence which, like other aspects of national defence, is a mundane, even if complex, craft. The need for military intelligence arises because no commander of troops can lead his men into operations without adequate knowledge of the terrain in which they have to fight and the strong and weak points of the enemy they have to encounter. Thus military intelligence is as old as warfare itself, although the methods of obtaining, analysing and storing it and the techniques used for ensuring its reliability have been changing. What was once a mostly manual effort with human agents engaged in gathering and transmitting information of use to the country's defence forces by a variety of means has now come to be electronically operated with the minimum involvement of the human element. Agents or spies in enemy territory have become passé with satellites and other means of prying into defence installations and hardware stores in vogue. But Gudgin contends that a purely mechanical intelligence establishment does not work; it has to be supplemented and corroborated by human agencies.

According to the author, "British military intelligence had, on the whole, a very good record during the first world war, its successes outnumbering its failures." Among the plus points was a legacy of the Boer war when British signals intelligence (SIGINT) established a listening and cipher-breaking section. It was used with equal success against the more sophisticated Germans in the First World War to listen in to German communications and obtain the order of battle throughout the campaign in France. The most decisive of the efforts was the correct prediction of the place and timing of the last great German offensive against Gough's Fifth Army in March 1918. It had put paid to the German offensive, which was already in its last stage. The failures, Gudgin says, was more due to the commanders disbelieving or ignoring Intelligence reports. The purpose of organised military intelligence is to act on the information gathered and analysed. The activity is institutionalised with that purpose in view so that military commanders do not weigh the accuracy of intelligence reports before undertaking operations. That is defeated when the reports, for whatever reason, are not acted upon. The British, incidentally, were well prepared for the war with the intelligence network in place.

A major failure, it was said, was the failure of military intelligence to anticipate the use of poison gas by the Germans in April 1915. It also happened in France, within a year of the outbreak of the hostilities, thus indicating that it was not a desperate step by part of the German war machine. Intelligence gathered from prisoners of war clearly suggested the use of poison gas by the Germans. There was also evidence of gas cylinders set up in German trenches. Still the French military authorities would not take the reports seriously rejecting the data as circumstantial evidence. In other words, it was not an intelligence failure as such, although the net result was the same.

Introduction of institutionalised military intelligence into India was as long ago as in the fading years of the 19th century when Major General E.F.Chapman became the second Director of Military Intelligence in the British army in succession to Lieutenant-General Henry Brackenbury, who built up the organisation as founder-director. Maj.-Gen. Chapman had spent all his army service in India, having risen to be the quartermaster-General (QMG) in Bengal. Before the establishment of DMI as a separate section QMG looked after intelligence also. Maj.-Gen. Chapman as DMI in the War Office brought his Indian 'outlook' to the organisation. The accent during his five-year term was preparing for a feared Russian invasion of India through the North-West Frontier Province (NWFP) as part of the "Great Game." As it happened, however, there was no Russian thrust into India whereas Europe and Africa were theatres of crises in the run up to the First World War. Until practically the British withdrawal from India in 1947, there was a Frontier unit in the India Section. Interrogation of Italian prisoners of war, internment of enemy nationals, press censorship and monitoring of political activity seen to be beneficial to Germany and Japan were among the tasks of the India Section, although the Home Secretary in the Viceroy's Executive Council was responsible for political intelligence.[5]

After independence intelligence worth the name was organised by the Home Ministry in collaboration with the police in the States. It was mostly political intelligence geared to keeping an eye on the activities, covert and overt, of radical groups and individuals. In the States what was called the Special Branch was allotted the work of snooping on political activities, including the activities of trade unions, students' unions and peasant organisations. The constables entrusted with the work were not specially trained for the purpose. Now there is a full-fledged intelligence section in the State police, very often manned by trained personnel. It replaced the earlier special branch. Besides the Intelligence Bureau of the Central Government also has operatives throughout India. Military intelligence has in the process become a part of the army operations with the Director-General of Military Intelligence (DGMI) heading the section. Unlike in Britain where there is a military intelligence corps with the Director of Military Operations (DMO) responsible for its functioning by combining both the tasks of intelligence and operations, in India the Director-General of Military Intelligence (DGMI) and the Director-General of Military Operations are separate entities. This has both advantages and drawbacks, which were experienced during the Kargil operations. Then the other two Services, the Navy and the air force have their own intelligence set-up, which entails special effort for coordination.

The report dealt at some length with alleged Intelligence lapses during the Kargil operation. The Congress party and its permanent president Sonia Gandhi made use of forged document purported to be a letter to the Chief of Army Staff from a commander of the forces in the Kargil area with a view to making political capital out the relatively heavy military casualties. A New Delhi weekly publication *Outlook*, carried the commander's letter the date of which had been changed to link it to the Kargil operations. When the army authorities decided to haul up the magazine the Editors Guild to India sought reprieve for its distinguished editor, Vinod Mehta.

Reverting to efforts for normalisation of India-Pakistan relations, the Kargil invasion constituted a cynical breach of trust represented by the visit to Lahore of the Prime Minister of India and the signing of the Lahore Declaration in February 1999. Prime Minister Vajpayee travelled to Lahore by bus at the invitation of his Pakistan counterpart, Nawaz Sharif, in a bid to normalise relations and open a new chapter in India Pakistan relations.

It came out soon after that Kargil instrusion was the handiwork of the then Pakistan army chief, General Pervaz Musharraf, to undo the efforts of Nawaz Sharif. Thanks to determined intervention by the then U.S. President, Bill Clinton, Pakistan had to concede the sneak military attack but Indian defence forces had to wage a tough military operation dislodge the intrudes, who were regular military personnel of the 'Azad' Kashmir light infantry. Pakistan would not even accept the bodies of its dead soldiers. Within the country the Kargil 'war' was the first televised military operation iwth the army authorities wisely allowing television correspondents into the bunkers of the defenders, in the case engaged in evicting the intruders. The transparency paid off and there were no takers for the adverse political propaganda. There was a groundswell of public support for the Government as evidenced by the overwhelming response to the Prime Minister's appeal for contributions to the national fund for the dependents of the Kargil martyrs.

Unfortunately, however, the Kargil Review Committe report-brought out in record time–did not receive the attention of the lawmarkers. There was no discussion on the report in Parliament, which struck the late J.N. (Mani) Dikshit, who later became National Security Adviser to the Manmohan Singh Government. He noted the callousness of the MPs while exhaustively reviewing a high-powered review committee into a military operation but also made its report public. In contrast, the Henderson-Brook report that probed that 1962 military debacle in the border conflict with China has remained under wraps.

End Notes

1. *From Surprise to Reckoning*, The Kargil Review Committee Report, December 1999, New Delhi, Sage Publications.
2. The report's description of the Kargil operations as 'fourth Kashmir war' is interesting because it includes only the first Pakistani invasion of 1947-48, the 1965 hostilities and the 1971 Bangladesh War but omits the Pakistani military intrusion in the Rann of Kutch also in 1965, which led to mediation and arbitration by the then British Prime Minister, Harold Wilson.
3. See *The Bear Trap* Muhamad Yousaf and Mark Adkin, *Ibid.*
4. Peter Gudgin, *Ibid.*
5. The then Home Secretary, Sir Reginald Maxwell, published a controversial report in 1943 alleging Congress complicity in violent activities during the Quit India movement. The report was called *Congress Responsibility for the Disturbances*, 1942 and led to a 21-day fast by Gandhiji detained in the Aga Khan palace, Pune. Gandhiji said it was in penance for the violence. The Communist Party of India was believed to have collaborated with the Government in compiling the report. The Communists first denied they had a hand in the preparation of the report but soon after started a counter-attack on their critics saying that Gandhiji and the Congress had not launched the movement and that Socialists and Forward Blocists were responsible for the violence. They dubbed them Japanese 'Fifth Column'.

21

Politics of Presidential Election

It was a pity that Captain Lakshmi the candidate of the Communists for Presidentship in the 2002 election should have described her rival, Dr. A.P.J. Abdul Kalam, as a nuclear scientist. Her ignorance of minutiae like the distinction between a nuclear capable ballistic missile and a nuclear weapon *per se* is understandable. But not her echoing an ignoramus headline writer in the *Indian Express* who cares more for alliteration than sense. The headline called Dr. Kalam the BJP's 'nuclear' option'. (When a Chattisgarh BJP leader Raman was elected chief minister of the State a newspaper called it 'Raman effect'!). That space science and avionics, which are Dr. Kalam's field of activity, are different from nuclear chemistry that deals with weapon production is too much for such people to grasp.

The essence of Dr. Kalam's vibrant personality is national integration, which he personifies and radiates. It stood out at his first press conference on his candidature. The saying that fools who came to scoff remained to pray was in evidence when compulsive BJP-bashers found him too honest, too straightforward and too truthful for their taste. Equally relevantly, when Captain Lakshmi and her mentor, Netaji Subhash Chandra Bose, were organising the Indian National Army (INA) to fight the British Indian army, the Communists denounced him as a Japanese agent and asked their cadres to 'fight the fifth column.' Captain Lakshmi, scion of the illustrious Ammu Swaminathan family, was then a nationalist. She has apparently picked up the Communist vocabulary and so-called anti-communalism from her daughter, Suhasini Ali, formerly Mrs Muzaffar Ali. Suhasini was not born in the early 1940's when the Communists–they had not split into two factions–collaborated with the Government in the name of waging a 'people's war' against fascism. They would denounce Netaji Subhas Bose and INA as Japanese fifth Column. Decades later, the CPI under the leadership of Inderjit Gupta and others owned the mistake and acknowledged Netaji's contribution to the freedom struggle, but not the faction–CPI(M)–of which Comrade Harkishan Singh Surjit and Yechuri Sitaram–a veritable Laurel and Hardy due–are permanent leaders.

Suhasini was a member of Parliament having been elected from Kanpur in 1996. She lost the seat to the BJP and had not been able to wrest it back twice. Opportunism is the driving force for the Communists picking Captain Lakshmi as their candidate after they could not find a full-fledged Muslim to project their 'secularism'. Contrast this with Dr. Kalam's observation that the Muslim label did not fit him as he considered himself an Indian, and a god-fearing human being, more importantly. It is an irony that the Forward Bloc, which owes its birth to Netaji, should go along with the Communists. More ironically the group which calls itself Janata Dal (Secular) with which nationalists like Madhu Dandavate and Surendra Mohan are associated kept the Communists' company during their opportunist odyssey.

Dr.Kalam's deeply religious and god-fearing approach to public life may prove a turning point in our more recent chequered experience of 'secularism' being reduced to a tool of vote-bank politics. His thinking and views bring a new insight to the much-misused cliche of secularism. Our second President, Dr.Sarvepalli Radhakrishnan had reinforced the pluralist approach of Hinduism to religion from a higher philosophical perspective 'The germinal conceptions of Hinduism', declares Radhakrishnan, 'are contained in the Vedanta standard. ... The Vedanta is not religion, but religion itself in its most universal and deepest significance'.[1] If the Constitution-makers had followed his writings to embed secularism in the Indian ethos and Hindu eclecticism and not the Western meaning of a non-denominational State, the problem could have been perhaps obviated.

Indira Gandhi added insult to injury when she added secularism to the Preamble during the 1975 'emergency.' Later in 1978 the Congress majority in the Rajya Sabha voted down an amendment of the Morarji Desai Government to define secularism as equal respect, protection and freedom for all religions. So the confusion persists with the secularist bogey being handy for garnering bulk Muslim votes and the BJP and its partners denouncing it as pseudo-secularism.[2] Hopefully, Dr. Kalam in Rashtrapati Bhavan will bend his immense energy and wisdom to clear the confusion and put secularism as a policy of the State not being identified with any religion or its rituals and treating all of them alike. Equality before the law can be thus re-enthroned.

Meanwhile, Dr. Kalam elevated the campaign for Presidential election from the low and cheap level of Captain Lakshmi dragging the Gujarat killings to embarrass the partners of the BJP, especially Mulayam Singh Yadav. He conceded Gujarat was a 'painful' experience and pleaded for compassion in politics. What a noble thought, even if it went over the heads of journalists out to flog the dead horse of Gujarat violence by raking up the demand for the removal of the controversial (Gujarat) chief minister.

Then came the former army chief, General V.P. Malik to show off his strategic wisdom and pick holes in Dr. Kalam's explanation of deterrence strategy. Ever since General Malik was criticised within and outside the army for his preference for an overseas trip while the country was engaged in hostilities with Pakistani intruders in Kargil, he had been smarting. So he would periodically find fault with his successor General Padmanabhan's handling of the crisis caused by terrorist attacks on the Jammu and Kashmir Assembly in Srinagar and later the Parliament House in New Delhi in December 2001. (The Kargil enquiry committee defended General Malik saying that the Chief need not be present for a division level action fought at Kargil). He had thus been smarting from inferiority complex. He would miss no opportunity to get into the limelight either by picking holes in General Padmanabhan's masterly mobilisation of defence forces along Pakistani borders in December 2001 or with Dr. Kalam's enunciation of nuclear deterrence strategy. To revert to the Presidential election campaign, it could have been less ugly if the outgoing head of State, Dr. K.R.Narayanan, had not objectively helped those opposed to the Government. The opposition parties, especially the Congress party, wanted to use the Presidential election as a plank to spread disarray among the supporters of the NDA and embarrass the Government. The then Prime Minister had conveyed to Dr. Narayanan the decision of the National Democratic Alliance (NDA) not to support him for a second term. That was on 30 May 2002. According to the *Hindustan Times*,[3] two days earlier, that is on 28 May, Sonia Gandhi requested Dr. Narayanan to seek re-election implying her party's support. He did not mention it to the then Prime Minister nor did he say whether he would contest in the teeth of the NDA stand. It was said he was keeping an 'open mind.' The stance continued for nearly twelve days when he finally threw in the towel. During the 'open mind' period, leaders of the Congress party, the Communists and others had been meeting him almost daily to persuade him to enter the election fray. They would also announce that Dr.Narayanan was not unwilling or that 'Barkis was willing,' to quote a CPI leader, Bardhan! That meant that the incumbent President was spoiling for a confrontation with the Government in office. It was a no-risk tactic for him because if defeated he would have retired and collected his pension. If, on the other hand, he had won it would have landed the NDA Government in the lap of Opposition disruption of Parliament proceedings, breakdown of law and order and even violence. In neighbouring Bangladesh, similar tactics had thrown out the Shaikh Hasina Government. Dr. Narayanan's role, primarily to help the Congress party block the candidature of Dr. P.C. Alexander for Presidentship laid open his record in Rashtrapati Bhavan to scrutiny from the point of impeding the incumbent Government.[4] Dr Alexander incidentally, is a richly experienced administrator widely respected for his professional integrity.[5]

As for Narayanan's record as President it was marked by frequent pinpricks against the Vajpayee Government, very often needlessly. His constant butt of criticism was market economy in the course of which he would quote Jawaharlal Nehru who after a period of centralised planning landed the economy in stagnation and corruption. It got aggravated during the tenure of his daughter Indira Gandhi, who made a fine art of misusing power and resources for personal aggrandisement and enrichment. Making snide comments on the Government's actions, both right and wrong, was another Narayanan trait. A rather more embarrassing occasion was Dr.Narayanan's implicit criticism of the US when its then President, Bill Clinton, was on a State visit to India.[6] Personally, it is galling to write against Dr. Narayanan because of my fascination for his alma mater, the London School of Economics (LCE). A student of the great Harold Laski, Dr. Narayanan has been different from the general run of Oxbridge products preponderant in the Services then. It was said Nehru also liked him because he was different from the run-of-the-mill foreign educated Indian bureaucrats, although Nehru himself had studied at Cambridge. Dr. Narayanan belongs to a Dalit family of Kerala of which at least one member, Kuttimalu Amma, his aunt I think, was a freedom fighter and also a member of the Constituent Assembly.

Narayanan was Indian ambassador to the US in the 1980s when I was associated with the Peace Studies Programme at Cornell University. He had visited Ithaca, the seat of Cornell University in north New York State of course, not for our sake but because there were several friends of India in the Faculty there. But my wife and I had a brief meeting with him over a cup of coffee. When Dr. Narayanan was a member of the Rajya Sabha, I would often meet him in the Central Hall with a perennial request for an article for a short-lived fortnightly publication I was editing. After he became President, prudence demanded that I did not show off or capitalise on my acquaintance with him and I observed it meticulously. I would also go out of the way to embellish his controversial broadcasts in scripts for All India Radio. In short, there is no animus against him as far as I am concerned. It was understandable that he should be partial to the Congress party and voice his loyalty to Nehru in public pronouncements. But his soft corner for Sonia Gandhi — whose association with Indian politics is not edifying — was the limit. He had allowed himself to be 'conned' by her – so to say — when she claimed the support of 272 MPs in the Lok Sabha and made him invite her to form Government in 1998. He was also burdened with an IAS officer with a corkscrew mind as secretary in the first few years of his tenure.[7] Later, Dr. Narayanan helped the officer climb the ladder both at home and abroad.

Critics of the NDA also questioned its decision to overlook the incumbent Vice-President, Krishna Kant's claim to be elevated. There is neither a rule nor even a convention to that effect. Better persons, in all respects, than Krishna Kant did not make it to the Presidency after being Vice President. They include Justice Hidayatullah, an integrated personality, a great judge and hard-working Vice-President. Rule of law was central to his striking character but the Congress party and Indira Gandhi could not countenance his independent spirit. Similarly, Dr. Gopal Swarup Pathak, formerly of the Allahabad High Court retired as Vice-President. It was a pleasant surprise to see Dr. Pathak among the voters — shedding his VIP status —who lined up to vote in the Lok Sabha elections in 1977. No need to add that he was among the critics of the 1975 'emergency.' Then there was B.D Jatti, who died in June 2002. Jatti was also acting President. He had fallen out with Charan Singh, the then Union Home Minister, when he refused to endorse an ordinance scrapping the legislatures in eight States, although the assemblies had outlived their term in many of them on account of an illegal amendment of the Constitution during the 'emergency.'

Finally, if one looks at the list of past Presidents, every one of them except illustrious scholars like Dr. Radhakrishnan and Dr. Zakir Husain, was a Congress party politician. Indira Gandhi had even drafted persons with dubious credentials like Fakhruddin Ali Ahmed and Zail Singh. That was even when the Congress had no ministry in most of the States from

Punjab to Kerala. Its share of popular vote even in the best of times had been about 40 per cent. Yet it had its way in tenanting the Rashtrapati Bhavan.

As has been noted elsewhere, none of the parties lost sleep at the loss of lives and property of Gujarat Muslims. Their only concern was to find and keep an issue on which all of them from the Congress party to the Communists could gang up politically to isolate the BJP and the NDA. That had been the recipe for the BJP not being able to do well in State assembly elections in the earlier two years, besides of course the incumbency factor. On the face of it, a Government engaged in economic liberalisation requiring imposition of levies and cutting down subsidies with a view to bringing down fiscal deficit cannot be popular. If the Congress party with Dr. Manmohan Singh as Leader of the Opposition in the Rajya Sabha had lived up to its responsibility of ensuring economic reform there would have been no problem. But Sonia Gandhi's indifference to India's economic development and lust for personal power were making governance itself a Herculean task. Parliament proceedings were being disrupted, day after day, on extraneous but vote-winning issues, legislation was barred and reform measures stymied. During three consecutive budget sessions — in 1999, 2001 and 2002 — the Lok Sabha proceedings were disrupted continuously for more than ten days. There was hardly any meaningful discussion on the demands for grants of important ministries and departments. The budget was passed hurriedly in late night sittings to meet the deadline. In the circumstances, there is need for a person like Dr. Kalam as the Head of State to inculcate values in public life and put an end steadily to vote-bank politics. If that happens, he will be the greatest President of India to date.

End Notes

1. *Radhkrishnan, A Biography*, Sarvepalli Gopal, *Ibid.*
2. see Dr. Subhash C. Kashyap, *An Introduction to India's Constitution and Constitutional Law*, *Ibid.*
3. May 29, 2002.
4. For a no-holds-barred attack of Dr. Naraynan's record as President see Arvind Lavakara, *Rediff-on-Net*, 8 Feb, 2000.
5. Dr. Pandinjarethalakat Cheiran Alexander, a distinguished civil servant, is a Syrian Christian of Travancore. Syrian Christians, incidentally, are Indian Christians owing their faith to St. Thomas, unlike later-day converts to

overseas churches when they set shop in India. Dr. Alexander, a brilliant IAS officer of Madras cadre, was principal secretary of Rajiv Gandhi when he was Prime Miniter. V.P. Singh, as short-lived prime minister, made him Governor of Maharastra when he replaced C. Subrahmaniam in 1980. It was said on behalf of the Congress party–though not officially–that the BJP was sponsoring P.C. Alexander for Presidentship with the 'sinister' objective of blocking Sonia Gandhi from becoming prime minister. The convoluted argument was that if Dr. Alexander was electred President, being a Christian, he wold block another Christian like Sonia Gandhi from being prime minister during his tenure, in 2005 when there would be next general election. But Sonia Gandhi was said to have renounced her religion at birth and become a Hindu after the public demonstration of her 'half-dip; in the Kumbh and, more relevantly, what about her great act of 'renunciation' when in 2005 she put Dr. Manmohan Singh as prime Minister instead of opting for the post.

6. It is unheard of that the Head of State of the host country openly criticises a visiting Head of State.
7. The President's secretary belonging in the Indian Administrative Service not only introduced blatantly anti-NDA Government observations in the speeches he drafted for Dr. Narayanan but also regaled in alerting friendly press correspondents about them.

Epilogue*

"The fault, dear Brutus, is not in our stars,

"But in ourselves…."

Cassius's admonition to Brutus becomes relevant in the context of the role which stargazing has come to play in India's political life. (It may also dispel the impression that this book, because of its title that India is star-crossed, lays store by a fatalistic belief in the power of the stars to shape nations' destinies.) If one looked back at the situation in the 1980s when the title of the book was conceived one would understand the reason for its assertion even if many might not go along with it. For instance, it had been widely reported that an astrologer had as long back as in December 1979 foretold that Sanjay Gandhi would die an unnatural death in June 1980. (The young man apparently ignored the prediction if he had heard of it.) When it came true the newspapers and periodicals started devoting more and more space to crystal gazing by the learned and the not so learned at the shape of things to come.

Politicians of all hues began to throng the diviners of destiny to find out what lay in store for them and their adversaries. Even the cocktail circuit of Delhi developed an astrological dimension. The result was a widely touted forecast that Indira Gandhi was passing through a critical period in her political life due to a malevolent configuration of the stars and that it would last until the end of the calendar year 1980. Being superstitious, unlike her father, Indira Gandhi had reportedly taken the foreboding seriously. Lesser leaders like Jagjivan Ram and Charan Singh had full-time astrologers in their entourages to guide them in their political actions. Even Morarji Desai, normally free of such irrationality, had clung stubbornly to the presentiment of a "holy" man on the fateful July 15, 1979, when he had to tender his resignation as Prime Minister.

---

* William Shakeshpeare *The Tragedy of Julius Ceaser.*

Six of his Cabinet colleagues had abandoned the sinking ship in the wake of large-scale defection by Charan Singh's supporters. Jagjivan Ram, regarded as the last political prop of the Government, was threatening to follow suit if Morarji did not step down at once. At a meeting of his supporters and well-wishers convened at his official residence that afternoon Morarji mulishly argued against resigning because "Baba" (holy man) from UP had predicted that he would last as Prime Minister for at least six more months. The *malaise* did not stop with believing in and perpetuating the superstition. It affected the timing and nature of political and administrative actions as well. (Indira Gandhi was believed to have put off reshuffling her Cabinet until the propitious time for the exercise). Even the "policies" of political parties were determined by such considerations. For instance, early in September 1980, Yeshwantrao Chavan, until then regarded as Indira Gandhi's archenemy in the rump Congress, suddenly and without any provocation delivered himself of high praise for her leadership and policies. According to political pandits, it was a precursor to Chavan crossing over to Indira Gandhi's side. (The celebrated cartoonist, R.K. Lakshman, immortalised the event with a cartoon, which showed a beggarly Chavan rendering a hallelujah in front of a fortress -like residence of the Prime Minister.) What had prompted Chavan to do so? Political analysts who claimed to be close to him said it was to get back to the proximity of the power centre because Chavan calculated that when misfortune struck Indira Gandhi in the next few months being near to her would promote his chances of succeeding her. If, on the other hand, he remained in the wilderness called opposition he would miss the opportunity. The same urge seemed to have seized others believing themselves to be in the line of succession.

Among them, the then Railway Minister, Kamlapathi Tripathi, the oldest member of Indira Gandhi's 1980 cabinet began to girdle up his loins to mobilise his supporters for the expected trial of political strength. In the assessment of Tripathi's admirers, he had the advantage of belonging to Uttar Pradesh which till then provided three of the four Indian Prime Ministers. He was also a Brahmin, which made him acceptable to all those resisting the Jat upsurge, especially the Harijans and other minorities, even though he was extremely hidebound in his outlook and could compete with Charan Singh in conservatism on social issues. Like Charan Singh, Tripathi was also once Chief Minister of Uttar Pradesh. His vision too was limited to the region of his birth, holy Varanasi. A Hindi scholar, he was a loud patron of Sanskrit, astrology and other forms of ancient lore. He was also the editor of the State's oldest and most respected newspaper, *Aaj*. Whether it was due to his age – which was more than 70 – or some other reason, he had a flair, frustrating for the victims but amusing to others, of forgetting peoples' names and faces. Senior officials in the Railway Ministry told me that he would not recognise them, much less remember their names or designations even after they had met him four or five times in the day. He would stare vacantly or peer at them as if the cat had brought them in. Like many other UP and Bihar politicians of his vintage, Tripathi liked his admirers to touch his feet while he squatted on cushions with his feet up on the sofa. He was not articulate, not merely because of his habit of spluttering, which sounded like stammer. He swallowed words and those he spat out irregularly, like a fountain in dis-repair, did not normally make sense. The technical term for the disability is "anacoluthon": the sentence that careers around several corners and finally lands in a ditch, its wheels spinning unintelligibly. All that you get is a mouthful of spit on your face if you are too close to the dignitary. Still, he could be the Prime Minister of India if the stars so ordained. If Soniaji's sycophants could want her to be twenty-five years later why couldn't Tripathi, even if he did not marry into the ruling family.

Although I had resigned as PIO in January 1980 as soon as Indira Gandhi resumed her Prime Ministership after a three-year interregnum, I was not relieved of my duties until April 1980. Thus I had to call on Indira Gandhi's new ministers like Giani Zail Singh, Kamlapathi, Vasant Sathe and friendly and upcoming Krishna Chand Pant, besides veteran PV Narasimha Rao. At my only encounter with Kamalapthi, I failed to touch his feet and there was nothing much he had to say to me. I formally told him that if the Railways had any special task for the PIB we were at their service. He couldn't care less because the Railways was the least attention-drawing among his interests which included politicking, astrology and gossip.

Talking of feet touching, "Babuji" (Jagjivan Ram) — bless his Soul — also liked his feet to be touched. In his case, it seemed to be born of an urge to disown the perceived social inferiority of his caste. During the 'emergency', he was Indira Gandhi's agriculture minister. There were rumours that, having fallen from grace, he had been kept under house arrest. So when he visited London in 1976 on his way to Rome for a meeting of the Food and Agriculture Organisation (FAO), I met him there to sound him out on his position in the government. (I was then a research associate at the International Institute for Strategic Studies in London). Apparently, guessing my intention, Babuji put me off deftly when I said there was much criticism in the British Press of the 'emergency' and rumours also floated about cabinet ministers in disgrace. He said four persons had touched his feet since morning and they were all Brahmins! Unfortunately, I was not one of them.

Poor memory or senility had never been a disqualification in our public life. Hafiz Mohammed Ibrahim who was rewarded with Governorship of undivided Punjab after he lost a Lok Sabha by-election to Acharya Kripalani in the late 1950s was none the worse for it. According to a story still recalled in Chandigarh, Hafiz Saheb was asked by the Congress 'High Command' to dismiss Lala Jagat Narain who was a Cabinet minister in Punjab and who had fallen foul of the leadership by his defiance of its directives. Prompt action was needed to nip in the bud growing dissidence in the party centred round Jagat Narain. So late one night the then Congress President, U.N. Dhebar, personally telephoned Hafiz Saheb and told him that it was Nehru's wish that Jagat Narain should be dismissed forthwith. Hafiz Saheb promised to do so without any ado or doubt. Twenty-four hours passed but nothing happened. News leaked out from New Delhi that Jagat Narain had been dropped from the Punjab Cabinet remained to be confirmed in Chandigarh. Meanwhile, Jagat Narain who knew that his days as minister were numbered was making the most of the discomfiture of the "High Command". Exasperated, the Congress President again called the Governor the following night. Hafiz Saheb had no hesitation in confirming that Jagat Narain had not only been sacked but had also been hounded out of his official residence early that morning. "But why didn't the radio and the newspapers report the news?" asked the Congress President.Hafiz replied that he had no answer for that question. "It was duly notified to all concerned," he added. "What do you mean 'to all concerned'?", the Congress President persisted, with his blood pressure rising. "Was it given to the press?" Hafiz Saheb promised to ascertain the details from his secretary who shifted the responsibility to the director of information. The director, a lowly official relatively, admitted that he did not issue a press release on Jagat Narain's removal from service. Why, demanded the Governor. Not further interested in the triviality of an official explaining his dereliction of duty, he called the Congress President in New Delhi and after telling him cryptically that the director of information had admitted that he did not issue a press release on Jagat Narain's dismissal, let the subordinate face the music from the party president.

The poor director of information, sweating from every pore of his body, started explaining that it was not customary to issue press releases on the appointment and dismissal of employees like the gardener. "Gardener?" shouted the Congress President. "Who is the gardener?"

"Jagat Narain, Sir, who was dismissed by the Governor early this morning," the official politely answered. Now it was Hafiz Saheb's turn to sort out the matter. He did not know who Jagat Narain was though he had been a Cabinet Minister and had met him several times. He simply conveyed the Congress President's directive to his officials and saw to it that Jagat Narain was forthwith removed from service. If it was not the right Jagat Narain it was not his fault!

Reverting to star gazing, Raj Narain who had been dismissed as health minister of the Janata Government for bad mouthing his ministerial colleagues was Charan Singh's principal lieutenant. He was also a great believer in astrology and tantriks. He wanted the Railway Minister Madhu Dandavate to issue to a tantric a first class railway pass for travel all over the country, along with a companion. Dandavate promptly said 'no, nothing doing.' Another legacy of the Raj Narain-Madhu Limaye period (1977-79) was also in evidence in New Delhi. It was the weapon of character assassination by slinging mud. Printed pamphlets and cyclostyled broadsheets were in circulation giving the low down on the private lives of Indira Gandhi and some of her associates, notably the Brahmachari (literally celibate in Hindi). Indira Gandhi's spiritual guru and mentor was known by the title). Such vilification of political opponents was unknown at the national level until 1969. During the Presidential election that year an illustrated pamphlet defaming Sanjiva Reddy was published and distributed among members of the electoral college for the election of the President. It had also figured in the hearing of the petition challenging V.V. Giri's election. It was alleged that some "progressive" supporters of Indira Gandhi were responsible for its publication but she did not utter a word of condemnation of such tactics. It might not have been the work of her supporters but as the Prime Minister of the country she had a moral duty to disown and stem such tactics. Giri did not like my pleading with him to make the Government find the authors of the publication and bring them to book. He tried to take shelter behind the Supreme Court opinion that the pamphlet did not influence the outcome of the election. He burked the moral issue, intentionally or otherwise.

The purpose of this somewhat rambling flashback to the Janata years was to show the recrudescence of dirty tricks in the country's political life. Such methods may not be effective in accomplishing the power political purpose for which they were claimed to have been used. Giri would have won the 1969 Presidential election even without the steamy pamphlet against Sanjiva Reddy. The Janata Government might not have survived its internal contradictions even if the bedroom exploits of Suresh Ram (Jagjivan Ram's son) with a Jat girl had not been captured in colour and circulated far and wide. Indira Gandhi was never the worse for the mud slung at her. But the tactics do not die. They proliferate. The Machiavellian dictum — (*e meglio che noi lo facciammo a lui che lui a noi*) meaning It is better we do it to him than he to us — operates. Indira Gandhi lacked the moral courage in 1977-79 to put her foot down on such tactics and resist the temptation to cash in on the situation created by such methods. Her opponents either consciously promoted such campaigns or just imitated her. Even if the ultimate outcome was not favourable to the political opponents using such methods, he or she could always derive comfort from the destruction of the other party's reputation. In the process the system is devalued and the people lose faith in politicians of all hues, as they have already, if political talk shows on commercial TV channels are an index. There is no Jayaprakash Narayan to raise his voice and take up cudgels against such practices. So it is left to 'small' men and women to do the battle while being steadfastly resistant to decline of values in public life. Already there is a growing feeling among the youth of the country that the democratic system as it operates in India is fraught with poor quality governance, waste of time and money and corruption and associated evils.

In this context, a young man made a pointed reference to the Liberhans Commission set up in December 1992 under a distinguished High Court judge to go into the demolition of the Babri masjid at Ayodhya that year. The Congress party Government of P.V.Narsasimha Rao established it soon after the outrage. Even if the commission had started functioning only about a year after its formation – due to lack of necessary infrastructure – it is still dragging its feet in 2005. Setting up the commission was a knee-jerk reaction of the Narasimha Rao Government, which felt cheated by the then U.P. Chief Minister, Kalyan Singh. Kalyan Singh had solemnly assured the Central Government, the Supreme Court and the National Development Council that all steps would be taken to prevent any damage to the Babri structure. Necessary para-military forces of the Centre had been sent to the area to assist the local administration. First, Kalyan Singh had allowed thousands of so-called kar sevaks to converge on the area. That there were plenty of vandals and thugs among them was obvious. They did not need instigation by anybody. Either they had been paid to pull down the disused mosque or they had taken a vicarious pleasure in doing it. Secondly, Kalyan Singh did not use the force at his command nor did his government allow the Central reserves to go to the site of the vandalism. I happened to be with Atal Behari Vajpayee at his Raisina Road residence in New Delhi a few days after the vandalism when he got a call from Kalyan Singh in Lucknow. I overheard Atalji bluntly tell Kalyan Singh that even if it had resulted in heavy casualties he should have used force to quell the mob and prevent the demolition. Atalji was then Leader of the Opposition in the Lok Sabha .A senior advocate of the Supreme Court, K.K. Venugopal, was with him to discuss the defence of Kalyan Singh and others.

The Narasimha Rao Government lasted for three more years during which there was niggardly progress, if at all. That nothing tangible or conclusive would emerge from the commission was evident. Still, the Government went on extending the life of the commission year after year. The two United Front Governments that followed from 1996 could have done it during their combined two-year tenure. They did not. The successor BJP-led Government could not have extinguished the commission during the last five years because its leaders were indicted in the chargesheet before the commission. So the commission has been getting annual extensions .The net upshot of the costly exercise has been periodical hype when a BJP leader or a minister deposed before it. The *amicus curie*, a senior Supreme Court advocate, would try to twit them during the cross-examination and there wuld be momentary titillation among those who felt that the accused were guilty. Of course, there would have been embarrassment for the NDA Goverment if ay of its ministers had been held accountable for the crime in the commission findings ultimately but the so-called judicial inquiry by the Banerjee committee set up by Laloo Yadav into the Godhra train outrage did not shake the world. Not did Laloo and his supporters gain much by using it in the recent Bihar State assembly election campaign. Such 'judicial' findings would not add much to the Congress party's refrain that the BJP had a hand in the Babru demolition. If, on the other hand, the commission, gave them a clean chit the critics of the BJP would disbelieve it. Above all, a Bench of the Allahabad High Court at Rae Bareilly had been simultaneously hearing criminal cases against the same leaders on the same issue. The CBI is the prosecutor. The result is so much avoidable expenditure of time and money and criminal diversion of government and public attention – for no other purpose than providing an additional forum for trading charges on an issue flogged to death already. As far as Advani is concerned both late Girilal Jain in his writings on the subject in the *Times of India* and Mark Tully in his book on India have made it clear that he did not instigate the demolition of the mosque -like structure. Girilal had even noted Advani's anguish when the structure was brought down. Is this how democracy should function, the young man asked?

Index

D

H

J

K

O

Q

R

T

Y

Z

DEVELOPMENT OF LADAKH HIMALAYAS
Recent Researches

Editor

PREM SINGH JINA

KALPAZ PUBLICATIONS

Delhi–110 052

DEVELOPMENT OF LADAKH HIMALAYAS
Recent Researches
(Tourism, Defence, Himalayan Studies)

Rs. 790

ISBN: 81-7835-095-5

Published in 2002 in India by
Kalpaz Publications
C–30, Satyawati Nagar
Ashok Vihar Phase–III
Delhi–110 052
E-mail: Kalpaz@hotmail.com

Lasertypesetting at: Varsha Graphics, Delhi
Printed at: Mehra Offset Printers, New Delhi

Dedicated to

Prof. Maya Ram

Mrs. Manju Jina

and

Manvender Jina

Contents

Preface

Ladakh 'The Abode of Nature' was once the kingdom of ancient races viz. Mons, Dards and Tibetans. It is believed that—the Indo Aryan Mons from across the Himalayan range, the Dards from the extreme western Himalayas, and the itinerant nomads from the Tibetan highlands had their early colonies in Lower and Upper Ladakh respectively. Today we have Buddhist and Muslim culture in dominance. There are indeed Indo-Aryan culture in a few pockets but this culture is influenced by both Buddhist as well as Islamic culture that is, the Dokpa villages which are in Kargil district are influenced by Shia culture of Islam and villages those are under Leh district are influenced by Mahayani Buddhist culture.

Ladakh, the gateway to the Central Asian countries, once served as an important trade and transit centre of central Asian countries. Numerous caravans carried exotic merchandise comprising silk, brocade, carpets, felts, tea, poppy, ivory, etc., to Leh and after exchanged these with other traders returned to their destination-China, Tibet, Yarkand and Kashmir. Now, since 1974 summer travellers of European countries have replaced traders of past and Ladakh has regained its importance as centre of travel-related activities.

The present volume is the product of thirty three chapters written by eminent scholars of Ladakh. Dr. Prem Singh Jina is the main contributor, he has written sixteen chapters on various topics— 'Paintings in Phyang monastery of Ladakh', 'A look at Bhoto society in Ladakh', 'Tourism and changing environment', 'Sindhu Abhyaan (Sindhu Darshan)', 'Rinpoches on Ladakh', 'Lamas of Ladakh', 'Gesar Epic of Ladakh', 'Dards of Ladakh and its adjoining areas', 'Monasteries of Ladakh', 'A Case Study of Tashi Ga-tsal Monastery of Choglamsar', 'The Ecology of wild life of Ladakh', 'Grazing free and Begari System in Ladakh' 'Life-Style of Changpas of Chang-Thang in Leh-district', 'Morup, Namgail a famous Ladakhi Artist', 'Famous mGonpa dkar-brgyad in Nubra valley of Ladakh', 'Bhoti and Arabic influence upon Dok-culture of Ladakh', and 'Ancient trade route via Balu-mkhar to Central Asia'. In addition to these he has written six chapters with the help of others scolars— 'Dok-pa', An Aryan Race of Ladakh', with Jamyang Gyaltsan, 'Ladakh' Before and During the Indo-Pak war (1947) with Rev Konchok Namgyal, 'Historical Background of Ayu Kalon of Ladakh', with the help of Tsering Sonam', 'Origin and growth of Ladakhi Medicine (Amchi) System along with Dr. Thinles Yangzor', 'Buddhist Art in Ladakh', 'A Case Study of Sumda Valley', with Tsering Tundup Gojing Pa and 'Some rock, stone, wooden sculptures of Ladakh', with Mrs. Manju Jina, and 'Buddhist Monasteries in Ladakh', with Jamyang Gyaltsan. He also translated two chapters— 'Hemis Tsechu of Ladakh' of Jamyang Gyaltson and 'Chortens of Ladakh' of Tsering Sonam.

Dr. Sonam Angchok has written on 'Physical Fitness Norms for High and Higher secondary students of Ladakh'. In his paper he used Modified Fleishman's Physical Fitness Test Battery. Dr. Saxena highlighted the travel account of Izztoollah, travelled Ladakh during 1812-13. Dr. Lobzang Tsewang has contributed two papers, 'Bhoti in Himalayan Culture : A Case Study of Ladakh', and 'Preservation and promotion of cultural Heritage of Himalayas region. 'A special reference to Ladakh Himalaya'. In his first paper he emphasised the importance of Bhoti language in the development of Buddhist culture and religion. Henceforth, he favoured to recognise Bhoti language under Indian Constitution. In the next paper he gave the detail picture of Ladakhi culture. Prof. Dembi read the Kharoshti inscription discovered by Francke near a bridge at Khaltse and proved that Kushana conquest Ladakh 2nd century A.D.

Abdul Ghani Sheikh made a descriptive study on wild life of Ladakh and in his paper he said :

"The wild life of Ladakh with its fascinating landscape and background have great attraction for the tourists".

He suggested Government should arrange exhibition of wild animals at their habitats which would promote. "Shooting with Camera" instead of with the gun.

Father C.D. Sebastian, presented his paper on 'Sa-skya-pa order and Ladakh'. He gave detail historical facts of Sa-skya-pa order and explained how this order introduced in Ladakh.

Prof D.D. Sharma made Linguistic Approach and contributed his paper on 'Linguistic Approach to Cultural Analysis of Ladakh Himalayas.' He also studied Ladakhi culture through the angle of language. He used linguistic terms in order to explain Ladakhi culture, social customs, rites and rituals.

Thus, the present volume is the outcome of thirty three papers written by different scholars in various fields of Ladakh. I hope this book will be useful for readers and research scholars of India and abroad who are interested to do their research work on Ladakh. Besides, it will become a guide tool for tourists who want to see Ladakh more correct and accurate.

Dr. Prem Singh Jina

Acknowledgements

I owe a deep sense of gratitude to Prof. Maya Ram, Retd. Director, U.P. Higher Education and Dr. R.S. Tolia, Principal, Secretary Uttaranchal whose keen interest in my study on Ladakh has always been source of inspiration.

I must thank Pt. Gautam Kaul, A.J., Director General, (Retd.), Indo Tibetan Border Police, New Delhi for moral support. I am grateful to Prof. D.D. Sharma, Jawaharlal Nehru Fellow and Prof. B.K. Dembi, Retd. Director for Central Asian Studies, Kashmir University, Kashmir for rendering help as and when required.

I would fail in performing my moral duties if I forget to mention Mrs. Manju Jina, Principal, Hira Convent School, Haldwani, who helped me in various ways is completing this book.

I am grateful to Abdul Ghani Sheikh, Prof. B.K. Dembi, Fr. C.D. Sebastian, Prof. D.D. Sharma, Jamyang Gyaltsen, Rev. Konchok Namgyal, Dr. Lobzang Tsewang, Mrs. Manju Jina, Dr. Sonam Angchok, Dr. S.C. Saxena, Tsering Sonam, Dr. Thinles Yangzor and Tsering Tundup Gojing Pa for contributing their learned papers for the present volume.

I am also grateful to the authors by whose thought and works, I have benefited immensely.

My thanks are due to Kalpaz Publications, Delhi, for bringing out this book in a short time.

Dr. Prem Singh Jina

List of Contributors

1. Abdul Ghani Sheikh,
   Yasmin Guest House,
   Leh-Ladakh—194101
2. Prof. B.K. Dembi
   Former Director,
   Centre for Central Asian Studies,
   Kashmir University, Kashmir.
3. Fr. C.D. Sebastian, mst.
   St. Peter School,
   Chushod, Leh-Ladakh
4. Prof. D.D. Sharma
   Former Professor and Head
   Sanskrit University,
   Punjabi University,
   Chandigarh
5. Jamyang Gyaltsen,
   Central Institute of Buddhist Studies,
   Choglamsar, Leh-Ladakh—194104
6. Rev. Konchok Namgyal, Reader,
   Central Institute of Buddhist Studies,
   Choglamsar, Leh-Ladakh—194104
7. Dr. Lobzang Tsewang,
   Central Institute of Buddhist Studies,
   Choglmsar, Leh-Ladakh—194104
8. Mrs. Manju Jina,
   Principal Hira Convent School,
   Bhagat Des Raj Colony,
   P.O. Bari Mukhani, Haldwani, Uttaranchal.

9. Dr. Prem Singh Jina,
   Central Institute of Buddhist Studies,
   Choglamsar, Leh-Ladakh—194104

10. Dr. Sonam Angchok,
    Central Institute of Buddhist Studies,
    Choglamsar, Leh-Ladakh—194104.

11. Dr. S.C. Saxena,
    Central Institute of Buddhist Studies,
    Choglamsar, Leh-Ladakh—194104

12. Tsering Sonam
    Central Institute of Buddhist Studies,
    Choglamsar, Leh-Ladakh—194104

13. Dr. Thinles Yangzor,
    Central Institute of Buddhist Studies,
    Choglamgar, Leh-Ladakh—194104

14. Tseing Tundup Gojing Pa
    Central Institute of Buddhist Studies,
    Leh-Ladakh—194104.

Introduction

Ladakh, the northernmost region of India consists of a high-elevation dry land of rocky mountains and open plains north of the main Himalaya and south of the Karakoram mountains in the state of Jammu and Kashmir.[1] During olden days it was popularly known 'Kie-chha'. This name was given by Fa-Hien, who visited this part of the world in 399-400 A.D. Some historians have an opinion that during third or fourth century people who lived in cold arid valleys surrounded by snow mountains and totally dependent upon snow water, were called 'Kie-chha-pa'. Probably Fa-Hien was influenced by this word. Moreover, one may not firmly relate this word 'Kie-chha' only for Ladakh, it would be used for other regions of Central Asia. However, through Fa-Hien's travelogue it is easily understood that in those days travellers or traders came to Ladakh via two routes:[2]

(1) The western route through 'Kukyar'
(2) The southern route via 'Rudok'.

In seventh century A.D. Hiuen Tsang passed through Ladakh. He called it 'Mo-lo-pho'. According to him, it was

"A country probably situated about three hundred miles in the north of Shimla called 'Mo-lo-pho'.[3]

In my opinion 'Mo-lo-pho' was later corrupted into 'Mar-yul'. During 10th century A.D. Tibetan scholar Lo-tsa-va Rin-chen-bzang-po visited Kashmir via Ladakh. He used 'Mar-yul' for Ladakh and constructed many chortens and temples throughout in western Tibet including Mar-yul.

Besides 'Mar-yul', Ladakh was also known by different names, for example, Sanskrit Pundits called it 'Huna Desh' and Kashmiri scholars pronounced it 'Bhutan'.

During 16th century western explorers started visiting Ladakh. They renamed Ladakh in their own ways, e.g., some called it 'Land of lamas' and others 'Western Tibet', etc.

After independence Ladakh became an integral part of India and remained under Jammu and Kashmir state, however, known by 'Ladags' which later got gradually corrupted into present name 'Ladakh'.

Thus, till 10th century A.D. Ladakh was under 'Naris-skor-sum' which comprises three provinces: La-dwags (or Mar-yul), Gu-ge (pron. Kuke) and Pu-hrang (pron. Purang). Later during the 19th century Central Tibetan Government had taken Guge and Purang provinces (except Menser village). In 1962 China occupied major portion of Ladakh, thus present Ladakh has only 1/3 area of the Greater Ladakh.

In 1947 the British Government finally quit India together with the Princely states of India. Seizing this opportunity, Pakistan mounted a major military offensive upon the state of Jammu and Kashmir. On 24th October 1947 His Highness Maharaja of Jammu and Kashmir Riasat appealed to Government of India for military help and to include J&K state under Indian Republic. On 27th October 1947 the accession of J&K state in India was accepted by the Government of India. Three days later Indian troops were airlifted to Srinagar. It took not much time to repel the enemy. Then with Kashmir, Ladakh also came under the administrative control of Indian Government. Pakistan did not digest this incident and occupied Skardu and Gilgit region from J&K state. Since then Ladakh is surviving strategically as an important frontier of India.

Today the administrative system of Ladakh is looking by the I.A.S. officer till 1980 the I.A.S. officer appointed as a Deputy Commissioner, thereafter it divided into two separate districts: Leh and Kargil; subsequently administrative powers were also divided between two Deputy Commissioners.

In 1989, Ladakh Buddhist Association agitated for S.T. Status of the region, which was eventually granted by Central Government. The State Government later made a notification under the State Constitution on 7th October 1989 vide GSR 882 (E) by the order of President of India Shri R. Venkatraman declared Ladakhis 'Scheduled Tribe' with this success in 1993, Ladakh Buddhist Association again agitated against State Government's unfavourable attitude towards Ladakhies. This time Ladakh Buddhist Association decided to start a joint agitation with Ladakh Muslim Association for Ladakh

Autonomy. This agitation lasted for about one year. At last the President of India accepted their demand and on 9th May 1995 he approved the 'Ladakh Autonomous Hill Development Council Act'. The Act envisages at Autonomous Hill Development Council for each district: Leh and Kargil, and an inter-district advisory council for the Ladakh region as a whole which the State Government may constitute in consultation with the Councils of Leh and Kargil. But people in Kargil district did not agree to form Kargil Autonomous Hill district Council. Moreover, Buddhists in Leh district were happy with the Government's decision to form Ladakh Autonomous Hill Council in Leh District.

On 3rd September 1995, 30 councillors took oath. Among these councillors 26 were elected and four were nominated by Governor of Jammu and Kashmir state. The oath ceremony was witnessed by the Governor K.V. Krishna Rao. Later councillors elected Thupstan Chhewangas Chief Executive Councillor. He thereafter nominated four executive councellors named : Rev. Kyabji Thiksey Rinpoche, Rigzin Jora, Akbar Ladakh and Sonam Dawa. Rev. Kyabji Thiksey Rinpoche later resigned due to some differences with Ladakh Autonomous Hill Development Council's senior executive councillors. Tunchup Sonam was given Executive Councellorship in place of him. In the following year on 28th June. 1996 Akbar Ladakhi passed away. The absence of two senior leaders of Ladakh was a great setback to the Council. Thus, the Hill Council was not able to get sufficient financial assistance from state Government in order to develop Ladakh economy. The state's unfavourable attitude for Hill Council's function created tense atmosphere. However, to get the political support from Ladakh Dr. Farooq Abdullah favoured the nomination of Rev. Thiksey Rinpoche for Member of Parliament (Rajya Sabha). Finally in April 1998 Thiksey Rinpoche became M.P., later Dr. Farooq Abdullah decided to give support to Atal Bihari Vajpayee Government at the Centre. His son omar Abdullah was taken in as Union Minister.

In June 2000 Dr. Farooq Abdullah alarmed the Central Government for the state autonomy that is seeking restoration of the pre-1953 position in Jammu and Kashmir. In Ladakh all the senior Congress leaders and the Ladakh Buddhist Association did not favour the pre-1953 position of Jammu and

Kashmir State. However, they asked the Central Government to grant Union territory status to Ladakh in order to keep the distinctive ethno-cultural identity of Ladakh.

Notes and References

1. Fox, Joseph, L., Norbu Chering and Chudawat, Raghunandan, S; 1991, 'The Mountain ungulates of Ladakh, India', In: *Biological Conservation 58,* elsevier Science Publisher Ltd., England, pp. 167-190.
2. Kapur, Teg Bahadur, 1987, *Ladakh: The Wonderland,* Mittal Publication, Delhi, pp. 1-2.
3. Jina, Prem Singh, 1996, *Ladakh: The land and the People,* Indus Pub. Co. and Kapur, Teg Bahadur; *op. cit.*

PART I
Culture, Language and Religion

1

Linguistic Approach to Cultural Analysis of Ladakh Himalayas

D.D. Sharma

It is of general knowledge that every cultural activity, major or minor, has a definite linguistic term to denote it. Etymological terms serve as an epitome of the form and the function of the cultural elements or objects for which they stand. The language, an account of its conservative character, preserves and transmits them faithfully from one generation to another. As such it is the most trustworthy repository of the cultural heritage of speech community.

There are many social customs, rites and rituals of the tribals which otherwise have become a thing of the past, but are still traceable through their linguistic terms. But before coming to the problem it may not be inapproprite to say something about the basic nature of culture and language in general. This would not only give us insight into these two fundamental components of our social life but also will better equip us to appreciate the analysis.

Culture, though abstract in itself, manifests itself through the visual and concrete, e.g., art, architecture, paintings or religious performances.

It is, like language, a socially acquired knowledge. In both the cases the acquisition of this knowledge is either by direct instruction or by watching the behaviour of other members of the community. Cultural heritage is in many ways distinct from biological heritage. In a given society, in order to be acceptable to its other members one has to operate within the traditionally established social norms. Thus 'Culture' is a knowledge which we learn from other people, and language becomes a potent vehicle to preserve as well as to transmit the cultural knowledge to members of the speech community.

There is an intricate relationship of language and culture which can be decided by socio-linguistic terms, largely manifested through various terminological and non terminological expressions. No doubt, speech has relatively high autonomy, but culture could probably not originate without language and language could be nearly empty without culture.

Language and society can not be separated. Language has its relevance with its society, Thus, it is so intricately interwoven in the texture of society that one cannot think of a society without a language and of a language without a society. The two are quite inseparable and co-existent. Any change in one is bound to bring a consequent change in the other.

A language, besides performing its function of verbal or written communication also serves as means of communicating the socio-cultural aspects and historical information of its speakers. It being the principal vehicle of social communication its socio-cultural oriented study is a very reliable source of knowledge of the past and present socio-cultural setting of the speech community concerned. Besides, it has also been noticed that not infrequently, such a linguistic information is a perfectly trustworthy evidence to determine the earlier history of the speakers of the language who otherwise have no record, whatsoever, of their past. A language based socio-cultural study, sometimes also provides clues even of the people who otherwise have totally disappeared from a particular region.

However, study of various terms and modes of address and greetings or of kinship terms is an important source to understand the socio-cultural ethos of the speech community concerned. For instance, prevalence of identical kin terms for maternal uncle, father's sister's husband and father-in-law (e.g., *azang* in Ladakh) and for the maternal aunt, father's sister and mother-in-law *(ane)* is a pointer to the cultural facet of the Ladakh Himalayas in which cross-cousin marriage is or was a socially sanctioned system. Further, the mode of address as between sister and brother and the father of the boy and the mother of the girl and vice-versa confirms the prevalence of this system in this region.

The peculiar marriage custom of Ladakhis where the father of the boy leave him to stay with the joint family or may leave parents house and parents along with unmarried children and stay in a newly build house. This indicates that newly married woman, (i.e., wife of son) holds a superior position than the parents of the boy.

A Socio-linguistic analysis of euphemistic expressions and linguistic taboos also is a potent source of a given speech community. The former are a point to the ethical or moral outlook of its members towards certain objects and acts, and the latter have the potentiality of unfolding the mysteries of the superstitions and beliefs that the speech community has nourished or inherited. In this regard, an equally important but still unexplored linguistic area is the analysis of social code terms which contain, in a very subtle form, the deep rooted socio-cultural traits and practices of the speech of the community concerned. For instance, swearing trinity of gods, *konchok sum* by the Buddhists of Ladakh is a clear indication of their association with the Buddhist culture of the region.

Now coming to the real problem of Buddhist culture in Ladakh, it may be pointed out that though Buddhism as a religion discipline has its specific dimensions with regard to metaphysical considerations and religious practices, yet the same is not true of the cultural traits of its followers.

The history of the spread of Buddhism tells us that in its outward journey it was embraced by people belonging to different racial and social groups and climatic conditions, already having their respective socio-cultural bases. Under the circumstances the cultural milieu of all the followers of the Buddha could not be uniform. The uniformity, of course, could be at the level of religious practices, art and sculpture, though there too, the geographical impact on these patterns cannot be overlooked. The local cultural variations are observable both in their visual forms and abstract concepts.

Here we will study linguistic manifestation of the Buddhist culture in the Ladakh region. Lets take socio-cultural facets—

Socio-Cultural Facets

When all the other means of treatment of a sickman are exhausted and he is on the verge of death, a lama prepares an effigy of the dying person and attires it as male or female as the case may be. After performing a ritual it is taken as in funeral procession along with lama musical instruments to a cross road during night. There while consigning the dummy to flames a man cries loudly that "so and so" is very sick and should be cured. After that they return home with a trust that the death has been averted and the sick will be alright.

The other term related to a post-death ritual is Lamaston. Among Buddhists of Ladakh the dead body of a person is not cremated immediately. It is kept for there to seven days, depending on the status of the deceased. The corpse is kept in a sitting posture in a room with the soles touching the ground. During this period the lamas read the scriptures by the side of the dead. This ritual is known as Lamaston.

An equally important and related to post death rituals of the cultural life of Bodhis of Ladakh region is termed as Yang-khuk. Etymologically, yang means calling faith. Its object is to retain the prosperity which otherwise may go with the outgoing soul. It is performed by a lama at the time of the departure of a soul from a house. The term 'phowa' which belongs to post-death ceremony is one of the important term of the Buddhist culture.

There is a term 'Rik-sum-gompo' (Trinity of Lords) universally used by the Buddhists of Ladakh region. It stands for the trinity of Buddhist pantheon viz. Arya Manjusri, Arya Avalokitesvara and Arya Vajrapani. According to the tradition, the figures of this trinity representing yellow, white and blue colours, respectively, are either made of clay, or carved on stone, or wood, or are drawn on paper and put on doorheads to ward off the entrance of various evil spirits passing that way.

Similarly, there are a number of terms in Ladakh which are indicative of various cultural traditions, followed by the inhabitants of these regions. One of such term is 'Tsha-khang' standing for a particular type of structure raised to house the images and a little medallion figure of a lama, made of a little portion of his ashes mixed with clay. It can be compared with the tradition of 'pratimāgriha' (image room) of the kings of the solar dynasty, as referred to by the poet Bhasa in his Pratimā Nāṭku, like Tsha-khang, erection of Dung-tan in the memory of a dead person is another form of the cultural tradition of the Buddhists of the repository of the relics of an honoured person such as a lama, a king or a person of great importance. In case of a lama the relic could be his body as well, but in other cases it is their ashes only.

Another Linguistic relates to a post-death ritual 'Lamaston'. Among Buddhists of the Ladakh region the dead body of a person is not cremated immediately as said earlier. It is kept for three to seven days depending on the status of the deceased. The corpse is kept in a sitting posture in a room with the soles as 'En-dum chorten' the lateral meaning of which is 'En' discord' 'dum' binding/bringing together, thereby conveying the meaning 'an accord'. According to cultural traditions of Buddhism in this part of the country such a *chorten* is erected to commemorate the event of an accord of two disputing Bhikshu Sangha of Buddhism: structurally, it differs from the other types which are so common in Ladakh.

The cultural vocabulary of Ladakhi has another intresting term called 'mesol'. It is a ritual performed at the time of Losar as an integral part of it. According to the celebrations of Losar which start from the first day of the eleventh month of the Tibetan Calender, 'Lhato', the seat of family deity, is replaced daily with a new one called 'Lhasol'. Immediately after the 'Lhasol' a male member goes to the family with a big semi-circular cake of flour. He lights up a lamp on the grave and places small pieces of cake, meat and other eatables thereon. He loudly calls the names of the deceased members of the family where 'chang' and cakes are served.

It would be interesting here to make a mention of the terms which form the part of the cultural vocabulary of Ladakh dialect. These are Khang-chen (Lit. a big house). The currency of these two terms for 'house' is an indicative of prevalence of the cultural trait, known as primogeniture system, according to which the eldest son alone inherits the ancestral property. There the aged parents voluntarily give up their right to ancestral property, as soon as the eldest son is married, and retires to a nearby small house to live in, leaving the ancestral big house 'Khang-chan' for the eldest son who now becomes the sole legal owner of the ancestral property. Other sons and daughters either entirely become dependent on their elder brother or retire to the monastic order. As in other shapers of cultural life in the field of art-architecture, especially of temple architecture, sculpture or iconography, mural painting or scroll painting, liturgy or spiritual performances, too, there are hundreds of technical and non-technical terms which when analysed linguistically throw a flood of light on their contemporary religious-cultural practices in their territorial settings. Besides, a textuo-linguistic analysis of such terms occurring in ancient and medieval texts of the Buddhist literature, can be successfully exploited to draw a trustworthy picture of these objects of religio-cultural life in the given period of history. Moreover, a contextual analysis of these terms can also help us in assessing the relevance and impact of art and sculpture in Buddhism. Various technical terms relating to structures of *gonpas* and *chortens* (Chhortens), forms and postures of icons of various deities of the Buddhist pantheon. Size, form and colour of scroll paintings (Thangkas and mandalas) when studied in their respective contexts are sure to yield quite faithful result of these aspects of Buddhist culture in the past and the present. For instance, a structural analysis of the elements denoted by the terms *ghi, gya, wang, tal,* etc., in the preparation of a *mandala* can give us an inside into the spirituo-cultural aspect of these formations in spiritual performances in Buddhism. The eight terms standing for eight types of chortens in the Ladakhi traditions are indicative enough of their structural peculiarities.

The few examples of the cultural vocabulary of Bodhis of Ladakh region as explained above, are enough to draw the attention of scholars to explore this source of the cultural study of the tribes living in the interior part of India.

A Look at Bhoto Society in Ladakh

Prem Singh Jina

Ladakh has two districts : Leh and Kargil. Leh is dominated by Bhotos whereas Kargil has Muslims of Shia sect in majority.

Though Bhotos do not belief in caste system, we can see some social classes in their society viz. Kalon, Lonpo, Mon, Gara, Beda, etc. Mon, Gara and Beda families considered lower class. Higher class families generally don't allow them in their worshipping room, (i.e., *chot-khang*) where their family god or Pa-lha resides. Ribbach said that Bedas are considered as unclean person by the higher Buddhist families. He remarks :

"One must take special care not to provoke the Pa-lha (father god). He is terrible in anger. If an unclean person – a Beda – enters the house or even touches the hearth, or if by mistake someone burns an old rag, dog's excrement or something like that in the hearth then, the Pa-lha becomes angry. It costs the lamas a great deal of trouble - and the householder. Considerable expense to appease the god by offering prayers and exorcisms and thus restore peace."[1]

It is said that Mons came in Ladakh much earlier to Mongolian tribes, However, they had good number of colonies in Zangskar later Skide Nima Gon called some Mons from Zangskar, to play music. Mons accepted king's request. Mons were good musicians, therefore, King offered them land near Leh. In later centuries when Bhotos became dominant in Ladakh they did not like Mons' society, however they invited them in all auspicious occasion for playing music. This tradition still continues and Mons still remained at their lower position in the Bhoto community. Ribbach explains the Mons position in the following way :

"Mon called Chosphel from neighbouring village had come in late one evening. He was refused entry and had to wait outside for a long time away from the house. Meanwhile the first of the monks had a flat pan fetched for him and told Namgyal, I'll show you how to perform a fire—offering to conciliate the bad spirits. Namgyal had put all kinds of food leftovers into the pan—bread crumbs, flour, rice, bones, onions and salt. Glowing charcoal was placed on top so that the house was filled with a thick, stinking smoke. All the inhabitants of the house went down through the stable to the front door which the monk opened and then threw out part of the smoking contents of the pan over the threshold. The Mon, who still awaiting admittance outside, was allowed to step over the smoking contents of the pan, enter the house and carry out his business."[2]

Bedas and Mons both existed till 1981 when I came first time to Ladakh. They rambled around in tents for begging and also moved from village to village and played Daman and Surna for public. Bedas belong to both Buddhist as well as Muslim communities. However, Mons belong to only Buddhist Community. Mons in-fact are old tribes whereas Bedas came very late that is probably during 16th century A.D. when Jamyang Namgyal was the king in Ladakh.

According to another local legend that :

> "Once a Ladakhi queen fell in love with her Minister. This news when King heard, he immediately expelled his Minister and ordered him to live like a begger. He had to follow King's order. Later his descendants also got bound to live like beggers and Ladakhis called them Bedas.[3]

The third major lower group called Gara. They are normally blacksmiths and manufacture plough—scissors, arrow-heads, knives, axes, stones, etc.[4]

Besides, the following families of Buddhist Community are considered high class.[5]

1. King (or rGyal-po)
2. gzims-dpon
3. nan-gner
4. mk'ar-dpon

5. gner-pa
6. s'in-dpon
7. degs-dpon
8. dkor-dpon
9. yig-dpon

rGyal-po has the highest order in Bhoto community. In olden days rGyal-po was surrounded by officials gzims-dpon (Master of Chamber), he was the main speaker for king in audience; nan-gner presented the petitions of subjects before King; mk'ar-dpon was the incharge of order cleanliness inside the residence and acted as substitute (sku-ts'ab) of King and the Prime Minister when they were absent; gner-pa was the incharge of store; s'in-dpon procured and stored wood and coal from each district (or yul) of kingdom; 'degs-dpon weighed the incoming commodities; dkor-dpon was the incharge of religions objects and yig-dpon pinned the letters of rGyal-po; bka-blon, the Prime Minister and blon-po, the Governor.

rGyal-po, Co (or jo) and Lord families of Bhotos were considered first class families; bka-blon and blon-po, the second class families and the rest little lower but also come under sku-Drag.[6]

There is also a religious group who perform religious duties and are considered higher class in the Buddhist Community. These are :

1. Rinpoche
2. Lama
   (a) Gelong
   (b) Ordinary
3. Chomo

Rinpoche is also known as Tulku or Kushok. He is the head of the monastery and responsible for special rituals. Gelong is the senior lama and performs all kinds of rituals whereas other lamas and Chomos perform day to day rituals according to public needs Fig. 2.1.

Social Change

In olden days Polyandry was very common among the Bhoto community in Ladakh. Therefore many Buddhist girls remained unmarried. They had two options : either to become Chomo or

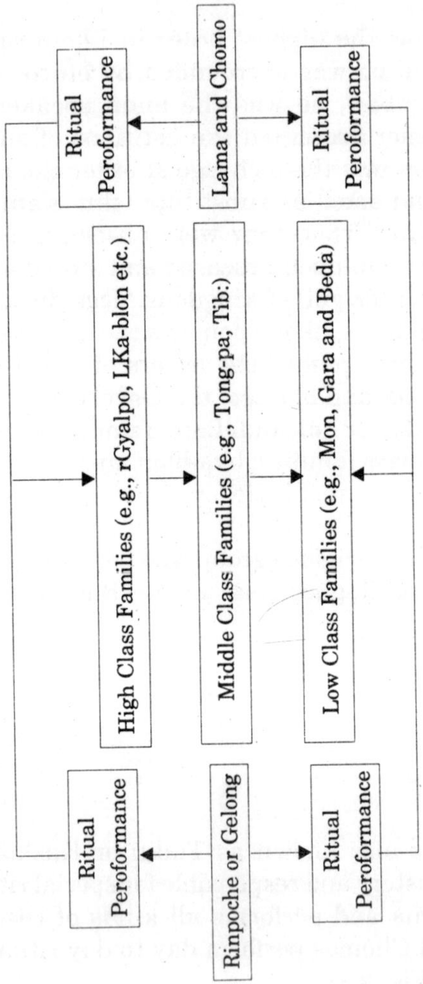

Fig. 2.1. Socio-cultural relations among Bhoto community in Ladakh.

marry with Muslim boys. This helped to increase Muslim population.

Leh was also trade centre of Central Asian traders. Muslim traders were then in majority. They came to Leh from Kashmir, Yarkand, Skardu and Turkistan. During trade affairs they had to stay at different Sarais at Leh for some days. On these occasions they happened to come in contact with young girls and later under Mutta Muslim tradition they married them. This tradition also increased Muslim population and the descendants of such marriages called Arghons.[7]

During Dogra period 1834-42 many Dogra soldiers married with Buddhist girls. Their offerings were called Ghulamzadas.[8] After Maharaja of Jammu & Kashmir state in 1871 permitted they were allowed to do any kind of private job. Later they were absorbed in the general public.

Today Ladakh is emerging as one of the best tourist stations in the world map because of Buddhist cultural identity. However experiences point at the following changes :

1. Polyandry system has been stopped to a great extent.
2. Inter-marriages are taking place. Higher class Bhoto families have now started to get married with middle class.
3. Lower class families without any hesitation are now ready to get married with Hindus.
4. Lower class Buddhist families are now gradually changing their traditional jobs and prefer to do white coller Government job and jewellery business.
5. Many learned lamas have change their traditional lama dress. They prefer to lead family life.
6. Marriages between Buddhist girls and Muslim boys have been decreased to the lowest minimum.
7. Child marriages have been decreasing day by day among educated Bhotos.
8. We find education awareness among Bhoto families.
9. The percentage of marriages have been increased by 2 to 3 per cent per year.
10. The custom of monogamy is being followed by the educated Bhoto families. They also prefer to have only two or three children.
11. Young generation likes to live western style.

12. Cultural clashes between old and young generation can be noticed.
13. Cigarette smoking, drinking, cyling and driving are popular among Buddhist youths.
14. Mountaineering, trekking, rafting, etc., are the newly emerging games.
15. Buddhist boys, lamas and even ladies are ready to become tourist guides.

Notes and References

1. Ribbach, S.H., *Culture and Society in Ladakh'* Tr. John Bray, Ess. Ess. Publication, New Delhi, 1986, p. 31.
2. *Ibid,* p. 173.
3. Jina, Prem Singh; *Ladakh: The Land and the People,* Indus Pub. Co. 1996.
4. *Ibid.*
5. *Ibid.*
6. *Ibid.*
7. Arghons : Families of half Casts (i.e., the offerings of Kashmiri or Yarkandi Muslim with Bhoto women).
8. Ghulamzadas : The slave, born. The theory was that being out of wedlock, under which it is usual practice that they used to receive their daily bread from J & K Maharaja Govt., and to give, unwillingly their labour in return viz. wool-cleaning Cf. Drew, Frederic : *Jammoo and Kashmir Territories* Cosmo Pub. 1971 (Reprint), p. 244.

3

Bhoti in Himalayan Culture : A Case Study of Ladakh

Lohzang Tsewang

The human being is a rational animal who has thinking power and with the help of his brain decides what is right and what is wrong for him ? He expresses his feelings, emotions and shares ideas with others. Thus the above experiences he can only communicate through language. The language is the outcome of combination, of letters (i.e., of vowels and consonants).

Man is not being satisfied only with simple expression of his opinions. However, he would like to keep his experiences, so that those may become a guideline for the coming generations. At this juncture script plays an important role and helps to preserve the culture and civilization of any community.

Buddhist logic also speaks about letter in the following way :

"A letter is sound which becomes basic unit to build up a name and word."

Thus the name and word consists of syllables which in fact are the combination of vowels and consonants. Therefore letter is the unit of words. But it can not be identified with script. The script has a wide concept because it is an image of the letters which is visible to eyes.

There are two types of scripts viz : pectorical and alphabetical. The second one is more convenient for recording the culture and civilization of a community. Thus, the letter, script and language are interrelated, human being experiences and thoughts may be recorded through them for a longer period.

As for the Bhoti language, it consists of four vowels and thirty consonants. This language has full capabilities to translate literature, philosophy and other subjects. Today we can see the following texts in Bhoti script :

(i) One hundred volumes of original Buddha's teaching,
(ii) Two hundred volumes of their commentaries composed by Indian Pandits, and
(iii) More than thousand volumes of Sungbum written by Tibetan great lamas.

H.H. Dalai Lama says :

"Nobody can get perfect and complete knowledge in Buddhism by any other language rather than Tibetan. So one must learn Tibetan language at first in order to do deep and vast study in Buddhism."

There is controversy among the Tibetan scholars about the invention of Tibetan or Bhoti script. Some scholars consider that before 7th century A.D. there was neither script nor grammar for Tibetan language, however, Tibetan people had only spoken language. Srong Tsan Gampo, the King of Tibet first thought about the script of Bhoti language. He therefore, selected brilliant boys and sent them to India to learn Buddhism and Grammar. Sombhota was the first Tibetan translator who sought admission in Nalanda University. He deeply studied Buddhism and Sanskrit grammar. Returning to his home land he met King Song Tsan Gompo. Who advised him to make script and grammar for Bhoti. He made two scripts : Uchan and Umed. The first script was later used in printing books and newspapers. The other was used in writing letters and in the offices. Besides, Sombhota composed eight books on grammar. At present only two of his books are available. It is hoped that the other six books possibly got lost during 9th Century A.D.

The other scholars' believe that Bhoti had script before 7th Century A.D., but it was in a fragmented form. Sombhota improved the existed old script into the present form of Bhoti script.

Today Bhoti is spoken by the people of Tibet, Bhutan and Pakistan in foreign countries. In India people of Himalayan region from Arunachal Pradesh to Ladakh use this language as their mother tongue. The root of regional and foreign Bhoti languages is same. However, we can understand little difference in pronunciation and usage of words. The written form is of course, the same.

Bhoti is known by different names such as Tibetan, Bhutani, Baltistan and Ladakhi. It seems that in some regions, the original Buddhist scripts are lost, as a result they borrowed words from other languages. This practice gradually isolated them from other communities by their mixed language form. Subsequently nothing much is written in their dialects.

This Bhoti got divided into many dialects and could not keep intact the original grammar of Bhoti. Hence it failed to get recognition in Indian constitution.

We all know that Buddhism was originated in India but later spread to neighbouring countries. But unfortunately it disappeared from its home country. However it is still preserved in its original form in Bhoti language. Therefore, it requires to be read. This can only be possible when it may get recognition by the constitution of India.

Bhoti is the national language of Bhutan and it has got recognition in China. Pakistan recognises it as its regional language then why Indian Government does not think about its recognition ? Bhoti fulfils all criteria which are required for the recognition but still fails to get recognition. Kashmiri which is not even having a script has got recognition.

Thus, if we want to preserve our unique culture and identity we must jointly struggle for the recognition of Bhoti language in Indian constitution.

4

Bhoti and Arabic Influence upon Dok Culture of Ladakh

Prem Singh Jina

Dok-yul is the Dard territory in Ladakh and is being influenced by Lamaistic and Shia Muslim culture. Earlier they were having close touch with Baltis and migrated from Brugdza adjacent to old Iran or Persia to the area near Gilgit.[1] When these Lamas settled down in Dok-yul, the Ladakh region got lamaistic culture. According to their oral tradition they came in small groups. Their ancestors were hunters who visited Dok-yul during their hunting tour. When they liked this place the other Dok-pas also migrated from Gilgit. According to Suniti Kumar Pathak :

"There had been three brothers with their families in Brugdza. One of them, in the course of hunting, reached the upper course of Sin (Indus) river, where the five villages namely Da, Hanu, Bema, Garkhun and Batalet (Batalic) are now located. That area was then full of wild jungles, and there were many game animals. The hunter and his associates had wooden footwear, as that was in use then, in the upper hills where snow, hard stones rocks and clay prevailed.

Those wooden footwear were made comfortable by putting cornhusks inside to protect their feet. In following the game they had to run up and down. Some cornhusks fell on the ground. Those hunters then left for home.

After some months they again visited the aforesaid area for hunting. They observed a few plants of corn growing there. They wondered how the corn were plants grew there. They had grown from the seeds which had been scattered here and there during their last trip. They were pleased to see that the area was fertile and decided to choose it for better inhabitation. The upper course of the river has several fountains, springs and nullas for drinking water even now. In due course they migrated from their old home of Gilgit valley. Since then, they have been the settlers in those five villages maintaining their original identity up till now."[2]

During their festival songs they sing folk songs in which they describe that how they migrated to Ladakh. The following translation of their one song makes clear that their ancestors were hunters and migrated from Gilgit.

"At Brushal and Gilgit;
One hundred youths appear.
In the fertile village of Satsil;
One hundred maids appear.
They form a great assembly at Gilgit;
The lion-king of Gilgit appears at the head of the dances.
Then all of you girls, twirl your heads; to greet us !
All you boys, clap your hands to greet us !
Hurrah for love ! well done, hallo !
On the Ambir pass it makes "tarag" !
Take the arrow then the bow, then
The arrow-shafts and the heads,
Oh boy that art clever at hiding !
Then, Oh boy, clever at climbing;
Then, Oh boy, who are clever at imitating
the antelope's cry;
Then, Oh boy, who are clever at getting out of right,
There is an ibex that can be seen, the ibex can be seen in a herd !
Now take the arrow; Oh boy
Then take the arrow – shafts and heads,
Oh boy that art clever at driving them together;
Oh boy that art clever at driving them heaps;
Thou that art clever at Singling out the best;
Thou that art clever at shooting them !
Offerings of flour, butter, milk and water
Must now be brought ! Honour of thee Oh God !
Now cut the flesh with a sharp knife,

Roadsted meat must be offered !
Cut it to pieces !
Give a mouthful to each of one hundred boys !
They will carry the meat in their pockets of leather;
They will give some to father and mother, Oh boy !
They will make presents of it to one hundred girls, Oh boy !
Now we have come to happiness and abundance Oh boy !"[3]

Similarly during marriage ceremonies the bride party asks many questions from bridegroom party and when satisfied with the answers, they allow them to bride's house. On this occasion questions and answers are being given in the following manner :[4]

The bride party puts questions : "who are you ? where do you come from ?"

On behalf of the bridegroom party, The oldest person among them responds : "We are the descendants of three splendid brothers. We have come from Brugdza, the sgo-ldan corner of Gilgit valley."

In Ladakh Dok-pas are being influenced by Bodhi and Arabic culture because the villagers of Da, Hanu, Darchik, Bema, Garkon, etc., are following Buddhism whereas Dras, Kargil, etc., people follow Shia sect of Islam. It is said in olden days during marriage or death ceremonies lamas and Aghas both were called to conduct the rituals.

Notes and References

1. Pathak, Suniti Kumar, 'The Dokpa ('Brog-pa) in Ladakh-remnant of the Aryans; In; *Ladakh Studies* News letter No. 8, Dec. 1996. p. 24.
2. *Ibid.*
3. Francke, A.H., The Eighteen Songs of the Bono-Na festival (Bono-Nayi Lu Athrungsh)", *The Indian Antiquary* Vol. XXXIV, 1905, Swati Pub. Delhi, 1985, p. 93.
4. Pathak, Suniti Kumar; *op. cit.*

5

The SA-sKYA-PA Order and Ladakh

C.D. Sebastian, mst

Introduction

The Sa-sKya-pa order derives its name from the Sa-skya monastery founded in 1073 (or 1071?) by dKon-mChog-rGyalpo. It got its name from the yellow colour of the scanty soil at the sight of its first monastery in western Tibet.[1] The first Sa-skya-pa masters promoted a great translating activity from Sanskrit and prepared ground for Bu-ston, a 13th to 14th century scholar who revised and translated texts in order to ascertain their authority and to eliminate the dubious versions. Under the abbot Phags-pa, in 13th century, the Sa-skya-pa enjoyed considerable political power. Phags-pa conferred initiation according to the *Hevajra Tantra* on Kublai Khan (founder of the Mongol dynasty in China) and in turn, was appointed TI-SHIH (Chinese-Imperial Perceptor) and was invested with authority to govern Tibet, though under the control of the Mongol Court.[2]

Early History of the Sa-skya-pa Order

Brog-mi, one of the most prominent among the bka-dams-pa order, with financial assistance from the local rulers of western Tibet, had set out for India and Nepal. Having studied Sanskrit extensively in Nepal, he pursued studies at Vikramsila under the guidence of the *Mahasiddha Santi-pa* who had written a commentary on the Hevajra Tantra. This text explains the experimental character of spiritual growth expressed in the symbols and images of femininity. However, Brog-mi received most of his teaching in Tibet from an Indian master, after paying him a considerable sum of money. Brog-mi later translated the

Hevajra Tantra in to Tibetan, and it became on the basic texts of the Sa-skya-pa order. This order, as has been mentioned above, is named after the place where one of Brog-mi's disciples dkon-mChog-rGyal-po of the Khon family established around 1073 A.D. The monastery lies on the trade route linking the Nepal valley with the rich agricultural area around Shigatse, with further extension with the pastoral lands that supply the order with butter and wool. The trade and the natural resources contributed to the growing wealth of the areas dominated by the Sa-skya-pas.

dKon-mchog-Rgyal-po's son and successor, the great Sa-skya-pa, Kun-dGa-Sning-po (1091-1150), formulated the tenets of this school, which became to known LAM-BRAS ("the path and its fruition"), and ultimately can be traced back to another Indian Mahasiddha, Virupa. Supported by wealthy land owners and using his own organizational capacity Kun-dGa-sNing-po laid the foundation for the greatness of the Sa-skya-pas. Eventually, they were granted sovereignty over Tibet by Kublai Khan of Yuan dynasty[3]. Thus they were politically powerful also for a short period of time.

The Cult of the Sa-skya-pa

dKon-mChog rGyal-po claimed inspiration from the celestial Bodhisatva of wisdom, Manjusri, through the Indian sages ranging from Nagarjuna to Vasuputra. And he mixed together the *old* and the new Tantras, calling his doctrine the new-old occult mystery of the deep insight. Its mystical insight is called the "fruitful path". Its special gospels are Nagarjuna's *Avatamsaka* and Vasubandhu's *Paramartha.*

Its tutelary demon is Vajra-Phurpa, for whose and other demonist worship, it borrowed the Ning-ma books *Dorje Phurpachai Choga,* and from the newer schools were taken Dem-Chok, Dorje, Kando, Den-zi, Maha-maha-ma-yab, Sangya to pa and *Dorje dutsi.* The denominal guardians are "the Guardian of the Tent' and "the Face-Lord". Its hat is Sa-zu. But now recept in a few externals it is practically undistinguishable from the Ning-ma-pa.[4]

The Meaning of the Sa-sKya-pa System

The Sa-sKya-pa system is also called the "Paths of its fruit" *(Lam-bras).* The Buddhist path as presented here evolves in three stages:

(i) the actual moment, the particular existence, the actual disposition in which the seeker finds himself.

(ii) these road to be followed, the path on way, during which he learns and understands what is to be accepted or rejected, and the mystical experiences that are realizable with the help of various form of meditations and yoga;

(iii) the fruit, on the result, the attainment of the Buddhahood. This experience can be attained through meditation while travelling on the path or during the intermediate stage between death and a new life.

This is the actual meaning of the system. These three stages are included in this *lam-bras.*

The Philosophical Standpoint of the Sa-sKya-pa

In Tibetan Buddhism, everything is centred on the *Sems* (Sanskrit *citta*), the mind element. It is exalted in a body of sublime knowledge, and thus, through successive moments, can be transformed into the diamond body, that is, the Buddhahood. This *Sems* is not only a mind element, it is also light, and it is precisely on the question of the relationship between the two-the mind element and the light that notable differences among the various Tibetan schools become evident and apparent.[5] The Sa-sKya-pa system considers light as a specific characteristic and distinguishable feature of the mind element. But for the dGe-lugs-pa, the light is *Sem's* very nature.

There was no aspect of Buddhist Philosophy with which the Sa-sKya-pas did not deal with. They made an important attempt to classify the Tantras, that is, the tantric scriptures, much before that of mKhas-Grub-rJe between the 14th and 15th Century. They had the Philosophical accumen, in the early days of Sa-sKya-pa order, to dive deep in the vast ocean of Buddhist reasoning. The Sa-sKya-pas established branches in many part of Tibet and gave rise to a subsect, the Ngon-pa, founded by Kung-dga bZang-po in 1429.

Contribution of the Sa-sKya-pa in the Field of Philosophy and Literature

Apart from their involvement in political struggles, the scholars of the Sa-sKya-pa order were most active in the field of philosophy and linguistics. bSod-nams rTse-mo (1142-1182) worked on classification and systematization of Tantric literature.

Grags-pa rGyal-mTsan (1147-1216) authored the first history of the early development of Buddhism in Tibet. He also wrote on Tibet medicines and treatments. Sa-skya-scholar Kung-dGa rGyal-mTsan (1182-1251) wrote on grammer, poetry and logic. His monumental work, the famous *Tsad-ma-Rig-pai Ster* is a distinct and remarkable development of Buddhist logic "beyond Dharma-Kirti's *Pramanavarttika*" from which it starts. Phags-pa, a versatile writer on every conceivable topic in Buddhism, not only wrote stylistically elegant letters to the Mongol princes, but also devised for the Mongolian language a script that goes by his name. A truly in independent thinker in this order was Rong-ston Smra-bai Senge (1367-1449) who joined the order from a Bon-po family.[6] He authored sixty four exegetic and didactia works. Thus, these are the prominent among the Sa-sKya-pa contributions to the ever widening horizon of Buddhist thought and literature.

The Sa-sKya-pa Order in Ladakh

The arrival of the Sa-sKya-pa order in Ladakh and its establishment was during the first half of the 16th century by Lama Thung-pa Dorje.[7] This is Matho Monastery. But it was almost destroyed during the war between the Muslim invader and the Ladakhis in the late 16th century. After a couple of years of this devastation, Lama Choskyi Lodos renovated the monastery and restored its activities.[8] At present Matho Monastery is situated in the same place where it was established, at a distance of 26 kms. south-east of Leh on the other bank of the Indus, with its majestic and ancient vestige. There are around thirty-five inmates, both the monks and the novices. This is one of the important monasteries in Ladakh.

(i) Matho Monastery. At present one can notice in the Matho Monastery that near the chapels, which were renovated for the visit of Sa-sKya Tri-zin Rinpoche is a small room which is very worth-mentioning. The room, called Gonkhang, is filled with 50 cm high grain from the first harvest for this room. The room has a special significance, during the two-day Nagrang festival (at the Tibetan New year in February) and a one day festival on the eighth day of the second Tibetan month (usually in March) called the *Nyis-pe Tses-rGyat.*[9] In the monastery prayers and worships are regularly conducted and the monks are serious about their religious practices and exercises.

(ii) Importance of Matho Monastery. Matho Monastery is famous among the Ladakhis due to its oracle. The *Lha-ba* of Matho is a priest and he lives in the monastery. On special days (in winter on the eighth day of the second month according to the Tibetan calendar) the oracle runs all over the nearby mountains and on the edges of the monastery building with swift motion causing fear and wonder in the people gathered. He is blind folded and sees only with a parting on breast and back. The oracle speaks to the people by a small spring at the foot of the monastery mountain. The people come from far and near for this festival. The people have got tremendous faith on the oracle. On oracle day one can notice the religious fervour of the Ladakhis. People from all walks of life, irrespective of age and sex, gather in the monastery for this festival.

Concluding Observation

The Sas-sKya pa order had been very powerful and vibrant, both politically and philosophically, once upon a time in the annals of history. But now it does not express that vigour, when one compares it with that of other orders of Tibetan Buddhism. Yet one cannot deny the fact that the Sas-sKya-pa order is equally alive with other orders. With regard to the spread of monastic orders in Ladakh, one can notice that other orders have spread more extensively than that of the Sa-sKya-pa. Apart from the Ka-dam-pa order which represents the older order, so become established and rooted in the soil of Ladakh is that of dGe-lugs-pa. The fact that, these, particularly, the Sa-sKya-pa and the more powerful of the Ka-gyu-pa or Kas-gyua-pa schools, had not established themselves in Ladakh, may indicate that how far Ladakh was independent of central Tibet in the 13th and 14th centuries. Again, the lack of great following, unlike others orders, in Ladakh may also indicate to what extent Matho monastery is economically and politically powerful. These are a few assumptions only, which one is prone to make. But the Sa-sKya-pa order is of parmount importance to a student and researcher in Tibetan Buddhism.

Notes and References

1. Austine Waddel, "The Sects of Lamaism", in *Encyclopaedia of Tibet,* Vol. 4, S.K. Sharma and Usha Sharma (ed.) (New Delhi : Anmol Publications, 1996, p. 145.
2. Herbert Guenther, "Buddhism in Tibet", in the *Encyclopaedia of Religion,* Vol. 2 (New York: Macmillion Publishing Company) 1987, p. 409.
3. *Ibid.*
4. Austine Waddel, "The Sects Lamaism", p. 148.
5. Herbert Guenther, *"Buddhism in Tibet",* p. 409.
6. *Ibid,* p. 410.
7. Prem Singh Jina, *Ladakh : The land and the people* (New Delhi : Indus

   a- a- a- Publishing Company,) 1996, p. 227.
8. Margret and Rolf Schettler, *Kashmir, Ladakh and Zanskar* (Berkeley : Lonely Plannet Publications) 1985, p. 160.
9. *Ibid,* p. 162.

6

Preservation and Promotion of Cultural Heritage of Himalayan Region : A Special Reference to Ladakh Himalayas

Lobzang Tswang

The Condition of Buddhistic Culture in Ladakh Before Rinchen Zangpo

Ladakh is one of the Himalayan regions, mainly situated along the banks of the Indus river. The history of Ladakh before 10th Century A.D. is shrouded in mystery as we do not have any authentic information whether Ladakh was an independent country or ruled by another country's ruler. Besides, history tells us that Lhachen Palgi Gon was the first king of Ladakh in 10th century A.D. He was descendant of Tibetan monarchy. However, we can not deny this fact that before 10th century A.D. Ladakh was divided into many small petty kingdoms and ruled by several dukes. Therefore, the period before 10th century can be recognized as Dukes period.

The present population of Ladakh is the consequence of a long process of blending three different races viz : Dard, Mon and Tibetan. A.H. Francke said:

"Present population of western Tibet is the result of a long process of blending of at least three distinct peoples two of which are of the Aryans stock whilst one of which is numerically superior to the other two, is of Mongolian origin. The Aryan nations are, the Dards of Gilgit and the Mon is North Indian (perhaps from Kashmir). The Mongolian is the Tibetan origin."[1]

There are certain local customs and habits which are neither Buddhistic nor Tibetan in character. For instance, Ladakhi people make Ibex images of flour and decorated them on the wooden shelves in order to celebrate New year festival called 'Losar'. Such images of Ibex also being made on the birth day of a baby. Ibex images are considered auspicious sign for Ladakhi Buddhists. Therefore we find Ibex carving on rocks and large stones throughout in Ladakh. Pettech says, ".... this may disclose an early totemistic cult having the Ibex as the sacred animal."[2]

Some historians belief that Buddhism flourished in Ladakh before 7th Century A.D. Jame Legge and Alexander Cunningham said that in 5th Century A.D. Chinese traveller Fa-Hien visited India. While visiting India he came to Ladakh after crossing the Karakoram range from Khotan and travelled to Ghandhara via Skardo. He saw Buddhism was flourishing in Ladakh. Cunningham says :

> "Buddhism was the prevailing religion of Ladakh from the conversion of the people by Ashoka's missionaries down to early A.D. 500 when Fa-Hien visited India. At that time he found Buddhism flourishing in the little state of Kia-chha or Ladakh as well as Khotan and other small states to the northward of the Tsangling of Karakoram."[3]

In fact, the Kushan dynasty ruled northern India including some parts of central Asia. Kanishka also is said to have ruled over Ladakh. This event is confirmed by carving images on the rocks in Ghandhara style. Besides we find many inscriptions on the rocks in Kharoshti lipi. It is obvious that when Sharvastivadi Buddhism spreaded throughout in Central Asian countries, Ladakh was too influenced by this. Prof. Snellgrove says :

> "It would seem very likely that Buddhism first appeared in the Ladakh from Indian side long before the Tibetan rulers of western Tibet gave it so great impetus. But of this early pro-Tibetan Buddhism period very little remains from approximately the 1st century B.C. to 5th Century A.D."[4]

As said above the Sharvastivadi Buddhism was very popular in Kashmir and Gandhara before 10th Century A.D. In those days Ladakh was the trade centre and had trade links with Kashmir, therefore, Ladakh was influenced by Sharvastivadi Buddhism.

The opinion of some scholars is that before the introduction of Tibetan form of Buddhism in Ladakh, the people of this region practised Bon religion. Francke found some religious instruments and old paintings by excavation of ruined monastery at Lamayuru which belonged to Bon religion. Francke says :

> "Those ancient gates with four doors and the mysterious temple at Lama Yuru are apparently all of Bon-Po origin; but they are erected in the days when Bon-po religion was largely influenced by Buddhism and Hinduism."[5]

During the period of Rinchen-Zangpo

Lo-Tsa-Wa Rinchen Zangpo is regarded as the father of Buddhist culture in Ladakh. He came in 10th Century A.D. and gave precious contribution for spreading Buddhism in Ladakh. Before Rinchen Zangpo the condition of Buddhism was still to be explored fully. But the people of Ladakh might have faith in Buddhism. Rinchen Zangpo built many shrines and stupas throughout in Ladakh. He established a learning centre of Buddhism at Nyarma near Leh. He invited many eminent scholars from Kashmir to teach Buddhist doctrines. These are confirmed by his biography. Rinchen Zangpo did not introduce any new religious order, because he became a disciple of Indian Pandit Dipankara Srigyana, as such, his centre and shrines occupied by Kadampa sect which was founded by Atisa. Tashi Rabgias say :

> "The foundation of Ladakhi culture was laid down by Lama Lo-Tsa-Wa Rinchen Zangpo. He is known as a father of Ladakhi culture, but did not introduce any new religious order followed by his disciples. Because he was the follower of Atisha. Therefore, his monasteries and shrines were occupied by Kadampa sect."[6]

Rinchen Zangpo translated various Buddhist scriptures from Sanskrit to Tibetan which are preserved in Kangyur and Stangyur. He also translated many medical texts. He was a skilful physician. His translation works in the field of medicine are the source of inspiration for the Tibetan Medicine practitioners.

Rinchen Zangpo was known as the expounder of new Tantra system. Thuhu-Kan-Chas-Kyi-nima says :

> "It is regarded that the translation of new Tantra was started from translator Rinchen Zangpo. He became the expounder of the teaching of new tantra. Thus we can say that it was only Rinchen Zangpo's efforts which gave birth to new system of Tantra."[7]

Marpa was a contemporary of Rinchen Zangpo. Both were the disciples of Saint Naropa. Marpa Lo-Tsa-wa also contributed his valuable efforts in the propagation of Buddhism in Ladakh. He spent many years together in Zangskar province and built Stongde monastery there. Besides some other Buddhist scholars alongwith Rinchen Zangpo worked in the propagation of Buddhism in Ladakh, for example : In the later age of Rinchen Zangpo; Lo-Tsa-wa Phagspa Sharab of Zangskar and Balti Lo-Tsa-wa Wangchuk Tsultim helped in order to spread Buddhism throughout in Ladakh. Thus we can say that the present form of Buddhism which is still in genuine form in Ladakh, of course, through the continuous strife of teachers and translators of Buddhist scholars.

After Rinchen Zangpo

Today four major Tibetan forms of Buddhism are in practice among the people of Ladakh. These sects have their own monasteries and centres in this region. All the Buddhist Kings of Ladakh also patronised them and gave equal chance to propagate Buddhism in this province. They also encouraged the practice to send young novices to central Tibet for higher studies in Buddhism and its philosophy. After completing their studies in Tibet Ladakhi monks returned to their respective monasteries in Ladakh and enriched the traditional monastic system of Mahayana Buddhism. The details of the four sects are as follows :

1. Ningma pa order is the oldest sect founded by Indian saint Padma Sambhava in 7th Century A.D. He built Samyas monastery in Tibet based upon Andantapuri model. This order gradually spread in Tibet and its neighbouring

countries in 17th Century A.D. Padma Thinles of Ningma pa sect visited Ladakh. Deldan Namgyal (Namgial) was then the King of Ladakh. During his stay in Ladakh he built a small monastery and established Ningma pa. This tradition influenced Ladakhis and very soon got its good hold in Ladakh. Today Ladakhis believe that in early days Padma Sambhava visited Ladakh and subdued those demons who were obstructing the Buddhist culture in Ladakh.

2. Kargyudpa order was founded by Marpa Lo-Tsa-Wa in 11th Century A.D. in Tibet. This order was first introduced in Ladakh by saint Gial-Wa-God-Tsangpa who sanctified several caves and hermitages in this region in 13th Century A.D. This order was further strengthened by saint and famous traveller Stagtsang-Ras pa in 16th Century. He built the great monastery of Hemis during the reign of King Singe Namgyal (Namgial).
   In early 16th Century great teacher Chorje Danma was invited by the king Jamyang Namgyal (Namgial) and introduced Digung Ka-rGyud in Ladakh. Later this order became one of the dominant sects in Ladakh.
3. Sa-skyapa order was founded by Kho-dkonchog-Gyalpo in early 10th Century in Tsang provinces of Tibet. This order gradually spread upto China and Mongolia. In 15th Century Lama Dungpo Dorje of Tibet came to Ladakh during the reign of King Takpa Bum lde. Under the patronage of the king he built a monastery at Matho village. Great number of Ladakhis then were inspired by his teachings and adopted Sa-skya order.
4. Gelukpa order was founded by great reformer Tsong-Khapa of Tibet in 15th Century. This order was moderate from old Kadampa sect founded by Indian saint Atisha in 11th Century in Mangris. In 15th Century A.D. Sherab Zangpo of Stagmo village came to Ladakh. Later with the help of King Takpa Bum lde he was able to propagate Gelukpa order in Ladakh and built a monastery at Stagmo village. Lhawang Lotos, thereafter popularized this order in Ladakh.

Thus, the legacy which we inherited from ancient times is

still kept intact and all the noble traditions belonging to the different sects are flourishing very well in Ladakh.

Present Condition of Buddhist Culture in Ladakh

Ladakh is one of the regions where Buddhistic culture has interruptedly survived. Buddhism is practiced in day to day life by the people of Ladakh. The monasteries are the treasure house where one can have a glimpse of different Buddhistic arts preserved since Rinchen Zangpo. Alchi Choskor is the good example of such treasure where 11th Century A.D. old frescoes paintings are still preserved.

The gilded statue was raised at Shey palace in 17th Century by the King Daldan Namgyal (Namgial). It is one of the biggest Buddha images in Ladakh as well as in Tibet. There are number of stupas made of silver and other metals. These contained invaluable relics and were studded with various precious stones. The chapels and assembly halls in the monasteries are orderly decorated with beautiful scroll paintings.

Every monastery in Ladakh has a rich library on the topics of religion, philosophy, literature and arts. Each big monastery has Ka-gyur, Stangyur and different Sungbums. These religious books had been brought from Tibet. Some monasteries have even old blocks for printing. These blocks were brought from Tibet. There are many old hand written books in some monasteries. These books are written by silver and golden ink and black lacquered papers of two edges with decorated Buddha figures on each leaf are used.

In Ladakh one can acknowledge rows of the Mani walls at both sides of roads in the various places. These Mani walls are decorated with pieces of stone plates carved with famous mantra "Om mani Padme Hum". In Ladakh devotees chant these sacred mantra while circumambulating round Mani walls. This is because of the Mahayanist belief that recitation of Mantra and to take round of Maniwalls may lead the people to higher realm in the next life.

Today Government of India is seriously thinking of the preservation and development of Mahayani Buddhist culture in Ladakh. In this connection Central institute of Buddhist Studies is doing a remarkable job. This institute is fully financed by Central Government. Recently Central Government sanctioned to open monastic schools at the different monasteries under the direct control of Central institute of Buddhist studies, Leh-Ladakh. In order to preserve the above motive the State Government also allowed Bhoti language teaching facilities in state Govt. schools.

Ladakh today is stoopping towards modernization, the young generation in Ladakh is too deeply influenced by this modernization or rather to say western culture. However, they are still intact with their indigenous Ladakh culture. Tourists from west visit Ladakhi Buddhist monasteries in good number. The monasteries are also benefited as they get good amount from them in terms of donation, which is used for the construction of new or larger shrines installations larger statues of Buddha and other deities.

Conclusion

Buddhism in Ladakh faced many difficulties but still survived. Dogra reign in Ladakh was a great setback for Buddhism. During this period Buddhist culture was destroyed badly, several monasteries were looted, silver and gold statues were carried to Jammu. However, Dogra could not subdue the spirit of Ladakhis. Thereafter many Buddhist saints visited Ladakh and helped in the protection of Buddhist culture. For instance, Lama Tsultim Nima who came in Ladkah during Dogra period and revived Buddhism by his valuable preachings.

At present Mahayana Buddhism is preserved as a living faith in Ladakh. It cannot be said how far our teachers will be able to spread this religion throughout in Himalayan regions, but there is Tibetan language through which we can put together all the Himalayan people into one stream. Because Buddhist doctrines, particularly Sutrayan and Tantrayana system can only be available in this language.

At last but not the least it can be that the preservation and promotion of Buddhist culture depends upon the interest of local government and the people. In order to give strength to this culture the Government must think about the establishment of good learning centre, rich library, etc. We should therefore, be aware and always be ready to preserve the Buddhist culture not only in Ladakh but throughout in Himalayas.

Notes and References

1. Franckes, A.H. : *A History of Ladakh* Sterling Pub. New Delhi, 1977, p. 57.
2. Lucciano, Pethech : *The Kingdom of Ladakh*, p. 164.
3. Cunningham, A : *Ladakh : Physical, Statistical and Historical*, pp. 350-57.
4. Snellgrove, David : *The Cultural Heritage of Ladakh*, Vikas Publishing House, New Delhi.
5. Francke, A.H. : *Antiquities of Indian Tibet*, pp. 96-97.
6. Tashi Rabgias : *History of Ladakh,* p. 80.

7

Buddhist Monasteries in Ladakh

Jamyang Gyaltsan
and
Prem Singh Jina

Ladakh is situated at the north of Jammu and Kashmir State of India, surrounded by high Himalayan mountain ranges. The Indus river flows in the middle and irrigates the large portion of agriculture land. During summer the whole valley gets converted into laush green belt, but in winter season due to heavy snow fall the surface transport gets blocked for about seven months.

Buddhism is the oldest religion of Ladakh and entered into Ladakh during 2nd Century A.D. King Kanishka propagated Buddhism in Ladakh. He sent Buddhism missionaries to Central Asian countries via Ladakh. In Zanskar he constructed Kanika Chorten. During 6th to 7th century A.D. Ladakh was influenced by Gandhara art through Kashmir. Thus, before the development of Buddhism in Tibet, it had already flourished in Ladakh. Thereafter during 10th century when Ladakh had established its political and religious relations with Tibet. Mahayana form of Buddhism entered into Ladakh and many monasteries according to the different sects established. Here follows the details :

Monasteries

Monasteries are the religious centres of Buddhists. According to Vinaya Pitak, "Gonpa (monastery) should be constructed at least one 'Kosa' (i.e. about 1 km.) away from the inhabited area".

Therefore, Gonpa means 'Vihara', but sometimes people get confused between 'Vihara' and 'Temple'. In 'Vihara' there are many temples. For example, Thikse Gonpa is a 'Vihara' and

'Alchi' is a temple where Buddhist statues are placed but does not have accommodation for monks.

Buddhist history tells us that Anatpindak constructed first Buddhist monastery in 'Jetvana' for Buddha and Sangha. During 8th Century A.D. Padmasambhava and Acharya Santarakshita constructed many monasteries in Tibet. Samyas was the first monastery constructed by Padmasambhava in Tibet. King Thri-Srong-aLde-Tsan of Tibet also patronized Buddhism and helped its propagation in Tibet.

During 11th Century A.D. Rin-chen-Zang-po constructed first monastery at Nyarma in Ladakh. It is said that the Dukhang of this monastery was so big that at a time about one thousand monks could sit together for prayer, sometimes they had debate classes in which hundreds of Lamas participated. It is now ruined. Padmasbhava was the key founder of Ning-ma-pa sect in Tibet. Besides, he propagated this sect throughout in Tibet and Ladakh. He visited many places in Ladakh viz. at Pho-kar-zong in Kargil, Dak-thok monastery at Sakti.

During 12th Century Marpa also helped in the propagation of Buddhism in Tibet and its surrounding areas. He was the founder of Kargyud pa order and visited India three times, under his guidance Naropa studied Tantrik Vidhyas. After returning from India he spent most of his time in preaching Buddhist doctrine. Melaraspa was his obedient student who spread his teaching under Kargyud pa order throughout in Tibet and its adjoining areas.

In 1170 A.D. Lama Marpa visited Zanskar and established Stong-lde monastery. Thereafter many Buddhist Siddhas visited Ladakh; popular among them were Siddha bZhad-pa who visited Zanskar in 1170 A.D.; Siddha God-Tsang-pa came in Ladakh during King Tashi-Gon. In 1225 A.D. he went to the rock cave upper side of Hemis Monastery and went for meditation for several years.

During King Singe Namgyal, Lama Stag-Tsang-Raspa visited Ladakh and helped in the construction of Hemis, Wan-la, Miru, etc., monasteries. The Dukhang of Hemis monastery was named after him. The second incarnation of Stag-Tsang-Raspa was Choskye Dorje who constructed Dukhang Barpa in the same monastery. He also sponsored for making golden Buddha Statue of 12 feet. Thereafter Gyal-sras Rinpoche constructed third Dukhang which is popularly known as

Dukhang. At present about fifty-four sub-Gonpas and Choskors are under Hemis Monastery.

Chemday Monastery

In Ladakhi language it is pronounced as 'theg-chog rDe-chen-gLing'. It was constructed by De-Ldan-rNamgyal with the help of Lama sTag-Tsang-Na-wang-Gya-Cho just a few years after the death of King Singe Namgyal in 1644 A.D.

Stagna Monastery

This monastery derived its name from two words 'Stag' and 'Sna' meaning thereby 'Tiger' and 'Nose' respectively. Therefore, after the Tiger's nose like hillock on which the monastery is established called Tiger's nose or Stag-sna (= Stanga) monastery.

According to Tibetan tradition this monastery is named as Dongdin. It was established in 1618 A.D. by Chos-je-mug-jin. Marbal statue of Avalokitesvara is a most popular statue of this monastery. The following monasteries are under its control.

1. Mud → (Changthang region)
2. Bardan
3. Stagremo — In Zanskar region (Ladakh in J&K State)
4. Zong-khul
5. Guru-Ghantal
6. Dag-Phug-ling
7. Ling-tup
8. Sasuk
9. Yar-Zong. — In lahul region (Himachal Pradesh)
10. Lab-cang
11. Zo-ling
12. Kar-dang
13. Tinam
14. Skyang-nang

Phyang Monastery

In Tibetan language this monastery is known sGang-on-Tashi-Chos-zong. It was founded by Lama Chosje ldan-Ma-Kunga-Tags-pa in 1515 A.D. When Tashi Namgyal was the King of Ladakh. Thereafter Tsewang Namgyal constructed Gonkhang of this Monastery. There are many old statues in this temple. Later a new structure of this monastery was made during King

Jamyang Namgyal period. It has following main branch monasteries under its control.

1. Lamayuru
2. Shang
3. Sachukul
4. Skyurbuchan.

Lamayuru Monastery

In the eleventh century A.D. it was founded by Lo-Tsa-wa Rinchen Zangpo. The old Lha-Khang Singe-sGang-Lha-Khang is still preserved ancient traditional art. It has about 31 sub-monasteries.

Kor-Zok-monastery

It is located in Chang-Thang near Tso-mo-ri-ri, Lama Kunga Lotos Ningpo founded this monastery in 1851 A.D. Rusod pon, the head of Rupsho and Tsering Tashi of Chang-Thang helped in the construction of this monastery and installed copper with golden polished statues and silver Chortens.

The Du-Khang of this monastery has an important Buddha statue in which Buddha bones (or Asthiyas), Buddha's teeth, and Bodhisattava Karivansha's bones are placed.

Mang-to Monastery

It is situated on the hillock of Mang-to village Mang-to means 'A happy village'. The name of this monastery also derived after village. The Tibetan name of this monastery is 'Thupstan-Shaling-Choskhor'. It was constructed during King Takpa-Bum-lDe (1400-1440) A.D. period with the help of Lama Tung-pa-dorje-Palzang.

Mang-to belongs to Sa-skya order. This sect was founded by Kon-chog Gyalpo who in 1073 A.D. constructed 'Chang' monastery and 'Bhikshu Sangha' in Tibet. During 15th Century A.D. when Lama Tung-pa Dorje Palzang came in Ladakh, the two deities also came to Ladakh. During annual festival they perform oracle. On this occasion people gather and ask different questions from them.

Gon-khang of this monastery is the oldest temple. It has many old statues and paintings. The following monasteries are taken under its control.

1. Skyid-mang
2. Kurgon of Leh
3. Kurgon of Igoo.

Lha-Khang-Sarop

This monastery is situated in stagmo village. It was constructed by Stod-Sherab-Zang-po in 1427 A.D. and was the first Gelukpa order monastery in Ladakh. Later in 1430 A.D. sPon-Paldan-Sherab constructed Thiksay monastery. In the Gon-khang of this monastery Vajra-Bherava statue is the main attraction. It is 16 feet in height. It has one branch Gonpa Deskyid in Nubra which was constructed by Sherab Zangpo in 1433 A.D.

Spe-Thub-Monastery

The Tibetan name of this monastery is Ga-lDan-Tar-rGyas-Ling. It was constructed by Lama 'Tha-vang-lotos' in 1432 A.D. He brought copper and gold mixed metal twenty one statues from Tibet. The Pal Sri-Devi (or Jigchet) looks like Kali Devi and placed in Gon-khang. According to Buddhist tradition Jigchet is one of Dharmapala. The following monasteries are under its control.

1. Gurphug Gonpa
2. Sabu Gonpa
3. Sankar Gonpa

Likir Monastery

The Tibetan name of this monastery is 'Lhu-Khyil' means 'Nag'. 'Lhu-Khyil' is the name of village situated below the hillock. The Monastery is situated on the hillock and the monastery received its name after the name of village.

Lama Drub-vang-chos-rje' in 1115 A.D. founded this monastery when Lha-Tsan-rGyalpo was the King of Ladakh. The Monastery so followed this tradition. rJe-Tsong-kha-pa and Avalokitesvara are among its popular statues. The monastery has the following monasteries under its control.

1. Karsha
2. Stong-lde
3. Rangdum

(In Zanskar region, Kargil district of Ladakh)

4. Mune
5. Phug-thal

Rizong Monastery

This monastery is also known with 'Shad-sGrub-gLing' means a place suitable for meditation. It was constructed by Lama Tsultrim Nyima in 1831 A.D. This monastery has strict Vinaya rules. It has many statues and stupas. The 18 feet high stupa and Buddha statue of Dukhang are some of the important one.

Lama Tsultrim Nyima also constructed Samstan-ling Monastery in 1842 A.D. in Nubra valley. Like Rizong this monastery also follows Vinaya rules strictly under Gelukpa order.

Conclusion

Buddhism entered Ladakh through Kashmir in 2nd Century A.D., after 10th Century A.D. four sects of Buddhism spread in this region. In each monastery one can see a good library in which 103 sets of Kangyur (i.e., Buddha Teachings) and Stangyur of 225 texts written by Indian Acharyas viz. Acharya Nagarjuna, Leeghnag, Asang, Santidev, Dharmakirti, Sakyashribhadra, etc. These scholars have written commentaries on Buddha teachings. Besides, there are many important books written by Tibetan and Ladakhi Scholars.

8

Hemis Tsechu of Ladakh

Jamyang Gyaltsan (Tr. P.S. Jina)

In Ladakh Hemis festival is popularly known as 'Hemis Tseschu'. It was first time celebrated by Hemis monastery under the direction of Gyalsras Rinpoche Mipham Tsewang. Since then it became tradition and organised by the monastery every year during summer (i.e. in between May and June). According to Tibetan calendar it starts from 6th day of the 5th month of the year. On this day Lamas from Chemde and Hemis gather at the main 'Dukhang' of Hemis monastery for the arrangement of necessary materials.

On the next two days (i.e. on 7th and 8th day) lamas gather on the roof of 'Dukhang' and perform ritual activities related with 'Istha Dev' (i.e. ferocious and silent deities). On 9th day they worship 'Casum' and in the evening of the same day practice Cham without mask.

On 10th day early in the morning (i.e., 5 a.m.) lamas enter in the monastery in raws and decorate 'Thankas' of Dukpa Rinpoche for exhibition.

Tantric Dance

The festival then finally starts on 10th morning and lasts for two days (i.e., 10th and 11th day). Here follow the details :

On First Day

On this day lamas wear colourful dress and masks of the different deities, thereafter they perform Cham in the following manner.

1. Janag or Cham-Skor-sum. Lamas wear Janag dress and then come to Chamra for Cham.

2. Rak-Bag-Chutug. This time lamas wear Vajra Guru marks and dresses, and come to the Chamra for dance, during this dance they chant 'Vajra Guru' mantras.

3. Katin-Chen-Chutuk. On this occasion sixteen 'Anugrahas' alongwith eight gurus enter in Chamra and sit at their allotted seats. Soon after four 'Mahe Suras' enter and after saluting their gurus they dance before them. Next four 'Maha Suras' also do the same job and dance. Finally at first eight gurus stand for dance then 'Anugrahas'.

4. Dukhang. Immediately after the break some lamas go to Dukhang to exhibit 'Jing-Skyong' thankas then lamas who wear 'Jing-skyong' masks come for dance.

5. Turdak Zee (Four Samasanathipati). After 'Jing-skyong' four lamas with Samsanathipati costumes come for dance.

6. sGoma-Zee (Four Dawarpala). Four lamas who wear Dawarpala dress, then come for dance.

7. Che-chog-Guru-Nagpo-Na. (Five Param Mahakarona avatars) :

This time five lamas in 'Che-Chog-Guru-Nagpo' dress come for dance and during dance they kill a lama who wears 'Jansha' dress. It is said 'Jansha' was a enemy who committed 10 sins.

8. Chog-len-na (Ganas). Now five lamas of 'Ganas' costumes come for dance and cut enemy effigies into small pieces which they throw in different directions. Soon after, 10 lamas wearing king dress join with them and dance together.

After the Ganas Cham first day function comes to an end.

On Second day

According to the Tibetan calendar on the eleventh day of fifth month of the year lamas get up early in the morning and offer prayer to Gonpa deities alongwith monastic instruments viz Gyaling, Tung, etc. Later they hang 24 feet high Rinpoche Mipham Tsewang's Thanka along front side of monastery wall. Then they start second day function in the following manner :

1. Janag. Lamas wear 'Janag' dress and come to Chamra for Cham.

2. Gyalpo-Pekar. In the Dukhang of the monastery lamas decorate the Gyalpo-Pekar Thanka. This thanka is a precious one and is made of pearls and silk cloths. One lama then wears

King Pekar costume and carry various religious articles. But as he reach at the door of Dukhang some people play a drama and request to remain in Dukhang till Horse, Yak, Sheep, Goat and Dog complete a roud of Dukhang. Spectators enjoy to see this drama.

3. Acharyas. Then lamas who wear Acharyas dress and mask come in a circular way.

4. Maning Sum (Matidah). Thereafter three naths come to chamra alongwith a big team of Sangpa-zee (4 Tantriks), two Guchangs, four Lamas, four women and four Stakshar. They all together perform Cham.

5. Two Acharyas. This time two Acharyas of Hemis and Chemde monasteries come to Chamra. They perform Cham alongwith two dance organisers. During Cham they perform Serkem rituals.

6. Mahe Dongchan, Dwarpalika and Dwarpalas. This time 'Mahe-Dongchan' first appear in Chamra later four Dwarpalikas and four Dwarpalas come, they all dance together. During the course of Cham they kill their enemies and throw their pieces to the different directions.

7. Hashang and Hatugs. Now four *sevaks* come with incense pot, musical instruments such as-rNa, Bugzal, etc. Hashang and Hatug follow them. During Cham Hashang offer fruits and give philosophical teaching to Hatug. When Hashang finished his teachings, he alongwith Hatug starts dancing later offer Khadaks to Rinoche's throne.

With Hashang and Hatug Cham the second day function comes to an end.

Hemis festival is popular among Ladakhis as well as in foreign countries. However, Telo Tsechu has especial importance, it falls every year after a gap of 11 years. Following are some of its features :

1. On this day Padmasambhava was born on lotus flower in 'Dhanakosha' (Urgyan) region.
2. On this day King Indra Bodhi of Urgyan fulfilled his desires and received god's blessing and a son. The story of this incidence is as follows :

Indra Bodhi was the King of Urgyan (Udyana). He had all sorts of things but no son. Therefore, he always worshipped god, and donated money to the poor. One day he had no money in his treasury, he ordered his businessman Norboo Zangpo to go to sea and bring jewels. Norboo Zangpo went into the sea and brought jewels. Before receiving these jewels King Indra Bodhi offered prayer to jewels. Suddenly through his one eye he saw strange light and many rainbows. He called his minister and asked about this strange incident. Minister replied, "His excellency ! In money island one eight years boy appeared on lotus flower. He may be your son".

"You are right, last night I saw similar dream. Therefore go and bring him in the palace".

The minister went to the island and brought the boy to the palace. When the King saw the boy, he again received a strange light. So, he offered prayer and welcomed him in the palace. Later in a function he offered his throne.

3. On this day guru defeated five hundred 'Mustag' sastas in south 'Thagnagar'. As a result he was known Singhe Dadog (i.e. Guru Singhanath). Thereafter, he went towards 'Lakha' in the south-west of 'Gung-Thang' country.

Notes and References

1. Guru-Tsan-rGyat :
   (a) Padma Jung-nas — Guru Padmakar
   (b) Padma Samvhav — Padma Sanbhav
   (c) Lodan Chog-sret — Dheemat Varauci
   (d) Padma Gyalpo — Padam Raj
   (e) Nyima otzer — Adhiyamah
   (f) Shakya Singhe — Shakya Singh
   (g) Singhe Dadul — Singhnad
   (h) Dorje Dolot — Vajra lila
2. Guru Tagpo-Na (Five ferocious Teachers) :
   (a) Buddha Thot theng tsal —Vikram Buddha Kapal Mala
   (b) Padma thot-theng tsal —Vikram Padma Kapal Mala
   (c) Vajra thot theng tsal —Vikram Vajra Kapal Mala
   (d) Karma thot theng tsal —Vikra Karam Karma Kapal Mala
   (e) Ratna thot deng tsal —Vikram Ratan Kapal Mala.
3. King Messenger or 'Sevak'.

9

Chortens of Ladakh

Tsering Sonam (Tr. Prem Singh Jina)

Introduction

Chorten is the combination of two words 'Chod' and 'rTen' means 'worship' and 'Base'. Therefore, it signifies 'A base of worship' or 'A worship place'. While constructing the Chorten the following things are being placed inside it.

1. Religious Books
2. Ash of dead body or a bone segment of renowned person or well-know Lama or Rinpoche's dead body.
3. Small pieces of precious things/metals.
4. Small quantity of food stuffs/food articles.
5. Mantras/religious scripts.

Thus, chorten is a religious Buddhist monument. According to Buddhist scholars those who take round from right side get 'Punya' or attain freedom from this illusioned world.

Who Builds the Chorten

In Ladakh the spon mainly build the Chorten. He may be a Lama or layman and is fully responsible to decorate it according to Buddhist tradition. Sometimes a person other than spon may build the same.

Place for Chorten

Chorten should be constructed at an impietius, ghostious and inauspicious place, so that after the construction of Chorten it may become free from ghosts or evil spirits.

Chortens are also being constructed along roadside or near monasteries, so that people may take round of it and offer their prayers. In olden days criminals were asked to contract Chortens and engrave 'Om Mani Padme Hum' or other Buddhist mantras on stone plates. This kind of punishment would change their future activities and later spend their rest period in religious deeds.

Reasons for the Construction of Chorten

The reasons for the construction of Chortens are as follows:

(i) To protect human beings from the infectious diseases.
(ii) To protect the region from any kind of natural calamities, viz., flood, landslides etc.

Rituals Performed before the Construction of Chorten

Before the construction of Chortens, Lamas purify the place by rituals and read the following texts :

1. Ten-Drel-Snyingpo
2. Yang-sal
3. Sa-dak-do-ji
4. sDergyad-Ser-Kem.

Lamas perform rituals according to the kind of Chorten. For example, for the construction of Namgyal Chorten, they perform the rituals of Namgyal ma; for Sku-Dung Chorten, the rituals will be of Buddha. Similarly, a Chorten of honourable Lama (i.e., in which honourable Lama's bones are placed), the rituals will be according to Lama.

Chorten has following main parts :

1. Upper Part
2. Middle
3. Base
4. Singh-thri

The seeds of 'sku-Sung-Thugs' that is 'Kaya', 'Vaka' and 'Chitta' are being placed in the upper portion of the Chorten. 'Ring-cell' and small pieces of precious articles are placed in the middle portion. 'Ring-cell' is a precious liquid, automatically flows from the bones of respected Lama or Rinpoche. Normally it flows from the bones of head and near the heart. It looks like white pearl and is of considerable value for worship. Besides, the following things are placed in the lower portion of the Chorten.

(a) Small pieces of five precious metals, viz., gold, silver, diamond etc.;

(b) Different medicinal hurbs;
(c) Small portion of foodstuffs; and
(d) Some pieces of valuable cloths.

Chorten has a Singh-Thri, above where 'Pung-pa' is being made in which some traditional weapons put by the people. In fact, are it is like *'Kalash'*. After the completion of Chorten, Lamas perform ritual ceremony called *Rab-Nas* (Pran Prathisthan) for its long life.

There are many kinds of Chortens but the following eight Chortens can be seen throughout in Ladakh.

1. Pad Spung
2. Chang Chub
3. Tashi Gomang
4. Chos Thrul
5. Lha bab
6. En dum
7. Namgyal (rNam rGyal)
8. Nyang Das

Pad-Spung Chorten

Maharaja Suddhodhan constructed this Chorten on the birth of his son Siddharth at Kapilvastu. It is said that when prince Siddharth was born he walked seven steps and after each step a lotus flower bloomed. This Chorten was constructed accordingly and lotus flowers painted on five 'Pand-Rim' which is the mark of identification Fig : 9.1.

Chang-Chub Chorten

When Buddha got enlightenment under Bodhi tree on 'Purnima', the news immediately spread in every corner of the country like sun rays. As King Bimbisar heard about this, he immediately decided to construct 'Chang-Chub' chorten. He knew that Buddha would now work for the welfare of human beings and help them to get freedom from the illusion world through his love and compassion Fig. 9.2.

Tashi Go-Mang Chorten

After the attainment of Buddhahood, Buddha thought to preach to human beings. He went to 'Margdev' near 'Kashi' from Gaya and preached to his five closed 'Bhikshus' about 'Four noble truths' and 'Eight noble paths'. This was the first 'Dharma

Chakra Parvartan'. Later his five closed disciples constructed 'Tashi-Go-mang' Chorten. It has many doors which is the symbol to allow all class of people. After joining the 'Sangha' they get equal status as other Bhikshus have Fig. 9.3.

Chos-Thrul-Chorten

This Chorten constructed by Lichavies at 'Jeitvan'. It is said that when Buddha defeated all 'Sasthas' through his spiritual power, then they came to his shelter and became his followers. This Chorten is the symbol of this incident. The 'Kimrim' of this Chorten is slightly smaller than the other Chortens Fig. 9.4.

Lha-Bab Chorten

Siddharth's mother Maya Devi died just after seventh day of his birth. When Siddharth attained Buddhahood he thought to meet his mother. Hence, with the help of his spiritual power he took birth in heaven and seeked his mother. Later King of Magadh inquired about Buddha, he did not get a favourable answer, so, he went to Ananda and asked him :

> "Please tell me about Buddha. I did not find him anywhere. I can not live without him".
>
> To know the eagerness of King Bimbisar, Anand said, "Don't worry, I'll inform you about him very soon".

Then Anand went to heaven through his 'Siddhi' power and met Buddha, and requested :

> "Guruji ! all human beings in the human world are suffering. They can not live without you. Therefore, return to human world and solve their problems."

Buddha said, "Anand ! you may return soon to human world and inform people that Buddha will be coming very soon".

Anand returned to the human world. He informed all the people who were gathered near his residence that you could now very soon see your beloved Buddha. Thereafter Buddha appeared before them. Bimbisar and other gathered people became very happy. This was a precious occasion and Bimbisar immediately constructed a Chorten in the memory of this incident, which was later known as 'Lha-Bab' Chorten. It has ladders in the middle of four directions i.e., "North, South, East and West". (Fig. 9.5)

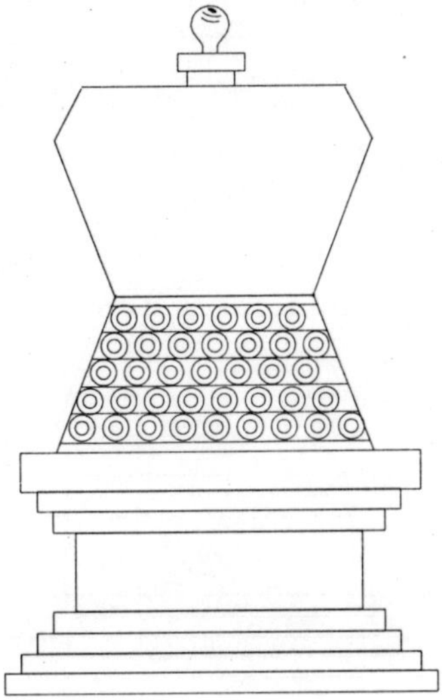

Fig. 9.1. Pad-Spung Chorten.

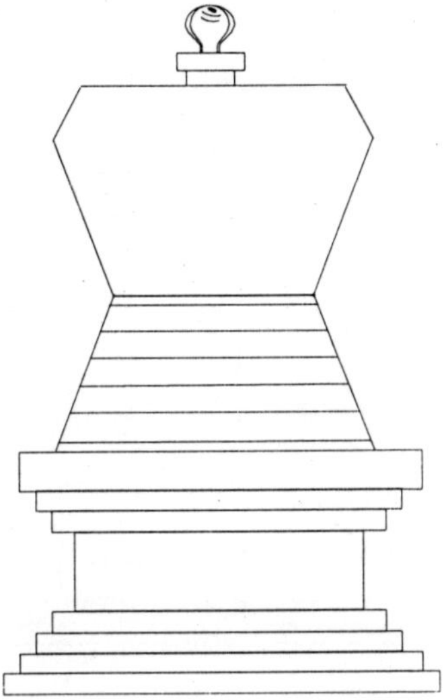

Fig. 9.2. Chang-Chub Chorten.

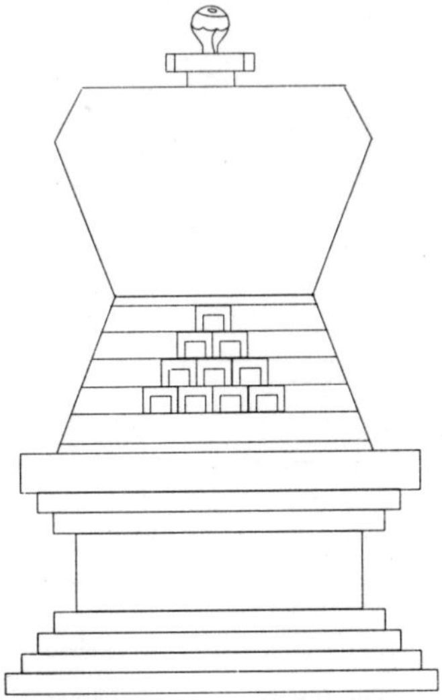

Fig. 9.3. Tashi Go-Mang Chorten.

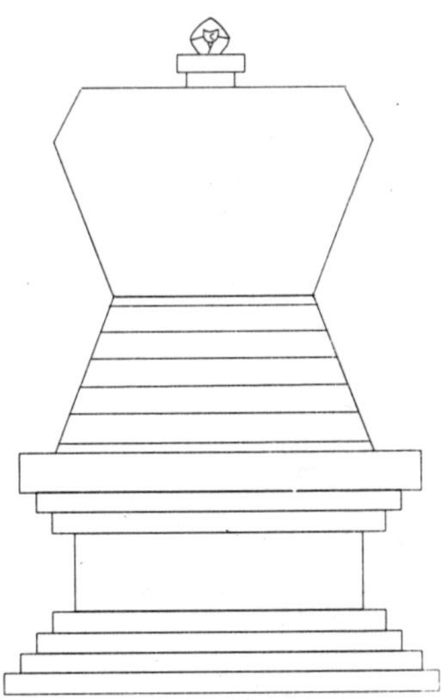

Fig. 9.4. Chos-Thul Chorten.

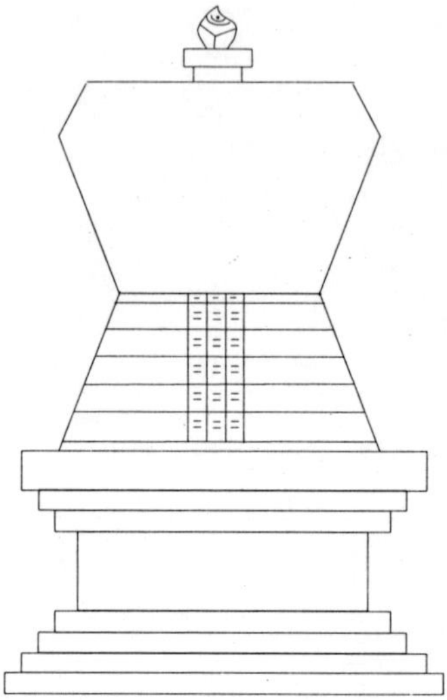

Fig. 9.5. Lha-bab Chorten.

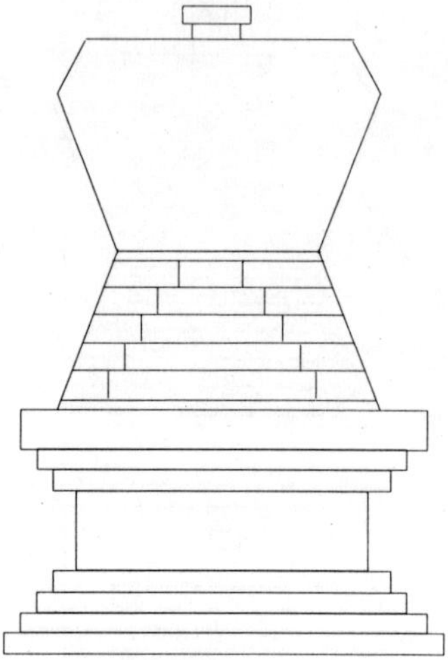

Fig. 9.6. En-dum Chorten.

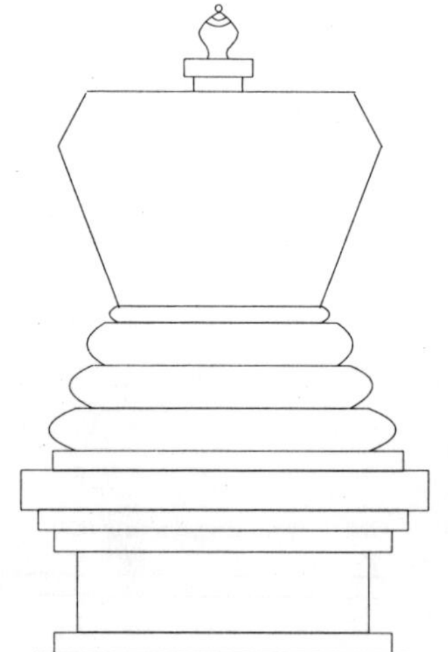

Fig. 9.7. Namgyal Chorten.

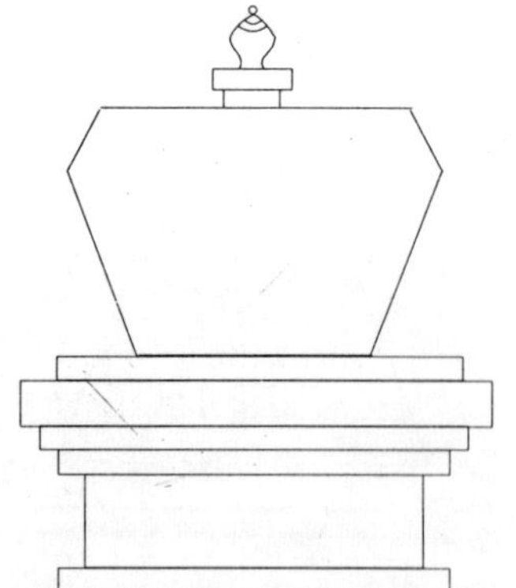

Fig. 9.8. Nyang Das Chorten.

En-Dum Chorten

After Buddha Parinirvana, Bhikshu Sangha lost their moral status, they divided into various classes. On hearing this Sariputra and Modgalyan felt sorry. They tried to reunite them and solved their difference. Later they constructed a Chorten at 'Rajgiri Deepvan' in the memory of this incidence which thereafter was popularly known as Nyen-Dum or En-Dum Chorten. It has eight 'Kons' and 'Lagh kons' Fig. 9.6.

Namgyal Chorten

When Buddha expressed his desire to take parinirvana, his pupils felt sorry. They requested him not to take nirvana. Buddha then decided to stay some days more with them. On hearing of this decision Bhikshus became happy and under the leadership of 'Go-mi-cum-da' they constructed a Chorten which later was known as Namgyal Chorten. It has round 'Pang-rim' Fig. 9.7.

Nyang-Das Chorten

It was constructed by King Ajatsatru at Kushinagar in the memory of Buddha. It has 'Pung-pa' on 'Singh-Thri' but no 'Pang-Rim' (Fig. 9.8).

Besides, one can see three chortens together with three colours (i.e., Yellow, White and Blue) at many religious places of Ladakh. In Ladakh these are popularly known as 'Rig-Zum-Gon-Bo'. Sometimes people pronounce them as – Namgyal, Chang-chub and En-dum Chortens. These Chortens are being constructed in the memory of three 'Naths'—

1.	Sku-yi Rigs	- 'Related to Kaya'	- Manjusri
2.	Sung gi Rig	- 'Related to Vaka'	- Avalokitesvara
3.	Thuks ki Rigz	- 'Chitta'	- Vajrapani.

10

Famous mGon-Pa dKar-brgyad in Nubra Valley of Ladakh

Prem Singh Jina

Nubra valley lies along the banks of the Shayok river and its tributary. To reach Nubra one has to climb 18,380 ft. Then descend downward to 10,000 ft. Fig. 10.1.

Leh	—up→	Khardong-La	—down→	Nubra Valley
11,500 ft. (District headquarter of Leh)		18,380 ft.		10,000 ft. (average)

The valley consists of two rivers—Nubra and Shayok. The Nubra river, flows from the north-north west and Shayok river, flows through the other portion of the valley. At the junction of the rivers the valley of the Shayok is some four miles wide, whereas the Nubra river is from two to three miles.[1]

At the two sides of the valley lie the habitable parts. It has comparatively high density of forest area of Ladakh region. The spaces occupied by the villages are green and pretty. But nonetheless monasteries have their own importance in Buddhist society and culture mGon-pa dKar-brgyad (or eight mGon-pos) have of course unique place not only in the monasteries but in the Buddhist religion. According to Dr. Prem Singh Jina, "mGon-po is called Mahakala in Sanskrit. In fact, a dharmapala who has two sides to his character—death and to give richness.[2] Besides, the above, mGon-pos are carved on the high mountain rocks in the Nubra valley. The following song is associated with them :

Text

mtha na ri bo bskor yod
nai skye yul ldum ra
dnual gyu mdog chag syod
gzigs san lha yul bar ma
rii bkra shis rtaks brgyat
mgon po dkar brgyad ran byon
rii bkra shis rtaks brgyat
mgon po dkar brgyad ran byan

...(1)

yas su yar mai mgon po
you du sham me mgon po
pa mg mgon dkar mgon po
byam chan byam pa mgon po
hor dan sogs poai khag gnon
ldum ra yons kyi bsun ma
hor dan sogs poai khag gnon
ldum ra yons kyi bsun ma

...(2)

bde skyid phyags drug mgon po
lag byun dbye bai mgon po
ron mdo pa deai mgon po
chu mig brgya dan rgya ca
nad rig kun la phan pai
dur sman snai chu don
nod rig kun la phan pai
dur sman snai chu don

...(3)

shar na bsam bstan glin dan
lho na bkra shis chos glin
nub ma byams pai lha khan
byan na dhen sa dag pa
ldum rai mi man chan ma
thug rze rgyans na gzig shig
ldum rai mi man chan ma
thug rze rgyans na gzig shig

...(4)

bham phyen lead rse mdun
sku mkhad thog chad mgon pa
mdun du rha mgriri mgon pa
grer dun sha sha blon pa
sku hs ablon pai byin dlabs
ldum ra yons la khyebs so

...(5)

nai skye yul ldum ra
gzigs san gras rten khayad can
Aa bi me me kungyi
yug srol thun abrea bzan po
ma nyams kons phel bor cig
ldum rai stag shar azum po
ma nyams kuna phel bor cig
ldum rai stag shar azam po

...(6)

Translation

Nubra, my motherland,
surrounded by snow cap mountains
sometimes looks silver like white,
turquoise like blue
infact the scene looks like heaven,
how nice these tashi kargyat,
eight gonpos,
shining in the mountains ...(1)

the right yar gonpo,
the left shyam gonpo
panik Gonkar gonpo
cham chen cam sa gonpo
these are protectors of
hor and Mongolia
hey gonpo ! please protect
us from evil spirits ...(2)

Deskyid chag dug Gonpo,
lag Jang Aeve Gonpo,
may purify the land,
the two hundred springs

may remove 424 disease,
the rang ton rikpo nector,
may remove ignorance, ...(3)

the East Samstan ling
the west Tasis chos ling
the North maitreya Lhakhang,
the south grand palace
may gods of these
bless and give compassion ...(4)

the pious Camsham village of Nubra,
seven storeyed palace of Camsham,
sten din gonpo, the main deity
may spread prasad to devotees ...(5)

my mother land Dumra
preserve traditional old culture
the youngsters of Nubra
gather here to celebrate
and spread your culture ...(6)

References

1. Drew, Frederic (1976), 'Jammoo and Kashmir Territories', Cosmo Pub., New Delhi, pp. 271-72.
2. Jina, Prem Singh, 2000; Murals of 'mGon-po' in Gon-khang of Phyang Monastery of Ladakh', In : 'Ladakh : Past and Present', Gyan Publishing House, New Delhi, p. 127.

11

Monasteries of Ladakh : A Case Study of Tashi Ga-tsal Monastery of Choglamsar

Prem Singh Jina

Ladakh in general and Leh district in particular is a centre of Mahayana Buddhism. Buddhist monastery can be seen at each Buddhist dominated village. In big monasteries hundred Lamas at a time can stay, but a small or village monastery has accommodation for a few lamas only.

In Ladakh monasteries are often situated on high hillocks or on an isolated mountain spur 1 to 10 kms far away from the inhabited areas. Spituk, Phyang, Thiksy, Shey, Stakna, Hemis, Matho, Rezong, Tiya, Timogang, Wakha, Lamayuru, Deskit, etc., are some of the monasteries situated on isolated hillock. In fact, monasteries are the most conspicuous buildings and have Buddhist Cultural background. For example, at the entrance of these institutions one can see prayer cylinders fixed with vertical axis, turning on a pivot, furnished inside with a paper on which holi Bodhi scripts, mantras viz. *Om mani Padme Hum*, etc., are written. Ladakhi Buddhists have strong belief that if one revolves the prayer wheel, he would get 'Punya'. Thus, revolving of the prayer wheel is reckoned as an act of devotion. The larger and heavy prayer cylinder wheel has attached rings through which the devotee gives a good impetus to his prayer. Sometimes prayer cylinders are kept moving through water flow. In olden days such prayer cylinders were very common now they are in few number. One such prayer cylinder is seen at Shey village. It is 6 feet high and 4 feet in diameter. Besides, one can see various shapes and sizes of Chorten at the surroundings of monasteries. Normally each monastery has the following temples.

1. Du-Khang
2. Gon-Khang
3. Dolma-Lha-Khang
4. Kangyur-Khang
5. Maitreya-Khang
6. Zims-Khang

Du-Khang

Here lamas of the monastery gather and offer their prayer together. At one side along the wall images of Rinpoches and Buddhist deities are placed. It also has thankas and wall paintings which attract tourists in various ways.

Gon-Khang

This temple has various forms of Gon-pos images with tantric forms.

Dolma-Lha-Khang

It has 21 statues of various forms of Dolma.

Kangyur-Khang

This temple has some Buddhist statues, but has good collection of Buddhist texts called Kangyur consisting of 101 volumes.

Maitreya-Khang

It has Maitreya statue besides other Buddhist images. Maitreya is the main statue of this temple, named after Maitreya-Khang.

Zims-Khang

This room is being allocated to the head of the monastery or Rinpoche. Monastery has a group of temples and 'Tashaks' which may vary according to its sect and function. It is a centre of rich cultural heritage. Each temple is being decorated by thangkas and wall paintings of Padmasambhava, Indian Buddhist Scholars, Tibetan Buddhist Scholars, Avalokitesvara, Gon-pos, Dolmas, Deities of Tantric Buddhism, Mandalas of different Buddhist deities, etc.

Besides, it has hundred acres land which were given by the Kings of Ladakh. For instance, King Singe Namgyal gave his full support to Hemis Monastery and donated land at every valley of Ladakh. Similarly his father Jamyang Namgyal encouraged Drigung Kargyud pa order in Ladakh.[1]

In Ladakh every Buddhist family is deeply associated with the monastery and on demand work for the monastery welfare. A. Cunningham in 1850-52 A.D. made a survey of Ladakh and found that out of 4000 Buddhist households 2400 were given assignments for the monastery activities.[2] No doubt he saw Lamas cultivate monastery land. But often monasteries had given their lands on rent to villagers, this practice still continues. Dutta remarks;

"The lands of monasteries were cultivated by the working Lamas and often these were given to farmers on *metayer* basis, that is the tillers handed over half the produce to the monasteries and were exempted from taxation and *begar* or free carriage."[3]

Source of Income

Normally a monastery has the following source of income :

1. Land
2. Alms/Donation
3. Festivals
4. Grant
5. Rent and Land possession of poor people
6. Rituals.

Land

It is the primary source of income. Table 11.1 shows the details :

TABLE 11.1

Land Area of Some Selected Monasteries in Ladakh

S. No.	*Name of the Monastery*	*Area of Land (Acres)*	*Rank of the Monastery*
1.	Hemis	1998.3	1
2.	Thiksey	1307.8	2
3.	Likir	263.3	8
4.	Phyang	360.0	7
5.	Chemray	375.8	6
6.	Spituk	582.8	5

(Contd.)

(Contd.)

7.	Lamayuru	234.5	3
8.	Rezong	496.4	11
9.	Stakna	576.7	4
10.	Matho	242.1	9
11.	Karsha	239.9	10
12.	Dakthok	40.3	13
13.	sTakrimo	64.3	12

Source : Ahluwalia, H.P.S : *Hermit Kingdom Ladakh,* Vikas Pub. New Delhi, 1980 p. 78.

Alms/Donation

In olden days Lamas used to visit different parts of Ladakh. They begged for cash or kind for monasteries from laity. During summer they received good donation from traders. Nowadays people donate cash and kind to monastery during special occasion when monastery organises Puja.

Festivals

Festivals are held annually at each big monastery of Ladakh, famous among which are Hemis, Phyang, Lamayuru, Dakthok, Spituk, Matho, etc. On this occasion large number of people including tourists visit. They charge entrance fee from foreigners and earn income Rs. 10,000 to Rs. 40,000 annually.

Grant

In olden days kings of Ladakh had made numerous efforts to donate lands and grants to monasteries. Nowadays Ladakh has 'Ladakh Gonpa Association' through which they get annual grants. The Department of Culture, Ministry of Tourism and Culture, Govt. of India, New Delhi gives lump-sum grant to the Association. Sometimes, monasteries through their welfare societies get grant directly from the Ministry.

Rent

Off late, monasteries have constructed cement buildings at Leh and its adjoining areas which they give on rent and get good income.

Besides, in olden days monasteries provided loans to poor people—after mortgaging their lands. According to *Imperial Gazetteer;*

"When the debtor is hopelessly involved, the monastery takes possession on half of his land for a period of three years. The land is restored to the debtor and his debt written off. The monastery will never sue a debtor, nor his land permanently for debt."[4]

Monastic System

Each monastery has the following authorities who look-after the monastic system.

1. Rinpoche and Head of the Monastery.
2. Lhopon
3. Chamspon
4. Chagzot
5. Nyerpa
6. Nyerchhen
7. Phi-Nyer
8. Umzat
9. Chos-timba

Rinpoche

He is the incarnated Lama known as Kushok and Head Lama of the monastery, All monastery's activities follow according to his instructions.

Lhopon

He is next to the Rinpoche and acts as a Deputy Head Lama of the monastery.

Chamspon

He is the director of Cham, under his direction Lamas of the monastery learn Cham. He selects Lamas for the annual festival out of the trained Cham dancers.

Chagzot

His duty is like manager of any business concern. He looksafter the temporary affairs of the monastery.

Nyerpa

He keeps monastery records, looksafter the store and keeps ready the cash book.

Nyerchhen

He assists the Chagzot.

Phi-Nyer

He lookafter monastery land and agricultural affairs.

Umzat

He starts the daily prayers in the monastery. All the present Lamas read Buddhist texts according to his instructions.

Chos-timba

He controls newly admitted Lamas during Lamas meeting. However, it is said during olden days Chagzot of the monastery had special powers. He then entrusted to lookafter the administration of the monastery and kept his eyes open on the following activities :

1. Agricultural activities on monastery's land.
2. Traders' activities who passed through monastery's land.
3. Rent collection activities from the tenants.
4. Lamas who went out for begging for monastery.
5. Advancing money/grain to needy persons.
6. Lamas activities who were deputed for military duty.

One Lama officer known as 'Kharpon' also appointed on special duty who looked after the monastery defence force. Under his command some Lamas get deputed for the construction of forts near monastery.

Sects

In Ladakh all four sects of Buddhism have their monasteries. They belong to bKa-rGyud-pa, Ningma-pa, dGe-lungs-pa and Saskya-pa. However, western scholars divided them according to the colour of their caps which they wear during ritual ceremonies like-Red sect and Yellow sect. dKa-rGyud-pa monasteries come under Red-sect and others belong to yellow sect.[5]

Migration

After 1947 Indo-Pak war many Ladakhis migrated towards Leh and its surrounding areas from the border. This trend was continued again during the 1962 Indo-China war, 1965 Indo-Pak War and in 1971 Indo-Pak War. As a result many new colonies and settlement areas near Leh developed. Choglamsar Colony near I.T.B.P. Camp is one of the examples where Buddhists from the different parts of Ladakh came and settled down. As they belong to different villages and Buddhist sects, it was difficult to build four sect monasteries at one place. Therefore they decided to build one common monastery in 1992 and named it as Tashi-Ga-tsal. And according to decision each big monastery would send a 'Pujari' to this monastery for at least one year. In 1994 Tashi-Ga-tsal started its function and following monasteries decided to send a 'Pujari'.

1. Spituk (Leh)
2. Phyang (Leh)
3. Thiksay (Leh)
4. Chemday (Leh)
5. Dak-Thok (Leh)
6. Nyoma (Chang-thang)
7. Shachukul (Chang-thang)
8. Stakna (Leh)
9. Matho (Leh)
10. Likir (Leh)
11. Lamayuru (Kha-la-che)
12. Samstanling (Nubra)
13. De skit(Nubra)
14. Lingshet
15. Rangdom(Zanskar)
16. Karsha (Zangksar)

Statues

Tashi-Ga-tsal is a new monastery, like other monasteries it has one big statue of Buddha of 7 feet in height and 3½ feet wide. This statue is placed in glass covered compartment Fig. 11.1.

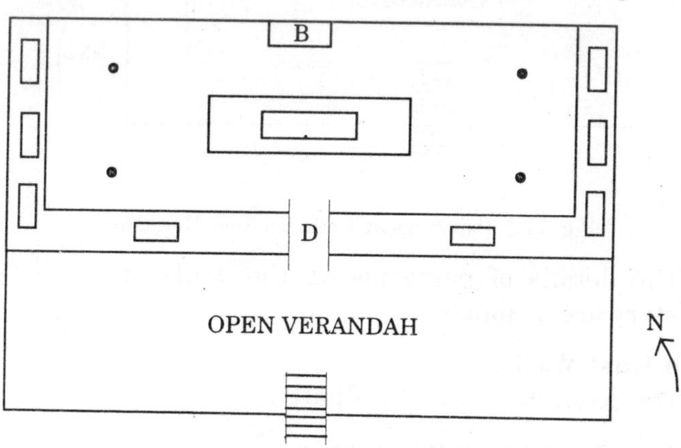

Fig. 11.1. Statue of Buddha in Tashi Ga-Tsal Monastery.

[B] = Buddha; • = Pole; [ ] = Window; |D| = Door; |≡| = Ladder

The Buddha statue is in a sitting posture with Bhumi Sparsha mudra.

Paintings

The monastery has 24 paintings of Arhads and Dolmas. These paintings are on hard board and pasted on the three side walls of the monastery (Fig. 11.2).

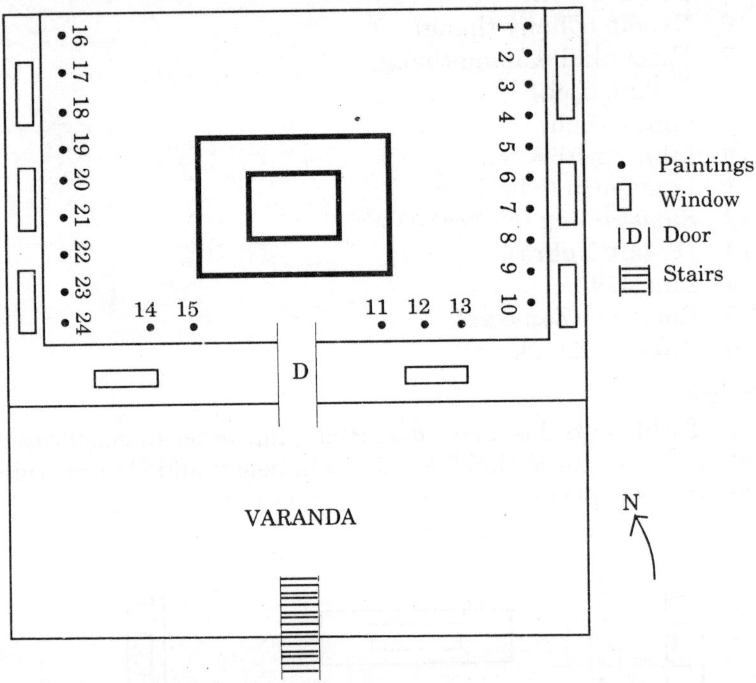

Fig. 11.2. Paintings in Tashi Ga-Tsel Monastery.

The details of paintings on the walls of Tashi-Ta-tsal monastery are as follows :

North-East Wall

The paintings on this wall are :

1. rje-jsun-cham-ba mgon-bo
2. Ba-ku-la-na-mo
3. sras sgras can aZin

4. Lam phan brtan la na mo
5. Phara-rha-za-va-sot snams la na mo
6. gNas brTan lin brtan la na mo
7. gNas brtan klu yi sde la na mo
8. Slabs gsum lam bston sbe byed na mo
9. gNas can ser bjugs mi byed na mo
10. sbyin bdog chen vo ha shan na

Paintings on South-West Wall :

11. Nr-rgyun-ma
12. rGyal po chen po yul aKhor-strung
13. rGyal po chen po Phags skyes
14. rGyal po chen po rNam-thos-sras
15. Dol-Kar

Paintings on North-west Wall

16. dGe-snyen dnyar-ma-ta
17. bha-ra-dha-za-dser-can-mchog
18. sPon-va-bDun-ldan-bzang-po
19. gNas-brtan-rdo-rje-moai buai la
20. dNos-drub adod-ajo-gser-becu-
21. sde snod gsum-a jin-dus-ldan
22. aPhags nor bDun-lDan nagas na gnas
23. srid-jiai zigs aphog ma pham
24. aPhangs pai gnas-brtan yang-lag

Notes and References

1. Datta, C.L., : *Ladakh and Western Himalayan Politics*: 1819-1848, Munshiram Manoharlal Pub. New Delhi, 1973, pp. 27-28; Francke, Antiquities-II', p. 110, Seven Hedin, *Trans-Himalaya : Discoveries and Adventures in Tibet-II*, p. 63 and Knight, *Three Empires*, p. 193.
2. Cunningham, *Ladakh*, p. 270 & Datta, *op. cit.* p. 28.
3. Datta, C.L., *op. cit.* p. 28, Hutchinson, G.E., *The Clear Mirror: A Pattern of life in Goa and Indian Tibet*, p. 87 and Knight *op. cit.* p. 200.
4. IGI (1909), *Provincial Series,* XVI, p. 101, Datta, *op. cit.* p. 200.
5. Datta, op. cit. p. 29, Drew, J&K Territories, p. 256, Lyall, Kangra *Settlement Report* p. 129, W.S.R. Hodgson, *Twelve years of a Soldier's Life in India,* p. 111. Knight *op. cit.* p. 129, IGI, 1909 Provincial Series, XVI, p. 99.

12

Paintings in Phyang Monastery of Ladakh

Prem Singh Jina

Introduction

Phyang monastery is located 24 kms. in the east of Leh town of Ladakh region. This monastery is one of the important learning centres of Drigung Kargyud-pa order in Ladakh. Many renowned Lamas are engaged to give instructions to young Lamas about Buddhist Art such as—Mandala, Cham, Music, Sculpture, Painting and Philosophy before being initiated into techniques of meditation and strict discipline for self-realisation. Thus, we can understand that the above monastery is a media of balanced blend of manual, intellectual, spiritual and the initiate move from one level of learning 'Vidya' to 'Mahavidhya' and untimately to 'Bodhvidhya'.

Paintings in the Gon-Khang Temple of Phyang Monastery

Wall Paintings on the Right Side Wall Along the Door

(i) Male and Female Yabyun. The Green colour female holds Tikuk while black colour male holds swords and trishuls of its four hands.

At the border traditional Kargyug-pa order Lamas are seated with their traditional Lama dress. The seventy five Srinath, Skyabgon and Du-Su-Canaga are seated lower side of the border.

(ii) Vajrapani. He holds snake and dorji, and wears a garland of human skulls across his body. He is in standing posture on flat lying Naga.

Paintings on the Wall Above the Door

(i) Chering ma (Tsering ma). She is seated on lion and holds a pot and *vajra*.

(ii) Dharma Dakini. She wears a crown and is seated on horse; holds 'Damaru' in her right hand and skull of jewels in left hand.

Lamas of the Phyang monastery believe that Dharma Dakini is the main goddess and is popularly known as Achi Chordon (or Chaskyi Dolma).

Paintings on the Left Side Wall Along the Door

(i) Danti Mahakala. He is popularly known as Gonpo Ping, standing with two white sticks across his body. The whole picture of Danti Mahakala is being covered by a mandala of fire.

(ii) Male and Female Mahakala. Male is coloured blue, holds skull, sword, Tikuk and skull trishul, trampling a man at his feet.

Paintings on the Northern Wall

(i) Four Hand Red Mahakala. He holds sword, Tikuk, skull and four vajras trishul; trampling a man at his feet.

(ii) White Mahakala. He holds trishul, *kalash* (pot) and skulls made four vajras, trampling a man at his feet.

(iii) Four Hand Single Mahakala. He holds sword, Tikuk and vajra; with skull garland across his body and seated on tiger skin. This figure is covered with animal kingdom viz : elephant, lion, pig, birds, sheep, garuda, men and ckara Sambhara dev.

(iv) Male Female Hevajra. He is of blue colour with seven heads and 14 hands; wearing skull garland which passes through his body, trampling two devils at his feet. This figure is covered by fire mandala.

(v) Chakrusambhar (Pron. Heruka). He is exhibted in the joint male-female form consisting of seven heads and 14 hands, wearing skull garland and elephant skin.

He holds tikuk, axe, skull, etc., and trampling two men at his feet.

Paintings on the Eastern Wall

(i) Melarepa. He wears *'Janeu'* (religious code) and depicted in 'Savara' posture.

He is surrounded by his disciples e.g. lama Raschungpa and Takpo Lharje. The main disciples.

(ii) Tilopa. He is depicted above the Melarepa mandala.

(iii) Naropa. He is also depicted above the Melarepa mandala.

(iv) Kargyud Lamas. There are many Kargyud pa order Lamas depicted above the Melarepa mandala.

(v) Sakyamuni Buddha. He is seated in 'Bhumi Sparsha Mudra', holding begging pot. Mogali and Sari Putras are standing at his right and left sides.

There are Indian Pundits and others such as Manjusri, Metreya, Nagarjuna, Asanga, etc., are depicted above the Sakyamuni Buddha figure.

(vi) Tantrik Buddha (Pron. Vajra Dhara. Tib. Dorje Chang). He holds Vajra and bell. Metreya and Avalokiteshvara with 'Upnishat' in eight forms of Bodhisattva are depicted at his left and right sides.

(vii) Skyoba Rinpoche (Ratna Shri). He is the founder of Dregung Kargyad-pa order and seated in a 'Bhumi-Sparsha' position. His main disciples are Kunga sherab Jungnes and Traspa Jungnes are standing at his left and right sides.

Above the Skyoba Rinpoche-Amitayu and kargyud-pa order Lamas are depicted along with eighty Siddhas.

At the lower side of Skyoba Rinpoche-Avalokiteshvara, white and green Vajrapani, 'Svara-Svati, gods, goddesses, etc., are depicted.

Paintings on the Southern Wall

(i) Tushkhor Guhya Samaj. This male and female joint painting is depicted in samadhi posture. Male figure of blue colour has three heads. Female figure also has three heads. Both together have twelve hands and hold wheel, lotus, vajra, sword, etc.

(ii) Male and Female Yabyum (Kalcakra). The standing yabyum consists of male and female joint figure. Male represents blue colour and female has yellow colour. Both together have thirty-two hands and are seen holding tikuk, bow, vajra hammer, wheel, sun, axe, bangle, etc., and trampling two men at his feet.

The above Kalcakra painting is covered by mandal of vajra and fire.

(iii) Single Mahakala. He has five hands, decorated by elephant and tiger skins, wearing snake garland, holds trishul, rope, *damru, tikuk,* skull, etc., and is seen trampling devil who has trunk like elephant.

(iv) Male and Female Yabyum (Mahakala). He has blue colour, has *tikuk,* skull, sword and trishul and is seen trampling a devel at his feet.

Besides, all the four walls have kargyud-pa order traditional Lamas at the upper border and spalgon dun-chu-tonga (i.e., 75 god and goddesses of Buddhists) are depicted with their animals.

Thus, there are twenty major wall paintings on the walls of Gonkhang. Following are the details :

1. On the right side wall along the door	2
2. On the wall above the door	2
3. Left side wall along the door	2
4. On the northern wall	5
5. On the eastern wall	4
6. On the southern wall	5
Total	20

Measurement of Gonkhang Walls

1. *Right Side Wall*

(a) Along the door length 8'7"
(b) Height 6' (approx.)
2. Left side wall length along the door 7'5"
3. Door
(a) Height 4'5"
(b) Length 3'5"
4. Northern wall length 19'6"
5. Eastern wall length 19'3"
6. Southern wall length 9'8"

Distribution of paintings in Gonkhang is shown in Fig. 12.1.

Paintings in the Tsokhang Temple of Phyang Monastery

Outside wall along the right side of door

Guardians. Two guardians of the monastery are represented in wrathful forms.

Outside wall along the left side of the doors

Guardians. Two guardians of the monastery are represented in wrathful forms.

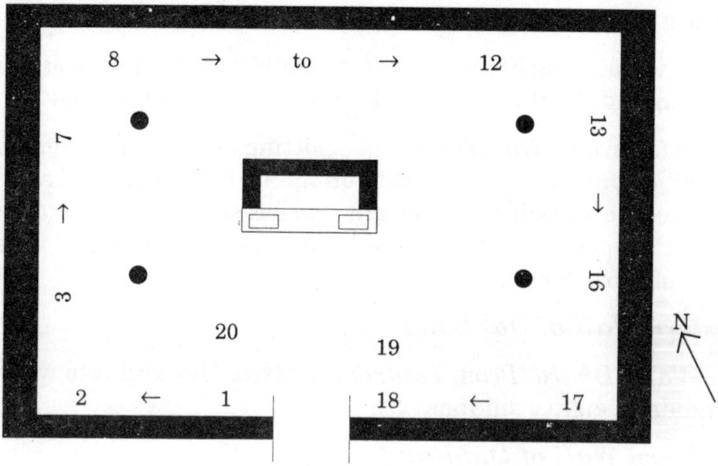

Fig. 12.1. Gonkhang in Phyang Monastery.
• = Pole; | | = Door; ▭ = Window; ■ = Wall; 1 → 20 = Paintings.

Southern wall of the Dukhang

(i) Tonyot Duba (Pron. Amogsiddhi). He is seated with the mandala of gods and represented in green colour.

(ii) Amitabh. He is seated in heaven, surrounded by gods, representing in red colour; blue colour vajrapani and white colour Avalokiteshvara are painted in his left and right sides. Besides, many Boddhisattavas are painted at the surrounding mandala.

(iii) Akshobya. He is in sitting posture, representing in white colour, red colour Metreya and blue colour Manjusri are standing at his right and left sides. 35 Buddha in mandala surrounded him.

(iv) Choje Denma Kunga Trakpa. He is in sitting posture, representing red colour, two Boddhisattavas are exhibited at

his right and left sides, and surrounded by kargyud-pa order traditional lamas mandala.

(v) Jabtung Nawang Namgyal. He is in sitting posture. He was the teacher of Choje Denma Kunga Trakpa who founded Phyang monastery.

The painting of Jabtung Nawang Namgyal is surrounded by the mandala of traditional Lamas of Kargyudpa order.

(vi) Skyoba Rinpoche. He is in sitting posture representing in red colour. Kunga Sherab Jangnas and Kunga Trakpa Jungnas are standing at his right and left sides. The portrate of Skyoba Rinpoche is surrounded by 10 direction Lhas and three Kalas of miracles.

Western Wall of Dakhang

Vajra Dhara (Pron. Tantrik Buddha). He exhibited with a mandala of eighty siddhas.

Northern Wall of Dukhang

(i) Padma Sambhava. At this left and right sides of Padma Sambhavas Khando Yeshey Chogyal and Lhacham Mandariva are standing. The above figure of Padma Sambhava is surrounded by traditional Kargyudpa Lamas.

(ii) Dipankara. He is in sitting posture represented by red colour. Dom stonpas (or Upasakas) are sitting at his right and left sides. The whole mural is covered by traditional kargyud-pa order lamas.

(iii) Amitayu. He is in sitting posture represented by blue colour. White colour Boddhisattavas are standing at his left and right sides. The Amitayu figure is surrounded by Boddhas and Boddhisattavas.

(iv) Medicinal Buddha. He is in sitting posture represented by blue colour. White colour Boddhisattavas are standing at his left and right sides. The figure of Medicinal Buddha is surrounded by Buddhas and Boddhisattavas.

(v) Manjusri. He is in sitting posture. Vajrapani and Avalokiteshvara are exhibited at his right and left sides. Manjusri figure is surrounded by 16 Sravakas.

(vi) Avalokitesvar. He is represented by white colour and surrounded by traditional Boddhisattavas.

(vii) Vajrapani. He is surrounded by traditonal Boddhisattvas.

(viii) Vajradakini. She is surrounded by traditional Lamas of Kargyud-pa order.

(ix) Vajra Varahi (Pron. Dorje Phagmo). She is in white colour.

Eastern Wall of the Dukhang

(i) Wheel of life. It is decorated beautifully in which human beings *'Karmphala'* have been exhibited.

(ii) Mahakala. He has four hands with Mahakala holding skull and Tikuk.

(iii) Cakra Sambhar. He has many hands holding different weapons such as axe, tikuk, etc.

(iv) Kalackara. The kalackara mural consists of male and female figures.

(v) Ghuya Samaj. This mural belongs to Buddhist tantra.

Thus in Dukhang 23 murals are exhibited on inner side of the walls whereas four murals are depicted outside on the wall along the door. The details are shown as follows :

TABLE 1

Number of Murals on Dukhang Walls

Sl. No.	*Particular*	*No. of Murals*
1.	Outside wall along the right of the door	2
2.	Outside wall along the left side of the door	2
3.	Southern wall (inner side)	8
4.	Western wall (inner side)	1
5.	Northern wall (inner side)	9
6.	Eastern wall (inner side)	5
	Total	27

Postures of Buddhist God, Goddesses and Buddhist Scholars

1. Guardians	Wrathful
2. Tonyot Duba	Teaching
3. Amitabh	Meditation
4. Rinchen Jungnas	Bhumi sparsha

5. Varocana	Bhumi sparsha
6. Akshobya	Teaching
7. Chorje Danma	Teaching
8. Jabtung Nawang Namgyal	Teaching
9. Skyoba Rinpoche	Bhumi sparsha
10. Dipankar	Teaching
11. Amitayu	Meditation
12. Medicinal Buddha	Bhumi sparsha
13. Manjusri	Teaching
14. Avalokitesvara	Compassion

Names of Painters Engaged for Painting Works

Sl. No.	*Name of Deities / paintings*	*Name of Painters*
1.	Tonyot Duba	Wok Sumpa Skyap
2.	Amitabh	Alchipa Tondup Paljor
3.	Varocana	Likir pa skyab
4.	Chorje Dhanma Kunga Trakpa	Phyang-pa Ganu
5.	Jabtung Nawang Namgyal	Phyang-pa Ganu
6.	Dipankar	Spanba
7.	Medicinal Buddha	Spalgun Tsering
8.	Manjusri	Spituk-pa Tongdup Lakpa

The above painters were probably engaged for painting works in the Phyang monastery during 16th Century A.D.

The details of paintings are shown in Fig. 12.2.

Seats of the Monks of Dukhang

During worshipping occasions monks sit in four rows in Dukhang (Fig. 12.2).

Paintings of Kabyat-Khang of Phyang Monastery

Right side outer wall along the door

Guardians. Two Guardians are exhibited in ferocious forms.

Left side outer wall along the door

Guardians. Two Guardians are represented in ferocious forms.

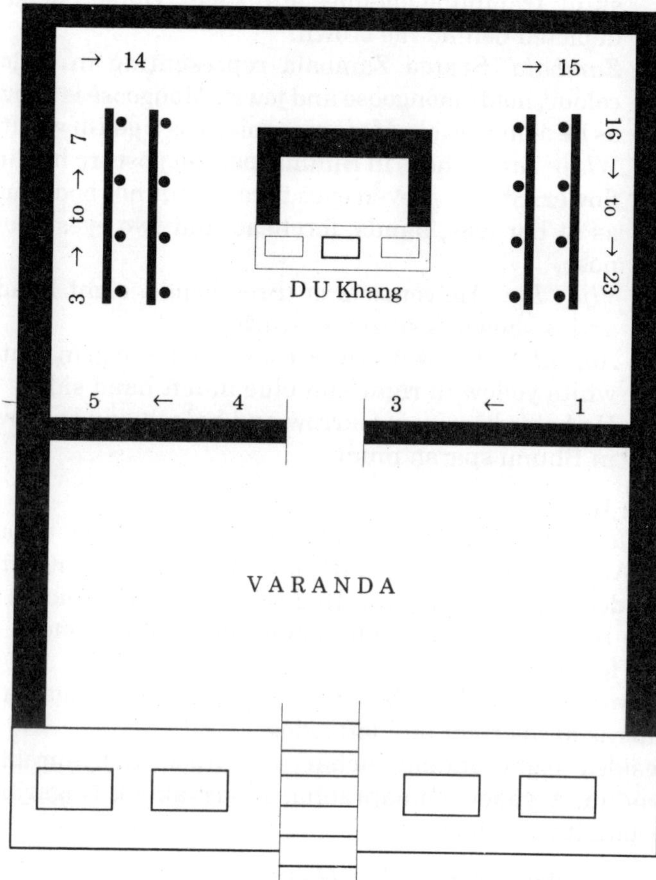

Fig. 12.2. Wall Painting in Dukhang of Phyang Monastery.
▭= Window; | | = Door; |≡| = Ladder; :| = Monks seat; ▬ = Wall;
1 → 23 = Murals.

Left side inner wall along the door

Vajrasattavas. There are five Vajrasattavas which are depicted at the portion of the row.

Left side inner wall along the door at lower row

(i) *Bechi Kundala.* He is in sitting posture.

(ii) *Hyagiva.* He is standing with skull, garland and represented in red colour; holds trishul, rope and skull; trampling enemies at his feet. Horse's head is depicted behind his crown.

(iii) *Zambala.* Seated Zambala representing in yellow colour, holds mongoose and jewel. Mongoose is shown as he omits jewels. He is recognised as a god of wealth.

(iv) *White Tara.* She is in Bhumi sparsha posture holding flower. She has seven eyes throughout her body such as at her legs, hands, forehead and two eyes above nose.

(v) *Vijay Dev.* He consists of three heads, eight hands, and is shown is sitting posture.

(vi) *Amitabh.* He is with three colour bodies e.g. in centre white yellow in right and blue in left hand sides. He holds bow, vajra, arrow and kalash and is shown in Bhumi sparsh mudra.

Left Side Wall

Medician Buddha. He is represented by blue colour, carrying Arura leaf at his right hand and begging pot at left.

Besides, eight meditating Buddhas are also depicted at the above Buddha's right and left sides along with some of 35 Buddhas' form.

Sakyamuni Buddha. He is represented with Mongali and Sari Puttras at his right and left sides.

Besides eight Indian Acharyas: Atisa, Sakyaprabha, Vasubandhu, Aryadev, Gunaprabha, Dharmakirti, Nagarjuna and Deeghnath are depicted.

Painting on Wall in Front of Door

Buddha. He is represented along with Mongali and Sari Puttras.

Paintings on the Wall Right Side of Kabyat Khang Temple

(i) *Manjusri.* It is represented in red colour.

(ii) *Avalokitesvara.* It is represented in white colour and shown in sitting posture.

(iii) *Vajrapani.* Two Vajrapani murals are represented in blue colour. They are wearing five crowns, each holds vajra and rope of snake.

The above Vajrapani murals are being covered by a mandal of fire.

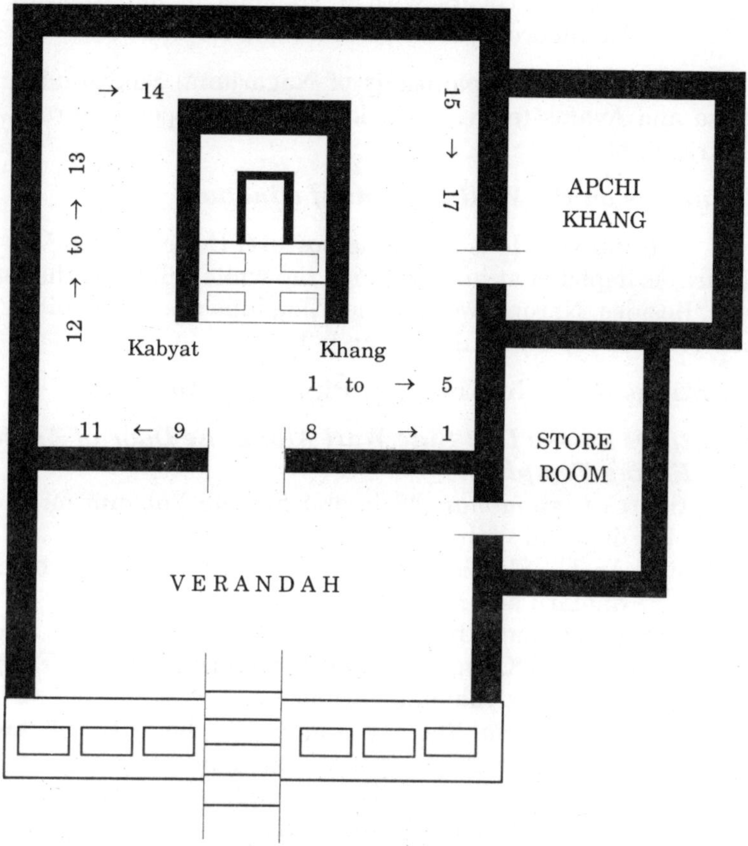

Fig. 12.3. Paintings at Kabyat Khang.

▭ = Window; |≡| = Ladder; ■ = Wall; 1 → 17 = Wall Paintings; | | = Door.

The details of painting in Kabyat Khang are shown in Fig. 12.3.

Paintings at Namling of Kabyat Khang in Phyang Monastery
Left side wall of the window

(i) *Four Hands Mahakala.* Blue colour Mahakala wearing skull garland and lion's skin, and holds sword, skull, trishul and axe.

(ii) *Cakrasambhar.* Male and Female Yum is standing

posture, covers with a mandala of four dakinis : Khandoroya, Lame, Aakini and Rupini.

There are some paintings of Nagarjuna, Sakyabuddha, Atisa and Avalokiteshvara depicted on the upper side row of Cakrasambhar.

Paintings on the Wall in front of window

(i) Ratnasri. He is in sitting posture. Dorje Chang (Vajra Dhara) is depicted at his right side top while Tilopa at the left side. Besides, Naropa, Marpa and Phagdupa are also exhibited at right side top and Milarepa on left.

Paintings in Apchi Khang in Phyang Monastery

Paintings on the Left Side Wall Along the Door of Apchi Khang Temple

(i) *Cakrasambhar.* Male and Female Yabyum form is depicted with four dakinis.

(ii) *Apchi.* She is riding on blue colour horse; holds damaru and jewel at her hands.

She is surrounded by Ishe Khando, Tamchik Khando, Angi Khando and Shaja Khando with their respective animals. These animals are—horse, yak, and garuda.

(iii) *Chering ma.* She is riding on lion, holds *kalash* and *vajra.* The Chhering ma is surrounded by mandal of four Chhering mas. They are riding on their animals, lion, dragon, horse and tiger.

(iv) *Vajrapani.* He is depicted at the corner of left side temple wall.

Paintings on the Wall Towards Window in Apchi Khang

Upper Row

(i) *Ming go Devi.* She is beautiful decorated on the upper side wall is Apchi Khang.

(ii) ***Pehar.*** He is riding on elephant like Padmasambhava he is depicted as to convert wicked men to laymen.

(iii) ***Chupe Lhu (Nagraj).*** He is riding on horse, holds mirror and five colour flag.

(iv) ***Sogera can.*** He is riding on horse, holds vajra castle at his one hand and storma at the other.

(v) *Parla.* He is riding on horse, holds flag attached on an arrow and jewels with flag at top.

(vi) *Rahul (Khyab Jug).* He is depicted by ten faces :

Right side—Three white	
Left side—Three green	Consisting three eyes at
Centre—Blue	each face (or head)
Just above—Blue	
Main—Blue	

This figure of Rahul is rolled by snake; holds bow, arrow snake and flag. He weared one crow type crown.

Lower Row

(i) *Dharma Pala.* He is riding on horse, wearing cap with flag, holds jewel in his one hand and rope in other.

In the picture Dharma Pala is shown as if he is running after his enemies and killing them by his rope and jewelen.

(ii) ***Cug na Namgyal Karmo.*** She is of white colour, riding on white horse, holds garland at her right hand and *kalash* at her left.

(iii) ***White Spenmo Devi.*** She is riding on deer type animal, holds flag at her one hand and garland at her other.

(iv) ***Changpa.*** He is similar to Brahma riding on white horse, wears turban; in the middle of his turban a 'Bruel' is fixed. He holds sword, in his right hand and rope in his left hand.

(v) ***Thangla.*** He is riding on white horse, holds round cap at his one hand and animal tail with flag at his other hand.

The details are shown in Fig. 12.4.

In sum the Phyang monastery in Ladakh consists of a good collection of scrol paintings (Thankas), wall paintings as well

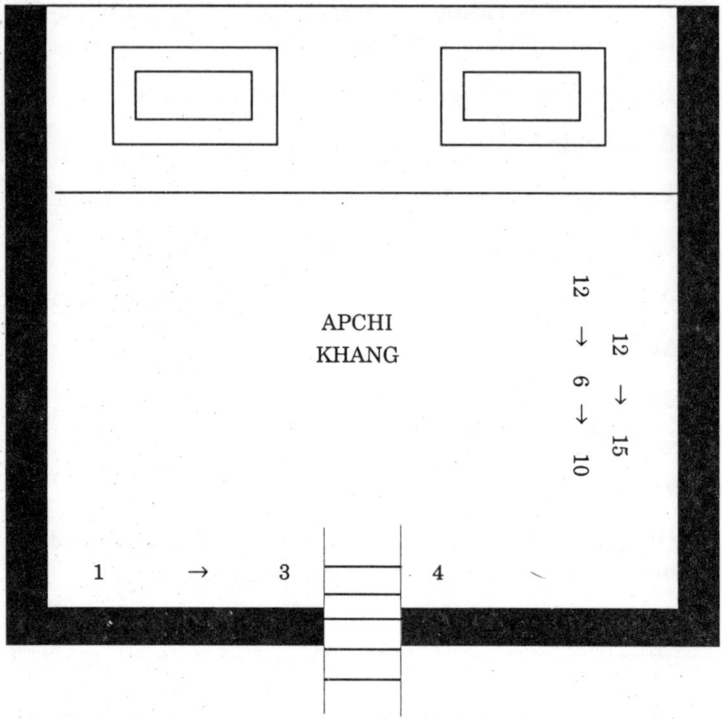

Fig.12.4. Paintings in Apchi Khang in Phyang Monastery.

| | = Door; ▭ = Window; ■ = Wall; 1 → 15 = Wall Paintings.

as religious books of thousands volumes. The statues of Buddha, Padmasambhavas, Gopos, etc., are equally important.

Note: This paper is based on the project 'A Study on the Murals in the Phyang Monastery of the Western Himalaya', Financed by the Indian Council of Historical Research, New Delhi; During 1996–97.

13

Buddhist Art in Ladakh : A Case Study of Sumda Valley

Prem Singh Jina
and
Tsering Tundup Gojing Pa

During 10th Century A.D. Rin-Chen-zang-po extensively visited many parts of West Tibet. He then with the help of Kashmiri Arts constructed around 108 temples. In Sumda valley he constructed two temples—Sumda Chung and Sumda Chenmo. In this study the details of these monasteries will be discussed.

Approach

Sumda valley is difficult to approach from Zanskar (Zangskar), however it can be approached from Leh after travelling along the left bank of Indus river. Rohit Vohra says :

"The Sumda Chen area is difficult to approach from central Zanskar and the most appropriate access routes are from the river Indus. The easiest of these is from Alchi over the Tagpa (sTag-pa) La by following a track along the left bank of the Indus and then over the Zanskar river."[1]

T. Skorupski also visited Sumda area during 1976. He gave a good description about the routes from Zanskar and Leh. He felt travelling over frozen Zanskar river is easier than the other routes, he remarks :

"Travelling is easier during the winter months when Zanskar river is frozen over, permitting crossing at several points."[2]

Nowadays there is weekly mini bus service from Leh to

Sumda. The bus is available from Leh in morning of every Sunday for Sumda-do. The journey between Leh to Sumda-do is 48 km. and Rs. 45 per person is the bus fare, thereafter 2-3 hour on foot journey upto Sumda and Sumda Chen.[3]

The details are as below :

1.	Leh to Sumda-do per person fare	by mini bus	48 kms.	Rs. 45/-
2.	Sumda-do to Azang village	on foot	04 kms.	—
3.	Azang village to Sumda Chung	on foot	16 kms	—
4.	Azang village to Sumda Chang Chen (Chenmo)	on foot	10 kms	—
5.	Sumda-do to Sumda Chenmo	on foot	14 kms	—

Note. The mini bus fare was recorded in the month of September 2000.

The location of Sumda Chung[4] and Sumda Chenmo can be more clear by the Fig. 13.1.

The study of this paper consists five villages :

1. Sumda-do
2. Azang
3. Sumda Chung
4. Sumda Chenmo
5. Chiling

Except Sumda-do all the other villages have cultural importance in the Buddhism of Ladakh. For illustration Azang village is famous for the birth of Nastan Dorje. It is said that Nastan Dorje was the head Lama of Rezong monastery born in Saspol village as Khanpo and at present 60 years old.

Sumda Chung has a monastery constructed by the Rin-chen-zang-po. This temple has a Varocana statue along with many old statues of Boddhisattvas and paintings of Buddhas on the side walls.

Sumda Chenmo has 10 houses of Buddhists with 90 Buddhists residing. This village is famous for Locava temple known Galdan Tsewang.

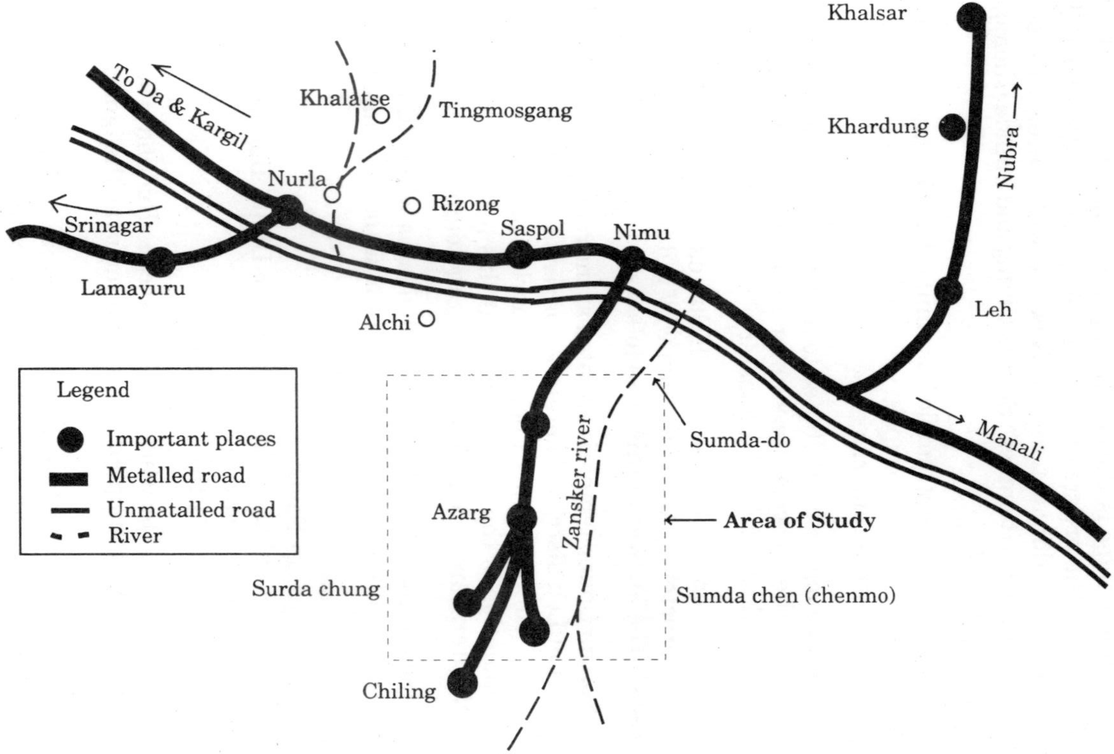

Fig. 13.1. Sumda chung and Sumda chenmo villages in Sumda Valley.

Chiling village is the centre of goldsmiths. It is said that in olden days the artists of Chiling village were called for the decoration of Buddhist temples. Now we will concentrate on the study on the two temples : Sumda Chung and Sumda Chemo.

Sumda Chung Temple

The Sumda Chung temple has similar frescoes and statues as Alchi Chos-kor. T. Skorupski visited this temple in 1976 and made the following remarks :

> "The monastery is attributed to the time of Rin-chen-bzang-po and the frescols are similar in artistic influence and skill to those of Alchi monastery."[5]

Now the question arises that if Sumda Chung has similar artistic character as Alchi has then why is it not famous among tourists ? The answer of this is as follows :

1. Sumda Chung temple is situated at the remote inaccessible part of Leh district. Therefore, tourists can not visit there easily. However, only 1 per cent tourists of the total tourist population of the year of Leh visit this temple.
2. No literature is available about this temple.

Besides, Sumda Chung is a small villages where Rin-Chen-zang-po made only one shrine. The main statues of this temple are :

1. Varocana (in the middle) 2. Aksobya (in East) 3. Ratna Sambhava (in south) 4. Amitabh (in west) 5. Amogshidi (North)	Five Dhani Buddhas

1. *Varocana.* The white colour Varocana Buddha is seated on lion throne. Worshipping this statue removes the ignorance of human beings.

2. *Aksobya.* Aksobya Buddha has vajra in its hand and seated on elephant throne. It is blue in colour and helps to remove the hatred from the minds of human beings.

3. *Ratna Sambhava.* It is yellow in colour, with jewels in its hand and seated on horse throne. It helps to remove the anger of human beings.

4. *Amitabh.* It is red in colour, with lotus in its hand and seated on peacock throne. It helps to remove the attachment of human beings.

5. *Amogashiddhi.* It is green in colour with sword in one hand and seated on Garuda throne. It is said that by seated worship of the Amogashiddhi one may remove jealousness Figures 13.2 and 13.3.

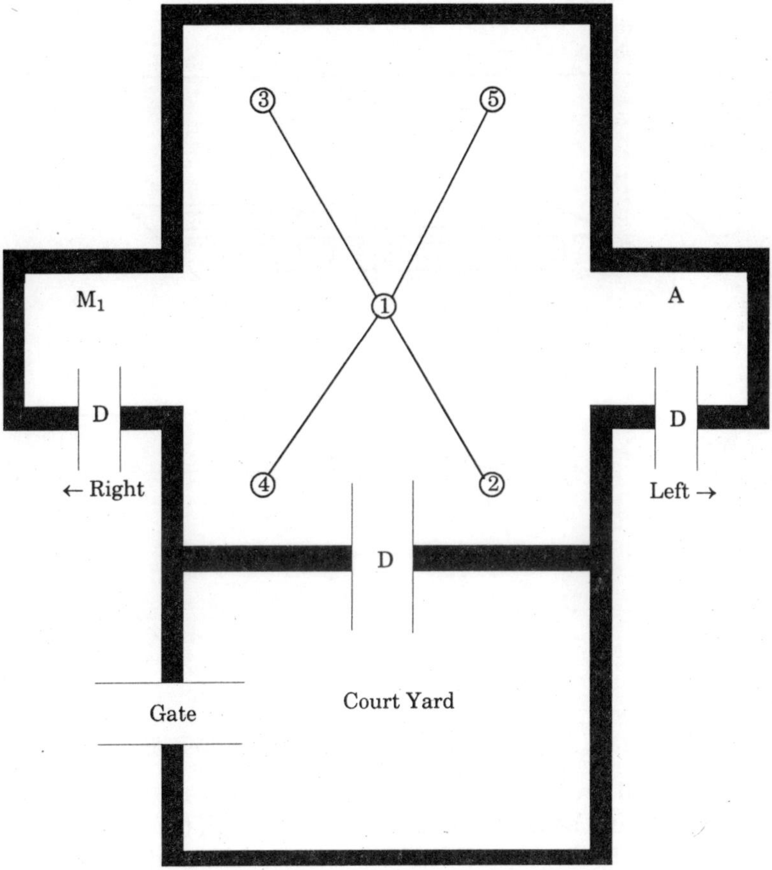

Fig. 13.2. Statues in Sumda Chung Temple

Key to Figure 13.2

1. Varocana (Centre)
2. Ratna Sambhava (South)
3. Amogshiddhi (North)
4. Amitabh (West)

5. Akshobhya (East)

M_I—Maitreya green coloured Statue of two storied in height.

A—Avalokitesvara white coloured Statue of two storied in height
D—Door
1. Varochana
2. Ratnasambhava
3. Amogshiddhi
4. Amitabh
5. Akshobhya

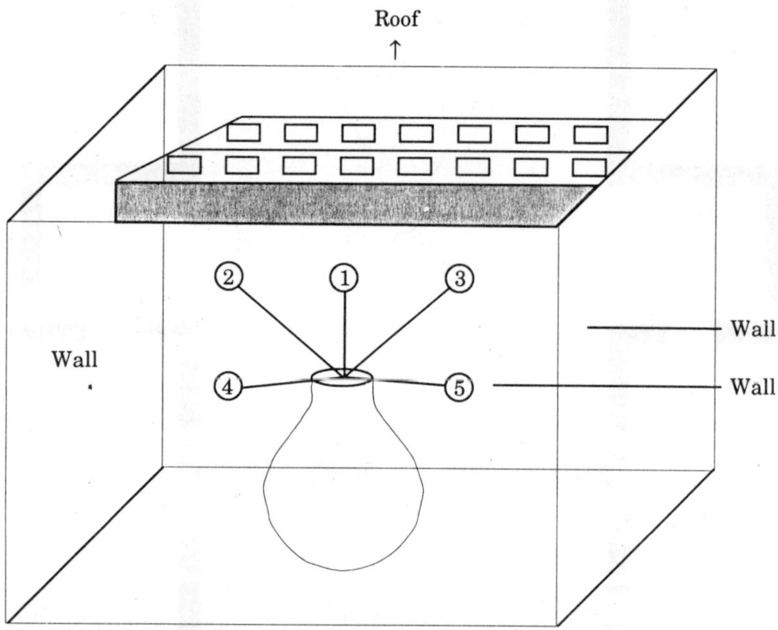

Fig.13.3. Position of Statues in Sumda Chung Temple.

Fig. 13.3 reveals that Five Dhani Buddhas are based with small vessel and affixed with side walls through threads which pass through their respective holes made at the middle of each statue. The structure looks like a flower pot. Besides the above there are many statues of gods and goddesses in the temple. These statues are not supported with the walls but are attached with the walls with the help of threads which pass through the holes on the back side of the statues. See Fig. 13.4

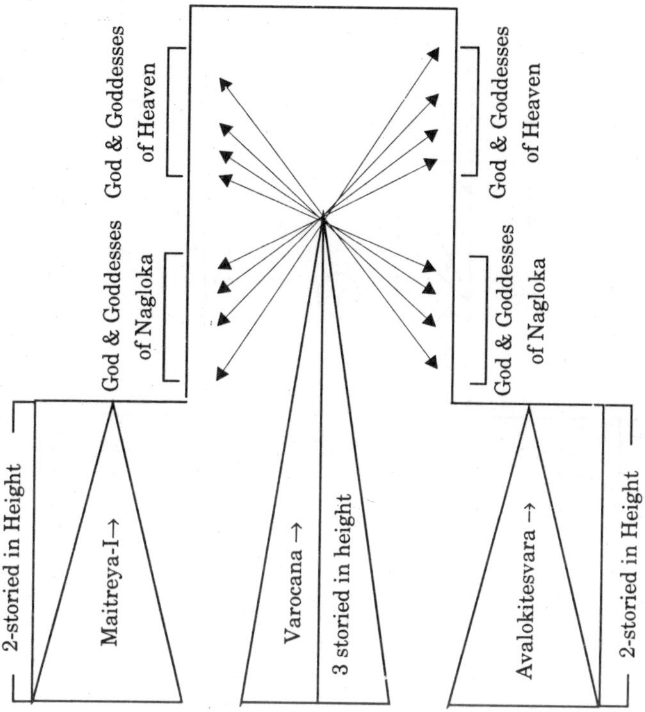

Fig. 13.4. God and Goddesses statues in Sumda Chung.

Fig. 13.4 reveals that :

1. Varocana statue is about three stories in height.
2. The left and right Maitrey a statues are about two stories in height.
3. The gods and goddesses on the upper side seemed as if they are welcoming Varocana in heaven.
4. The gods and goddesses on the lower side seemed as if they are inviding Varocana in Lhu youl (Nag loka).

The gods and goddesses of the Sumda-Chung are not attached with the walls but they are hanged in support of thread with the side walls as shown in the Fig. 13.5.

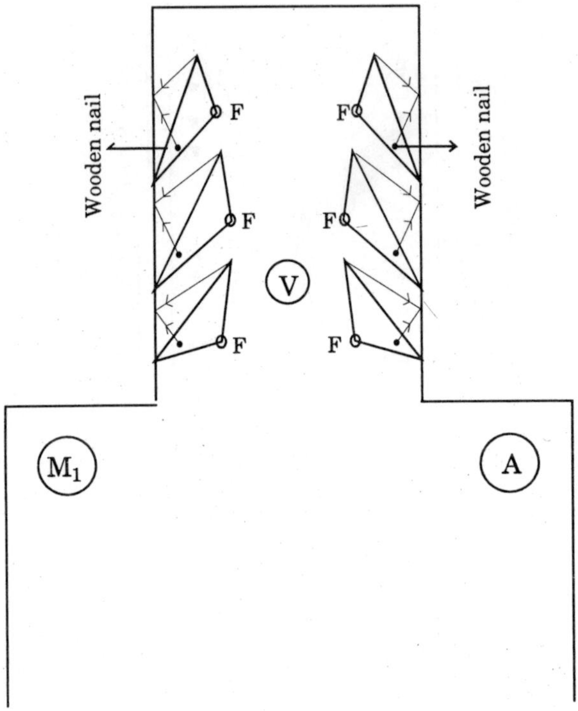

Fig. 13.5. Position of God and Goddesses in Sumda-Chung

V. Varocana :

M_1 : Maitreya (Green colour)

A: Maitreya (White colour)

F: Face of the god and Goddess

Fig. 13.5 indicates that the gods and goddesses are hanged on the walls of the temple through the holes which are in the middle of these statues. The faces of these statues are towards Varocana as if they are inviting Varocana to their respective *lokas*.

The Sumda-Chung temple has beautiful frescoes of Five Dhani Buddhas and one thousand Buddha mandal Fig. 13.6.

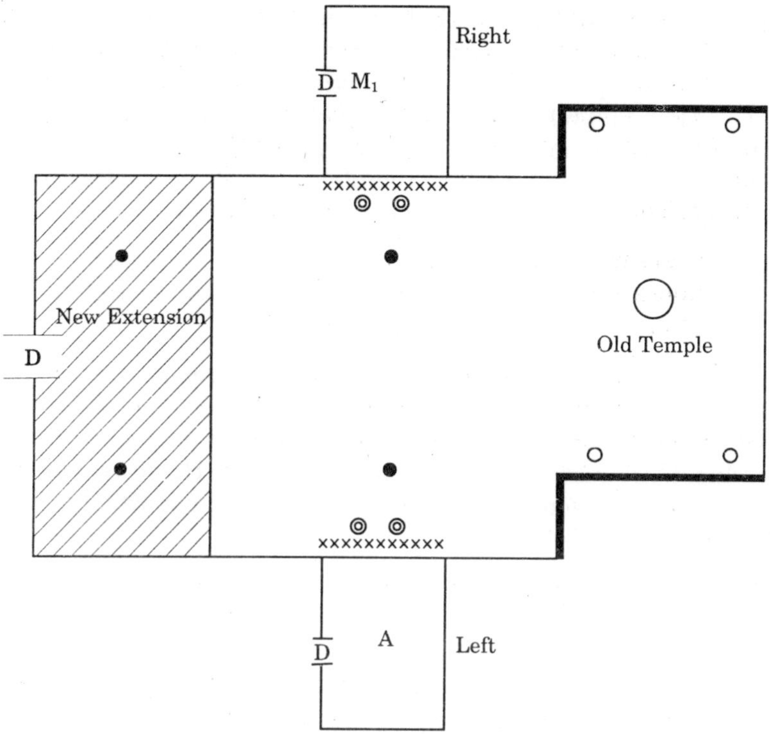

Fig. 13.6. Wall Paintings in Sunda-Chung.

Old temple : Constructed by Rin-chen-zang-po
New extension : By stag-sang-raspa

O : Dhani Buddha statue
o : Varocana
• : pole
◎ : Dhani Buddha painting
× : 500 Buddha at one side of wall
▨ : Extension portion
M_1 : Maitreya Statue
D : Door
A : Avalokitesvara

Historic Beliefs

It is said that after the construction of Sumda-Chung temple, Locava Rin-Chen-zang-po felt the need of its preservation from the enemy. Therefore, he said to his followers to cover the temple with soil and stones so that the enemy could not trace it and it could be saved. Later the temple was being covered with stones, soil, etc., and a small cave made through which a person could go upto the base of temple for lighting the lamp regularly. The duty of lighting the lamp at temple was given to Khagchan-pa (Tib. : Khang-Chan-pa) family of the Sumda-Chung village.

After 500-600 years Tibetan Government sent a letter to the head Lama of Hemis monastery in which was mentioned about the construction secret temple in Ladakh by the Rin-chen-bzan-po. The matter of the letter was as follows :

> "There is a famous temple at the west of Leh which is still underground. Therefore to search this temple and inform the government accordingly."

The head Lama probably 1st Stag-sang-ras-pa ordered his men to search the underground temple. His men went to Sumda and its neigbhouring villages to locate the said temple but failed to find it. After sometime when they returned to Hemis monastery without any favourable response, then a lama of Khang-Chen family informed that:

> "He saw a cave in his village Sumda-Chung, where one member of his family daily goes to light up the lamp somewhere inside the cave. In my opinion there may be a temple and possibly it would be the same temple as mentioned in the letter of Tibeten Government addressed to the head lama of the Hemis monastery. Therefore exavation is required to find the reality." Fig. 13.7.

The head lama of the Hemis monastery was fully agreed with the lama and deputed him alongwith some more lamas for the excavation work at the proposed site. After the excavation they found a temple which had five Dhani Buddhas statues Fig. 13.8. When the excavation work was completed, Stag-sang-ras-pa visited the temple. He was surprised to see the statues of five Dhani Buddhas which were partially supported with the vessel at their base. He asked :

"How these big statues are based with such a small vessel?"

Lama replied, "I don't know but if you will toss a coin it will come to vessel."

Stag-sang-ras-pa tossed a coin which directly came down to the vessel. Then he confirmed that the vessel in the temple was placed in such a way that the centre of gravity of each Dhani Buddha passed through the vessel.

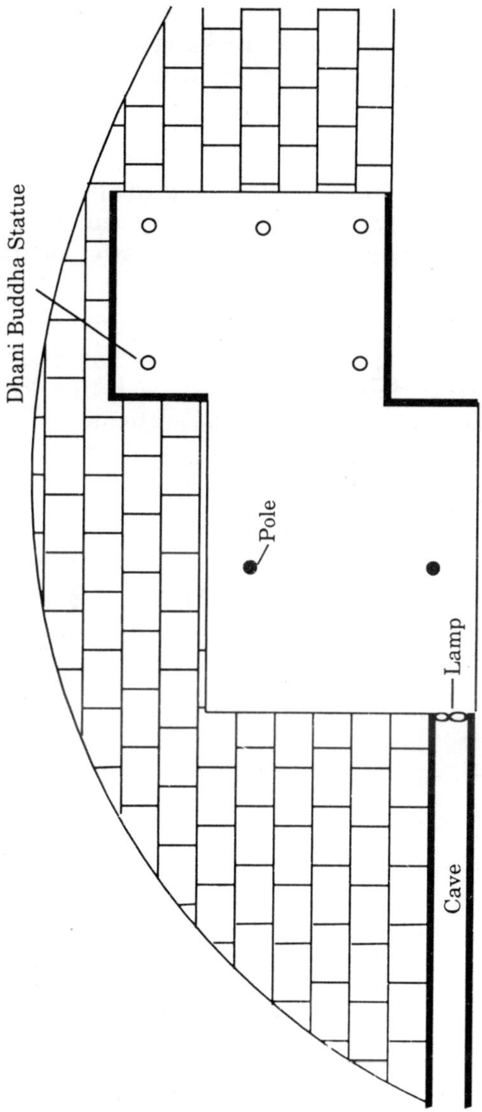

Fig. 13.7. Old Sumda-Chung temple.

Later Stag-sang-ras-pa ordered his men to extend the Du-Khang and construct two more rooms for the Maitreya and Avalokitesra. After the completion of the new rooms at the temple, Stag-sang-ras-pa asked Khangchun-pa family to look after the temple and wrote the following letter :

> "The Khang chun-pa family will look after the Sumda-Chung temple and preserve all related documents."

Now the question, "why Stag-sang-ras-pa felt to once again give the responsibility for looking after the Sumda-chung temple to Khangchun-pa family only ?" The answer of this question will be like this :

In those days it was very difficult to come to Sumda-Chung temple on foot from Hemis. Therefore viewing this fact Stag-sang-ras-pa probably felt that the temple would be better looked by the Khangchun-pa family than the monks of Hemis.

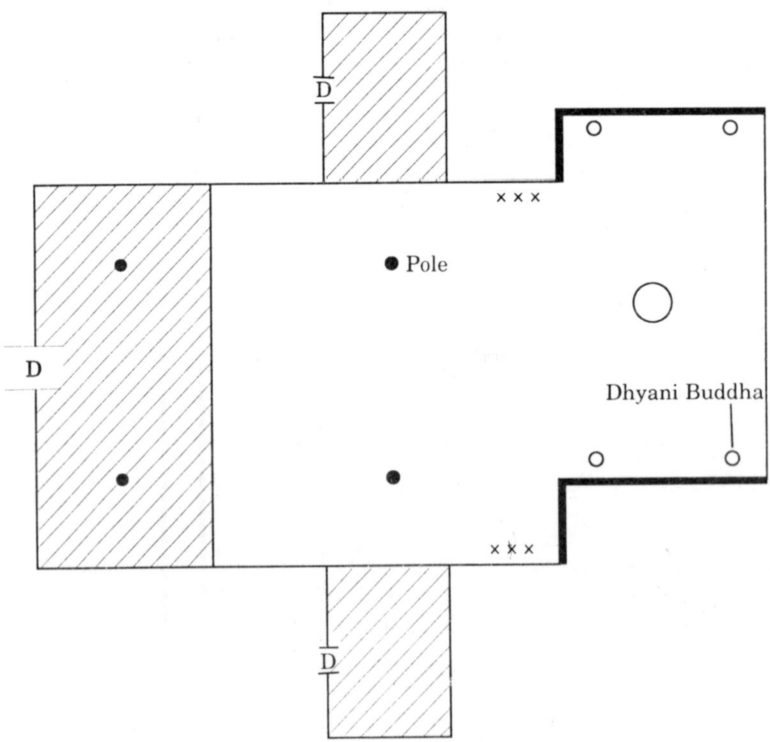

Fig. 13.8. New and old portion of Sumda-Chung temple.
××× = God & goddess (deities)

Since then from the period of 1st Stag-sang-ras-pa Khang-chung-pa family was keeping the records of the Sumda Chung and properly looking after the day today activities of the temple.

Eight Ruined Lha-khangs

There are eight Lha-Khangs nearby the Sumda-Chung temple. Except one Lha-Khang which consists of five Dhani Buddha frescoes in mandals shape, rest are completely ruined. However, all these Lha-Khangs are of the Sumda-Chung temple period. Fig. 13.9 shows the details :

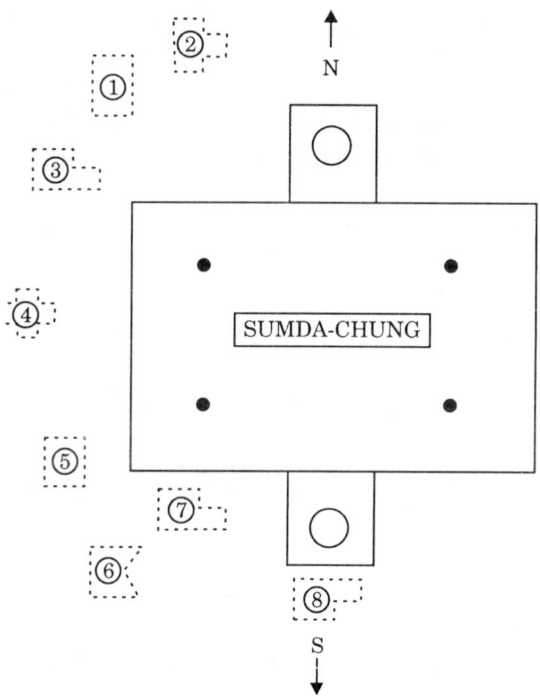

Fig. 13.9. Eight ruined Lha-Khang near Sumda-Chung.

Chotbul

According to the Tibetan Calendar in the 10th month Chotbul festival is annually organised by the Sumda-Chung temple. On the occasion people come for worship from Sumda-Chenmo, Azang and Chiling villages. This festival lasts for four days (w.e.f. 13 to 16 dates of the month). Besides people from the other parts of Ladakh come here and light the lamp. All pilgrims bring local butter (Demo milk butter). However, to light the lamp at the temple the Khangchen-pa gives instruction to his fellow villagers to bring a certain scaled butter only turn by turn. At the last day (i.e., on the 16th of the 10th month) Lamas complete all rituals in the temple. Thereafter they make *torma* and throw it outside the village. In the *torma* throwing procession two persons carry torma and others particularly Lamas chant mantra and play religious music. They all carry the torma up to that place which is selected according the direction given by the Onpo. Normally this place is about half a km. away from the temple. Nowadays Lamas burn the torma at the selected place with ritual performance. In the evening pilgrims and villagers gather near the temple and organise traditional music and dance programme. On this day they sing and dance with full gaitey and joy.

Festival of Avalokitesvar

In the 8th, 14th and 15th day of 1st month of the Tibetan calendar, villagers of the neighbouring places come for worship at the Sumda-Chung temple. During the course of worship they chant Avalokitesvar mantra in the presence of the Lama. Many pilgrims on this occasion also come from the other different parts of Ladakh. They pray to give them pardon for their ignorant deeds and encourage them to do good works in the future.

Now we will discuss about the Rin-chen-zang-po's another temple at Sumda-Chen (Chenmo).

Sumda-Chen (Chenmo)

Sumda-Chen (Chenmo) temple is 62 kms. away from Leh towards the west and popularly known as 'Galdan Tsewang' temple. It is about one thousand years old. Near the temple 10 houses have about 90 residents. The details are shown in the following Fig. 13.10.

Sitpe Dokpo

The Sumda-Chenmo temple is also known Sitpe Dokpo which means Kalacakra. When Galdan Tsewang attacked and destroyed many villages in Ladakh, he came to Sumda Chenmo via Chiling and destroyed the temple but did not carry any statue. The temple has one main statue of Pyagar Gyal po of

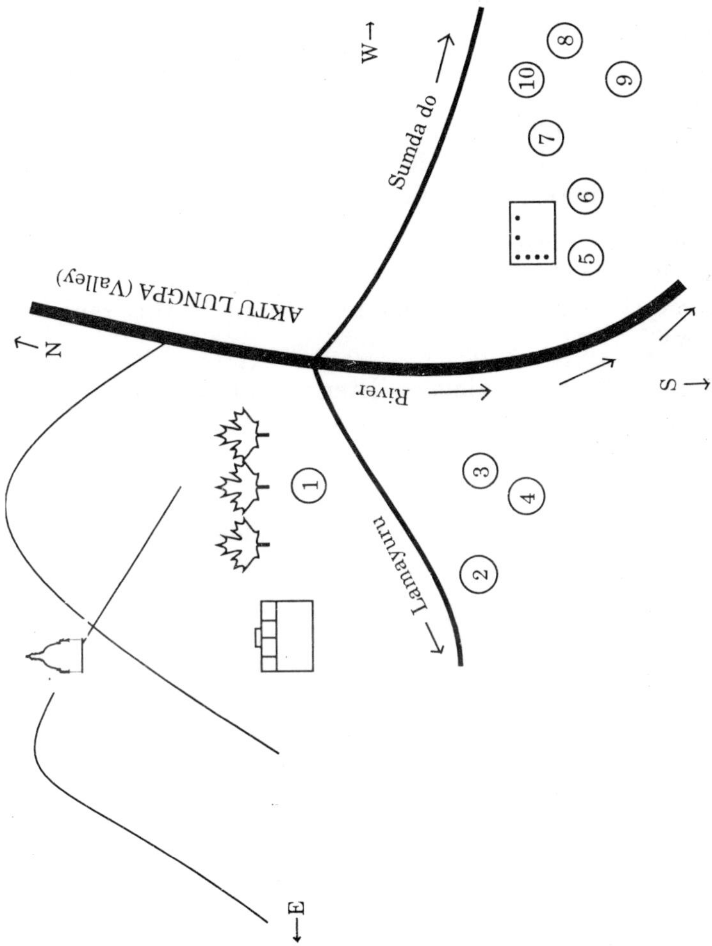
AKTU LUNGPA (Valley)
Sumda do
Lamayuru
River
N
S
E
W
1
2
3
4
5
6
7
8
9
10

Fig. 13.10

one foot in height. It is made of pure gold. Besides, there are many gold and silver worshipping items, but all these were covered by the soil, stones and woods during the collapse of temple.

Historical Belief

According to local people, eight years ago a British citizen Tim visited Sumda Chenmo. As he came to known about the golden Pyagar Gyalpo statue, he visited the site and decided to excavate the temple area. He went to villagers for help and tried to explain them and said :

> "He would like to excavate the Sumda-Chenmo temple site for Pyagar Gyalpo statue made of gold. Later he would place the same in the temple, help me in this religious work."

Sumda-Chenmo villagers listened to him carefully, but refused to give him support in this task. Mr. Tim then returned to England. After some years he again came to Sumda-Chenmo village and said :

> "I want to excavate the Sumda-Chenmo site and re-establish the temple in its traditional form."

Sumda-Chenmo villagers replied :

> "If you start renovation works at the Sumda-Chenmo temple site, you must follow the following conditions : (1) to take the permission from the Head lama of Hemis monastery Rev. Tag-sang-res-pa, (2) No Sumda-Chenmo villager should be harmed directly or indirectly."

In 1992, Mr. Tim went to Hemis monastery. He met Rev. Stag-sang-res-pa and Duchen Renpoche and asked to give permission to renovate the Sumda-Chenmo temple in Sumda valley. Rev. Stag-sang-res-pa said : "Before giving the permission I would like to visit the site." But as he reached near the temple, dusty storm blew dangerously and he was unable to see the site. Thereafter Rev. Stag-sang-res-pa said :

> "Pyagar Gyalpo is the main protector deity of my Hemis monastery, if the deity did not allow me inside the temple, how can others be allowed inside the temple ?"

Thus, Mr. Tim was not allowed to do any works at the temple site. Though he was ready to bear all expenses of rituals for Pyagar Gyalpo deity and for the road construction from Sumda-do to Sumda-Chanmo temple.

Statues in the Sumda-Chenmo Temple

Temple has one wooden Maitreya and 12 small statues, for details see Fig. 13.11.

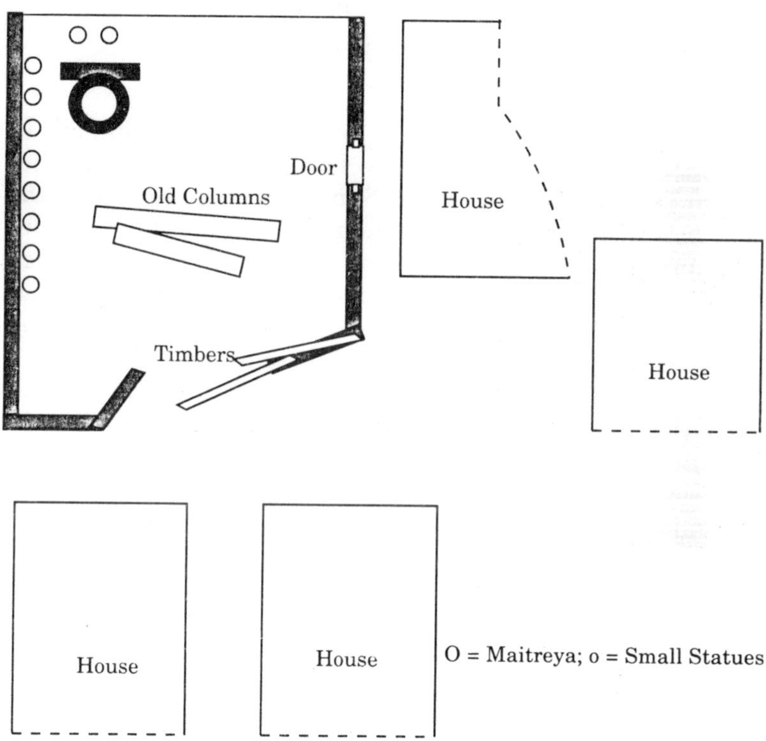

Fig. 13.11. Sumda-Chenmo temple and nearby houses Cf. Vohra, Rohit; Dating of a Maitreya Relief of the mid-8th century; from Sumda Chen, South Asian Studies, 9, 1993 pp. 97-103.

In the Sumda-Chenmo temple Maitreya is the important statue. It is carved on a juniper trunk and has the following measurements :

Height : 2.70 m.

Breadth (through the middle of the chest)	: 1.82 m.
Chest breadth	: 53 cm.
Width of both Arms	: 40 cm.
Width of Back	: 62 cm.
Height leg below back side	: 1.40 cm.
Height lip (upper) to head	: 66 cm.

When Galdan Tsewang destroyed all important monuments of Ladakh, the people of Sumda valley thought that Galdan Tsweng could not reach Sumda-Chenmo temple as the route between Leh to Sumda-Chenmo was very difficult. But their imagination was wrong and Galdan Tsewang reached Sumda-Chenmo. He destroyed the temple and threw all statues outside the gallery. The big Maitreya statue later in 1968 placed inside the temple after performing all traditional rituals.

The small statues are also equally important. However, it seems that these statues are fixed through wooden nails with the walls.

Now the temple is in a ruined condition, we can see only stones, juniper trunks (poles) and destroyed stone walls there.

Notes and References

1. Vohra, Rohit : 1993, *Dating of a Maitreya Relief of the Mid-8th Century : from Sumda Chen',* South Asian Studies; p. 98.
2. Snellgrove, D.L. and Skorupski, R. 1980, *'Cultural Heritage of Ladakh,'* Vol. 11, Aris' & Phillips, London & quoted by Rohit Vohra, 1993 *op. cit.*
3. Sumda Chung : Sumda Chango.
4. Sumda Chen : Sumda Chenmo = Sumda Chang Chen.
5. Snellgrove, D.L. and Skorupski, R. 1980 op. cit. p. 15 and quoted by Rohit Vohra, 1993, *op. cit.*

PART II
Tourism

14

Meer Izztoollah's Visit to Ladakh during 1812-13

S.C. Saxena

The travel account of Izztoollah for Ladakh was in Urdu, it was translated by R.D. Henderson and was printed in 1872 at the Foreign Department Press Council House Street.[1]

Meer Izztoollah was a famous adventurer, he had travelled many places in Central Asia. The route from Kashmir to Tibet was very popular during the Eighteenth and Nineteenth centuries. Tibet was then known by 'Khituh-i-Kashmir' among Kashmiri Muslim traders. Meer Izztoollah was the first Muslim adventurer in Kashmir who had narrated his travel account in Urdu. He travelled from Ladakh from Kashmir during 1812-13. Here follows some interesting information which he was able to explain about Ladakh.

1. ***Matayan.*** A village is on the right bank of the river of Lesser. Tibet called Matayan. It is inhabited by Soonnee Mohammedans.
2. ***Diras.*** Diras is situated on the banks of Thibet river. The villages between Matayan and Diras are of the most wretched description—About a year before the date of our visit 300 men of Dardee tribe had attacked and plundered Diras, and carried away as prisoners 250 of the inhabitants, who were sold as slaves. Since that time a force of 50 match lock men under the son of Malik Ukrum have by the order of the ruler of Kashmir been stationed here for the protection of the road and village. Malik Ukrum receives from the Raja of Thibet an allowance of half the revenues of the villages between Matayan and Diras.

The Dardees above mentioned are an independent tribe who inhabited the hills which were three or four days journey north of Diras. They have their own Dardee language but speak Pashtoo also. It is said that there is a route through the Dardee country of Budukhshan, by which that city can be reached from Kashmir in ten days.

3. ***Kurchoo.*** Kurchoo is small district like Diras containing many villages close together, situated on the left bank of Thibet river. The houses are well built and clean. The inhabitants are Mohammedans of the Sheat sect. We arrived here on the 24th of September 1813. Seven Kroh from Diras is a halting station for caravans. One 'Kroh' from Kurchoo is the small village of Brook.
4. ***Thirispown.*** It is situated two 'Kroh' from the left bank of the river. Inhabitants of the village are Sheas. Houses are built in Thirispown. Five or six villages are passed in the stage. A large village called Hurun is lying on half way.
5. ***Pashkum.*** The inhabitants of Pashkum are Sheas. The name of the Raja of this place is Mohammed Ali Khan. He is also a Sheas Muslim. He is a feudatory of the Raja of Thibet. He is married to a sister of that sovereign and has compelled his wife to adopt the Mohammedan religion. One of his sisters is married to the Raja of the Thibet whose faith she has embraced. Several villages are passed road. The largest of which is Minjee. It is two 'Kroh' from the last stage.
6. ***Mulbec.*** Near the Mulbec village at 6 'Kroh' is a hill consisting of one entire rock. On the summit of which is a fort and a monastery of Lamas. There also the idols are prevented. An immense idol is close to the village which is twice life size and carved out of the solid stone, but by whom it is not known. The ruins of Sarai which was built by Ibraheem Khan are still visible here. The inhabitants of Mulbec are not Mohammedan, but follow the religion of Thibet. The 'Junior Kahlon', to whom belongs the whole territory between Diras and this place. Loochum, Sargoor, etc.
7. ***Hunskoot.*** It is inhabited by the people professing the religion of Thibet. Several villages are passed on the road. The names of some are Wukh, Tukhchuk, Khoorpoo, etc.

8. ***Lamayooroo.*** This village has a lama monastery. Several villages are passed on this stage.
9. ***Khuluch.*** A bridge over the river at Khuluch which was built by Ibraheem. It still exists. Khuluch is on the right bank of the river. Formerly the road to this place was merely a mountain path. It has lately been improved by one of the Lamas who has constructed bridges where required.
10. ***Saspowl.*** Saspowl is a flourishing village. It is two 'Krosh' from the last stage of the large village of Noorullah and 3 'Kroh' from Noorullah again is Himchee. A medicine[2] the staple food of the inhabitants of Tibet is "suttoo" or parched grain reduced to meat and made with paste. This they eat without any sweetening. Their favourite food is "Suttoo" in which meat is cooked. The higher classes eat rice. All classes of society are dressed in woollen cloth. The poor wear sheep skin coat and a black cap in winter. The leather is worn on one side so as to cover one of the ears. Their boots are undressed high each half way up the half and are lined with woollen cloth. They wear their hair plaited into a tail, which hangs down the back. Their upper garments are somewhat similar in shape to those worn in India, but are made in one piece, women wear in their hair strings of turquoise, Cornelian coal or pearl heads.

    In consequence of the difficulty of getting a decent living out of the land an abominable custom, which however is not sanctioned by their religion, prevails among the lower classes of three or four brothers being married to one woman. All the children born of such a marriage belong to the eldest brother. The oldest son has the power of dispossesing his father of his property to the exclusion of the other sons.[3]
11. ***Neemuch.*** Two or three villages are passed on this stage the largest of which is Boozgoo. Three 'Kroh' from Neemuh. There is a large town of Leh.
12. ***Leh.*** Leh is the largest town in Thibet. It is situated on the right bank of the Sanspoo river. The road for Leh is good. The country in which Leh is called here Ladakh and by Kashmeerees, Bootun, the name is given to the inhabitants by the latter is Boot. In Persian and Turkish

the country is known by the name of Thibet which is Turkish signifies in consequence of the abundence of that article exported thence.

Between Diras and Matayan the country produces wheat, cotton and barley. Beyond the latter place no cotton is grown. In neighbourhood of Leh wheat is harvested in October. There is only one crop in the year. Indian corn and pulse do not grow here. The turnips of Leh are sweet. Between Matayan and Leh water is bad. The water of Saspoo river is good. There are no wells in country and all people drink water from springs and mountain.

Notes and References

1. A brief account of travel in Central Asia by Meer. Izztoollah in the year 1812-13, translated by R.D. Henderson, attached to the Foreign office, Govt. of India.
2. The medicine is called Kubr, much used by physicians of the Greek School, is also procurable here.
3. The total grain produce of Leh is estimated at 5000 Khaswars per annum. No tax is levied on produce but a yearly tax is paid by each proprietor in proportion to the account of land held by him. For the purposes of this tax the land is not measured, but the amount to be paid is determined by the water advantages possessed by each proprietor. Thus one is estimated to have command a sufficient amount of water to turn one flour mill, another half that quantity, and a third sufficient for the irrigation of his land for so many days, and so on.

   In Leh houses are built of stone or unburnt brick, they use the beans of poplar wood. There are more than a thousand houses in the Leh town, most of them three or four stories. Among the Mohammedans of Kashmeer and Thibet members of both are Shea and Soonee are be found.

15

Sindhu Abhyaan (Sindhu Darshan)

Prem Singh Jina

Sindhu is as sacred as Ganga and Yamuna, yet it could not become popular. The reason could be due to its existence in high mountains. It flows from the mouth of lion and lofty mountain near holy Mansarovar and enters Indian territory at Dam-chok. It later flows through the sandy plains of Chang-Thang valley then passing through the central valley of Leh area thereafter flows via Lemo (Snye-mo) Khalatse, Dahanu, Batalik valley then enters the territory of Pakistan. Thus, in India it flows through high mountain valleys right from Chang-Thang, Leh (Central) Lower Ladakh and Batalik.

Therefore, to know the importance of Sindhu river Hon'ble Home Minister Sri L.K. Advani decided to organise Sindhu Abhyaan in 1977 for the first time at Leh. In 2000, Sindhu Darshan festival was inaugurated by the Prime Minister, Sri Atal Behari Vajpayee at Shey village, 15 kms. from the Leh town on 7th June, 2000.

On this occasion almost the entire top brass of administration came to Leh much earlier to make necessary arrangements for the Prime Minister. Chief Minister Dr. Farooq Abdullah and Chief Secretary Jammu and Kashmir state arrived on 6th June morning and gave on the spot instruction to the district authorities for making elaborate arrangements for the occasion. Chief Minister Dr. Farooq was briefed about the arrangements made at Leh and Shey, the village on the banks of gushing blue Sindhu river. Minister of State for Housing and Urban Development of J&K State Kushok Tokdan Rinpoche, Chief Executive Councillor, LAHDC Mr. Thupstan

Chhewang, Kushok Thiksey and Mr. Ghulam Hassan Khan both Members of Parliament were also present.

Thus, on Monday 7th June, 2000, the moon-land at an altitude of 11,500 ft. in Jammu and Kashmir State received a host of devotees from various parts of the country mostly the Sindhis. Among the national leaders who were present at the bank of Sindhu river near Shey village were as below :

1. The Governor Jammu and Kashmir, Mr. Girish Chandra Saxena.
2. Governor of Goa, Mr. Fazal.
3. Chief Minister of Jammu and Kashmir Dr. Farooq Abdullah.
4. Chief Minister of Himachal Pradesh, Mr. Prem Kumar Dhumal.
5. Union Minister of State for Civil Aviation, Prof. Chaman Lal Gupta.
6. Union Minister of State for Railways, Bangaroo Lakshman.
7. Former Indian Ambassador to Mongolia Rev. Kushok Bakula.
8. Bhartiya Janta Party General Secretary Mr. Narinder Modi.
9. Uttar Pradesh Bhartiya Janta Party Chief and Minister Mr. Om Prakash.
10. Maharashtra Minister, Mr. Hussain Dalaai.
11. Jammu and Kashmir Tourism Minister, Mr. S.S. Slathia.
12. Minister of State, Mr. Qamar Ali Akhoon.
13. Kushok Tokdan Rinpoche.
14. Mr. Ghulam Hassan Khan Member of Parliament, and
15. Mr. Thupstan Chhewang, Chief Executive Councillor, LAHDC.

Besides semi civil police and military officers, prominent citizens and a large number of Ladakhis were present.

As said earlier, Sindhu river originates from Kailash Mansarovar and flows down to Pakistan after traversing through a large clunk of Ladakh, which is a cold arid zone but has rich Mahayani culture, Buddhist monasteries, Mani and Stupas. This land of monks known for its peaks changing shades, and now the *Karambhoomi* of India's war heroes who wrote heroic history by their blood on high mountain snow clad peaks making the nation proud.

The Sindhu, was referred as Hindu by Parsian speaking

people but when Muslim rulers came in power they used Hindu for Sindhu and finally Hindustan was derived from Sindhu. When British ruled over Hindustan, they used Indus for Sindhu and thereafter India was derived from Indus. Thus, the Indus from which India derives its name, is the latest. If Batalik and Mashko valley in Kargil created nation wide awakening for strengthening the unity during operation Vijay, the Sindhu festival also known as Sindhu Abhyaan had emerged as symbol of national integration.

In fact, Mr. L.K. Advani himself a Sindhi visited four years ago at the Sindhu site at Choglamsar, 8 kms far from Leh, and thus started the Sindhu Darshan Abhyaan starting from a handful of Sindhis.

The Union Ministry of Tourism in collaboration with the Jammu and Kashmir Tourism also decided to promote Ladakh as a tourist destination linking it with great India-civilization— Indus valley civilization – that comes live during visit to this fairyland. It was on the banks of this river, from times immemorial, a civilization had flourished the Indus valley civilisation making every Indian proud. Therefore, keeping the great historic importance, the Prime Minister was overwhelmed and after touching Sindhu Atal Behari Vajpayee aptly said :

"Some people queried about the existence of Sindhu in India as described in our national anthem but little did they know that it flows on our soil in Ladakh."

"How great must be the feelings of Sindhuputra today." Wondered Home Minister L.K. Advani who rediscovered Sindhu is a great trip to Leh in 1995. Since then it has been the pilgrimage for Sindhis who during pre-partition era used to worship its Sindh in present in Pakistan.

On 7th June 2000, the joyous Sindhis converged from 14 states of the country to join the Sindhu Abhiyaan. Prime Minister Atal Behari Vajpayee opened it by performing 'pujan' and hoisting the tricolour amid chanting of slogans "Bharat Mata Ki Jai". This was followed by Baharana worship of water deity, with a group of 20 artists in Sindhi costumes carrying water from different parts of the country dancing to the rhythm of drums and immersed it in the Sindhu, a unique union of holy rivers.

A strong crowd of about 7,500 dominated by Ladakhis in their colourful attire witnessed it. To cap it further, a Sindhu ballet by the famous Anila Sunder followed.

The occasion was marked by immersion of Brahmaputra water brought by Arunachal Pradesh Chief Minister Mukut Mithi, Brahmaputra and Sindhu rivers rise from the same source in Manasarovar.

The highlight of the festival was the presence and active involvement of all religions organisations, Ladakh Buddhist Association, Muslim Association, Anjuman Imamjia, Christian Association, Hindu Trust and Citizen Council, Leh.

On the occasion of inaugurating Sindhu Darshan Festival – 2000 at Leh on 7th June 2000, Prime Minister said "Let gushing Sindhu flow friendship to Pakistan." He renewed India's earned desire for friendship with Pakistan expressing confidence that "Our endeavours in this regard would succeed though it may take time." He said "India need not reiterate its yearning for friendship from the core of our hearts."

Wishing to see Sindhu as a river of friendship, he hoped its currents will carry the message of peace, brotherhood, cooperation and tranquility wherever it flows. He said :

> "Sindhu, symbolised 500 year ethos of great Indian civilization and its rediscovery will strengthen emotional integration in the country."

While quoting Rig Veda he said : "Sindhu it might surpasses all the streams that flow – His roar is lifted up to heaven above the earth, he puts forth endless vigour with a flash of light, even as cows with milk rush to their valves, so other rivers roar into the Sindhu. As a warrior king leads other warriors, so does Sindhu lead other rivers. Rich in good steed is Sindhu, rich in gold, nobly fashioned rich in ample wealth."

Prime Minister felt the need of road communication in order to promote tourism in Ladakh. He said, the festivals like Sindhu Darshan would promote tourism in Ladakh region and give a fillip to its art and crafts. He stressed for creating countrywide awareness about Ladakh's rich art, culture and ethos. For promotion of tourism round the year, he said dependable road communication is necessary. In this connection he mentioned about the Rs. 500 crore tunnel project at Rohtang Pass. About the Rohtang tunnel he said:

> "The Rs. 500 crore tunnel project at Rohtang Pass would be completed in seven years. It will be immensely beneficial for development of Ladakh region also besides meeting defence requirements. The road link between Ladakh and Himachal Pradesh will integrate the people of two neighbouring states."

Referring to the plan of Union culture ministry for promotion of culture in Ladakh, he said :

> "In order to promote culture a beginning had been made by laying the foundation stone of ambitious Sindhu cultural centre. The centre will go a long way in creating world – wide awareness about Buddhism."

Before the Prime Minister, Home Minister L.K. Advani, J&K Chief Minister Farooq Abdullah, Union Minister for Tourism and Culture, Mr. Anant Kumar, Chief Minister Arunachal Pradesh, Mr. Mukut Mithi also spoke on this occasion.

While speaking, Home Minister Mr. L.K. Advani wished that someone like General Parvez Musharraf had dipped his hands in Sindhu at Sakkar Barrage this morning when Atal Behari Vajpayee touched the sacred water here (at Shey village in Leh district) to have feel of friendship. He said :

> "That is not possible right now as some elements there (Pakistan) have not reconciled with the decision of Jammu and Kashmir and its people to accede to India by rejecting 2-nation theory,"He added.

> "If Vajpayee's sentiments of friendship were negatively responded by Pakistan, the smooth hands of his friendship could be stronger enough too. However, the Sindhu would emerge as a river of Indo-Pak friendship."

Mr. Advani further said:

> "The Sindhu festival will flourish as a national movement giving fillip of national integration."

About Sindhi language he added, the tireless efforts of Mr. Vajpayee who as a parliamentarian moved a private member's bill in Lok Sabha way back in 1957 for incorporating Sindhi language in the 8th Schedule of the constitution. Attributing it then is an injustice to Sindhis.

The Union Minister for tourism and culture, Mr. Anant Kumar, announced Rs. 3 crore for Sindhu cultural centre to be set up near Shanti stupa in Leh about the centre he said :

"The cultural centre will have a library, a museum and an open air auditorium." He added.

"The Sindhu Festival will give boost to tourism in Ladakh,"

Mr. Mukut Mithi Chief Minister of Arunachal Pradesh said :

"He has brought with him a message of friendship, national Integration and brotherhood." He added :

> "Sindhu is an identity of Indians which has unfolded a great civilisation. The Brahamputra and the Sindhu rose from the same origin in Mansarovar, these two great rivers have brought us together with the isolation of the people of his state and Ladakh due to rugged terrain, backwardness etc. and subsequent joining in the mainstream."

Speaking on the occasion Dr. Farooq Abdullah said :

> "A day will come when barriers between India and Pakistan will be removed and the people of both these countries would visit each other."

On this occasion Dr. Farooq Abdullah announced a piece of land in Leh on Sindhu bank for the construction of Sindhu Ghat. He said similar Ghat should be constructed at Damchok, the entry point of Sindhu in India. He described Sindhu as mother of Indian constitution.

On the occasion Prime Minister flagged off a Sindhu expedition from Damchok to Batalik. He also released a CD-ROM on Indus containing thousands of photos of Sindhu with sounds of gushing river. The function at the bank of Sindhu near Shey village came to an end with the recitation of *Vande Matram* by the artists of songs and drama division.

In the afternoon of the same day Prime Minister returned to Delhi.

There was in the programme schedule that Prime Minister would inaugurate the Ladakh Autonomous Hill Development Council (LAHDC) complex. But Prime Minister returned to

Delhi due to unavoidable circumstances. Union Home Minister Mr. L.K. Advani inaugurated the above complex. He favoured devolution of powers to help speeding up the development process at the regional level. He said :

> "Power should flow from Delhi to Srinagar and from Srinagar to Leh and Jammu."

Mr. Advani spoke eloquently about the democracy taking roots in the country and said the system was attained over 50 years ago, the people of the country did not get Suraaj (good governance). He said after attaining Swaraaj, we should strive for the attainment of Suraaj.

Responding to the demand of Ladakh Autonomous Hill Development Council for one time special financial assistance from the centre, the Home Minister assured that he would take up the issue with the Planning Commission and the Union Finance Ministry. He concurred with the demand for an all weather surface communication for the economic uplift of Ladakh region and said apprehensions expressed by LAHDC about the feasibility of a tunnel at Rohtang la will be considered before taking a final view.

The Home Minister complimented the people of Ladakh for making the Sindhu Darshan Festival a grand success and irrespective of their faith, he added during the course of cultural programme at the time of Sindhu Darshan. Sindhis were chanting songs of 'Zhulelal'. In the Sindhu society 'Zhulelal' has a special respect. 'Zhulelal' is the 'Istha Dev' of Sindhis. 'Zhulelal' is in every nook and corner of Sindhi society. Therefore, while welcoming any person Sindhi pronounced 'Zhulelal'. Finally he thanked for the overwhelming response of the people of Ladakh.

Earlier the Chief Executive Councillor Ladakh Autonomous Hill Development Council Mr. Thupstan Chhewang, while welcoming the Home Minister said the people of Ladakh feel secured in secular and democratic India. He said the people of Ladakh have offered supreme sacrifices to uphold the integrity of the country and would not hesitate to do so if the situation so demanded. He added that the Planning Commission should give special grant to Ladakh for the grass root level development. Ladakh needs financial assistance for the infrastructure development, village development and other basic requirements of villagers. He further said :

"There is a quite shortage of power, in the State Assembly Nemo Bazgo power project was discussed. If financial assistance through National Hydel Project may be given, it would solve some problem in this direction." He added :

"For the overall development of Ladakh road communication is essential. In this line Leh-Spiti road should be constructed. If this road will be constructed in Leh then there would be direct link with Delhi as in Ladakh we have road up to the last village Korzo. From Spiti side road is already constructed up to Cigdar. Therefore, if Karzo and Cigdar will be linked by road which is about 80 Kms, Leh will be linked with Delhi throughout the year. No doubt there is one pass Parang La (18,000 ft.) which lies in between. So, if we consider Rohtang tunnel, Ladakh will not be benefitted with this because in between Lahul and Leh there are four passes; Baralacha Taglungla are snow capped passes and this road can not be opened throughout the year. In my opinion Lahul even may not be benefited. About Bodhi language he said :

"The Centre should include Bodhi language in the 8th Schedule of the Indian Constitution and regretted that funds could not be made available to Ladakh Autonomous Hill Development Council for micro hydel projects."

The Union Home Minister Mr. L.K. Advani also layed the foundation stone of Sindhu ghat in Shey near the Sindhu Bank on 7th afternoon. On this occasion he expressed optimism about easing of tension between India and Pakistan and said if German wall could collapse there is no reason why two neighbours could not become friends. He added who knows one day Parvez Musharraf may feel like having Sindhu Darshan. The rediscovered river has emerged as a symbol of national integration, peace and friendship.

Emphasising the need for cordial Indo-Pak relations, he referred to the Deendayal Upadhayay and Ram Manohar Lohia's joint statement of their concept of confederation of the two nations and said that what the two leaders had envisioned could be reality some day. This is what the erstwhile Jana Sangh used to talk about Akhand Bharat. He added :

"Sindhu Darshan will create awareness about the uniqueness of the land and potential for domestic tourism of Ladakh region. The beauty of Leh and other areas in this region are still unknown. Therefore, Sindhu festival will motivate people to visit Leh and Leh becomes their other destination for pilgrimage."

In the evening thousand of people gathered in the polo ground near D.C. office Leh to see world's renowned artists performing. The classic dancers came from various parts of the country.

"It is a great occasion to see highly decorated and talented artists thronging Leh to perform during the Sindhu Darshan," said Mr. L.K. Advani.

"People of this country had got a God sent opportunity to watch famous classical dancers perform," acknowledged Dr. Farooq Abdullah.

The scintillating Kuchipudi dance by Raja and Radha Reddy, Kathak by Uma Sharma and Sunhana Narayan and Bharat Natyam by Kanika Srinivassam marked the cultural evening.

Kinnaur folk dance, Chabskyang and Shondol dances by Ladakhi artists Manipur dance by Singhjeet Singh and Charu Mathur and several dances from Arunachal Pradesh were the other highlights of the cultural evening.

The 3-day festival of Sindhu Darshan came to an end with the cultural programme.

In the meanwhile to keep the cultural identity of Ladakh the Ladakh Buddhist Association gave a memorandum to Prime Minister Atal Bihari Vajpayee demanding to give Union Territory status to Ladakh. Therefore, many Buddhist activists were also seen wearing badges which read "we want U.T."

The L.B.A. President Tsering Samphen said, "The Government should appreciate the heterogeneity of Jammu and Kashmir. Political arrangement should take into account the aspirations of the people of all the three regions—Ladakh, Kashmir and Jammu. Therefore, lasting solution lies in trifurcation of the state." He at the end warned the Government against any action for restoration of the pre-1953 position. The

District Congress Committee (Leh) also opposed the idea of restoration of the pre-1953 position. P. Namgyal, former Union Minister said :

"It must be done after separation of Ladakh and Jammu from the valley. Otherwise, the problem that confronts the valley will crop up in Ladakh."

In conclusion, Sindhu Darshan Festival came to end at Polo ground with full success of classic dances. This was a memorable event which will live in the memories of the people of Ladakh for a long time. The national level festival had been designed to boost tourism here in Ladakh which inturn would improve the economy of the region. The above Festival is organised each year from 1st June to 3rd June.

References

'Advani for Confederation of India, Pak-Farooq's call to ease Indo-Pak tension', *The Kashmir Times,* 8 June, 2000.

'Advani for devolution of powers at all levels, *The Kashmir Times,* 8 June, 2000.

'Farooq in Leh to oversee PM's Visit', *The Kashmir Times,* 6 June, 2000.

'Leh tunes-up on six Indian classical dances', *The Daily Excelsior,* 10 June 2000.

'PM extends hand of friendship to Pak-Sindhu will flow message of peace and cooperation', *The Kashmir Times,* 8 June, 2000.

'Samyukta Koshal,' Sindhu', paper read on the occasion of Sindhu Festival on 1997.

'Sindhu Darshan', A Festival of Unity', *The Kashmir Times,* 9 June, 2000, p. 3.

16

Tourism and Changing Environment of Ladakh

Prem Singh Jina

I

Ladakh, a landlocked region of Jammu and Kashmir State in the lap of western Himalaya, is exposed to accelerating environmental changes. Although change is inevitable and desirable when it improves the living conditions of local inhabitants, a methodology of change must be examined in consistence with the preservation of unique flora and fauna, spectacular natural beauty, and distinctive culture of this area.[1] The slow but gradual changes are affecting the natural environmental conditions, economy and human society. An appraisal of various aspects of change reveals that tourism and economic developments are creating disharmonies in the eco-systems. The disturbances in the environment do not mean that we should arrest the change, changes should be accepted and hence, instead of arresting the changes which are taking place in the mighty mountain chain that possess immense potentials (i.e., in the form of hydel power, irrigation, raw materials etc.), we must find out a way of change while realizing the latent potential powers for human welfare. Different ethnic stocks[2] live in this small region having diversified problems due to complexity of change, as experienced during the last five decades.[3]

Man is everywhere the principal agent of change. With rapid increase in population and their unending needs, man pressed up a limited available resource and inroads into the mountains. Extention of plantation, agriculture development building up hydro-electric power stations, laying out of new roads and buildings are taking place at the cost of depleeted cultivated areas in and around Leh and Kargil towns of this region. The mountainous region such as Ladakh could not accommodate the suddenness of these changes. With the increase in population, the supporting capacity of land along the Indus catchment and Suru river had decreased. The rearing of sheep has correspondingly decreased. Not only this, pasture grounds near the villages and even the in Chang-Thang sub-division have been decreasing in every decade.

The physical layout until 1940 did not allow much socio-economic and environmental change in Ladakh. In later period the communities here were not excluded from the benefits of developments, but the communities who were professionally traders and by religion Muslim got chance to marry with the young girls and settled down in Leh and its surrounding villages. They were Yarkandi and Kashmiri Muslims who made temporary 'Nikahs' (marriage) with the Buddhist girls and gradually became the owners of Buddhist land and other immovable properties. Today the offsprings from Ladakhi Buddhist ladies with Yarkandi or Kashmiri Muslim men are called Argons and have a good population in and around Leh.

When developments through Five Year Plans and financial-cum-technical assistance from Indian government reached Ladakh, some partial infrastructural changes took place, but such financial assistance could not assist the cultural activities and hence shocked the Ladakhi culture as more and more Ladakhi educated boys and girls were given Government jobs, this caused the rich and poor gap. To maintain the minimum living standard poor Buddhist ladies either went for labour jobs or started to sell 'chang' (cheap beer).

Another severe jolt was felt by the people of Ladakh in 1962; when the Sino-Indian Border dispute completely stopped the flow of trade with Tibet through the high land route passes. Thus, Indo-China Border dispute and war caused a sudden unexpected change in the economy of Ladakh. During this period many males joined the Army or partially engaged with the Indian Army. Indian Government was then mainly concentrated to fulfil the demands related with defence. Civilian problems were ignored. So, Ladakhis limited their activities within their village communities.

After 1962, when peace returned on at Indo-China Border; Government of India paid more attention towards the Ladakh border, because in 1962 war China occupied a large portion of Indian territory. As a result Indian Army made its permanent settlements in Ladakh at different altitudes. Consequently, wide scale road construction work was started in order to link the main Army and Para Military forces camp with the sub-sector headquarter at Leh. Viewing the developmental activities in Ladakh, some more Central and State Government departments opened their offices in Leh. This time again Ladakhis had good job opportunities in Government offices and to improve their living standard. Thus, migration from villages to Leh and its surrounding areas took place in order to get education and to search for Government jobs by the educated Ladakhi mass.

In 1971, Ladakh again faced war, this time Indo-Pak war took place. In December 1971, Pakistani troops started firing from the border, as a result heavy shelling took place from both sides. In Nubra valley severe fighting lasted for about a week and India reoccupied its five villages viz. Bogdang, Turtuk Tyakshi, Parchathang and Thang from Pakistan. In Kargil, India made its position strong. Ladakhis as a result of border dispute again suffered a lot. In brief if we examine the Ladakhi socio-economic conditions since Independence up to 1971, Ladakhi faced four wars three against Pakistan and one against China, with the result Ladakhis had been struggling for several years in order to adjust them in their normal life.

In 1974, Ladakh was opened for foreign tourists. Hundreds and thousands of tourists annually visiting Ladakh. The influx of Indian and foreigners influenced Ladakhi culture. Younger generation adopting western culture fast along with Hindustani habits.

Now Ladakhis who before 1971 were influenced by Army culture suddenly got influenced by western culture on one side and on the other by adopting Indian culture stopped their traditional system of polyandry. This suddenly increased Ladakhi population and agriculture-vegetal cover. Such rapid changes effected the ecology of Ladakhi region, and hence the micro-climatic conditions are changing gradually. The unexpected heavy snow fall on 14th December 1986 at Zojila, three days continuous rainfall in September 1988, snow, fall on the second week of May 1993. Severe cold during December to February 1994, very hot days during summers in 1995 and still continuous hot and dry days in 1998, are some instances which show how the environment of Ladakh is changing slowly and steadily. Therefore, if the present trend continues in future too, there would be a great danger to the Ladakh ecology. Hence, there is an urgent need to follow a conservation policy for environment of Ladakh as the rational use of the environment to provide a high quality of living for mankind. Since the tempo of development has to keep up with the help of advance technology, the only realistic solution to the problem of environment lies in setting apart sizeable natural area in representative habits, to preserve some of our ecosystems in pristine condition as benchmarks for conservation of the environment.[6]

II

Ladakh has an area of 97,010 sq. kms. is situated in between 32° and 25° north latitude. It constitutes the northern most part of India where the altitude above mean sea level of inhabited places varies from 8,000 ft. near Kargil to around 14,000 ft. in some places in Chang-Thang. Because of higher altitude location, the climatic condition of Ladakh is very harsh tough, unexpected cold and dry. The eighty per cent region is mountainous, therefore causing heavy snowfall in winters and remained cut off from the rest of the world for about six months of the year.

The annual precipitation in Ladakh varies from 5 cms. in Leh district to about 20 cms. in Zangskar tehsil of Kargil district. Sky in Ladakh remains clear on most days, this results strong in strong solar radition and offers warm days even in winters when night temperatures drop as low as upto – 40°C in some places of Ladakh. Summer season is pleasant and sometimes days of this season are very hot when temperatures during July increase upto 36°C, however, nights remain cool throughout the year.

Indus is the main river of Ladakh, but it is not so big that it can be used for transportation. Therefore, transportation for Ladakh is through road and air. Before 1947 Ladakh could be approached by road only. Routes through Zoji-la and Baralacha were popular among traders and visitors. These were the life line of entire Ladakh through which all processes of development was followed. When roads closed before October due to heavy snow fall at Zoji la and Baralacha, the life of Ladakhis seemed to be dead. Today Ladakhis are fortunate they can go to Srinagar, Jammu, Chandigarh and Delhi even in winters by Airlines. Indian Airlines nowadays is operating flights for these places. During summers Indian Airlines operates daily flights for tourists. Similarly, Himachal Roadways and J&K Roadways operate bus services from Srinagar, Manali and Delhi. Besides, private tour operators also render their services for tourists. Now Delhi Government is also thinking to start 'Sindhu Yatra' bus service from Delhi to Leh. Taxi operaters also frequently operate taxi services from Manali to Leh and vice versa. They render their services within Ladakh for sight-seeing, and help tourism in Ladakh.

III

Although many foreign missionaries had started coming in Ladakh since long back but after 1974 Ladakh has been emerging as a international tourist centre. The following statements give evidence of the tourist traffic in Ladakh.

1. When Government of India opened Ladakh for foreigners suddenly foreigners who were in Kashmir valley visited Ladakh in summer 1974, in the next following years their percentage increased drastically in 1978 as compared to 1974.
2. Percentage of foreign tourists decreased to 1.4% in 1986 as compared to 1982, however, total tourist percentage increased slightly during this period. This was because of disturbances in Kashmir valley, and due to the cancellation of flights from Srinagar to Leh in which foreigners had booked their tickets well in advance.
3. The terrorist activities in Kashmir valley and Ladakh Buddhist Association movement in Ladakh for declaring Ladakh Scheduled Tribes caused a severe setback to tourism, foreigners were reduced to only 4,738 in 1990 as compared to 12,608 in 1986 and the total tourist percentage beings decreased to 58.15 in the same period.

Table 16.1 shows the last 18 years tourist trend in Ladakh

TABLE 16.1

Percentage Increased and Decreased of Tourist Traffic in Ladakh (1970-97)

Sl. No.	*Year*	*No. of Foreign Tourists*	*(+) % increased (–) % decreased*	*Total Tourist*	*(+) % increased (–) % decreased*
1.	1990	4,738	—	6,738	—
2.	1991	8,014	(+) 69%	9,055	(+) 34%
3.	1992	13,580	(+) 69%	16,018	(+) 77%
4.	1993	12,401	(–) 09%	14,401	(–) 10%
5.	1994	15,369	(+) 24%	17,499	(+) 22%
6.	1995	12,391	(–) 19%	17,985	(+) 3%
7.	1996	13,036	(+) 05%	16,573	(–) 08%
8.	1997	12,813	(–) 02%	16,801	(+) 1.3%

Source : Compiled from the tourist office, Leh–Ladakh.

Table 16.1 reveals that :

1. In Ladakh foreign tourist traffic is far more than the domestic, it has 75 per cent average per year.
2. Due to disturbances in Ladakh tourist percentage decreased to 9 per cent among foreigners and 10 per cent among the total tourists.
3. In Ladakh during 1995 at the border cross firing foreign tourist traffic suddenly decreased to 19 per cent, however there was no change in domestic tourist traffic. The percentage decreased among foreigners because of fast net work of information technology in foreign countries, through which as travel agencies in their respective countries got the information about the heavy artillery shells had been fired by the Pakistan Army in the Nubra sector of Indian territory, they immediately cancelled their tour programme to India, however, such information did not get much impact upon domestic tourists.
4. In 1997 Pakistan during summer started heavy artillery shelling at Kargil town, located between Srinagar and Leh Highway. This news was immediately spread throughout the European countries, as a result foreign tourists percentage decreased by 2 per cent as compared to 1996.

In Ladakh the demand of tourists between November to April is very low. However, first time tourist sets in with the opening of Srinagar-Leh road in the month of May. In the June and July it is increased considerably due to Hemis Festival, a popular festival of Lama dance in Ladakh. At the end of July with opening of Manali-Leh road and increasing of the number of flights, the tourists demand culminates in August. In September tourists demand retreat and in December tourist's season terminates (Table-16.2).

TABLE 16.2
Seasonal Spread of Tourists Demand in Ladakh (1997-98)

Sl. No.	*Month*	*Tourist Arrival (1990)*	*(1997)*	*Percentage of the total (1996)*	*(1997)*	
1.	January	38	29	0.23	0.17	
2.	February	50	33	0.30	0.19	
3.	March	84	65	0.50	0.39	
4.	April	203	177	1.22	1.05	
5.	May	492	369	2.97	2.20	
6.	June	2,140	1,941	12.91	11.55	
7.	July	6,100	5,960	36.80	35.47	Peak
8.	August	5,400	5,311	32.58	31.61	
9.	September	1,592	1,847	9.6	10.99	
10.	October	359	899	2.17	5.35	
11.	November	80	84	0.49	0.50	
12.	December	35	86	0.211	0.51	

Source : Compiled from the tourist office, Leh-Ladakh.

Table 16.2 reveals that July is the peak season of tourism in Ladakh. During this period all the other parts of India have rainy season, therefore, Ladakh is best for tourists, here climate is much pleasant and free from rain, the roads from Srinagar and Manali are also opened during these months, this adds to the tourist inflow to Ladakh which about forty three per cent by road Table : 16.3.

Table 16.3 reveals that tourists come to Ladakh by road from June to October, thereafter the road remained closed till May. So, Ladakh has only five months tourists season, which starts in the months of June and terminates at the end of October every year.

TABLE 16.3
Tourist Arrival by Air and Road to Ladakh (1996-97)

Sl. No.	*Month*	*Tourist Arrival in 1996*		*Tourist Arrival in 1997*	
		Road	*Air*	*Road*	*Air*
(1)	*(2)*	*(3)*	*(4)*	*(5)*	*(6)*
1.	January	—	38	—	29
2.	February	—	50	—	33
3.	March	—	84	—	65
4.	April	—	03	—	177
5.	May	—	92	109	560
6.	June	555	1585	712	1229
7.	July	2940	3160	3083	2877
8.	August	2845	2555	1965	3346
9.	September	707	885	483	1364
10.	October	59	300	189	710
11.	November	—	80	—	84
12.	December	—	35	—	86

Sources : Compiled from Tourists office Leh-Ladakh.

In 1996, 43 per cent of total tourists visited Ladakh by road and 51 per cent by air during June to October month. Therefore, during this period 93 per cent of the total tourists came by air and road, if we compare the same in 1997, we find, 38 per cent of the total, tourists visited Ladakh by road whereas 57 per cent visited by air. Thus, 93 per cent of the total tourists visited by air and road. In 1998, between May to July 5072 tourists came to Ladakh, but no tourists arrived by road till then, though Srinagar-Leh road opened for traffic, however, Pakistani troops had fired at least 150 artillery shells on Kargil and its adjoining areas. Most of the residents from these areas had fled to safer places following heavy shelling across the border. However, many Indians and trucks came to Leh at their own risk. In 1997, 24 per cent of the total Indian tourists visited Ladakh out of these, 25 per cent visited by road. Here follows the details in Table 16.4.

TABLE 16.4

Domestic and Foreign Tourists Arrival Statement During 1997

Sl. No.	*Month*	*By Road*		*By Air*	
		Domestic Tourist	*Foreign Tourist*	*Domestic Tourist*	*Foreign Tourist*
1.	January	—	—	—	29
2.	February	—	—	—	33
3.	March	—	—	15	40
4.	April	—	—	45	132
5.	May	69	40	50	210
6.	June	101	611	583	696
7.	July	280	2803	543	2334
8.	August	450	1515	746	2600
9.	September	80	403	573	791
10.	October	40	149	398	312
11.	November	—	—	38	46
12.	December	—	—	30	56

Source : Compiled from the Tourist office Leh-Ladakh.

Table 16.4 shows that during July and August both road and Airways operated their best services for tourists. During this period, 2019 Domestic tourists and 9,252 foreigners visited Ladakh.

In 1995 to increase tourism some new places viz. Nubra, Dha-Hanu, Tangtse, and Pangong lake were opened for foreigners, but due to high taxi fare these areas did not become popular among them (Table 16.5).

TABLE 16.5

Statement Showing Number of Foreigners Visited Nubra, Dha-Hanu, Tangtse, Tsomoriri and Pangong During 1995-97

Sl. No.	*Year*	*Nubra*	*Dha-Hanu*	*Tangtse*	*Tsomoriri*	*Pangong Lake*
1.	1995	501	115	180	134	—
2.	1996	486	291	—	17	—
3.	1997	26	12	—	14	57

Source : Compiled from the Tourist office, Leh-Ladakh.

Table 16.5 indicates that foreigners were interested to visit Nubra, Dha-Hanu and Tsomoriri lake. On an average (1995–97) 2.7 per cent of them preferred to visit Nubra, 1.06 per cent to Dha-Hanu and 0.44 per cent to Tsomoriri lake. In case Taxi rates were reasonable, the percentage of foreigners might be increased up to 10 to 20 per cent.

IV

To increase tourism the following recommendations could be considered :

1. Jammu and Kashmir Tourism Department should open Tourist guest houses along the country side, it will increase rural tourism and trekking.
2. Private Airline services are urgently needed because Indian Airlines has monopoly in Ladakh. Besides, the Indian Airlines' staff behaviour with passengers is rough enough.
3. They should open more Foreign Exchange counters in Leh.
4. During tourist season, there should be regular electric and water supply in Leh and its vicinity areas.
5. More restricted areas may be opened for tourists, the J&K Road Transport bus service facilities should be open for them.
6. Taxi rates are very high, therefore, necessary steps may be taken to normalize their rates for the countryside tourist places. The J&K Road Transport should conduct sight-seeing tours.
7. In order to promote tourism during off season, the Indian Airlines should give some concession in tickets for visiting Ladakh.
8. Indian Airlines should operate more flights from Delhi, Chandigarh, Jammu and Srinagar to Leh throughout the year or at least from May to December.
9. Update Telecommunication services and up grade the Travel Agencies services.
10. There is only one Post office, in Leh. The number of post offices should be increased.
11. Government should open Kailash-Mansarovar route from Leh for pilgrims.
12. Necessary arrangements are needed to open Manali-Leh road in May.

13. Indian Airlines should give L.T.C. Concession schemes for Domestic tourists who are interested to visit Ladakh during off-season.
14. Time to time J&K Tourist Department should advertise the cultural heritage, mountaineering and water rafting facilities of Ladakh.

Notes and References

1. Jina, Prem Singh : *'Tourism in Ladakh Himalaya'*, Indus Pub. Co., New Delhi, 1994.
2. Jina, Prem Singh : *'Ladakh : The Land and People'*, Indus Pub. Co., New Delhi; 1996.
3. Jina, Prem Singh (ed.) : *'Recent Researches on the Himalayas'*, Indus Pub. Co., 1997.

PART III
Wild Life

17

The Wild Life of Ladakh

Abdul Ghani Sheikh

Ladakh has one of the richest faunas in the world. Its arid deserts and high mountains are rich habitats of wild life. The range of the species of wild life is wide and varied. It include wild yalk, wilds ass, snow leopard, lynx, wild cat, wild dog, fox, wolf and different species of wild goats and sheep viz; Ovis ammon, urial, bharal, antelope, ibex, ovispoli, stag, marlchor, Tibetan gazelle, etc. Some of these species are now extinct and some are rare or are being treated as endangered species.

Therefore, considering the richness of wildlife in Ladakh, European travellers and sportsmen had described Ladakh as "Sportsman's Paradise" and till the end of 19th century Ladakh was very much popular among hunters for its variety of wild species. Not only this, even some wild animals are named after them. The Ovis ammon is also called Hodgson's sheep. The Onis poli as known is Marco Polo's and Urial as Vigen's sheep. Similarly, a specie of hare has been named as Stolizilka's mouse hare.

Traditionally some old songs of Ladakh also gave suitable place for wild life. These songs reflect that in ancient times Ladakh region was teemed with wild life. In those days herds of wild animals prowled as they were indispensable for the survival of early settlers, who hunted them for their food. Their horns, hair and wool were considered sacred. Particularly, the ibex assumed the significance of a deity for certain clans. For example, early settlers have carved the images of wild life and hunters with bow and arrows on the rocks, which are seen in some parts of Ladakh and Baltistan. Besides, some folk songs are also prevalent in Dard villages in which they describe about hunting scenes of ibex. Arthur Neve, an English doctor on visiting Ladakh at the end of the 19th century said that at Dard village Da-Hanu, some men and women recited songs to him. The Dards headmen told that they sung about the old hunters who went after the ibex and stalked them up the mountains and shot them with bow and arrow. They remembered their forefathers who had come from Gilgit and were great hunters and brave warriors. Dr. A.H. Francke thus translates an ancient song of Ladakh about hunting :

"Take the arrow, then the bow, then the arrow-shafts and the heads,
Oh boy that art clever at hiding;
Then, Oh boy, clever at climbing;
Then, Oh boy, who art clever at imitating the antelope's cry
Then, Oh boy, who art clever at getting out of sight,
There the ibex can be seen, the ibex can be seen in a herd
Now, take the arrow Oh boy,
Now, take the bow Oh boy,
Then take arrow-shafts and heads,
Oh boy, that art clever at driving them together,
Oh boy, that art clever at driving them to heaps,
Thou art clever at singling out the best;
Thou that art clever at shooting them;
Offering of flour, butter, milk and water,
Must now be brought; Honour to thee, Oh God;
Now cut the flesh with a sharp knife
Roasted meat must be offered,
Cut it to pieces;
Give a mouthful to each of one hundred boys,
They will carry the meat in their pockets of leather
They will give some to father and mother, Oh boy,
They will make parents of it to one hundred girls, Oh boy
Now we have come to happiness and abundance, Oh boy"

Some places in Ladakh are also associated with wild life. A village is named as 'Lingshet' which means "Haunt for Sports". A village in Zanskar (or Zangskar) is known as Himaling or Hunter. It is said that a Ladakhi ruler in the 15th century was very fond of partridge and was known as partridge eater. His real name has erased from the pages of history and obliterated from pubic memory. In those days the game birds like partridge, snow partridge, godwall, the sinew, etc., were found in abundance in Ladakh. During snowfall in winter, the partridges came down from mountains to the human habitated areas including the Leh town and were caught in large number. Now, their number has considerably depleted and none is seen in the vicinity of the Leh town.

Following establishment of Dogra rule in Ladakh in 1836. The European sportsmen started to come to Ladakh for hunting. Their number gradually swelled which continued till independence of India. The hunters and visitors had to obtain permission from the British Resident station at Srinagar for travelling to Ladakh. However only a specified number of hunters were issued licences in view of the paucity of resources in the region. In this connection Lt. Colonel Sir Reginald Rankin highlighted some points in his book entitled, *A Tour in the Himalayas and Beyond* :

"In 1895, 400 sportsmen went up into Ladakh and Baltistan from Srinagar. This year (i.e. 1898) my licence was numbered 64 and I am certainly the very last of those going in".

In this way the State Govt. had framed rules for hunting. A sportsman could kill upto 6 ibex, 2 ovis ammon, 4 urial, 4 bharal, 4 antelopes and 2 gowa or gazelle. The lengths of the horns of the species of prey had been specified under these rules. For an ovis ammon, it was fixed 45 inches. For ibex, bharal urial, antilopes and gazelle, the lengths of the horns had been identified 35", 25", 24", 22" and 10" respectively.

Colonel Reginald writes that local hunters did not stick to the prescribed number and killed wildlife indiscriminately. According to him, a man had killed at least a couple of hundred markhor to his own rifle. In the dead winter the natives drove the ibex with dogs and later killed a dozen a day.

During British regime many high-ranking British army officers visited Ladakh for hunting, some of these including General Kinloch, General Macintyre, Colonel Durand, Col. Ward, Col. Heber, Col. Markham and Lt. Colonel Reginald have written books about their sports adventures in Ladakh. Many writers have embellished their books with the photographs of the heads and horns of wild life killed by them, which constituted prized trophies. Some British army officers decorated their drawing-rooms and houses with these trophies. Some of them offered trophies to museums, following are some examples.

There is a head and horns of a urial and a stuffed wolf of Ladakh in the British and Calcutta Museums. Following are some bags of animals which the western sportsmen gave to the museums or elsewhere.

1. Edger phelps and Gerry Milne's bag consisted of 7 yaks, 27 antelopes, and 2 bharal.
2. Henry Zouch Durrah bag had weight of ten mounds and twenty seers, which included 4 ibex, 3 red bear, 4 antelopes, 3 Tibetan gazelles, 2 ovis ammon and one each of markhor, urial, stag and black bear.

With the arrival of modern technology, improved rifles were manufactured in European Countries, as a result European sportsmen proved deadly to wild animals and they moved to less accessible areas of the Ladakh region. After killing the animals they first skinned and to preserve the horns and skins from decay kerosene oil, carbolic acid, bees wax, turpentine, castor oil, etc., were used.

Therefore, past practice of hunting in this region made extinct some species like stag, markhor and others such as antelope, wild Yak, Ovis poli and gazelle.

Again if we ask questions whether local hunters had any contribution for the promotion of hunting in Ladakh. The answer could be yes as European sportsmen utilised their services while hunting games. Here follows some references :

In his book entitled *Trans Himalaya,* Sven Hedin has described his hunger, Tondup Sonam as 'Grand Courts Hunterman", who accompanied him in his long expedition Tibet.

Arthur Brinckman has devoted several pages in his book *Rifle in Kashmir* in praise of his Ladakhi hunter named Paljor for his sharp sense of humour and cheerful disposition.

Admiring Rassul Galwan for his performance Edger Phelps writes;

> "It was most fortunate in getting an Arghon Rassul Galwan who was with me twice before, to again as headman. His accomplishment, over and above, the general superintendence

of the outfit, included rifle cleaning, skinning and waiting at table".

A.E. Ward in his book entitled *The Tourists and Sportsmen Guide to Kashmir and Ladakh,* 1896; writes:

> "Most of the old fashioned Ladakhi Shikaris are still to the fore, and a few new are taking up the trade. They are often hard-working and honest but have no idea of managing a camp".

Hence after reviewing the hunting game, practices in Ladakh, the J&K Government revised the rules and regulations about hunting of wild animals in 1888. It has mentioned about local experienced hunters and the European sportsmen had been advised to avail their services. Thereafter, wild animals who had danger from hunters could be seen easily along the routes. Here follow some examples :

Frederic Drew who was governor of Ladakh during seventies of last century watched 300 wild asses in a single day in Changthang *illcqua* (region) of Ladakh.

Colonel Durah counted 136 wild asses near Hanley village in 1890 and at another place, he saw a herd of 30 gazelles.

Hamilton Bower came across as many as a hundred wild Yaks in a day sometimes during his trip in 1890.

Even today, the trekkers come across herds of wild sheep, goats, hares and sometimes the rare snow leopard in the interiors of Ladakh.

Again if we go back to 1947 or before it is understood that some enroute villages between Srinagar and Leh were homes of ibex and other wild goats and sheep. Arthur writes in 1895 that Urial came from the mountain recesses and grazed in number of the plains above Saspol and Nimu (Leh-Srinagar enroute villages). The natives hid in stone enclosures and shot them when they came within easy range Later Arthur encountered herds of wild sheep/goats and many hares on this route during 1950s when the vehicular road had yet not been constructed.

In post-independence area as said earlier like during British period Ladakh witnessed in indiscriminate and ruthless hunting, poaching and staking at least for two decades leading to near decimination of many species of wild life. The rest moved to higher and inaccessible areas. Now these enroute villages are being bereft of wild life. Moreover, wild life are more common than the domestic animals. For example, a grown up wild sheep and goat are just equal to a Ladakhi pony. Here follows some general information about various wild animals.

Ovis Ammon

It is known as Nyan in Ladakhi and one of the most famous wild goats and has been described as the 'father of all flocks' on earth. It is also known as Tibetan argali. The horns of this animal are so enormous that they make his head almost too heavy for him in old age. A hunter Arnold Pike killed a Nyan which had 57 inches long horns with 18¾ inches girth, which is a record to this date. Colonel Fred Markhon observed that Ovis Ammon a hardest animal as he remarks :

"Ovis Ammon are by far the hardest to kill of all the animals that he had to deal with".

Major General Mycentrine awarded 'Blue Ribbon' for hunting of Ovis Ammon. He says :

"Whosoever hunts an Ovis Ammon he wins the highest honour of the 'Blue Ribbon' for Himalayan sports."

Urial

In Ladakhi it is called Shapo. Its habitats are in the upper Indus valley of Ladakh along the edge of the mountains. According to Dr. Joseph L. Fox an Ecologist and Zoologist from Norway, there are an estimated 1500 Urials in their upper Indus valley habitats.

The average length of a Urials' horn is 28 inches. The maximum recorded length is 37.75 inches and 11.5 inches. It was becoming endangered specie, but now its number is swelling due to ban on hunting.

Ram

The largest ram on record weighted 280 lbs and measured 46 inches at the shoulder and 64 inches across. The average length of the horn is 42 inches.

Bharal (rNapho)

It is also know as Ovis Nahure and blue sheep. It looks half sheep and half goat in its appearance and is marked by distinctly from other wild sheep. The largest horns recorded are 32.1 inches with 13 inches girth.

In summer, the bharals ascend to the elevation of 18,000 feet above. In winter they descend to 1000 feet. At the slightest whiff of danger, they retreat to stiff cliffs. The male bharals have black markings on the face, chest and legs and sometimes can be seen in the company of ibex. It is the most common prey species of the snow leopard in Ladakh. Hunters praised its flesh taste.

Ibex (Riddags/Skin)

The Ibex is a graceful wild goat with beautiful horns. It is a sweet-footed animal. The image of the ibex represents the badge of Ladakh Scouts and Gilgit Scouts. Its average weight is 200 lbs and length of horn has been measured 44 inches.

The Tibetan Gazelli (Gowa)

The Tibetan gazelli was always been rare in Ladakh. It is found at a few spots near Hanley and other western locations. Colonel Darah had watched a head of gazelli in Changthang sub-division of Leh district of Ladakh region.

Ovis Poli (Marco Polo's Sheep)

It is rare in these days and restricted to Depsang and Karakoram ranges. Moreover, it was quite a popular specie in Ladakh as A.E. Ward has described Ladakh the 'Country of the Ovis Poli' in his book published in 1896. Marco Polo, who was a well-known explorer had watched this animal in Pamir. The biggest horn of an Ovis Poli on record measured 70 inches.

Markhor (Rapochey/Rawachey)

Like stag, Markhor is presently extinct in Ladakh. In Persian language Markhor means snake-eater. It is said that it eats snakes. In past, Dards displayed skin of Markhor at their houses to scare the snakes. It cannot tolerate snow like other wild goats and sheep, therefore it comes down to low ground in winter and becomes vulnerable to hunters.

Antelope (Tsos)

A fully grown male antelope stands 30 to 35 inches at the shoulder and weighs between 80 to 100 lbs. Its fine wool is called shahtoos and sells at the price of gold. Shawl is woven from shahtoos which costs over fifty to sixty thousand rupees. Till recent past antelope's horn was used for digging to sow wheat and barley and to unite knots of rope by the farmers. They tie it with their sash. The nomads utilised it as tent pegs.

In Ladakh, antelopes are found in the arid lands of Dolat-Beg, Uldi, Aksai chin and Chang-chhenmo. In winter they migrate to the Chinese side of border and in summer move back to Indian side. For its precious fine wool, they are being indiscriminately killed by the unscrupulous hunters. Hence, it is presumed that their number does not exceed more than few hundered.

Snow Leopard (rChan)

The snow leopard is a beast of prey. It lives on high mountains. J.N. Ganhar in his book *The Wild Life of Ladakh* writes that it stands about 24 inches at the shoulder and of his total length of about 6½ feet, the tail accounts for nearly a half. The snow leopard has nocturnal habits and prowls in search of prey during night.

The farmer are extremely scared of the snow leopard because it spells disaster to their sheep and goats. It steals into the pen through the sky light and kills the sacred sheep and goats one by one sucking their blood. Finally it becomes too heavy and dizzy to move out and is clubbed to death by the villagers.

Wild Yak (Dong)

Wild yak is a precious and strong animal. A fully grown male wild yak may well exceed 1000 lbs. Its horns are 36 inches long and in the middle circumference they are 14 inches thick. A.E. Ward had measured a Yak of 16 hands height with horns 29 inches × 30 inches by 14 inches in circumference and length of neck and body 7 feet. It is found in Chang-Chhenmo and Aksai Chin areas of Ladakh. Describing about his ferociousness and strength, Mirza Hyder Dughl writes in *Tarikh-e-Rashidi* that it kicks up his prey twenty metres high above the ground and before reaching the ground it expires. He watched wild yak in Ladakh during his onslaught in 1532.

A Russian visitor N.M. Prezwal had drawn an analogy of yak hunting and a duel with Spanish bull. Therefore, wild yak is a dangerous animal and even a wounded yak is very aggressive and pounces upon its assailant instantly. Himalton Bower writes that he had never known one which charges, even when wounded and with his assailant in view. He further writes that the Yaks are extremely easy to stalk, their sight not being nearly as cute as that of most wild animals. Their powers of scent are, however, fairly good. In brief, the European sportsmen often visited Chang-Chhenmo exclusively for hunting of wild yaks.

Wild Ass (rKyang)

Skiyang (rKyang) is a swift-footed and shy animal. It is found in Changthang. With a slight whiff of human voice and danger, the entire herd of the wild asses scampers and disappears. There are evidences of domestication of this animal. According to J.N. Ganhar, a Russian Nazaraff had tamed a wild ass. Nazaraff had travelled Ladakh in the nineteen thirties. Similarly a Ladakhi also tamed a wild ass and kept it with the domesticated asses but it did not survive long. However, after cross-breeding a mare with a wild ass, a progeny was produced in Ladakh.

Lynx (Ei)

Lynx is cat like in appearance. It measures from 35 to 40 inches in size and the tail is of six inches. A.E. Ward who visited Chang-chhenmo found the Lynx and he measured a lynx 42 inches in size and tail 8 inches.

Bear (Denmo)

The bear hibernates from November to April. It is generally vegetarian and is found in Drass and some inhabitable villages of Ladakh.

The dwindling numbers of bear have not picked up due to a strange reason. The villages where bears found are crisscrossed by a host of streams. It is said that after giving birth to children, normally numbering 4 to 5 the she-bear moves across the stream carrying her children one by one. After crossing the stream, the she-bear puts the child on ground and places a boulder over it, probably with the idea to safeguard it from the beasts of prey and gets back to carry another child on reaching across the stream, she places a heavy stone over it. Finally, when she crosses the stream with last child and removes the boulders only to find them dead under the burden of heavy stones. Thus, only the last one child survives.

Besides, wild dog *(khizig)* and wild cat inhabit the arid desert of Ladakh. In olden days gold digging ants were found in Ladakh. As the Greek historian Herodotus has described about it in Dards inhabited areas in Ladakh. They dug gold out of the earth making deep burrows for themselves. It has a ring of myth and legend. Actually, the gold digging ants were marmots which are found in Ladakh in abundance and live in deep burrows.

The Jammu and Kashmir Government has put a ban on hunting, poaching and stalking of wild life in the State. J&K Wild Life Protection Act was passed in 1978, which envisages various rules and regulations for protection of wild life.

In Ladakh sanctuaries have been set up for ibex and other wild goats and sheep. In recent years, the number of wild life has considerably increased in the region.

Some species were on the brink of extinction, but timely action has saved these species from annihilation. There has been a long-standing proposal to establish a Wild Life Park in the region but it has yet not matured for want of fund.

In conclusion, the wild life of Ladakh with its fascinating landscape and background are of great attraction for the tourists. J.N. Ganhar has suggested to arrange exhibition of wild animals at their habitats which would promote "Shooting with the Camera" instead of with the gun.

Notes and References

Bower, Himalton : *Diary of a Journey Across Tibet*, 1894.

Brinckman, Arthur : *Rifle in Kashmir*, 1862.

Darrah, Henry-Zouch : *Sports in the Highlands of Kashmir-8 months Trips in Baltistan and Ladakh*, 1898.

Drew, Frederic; *Jammu & Kashmir Territories*, 1875.

Dughlat, Mirza Hyder : *Tarikh-e-Rashidi* (English version by E. Denison Ross, 1532).

Fox, Joseph : *Ladakh Melong*, Journ. Aug. 1998.

Francke, A.H. *Ladakhi Songs*, 1906.

Francke, A.H. : *History of Western Tibet,* 1907.

Ganhar, J.N. : *The Wild Life of Ladakh*, 1979.

Hedin, Sven : *Trans Himalaya* 1909.

Lydekher, R : *The Game Animals of India, Burma, Malaya and Tibet*, 1907.

Markhon, Fred : *Shooting in the Himalayas*, 1854.

Mycentrine, Major General : *Hindukush.*
Neve Arthur : *Thirty Years in Kashmir*, 1913.
Phelps, Edger : *Yak Shooting in Tibet*, 1900.
Rankin, Reginald : *A Tour in the Himalayas and Beyond*, 1895.
Sheikh, Abdul Ghani : *The Famous Wild Animals of Ladakh* Urdu. Journ. Tamir, Srinagar Dec. 1976.
Ward, A.E. *Tourists and Sportsmen's Guide to Kashmir and Ladakh,* 1896.

18

The Ecology of Wild Life of Ladakh

Prem Singh Jina

Ladakh is a home of some endangered species viz. wild Yak (Bos grunniens), Tibetan Antelope (Pantholops hodgnoni) and Tibetan Gazelle (Procapra picticandata). All these animals can be seen easily at the altitude of 15,000 to 16,000 feet from the sea level.

Besides some migratory birds like-Black-neck crane, ducks, etc., are also endangered species. They migrate from Siberia to Chushul, Thomo-riri and some parts of Chang-Thang of Leh district during summer season and before October they return.

At the Chang-Thang Sub-Division of Leh district of Ladakh region Kiang and Tibetan Argali (Ovis ammon hodgsoni) are very common. The Kiang (wild ass) are thousands in number in between Chushul and Nyoma belt. This animal is like mule, brown in colour with white under the belley, a dark stripe down the back.[1] On the other hand, Tibetan Argalis are commonly seen only in the most remote and inaccessible places. Ibex, Bharal, Urial, wolf and snow leopard are widespread. Bears can be seen only in Zangskar region whereas Fox, Marmot, Hare and Weasel are commonly seen along the passes like Thaglang-la, Khardong-la Chang-la, etc. During winter season these animals come down at the vicinity of villages or sometimes near the settlement areas.[2]

Ladakh was famous for hunting till in 1947, shooters came here for shooting wild animals. For hunting, they had to take the permission from the Game warden in Srinagar, who allowed to hunt animals in two blocks: Ammon and Sharpu. For Ammon block hunters had to take the permit during 16th July to 14th

October (Appendix – 1) : The following areas were included under Ammon block.

1. The water shed of the Koyul river up to Indus.
2. The Hanle river basin.
3. The tributaries of the Indus between the Puga and Hanle rivers.
4. The basins of Tso-Moriri lake.
5. The watershed of Zara and Rukchen rivers.
6. The watershed of Markh river.
7. The Changchenmo.
8. The triangular area up to Choosbal.

For Sharpu Block hunters had to take the permit during 16th April to 15th July every year. This block had the following areas (Appendix-1).

1. The Igu and Chemra nullah
2. Umal and Nimu
3. Bazgo and Myel
4. Likir and Saspol
5. Dumkhar and Hanu
6. Hemis-Shukpa and Khalsi
7. The watershed of the Zangskar
8. Rampakh
9. Masho
10. Shera and Lockchey
11. Kamdok

The shooters had to pay licence fee for shooting game which varied between Rs. 15 to Rs. 175 (Appendix – 2). They were not allowed to go beyond the hunting rules. Under rules no hunter was allowed to shoot any animal before sunrise and after sunset. Hunters could shoot the following animals (Appendix 3) :

1. Markhor of any variety 45"
2. Ibex 35"
3. Ovis ammon 38"
4. Shapu 24"
5. Bharal 23"
6. Tibetan Antelope 22"

7. Tibetan Gazelle 10"
8. Kashmir stag 35"

Therefore, during British period every year hundreds of British shooters came to Ladakh for hunting. As a result by the end of 1947 animals : Ibex, Ovis ammon, Shapu, Bharal, Tibetan Antelope and Tibetan Gazelle had suffered a great extent. Later the State Directorate of wildlife passed Protection Act, State Forest Department also imposed strict ban on wildlife hunting. Today due to the Wildlife Protection Act the number of these animals have increased considerably. The following conditions also are helping to increase their population.

1. The sparsely distributed human population.
2. The location of most settlements in major river valleys have left large areas available for wildlife.
3. Some particularly inaccessible valleys are so rarely disturbed that they can be regarded as a kind of natural sanctuary.
4. Buddhist prohibitions on hunting have meant that hunters in Ladakh are traditionally low.

No doubt there would be some illegal hunting, but it is only to a small scale (Fig. 18.1). Hence wildlife protection factors are comparitively more than the harming factors. And the wildlife population recovered its position in those pockets where they had suffered by overshooting. Wildlife Protection Act does not imply an increase in the wildlife population but its main emphasis is to improve the quality of life which depends upon resources, knowledge, altitude and conservation. The quality of wildlife can be analysed by the following equation.[4]

$$QL = \frac{R + K \pm A + C}{P}$$

where QL = Quality of Life
R = Resources
K = Knowledge
A = Altitude
C = Conservation
P = Population

The control growth of wildlife helps human beings in the following ways :

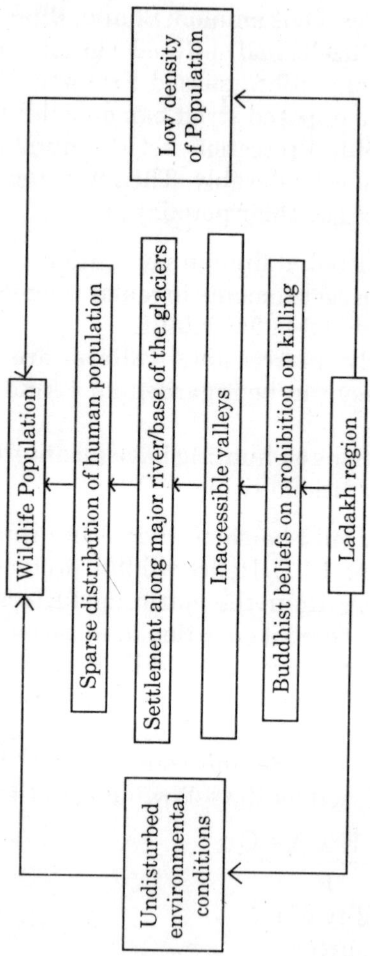

Fig. 18.1. Environment Factors and Wildlife Protection in Ladakh.

1. To improve crop/fruit production by pollination.
2. To improve soil quality and soil tillage.
3. To keep natural regulation of plant and animal population under sustainable conditions.
4. To keep regulation of water resources.

When we disturb the natural eco-system and keep on protecting wildlife animals, their number increases beyond the carrying capacity of available resources. Then they would definitely harm human beings and graze their crop fields. For example, in Chang-Thang sub-division of Leh district Kyang's (Equus Kiang) increasing population becomes a great problem as they come in groups at night in the settlement areas and graze their crops. Therefore, Chang-pas have been facing severe loss in crop production and shortage of good pasture cover. However, wire fence is being suggested to protect Kyangs activities but it is a costly affair.

To protect wildlife, a wildlife Advisory Board was constituted under the Wildlife Protection Act of 1978. Under the direction of this Act Hemis National Park was established in Ladakh. It has an area of 3350 sq. km. The following wild animals can be acknowledge in this Park (Map 1).

Snow Leopard (Panthera India) : It is a beautiful animal like cat but bigger than a cat with a luxuriant coat, relatively small head and very long tail. It is able to leap horizontally as much as 50 feet. During summer it moves to high mountain meadows between 8,800 ft. and 19,700 ft. In winter it comes down to 5000-6,000 ft Bharal or Blue *(Pseudois nayaur) :*

In Ladakh people call it Napo. According to size and shape it is similar to Ladakhi Urial and has slightly shorter legs. It changes its colour according to climatic condition, in summer it looks brownish-grey and bluish-grey in winter. Generally it moves in herds averaging 5-20 in number, but sometimes this number increases upto 200-400. It is found in open slopes at an altitude of 11,500-18,000 feet, sometimes as high as 21,500 feet. Earlier bharals were classified as genus Ovis. Now Zoologist believe that they are goats and should place them in genus Capra.

Ladakh Urial or Shapo (Ovis Vignel Vignei). It is one of the largest Urials with most fully developed neck ruff, over all colour is raddish. A dark band separates the belly from the upper body. The male have a white bib, a black neck ruff and a greyish saddle patch in the winter coat.

Ibex (Capra Sibirica). A big male stands 40 inches at the shoulder and weigh 200 lbs, its coat is thick and woolly in winter being shed in early summer. Colour is variable, ranging from pale brown to dark brown with a darker dorsal stripe, and often a lighter saddle patch and whitish neck patch. Generally darker in summer than in winter.

Nyan or Argali or Giant Sheep (Ovis Ammon). Argali is the largest and most spectacular of the world's wild sheep. It has weight as much as 400 lbs (180 kgs) and stands as tall as 48 inches at the shoulder.

The Dhole or wild dog (Cuon alpinus). It is like domestic dog and very distinctive in its red coat which varies with season and locality.

Marmots (Marmota babak). It has squad built, short tail and very small ears and lives at altitudes ranging from 13,000 to 18,000 ft. in large colonies excavating deep burrows in which they hibernated through the winter. With the coming of spring they emerge and feed on roots, leaves, grasses and the seeds of various plants.

Golden Eagle (Aquila Chrysaetos). Resident vulture, 90-100 cm. found in rugged high mountain country between 1800 m and 5000 m.

Lammergeier or Bwlearded Vulture (Gypaetus Barbatus). Resident vulture, 122 cm in size finds in Himalayas and associated northern mountains. Normally at an altitude of 1200 to 4200 m, soaring to over 7000 m.

Chukar Partridge (Alectoris Chukar). Resident Partridge around 40 cm in size found on rocky hillsides with grass and sparse bushes, at an altitude of 1000-5000 m.

References

Jina, Prem Singh : *Ladakh : The Land and the People,* Indus Pub. Co. New Delhi, 1996

Mallon, David & Prodon, Roger : Ecology and Conservation in Ladakh : In : *Recent Research on Ladakh* 4 & 5, 1995, pp. 111-112.

Sagwal, S.S. : *Ladakh : Ecology and Environment;* Ashish Pub. New Delhi, 1991, p. 73.

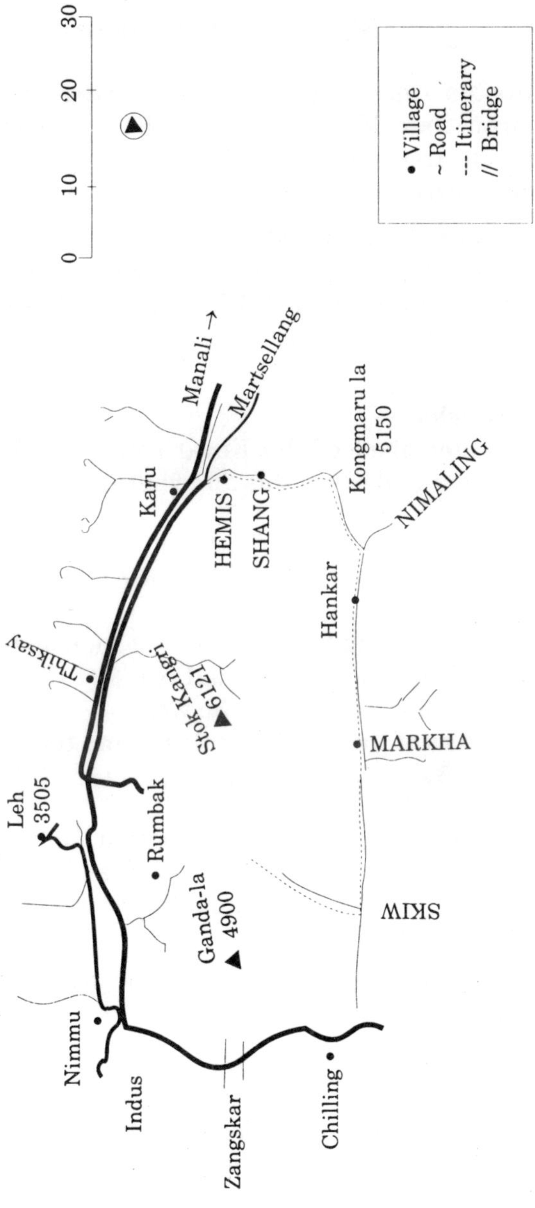

Map-1. Hemis National Park.

ANNEXURE 1
Big Game Shooting Areas

(1) Baltistan (including Skardu and Kargil tehsils) where Sharpu, Ibex, Markhor and Red Bear are found.
(2) Ladakh area where Tibetan antelope, Tibetan gazelle, bharal, ovis ammon, wolf, snow leopard are found.

Ammon and Sharpu Blocks

The following are the Ammon and Sharpu blocks available for booking during 1st period (16th April to 15th July) and 2nd period (16th July to 14th October) and others as stated are not available.

Ammon Blocks

(1) The water shed of the Koyal river upto Indus—Koyal confluence and below this all tributaries of the Indus upto Dungti;
(2) The Hanle river basin (south of);
(3) The tributaries of the Indus between the Punga and Hanle rivers;
(4) The country lying between No. 2 of Ammon block and 3 of Sharpu block on the east and No. 3 of the Sharpu block and 4 of Ammon block on the west;
(5) The basins of the Tso-Moriri lakes and the Phirsi Nullah;
(6) The watershed of Markha river;
(7) The Changchenmo;
(8) The triangular area upto Choosbal on the north, the frontier on the east, the Choosbal and Chamatnag Foo watershed on the west and Indus on the south from Chamatnag to Dungti.

Besides the above, there are other blocks which are not available for shooting :

(1) The tributaries of Indus from Demchok to Koyul.
(2) The Hanle river as far as the south of the Hanle monastery.
(3) The basin of the salt lakes and tributaries of the Indus between (and including) the Puga river as far as the water of the Tiri Foo.
(4) The Tiri Foo and the country lying to the north bounded

by the Indus in the north and east, the Leh-Kulu Road on the west and watershed of Tsokar Came plain on the south.

(5) The Kharnak Nullah.

Sharpu Blocks. (1) The Igu and Chimre Nullah; (2) Urival and Nimmu; (3) Bazgo and Myel; (4) Likar and Suspul and Woleh Drokpa; (5) Damkar and Hanu; (6) Hemis-shukpa Narlah and Khalsi; (7) The watershed of the Zangskar and Markha river but including Shew Nullah; (8) Rampakh; (9) Masho; (10) Shera and Lockchey; and (11) Kamdok.

Besides the above, these are other blocks which are generally not available for shooting (1) Nang and Sabu (2) Phyang and Tara, (3) Hemiskot and Wanla, (4) Illuchi and Lardu, (5) Stok and Shang.

ANNEXURE 2

Sport Licenses

No. I of Rs. 175. This is available from 15th March to 15th November and permits to kill 2 markhor, 3 ibex, 2 sharpu, 2 ammon, 4 bharal, 3 Tibetan antelope, 1 Tibetan gazelle, 2 Kashmir stag, 4 serow, 2 brown bear, 4 tehr, 4 goral, small games vide item No. 19 (Appendix 3) of the rules of hunting and black bear, pigs and leopards with no limit.

No. II of Rs. 55. This is available from 15th March to 15th November and permits to kill black bear, leopard and pigs with no limit.

No. III of Rs. 105. This is a winter license available from 16th November to 14th March and permits to kill 2 markhor, 2 ibex, 2 sharpu, 3 burhel, 3 Tibetan antelope, 1 Tibetan gazelle, 1 Kashmiri stag, 1 serow, 3 tehr, 2 brown bear, 3 goral, small games subject to rule 19 of the rules of hunting (App. 3) and under license No. V and black bear, leopard and pigs with no limit.

No. IV of Rs. 50. This is available from 16th November to 4th March and permits to kill 2 ibex; and 2 sharpu in Baltistan and lower Ladakh, 2 burhel and 2 sharpu in upper Ladakh, 4 sharpu in Astor and Bunji; 1 brown bear, 2 black bears, 1 ibex in Gurais valley and also small game under licence No. V.

No. V A of Rs. 70. This permits to shoot peasants, chikor and partridges from 1st October to end of February, geese, duck and teal from 16th September to 31st March.

No. V B of Rs. 42. This is available for 2 months from the date of issue and permits to kill all games vide license No. V A.

No. V C of Rs. 70. As in V A (see above) but permits to use punt and long guns for killing wild fowl.

No. V D of Rs. 15. This is available for 15 days and permits to kill all small games vide license No. V A.

No. VI of Rs. 70. This is a special license and permits to kill one musk deer (rare case).

No. VII of Rs. 40. This is a license for trapping all vermins.

Remarks

No one can hold more than one license (1 to V). Holders of license (1 to V) can kill Ram Chikar between 16th September and 1st May, pigs on left bank of the Jhelum above Srinagar and on both sides below Srinagar but 5 miles away from the Rakhs and can shoot leopards including ounces, wolves, foxes, martens and other vermins.

License No. III can be exchanged with No. 1, No. V A with No. 1 or III, No. V B with No. V A., No. V D with V A or V B after payment of the difference. No refund is permitted.

ANNEXURE 3
Rules of hunting in Kashmir

1. Sportsmen are requested not to shoot before sunrise and after sunset.
2. Sportsmen are advised to engage only registered *Shikaris*.
3. No one is allowed to shoot in the Satte Game.

   Reserves or Rakhs without special permission of His Highness the Maharaja. The Rakhs are those of Dachigam, Khanmoo, Khrew, Tral-cum-Kherim and Panjar, Khel basin in Avantipur tehsil, Anchar Lake (Peth Kundel to Sangam). Hokar Sar Jhil, Hygam Jhil in Kashmir Province and Ramnagar, Keran, Kheri, Bahu, Mansar (Tunnel), Mansar (Sagoon), Sanu, Tandeh, Nehranal, Kotli, Thanoa, Janganoo Dalsar, Marh, Gurarh, Badyal, Mackwal and Agrachak in the Jammu Province.
4. No one is allowed to shoot in the nullahs mentioned here without permission from the Rajas concerned. The nullahs of Gandoos and Rumbak belong to the Raja of Khapallu; the Shigar, the Rondu and Kiris Nullahs and portions of the Mantho and Satpur Nullahs belong to the Rajas of Tolti and Skardu respectively. The Harcho Nullah belongs to the Raja of Astor. Permission is necessary for shooting in the Poonch territory from the Raja of Poonch.
5. No one is allowed to enter the Game Reserves without permission. Permission is however given for shooting to officials stationed at Srinagar, residents of Srinagar and to visitors in special cases. The game reserves are those (1) Achhabal Rakh (2) Ovra Rakh near Pahalgam (3) Chhatargul nullah in Sind valley (4) Dara area (5) The Nishat, Brain and Chashmashahi basin (6) Wangat Rakh in Sind valley (7) Khandi and Kharus Nullahs, in the Uri tehsil (8) The Pampur and adjoining hills of Kranchu cum-Sondahar and Maenboog (9) Mir Gund Jhil and (10) Kajnag and Kafir Kund areas including the Salkhala, the Moji and Shamashberry Rakhs. However, special permits are issued for these reserves by Game Warden for not more than three days in case of big game shooting.
6. No one is allowed to enter the Sanctuaries without permission. The Sanctuaries are those of (1) The Aijas

nullah, and Jhil in Bandipur district (2) Kushmul and Yimu basins in Baltistan (3) The Rajparin and Bewa basins in the Nawboog district (4) Soomjan and the Sapphire Mines nullah is Kishtwar (5) Askor nullah in Randu Baltistan (6) The old Rakh Chashmashahi (7) Pond near Sri Gauri Shanker in Kishtwar (8) The Shankeracharya hill from Gagribal point up to and including the basin above Pandrethan.

7. Bara-Singha in Ramban, serow in Bhadrawah and cheetal, musk deer, females of barking deer, thar, gural, peacock, heron, nilkanth (blue jay) in Jammu province are prohibited to be shot as they are scarce in those localities.
8. No one is allowed to shoot without a license.
9. Rewards are given for killing vermin to license-holding sportsmen by Game Preservation Department @ Rs. 10 for leopards (snow and common), Rs. 5 for leopards (cup), Rs. 10 for wolves, wild dogs, lynx; As four for carrion, crow and cormorant and other fish vermin. Also Rs. 5 may be given for others during damage on trout waters at the discretion of the Game Warden.
10. Rewards are also given on skins of animals when brought untanned. Skins are returned to license-holders.
11. Licenses should be returned on expiry of date. Sportsmen are requested not to kill more than the number of animals allowed.
12. Sportsmen are requested not to give presents to servants of the Game Preservation Department. Any act of disobedience on the part of servants should be reported.
13. Rates of the wages of the First class Shikaris are Rs. 30 to 35 plus ration allowed from Rs. 6 to Rs. 8 per mensem and those of Chotta Shikaris are Rs. 12 to Rs. 15 plus Rs. 5 ration allowance.
14. The wages of fifteen coolies are Rs. 12 plus Rs. 5 ration allowance, of camp permanent coolies, Rs. 10 plus Rs. 4 ration allowance, of camp permanent coolies, Rs. 10 plus Rs. 4 ration allowance.
15. The Shikaris licenses are not endorsed if they do not come to take their annual licenses to abide by the rules of the Game Preservation Deptt.

16. Sportsmen must report to the Game Warden all cases of serious injuries received by the Shikaris.
17. The shooting season for Kashmir stags is from 15th September to 15th March.
18. The season of Chakor, partridges and pheasants is from 1st October to February, that for wild fowl (geese, duck, teal) from 16th September to 14th April and for snipe from 1st September to 31st March. Rest months are breeding season in which shooting is prohibited.
19. The following dimensions have been fixed in case of big animals, under sized animals are not to be killed and if such are killed sportsmen are called to take license No. 6 for each animal shot—markhor of any variety 45", Ibex 35", Ovis ammon 38", sharpu 24", bharal 23", Tibetan antelope 22", Tibetan gazelle 10", Kashmir stag 35".

Source : Arora, R.C. : *In the land of Kashmir, Ladakh and Gilgit,* Jay Kay Book House, Jammu; 1940 (First Pub.); pp. 239-286. For Annexures—1, 2&3.

PART IV
History and Tradition

19

Dok-Pa: An Aryan Race of Ladakh

Jamyang Gyaltsan
and
Prem Singh Jina

Dok-Yul is 147 kms. far in the west of Leh. The inhabitants of this region are called Dok-pas, which means those whose livelihood is based upon sheep and goat rearing.

Geography

Dok-yul is in the Central part of Ladakh. It spreads 100 miles along the Indus Valley; 30 miles of its border touches Baltistan and the rest part to Leh region. Dok-pas have their villages at the narrow valleys along the Indus river, surrounded by snow capped mountains. During summer the sun shines brightly as a result the snow of the mountain peaks melts and water flows towards their villages and irrigates their lands.

Dok-pas have following villages :

1. Bal-Dres
2. Batalic
3. Bema
4. Che-che-thang
5. Dhu-li-chan (culi-can)
6. Da
7. Dra-Dra-do
8. Drg-gurche
9. Gabis
10. Ganogs
11. Ganogs-sha
12. Darchigs

13. Garkon
14. Hanu Yogma
15. Hanu Gongma
16. Hardas
17. Hundo
18. Hun-ten-gun
19. Kan-yung-che
20. Khebar
21. Lha-ste-Gyas
22. Lhan-char
23. Morol
24. Notican
25. Sana-che
26. Saneed
27. Sarche
28. Seng-kar-mo-gram
29. Silmo
30. Yardoldas

Vegetation

The climate of Dok-yul is comparitively warmer than the other parts of Ladakh. It has dense vegetation with variety of herbs, shrubs and trees viz. Shukpa, Stagpa, Umbu, Seva, Skyerpa, Spenma, Kangtakari, Askuta, Garma, Sow, Yulad, Kumant, etc. Under Horticulture Dok-pas grow-apricot, halman, rassing, black and green grapes, walnut, apple, gilas, etc. There are many kinds of flowers such as, Soklo, Skalzang, Pomsyu, Chabo, Guchegas, Gyas, etc. They produce two crops in a year and grow-nas, cha, gyabras, buck wheat, mustard, maize, razma, masoor, urad, karze, etc., and carrot, cauliflower, cabbage, onion, potato, tomato, etc., among vegetables.

History

The ancestors of Dok-pas migrated from Central Asia and first settled down along the Indus belt near Gilgit. Thereafter they elected one person among them as a King of Gilgit and gradually started cultivation. In 736 A.D. King Thri-lde-gung-stan (Tib. Khri-lde-gung-bStan) of Tibet sent marriage offer of his daughter to the King of Gilgit Ma-ō-Eing. This offer was welcomed by Ma-ō-Eing who married his son with the daughter of King of Tibet. Then cultural relations were established between

Tibet and Gilgit. Unfortunately after some years internal disturbances took place in Gilgit. As a result villagers of Gan-Grum and Sacel migrated to Baltistan under the leadership of Singhe, gradually they came to 'Ganogs', and settled down at the upper part of 'Da' village in Ladakh, later some more Dok-pas also migrated to Ladakh under the leadership of three brave personalities of 'Rumras village'. But they did not get sufficient fertile land in Dok, therefore they came to Galo, Melo and Dulo villages.

Thereafter the migrated Dok-pas passed their time happily. They had their gods and goddesses and in all the important occasions they joined and danced with them. This tradition continued till the ninth generation of Singe. Later gods and goddesses left Dok-Yul because of the misbehaviour attitude of a Dok-pa. Here follows the details :

On an occasion of Harvest festival, gods and goddess were dancing together with Dok-pas. One Dok-pa then was not able to control his sexual desires and kissed a goddess. This shameful incidence immediately got sharp reaction and immediately all gods and goddesses left the human world.

One can still see the remains of gods and goddesses at the upper side of Dok-pas inhabitation surrounded by high mountain ranges. Their dancing ground had big flat standing stone plates boundary. Here grove still does not allow to grow any kind of vegetation. However from the remains we can make the following statement :

(i) The dancing ground might be known with 'Khudu'.
(ii) In the dancing ground, musicians were given special honour, as their sitting place was covered by stone plates boundary.
(iii) Gods and goddesses lived at the upper side of Dok-pas inhabitation who on the request of Dok-pas came down to the dancing ground and danced with them.

Early Life

The ancestors of Dok-pas were nomades who moved one place to other in search of pastures and worshipped nature like mountains, water, sky etc. According to Dok-yul Chronicles :

> "Their ancestors worshipped nature and believed that nature had powers to save them from evil spirits and help

them for good deeds. To please such powers they sacrified goat on a special occasion".

Dok-pas preserved their old tradition. Every year they sacrificed goats on their feasts and festivals. They mostly sacrificed he-goats. Harvest festival is the most popular festival. On this occasion they sacrifice he-goat to Lha-boy. One Dok-pa is especially deputed for this purpose, who before sacrificing the goat to 'Lha' does not take meat, wine, onion, garlic and other non-vegetarian food.

Agricultural Life

The ancestors of Dok-pas were hunters who at first came to Dok-pa in their hunting tour. When they saw water sources and fertile lands their leader decided to migrate here. One Dok-pa then experimentally sprayed food grain seeds. During autumn, they again visited Dok-pa for hunting and were surprised to see ripped food grain plants. Soonafter, they migrated to Dok-sa and its neighbouring areas in groups. Thereafter this whole area was popularly known as 'Han-Dang-Sman', means 'Areas where food grains do not require much care at their production'. Later, during the course of years their population increased three to four times. Therefore, they shifted towards the Indus river belt. In this way their settlements were divided into two portions : upper Dok-pa and Lower Dok-pa, the upper portion of the land known as 'Upper Hanu' and the other 'Lower Hanu'. There is one Dok-pa song in this regards :

Texts

"Samid-sa-chugs vayed, Duboro Taru ne so decan"

Translation

"The upper valley of Hanu is Samid.
The Samid valley was the first Dok-pa village,
Then two more areas were cultivated.
(These were) later popularly known with Sukhi village.

It is an interesting story about 'Da' village. Here follows the details :

Once Dok-pas ancestor Singhe came to Dok-yul for hunting. When he did not find any animal, he became upset and angrily shot an arrow to the rock near Samid village. It was so powerful that it not only struck the rock but went several meters inside and formed a tunnel. After this incident many Dok-pas who came to see this tunnel, later settled down there and named the village after the powerful arrow "Da". Gradually more Dok-pas migrated from Gandun towards 'Da' region and settled down near 'Da' called Garkon. In this way Dok-pas migrated at Da and Garkon in three groups: Gala, Malo and Dula from the same region. So, there is not much difference in their languages.

Similarly more Dok-pa groups migrated to Dok-yul and formed 'Gashopa', 'Trango', 'Kukso', 'Gis', 'Cigs', etc., villages. About the Gis, Cigs and Culi-Can, the Dokpas say the following story:

> "Once a Garkon lady gave birth to seven sons, who later became leaders of their communities. They before migration came to Dok-yul in search of suitable agricultural and pasture lands. They saw Gis and Cigs areas for their communities. Thereafter, on the advise of their leaders Dok-pas came in Dok-yul and settled down at 'Gis' and 'Cigs' villages".

After sometime, some more Dok-pas migrated to 'Culi-Can which is named after the good apricot production. Here follows the details :

"Once a lama was constructing a canal near Garkon through his spiritual power. After few days when water was flowing in canal, he threw an apricot nut in it. The water current was fast enough to carry it up to Da-Hanu area. Here it mixed with soil and in the presence of sun-heat and moisture it grew up to apricot plant. When fruiting season started, this plant also had apricots which after ripening down on the ground, some of them even fell through water travelled further ahead and thus helped to grow new apricot plants to the whole region, and named as 'Culi-Cen'. That is : (Culi = apricot, 'Can=area)."

Beliefs

Though gods and goddesses left Dok-yul, yet Dok-pas did not forget their blessings. They continue the practice to worship them alongwith ghost spirits. In their society 'Ozha' is recognised as a doctor. He with the help of ghost spirit removes all kind of problems of the society or individuals.

Religion

Dok-pas are influenced by Islam and Buddhism. Here follow the details :

In 17th century A.D. many Buddhist Monks came to Dok-yul from Kinnaur via Spiti and preached Buddha teachings to Dok-pas, which influenced them to follow Buddhism. Thereafter, with the help of monks they constructed monasteries and Chot-Khangs at their houses.

In 1850 A.D. Rev. Konchog Wangpo came in Dok-yul and gave his preachings on Buddha teachings. He later helped Dok-pas in the construction of monasteries each in Hanu-Gongma, Hanu-Yogma, Garkon, Darchik (Dang-chigs) and Sanche (sa-na-ce).

Rev. Konchog Wangpo belonged to Lamayuru Monastery, then the well known monastery in Ladakh. He whole heartedly gave his full time in the propagation of Buddhism. On his request, the head Lama of the Lamayuru Monastery sent Kom-Nyer to Dok-yul monasteries, who not only performed rituals at the monasteries, but on the request of Dok-pas performed rituals at their Chot-Khangs. Thus, with the dedicated service of Rev. Konchog Wangpo a tradition of observing fast on 'Amavasya' and 'Purnima' every month was popular among Buddhists in Dok-yul. In this way Rev. Konchog Wangpo played a dominant role in the propagation of Buddhism in Dok-yul till 1871 A.D.

After the Parinirvana of Rev. Konchog Wangpo, Shia Muslim missionaries came to Dok-yul. They also preached Islamic teachings to Dok-pas. Many Dok-pas from Ga-Nogs, Ga-Ris, Morol, Seng, Karmo, Silmo, Cu-li-can, Shas-che then got converted into Muslims.

Harvest Festival

Harvest festival is the popular festival among Dok-pas which they celebrate every three years. Among Ladakhis it is known as 'Bonona' and lasts for five days. During this festival Dok-pas from Garkon, Da and Ganogs villages come and dance full of joy and gaiety.

Before the celebration of this festival, one Dok-pa boy is chosen as Lha. He wears white clothes and is allowed to go to meditate at the hillock for seven days. During this period he does not eat meat, onion, garlic, etc. On the seventh day god's spirit enters in his body and he acts like Lha. Immediately after this moment one deputed Dok-pa sacrifices he-goat in his honour and brings him to the dancing ground. At the ground Lha under the specific tree offers prayer, burns Shukpa leaves as incense and purifies the atmosphere. After prayer, Lha changes his dresses and returns to his house. Then the assembled Dok-pas start dancing with the Ladakhi songs and music. On the first day ladies are not allowed to dance, later they freely dance with them.

Language

During the festival Lhadrakh speak 'Mirano' and sing 25 songs. Today the number of Lhadrakh are decreasing year after year, because it requires lot of practice to enable them to sing continuously during the festival. Normally the Lhadrakh practice 'Bonona' songs for fifteen days before its commencement.

Dress

During festivals Dok-pas wear colourful dress. Their ladies wear white and black woollen clothes. They decorate their caps by needles, flowers, soklo, white buttons, silver coins, etc.

Polyandry/Polygamy

Polyandry system still exists in few villages of Dok-yul, however, polygamy can be seen comparatively in greater number. In Dok-yul one person can have up to four wives, and have more than fifteen children, e.g., The Sogpo-pa family of Samad village has fifteen children and Dang-Chig family has twenty one children.

Funeral

Earlier the Dok-pas burried their bodies. But after King Singe Namgyal, some families such as : Gyalpopa of Henasku, Onpopa of Lteva and Bhotpa and Skyindhelpa of Skurbuchan villages came to 'Da' and stopped the burrying tradition. Since then the Dok-pas cremate their dead bodies and call Lamas to perform funeral rituals. After the cremation they give the caps of dead person to Lamas and divide his property among villagers.

Birth Ceremony

On the occasion of child birth, villagers keep themselves away from the concerned family for about one month. A Lama is then called to purify the concerned family house. Thereafter, they celebrate the birth day ceremony. On this occasion Lama gives name to the newly born baby. In case after the child birth, any person in the family dies the child named 'Mi-Skik-kan'. If child birth takes place on 'Purnima', it is named 'Gang-dud'. In other cases Lama gives name accordingly to the religious text or *pothi.*

20

Dards of Ladakh and its Adjoining Areas

Prem Singh Jina

There is nothing known about the period of Dards migration towards Indus Valley. However, it is certain that they came in many batches and established their colonies at Skardu, Dras, Da, Hanu, Darchik, Bema, Garkon, Beyong, Chorbat pass, Shigar, Shingo, etc.

According to a Ladakhi legend the ancestors of Dards migrated from Gilgit and settled down in lower Ladakh. Frederic Drew also agrees with this statement and says :

"The heading of Central Ladakh, are some villages inhabited by Dards who follow the Buddhist faith; who, through remanants left by a wave of immigration from the direction of Gilgit, have so much amalgamated with the Bhots that they obey the Lamas as spiritual leaders. The following places—villages and hamlets are inhabited by the Buddhist Dards: Gurgur-do, Sanacha, Urdus, Darchik Garkon, Dah(Da), Phindur, Baldes, Hanu (Hanu) Lower and Upper.

Even though they did not come from the direction of Gilgit they have a tradition and many circumstances of language and manners which show that in spite of their being Buddhist in religion they are one in origin. Probably a small number reached their present seat and settled there, separated from the main mass of their tribe-brethren. During earlier times the Dards were converted to 'Muhammedanism so that the transition from their ancient faith to Buddhism was not difficult. At that time the neighbouring Baltis also may still have been Buddhist. Later, when Dards had become Muhammedan, they spread again in this direction, and the newcomers have joined on with, or become next-door neighbours to, the earlier migrants. In a greater number of villages above enumerated a truly Dard language is spoken. In the Hanu side valley the people have lost their original language and speak only Tibetan Ladakhi."[1]

The Buddhist Dards in Ladakh have been influenced by Buddhism but do not have any resemblance with Tibetans. Though their faces are entirely different from Tibetans, but on the other side their language has little variation than the Muslim Dards of Dras, Astor or Gilgit. They are taller than the average Ladakhi and Tibetan but not as fine as the Dards of Dras and others. Frederic Drew remarks :

"Buddhist Dards (of Ladakh) have little or no trace of Tibetan on their faces; the two races have not mixed, or not much mixed; their face is Aryan, but not a fine stamp of Aryan; their noses are small, though often slightly hooked, their chin is narrow. In stature they are taller than the average Ladakhi, but they are not such fine men as the Dards of Dras, Astor, or Gilgit. They wear the pigtail as the Ladakhis do, and their dress is the same as theirs, including the drooping cap."[2]

The villagers of Da have the following opinion about their ancestors migration to Ladakh :

"Once their Mangspon[3] Gil-Singhe[4] was on a hunting tour. He then shot an arrow from Mal-Mal Khatu[5] to a rock of 'Da' village. The arrow was so powerful that it not only stuck the rock but went inside the rock for several meters. Thereafter, the village got its name 'Da' which means a village where a powerful 'Da' (or arrow) struck the rock."[6]

Gil-Singhe was the Dard leader and belonged to Gilgit.[7] He along with his followers came out from Gilgit in search of wild animals for hunting. He was happy to see the soil fertility of Da, Hanu and nearby villages, so he decided to settle down in these villages.

As mentioned earlier, Dards did not originate from Gilgit. Before the settlement at Gilgit they had been coming to the upper side of Indus along with the troops of Alexander. During the course of time they settled down at Gilgit, Astor, Bawanji, Punial, etc., along the Indus. Therefore, they are closely related to Dravids of Indus valley. The Dard word might be corrupted from Dravid as follows.[8]

Dravid ≥ Darad
Darad ≥ Dard

Ethnologically Dards are the Indo-Aryan stock and have Greek blood. Herodotus said :

"There are people settled in Indus valley, gold dust producers, have good connection with Greeks."

Therefore, in olden days Dards might be engaged in gold-dust business. In those days, they came to the areas where gold dust was available and in winter returned to Gilgit, Astor, etc. Perhaps, Zangskar in Ladakh would be the place from where they collected gold dust.

Physique

Dards can easily be distinguished by their fine features. They are sharp-featured, tall with relatively long head; the nose is aquiline sometimes straight like Kashmiri. Frederic Drew says :

"They are broad-shouldered, moderately stout-built, well-proportioned men. They are active and enduring. They are good as mountaineers, and those who have been used to act as porters are strong and quick in work; but in some parts they have never been trained for coolies work. In face they can in general hardly be called handsome, but still they have a rather good cast of countenance; their hair is usually black, sometimes brown; in complexion they are moderately fair, the shade is sometimes, but not always, light enough for the red to show through it. Their eyes are either brown or hazel. Their voice and manner of speech is somewhat harsh."[9]

Habits

Buddhist Dards may be taking bath, but 1871 when Frederic Drew visited Ladakh, he acknowledged that they never take bath or hardly took bath. He remarks :

> "(Buddhist Dards) are a dreadfully dirty people; their faces are blotched with black dirt, which they never think of removing. As a means of purifying, instead of washing, they burn twigs of pencil-cedar and let the smoke and the scent from it come over them and inside their clothes; they do this before eating, not perhaps generally but on feast days, and at other times when they think purification to

> be necessary. Their women, who are not shy of being seen, surpass even the men in dirtiness."[10]

Now changes have been taking place with no infrastructure having changed. Dard region is opened for foreigners. As a result they are now changing their habits. Their children are getting modern education, many of them are taking education in Jammu and even in Delhi University.

Customs

Dards do not breed fowls and rear cows, nor eat their eggs and drink milk. They depend on goats for meat and milk. For evidence one can find a large number of skulls and horns of goats at their worshipping places which they had sacrificed to please their god and goddess. This tradition is still preserved. This indicates that their ancestors were animists.

Buddhist Dards in Ladakh belief that if they drink cow's milk, it may cause 'Anethema'. And it may be more serious in case of women. They also believe that if any Dard by mistake drinks cow's milk or uses its products, his god will be displeased and his family members will come under the grip of red boil disease. The same feelings also have come among the Dard Muslims, as Drew says :

> "There is a peculiarity of manners most strange and curious attaching to some of the Dards. It belongs especially, perhaps even, to this shin caste. The thing is this; they hold the cow in abhorrence; they look on it in much the same way that the ordinary Muhammedan regards a pig. They will not drink cow's milk, nor do they eat or make butter from it. Nor even will they burn cow dung. Some cattle they are obliged to keep for ploughing, but they have as little as possible to do with them; when the cow calves they will put the calf to the udder by pushing it with forked stick, and will not touch it with their hands."[11]

However, the cause given by Joldan about forbidding cows also seems correct, as they are having traditional feelings that they should not rear cow. Joldan explains the above reason in the following way :

> "The main reason for forbidding cows, is the geography of the area. Beyond Da, to the west, the Indus gorge gets narrower and the mountains on both sides steeper and higher. At several places in Da, the width of the village is hardly more than that of a football field. Such terrain is not good for the clumsy cow and besides, feeding them in winter would be a problem. On the other hand, the sure-footed goat could go to feed itself anywhere in the mountains."[12]

In olden days all Dards buried their dead like Egyptians and offered water, wine, food and clothing to their relatives. Their graves were small vaults of walls and covered with slates. In these graves they placed the dead person's belongings such as ornaments, clothes etc. Bows and arrows were also consigned to their graves so that dead relatives bodies could be protected from evils. Ahluwalia says :

> "They, bury their dead as if they were pharaohs from Egypt's ancient civilization. They fill earthen or metallic pots with fine wine and food, depending on their financial status, for the journey into the next world. Bows and arrows are also placed near the dead to protect them from wild animals and other dangers in the course of this onwards journey. Drogpa (Dokpa) graves are distinct from Muslim graves. These are just stone walls about a metre high around the dead body which is placed on the ground and covered with slated stones."[13]

Today changes are taking place in Dokyul. Buddhist Dards now cremate the dead like Hindus.

Marriage

The marriage ceremony is arranged by the consultation of parents and relatives of both sides. Therefore, it includes a number of stages before reaching the final decision. For instance, the parents of boy want to marry his son, they will send the maternal uncle and close relatives of boy to go to the girl's parents. In case girl agrees for marriage, marriage feasts continue for several days. According to Dard's custom, marriages outside the village are not allowed. As Ahluwalia remarks :

> "When a boy is to be married, he has to find his bride from one of the Drogpa (Dokpa) village only. If anyone marries

> outside the village, he is disowned by the community. For marriage the groom's maternal uncle takes a needle and thread to bride's house and gifts of butter and 'tsampa' while negotiating the matrimony. The significance of carrying the needle to bride's place could not be ascertained from them. After the marriage has been finalized, the bride's mother gives rings and ornaments to her daughter. These ornaments are mostly of silver and made in the village itself. When the girl comes to her husband's place a community feast takes place. The entire village joins the dancing and singing programme which goes on for three days during which they drink 'Chang' and enjoy themselves."[14]

Dress

They cover their heads with Kullu style colourful caps decorated with wild flowers. Their clothes are made from home-spun wool sheared off from their sheep and coloured beautifully. They wear woollen dresses like Kullu and Kyelong people, but little bigger and broader to accommodate flowers and decorative items. Their ladies mostly decorate their Caps by rows of barley grain, flat round beans and rows of needles, silver coins, buttons and cowery shells. During festivals Dards wear jackets over their Ladakhi-style long coat. The borders of the long coats are decorated by different designs.[15]

Today Dard ladies have started to wear cotton shirts shalwar, etc., and men wear pants, coat, etc.

Muslim Dards except few high class families wear woollen clothes. Drew remarks :

> "The dress of the Dards is woollen, except among the higher people, who wear cotton clothes for the summer if they can get them; the dress consists of pyjamas, Choga (or gown-coat), a waistband to confine this, and lastly, a cap and 'chaussure', both of peculiar construction. The cap is a bag of woollen cloth half a yard long, which is rolled up outwards at the edges until it gets to the size to fit comfortably to the head, round which the roll makes a protection from cold or form sun nearly as good as a turban. For their feet they have strips and scraps of leather put under and over and round the foot, and a long thin strip

wound round and round to keep all these in place. The head-dress is thoroughly characteristic of the Dards."[16]

Castes

Muslim Dards have five castes such as :[17]

(i) Ronu
(ii) Shin
(iii) Yashkun
(iv) Kremin
(v) Dum

Ronu caste among Dards is considered as the highest. Drew says :

> "In Gilgit country it is certain that a small number of families are of a caste called Ronu and that they are held higher even than the Shin."[18]

The Shin abhor cow rearing and fowl breeding. Frederic Drew remarks :

> "They hold the cow in abhorrence. In some places for instance, at Dashkin, 13 miles below Astor (now under Pakistan), where the people are Shin, they will not eat fowls nor touch them. They have no objection to cultivate tobbacco and red papper".[19]

The 'Yashkuns' are found in Gilgit and Astor. Their chief occupation is agriculture.[20]

The 'Kremins' act as potters, millers, carriers etc.[21]

The 'Dums' are the lowest of the four, and like Bedas, Mons and Gara of Ladakh.

Among Buddhist Dards by and large there is no caste system. However, the 'Kharo' are considered the low caste and Lhadrakh the higher one.

Heros of Dards

Dards of Dras, Gilgit, Skardu, etc., embraced Islam after the Muslim invasion during 14th century A.D. whereas the Dards of Da, Hanu, Bema, Darchik and Garkon did not accept this and gradually later accepted Buddhism. It is said that while migrating to Ladakh they first settled down at the higher pasture grounds called 'Dok' and got their name after this Dok-pas or Brok-pas.[22] Drew says:

> "Whenever the Dards are in contact with Baltis or with Bhots, these others call them Brokpa or Dokpa. The word Brok or Blok means in Tibetan a high pasture-ground, and Brokpa or Blokpa must mean a 'Higherlander'. The origin of this appellation for the Dards that they first came in contact with the Baltis by coming over the passes and settling in the higher parts of the valleys parts that perhaps had been left unoccupied."[23]

Buddhist Dards have preserved traditionally old stories of their heroes in ballads and hymns. The largest ballad among them belongs to Ge-Sar. According to them Ge-Sar was the son of heavenly god, who took birth as human life and removed the sufferings of human beings.[24]

Besides, there are many other heroes like-Dani, Melo, etc., who conquered many countries between Tibet and Mongolia. According to them :

> "Dani belonged to Sicili region and later migrated to Indus valley. He was a great warrior and conquered many countries in between Tibet and Mongolia later many of his people settled down near Indus Valley in order to get fertile land and good pasture grounds for their animals. Similarly Melo conquered many countries and also settled down in Indus Valley and founded Hand village."[25]

Festival

Dards have a grand Harvest festival which they celebrate at 'Da' and 'Garkon' villages at every third year interval during Autumn season or at the time of harvesting. On this occasion they sing 23 or 25 hymnals with music. Before the festival a young boy is chosen Lha-boy[26] by the Lhadrakh[27] who has to go to a hillock wearing oracle dress and meditate there for several days. During night he is allowed to sleep, so in late evening he comes down in a separate room but returns in the early morning to his place on the hillock for meditation.

On the festival day in the morning a man first sacrifices one or two goats near the rock, then he cuts it into small pieces for distribution after mixing with barley flour and butter. Thereafter a small procession leads to the hillock to carry Lha-boy to the dancing ground. The Lha-boy after putting off his oracle dress comes down to the ground and join with procession which passes through the path over the village. The Lha boy this time wears simply white woollen gown and a conical cap. He carries on incense pot and lead the procession. People also carry incense pot and play music in his honour. E. Joldan says :

"The Lapdrak (Lhadrakh, i.e., caretaker of the god), the village-headman and some others started dancing and then climbed to the rock to bring down the Lha. The boy in the meantime had changed into a white woollen gown and a conical cap. The Lha-boy came down, leading the small procession and carrying Phoks (the incense pot) and blowing every now and then on the charcoal which burnt the dry pencil cedar, emitting a curling smoke. The musicians were playing down below and a small party came dancing down the slope. After a dance on the field the procession went down in a single file to the square in the village. The Lha boy (then) placing the incense pot on a boulder (and) disappeared in the crowd."[28]

The dancing ground is permanently built in a circular shape under a huge walnut tree, surrounded by tall willows. Here Lha-drakh sing aged old hymnals, describing the migration of their ancestors. At night after four-five hours rest, he again recites the songs along with his colleagues. This time ladies also come forward and start dancing till late in the night when mass kissing starts and last an hour or so. This of course a good chance when young boys and girls choose their life partners.

The festival normally observed for five days in which all Dards from Da, Hanu, Garkon, Bema, Darchik etc. participate with full joy and gaiety. E. Jolden describes the festival scene in the following way :

"About 5.30 p.m. when the musician arrived, the Lapdark Lhadrakh (Lhadak) was somewhat cross on their being late. The recitation of the songs by the same persons started, as on the first day soon other men joined them and sitting down they sang to the accompaniment of music. Then the ladies who were larger in number joined, forming a sort of semicircle by themselves and some participated in the singing, which lasted for another half an hour. Sometimes while singing, the men swayed right and left and bowed down their head.

Recitation for the day ended and dancing began. By this time it was dark except for the half moon light which filtering through the tall trees made patches of darkness and light on the dancing floor. On the first day, drinking is strictly forbidden by tradition, but during the rest of the festival it is freely allowed but not on the dancing place. So, most of the young men were tipsy and dancing was brisker and then the mass kissing started. The whole show lasted for an hour. The dancing fantastic scene kept on playing on every night. The fourth and the final day of the festival coincided with death anniversary of their ancestral leader Gel Singe (Ge-Singhe), so all of them, at the dancing place put off their bedecked caps and observed a few minutes' silence in his memory."[29]

During the Harvest festival Muslim Dards from Kargil, Dras, Da-da-do, Culi-can also come to participate at the function. They are considered as their distant cousins. Though they have given up Dard dress and culture but still speak Dardi language.[30]

It is believed that during olden days the ancestors of Dards danced with the Lhas and Lhamos (god and goddess) in the Harvest festival. The Lhas and Lhamas then considered highest order personalities and looked after the religious affairs and did not intermerry with the commoners. Once a common Dard male tried to kiss a goddess. This incident annoyed gods they went to heaven and never returned to Dokyul.[31]

Lo-Dron Feast

This feast is given when one cycle of 12 years is completed. E. Jolden explains about this festival in the following way :

> "A unique tradition among the Brokpas (Buddhist Dards) is the celebration of Lo-Dron Feast. They follow the Tibetan Calendar of 12 years' Cycle-each year named after an animal such as dog, hog, monkey, dragon, etc., when a man says he has completed two Lo-Skors it means he is 24 years old, but the Brokpas, particularly the ladies, on completing the Cycle of 12 years celebrate in the village. Thus, everybody in the village knows all those persons who would be celebrating their Lo-Dron in a particular year. It is of special importance for girls completing their first cycle because they would be entering puberty".[32]

Losar

Buddhist Dards celebrate Losar after wearing their best

traditional dresses and come to the dancing floor in a procession. In 'Da' village they light torches made of wooden pieces tied round a stout stick and throw them at a particular place in village, with this the Losar festival comes to end.[33]

Notes and References

1. Drew, Frederic : *Jammoo and Kashmir Territories,* Cosmo Publication, Delhi, 1976, pp. 430-31.
2. *Ibid,* p. 431.
3. Magspon : (= Makpon : Chief of Dards).
4. Gil-Singhe : (Gil-Singe : He was the Chief of Dards who along with his followers migrated to Ladakh).
5. Mal-Mal-Khatu : Dancing place where Buddhist Dards dance for five days during their Harvest festival.
6. Jina, Prem Singh : *Ladakh: The land and the people,* Indus Pub. Co; 1996, p. 94.
7. Gilgit; Scholars pronounced Gilgit by different ways : Vigne says 'Gilgid', Dr. Leitner speaks of 'Gilgit or Gilit', Fredric Drew spells it as 'Gilyit'.
8. Mohi-ud-din, Akhtar : 'Identity of the Kashmiri People In: *The Journals of Central Asian Studies,* Vol 1, 1990, p. 62.
9. Dew, Frederic; *op. cit.* pp. 423-24.
10. *Ibid;* p. 431.
11. *Ibid;* p. 428.
12. Jolden, E. *Harvest Festival of Buddhist Dards of Ladakh and Other Essays*; Kapoor Brothers, Srinagar, 1985, p. 12-13.
13. Ahluwalia, H.P.S., *Hermit Kingdom Ladakh*, Vikas Pub. House, 1980 p. 114.
14. *Ibid.*
15. Jolden, E.; *op. cit.* p. 33.
16. Drew, Frederic; *op. cit.* p. 425.
17. *Ibid.*
18. *Ibid,* p. 426.
19. *Ibid,* p. 428.
20. *Ibid,* p. 427.
21. *Ibid.*
22. Brok-pas (: Brog-pas : Drok-pas : Highlanders) or who first settled down at the higher parts of Indus valleys.
23. Drew, Frederic; *op. cit.* p. 433.
24. Bedi, Ramesh : *Ladakh,* Brijbasi Pub. Co. Delhi, 1986, p. 3.
25. Jolden, E.; *op. cit.* pp. 28-29.
26. Lha-boy: Dok-pas choose a young boy who is active and belong to good family.
27. Lhadrakh = Lapdakh : He perform rituals like priest of Hindus.
28. Jolden, E. *op. cit.* pp. 28-29.
29. *Ibid.*
30. *Ibid,* pp. 30-31.
31. *Ibid,* p. 15.
32. *Ibid,* p. 16.
33. *Ibid.*

21

Lifestyle of Chang-Pas of Chang-Thang in Leh-District

Prem Singh Jina

Chang-Thang plateau lies on the North-East of Jammu and Kashmir State. It is strategically significant internationally bordering China to its north. The area is sparsely populated with small group of nomadic communities and some permanent settlements along the Indus river all called Chang-Pas.

The Chang-Thang of Ladakh region covers an area of about 60,000 sq. kms. In 1962 Indo-China war; the northern part of this area, the Aksai Chin was taken by China. Since then, the border between the two countries has been effectively sealed.

Because of its strategic importance the Chang-Thang region was closed to foreigners and outside development agencies. However, in 1987 due to political unrest in Srinagar it was decided to open the military road from Leh to Manali. This allows access to foreigners to the western edge of the plateau but access to the east of this road towards the Tibetan plateau is severely restricted. In the winter of 1992 and early 1993 talks were held in Jammu by the Jammu and Kashmir Department of Tourism with a view to de-restricting access to other parts of the Chang-Thang. According to radio reports, discussions were undertaken to open the lakes of Pangong Tso and Tso Moriri to small groups of tourists. Finally in 1994 the above two magnificent lakes, located at an altitude of about 5000 metres, were opened for tourists.[1]

The Chang-Thang plateau lies at an elevation of 15,000 ft. and consists of wide, open valleys interspersed with rounded, snow covered mountains of 20,000 ft. or more. Vegetation is sparse due to the high altitude and arid climate. Summer season also is cool and chilly, so no trees are present on the plateau. However, Chang-Pa who settled down along the Indus catchment can grow only one crop in a year; peas, potatoes and turnips are planted in the limited spaces of the narrow valleys called 'lunpas'. Water formed from the mountain snows forms small streams and the plateau is dotted with both fresh and salt-water lakes. The climate of the plateau is extreme with winter temperatures regularly falling below minus 40 degree centigrade. Even in summer snowfall can be recorded intermittently.[2]

Yak-hair Tents

Chang-Pas usually live in white canvas or black yak-hair tents and tend large flocks of sheep, goats and yaks. The livelihood of the nomads is based on selling meat, dairy products, such as cheese and butter, as well as the increasingly valuable pashmina wool.[3]

Trade

Today Chang-Pas are engaged in trade and pastoral activities, selling *'pashmina'* and wool to Ladakhis and Kashmiri, Himachal trades. From this income they buy rice, jaggery, flour and *tsampa*. Today these things are usually available at the nearby markets, but some decades ago when no heavy trucks or tippers were available, Ladakhi peasant traders with their donkeys and occasionally horses provided an essential link in the system. They carried loads of flour, *tsampa*, dried apricots, mustard oil and spices on their pack animals and exchanged these for *pashmina* and wool in Chang-Thang. In the nineteenth century this trade was in the hands of individual farmers from Central Ladakh, particularly from the banks of the Indus valley, whose lands were suitable for agriculture and whose produce they regularly took on their donkeys up to Chang-Thang. Bartering there in return for *pashmina* wool and salt, these peasants drove their donkeys down again to the valleys before snowfall. About fifty years ago Chang-pa themselves carried *pashmina*, wool, salt and *Khuloo* (Yak wool) on their sheep and goats backs to the Leh market and exchanged these for *tsampa*, jaggery, flour and dry apricots. Today they are not seen much at Leh or at surrounding markets.

However, they still maintain trade links with Leh butchers for the disposal of their old livestock, *pashmina* and yak wool.[4]

Chang-Pas thus have income from their animals. These animals provide milk, butter, cheese, meat, wool and hair. Butter which is indispensable to their daily diet, is, generally, never sold. Many other essential items of household use, such as clothing, boots, tents, ropes and bags are also made from these animals. Livestock also brings in cash to buy agricultural and manufactured products. Pashmina wool, which is the main important item taken from the soft underhair of Changra goats currently fetches Rs. 2000 per kg. in its raw state. Approximately 15,000 farmers and nomads produce about 30,000 kgs. pashmina wool per year in Ladakh. The wool is sent to Kashmir and Kullu in Himachal Pradesh where it is laboriously cleaned by hand spun and then woven into shawls. Sometimes Angora rabbit hair also mix in pashmina for making more white and soft shawl. In local market pashmina shawl costs Rs. 2500 to Rs. 3500 per piece. However, the export quality Cashmere pashmina shawls fetch Rs. 20,000 to Rs. 30,000 in London market.

Presence of Army and Para-Military Forces

Today Indo Tibet Border Police (ITBP) has four Battalions and Army has one core in Ladakh region. Both Army and Para Military forces have number of posts in Chang Thang region. As a result of these forces in recent years many roads were built by them. Thus, we can see a wide change in this region and this cause development.

Tibetan Refugees Presence

In March 1959 upheaval broke out in Tibet against the tightening rule of People's Republic of China and the Dalai Lama fled to Dharamsala, in India. Following this many Tibetan refugees poured into the Chang Thang area together with their herds. Initially, this did not lead to serious problems, but it did lead to economic ones, especially to shortage of pasture. Two years later China attacked India via Chang Thang in Ladakh region and occupied a great deal of this area. This brought further pressure on grazing resources, since it led both to a reduction of about 10 per cent in the pasture land available and to an increase in livestock pressure by about 40 per cent. The fact that the herds of the 'Tibetan refugees' are not controlled or co-ordinated by the Chang-pa 'goba' of different localities still leads to considerable overgrazing.[5]

Today we have noticed that Tibetan refugees are now trying to intermix with Chang pa society in Chang Thang, some of them have even got married with Chang pa girls. According to Dr. Prem Singh Jina :

> "The last few decades have also seen much social change in the region as a whole. The Tibetan refugees have had a tremendous impact on Chang Pa society. Many Tibetan refugees have married Chang Pa girls and thus become members of the Chang-pa society."[6]

It has been acknowledged that since couple of years some Tibetan refugees directly and indirectly were involved in pashmina wool smuggling. This cause wide fluctuation in the prices of raw pashmina wool and local Chang Pas sometimes get huge loss.

There has been also a rumour that smuggled pashimina wool traded illegally over the Chinese border had synthetic fibres. This caused adulteration and thus reduced the prices of pashmina.

Today there is urgent need to check the pashmina wool smuggling over the Chinese border in order to preserve the Chang Pa traditional pashmina wool trading business.

Seasonal Mobility in Relation to Altitude

Chang Pas move with their animals valley to valley and stay in *pulloos* while grazing their animals (Fig. 21.1).

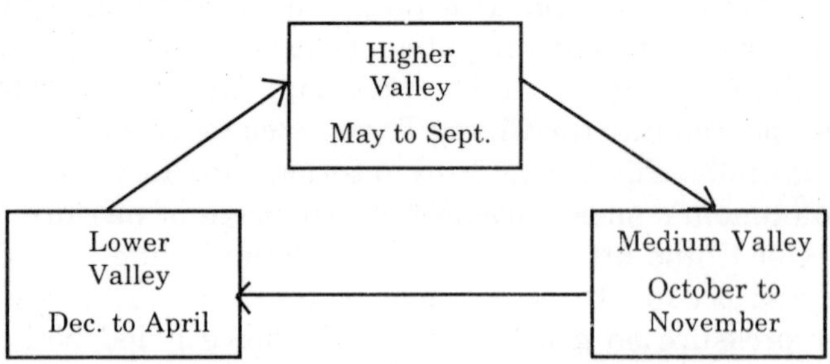

Fig. 21.1. Pattern of seasonal mobility in relation to altitude (taken from Jina 1999 : 99).

A Case Study of Chang-Pa of Kozok Area

Kozok area is about 90 kms. away from Nyoma. Here 100 families have about 400 Buddhist population which belongs to Dug-pa kargyud under Hemis monastery of Ladakh. 250 persons are above 18 years of age, out of which 52 per cent belong to male population, 150 persons belong to less than 18 years of age, in which 53.4 per cent are males.

Annual Grazing Cycle of Kozok Herds

In Chang Thang, Chang-pas move valley to valley with their animals and 'Rebos' in search of pastures. 'Rebo' is nothing else but tent, which is made of 'Yak' hair (Fig. 21.2). In Chang Thang 'Rebo' has cultural importance as each family has its own traditional name given to Rebo. Generally this name is based upon the head of the family that is father's name. 10 families are taken randomly for the study (Table 21.1).

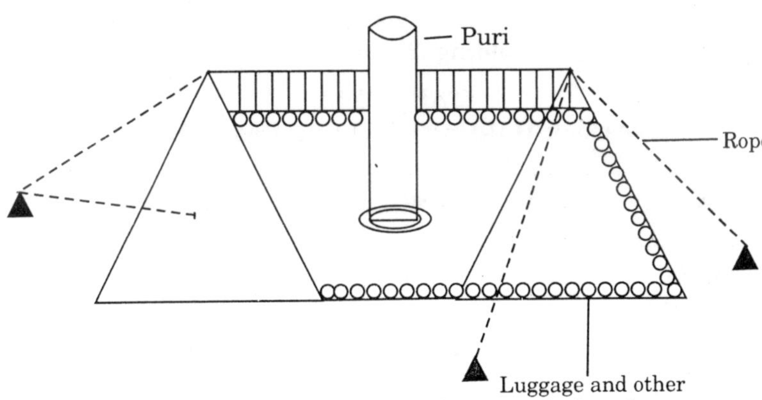

Fig. 21.2. Chang pa Rebo.

Table 21.1, reveals that Chang-Pas don't have big family size, this is because they have to move valley to valley in search of pasture, and under cold-arid climate with herds it is difficult for them to have big family size.

TABLE 21.1
Description of Ten Selected Families of Kozok

Name of Rebo	*Population*	*Male*	*Female*	*Male %*
Tswang Ka	8	4	4	50.0
Wang Chan Ka	5	3	2	60.0
Sonam Ka	9	4	5	44.4
Meme Angchok	3	2	1	66.7
Angchok Pol	2	1	1	50.0
Tashi Narboo	8	3	5	37.5
Namgyal Rigzin	6	4	2	66.7
Choro	8	4	4	50.0
Tundup Chun	9	5	4	55.6
Chemet Rigen	4	1	3	25.0

The percentage of male population is slightly high. Males normally go with herds and females look after children, kids, kitchen, milching, etc. In Kozok Chang-Pas do not have very big size of livestock holding (Table 21.2).

TABLE 21.2
Livestock Holding of Chang-Pas in Kozok

Name of Rebo	*Yak*	*Goat*	*Sheep*	*Demo*	*Total animals*
Tswang Ka	4	30	50	—	84
Wang Chan Ka	7	50	70	—	127
Sonam Ka	3	40	50	—	93
Meme Angchok	5	45	50	1	100
Angchok Pol	4	30	20	—	54
Tashi Narboo	5	60	50	2	117
Namgyal Rigzim	7	50	50	—	107
Choro	10	60	100	—	170
Tundup Chun	25	50	40	10	125
Chemet Rigen	3	25	40	—	68

Table 21.2, shows that in Kozok area Chang-pas have goat and sheep in good number. They rear big animals viz. Yak and

Demo but they are a few in number. Except the Tundup Chun Rebo no one has good number Yaks and Demo. Probably they use these animals for luggage carrying purpose.

Table 21.3 gives the Schedule of the Annual Grazing Cycle of Kozok Herds

TABLE 21.3

The Annual Grazing Cycle of Kozok Herds

Sl. No.	*Valley*	*Month*
1.	Tia Zung	January
2.	Tia Zung	February
3.	Tia Zing	March
4.	Ney Rong	April
5.	Ney Rong	May
6.	Ney Rong	June
7.	Young Lung	July
8.	Young Lung	August
9.	Phu	September
10.	Ma Lung	October
11.	Pal do	November
12.	Dhi Yee	December

The annual grazing cycle of Kozok area is fixed by the headman of Chang-pas. Besides, he is also responsible to allot pasture ground separately for big animals viz. yak, horse and demo.

Women and Livestock

Women have a dominant role in Chang Pa families. They usually collect goat milk and if needed make 'Churpe' from the 'Demo' milk. In addition women and children take care of animals when they return to rebo in the evening. Figures 21.3 and 21.4 show the method of standing and rearing mix yielding animals.

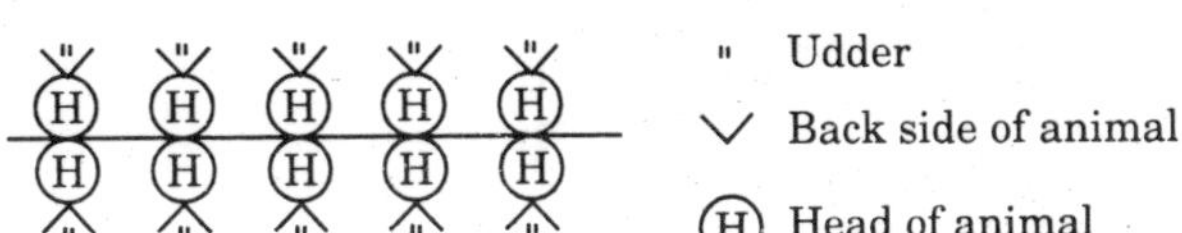

Fig. 21.3. Method to stand milk yielding animals while milching them.

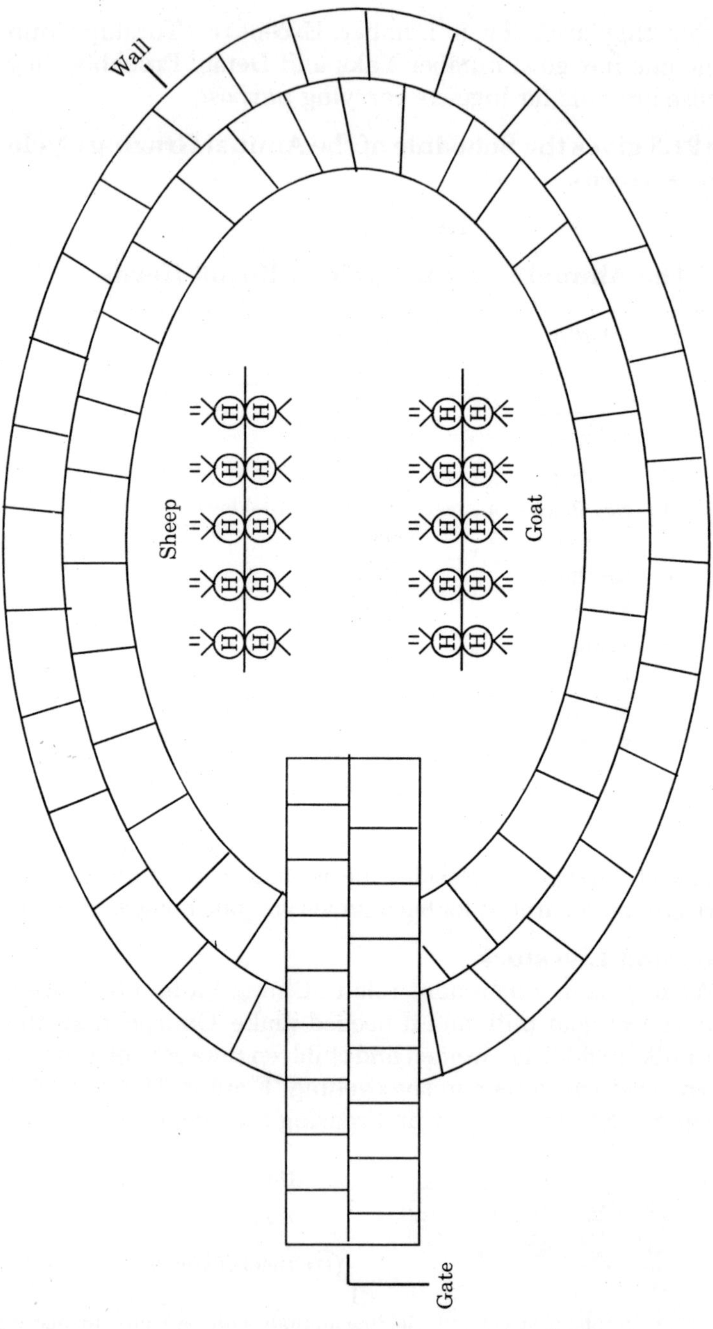

Fig. 21.4. Method of Rearing Sheep and Goats.
Symbols/keys are same as in Fig. 21.3

Problems of the Chang-pas in Chang-Thang

(a) Health. The extreme climate and conditions of the Chang-Thang sub-division make Chang-pa's life difficult. Besides the following health problems have been noticed among Chang-Pas.[7]

(1) Respiratory tract infections, this is exasperated by the cold climate and smoky tents.
(2) In summer diarrohea diseases are prevalent.
(3) Serious illness is most prevalent in winter.
(4) Infant child death problem occurs because of exposure.

(b) Education. In theory state Government made necessary arrangements to educate Chang-Pa children at their respective tents, in this connection Government provides primary school teachers. No doubt these teachers are Ladakhis, find the conditions too tough and normally take long leave or seldomly visit there. The main problem with trying to provide even basic educational services is that the nomads move their camps to new locations every two months so that building schools is impractical.

Secondly, each camp may be spread out over a large area as nomads often take their animals to satellite camps in side valleys, so that mobile schools in tents is the only practical solution.[8]

The educated Chang-Pas usually do not return to Chang-Thang region to help their parents in traditional life style.

(c) Lack of Pasture. Chang-Pas are dependent on nature for their livelihood. In recent years Tibetan Refugees due to their animal grazing cause overgrazing and thus make extinct pasture cover. Sometimes heavy snowfall also causes to destroy their animals.[9]

In brief, the Chang-Thang region is under severe pressure due to climatic, political, ecological, military and paramilitary presence, and due to the process of urbanisation. Youth generally migrate towards Leh and its adjoining areas. Thus, a conflict between young and old generations cause a stressful atmosphere. Besides, old Chang-Pas are trying to develop and adjust their livestock rearing to fit these pressure. Goat rearing continues to occupy an important place in Chang-Pa cultural identity. Though they follow sheep rearing alongwith yak and horse, the Chang-Pa goat rearing is still considered essential and profitable by them. Raising livestock remains a rational economic strategy when there is enough suitable manpower. Flocks are profitable as long as they are managed by their owners and these have access to adequate pasture land.

Notes and References

1. Report on the nomads of Rupshu and Kharnak submitted by ethnographic Audio Visual Archive (EAVA) and Leh Nutrition Project (LNP), April 1993.
2. *Ibid* & Jina, Prem Singh : 'The Chang-pa of the Ladakh Himalayas: some observations on their economy and environment', *Nomadic People* (NS) Vol. 3 issue 1, Köln (Germany), 1999, p. 96.
3. Cf. Report on the nomads of Rupshu and Kharnak *op. cit.*
4. Rizvi, J. 1985', *Peasant Traders of Ladakh. A Study in Oral History,* India International Centre Quarterly 12(1); 14-21 & Jina, Prem Singh (1999) *The Chang-pa of the Ladakh Himalayas : Some Observations on the their Economy and Environment,* op. cit.
5. Jina, Prem Singh (1999)', the *Chang-pa of the Ladakh Himalayas; Some Observations on their Economy and Environment, op. cit.*
6. *Ibid.* p. 103.
7. Report on the nomads of Rupshu and Kharnak, *op. cit.*
8. *Ibid.*
9. *Ibid.*

22

Historical Background of Ayou Kalon of Ladakh

Tsering Sonam
and
Prem Singh Jina

After the death of the most famous King of Ladakh Chosgyal Singe Namgyal,[1] his son Deldan Namgyal became the King of Ladakh. He ruled the country for twenty years from 1620 A.D. to 1640 A.D. During this period Mgarmo's son Kalon[2] Chosnit was the Prime Minister. He belonged to Ayou and married with Shema Zil Zom, a beautiful and charming lady, famous throughout in Ladakh for her graceful face. The King of Ladakh was attracted by her beauty, and decided to marry her. Therefore, he made a plan to murder his Prime Minister Kalon Chosnit.

After sometime according to the instruction of King Deldan Namgyal, some of his soldiers and officials hid near the Lion Gate of Leh palace. When Kalon Chosnit reached at the entrance Lion Gate and walking through the dark gallery, they started to throw stones on him. He got injured seriously. Fortunately he did not die. Then he escaped towards his residence Ayou in the east of Leh palace. After reaching at Ayou he stopped near a stream for washing the blood of his injured head. Soon after, the King's men also reached there and attacked again. This time Kalon Chosnit was unable to save his life and died on the spot.

After the death of Kalon Chosnit, King Deldan sent a delegation to Shema Zil Zom with a marriage proposal. Shema Zil Zom tactfully handled the situation and warmly welcomed the delegation. As the delegation offered the marriage proposal of King Deldan Namgyal, she accepted the offer but carefully put some conditions :

(i) that the King Deldan Namgyal should construct a Mani wall in the memory of her husband Kalon Chosnit.
(ii) that the King of Ladakh should wait till the completion of prayer wall, and he should not make any effort for establishing any kind of relation with her.
(iii) that she will only accept the offer of marriage with King Deldan when she personally witnesses the Mani wall which should be made according to her Payrak.

After hearing the conditions of Shema Zil Zom, the delegation returned to Leh palace and informed King Deldan about her conditions for marriage. The King ordered his people to construct a great Mani wall immediately. Hundreds of people were employed for the construction of Mani wall[3] which they constructed within a short time. Presently this Mani is behind the All India Radio Station, Leh; lying in between Deskit Tsal and New bus stand.

After the completion of the Mani wall the King sent his delegation to Shema Zil Zom with the proposal of marriage, she again played a trick and said:

"Your King did not ask me where to construct Mani wall and what would be the shape of Mani. So, she will not marry till the Mani is constructed according to her wish."

The delegation again returned to Leh palace and informed about Shema Zil Zom wishes. Later King ordered his people to construct the Mani according to Shema Zil Zom's Payrak[4]. As the Mani was completed the King sent his delegation to Shema Zil Zom to Ayou. But they did not find her at the palace. They searched and inquired about her whereabouts from the villagers. One villager told them she went to Igoo. The delegation went to Igoo. At Igoo Shema Zil Zom welcomed the delegation and offered them light refreshment with tea. She said, "I know you came here with the marriage offer of King. Don't worry, I am ready for marriage. But please allow me to take the permission from Tri Ratna."[5]

She then went to the Chot-Khang for offering her prayer to Tri Ratna.

The members of the King Deldan Namgyal delegation became happy to know Shema Zil Zom's decision. After some time she came out with a nun's dress. She cut down her hair and with simple behaviour asked the delegation to go to Leh palace. On seeing Shema Zil Zom in a nun's dress, the members of the King's delegation got surprised and thought how could they take a nun as a queen for the King. So, they left her at Igoo and returned to Leh.

When King Deldan heard all the story from his delegation about Shema Zil Zom, he felt sorry for his deeds and appointed her son as his Prime Minister and ordered to construct two Chortans[7] in the honour of Kalon Chosnit and Shema Zil Zom at both sides of the Mani wall. He also ordered to construct 'Pal-mKhar-dGu-thok' palace near his palace for Shema Zil Zom's son and his Prime Minister Kalon Shakya Gyatso.

The latest generation of the Ayou Kalon family is as follows.

Kalon Jamyang Namgyal
↓
Kalon Chemat's wife Ni-Ni
↓
Kalon Tondup Namgyal
↓
Kalon Tashi Phunchog
↓
Kalon S.K. Namgyal

Kalon Chemat married a very beautiful Tibetan girl who belonged to the Royal Cha-Rong family of Tibet. The present head of Drigung Kargyud pa sect. His holiness Skyab-Gon-Che-Tsang Rinpoche also belongs to the Che-Rong family.

Notes and References

1. Chosgyal Singe Namgyal (Chosgyal Singey Namgyal or Chosgyal Singey rNamgyal). He was the son of King Jamyang Namgyal and was a powerful King of Ladakh.
2. Kalon (Prime Minister). During King's reign Kalon was one of the main advisor of King. He was also having key administrative post.
3. Mani wall : This Mani Wall is 700 metres in length 15 meters in breadth and 2.8 meters in height.
4. Payrak : Ladies head ornament of Ladakhi Buddhists.
5. Tri Ratna :
   (i) Avalokitesvara
   (ii) Manjushri
   (iii) Metreya.
6. Nun : Cho-mo (in Ladkhi language). After Nun Shema Zil Zom renamed as Chon-Zad-ma.
7. Chortens (Stupas) :
   (i) Chang-chup-Chorten of 30 feet in height
   (ii) Namgyal Chorten of 300 feet in height.

23

Ladakh : A Part of Kushana Kingdom

B.K. Dembi

We have evidence of the Kushana conquest of Ladakh. This evidence is furnished by a brief but important Kharoshti inscription discovered by Francke near a bridge at Khaltse 50 miles from Leh on the Srinagar Leh Central Asian trade route. The inscription comprising of two lines read :

Line No. 1 : Sam 1 100 20 20 20 4 (III)

Line No. 2 : Maharajas Uvima Kavthisas (Kavusasa)

Anno 187 during Uvima Kavthisa, (also read as Kaufisas) is identified with Kushana ruler Vima Kadaphises the son and successor of the founder of the dynasty Kujula Kadaphises.[2] The name Uvima mentioned in the inscription is in agreement with Greek legend Voomo found in the coins of Vima Kadaphises. In the Chinese annals the name of the King is given Yen-Kao-Chen which corresponds to the name Vima Kadaphises found in the coins.

The most significant aspect of the inscription is the date which reads Sam 187. If this date is assigned to Scythe-Parthian era of 58 B.C the date of the inscription would be 129-30 A.D. This is the period when the famous Kushana ruler Kanishka was ruling who is now generally accepted to have ascended the throne in 78 A.D. and started an era which later came to be known as Saka era. Prof. Mukherjee on the basis of the dates mentioned in some inscriptions of the period which do not compare favourably with the generally accepted chronology of Kushana rules postulated another reckoning besides the Scytheo Parthian era having been in use in the period. According to the date of our inscriptions this according to Mukherjee is not stated specifically.[3] Sten Know quotes Dr. Van Weijk, according to his calculations the year 187 of the inscription corresponds to 103-4 A.D. How Dr. Weijk has arrived at this date is not clear.[4] Even if we take it to be correct again it would fall in the reign of Kanishka and not Vima Kadaphises. This has led some scholars to argue that the inscription in question does not belong to Vima Kadaphises but to some Scythian governor of Ladakh who ruled under the Kushanas of Kanishka's house in 130 or 103 A.D.[5]

Francke refers to another interesting feature of the inscription which lies in the fact that a portrait of a Kushana King just as it is given in many Kushana coins is found in the middle of the text.[6] However, it is argued that the drawing of the figure is so rough that it does not help us in identifying the King. There is no dispute about the figure being a Kushana figure since the figure is represented as wearing a typical Kushana dress.

Be what it may, whether the Khalstse inscription belongs to Vima Kadphises or to some Kushana Governor of Ladakh, this much is certain that Ladakh did form part of the early Kushana empire and the known history of the region should be dated from this period and not from the visit of Fahien to Ladakh as postulated by Cunningham. A branch of Kushana having entered Ladakh either from the valley itself or from Darel or Balor or Chilas where more inscriptions of Maharaja Kadhatphisa or Kadphises Uvimika were found by Prof. A.H. Dani and described by him in his Chilas. Kadphisa corresponds to Chinese Katpaisa which means "of honoured form".

Notes and References

1. Sten, Konow : *Corpus Inscriptionum, Indicarum,* Vol. II, Part-I, pp. 79 f. The 'Kavasasa is mine'.
2. *Ibid.* cf. Mukherjee, B.N. *Rise and fall of Kushana Empire,* Calcutta, p. 37; p. 567 n.
3. Mukherjee, B.N.; *op. cit.*
4. Sten, Konow; *op. cit.*
5. Sircar, D.C., *Age of Imperial Unity* (The History and Culture of Indian People) Bharatiya Vidya, Bombay, p. 139, f. n.1.
6. Indian Antiquary, 1929, p. 110.

24

Grazing Fee and *Begari* System in Ladakh

Prem Singh Jina

Begari System means : "A certain number of villagers are told to supply transport and certain periods are fixed for villagers or small groups of villages to maintain number of ponies at each state."[1]

The above system was enforced during Dogra reign and more emphasis was given to supply ponies at each stage. However, this system had merits and demerits. Here follows the details.[2]

Merits

Under this system villagers earned a good deal of money as there was limited number of livestock for transport and on the other hand ponies demand was very high. Thus, villagers sold their ponies when offered a good price.

Demerits

1. Due to the limited resources of Ladakh normally ponies at each stage were a few in number. But when trade season started ponies demand increased correspondingly. Thus to meet the demand the neighbouring villages sent their animals. But due to shortage of fodder many ponies died.
2. Because of the shortage of ponies during trade season especially in the month of Ashar and Sawan, the traders were normally detained at each stage for some days.
3. When local administration put pressure upon villagers to supply necessary ponies for transport, the villagers were bound to provide over worked animals. These animals were mostly disabled and unfit for further service. Therefore,

sometimes animals lost their life or suffered upto a great extent.

4. Begar system was unevenly distributed among the different villages. This unfair rule caused economic losses to few villages as they had to provide ponies during peak agricultural season.
5. Some groups of villages were required to remain at the stages in their entire strength, which seriously interferes with their agricultural operation.

Grazing Fee :[3]

1. It appears from the history of state settlements that the Durbar had always insisted on levying grazing fees in view of the grazing facilities and pastoral assets of Ladakh region.
2. There are extensive grazing grounds in Zangskar, a large number of ponies cattle and sheep were reared by the villagers and a substantial income was made by sale of the livestock. Under the circumstances, the state was clearly entitled to take grazing fees.
3. Grazing fees had not hitherto been taken in usual form. The *bahis* system of Sambat 1913 made the assessment that included 54 sheep and 100 worth of milk. However, *bahi* of 1935 shows that a pony was annually taken as 'nazar'. But these items were not repeated in the subsequent *bahis,* probably due to the fact that these were included as miscellaneous items which were merged in revenue proper in Sambat 1945.
4. Grazing fees were not levied on agricultural cattle, and Zos and yaks were exempted from this fee.
5. 04 annas tax was levied on every pony which was engaged in carrying load on the small trak in Zangskar. However, according to the Assessment Report of Zangskar 1909 it was suggested that the tax rates should be applied six paise for per head for sheep and goat. This would increase the income from grazing fees to Rs. 635-10-06. The grazing fees at half the above rates would give Rs. 318. Here follows the details :

Items	*No.*	*Rate*			*Amount*		
		R.	A.	P.	R.	A.	P.
Ponies	870	0	2	0	108	12	0
Sheep & Goats	13,381	0	0	3	209	01	3
Total	—	—	—	—	317	13	03

R = Rupee Note : Omitting fractions
A = Anna
P = Piese

Source : Assessment Report of Zangskar Ilaka in Ladakh district, 1909, Printed at Pioneer Press, Allahabad p. 21.

Grazing fees in Ladakh had an anomaly. The circumstances of the tax were stated in full length in Clarke's report which forms preamble of the State Council Resolution No. 23, dated 25th October 1901. The principal points may be summarized as below:

1. The grazing fees were formerly taken in kind in the shape of charas, positions, sheep and yaks. In 1941 Zar-i-Markab was realized to the amount of Rs. 704-12-03. This was apparently a tax on transport animals and besides this there was an item of Rs. 13 shown as grazing fees in Nubra.
2. A number of State sheep was mentioned by villagers in Tanktse and Rupshu Ilakas for which annas 8 per head per annum was realized under the head Qimat-i-Gosfandan, the total amount in 1941 were Rs. 540-11-06. This system continued in force till 1953, when on the report of the then Wazir-i-Wazarat a Moharrir Kahcharai was spent by the Governor of Jammu.[4]

The Moharrir carried out enumeration of the livestock and assessed grazing fees in Nubra, Khardung, Tanktse and Rupsh Ilakas.

Mr Clarke fixed the grazing fees demand at Rs 3,317-10-06 for Nubra, Khardong, Thaktse and Rupshu Ilakas. Since then Kah-charai fees continued to be realized on annual enumeration.

In 1958 the Kah-charai fees amounted Rs 3,784-04-00. By and large we can understand from the above studies that the Kah-Charai assessment was unfair and it was unreasonably distributed. Because no fees were taken in any of the prosperous villages along the Indus valley. The grazing areas in Rupshu,

Tanktse and Nubra were comparatively extensive, the villages in the Central Ladakh also had similar nallahs for grazing purposes. Therefore, it might be urged that the villages in Central Ladakh deserve special consideration in view of their services in connection with the Treaty Road. But similar services were rendered by villages in Nubra on whom the incidence of Kah-Charai was heavy. Again the villages in Tanktse and Rupshu Ilakas had to supply transport for the Lhassa Missions.

At all events the state was fairly entitled to receive grazing dues from every Ilakas in Leh Tehsil as well as from Zangskar, in view for the grazing done in long nallahs and hill sides for which no revenue was taken. At the same time the grazing fund in Ladakh was far inferior to that available in Kashmir and other parts of State, besides the compulsory service taken for the purpose of the Treaty Road and Lhassa Missions, etc. Grazing fees here should be lower than those obtaining in other parts of the state. At the conclusion the annual Malshumari system caused a good deal of harassment to the people, and provided opportunities for speculation to petty officials. Also enumeration of yaks and sheep in Ladakh was very difficult, as the animals were not kept in villages during the winter. Hence it was necessary that the demand in this connection should be fixed permanently for a term of years.

Notes and References

1. Chaudhri Khushi Mohamad : *Preliminary Report of Ladakh*, Rambir Prakashan Press, 1908, p. 25.
2. Assessment Report of Zangskar Ilaka in Ladakh district, 1909, Printed at the Pioneer Press, Allahabad, p. 21.
3. *Ibid.*
4. *Ibid,* 1908, p. 21.

25

Ancient Trade Route via Balu-mkhar to Central Asia

Prem Singh Jina

Till 10th Century A.D. Lamayuru monastery was recognised as a biggest monastery in Lower Ladakh. It had good relations with Tibet and its neighbouring countries. This monastery invited many Tibetan Buddhist scholars in Ladakh who later preached lamas and people of adjoining areas. In those days Dard tribes were in majority. So, Tibetan scholars also visited in their areas and preached them about Buddha's thoughts and his philosophy. They listened to them peacefully, some of them got influenced by Buddhism and became the followers of Buddhism. Dards who became Buddhists only spoke Dardi and did not know Tibetan. When Buddhist scholars asked them to inscribe something in Tibetan, they could not deny and inscribed what they knew from them. The following inscriptions are the examples.

Text No. 1[1]

Phaggi lola grib zhangsso

Text No. 2[2]

Phaggi Lo (la) brisso (ba?)

Text No. 3[3]

mthing brang yzhungalas khrungspai mdo thsong ytso khri shong 'abum ydugs (kyi) khungs sras stag

thsar rlabscan nyidkyis bzo
bayis dpe legste yun
te mi gyur Yyungdung (la) brten
pai mkar 'adila
la(g) par stsogpao

Roman Transliteration

No. 1

phaggi Lola krib mal zhangsso

No. 2

phaggi lo diso va

No. 3

thing dang zang las thung pai do song
yotsa thi shong bum jugs ki
thung sras stag
char labcan yid kis zo
gis pe legs pe yuh
te pe gur yungdrung ten
pe khar 'adila
lag par togs pal

Translation

No. 1

In the pig-year [this] cenotaph was erected

No. 2

Written in the pig-year

No. 3

This cenotaph was erected by Stag-Ythsar-rlabs – can himself, who is the chief son of Khri-Shong [srong?] 'abum – rdugs, the master of the trade in the Lower Valley, born in the middle past of the village of mthing-brang this is a good picture of the conotaph. It was carved as a land – print on this lasting and unchangeable fort which belongs to the village of Yyung-drung.

Explanation

1. The above inscriptions were inscribed in between 8th and 10th Century A.D.
2. During above period traders passed through the above region.
3. To lookafter the trade-activities one fort was constructed near Indus.
4. The above inscriptions were found at Balu-mkhar. Thus to look-after the trade activities at Balu-mkhar one custom-officer (or Custom house officer) also known Mdo-ytsong-ytso was appointed. His duty was to guard. Rope bridge across the Indus river.

5. There was another custom-house on the north side of the above custom house called Shogam-la, the customs pass.

The Function of Custom-House Officer

Custom-house officer levied taxes upon traders who passed through the bridge. The tax was apparently levied in kind from i.e. tea, beads, cowries and sometimes in the form of cash. The goods were probably carried across the bridge by men and the baggage animals had to swim through the river. Sometimes they were being dragged across with ropes.

Sometimes custom house officer thought to exchange horses at the stage and that a fresh supply of horses at the stage. No doubt the custom house officer made the above system but it seemed to be impossible either to exchange horses at every stage and that a fresh supply of horses was kept waiting for them on the other bank of the river; or to pass other side of the river through rope bridge.

The traders after passing through Balu-mkhar track to mThingmo-gang, Hemis-Shugpacan, Likir, Basgo, Leh then to Yarkand.[5] The details are explained below:

Balu-mkhar → Khalatse → mThingmo-gang → Tantse → Nyemo → Leh

(1) After Balu-mkhar traders next halt was Khalatse, then mthingmo-gang. The path between Khalatse and mThingmo-gang was 10 miles. Traders while following this path first travelled along the Indus river for a few miles, then ascended and crossed the plain. Further they descended the valley to mThingmo-gang.

(2) From mThingmo-gang traders came to Tantse via—Hemis-Shugpacan after travelling seven miles distance.

(3) Thereafter they came to Nyemo via Basgo then they moved to Leh. The distance thus covered between Tantse to Leh was around 28 miles. At Basgo traders travelled on the main road and at Nyemo they left the Indus river and ascended the sandy plateau upto 11,200 ft from Leh.

There were two routes from Leh to Yarkand (a) summer trade route via Khardung, Saser and Karakoram passes (b) winter trade route via Digar, Agham, Pakra, etc.

In brief, the inscriptions found in Balu-mkhar give us good information about past trade activities in Ladakh.

Notes and References

1. Francke, A.H. :Archaeological miles on Balu-mkhar in Western Tibet' In : " The Indian Antiquary; Swati Pub., Delhi, 1985, Vol.XXCIV, pp.203-211.
2. *Ibid.*
3. *Ibid.*
4. The Balu-mkhar inscriptions indicate that the custom-house officer at Balu-mkhar was appointed by the Lamayuru monastery which acted as a mini king in Lower Ladakh that is head of the monastery exercised the powers like king. Thus, the income collected by custom house officers from the Central Asian traders was deposited at the monastery.

   From the above inscriptions we may understand that during 10 century A.D. Ladakh was divided into a great number of petty Kingdoms. Lamayuru monastery was considered one of the big Kingdom of Lower Ladakh. This monastery had its full administrative control from Khalatse, Wanla, Skrubuchan to Da & Hanu area. Today we can still see its monastic control over the monasteries located in the above areas.
5. On the trade route from Kashmir via Balu-mkhar to Yarkand the following facilities were available for traders on the different stoppages:

   (i) Caravan Sarai
   (ii) Fuel
   (iii) Encamping ground
   (iv) Dak Bungalow
   (v) Dispensary
   (vi) Forest rest house
   (vii) Grass, grazing ground
   (viii) Supplies
   (ix) Transport.

26

Some Rock, Stone and Wooden Sculptures of Ladakh

Prem Singh Jina
and
Manju Jina

Rock and stone sculptures of Buddha are found throughout in Ladakh. The maximum numbers of images were being made during 7th-10th century A.D. Here follow some of them.

1. ***20 cm Deep Carved Five Buddhas at Spadum in Zangskar of Kargil District.*** On the slope of the ridge towards the river, a little below the Spadum town one can see a huge boulder of at least 12 feet in height and at the north of it there are five figures of Buddha in deep relief. All these images are facing towards the Spadum. Zangskarese called them rGyalba rigs lnga. They are much above life-size, and cover a space of at least six yards square. The figure of the Buddha in the middle represents Maitreya, and the four other Buddhas are said to belong to period much earlier to 10th century A.D.
2. ***Maitreya Sculpture at Sani in Zangskar.*** This Maitreya image was first time highlighted by David L. Snellgrove during his visit to Zangskar in 1974-75. The above image is about 2 metres high and belongs to 7th to 9th century A.D.
3. ***Sculptures at Changspa Near Leh Town.*** There are two main statues: Buddha and Avalokitesvara. The sculpture of Buddha is in standing posture. Two Bodhisattvas are standing at its right and left side. The Maitreya image which is on the right side of Buddha carries a vessel wheras left side Avalokitesvara holds a flower. Two Gandharvas are placed above these images.

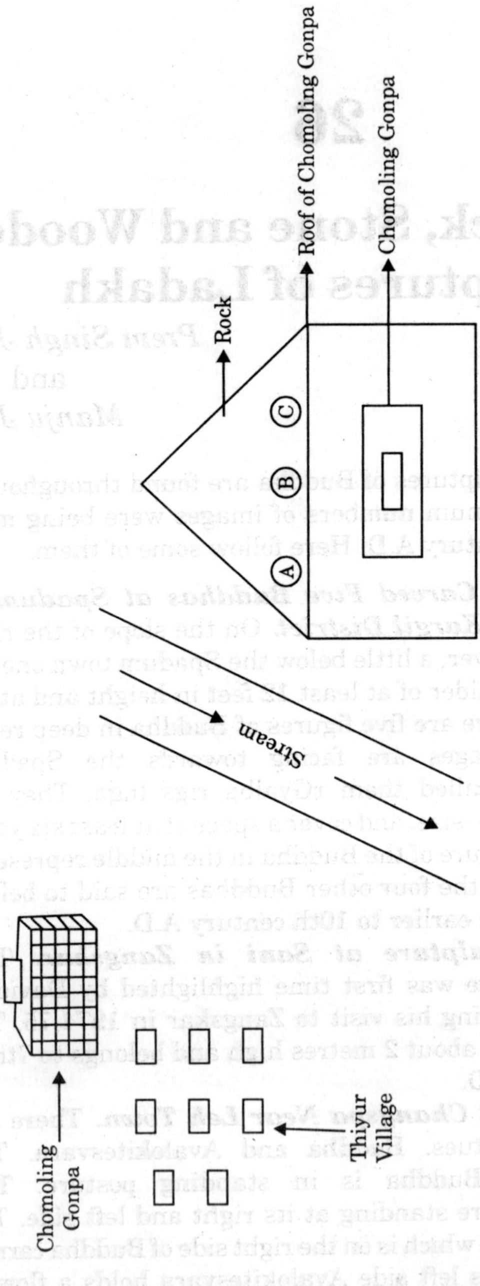

Fig. 26.1. Maitriya near Chomoling Gonpa (A), (B), (C) Maitreya images described.

4. ***Maitreya Sculptures near Chomoling Gonpa in Zangskar.*** About 2 km. from Chomoling Gonpa one can see three Maitreya sculptures on the rock right of stream Fig. 26.1.

Maitreya Sculpture A

(i) face: South of Ufti village
(ii) crown : Three
(iii) height : 10 feet
(iv) width : 4 feet

Maitreya Sculpture B

(i) height : 10 feet
(ii) width : 4 feet

Maitreya Sculpture C

(i) height : 10 feet
(ii) width : 4 feet

All the above sculptures of Maitreya are of 7-8th Century A.D.

5. Maitreya image at Hunder. In 1993 Dr Jina visited Hunder and near the Hunder temple below the bridge along the bank of stream. He saw a Maitreya engraved image on a big boulder. Ladakhis called it Me'me' rGyal-po. This image is caused on the soft rock, therefore, it is not clearly visible. However, it seems to be very old of a period even before 7th or 8th century A.D.

6. Me'me' Thuba image at Hunder (Nubra). There was another image of Me'me' Thuba just near the Maitreya at Hunder nalla below the bridge, but unfortunately it was not found. However, some villagers said that this image was destroyed by labourers while construction of a canal.

7. Chamba Jang Skyal Image at Tirche. The image engraved on a large rock lies just outside the village Tirch'e along the left bank of the Shyok. Measurements of this image are:

(i) Height : 10.5 feet
(ii) Wide along the chest : 4.00 feet

8. Chepak Met, Chamba, and Dolma Images Near Shankar Gonpa: There are four images of Chepak met,

Chamba, Dolma and one more Chamba images on stones are placed near Shankar Gonpa (Fig.26.2).

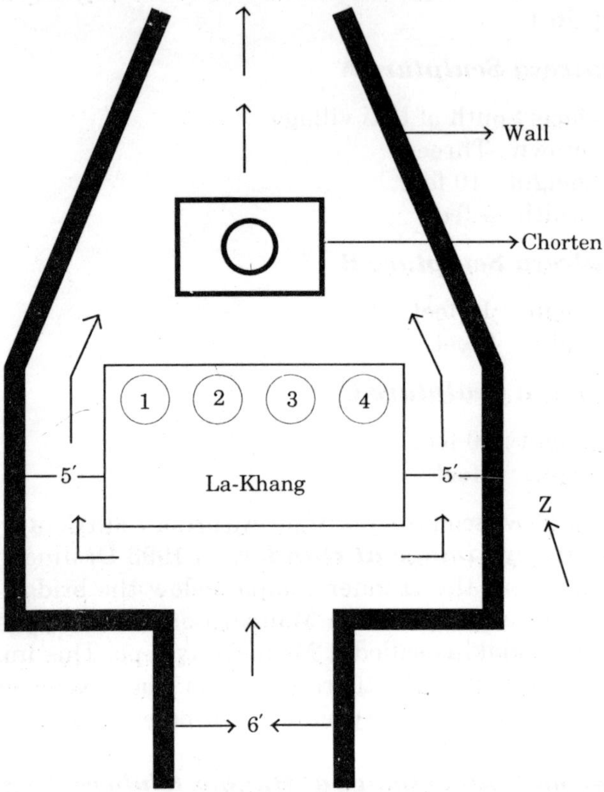

Fig. 26.2. Chepak Met, Chamba, and images near Shankar Gonpa.

(1) Chepak Met : Height 5'
width 2'3"

(2) Chamba : Height 4'6"
width 1'2"

(3) Chamba : Height 4"6"
width 2'

(4) Dolma : Height 3'9"
width 2'8"

The above images are of 9th-10th Century A.D.

9. Gyalva Chamba image in Chanspa (Leh). Near the source of spring water at Chanspa just across the metalled road there is one image of Chamba or Metreya Buddha with three coned crowns of about 9th-10th Century A.D. (Fig. 26.3).

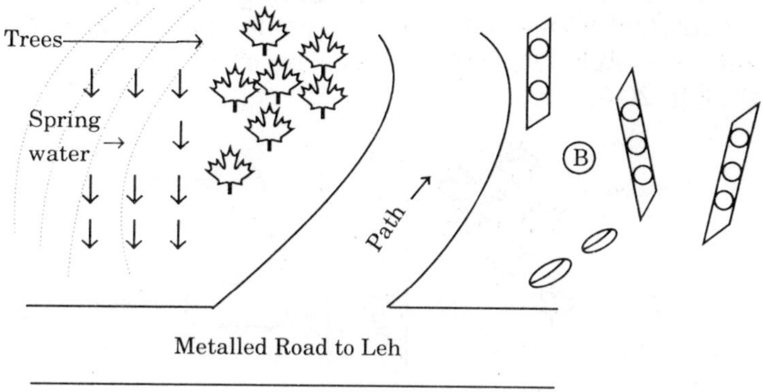

(B) Gya Chamba = Maitreya Buddha
Height : 4'
Width : 3'
Rounded name
Chortens

Fig. 26.3. Gyalva Chamba image in Chamba (Leh).

10. Three Coned Crown Maitreya Image Near Gong Guest House (Leh).

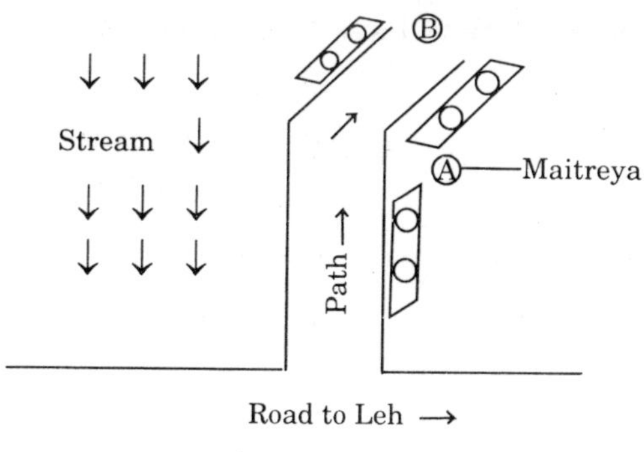

Chorten (B) Maitreya image.

Fig. 26.4. Maitreya image in Changspa.

In Changspa there is one more Maitreya image of 7th to 9th Century A.D. (Fig.26.4).

Maitreya Image : height 4'

Standing posture : width 3½'

11. Buddhas & Chorten Image at Chote Rantak (Leh). At Chote Rantak near Leh town on a stone Buddha and Chorten images are engraved. These images are of 9th to 10th Century A.D. (Fig. 26.5).

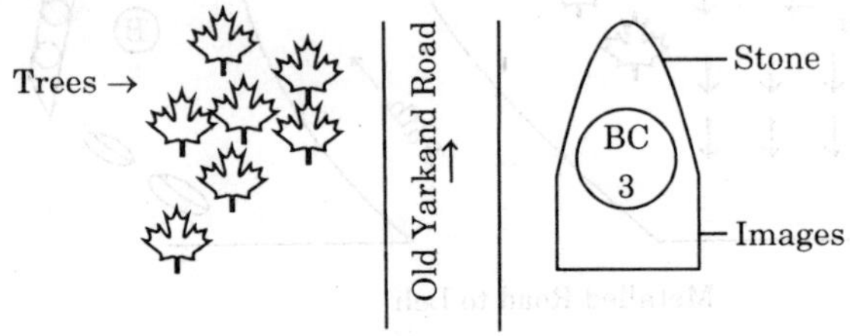

Fig. 26.5. Buddha and Chorten images at Chote Rantak.

BC 3 = (1) Buddha height 4'4" width 1'11"
Chorten on the other side (Upper side)—2'11" × 1'1"
At the lower side Buddha image 7" × 9"
(2) Second side Buddha 3"6" × 1'1"
(3) Third side Buddha 3'5" × 1'6"

12. Maitreyas Statues at Chorten Backside of SBI Leh. There are two Maitreyas statues at Kaa-Ling Chorten back side of SBI Leh road. One image is in standing posture and the other is in sitting posture. Both have five coned crowns (Fig.26.6).

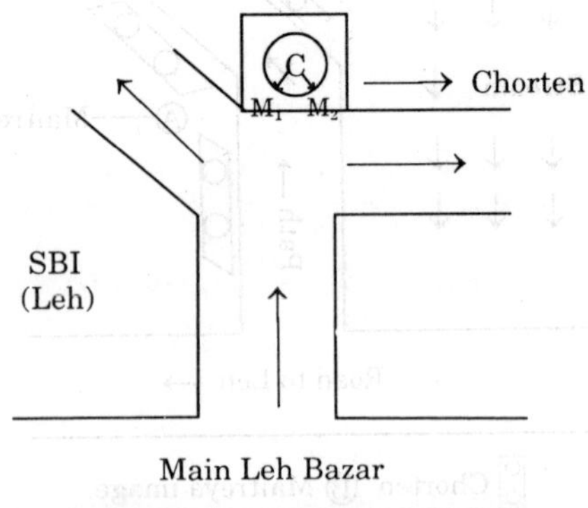

Fig. 26.6. Maitreya images at Leh town of 7th to 10th Century A.D.

Chorten.

M_1 Maitreya : height 2'
: width 1½'

M_2 Maitreya : height 3'
width 2'

Besides, there are many big images throughout in Ladakh popular among them are—Buddha image near Housing Colony, Maitreya images at Shey, Chamba at Mulbek and Maitreya at Kartse.

27

Ladakh : Before and During the Indo-Pak War (1947)

Prem Singh Jina
and
Rev. Konchok Namgyal

Ladakh Before 1947

Ladakh was one of the most backward region before 1947 it had no motorable road. Traders carried their loads on horses, sheep, goat, etc. Leh was the only town and market for exchanging their goods. During summer season trade routes were busy with traders who carried merchandise goods from India and its neighbouring countries. But during winter these routes seemed to be barren. Therefore, Ladakhis purchased all necessary items from traders and produced food stuff during summer and stored them for the sever cold winters.

Taxation

Ladakh was partially ruled by Britishers in 1896, and thereafter continued till independence. In those days British Government had one commissioner at Leh who looked after the trade activities and local administration. He imposed taxes on Ladakhis in the following manner.

(i) Zinis (Jinis). This tax was levied upon farmers. Under this tax system each farmer of Ladakh had to give prescribed quantity of his annual agricultural production to the government godown.

(ii) Mund*[1] *(Mun). British India Government under Commissionor's orders annually collected one *mund* from each farmer of Ladakh. However, farmers were not happy with this decision. And often one could hear the following remarks usually passed by one farmer to another:

"Kagale ! the fire wood bundle which you are carrying must be very heavy, because it goes to governmnet as Govt. Mund. Oh No ! our government now-a-days becomes cruel. How could we rid from this ? Om Mane..... Om..... Mane.....".

(iii) Anna. In Ladakh a farmer can produce only one crop in a year. The situation became serious when poor or low landholding farmers also were bound to pay tax in cash. So, they paid the tax after borrowing money from landlords on higher interest which they sometimes were unable to return in their whole life, later their generation faced additional loan burden.

The tax was 4 to 8 Anna/family/year[2] depending upon the family structure.

(iv) Bari. During every summer the British Commissioner along with his staff visited Leh. The local officers then ordered each family turn by turn to offer their services to him. Subsequently, Ladakhis on the way to Leh were ready for their services according to Bari[3] at each Dak[4] and Para[5]. And arranged horses for them if they asked for. For example-between Nurla and Leh. Ladakhis would then offer their free service at the following Daks and Para. (Table: 27.1).

Thus, lamas were also not exampted by the British Government. During the visit of British Commissioner and his junior officers they had to perform mask dance in their honour. And Ladakhis had to arrange 'Palki' at each 'Para' for their wifes and dogs.

Indo-Pak War

In 1947 India got independence, Jammu and Kashmir was then automatically included in the Indian Republic. Pakistan did not like this and attacked on India from Skardu side. Skardu tehsil then came under Ladakh district and had only a few soldiers there, even at district headquarter at Leh only some soldiers were on duty. Hawaldar Konchok Tandar of Phyang was among a few Ladakhis who was attached with Dogras at Zorawar fort, Leh. Thus, Pakistanis did not face any difficulty while entering in Ladakh and easily captured Indian territory upto Nimu.

Pt. Doloo was then at Education Department and posted at Leh. As he came to know about Pakistani's hostile activities

TABLE 27.1
The Details of Dak, Para and Lama dance between Nurla and Spituk on the Visit of British Commissioner

S. No.	*Dak*	*Para*	*Lama dance*	*Remarks*
1.	Nurla	—	—	—
2.	Rizong	—	by Rezong Monastery	—
3.	Saspol	—	—	—
4.	Likir	Horses may be asked	by Likir Monastery	Sometimes Palki has to provide
5.	Bazgo	—	—	—
6.	Nimu	—	—	—
7.	Taru	—	—	—
8.	Phyang	Horses may be asked	by Phyang Monastery	(a) Sometimes Palki may be asked (b) Lamas of Phyang Monastery welcomed them at Phyang Nala.
9.	Spituk	—	by Spituk Monastery	Lamas of Spituk monastery welcome them at Government garden.

and their entrance up to Nimu, he immediately sent all this information to government of India in Delhi. The government at first didn't take it seriously. However, later it sent troops to Ladakh via Lahul and Spiti. Hawaldar Nawang Mindol, Gyaltsen, etc., who were on duty at Leh passed this information to Pt. Doloo. He immediately arranged 50 horses and Yaks and sent them alongwith some Ladakhis to Gya, Miru, Rupshu and Kharnak. When Indian troops reached at Rupshu they were welcomed by Ladakhis and showed the path up to Leh. At Leh all Ladakhis including important personalities warmly welcomed Indian troops. Later, they immediately formed National Guard and Home Guard by Ladakhi Youths and gave them military training.

In the meanwhile the Govt. of India sent another contingent of troops under the command of Major Hari Chand via Zoji-la. This contingent had 30 Dogra sodiers. After reaching at Leh, Major Hari Chand divided the troops into two groups: Dogra ad Karja, and gave them intensive military training.

Construction of Leh Airport

When Pakistani troops attacked upon Ladakh, Sonam Norboo was posted as Junior Engineer at Srinagar Airport. He immediately marched to Leh with 5-6 rifles. After reaching Leh he took the responsibility for the construction of Leh Airport at Abi Chenme Thang. He employed labourers and started war level construction work and within a few months made temporary Airport for light aircraft landing. In 1948 Col. Thimaya and Air Commander Mehar Singh landed at Leh. Col. Thimaya addressed Indian soldiers and returned with Major Hari Chand. Thereafter Major Hari Chand came to Leh with 300 Gorkha soldiers by Air.

Pakistani Forces in Shyam

Indian defence was quite unaware of the sudden attack of Pakistani forces on Ladakh. Therefore, India had no sufficient forces in Ladakh and particularly at Pakistan border. Pakistani forces did not face any major fight at the border and easily reached up to Hemis-Shukpachan in Shyam area. At Hemis-Shukpachan India had one post in which some soldiers were on duty. Nayab Subedar of Chushod was among them. When the Pakistani troops marched ahead they opened fire on them.

Nayab Subedar fought bravely and at last lost his life. Thereafter Pakistani soldiers spread throughout the Shyam area, some of them even reached up to Taru mountains.

Battle at Taru

India had another post at the top of Taru mountains. As Pakistani soldiers advanced towards Taru mountains. Indian soldiers opened fire and a heavy battle took place. Indian army then had its base camp at 'Staskar Ce' government garden in Taru Village. At 'Pulucan' house they had a mess in which Ladakhis voluntarily offered their services and supplied food at their own costs to soldiers who were posted at Taru mountains.

The Taru battle lasted for a long period, therefore, Indian army faced severe ration shortage. Ladakhi Gonpas and rich people of Ladakh then arranged ration for them. Those who had milched cows carried them to Taru Tokpo Army mess for meeting their milk demand turn by turn. One day Phyang Naro's grandmother Palkit brought her white milch cow along with Phyang pa Konchok Namgyal. At the Army mess she felt happy to give her cow's milk to Indian soldiers. Addressing to them she said :

> "Today I am very happy to offer my services to the brave Indian soldiers who are fighting for the safety of our country."

Similarly Konchok Namgyal's brother Sonam Joldan was among those who offered his milk cow to Taru Tokpo mess.

Tseri Post

India had its main post at Tseri mountains when heavy battle was in progress. Ladakhi podders had great role to carry weapons to Tseri post. One day when Ladakhi podders were carrying weapons to Tseri post, the Pakistani army got this information and attacked on them. Tondup Paljor (Zokorpa) lost his life in this incident. Soonafter Pakistani troops gathered at Nimo and at night attacked on Kongka village. Thereafter, a hand to hand combat took place. Pakistani side recorded heavy casualty. At last only two Pakistani soldiers were left who later left the Pakistani post and ran away to an unknown place. Indian forces marched ahead and collected Pakistani dead bodies at one place and thereafter constructed Chortens on them. Indian troops then further advanced and recaptured all the posts from Pakistani army except Skardu and Gilgit area. In this war many Ladakhi civilians lost their lives, popular among them were Phyangpa Phunchok Tashi, Rigzin Angdus of Phokar, etc.

References

1. Mund = 40 kgs.
2. Aana = One Aana = 6 paise
   Four Aana = 25 paise
   Eight Aana = 50 paise
   Sixteen Aana = 100 paise (= One Rupee)
3. Bari : The labour who worked without asking any kind of wage.
4. Dak : It was the stoppage where Ladakhis were ready to offer their services for the British officers.
5. Para : One Para = 4 Daks.

PART V
Medicine

28

Origin and Growth of Ladakhi Medicine (Amchi) System

Prem Singh Jina
and
Thinles Yangzor

The Ayurvedic classics were written prior to the birth of Lord Buddha. Many medicinal plants were brought to India from the Himalayas in order to develop Ayurvedic medicines.[1] This system later influenced Buddha. Tibetan scholars believe that Buddha is indirectly connected to the knowledge of medicine because he cured suffering by his spiritual power.[2] After the *parinirvana* of Buddha, Buddhism suffered upto a great extent. Some Buddhist scholars wanted to improve Vinaya rules according to time while others disagreed. Moreover, Buddhism continued its hold in India as well as in the neighbouring countries. During Kushana period, i.e., 2nd century A.D. it had good hold in central Asian countries. But after the influence of Hinduism and Islamic culture, Buddhism drifted away from India and continued in Tibet and in neighbouring Himalayan countries. Tibet thereafter became the main centre of Buddhism. In 5th century Nyathi Tsenpo became the king of Tibet. During his reign two Indian physicians Vijay and Gajay visited Tibet. They practised there and imparted their medical knowledge. Later Gajay married one queen. His son Dungi Thorchog followed father's knowledge of medicine and gradually became an outstanding physician. He was appointed as the first physician of the king. His family lineage continued to 18th century when Yuthok Yonten Ganpo Sarma became the famous Tibetan doctor.[3]

Till Sinyen, the above tradition was as oral form. Lodroe Sinyen was the first person who introduced the medical writings in Tibet. His son Yuthok Drechi Becha visited India three times. During his period four medical *tantras* were translated from Sanskrit language.[4] Gradually this tradition spread in Ladakh and is popularly known as Amchi.

Here follows a list of medicinal plants which Amchi use in the preparation of medicines.

1. ***Tib.*** byi-bzung (Chi-zung)
   Bot. *Arctium leppa*

Properties :

Taste. Bitter.

Parts used for medicines. Roots, leaves and fruits.

Collection period. July-September.

Location in Ladakh. Every village near water banks. It cures fever, lung fever, gall-bladder stone, poison and pimples.

2. ***Tib.*** Aom-bu (Om-bu)
   Bot. *Myrkaria bracteata* (Royal)

Properties :

Taste. Salt mixed sweet.

Parts used for medicines. Leaves and inner parts of stem.

Collection period. July-October.

Location in Ladakh. All nallas in Ladakh.

It cures fever, poison, pimples, boil, swelling in foot (in Tibetan language called Boṃ).

3. ***Tib.*** Lug-mig
   Bot. *Aster souliei* (French)

Properties :

Taste. Bitter.

Parts used for medicines. Flowers and leaves.

Collection period. July-September.

Location in Ladakh. Khardong La top height 18,000 ft. to 18,500 ft.

It cures lung diseases, cough, fever and poison. It has cooling property.

4. ***Tib.*** Rgya-khur (Pron. gya-khur)
Bot. *Picris hieracioides* (L. Ssp. Fuscipilosus Hand, Mzt).

Properties.

Taste. Salt mixed bitter.
Parts used for medicines. Whole plant.
Collection period. July-September.
Location in Ladakh. Every village 1500 ft. to 16,000 ft.

It cures lung diseases, cough, chest pain, boil, fever and asthma. It has slightly heating properties.

5. ***Tib.*** Gan-rda-rba-dra
(Pron. gan-da-ba-da)
Bot. *Gnaphalium affine* (D. Don Sapi).

Properties :

Taste. Sweet.
Parts used for medicines. Whole plant.
Collection period. July-August.
Location in Ladakh. Khardong La and Zangskar tehsil of Kargil district, 15,000 ft. to 18,500 ft. from the SLV.

It cures liver, lung and stomach diseases/pain, boil, swelling at foot and infection by air. It stimulates the power of digestion and improves overall health.

6. ***Tib.*** glu-bdut-rdo-rze
(*Pron.* Lu-dut-do-ze)
Bot. *Adenophora lilifolioides* (Pax et. Hoffm).

Properties :

Taste. Sweet mixed with bitter.
Parts used for medicines. Whole plant.
Collection period. July-October.
Location in Ladakh. It is found in Shyam side, viz., Alchi, Sapi and Kargil districts.

It cures lung fever, cough, Arthritis and goitre diseases. It has cooling property.

7. ***Tib.*** Sao-lo-dmar-po
(Pron. Solo marpo)
Bot. *Rhodiola seera* (Prain Fu).

Properties :

Taste. Sweet.
Parts used for medicines. Roots.
Collection period. July-October.

Location in Ladakh. It is found in every village located in 15,000 ft. to 18,000 ft. from SLV.

It cures lung diseases, bleeding in cough, tuberculosis, asthma and leucoreas.

8. ***Tib.*** pa-yag-rca-ba
(Pron. payagca-va)
Bot. *Lancea tibetia* (Hook *f. et. Thoms*)

Properties :

Taste. Sweet-bitter.

Parts used for medicines. Whole plant.

Collection period. July-September.

Location in Ladakh. It is found in nallas of every village located 10,000 ft. to 13,000 ft. from SLV.

It cures tuberculosis, lung fever, poison, cough and asthma. It has cooling property.

9. ***Tib.*** sro-lo-smug -po
(Pron. so lo mug po)
Bot. *Solms laubachia* (sp.)

Properties :

Taste. Bitter.

Parts used for medicines. Roots.

Collection periods. July-October.

Location in Ladakh. It is found in high mountain passes, viz., Khardong La, Sapi, etc. Besides it is found in Chang-Thang area of Leh district.

It cures lung fever, cough and stops bleeding. It is cold in potency.

10. ***Tib.*** byiau la phug
(Pron. Chiu lo phug)
Bot. *Malcolmia africana* (L. R. Br.)

Properties :

Taste. Bitter.

Parts used for medicines. Seeds.

Collection period. July-September.

Location in Ladakh. It is found in Zangskar tehsil in Kargil district and Shyam side of Leh district.

It cures weak spleen, boil, swelling of hands and legs, chest pain, lungs diseases, tuberculosis and foot poison. And is cold in potency.

10. ***Tib.*** Skyer-pa
(Pron. Sker-pa)

Bot. Berberis dictyophylla Franch var epruinosa Schneid.

Properties :

Taste. Bitter.

Parts used for medicines. Fruits and fruit's peel.

Collection period. July-October.

Location in Ladakh. It is found on high altitude mountains (10,000 ft-16,500 ft.) viz., Khardong La, North Polo and Markha valley.

It cures eyes problems, small intestine fever, mouth infection, kidney fever, and dysentary or dyspepsia. It is cold in potency.

12. ***Tib.*** Khur Mang
(Pron. Khur mang)
Bot. *Taraxacum tibeticum* (Hand Mzt)

Properties :

Taste. Sweet with slightly bitter.

Parts used for medicines. Whole plant.

Collection period. May-October

Location in Ladakh. In every village lying in between 10,000 ft.-17,000 ft.

It cures ear problems, nerve infections, throat infection, breast and nipple infection, stomach and liver fever, bone infection, boil or *pitta* problems and jaundice diseases.

13. ***Tib.*** bre-ga
(Pron. De ga)
Bot. *Caspi arvene* (L.)

Properties :

Taste. Bitter.

Parts used for medicines. Fruits.

Collection period. July-October.

Location in Ladakh. Sapi side in Kargil district.

It cures lung infection, pimples, cough, kidney fever,

semen problem, leucoreas, joints pain. It stimulates the power of digestion.

It is cold in potency.

14. ***Tib.*** dres-ma
(Pron. Tes-ma)
Bot. *Iris ensata* (Thumb)

Properties :

Taste. Salty with slight bitter

Parts used for medicines. Seeds and flowers.

Collection period. July-August.

Location in Ladakh. It is found in high altitude mountains (10,000 ft. to 15,000 ft.) from SLV.

It cures throat infection, boil, fever, liver fever, pimples and viral infection. It also cures poisoning, stops bleeding from nose, blood vomitting and bleeding. It is cold in potency.

15. ***Tib.*** Spang-ram
(Pron. Pang ram)
Bot. *Polygrum sphaerostachyum* (Meism)

Properties :

Taste. Sweet mixed bitter.

Parts used for medicines. Roots.

Collection period. July-October.

Location in Ladakh. It is found in nallas of high altitude mountains (10,000 ft-18,500 ft) and in high passes such as Khardong la, Talung la etc.

It cures mouth infection, boil, teeth infection, fever, dysentery and Pyrrohea. It also cures burn-skin and stop poisoning. It is cold in potency.

16. ***Tib.*** hong leng
(Pron. hung len)
Bot. *Pierorrhiza scrophulariaegolia* (Pennell)

Properties :

Taste. Bitter.

Parts used for medicines. Roots.

Collection period. July-October.

Location in Ladakh. It is found in high altitude mountains (10,000 ft.-16,000 ft.) in Zangskar tehsil and Sapi in Kargil district.

It cures liver infection, control blood pressure, fever and stops poisoning. It helps in headache and consist of cold in potency.

17. ***Tib.*** Chu-rcai nag po.
(Pron. Churci nag po)
Bot. *Polygonum polystachyum* (wall)

Properties :

Taste. Chilly with bitter.

Parts used for medicines. Whole plant.

Collection Period. July-October

Location in Ladakh. Every where in Ladakh but mostly find along nallas.

It cures leg swelling, joint pain, boil, cuts and remove the excess of water storage. Churci nag po is cold in potency.

18. ***Tib.*** Gang-ga chung
(Pron. Gangachung)
Bot. *Gentiana H. Sm*

Properties :

Taste. Bitter.

Parts used for medicines. Whole plant.

Collection period. July-September.

Location in Ladakh. It is commonly Sapi in Kargil district.

It cures fever, cough, dysentery and tonsils. It is cold in potency.

19. ***Tib.*** rca mikharisa janpa
(Pron. Ca-this Jan-pa)
Bot. *Ixeris gracilis* (D.C.)

Properties :

Taste. Bitter.

Parts used for medicine. Whole plant.

Collection period. July-August.

Location in Ladakh. It is found in every village in Ladakh lying in between 10,000 ft-17,000 ft. from SLV.

It cures fever, *Pitta* infection, and stop poisoning. It helps to stop vomitting.

20. ***Tib.*** zangs-rci-dkar-po
(Pron.-*zans ci Karpo*)
Bot. *Galium spurium* (L.)

Particulars :

Taste. Sweet with slightly bitter.

Parts used for medicines. Whole plant.

Collection period. July-October.

Location in Ladakh. It is found near Zangskar in Kargil district.

It cures urinary infection, pain in bones, fever and stops bleeding from nose. It is normal in potency.

21. ***Tib.*** pha-ba-dgo-dgo
(Pron. pha ba go go)
Bot. *Cavatia Sp.*

Properties :

Taste. Chilly bitter.

Parts used for medicines. Whole plant.

Collection period. July-September.

Location in Ladakh. It is found in every village in Ladakh lying in between 10,000 ft to 17,000 ft from SLV).

It cures tonsils, cough, lung infection, fever and throat infection. It also stops bleeding from nose.

It is normal in potency.

22. ***Tib.*** yu-gu-shing-dkar-po
(Pron. yu gu shing kar po)
Bot. *Senecio dianthus* (French)

Properties :

Taste. Bitter.

Parts used for medicines. Whole plant.

Collection period. July-September.

Location in Ladakh. Markha and Sapi Valleys.

It cures foot swelling, fever, joint pain and itching. It is useful in dressing while accident.

It is cold in potency.

23. ***Tib.*** rca va
(Pron. ca va)
Bot. *Loydia serotina* (Reichb)

Properties :

Taste. Bitter.

Parts used for medicines. Whole plant.

Collection period. June-July.

Location in Ladakh. It is found in every village and high altitude mountains at the height of 10,000 ft to 18,500 ft from SLV. It is mostly found in Zangskar in Kargil tehsil and Khardong La in Leh district.

It purifies blood and gives strength to eyes. It helps to dry pus and stops the water formation between joints.

It is normal in potency.

24. ***Tib.*** Par pa ta

Bot. *Hypecoum leptcarpum* (Hook f. et. Thoms)

Properties :

Taste. Bitter

Parts used for medicines. Whole plant.

Collection period. July-August.

Location in Ladakh. Skati, Phyang, Nemo and villages lying between 10,000 ft. to 12000 ft from SLV.

It cures fever, lever infection and headache.

25. ***Tib.*** *Chu-rug-sbal-lag*

(Pron. *chu rug bal lag*)

Bot. *Halespestes sarmentosa* (Adns Kom)

Properties :

Taste. Sweet.

Parts used for medicines. Whole plant.

Collection period. July-September.

Location in Ladakh. It is found in Shey, Smalla and all water logged areas.

It cures pain between joints and foot swelling. It is normal in potency.

26. ***Tib.*** Nya lcae bas

Pron. Nya Cibs

Bot. *Spirogyra longata* (Vauch) Kuetz

Properties :

Taste. Bitter.

Parts used for medicines. Whole plant.

Collection period. July-October.

Location in Ladakh. Every where in Ladakh in water logged places.

It cures burned skin, dry up water at the injured parts and throat infection.

27. ***Tib.*** Khye Mig
Bot. *Hetropapus crenatifolius* (Hzt) Griers

Properties :

Taste. Bitter

Parts used for medicines. Flowers.

Collection period. July-September.

Location in Ladakh. It is found in Sapi and Khardong la lying between 11,000 ft. to 15,500 ft.) from SLV.

It cures lung fever and infection and is cold in potency.

28. ***Tib.*** Aa byag cher snon
(Pron. Aa cak cher snon)
Bot. *Meconopsis horridula* (Hook. f. et. Thom.)

Properties :

Taste. Bitter.

Parts used for medicines. Whole plant.

Collection period. July-October.

Location in Ladakh. It is found in Sapi and Zangskar tehsil of Kargil district.

It cures bone fever and back pain. It joins bone cracks and is cold in potency.

29. ***Tib.*** mche-ldum
(Pron. che-dum)
Bot. *Ephedra saxatilis* (Royle)

Properties :

Taste. Bitter like chilly.

Parts used for medicines. Whole plant.

Collection period. August-October.

Location in Ladakh. It is found everywhere in high altitude mountains of Ladakh lying between 10,000 ft. to 18,000 ft.

It cures cough, sneezing and shivering.

It stops menses and bleeding. It helps to get relief from tension and stops the excess water formation.

mche ldum is hot in potency.

30. ***Tib.*** byi rug ser po
(Pron. zee rug serpo)
Bot. *Nepeta cataria* (L.)

Properties :

Taste. Bitter like chilly

Parts used for medicines. Whole plant.

Collection period. July-September.

Location in Ladakh. It is found in every village in Ladakh lying in between 10,000 ft. to 13,000 ft. from SLV.

It cures cough, headach, fever, small pox, blood vomitting, throat infection and throat swelling. It also used for the treatment of blood diarrohea and stops the flow of blood coming out from nails. It is hot in potency.

31. ***Tib.*** rca mkharis zan pa

Bot. *Ixeris gracilis* (D.C.)

Properties :

Taste. Bitter.

Parts used for medicines. Whole plant.

Collection period. July-August.

Location in Ladakh. It is found in Nimo, Taru and at the surrounds of Leh.

It cures headache, liver infection and jaundice. It also helps in removing the infection in nervous system. It is cold in potency.

32. ***Tib.*** dvang lag

Bot. *Spiranthes sinensis* (Pers) *Ames*

Properties :

Taste. Sweet with bitterness.

Parts used for medicine. Roots.

Collection period. September-November.

Location in Ladakh. It is found in Nubra, Zangskar and Kargil.

It is useful for sex and health. It is a good tonic and purifies blood. dvang lag cures kidney and gall-bladder problems.

33. ***Tib.*** va sha ka

Bot. *Veronica ciliata* Fisch

Properties :

Taste. Bitter.

Parts used for medicines. Whole plant.

Collection period. July-September.

Location in Ladakh. Spituk, Shey, Thiksey, Chusod, Sabu and at the vicinity of Leh town.

It cures headache, blood pressure, fever, liver infection, piles and jaundice.

It is cold in potency.

34. ***Tib.*** bya rgod spos

(Pron. ca god spos)

Bot. *Delphiniun brunonia* (Um Royal)

Properties :

Taste. Bitter.

Parts used for medicines. Whole plant.

Collection period. August-September.

Location in Ladakh. It is found in high mountains of Nimo, Zangskar and Khardong la (12,000-15,500 ft).

It cures fever, poison formation, sneezing and skin diseases.

It removes itches and poison of snake bite. It alleviates *vayu.*

It is cold in potency.

35. ***Tib.*** abu su hang

(Pron. bu su hung)

Bot. *Hydrocotyle nepalensis* (Hook)

Properties :

Taste. Bitter.

Parts used for medicines. Whole plant.

Collection period. July-September.

Location in Ladakh. It is found in every village near nallas (10,000 ft. to 17,000 ft.)

It cures cough, boil, fever, stomach poison, dysentry, liver fever, pimples, diarrhoea and foot swelling. It improves digestive system.

It is cold in potency.

36. ***Tib.*** sum bcu tig

(Pron. sum cu tig)

Bot. *Saxifraga pasumensis* Marg et. shaw, f. Intgrifolia Jeeir

Properties :

Taste. Bitter.

Parts used for medicines. Whole plant.

Collection period. July-August.

Location in Ladakh. Zangskar tehsil of Kargil district (11,000 ft. to 15,000 ft.).

It cures cough, fever, liver poison, food poison and boil.

It is cold in potency.

37. ***Tib.*** sno-sprin

(Pron. Sno tin*)*

Bot. *Thalictrum foetidum* (L.)

Properties :

Taste. Bitter.

Parts used for medicines. Whole plant.

Collection period. June-September.

Location in Ladakh. All villages lying in 9000 ft. to 15,000 ft.

It cures high blood pressure (hypertension), fever, boils and pain between joints. It is useful for diarrhoea and is cold in potency.

38. ***Tib.*** stong-zil

(Pron. stongzil)

Bot. *Corydalis boweri* (Hemse)

Properties :

Taste. Bitter.

Parts used for medicines. Whole plant.

Collection period. June-September.

Location in Ladakh. It is found in Nimo and Zangskar (10,000 ft. to 16,000 ft. from SLV).

It cures stomach fever and diarrhoea.

It is cold in potency.

39. ***Tib.*** gsergi me tog

(Pron. ger gi metog)

Bot. *Hearpetospermam caudigarum* (wall)

Properties :

Taste. Bitter.

Parts used for medicines. Whole plant.

Collection period. August-September.

Location in Ladakh. Nimo, Likir and at the viscinity of Leh town.

It cures fever, poison formation, liver problems, boil, piles (seed pile) and jaundice. It stimulates digestive system.

It is cold in potency.

40. ***Tib.*** lcags tig nag po
(Pron. cag tig nag po)
Bot. *Gentianopsis paludosa* (Monro Ma)

Properties :

Taste. Bitter.

Parts used for medicine. Whole plant.

Collection period. July-September.

Location in Ladakh. It is found in Zangskar and Sapi lying between 11,000 ft. to 15,000 ft. from SLV.

It cures fever, hypertension, blood pressure, kidney and stomach fever and jaundice.

It is cold in potency.

41. ***Tib.*** spang- rgyan dakar po
(Pron. span gyan karpo)
Bot. *Gentiana algida* pall

Properties :

Taste. Bitter

Parts used for medicines. Flowers.

Collection period. July-September.

Location in Ladakh. It is found in Chang-Thang region in Leh district (13,000 ft. to 15,000 ft.).

It cures lung diseases, liver and stomach infections, boil fever, lung fever, cough fever, throat infection, chest pain and asthma.

It also cures vaginal and penis infection.

It is useful for itching and helps to stop excess of water formation while in fever. It is cold in potency.

42. ***Tib.*** ser po rgu drus
Bot. *Senecio scandens* buch ham

Properties :

Taste. Bitter.

Parts used for medicine. Whole plant.

Collection period. July-September.

Location in Ladakh. It is found in all villages lying 10,000 ft to 15,000 ft.

It cures fever, liver fever, itching, pile and boil.

It promotes eye sight and cures injured portion of the body.

It is normal in potency.

43. ***Tib.*** spang rcai rdo bo
Bot. *Pterocephalus hookeri* (Hook)

Properties :

Taste. Bitter.

Parts used for medicine. Whole plant.

Collection period. June-September.

Location in Ladakh. It is found in all villages of 10,000 ft to 15,000 ft.

It cures foot swelling, sneezing, fever, heart fever, blood fever. It is useful for pain between joints and works as pain killer.

It is cold in potency.

44. ***Tib.*** gzer azam me tog
Bot. *Chrysanthemum tatsienense* (Bur et. Franch)

Properties :

Taste. Bitter.

Parts used for medicines. Whole plant.

Collection period. June-August.

Location in Ladakh. It is found in all villages lying in between 12,000 ft. to 17,000 ft.

It cures pain between joints, infection in nervous system. It is very useful in bone crackes.

It is cold in potency.

Notes and Reference

1. Das, Bhagwan : *Tibetan Medicine : with special references and Yoga sataka,* Tibetan works and Archives, Dharamshala, H.P. 1976 (Re-print 1980), p. 3.
2. Khangskar, Lobsang Dolma : *Lectures on Tibetan Medicine*, K. Dhondup (ed.), Tibetan Works and Archives, Dharamshala; 1986, p. 4.
3. *Ibid.* p. 5.
4. *Ibid.*

The authors of this study are aware of their limitation to undertake this type of research work. There may be the possibility of controversies on the above research work. But this is the first research work of its kind, therefore, controversies may be welcome.

PART VI
Personality

29

Morup Namgial : A Famous Ladakhi Artist

Prem Singh Jina

Ladakh has rich cultural heritage. When Buddhism disappeared from Kashmir and rest of India, Ladakh turned towards Tibet for cultural and political relations. Many learned Lamas then invited in Ladakh for the preservation and development of Buddhist culture and religion. Consequently, Buddhist monasteries were established during 10th and later centuries according to the directions of concerned Lamas/Rinpoches. Thus, Buddhist society in Ladakh also influenced by the Mahayana Buddhist orders. Gradually Buddhist monasteries started 'Cham' (Lama dance) in their respective monasteries during winter season when people had no work in fields. They enjoyed to see Lama dance and chant 'Om Mani Padme Hum' mantra. Ladakhis also started to organise different festivals and functions. On this occasion they performed the following dances according to the function :

1. Tasok chemo
2. Kompa somsek
3. Koshen sches
4. Chabskyang sches
5. Mentok Padme sches
6. Tashispe sches
7. Nyope sches

Similarly they sang the following songs :

1. Sandi
2. Chos ho
3. Cu ho

4. Gang ho
5. Skyo ho
6. Son ho
7. Jak ho
8. Chang ho
9. Ghar ho
10. Gar ho
11. Jab ro

Such a rich cultural atmosphere of Ladakh influenced Morup Namgil who presented the following dances in the new form with possible acceptable changes.

1. Spavo
2. Cherches
3. Sondol
4. Aale Yati
5. Alo
6. Jingpa
7. Shon kalima
8. Tasis pa.
9. Zabro
10. Apo-Abi

The renowed Ladakhi artist Morup Namgail was born on 16th April 1947 in the village Wanla, 113 kms. from Leh. In a respectable Buddhist family known for its loristic knowledge, and was destined to be the muscial one in the family. As there was no school in his native village, he had to go to village Tingmosgang for schooling. Later he proceeded to Leh where he had been lucky to meet Khanpo Geshes Ishey Tundup and Shri Tashi Rabgais, the reknowned scholars and to work with them.

Morup Namgail is a versatile artist, gifted with a melodious voice, staging standardized dramas, superb dance performances. His talent flourished and he soon became the premier artist in Ladakh.

Just after the commission of All India Radio Leh, Morup Namgail used to present the Ladakhi music on casual basis and was declared as B-high vocalist by the Local Audition Board on 1st April 1972. On 23rd May 1977 he was appointed as an instrumentalist (Damyan Playon) and graded as B, and in view of his remarkable talent and capability the authorities of AIR promoted him to the post of music composer in 1991 and was soon up-graded as a composer grade 1st in 1994. Since then he has been controlling listeners by his super performance as producer, director, actor, singer, talker, writer, composer and narrator. On account of his varied talents and capabilities he has been entrusted different assignments in the Broadcasting media and his output is tremendous. His dramas and other productions are infinite, while his narration of talk tales have made many tales alive, his commentaries have made events vivid and memorable, may it be for sad or happy occasion, Morup Namgial is a name to be recognised on the field of performing arts and his Ladakhi language is nothing less than excellent.

Though his performance is with All India Radio, but he has become a household name not only in Ladakh but also in neighbouring areas of Lahul-Spiti, Baltistan, Tibet, Kinnour and other Himalayan areas as a singer, composer, play-writer, drama artist and an excellent producer of radio-features, documentary and dramas, etc. He is one of the most popular folk singer of Ladakh possessing a melodious voice. The kind of reputation and fame earned by Morup Namgial in such a short period is unparalled at least in Ladakh.

Besides, being a very versatile artist himself, he has played pioneering role in promoting folk-music and culture in Ladakh. He has been instrumental in establishing several cultural organisations. He has founded the Lamdon Social Welfare Society which has served as a model for other cultural and welfare society (organisation) being set-up in Ladakh over the years. The Lamdon Welfare Society was awarded the prestigious "National Award for Child Welfare" in the year 1989 from the President of India and Morup has been instrumental behind it. He has played a leading role in creating talented artists singer, etc., by his cultural promotional activities.

Morup Namgial experienced great concern for the extinction of the rich cultural and traditional folk dances, songs and music. As people had forgotten and lost their rich cultural heritage, he researched, collected and revived the dying folk lore of Ladakh.

It can be said with certainty that he is the unrivalled artist of this day and age. He is the only one who knows the Kesar

Saga, the national epic of Ladakh, Tibet and Baltistan and the rites and rituals of marriage and other ceremonies in their full details.

For his versatility as an Asian artist, he has been given awards by various academic cultural and social organisations.

In the year 1977 for the recognition of his contribution in the field of art and culture, he was awarded Gold Medal and Rs one lakh from the Government of Jammu and Kashmir State. In the year 1998 he was honoured by his Holiness Dalai Lama for making vivid and comprehensive commentary and programmes.

There is hardly any important programme on Radio Leh where he has not participated or there is not a single day that his programme is not broadcasted on the radio. As a social worker he has strained his every nerve for the preservation and promotion of myriad culture and traditions of Ladakh. He has founded societies for the promotion of culture in every village. He has rendered outstanding services towards the health and hygiene of the poor masses. For the old destitute people having nobody to look after them, he set a noble example by making homes for old, people.

Above all, he has done a yeoman's service for the communal harmony and peace among the different communities of Ladakh. Besides he has put an untiring efforts for the preservation of traditional costumes and promoting folk music and culture in Ladakh.

30

Rinpoches of Ladakh

Prem Singh Jina

Rinpoche is a reincarnated form of Lama. Therefore, it is a form of rebirth consistent with the Karmic view of existence. This particular elaboration is called Mahayana Buddhism. According to this tradition men destined for Buddhahood but reject total enlightenment in order to return to the world of sentient beings are helped along the slow path of salvation. In order to do this some take human form moving from one body to other in a continual series of predestined rebirths. Since any such deity transcends human existence when a person in who it is manifest dies, it enters another, usually a male child, there it remains throughout the individual's human existence, and when he in turn dies, the deity is again free to emanate in another infant, this can go on for an unlimited number of generations. The present Dalai Lama is the 14th in a series of reincarnation, emanations of the Bodhisattvas. Chanrazik (aPhyan-ras-gZigs) the Karmapa is the 16th in his line, and Drugchen is the 11th. But Ladakhi Tulkus and Rinpoches have much younger lineage, Kushok Bakula of Spituk monastery, Thiksay Rinpoche, Stakna Rinpoche, Togdan Rinpoche of Phyang monastery, Sras Rinpoche of Rizong monastery are among the popular ones who have been reincarnated three to four times in series.

As said earlier in Ladakh the reincarnated Lama is referred to as Rinpoche. The term Rinpoche means precious one. Tulku is a Tibetan word and spells as 'Sprul-Sku' or "Sprul" which means 'Transformation in the shape of 'Sku' means as 'Body of human being'. Thus, the incarnated Lama before expiring leave the some of his daily routine things through which his emanation is apparant. Therefore, after the 'Parinirvana' his devotees start to search his reincarnation through the following ways :

1. A dream of a devotee or kinsman about the recently deceased Rinpoche.
2. According to the dreams of parents which they received about Rinpoche.
3. According to the words which are uttered by the proposed incarnation of Rinpoche. Through the child, Lamas of the concerned monastery examine deceased Rinpoche's past life or habits. In case the child's habits are found similar to the earlier birth, then he is being declared as incarnate Lama.
4. The incarnate child recites passages from religious texts and chants beats and say prayers at the early age i.e. from three to four years.
5. The incarnate child's habits are entirely different than that of normal children. He is always inclined to play with ritual objects.
6. The incarnate child has amazing ability to identify texts and articles of his past life. He also remembers some people of his past life who were close to him.
7. The incarnate child instructs his mother not to pamper him, but to worship him as Lama.
8. He recognizes ritual things of his past life 'Kong-ma'.
9. He has marks at the same place of his body as he had in his previous life.

In Ladakh after the 'Parinirvana' of Rinpoche, the concerned Lamas immediately go to the high class Lamas for the consultation and inquire about the rebirth of their Rinpoche. Thereafter, they go out in the search of the child who possesses the habits of deceased Rinpoche. Sometimes, 'Lha-mo' or 'Lha' is also consulted in this regards. On the other side similar activities are being performed by the parents of the newly born child who has extraordinary memory. When both sides approach satisfy Head Lama of the concerned monastery, the child is then declared as Rinpoche and takes all responsibility for his education.

Sometimes the child incarnate is examined through the articles and people of his previous life whom he remembers most. Under this situation parents of the child contact the Head of concerned monastery along with articles. In case head lama is being convinced then he constitutes a Gonpa Committee in which senior Lamas of Rinpoche's past time become member. They examine the child, whether he is the incarnation of the deceased Rinpoche or not. In the examination process the Committee members mix articles which parents brought to monastery with other ritual articles. The child is than asked to select his articles. If he selects the right articles and replies the right answers of his past life, the Committee recommends him as Rinpoche. Accordingly, child's parents donate him to the monastery.

There is no need to re-examine the child by other high ranked Lamas. However, the details of the newly born Rinpoche need to be sent to His Holiness the Dalai Lama for final confirmation. After his confirmation, the child is recognized as Rinpoche without any doubt.

There is no caste and creed bar for the Rinpoche. But there is no Rinpoche who belongs to 'Beda', 'Gara' and 'Mon' families. The succession of a Rinpoche can be found in all classes other than the above. He can be discovered among humble peasants as well as in lofty noble households. Rinpoche is free to get education in any religious Buddhist Centre. Usually he chooses to take his own sect Centre for education, however after getting primary education, he is being allowed to go to other Buddhist Institutions for higher studies. During this period Lamas of his monastery excuse his absence with the feeling that he will return to serve them after acquiring higher knowledge.

Rinpoche is a high order Lama, therefore, for purification rites and other important substance activities his blessing is needed for magical effect. No doubt, Rinpoche can not perform every ritual, so Lamas in the area, undertake minor purification rites and domestic ritual services, but for this they take blessing and ingredients from Rinpoche. Bedsides, there is another common form through which Rinpoche of dispenses their powers which is in emulets. These emulets consist of simple bright red and yellow coloured threads knotted in the middle and acquire potency of Rinpoche's breath blessings.

Rinpoche usually does not attend the household rituals, viz., Choga, Skurim, Skangsol, etc. He undertakes a private ritual for the deceased in his own chamber, such powers accrue to a Renpoche by virtue of his incarnate status.

31

Lamas of Ladakh

Prem Singh Jina

Buddha's first admonition for Bhikkus was to go forth into the world and work for the welfare of people. Oh Bhikkus ! "he exhorted, "Go forth now, and wander from place to place, for the gain of the many, for the welfare of the many, out of compassion for the world, for the good, for the benefit and for all well beings."

The exhortation was the common attitude towards society of Sangha, the community of monks, from the time of Buddha. The monks are expected to work for the well being of all, not only human beings but all living things. The idea that Buddhism does not advocate that monks serve others but comprises a life devoted entirely is negated by Buddha's exhortation.

The missionary emissaries were sent to different parts of Asia by the meditation of King Asoka and after the third Buddhist council. Asoka inspired the idea to carry Buddha's message of service to others. It is said some Asoka missionaries also passed through Ladakh. While approaching Central Asia.[1]

The Kharosti inscriptions at Khalatse[2] indicate that Buddhism was introduced in Ladakh through Kashmir during 2nd century A.D. In fact, during this period of Kushana many Buddhist missionaries were sent to Central Asian Countries for the propagation of Buddhism. Gradually Buddhism spread there and till 7th Century A.D. maximum Central Asian countries adopted Buddhism. However, Bon had strong influence in Tibet. Therefore, Padmasambhava went there in 8th Century A.D. and started to build Samye Monastery. Bon-Chos didn't like it, as a result religious conflicts started. During day time Padmasambhava built the monastery through his tantric power but in night Bon-chos destroyed the same with his spiritual power. Then Padmasambhava decided to compromise with Bon-Chos with the condition that he would assimilate Bon gods and worship them alongwith Buddhist deities. Bon-chos agreed and Padmasambhava built Samye Monastery. In the monastery he assimilated Bon deities.

However, Padmasambhava, efforts were unable to influence Tibet by Buddhism fully. In fact, Buddhism spread its roots after the death of Lhang-dharma.[4] Later it developed very fast throughout in Tibet. Ladakh could not keep away from this development. Therefore, by 10th century it became a Buddhist Kingdom. Gradually, it had religious contacts with Tibet and Kashmir.

During 14th Century A.D. after the political triumph of Islam in Kashmir Ladakh had stopped its cultural and religious relations with Kashmir and turned completely towards Tibet. Ladakh then came under the influence of Mahayani culture. Monasteries, Chortens, Mani Walls, etc., were built during the course of this period, and Lamas held all good posts in the society. They were spiritual leaders, counsellers, etc. Thus exercising benevolent influence on the feudal system.

Today in the Buddhist society of Ladakh, Lamas have greater role to improve the social and economic condition. As under the Buddhist tradition, Lamas serve for the welfare of Buddhist community. They offer their services in order to overcome greed, hatred, ignorance or more succinctly all forms of craving that cause endless suffering in this cycle of birth and deaths. While rendering their spiritual service, people expect from them to solve their material problems as well. In the fields of Sociology, Economy, Education, Culture and Politics their help and guidance give encouragement to those who are involve in these fields. Thus, they have a unique position in the Buddhist Community and every aspect of Ladakhi life is partially or impartially influenced by them.

In Ladakh, Lamas have had practical wisdom to understand the spiritual growth of Ladakhis. They know that a healthy-material, social environment would be necessary to spread Buddhism. Sometimes, they exalted their scholarship in such a way that Kings or Ministers were influenced by them and they worked according to their wishes. By and large Lamas role in Ladakh was not only admired by Ladakhis but foreign rulers also appreciated them.

During 12th Century A.D. Buddhism almost disappeared from India. But in Tibet it was flourishing very well. Then Lamas of Ladakh did a wonderful task for the preservation of Buddhism in Ladakh. Monasteries of Ladakh sent them to Tibet for higher education, who after finishing their education in Tibet returned to their respective monasteries, thereafter they were deputed to educate young Lamas according to Tibetan pattern. Some of them were good artists who later decorated the monasteries according to Tibetan style. Figure 31.1 outlines the traffic of Buddhism to Ladakh before and after 10 century A.D.

Then, Ladakh got gradually influenced by Tibetan Buddhism and Ladakhi Villages were put under the control of different monasteries. To fulfil villagers religious needs one small Gonpa was established at each village according to the concerned monastery's sect.

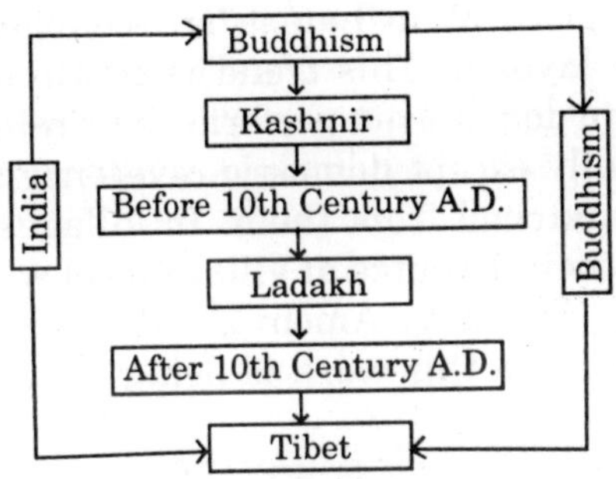

Fig. 31.1. Historical traffic of Buddhism to Ladakh before and after 10th Century A.D.

Therefore each Ladakhi Buddhist family is being associated with a monastery. And people on the advise of concern monasteries Lamas do all sort of work. The advise was related to issues like: when should they plough their lands, irrigate them and harvest ? Fig. 31.2.

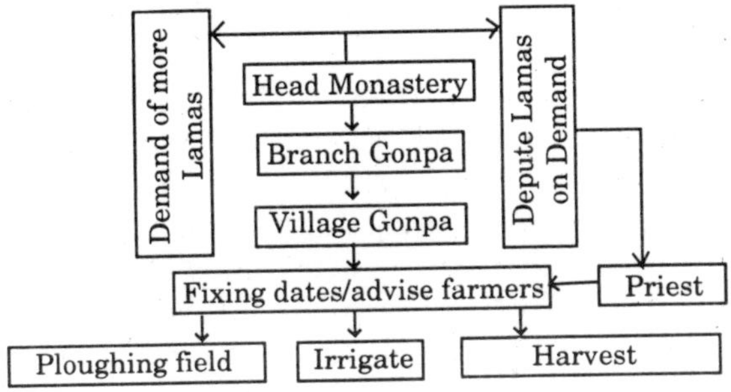

Fig. 31.2. The Flow Chart of monastic activities in Ladakh.

In Ladakh a Lama was not only considered as a good orator but he was consulted at the time of distribution of land, water and for the settlement of disputes. When the crop got infected by any disease, he was called for the treatment, even at the time of harvest his presence was needed. For this work Ladakhis offered a portion of their crop production and sometimes they gave cash. This practice still exists in all the Buddhist dominated villages.

Lamas were often considered as physicians, lawyers and religious leaders. They were teachers, their words became law and they were responsible for education, Nowadays some changes are taking place. Many Lamas have changed their Lama dress and become laymen. This trend is continuously taking place. Some of them do not even perform their religious duties. As a result gradually except domestic reverence all the other works are being snatched from them. In villages Lambardar now mostly settle their disputes at village level without taking the help of Lamas. Similarly Amchi is called for the medical treatment or sometimes this work is being done by M.B.B.S. Doctors.

Notes and References

1. Rigzin, Tewang & Prem Singh Jina (Tr.) : Religious Boddhi Literature in Ladakh; In : *Recent Researchers on the Himalaya,* Jina, Prem Singh (ed); Indus Pub. Co. 1977, p. 117.
2. Jina, Prem Singh : *Ladakh : The Land and the People,* Indus Pub. Co. 1996.
3. Bon-Chos: Religious head of Bon Religion.
4. Langdarma : Powerful King of Tibet and strong follower of Bon Religion.

32

Ge-Sar Epic of Ladakh

Prem Singh Jina

There are several legendary materials about Ge-Sar available in Central and Eastern Asia. It is said that during 8th Century oral form of Ge-Sar story telling the tradition was in practice in Tibet. People said the stories with Gru-gu (= Dru-gu). Thomas writes :

> "The Gru-gu Ge-Sar, residing in the northern quarter having until then, in resentment at commands shown rivalry. The demon Red-Face, army of Tibet was set in motion. As far as 'On-nu in the Gru-gu Kingdom the army forces of Tibet, set up the black tents and escorted the people. Their land overthrown into the Mon Territory.[1] They were discontented, relying upon evil men in the country. A terrifying leader (ded-dpon = Sarthavaha) being posted to garrison the country. The Gru-gu- Ge-Sar gave his submission as a servant of Tibet."[2]

Thus, Thomas believes Ge-Sar had his kingdom near Mon territory. However, Sarat Chandra Das said Ge-Sar country was situated to the northeast of Yarkand and to the north of Tibet.[3] According to Uray, Ge-Sar kingdom was lying in between Gandhara and Udayana.[4] Festgabe Hermann Jacobi had advocated a non-legendary Phrom Ge-Sar. E. Schlagintweit had referred Ge-Sar's information in the life of Padmasambhava. Rohit Vohra also agreed with Schlagintweit upto some extent and referred 'Padma-Thang-Yig' for the information about Ge-Sar.[5] Jina said, Ge-Sar was born in Smad-Mang-yul-de-chog-Norboo in Tibet and ruled the kingdom situated in between Ladakh and Tibet.[6]

Though scholars have different opinion about Ge-Sar kingdom, yet they have one opinion about the availability of Ge-Sar legend. The Ge-Sar stories were first time published in 16th Century in Mongolian language. Earlier its stories were very popular in oral form in Kokonor region. Chang-Skya was the popular story teller who preserved the oral tradition till its publication. In 1614 the Mongolian version of Ge-Sar stories became popular throughout in Mongolia. After one century gap I.J. Schmidt's translation of Ge-Sar stories from Mongolian language to German under the title 'Die Thatan Bogda Gessar Chan' came in European countries. Thereafter Peter Saiman Plas of Germany translated some more of its stories from Mongol to German. His publication came in 1770.[7]

Like Mongolia many Ge-Sar story tellers were available in Ladakh before 12th Century, but the stories were not well organised. In 1902 Dr. A.H. Francke put them in an organised way and produced its Ladakhi version with belief summary in English under the following titles.[8]

1. Prologue to Ge-Sar[9] Sagar Vocabulary and comments.
2. The story of Ge-Sar's birth.
3. The story of Braguna's marriage to Ge-Sar.
4. Ge-Sar's victory over the giant of the north.
5. Ge-Sar's journey to China and marriage with Gyudkon-ma-chognu.
6. Capture of a Braguma by the King of Hor.
7. Defeat of the King of Hor.

Here follows the summaries of some Ge-Sar stories.

Ge-Sar's Arrow[10]

Once Ge-Sar left his kingdom with his horse to kill a giant Churu-Lungtung. As he arrived at the giant's place, he saw his beautiful wife alone. He fell in love with her. Thereafter with her help he killed the giant and married his wife. Then both were passing their life happily. One day King of Hor invaded 'Ling' and carried away queen Schelochum Dugmo. When Ge-Sar came to know about this incident, he shot his efficient arrow 'Sed-Da-Yuron' on a reconnaissance fight to Hor. The arrow flew on and on, setting on fire eighteen Hor land valleys. At last it arrived in Hor capital and struck Hor palace. To see this the Hor King ordered his heroes to pull it out but they failed to do so. Then he requested his queen Dugmo. She stood up after taking a tiny piece of butter from the edge of the Chang pot, applied it on the top of the arrow and pulled it out gently with her right hand. Then after tying a 'Khatak' in a special knot over the feathers of the arrow she put it into the barley-filled pot and ordered to carry the pot to the royal Chapal's roof of King Kurgyal palace. In this way she saved the Hor Kingdom from the angry arrow of Ge-Sar.

Cho-Cho-De-Gu and King Kurgyal[11]

Once Bumar Lamstan stole Hor palace horse named Lame. Next day when Santa-meru did not find Lame, he got worried and went out from Hor in search of him. At last he reached Ge-Sar palace. He saw Agu Pale there. He inquired about the Hor horse from him. Agu Pale said he did not know about him but he could give some tricks through which Hor horse could be searched. Santa-meru heard of the tricks carefully then applied them accordingly. Soonafter he saw Hor horse Lame alongwith other horses. Santa-meru became happy to see this. He thanked Agu-pale and returned with Lame. After reaching Hor palace, he met King Kurgyal and advised him to invade on 'Ling' as Ge-Sar is not at his palace and he could easily capture queen Co-Co-De-Gu. King Kurgyal accepted Santa-meru's advise and invaded on Ling. Queen Co-Co-De-Gu was alone at her palace, so he caught her. But before taking her to Hor he made a marriage proposal. Queen accepted his proposal with the following conditions.

1. To build palace by Dung.
2. To eat all meat and butter of Ling Kingdom

King Kurgyal ate all meat and butter in 16 years and in the next eight years he built a big palace by Dung. When the queen saw this, she made a plan to cheat King Kurgyal. She gave all her ornaments to her female servant and asked her, when King Kurgyal would come for marriage you offer yourself. Therefore, King Kurgyal married with Co-Co-De-Gu's female servant and he carried her towards Hor. However, as he was crossing the Ling border, one old woman disclosed Co-Co-De-Gu's cheating plan. To listen this King became angry upon Co-Co-De-Gu's servant and immediately returned to Ling and forcefully carried Co-Co-De-Gu to Hor.

Abi Meme of Ting-Chur-Ming-Chur[12]

An old couple had a small land in Ting-Chur-Ming-Chur. During the ploughing season like others they also went to their field and sowed food grains. After sometime when they went to their field, they saw only one plant in the middle of the field. By the harvesting season it became a big tree. When they cut the tree, they were surprised to see the big size food grains in huge quantity. They did not get sufficient space to store them. So, they dug a big trench and stored them in it. After one year when the old man opened the lid of the trench, he saw many insects instead of food grains which were later converted into a beautiful baby.

The baby grew up very fast and was popularly known by name 'Dong-Sum-Mela-Snang-mo'. He had two dogs. One day his dogs captured one giant. As 'Dong-Sum-Mela-Snong-mo' saw this, he released the giant but giant did not go any where else, and became his servant. Later, on the advise of his guru he killed the giant into eighteen pieces and threw them in eighteen directions. Thereafter with these pieces a beautiful country Ling was formed.

When 'Dong-Sum-Mela-Snong-mo' grew up to be a young handsome boy, his parents thought of his marriage. They sent marriage invitation of his son to all neighbouring countries. As a result eighteen beautiful girls got ready for marriage. They came to Ling to see Dung-Sum-Mela-nong-mo. But as they saw him they all got pregnant and after nine months, eighteen babies were born from them who later constructed eighteen big rooms at the Ling palace. To decorate them they went for jewels in 'Pal-Chi-Pal-Dong' palace. Agu Pale among them reached first and brought all jewels to Ling. When other brothers reached there, they did not find anything and destroyed the 'Pal-Chi-Pal-Dong' palace into small pieces.

Sheperd Pa-Le-God-Po[13]

Pa-le-God-po was a shepherd. He after breakfast went daily to Dok with his animals for grazing. One day while he was grazing his animals in Dok, he saw two birds-white and black on the two mountain peaks. Soonafter they flew towards the valley and started fighting. Pa-le-God-po was enjoying a lot to see their fight. In the evening both flew to high mountains, Pale-God-po also returned with his animals to his house. Next day he left his animals at Dok and went to the same spot from where he saw two birds. This time he saw two Yaks instead of birds. One was black and another white. Like birds they also started fighting each other at the Dok. In evening he thought that the black Yak could kill the white so he felt pity upon white Yak thus he killed the black. Then the white Yak appeared in its real form of god Gyab-Jin and said to ask anything from him. Pa-le-God-po said, "He wanted to be a King of Ling Kingdom". Gyab-Jin said, "you will very soon be King of Ling". Then he disappeared.

Notes and References

1. Mon-territory : It was the territory of non-Tibetan people, usually associated with the western part of Tibet and the lower Himalayas.
2. Thomas, F.W. : Tibetan Literary texts and documents concerning Chinese Turkestan; Part-II, Vol. XXXVII. The Royal Asiatic Society, London; 1951.
3. Vohra, Rohit; *Early History of Ladakh : Mythic Lore & Fabulation;* In *Recent Research on Ladakh* 4 & 5, Motilal Pub. New Delhi, 1995, p. 217.
4. *Ibid* & Quoted from Uray, Geza. 1979, *The Old Tibetan sources of History of Central Asia upto 751 A.D.*
5. *Ibid.*
6. Jina, Prem Singh : Ge-Sar : A Great Epic (Hindi), *Seeraja* Vol. 2 (June-July) 1994, p. 17-20.
7. *Ibid.*
8. *Ibid.*
9. Ge-Sar (= Ke-Sar)
10. Joldan, E : *Harvest Festival of Buddhist Dards of Ladakh and other Essays,* Kappor Brothers, Srinagar, 1985, 85-90.
11. Jina, Prem Singh, *op. cit.*
12. *Ibid.*
13. *Ibid.*

PART VII
Physical Fitness

33

Physical Fitness Norms for High School Students of Ladakh

Sonam Angchok

Ladakh is known for its remotness, difficult terrain, cold desert, unique culture and tradition. Before 1947 it consisted of three Tehsils : Leh, Kargil and Skardu with a total area of 96,701 sq. kilometres, but following the Pakistan's tribal raids and Chinese aggression it lost 37,555 sq. kms. Now it has only 59,146 sq. kms. and two districts. Leh and Kargil with a population about two lakh.

The altitude in Ladakh varies from place to place by several hundred metres which affects the climate. In winter temperature touches as low as – 30°C (Leh and Kargil) and – 40°C in Drass whereas during summer season it increases up to 26°C (July and August). The relative humidity is also low and ranges from 31 to 64 per cent.

However, the whole Ladakh region is located at a high altitude. Therefore, the people remained isolated from outside world and survived on its natural environment. People therefore affected by this environment have less height and symmetry, shorter and flat nose, small eyes, longer ears, stout muscular body with dark complexion. Mr. Heratio also found the same complexion in his tribal belt study of India, according to him :

> "Almost all the tribal races have less height, less symmetry, broader and flatter face, shorter and flat nose, small eyes, longer ears, stout muscular body with dark complexion. The legs are disproportionately shorter and the arms are disproportionately longer."[1]

Ladakhis are fond of fair and festivals. Archery is quite a popular game and is organised as a fair in every village. The most popular sports of Ladakh are : Horse polo, archery, mountaineering, trekking, rock climbing, river rafting and ice-hockey. Though Ladakhis are international level skiers, mountaineers, archers and marathners, yet they need standard health and physical fitness. This chapter deals briefly with some norms of physical fitness for thirteen to seventeen year students of high and Higher Secondary Schools of Ladakh. A systematic and random sampling method is used for the collection of data. On the basis of random sampling 542 native and School going students in the age group of 13-17 years from twenty-five High and Higher Secondary Schools of Leh and Kargil districts were selected.

In order to establish Physical fitness norms Modified Fleshman's Physical Fitness Test Battery consisting of seven test items were used because of limitation of physical facilities. The Modified Fleshman's Physical Fitness Test has the following items—sit up, forward bend and reach, shot put throw, shuttle run, standing broad jump, 50 yard dash and 600 yard run/walk. Therefore, for establishing the reliability of the Modified Fleshman's Physical fitness test a sample of twenty five subjects was taken. The twenty-five subjects are discussed in the ..ng pages. The above test was repeated again on the same ..jects under similar conditions. The Pearson's Product Movement Correlation was later being computed between the two scores of performance of each items for each subjects. The reliability co-efficient is given in the Table 33.1 as follows :

TABLE 33.1

Reliability Co-efficient of Test-Retest Scores

Sl. No.	*Name of Test*	*N*	*Co-efficient of Reliability*
1.	Sit up	25	0.87*
2.	Forward Bend and Reach	25	0.97*
3.	Shot Put Throw	25	0.94*
4.	Standing Broad Jump	25	0.75*
5.	Shuttle run	25	0.67*
6.	50 Yard Dash	25	0.98*
7.	600-Yard Run/Walk	25	0.82

* Significant at .01 level.

Table 33.1 reveals that all the seven test items have a high reliability. However, to find out the significance of difference among the physical fitness of various age group of boys and to compare the standard of fitness analysis of variance (F-ratio) and in case of significance differences of existed at .05 level, Scheffes post-hoc test was applied.

Descriptive Analysis of the Fitness Variables

Descriptive analysis of the fitness variable for the five age-groups (13 through 17 years) have been presented in Table 33.2. Vide this table the abdominal strength of the 17 year old boys was the maximum with the mean value of 17.06, followed by 16,15 and 14 years old boys with mean values of 16.31, 16.49, and 12.47 respectively. Whereas, 13 year old boys were found with the lowest mean value of 11.28.

In case of trunk flexibility, the 17 year old boys mean value of 15.74 cm, whereas, 13 year old boys had shown the maximum flexibility with mean value of 10.05 cm. The 14, 15, and 16 years old boys were in between highest and the lowest their mean values being 11.18 cm, 14.01, and 14.33 cm, respectively.

The explosive strength of arm and shoulder was measured through Shot Put Throw test. It has been found that arms and shoulders strength of 17 year old boys was maximum with the mean value of 470.49 cm. On the other hand, it was minimum among 13 years old boys with the mean value of 398.66 cm.

The 16, 15 and 14 year old boys scored in between the lowest and the highest score with a mean value of 459.25 cms, 455.02 cms and 434.99 cms respectively.

For the measurement of explosive strength of the legs, Standing Broad Jump test was applied. The result of their performance indicated, that maximum explosive strength of the legs was exhibited by 17 year old boys, with mean of 183.03 cms, whereas 13 year old boys scored the minimum, with the mean value of 164.72 cms.

In case of agility, measured through Shuttle Run Test, the 17 year old boys have again performed better, as they clocked 10.06 sec. to complete to test, whereas, the 16 year old boys clocked, with mean value of 10.23 sec. followed by 15, 14 and 13

TABLE 33.2

Means and Standard Deviations of Physical Fitness Variables

S.No.	*Variables*	*Units*	*Age 13 years*		*Age 14 years*		*Age 15 years*		*Age 16 years*		*Age 17 years*	
			Mean	*S.D.*	*Mean*	*S.D.*	*Mean*	*S.D.*	*Mean*	*S.D.*	*Mean*	*S.D.*
1.	Sit Up	No./30 sec.	11.28	4.02	12.47	3.81	16.49	4.57	16.31	4.57	17.06	4.58
2.	Foreword Bend and Reach	Centimetres	10.05	2.62	11.18	2.69	14.01	2.67	14.33	2.56	15.74	2.69
3.	Shot Put Throw	Centimetres	398.66	87.97	434.99	86.17	455.02	72.64	459.25	78.65	470.49	73.56
4.	Standing Broad Jump	Centimetres	164.72	25.50	163.73	19.35	174.92	20.66	176.07	23.24	183.03	16.88
5.	Shuttle Run	Seconds	10.43	0.76	16.37	0.77	11.31	0.84	10.23	0.88	10.06	0.89
6.	50 yard Dash	Seconds	8.24	0.90	8.32	0.82	8.08	0.93	8.06	1.00	8.14	0.86
7.	600 yard Run/ walk	Seconds	163.41	23.14	162.73	25.22	155..01	24.00	151.44	23.92	152.59	25.01

years old boys, with a mean value of 10.31, 10.37 and 10.43 sec. respectively.

General speed was measured through 50-yard Dash Test. In case of speed the 16 year old boys exhibited the maximum speed, with a mean value of 8.06 sec. followed by 15, 17 and 13 years old boys with mean value of 8.08 sec. and 8.24 seconds, respectively. The minimum was shown by the 14 year old boys, with mean value of 8.32 seconds.

Similarly, cardio-vascular endurance was measured through 600 yard Run /Walk test. It has been observed that 16 year old boys possessed the maximum cardio-vascular endurance with the mean value of 151.44 sec. whereas, the 13 year old boys possessed the least Cardio-Vascular endurance with the mean value of 163.45 seconds.

There has been a significant difference among the various age-groups of boys in the scores of their Sit Up variable as the 'F' Value (28.17) which was found significant at 5 per cent level (Table 33.3).

TABLE 33.3

Analysis of Variance for Sit Up Age-Groups 13 to 17 Years

Variable	*Source of Variance*	*Degree of Freedom*	*SS*	*MS*	*'F'*
Sit Up	Between	4	2201.20	550.30	28.17*
	within	539	10491.74	19.54	

* Significant at 5 per cent level of confidence (F > 2.39).

To determine the actual difference in the group Scheffe's Post hoc Test was applied, the results of this test are shown in Table 33.4. The obtained results of the test is a significant difference in the performance of their dynamic strength of abdominal muscle from one age-group to the other age-groups as the difference between paired means in most of the age-groups is found greater than the critical ratios presented in the table against the means of each pair. The dynamic strength of abdominal muscle in 17 years boys was found the maximum 17.06 and 13 years the minimum 11.28.

TABLE 33.4

Paired Means and Difference Between Means for Five Age-group in Sit-Up Variable

13 *N = 58*	*14* *N = 74*	*15* *N = 143*	*16* *N = 169*	*17* *N = 98*	*MD* —	*CI* —
11.28	12.47	—	—	—	1.19	1.51
11.28	—	16.49	—	—	5.21*	2.55
11.28	—	—	16.31	—	5.03*	1.29
11.28	—	—	—	17.06	5.78*	1.43
—	12.47	16.49	—	—	4.02*	3.15
—	12.47	—	16.31	—	3.84*	1.16
—	12.47	—	—	17.06	4.59*	1.31
—	—	16.49	16.31	—	0.18	2.36
—	—	16.49	—	17.06	0.57	2.44
—	—	—	16.31	1706	0.75	1.07

* Significant at 5 per cent level of confidence.

The results of analysis of variance for dynamic flexibility of boys have been presented in Table 33.5.

TABLE 33.5

Analysis of Variance for Forward Bend and Reach Age-groups 13 to 17 years

Variaable	*Source of Variance*	*Degree of Freedom*	*SS*	*MS*	*'F'*
Forward	Between	4	1730.01	432.50	62.14*
Bend and Reach	Within	539	3736.62	6.96	

* Significant at 5 per cent level of confidence (F > 2.39.)

The results of Table 33.5 indicate that there has been a significant difference among various age-groups of boys as the obtained 'F' value was found to be greater than the table value of 2.39.

Scheffe's post-hoc test was applied to determine that in which age-group the actual difference in the Forward Bend and Reach efficiency among different age-group existed.

TABLE 33.6
Paired Means and Difference Between Means for Five Age-groups in Forward Bend and Reach Variable

13 *N = 58*	*14* *N = 74*	*15* *N = 143*	*16* *N = 169*	*17* *N = 98*	*MD* —	*CI* —
10.05	11.18	—	—	—	1.13*	0.90
10.05	—	14.01	—	—	3.96*	1.52
10.05	—	—	14.33	—	4.28*	0.77
10.05	—	—	—	15.74	5.69*	0.85
—	11.18	14.01	—	—	2.83*	2.21
—	11.18	—	14.33	—	3.15*	0.69
—	11.18	—	—	15.74	4.56*	0.78
—	—	14.01	14.33	—	0.32	1.41
—	—	14.01	—	15.74	0.73*	1.45
—	—	—	14.33	15.74	0.41*	0.63

* Significant at 5 per cent level of confidence.

The results of Scheffe's post-hoc test have been presented in Table 33.6. The results thus indicate that in each of paired means significant difference existed except in 15 years and 16 years of boys. The mean difference was found to be greater than the calculated critical ratio presented against each paired means in the table. Seventeen years boys were better than 13, 14 and 15 year old boys.

Table 33.7 shows the Analysis of Variance for Shot Put Throw age-groups 13 to 17 years.

TABLE 33.7
Analysis of Variance for Shot Put Throw-age-groups 13 to 17 Years

Variable	*Source of Variance*	*Degree of Freedom*	*SS*	*MS*	*'F'*
Shot Put	Between	4	228715.12	57178.78	9.31*
Throw	Within	539	3296695.1	6139.10	

* Significant at 5 per cent level of confidence (F > 2.39)

Reffering to the above table the 'F' value 9.39 has been found significant which indicates that there is a significant difference in the Shot Put Throw test among the various age-groups of 13 to 17 years old boys. To determine the five age-groups, where the actual difference existed, Scheffe's post-hoc test was applied. Table 33.8 shows the details.

TABLE 33.8

Paired Means and Difference Between Means of Five Age-group in Shot Put Throw Variable

13 *N = 58*	*14* *N = 74*	*15* *N = 143*	*16* *N = 169*	*17* *N = 98*	*MD* —	*CI* —
398.66	434.99	—	—	—	36.33*	26.87
398.66	—	455.10	—	—	56.44*	45.26
398.66	—	—	459.25	—	60.59*	22.89
398.66	—	—	—	470.49	71.83*	25.36
—	434.99	455.10	—	—	20.11*	44.20
—	434.99	—	459.25	—	24.26*	20.70
—	434.99	—	—	470.49	35.50*	23.40
—	—	455.10	459.25	—	04.15	41.98
—	—	455.10	—	470.49	15.39	43.38
—	—	—	459.25	470.49	11.24	18.90

* Significant at 5 per cent level of confidence.

The results of the Table 33.8 shows the Shot Put Throw efficiency for different age-group of 13 to 17 year old boys have been found significantly different in the performance of their throwing ability from one-age to the other-age group as in most of the cases. No significant differences were found in age-group of 15 and 14 years and 15 and 16 years, 15 and 17 years old boys. The 17 year-old boys possessed the maximum explosive strength in their arms and shoulders, whereas, the 13 year old boys possessed the minimum explosive strength.

Analysis of variance for Standing Broad Jump age-groups 13 to 17 years is shown in Table 33.9. The results of this table indicate that there has been a significant difference among the different age-groups of 13 to 17 year old boys in the score of their Standing Broad Jump variable.

TABLE 33.9

Analysis of Variance for Standing Broad Jump age-Groups 13 to 17 Years

Variable	*Source of Variance*	*Degree of Freedom*	*SS*	*MS*	*"F"*
Standing	Between	4	21621.94	5405.49	11.93*
Broad Jump	Within	539	243347.53	453.16	

* Significant at 5 per cent level of Confidence (F > 2.39).

As the obtained "F" value 11.93 was found significantly greater than the table value 2.37 required to be significant at five per cent level of confidence. Scheffe's post test was applied. The results are presented in Table 33.10.

TABLE 33.10

Paired Means and Difference Between Means for Five Age-groups in Standing Broad Jump Variable

13 N = 58	*14 N = 74*	*15 N = 143*	*16 N = 169*	*17 N = 98*	*MD* —	*CI* —
164.72	163.73	—	—	—	0.99	7.30
164.72	—	174.92	—	—	10.20	12.29
164.72	—	—	176.07	—	11.35*	6.22
164.72	—	—	—	183.03	18.31*	6.89
—	163.73	174.92	—	—	11.19	12.00
—	163.73	—	176.07	—	12.34*	5.62
—	163.73	—	—	183.03	19.30*	6.35
—	—	174.92	176.07	—	1.15	11.40
—	—	174.92	—	183.03	8.11	11.78
—	—	—	176.07	183.03	6.96*	5.13

* Significant at 5 per cent level of Confidence.

The results of post-hoc test (vide Table 33.10) on Standing Broad Jump test for various age-groups of boys have indicated that there was significant difference in the performance of their explosive strength (leg muscle) from one-age group to the other age-group. Maximum explosive paired means and difference between means for five age-groups in Standing Broad Jump Variable strength on the leg muscles was found in 17 year old boys followed by 16,15 and 13 year old boys. It was minimum in 14 years old boys.

The analysis of variance for Shuttle Run age-group 13 to 17 years shown in Table 11.

TABLE 33.11

Analysis of Variance for Shuttle Run Age-Groups 13 to 17 Years

Variable	*Source of Variance*	*Degree of Freedom*	*SS*	*MS*	*"F"*
Shuttle	Between	4	7.08	1.77	2.60*
Run	Within	539	367.75	0.68	

* Significance at 5 per cent level of Confidence (F > 2.39).

The above table indicates that the "F" value (2.60) is significant means that there has not been significant differences in the Shuttle Run Test among various age-groups. To determine, the age-groups where the actual differences existed, Scheffe's Post-Hoc test was applied. The result is shown in Table 33.12.

TABLE 33.12

Paired Means and Difference between Means for Five Age Groups in Shuttle Run Variable

13 N = 58	*14 N = 74*	*15 N = 143*	*16 N = 169*	*17 N = 98*	*MD —*	*CI —*
10.43	10.37	—	—	—	0.06	0.28
10.43	—	10.31	—	—	0.12	0.47
10.43	—	—	10.23	—	0.20	0.23
10.43	—	—	—	10.06	0.37*	0.26
—	10.37	10.31	—	—	0.06	0.46
—	10.37	—	10.23	—	0.14	0.21

(Contd.)

(Contd.)

—	10.37	—	—	10.06	0.31*	0.24
—	—	10.31	10.23	—	0.08	0.44
—	—	10.31	—	10.06	0.25	0.45
—	—	—	10.23	10.06	0.17	0.19

* Significant at 5 per cent level of confidence.

It is observed that from Table 33.12 that only in two age-groups, in the paired means significant differences existed.

Table 33.13 shows the analysis of variance for 50 yard Dash age group 13 to 17 years.

TABLE 33.13

Analysis of Variance for 50 Yard Dash age-groups 13 to 17 Years

Variance	*Source of Variance*	*Degree of Freedom*	*SS*	*MS*	*'F'*
50 Yard	Between	4	4.61	1.15	1.35
Dash	Within	539	458.79	0.85	

The results reveal (Vide Table 33.13) that the various age groups considered in the study did not show significant differences on the 50 yard Dash. The obtained "F" value was found less than the required table value of 2.39.

For 50 yard Dash test, since the 'F' was not found significant post-hoc test was not applied.

TABLE 33.14

Analysis of Variance for 600 Yard Run/Walk age-groups 13 to 17 Years

Variable	*Source of Variance*	*Degree of Freedom*	*SS*	*MS*	*'F'*
600 Yard	Between	4	11148.32	2737.09	47.00*
Run/Walk	Within	539	31856.93	593.20	

* Significant at 5 per cent of confidence (F > 2.39).

The above table indicates that there has been a significant

difference among different age-groups of boys, as the "F" value (47.00) was found to be greater than the table value of 2.39.

To determine the age-groups, where actual difference existed, Scheffe's post-hoc test was applied. The results of post-hoc test have been presented in Table 33.15.

TABLE 33.15
Paired Means and Difference Between Means for Five Age-groups in 600-Yard Run/Walk Variable

13 *N = 58*	*14* *N = 74*	*15* *N = 143*	*16* *N = 169*	*17* *N = 98*	*MD* —	*CI* —
163.41	162.72	—	—	—	0.69	8.33
163.41	—	555.01	—	—	8.40	14.07
163.41	—	—	151.44	—	11.97*	7.11
163.41	—	—	—	152.59	10.82*	7.88
—	162.72	555.01	—	—	7.71	13.73
—	162.72	—	151.44	—	11.28*	6.43
—	162.72	—	—	152.59	10.13*	7.27
—	—	555.01	151.44	—	3.57	13.05
—	—	555.01	—	152.59	2.42	13.48
—	—	—	151.44	152.59	1.15	5.87

* Significant at 5 per cent level of confidence.

Table 33.15 of the post-hoc test shows that there has been a significant difference at 5 per cent level of confidence from one age-group to the other age-group of school boys in their 600 yard Run/walk ability in most of the cases. Maximum (151.44) cardio-vascular endurance was observed in 16 year old boys, whereas, minimum (163.41) was found in 13 year old boys.

Conclusion

The following conclusion was drawn from the above analysis.

1. Percentile norms for seven test battery were developed and found suitable to assess the Physical fitness level of High and Higher Secondary male students of Ladakh belonging to age-group 13 to 17 years.
2. The Physical fitness level of 16 and 17 years boys were superior to all other age groups. They were found

significantly superior to 13 and 14 years old boys in abdominal strength, flexibility, explosive strength, agility and cardio-vascular endurance.

3. No significant differences existed among 15 year old boys with 17 and 16 year old boys at .05 level of confidence. Similarly no significant difference was found between 13 and 14 year old boys in almost all the Physical fitness components except in trunk flexibility and explosive strength.

Recommendations

Physical fitness testing is an important aspect of the Physical Education Programme. It is through the evaluation of the test results that fitness needs of individuals, present level of fitness, success and failure of performance are adjusted. Norms provide the criteria with which test results may be interpreted and compared, meaningfully and reasonably.

1. It has beeen observed that no significant differences were found in age-group of 13 and 14 years old boys. Thus, a systematic and scientifically developed Physical Fitness Programme would help to increase the fitness level of Ladakhi people.
2. Fitness evaluating test batteries such as one used in the present investigation, may be implemented in all the government schools of Ladakh.
3. A list of selected exercises and instructions for their execution be prepared in the form of a "Fitness Scheme Booklet" which then be supplied to all the government schools. These exercises should be performed by all the students on a regular basis during the school hours.
4. A similar study should be taken to assess the fitness level of girl students of Ladakh.
5. A longitudinal study can be undertaken to assess the fitness of youth every five years. This will help to frame new fitness norms.

Notes and References

1. Fleishman, A.Edwin (1964), *The Structure and Measurement of Physical Fitness,* Englewood Cliffs and Prentice Hall.
2. Gazetter of J & K (1974), Vivek Pub.
3. Haratio, Bicken Staff Rowney (1974), *The Wild Tribes of India,* B.R. Pub. Delhi, pp. 209-10.

Bibliography

Bedi, Ramesh (1986), *Ladakh,* Brijbasi, Pub. Co., New Delhi.

Chaudhari Khushi Mohamad (1908), *Preliminary Report of Ladakh,* Ranbir Prakashan Press.

Cunningham, A. (1970), *Ladakh Physical, Statistical and Historical with Notices of the Surrounding Comprises* Sagar Pub. Delhi.

Das, Bhagwan (1976), *Tibetan Medicine with special reference to Yoga Sataka,* Tibetan Works and Archieves, Dharmshala, H.P.

Datta, C.L. (1973), *Ladakh and Western Himalayan Politics: 1819 – 1848,* Munshiram Manoharlal Pub., New Delhi.

Drew, Fredric (1976), *Jammoo and Kashmir Territories,* Cosmo Pub. Delhi. 1895.

Dughlat, Mirza Hyder, *Tarikh-e-Rashidi* (English Version) by E. Denison Ross, Lahore: Book Trader.

Fox, Joseph, L. (1998), *Ladakh Melong* (Bilingual, Journal), Leh.

Fleishman, A. Edwin (1964), The *Structure and Measurement of Physical Fitness,* Englewood Cliffs and Hall.

Franke, A.H. (1906), *Ladakh Songs,* Scandinavian Alliance Mission Press.

Franke, A.H. (1977), *History of Western Tibet,* Sterling Pub., New Delhi.

Franke, A.H. 1982, *Antiquities of Indian Tibet,* S Chand Pub., New Delhi

Ganhar, J.N. (1979) : The Wild Life of Ladakh.

Gazetteer of J & K (1974), Vivek Pub. Delhi.

Haratio, Bicken Staffe Rowney (1974): *The Wild Tribes of India,* B.R. Publication, Delhi.

Herbert Guenther (1987), 'Buddhism in Tibet', in the *Encyclopaedia of Religion,* Vol. 2. (New York: Macmillan Publishing Company).

Jina, Prem Singh, 1981, 'Ladakh Aur Paryatan (Tourism in Ladakh), In : first National Conference, CIBS, Leh (Ladakh).

——1983, Foreign Tourists and their Impact on Ladakh, In IIIrd National Conference, Ladakh Prabha (3), (IBS, Leh.

——1983, Boudh Bikshus of Ladakh, In : Proceedings of All India Conference on Buddhist and Jaina Monasticism, Deptt. of Buddhist Studies, Delhi University, Delhi.

——1984, The Foreign Tourist Traffic in Ladakh Himalaya; In : *Research and Development of Himalaya* (Problem Oriented Studies), Vol. 3(I), Nainital.

——1984, Buddhism in Ladakh and World Peace, In : 10th International Buddhist Conference on 'Buddhism and World Peace', Japanese Temple, Bodh Gaya, Vol. X.

——1986, A Brief Introduction of Ladakhi Gonpas, In : All India Conference Kashmir University, Srinagar, Deptt. of Centre for Central Asian Studies; Proceed, Ladakh Life and Culture.

——1986, A Survey of Buddhist Community in Ladakh Himalayas, In : 12th International Buddhist Conference on Buddhism and Social Harmony, Japanese Temple, Bodh Gaya, Vol. XII.

——1986, 'Pasture Land of Leh and its effect on Ecology', In: National Workshop on Nature Conservation, Trishul, Leh-Ladakh.

——1986, Socio-Economic and Cultural Relations between Ladakh and Lahul-Spiti, National Conference, Keylong.

——1986, Ladakh Ki Sanskriti me Stok Rajvans (Hindi), *Culture* (Quarterly Journal), Delhi.

——1986, Pasture Land of Zangskar and its effects on Ecology; National Seminar-cum-Worshop on 'Development of the Cold Desert of Ladakh,' Desert Development Agencies Leh and Kargil.

——1987, *Leh Tab aur Abb* (Hindi); *Navneet* (Hindi Digest), Bombay.

——1988, Monasteries in The Economy of Leh-Ladakh; In: All India Conference on Buddhist Monasteries of Himalayan Region Various Aspects; CIBS, Leh.

——1988, Bodh Dham Leh-Ladakh (Hindi), *Hindu Chetana*, Vol.7, New Delhi.

——1988, Ladakhi Rajao Ka Bodh Dharam me Yogdan (Hindi), *Hindu Chetana;* Vol.10.

——1989, Eco-Environmental Study of Tourism in Ladakh Himalayas, All India Conference; Kashmir University; Srinagar.

——1989, Losar in Himalayas; Proceeding of All India Conference Himalayayi Sanskriti-2; Shimla.

——1990, Buddhism and Human Values in the History of Ladakh Himalayas; In : International Buddhist Conference, Japanese Temple, Bodh Gaya, India.

——1990, The Pashmina Economy in Ladakh Himalaya, *Yojana* (English); December, Delhi.

——1990, Pasture Ecology of Leh, Ladakh, In : Internale's Kolloquium, Hernlul Heraugegeben und redigiest Vom Lydia Lcke-Schwelbe Und Gudrun Meier 'Wisseneschaftsgeschichte und Gegenwartige Forschungen in 'Nordwest-Indian, Steatliches Museum Fur volker, *Kunde Dresden Forschungsstelle,* Vol. 9, Bis 13, Marz, 1987.

——1991, Ladakh me Bodh Kala Ka Udya aur Vikas, *Seeraja,* Vol. 6, Feb. March.

——1992,Ladakhi Shirobhusa—Perakh (Hindi), *Seeraja,* vol.6. Feb-March.

——1992, *Ladakh Ki Mahila Prasasak Putith Wangmo; Hamara Sahitaya;* Usha Viyas (ed.); J&K Academy of Arts, Culture and Languages, Jammu.

——1993, Impact of Tourism on Ladakhi Society and Culture; In All India Conference, J.N.U., New Delhi.

———1993, Impact of Tourism on Ecological set-up of Ladakh Himalaya, In : International Conference on Ladakh Studies (Sixth Collquium).

———1993, Poultry Industry in Ladakh, *Himalaya Today*, Sept., Vol.IX, No. 6 2&3, Feb.

———1993, Buddhism in Ladakh and its Approach to Material World, In: International Buddhist Conference, Japanese Temple, Bodh Gaya.

———1994, Tourist Industry in Ladakh, *Himalaya Today,* Vol.V, No. 2, Jan –March.

———1994, Bhikshunis in Ladakh (Nuns in Ladakh): In : International Conference Proceed, Keylong (H.P.).

———1994, Kesar: A Great Epic (Hindi); *Seeraja,* Vol. 2, (june-July), Jammu.

———1994, *Tourism in Ladakh Himalaya,* Indus Publishing Company, New Delhi.

———1995, Phyang Monastery of Ladakh, Indus Publishing Company, New Delhi.

———1995, High Pasturelands of Ladakh Himalaya, Indus Publishing Company, New Delhi.

———1996, *Ladakh: The Land and the people,* Indus Publishing Company, New Delhi.

———1997, *Recent Researchers of the Himalaya,* Indus Publishing Company, New Delhi.

———1998, *Tibetan Manuscripts and Inscriptions of Ladakh Himalaya,* Sri Satguru Publication Delhi.

———Jina, Prem Singh, 1999, *Some monasteries of Drigungpa order in Central Ladakh;* Sri Satguru Publications, Delhi.

———1999, *Changing face of Ladakh Himalaya,* Om Publication, Faridabad, Haryana.

———1999, *Lamayuru monastery of Ladakh Himalaya,* Om Publication Faridabad, Haryana.

———1999, History of Education and Growth in Ladakh, paper presented in the International Conference, IALS, Leh.

——2000, *Ladakh: Past and Present,* Gyan Publishing House, New Delhi.

——2000, Rinchen bzangpo's Contribution in Buddhist Art: A Case Study of Sumda Chung and Sumda Chanmo (Ladakh), Papers presented in National Conference, CIBS, Leh Ladakh.

——2000, Alchi a Buddhist monument in Ladakh, paper presented in International Buddhist Conference, Bodh Gaya.

——2001, *Religious History of Ladakh,* Sri Guru Publication, New Delhi.

——2001, *Ladakh Ki Kala Avani Sanskriti,* IGNCA, New Delhi.

Jolden, E. (1985); *Harvest Festival of Buddhist Dards of Ladakh and other Essays,* Kapoor Brothers, Srinagar.

Khangskar, Lobsang Aolma (1986): Lectures on Tibetan Medicine', K. Dhondup (ed.) *Tibetan works (Archive), op. cit.*

Lucciano, Pettech: *The Kingdom of Ladakh.*

Lydekher, R (1907), *The Game Animals of India, Burma, Malaya and Tibet.*

Markhon, Fred (1854) : *Shooting in the Himalayas.*

Mycentrine, Major General: *Hindukush.*

Pathak, Suniti Kumar (1996) 'The Dokpa ('Brog-pa) in Ladakh—remnant of the Aryans', In : *Ladakh Studies* News Letter No. 8.

Phelps, Edger (1900): *Yak Shooting in Tibet.*

Rankin, Reginald (1895): *A Tour in the Himalayas and Beyond.*

Rizvi, J. (1985), *Peasant Traders of Ladakh—A Study in Oral History'*/India International Centre Quarterly 12(1): 14-21.

Sharma, S.K., and Sharma, Usha (ed.) 1996, *Encyclopaedia of Tibet;* Vol. 4.

Sheikh, Abdul Ghani (1976), 'The famous Wild animals of Ladakh', *Urdu,* Journs : Tamir, Srinagar.

Snellgrove, D.L. & Shorupski, R; (1980) : *Cultural Heritage of Ladakh;* Vol.II, Aris & Phillips, London.

Vohra, Rohit (1993), *Dating of a Maitreya Relief of the Mid-8th Century: from Sumda Chen,* South Asian Studies.

Ward, A.E. (1896), *Tourists and Sportsmen's Guide to Kashmir and Ladakh.*

Index

C

D

S

U

V

W

Y

Z